The Railroad in American Fiction

The Railroad in American Fiction

An Annotated Bibliography

GRANT BURNS

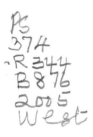

McFarland & Company, Inc., Publishers
Jefferson, North Carolina, and London

LIBRARY OF CONGRESS CATALOGUING-IN-PUBLICATION DATA

Burns, Grant, 1947–
The railroad in American fiction : an annotated bibliography / Grant Burns.
p.   cm.
Includes bibliographical references and indexes.

ISBN 0-7864-2379-X (softcover : 50# alkaline paper) ∞

1. American fiction—Bibliography.   2. Railroad stories—Bibliography.
3. Railroads in literature—Bibliography.   4. Railroad travel in
literature—Bibliography.   I. Title.
Z1231.F4B88   2005   016.813008'0356—dc22   2005015328
[PS374.R344]

British Library cataloguing data are available

Cover photograph © 2005 Brand X Pictures

Manufactured in the United States of America

*McFarland & Company, Inc., Publishers
Box 611, Jefferson, North Carolina 28640
www.mcfarlandpub.com*

For my father, Francis M. Burns,
a railroader from 1931 to 1975

ACKNOWLEDGMENTS

I am grateful to librarians and special collections curators around the country for their prompt and congenial assistance in helping me verify and complete citations to a number of stories in hard-to-find magazines. In this effort, e-mail is another tool that my bibliographic predecessor, Frank P. Donovan, Jr., could not have imagined. What a satisfying afternoon it was, for example, when only a few hours after I had in modest hope sent requests for information on approximately a dozen elusive citations to librarians at the Kent State University Libraries' Department of Special Collections and Archives, and the Browne Popular Culture Library at Bowling Green State University, I received complete details from librarians at those two institutions on all those elusive citations!

Many thanks go to Lesa Quade, of the interlibrary lending unit at the Frances Willson Thompson Library, University of Michigan-Flint. Lesa was an ever-willing and resourceful seeker of obscure and scarce books. Thanks, too, to Thompson Library Director Robert L. Houbeck, who cheerfully tolerated, and even encouraged, my long preoccupation with this project.

Special thanks go to my wife, Stephanie, who accepted my time-consuming obsession without complaint, and who acted as though it did not bother her a bit when I had the dining room lined for many months, not very neatly, with stacks of *Railroad Magazine*, photocopied stories, heaps of note cards, random debris, and piles of books from multiple libraries. She is, of course, a woman who finds considerable satisfaction in joining me with a cup of coffee to sit by the railroad tracks in pleasant weather to watch the passing trains, so patience on this point came naturally to her. Thanks also to my son, Steven, who knows more about railroading than I ever will, for his helpful suggestions and encouragement.

In short, I could not have done this job half as well without the willing help and accommodation of all of these people. I hope that the bibliography does their forbearance and good will justice, and that readers interested in exploring American fiction of the railroad find here many routes to enjoyable and rewarding reading.

GB, July 2005

CONTENTS

PREFACE

The Bibliography's Scope

A comprehensive bibliography of adult American railroad fiction, and fiction featuring the railroad, would prove far longer than this one. I have attempted to provide a bibliography that, although short of comprehensive—listing every discoverable instance of this fiction in books and periodicals—is at least representative, featuring work from the 1840s to novels and stories published in this century. I have leaned toward substance rather than quantity. In some respects, more is better, but I have never been a great devotee of "annotated" bibliographies that provide scant information on the content of the material listed. I am writing for readers who share my interest in knowing enough about the work in question not only to be able to judge whether it may be worth seeking and reading in the flesh, but in obtaining enough information about the work through the annotation that they have some reasonable sense of the work as a whole.

When someone tells me about a film, or a novel, I want to know enough about what happens in it, enough about its characters, and enough about the ideas it represents, to believe that I have received something with a little meat on its bones. It is simply not enough to say of Sinclair Lewis's *Main Street* (Entry 459) that "It's a book about a librarian who takes the train to Minnesota and wishes she were back in Chicago." As well as giving a reasonable sense of the individual works through their annotations, this bibliography aims, through the cumulative effect of the annotations, to present a reasonably-detailed picture of the railroad in American fiction. The reader will, of course, have to do a good deal of the work in making that picture come into focus.

Leading writers of railroad fiction—Harry Bedwell, Frank L. Packard, Frank H. Spearman, Cy Warman, and A.W. Somerville—receive extensive attention. The second tier of authors who wrote for the pulps are represented in sufficient entries to give the reader an idea of their work. I have included few pulp writers whose work does not rise at least to the level of E.S. Dellinger's or John A. Hill's; there are many who still languish—and probably always will, until the paper crumbles to dust—in the yellowing pages of old issues of *Railroad Stories* and *Railroad Magazine*.

Identifying fiction by topic in mainstream and literary magazines involves challenges. In both categories limited access due to poor or non-existent indexing presents obstacles. I have wrestled with some of these obstacles, skirted others, and yielded when apparently inevitable to the rest. Whatever the limitations that lay in the path of this compilation, readers should find here many stories in a railroad vein of which they were previously unaware.

The identity contest between fiction and fact in railroad writing is not always easy to judge. Some of Cy Warman's pieces, for example, could fall into either category, as might some others that made the cut and find themselves in the bibliography. Some others did not make that cut. Herbert E. Hamblen's interesting 1898 book, *The General Manager's Story*, is sometimes embraced as fiction, but Richard Reinhardt, who has researched railroad literature of the era, clearly categorizes Hamblen's work as autobiography; hence, it does not appear here.

Entries for novels should furnish some welcome finds, and, I hope, few disappointments. One consideration led to a long-running internal debate: To what extent should the bibliography include novels that are all but impossible to find? Not infrequently, a novel noted in Frank P. Donovan, Jr.'s 1940 bibliography of railroad fiction, or mentioned in a journal article, proved extant in only a tiny handful of libraries across the country; some of these novels are accessible neither through interlibrary loan nor through online full-text sources. Did I really want to stimulate readers' appetites with a menu of books from which some items were not available from the kitchen? I solved this problem with courageous vacillation: Sometimes I included the book; sometimes, I did not.

The bibliography excludes work primarily intended for children. A large body of writing occupies this area, but someone else will have to tend to it. It also shuns romance fiction, and, with a very few exceptions, specifically religious fiction. Other genres—science fiction, mystery, horror, crime, Westerns—are represented. Speaking of Westerns, contemporary mass-market potboilers receive but limited attention. Works by American writers set in foreign countries qualified for inclusion if they seemed to concern an American character or characters in significant ways (it

was not always easy to tell); if they did not, they do not appear in the bibliography.

Citation Notes

For works with more than one publication cited, the first noted in the entry is the one I used. When I could identify a full periodical citation for a story, I included it; if I could not discover it all, I noted as much as I was able to find, even if that amounted to no more than the name of the periodical. When I could identify more than one publication source for short stories, I included that information in the entries. For entries freely available on the Web in the *Wright American Fiction* project, I included the Wright URL in the citation.

The Subject Index

This bibliography's subject index is a limited guide to topical concerns appearing in the novels and stories under consideration. The index in no sense reflects an evaluation of the full extent of concerns embodied in the works of fiction listed in the bibliography.

A Note on Jargon

The most railroadly (to invent a term) of railroad fiction, that appearing in the pulp magazines, frequently turns loose a stream of jargon on the reader. Now and then an alert pulp writer is well aware of this tendency, and turns it to his story's advantage. Harry Bedwell's "Priority Special" (Entry 58), for example, works in an amusing little subplot concerning a veteran railroader's befuddling an Army major with a cascade of terminology readily understood by any railroader or railfan, but that would leave most lay readers, like the major, scratching their heads.

Every line of work has its jargon; railroad jargon is a particularly rich vein of occupational language. In this bibliography, however, I have made every effort not to use railroad jargon. I have even sidestepped using such a ubiquitous term of railroad fiction as "hogger" (for locomotive engineer). Avoiding colorful language is not agreeable, but better to avoid it than to confuse the reader new to the subject, or, worse, wear him or her out with repeated explanations.

And a Note on the Disappearing Stuff of History

When I compiled this bibliography, I enjoyed the use of research tools that Frank P. Donovan, Jr., would have greatly appreciated, and I hope that I have used them at least approximately as well as he would have. Today's researcher does not have every advantage, however. One obstacle that hinders every investigator of American popular cultural history is the way that its published artifacts are disappearing. With a few institutional exceptions, American librarians and archivists have not done an outstanding job of collecting and preserving the documents of popular culture. Any reasonable analysis of a people's social life and customs leads to what one might believe is an inevitable conclusion: To understand the way people live and think, it is helpful to understand their popular culture. It is not possible to understand popular culture without experiencing its products. Popular music, literature, art, and other aspects of popular culture reveal people and their times in ways that nothing else can.

In spite of this inescapable and, one would think, obvious, truth, the researcher diving deep into American popular culture's history finds many dry pools. Even today, as publications like *Railroad Man's Magazine* are busy falling apart in the few

libraries that own them (as the magazine's editor, Freeman Hubbard, observed, that acidic pulp paper eats itself alive in a painfully short time), too many librarians continue to give short shrift to the idea that preserving today's popular work is a favor to tomorrow's student.

Many of the magazines that furnished stories for inclusion in this bibliography are extremely difficult to find in libraries— or anywhere else that is publicly accessible. I am fortunate to live within walking distance of the Michigan State University Libraries' Popular Culture Collection. Inspired by the American literature teacher Russel B. Nye, whom I was fortunate enough to have as a professor many years ago, this collection proved an invaluable source of material for this bibliography.

Other special library collections also enabled access to material otherwise close to impossible to track down. They included the collections of the Lilly Library at Indiana University, and the Special Collections Library of the University of Michigan. The Library of Michigan, Michigan's state library, is an answered prayer for any researcher delving into 19th and early 20th century American periodicals. There in open stacks one finds long runs of such great American magazines as *Scribner's, Century Illustrated, McClure's*, and many others, where now-forgotten popular writers rub shoulders with the giants of American literature.

From the point of view of anyone concerned about preserving the material links to the past that themselves facilitate spiritual links to those who occupied that time, the growing problem of access to popular periodicals in their original form is a serious matter. Expanded access to these publications through the burgeoning of online full-text would certainly be welcome. A project that does for popular periodicals what the *Wright American Fiction* collection, a Committee on Institutional

Cooperation product hosted by the Indiana University Digital Library Program, does for a major segment of 19th-century books would be a boon. One looks forward eagerly to Google's plans to cooperate with the University of Michigan, Harvard University, and several other institutions in making millions of books and other items freely available online.

This eagerness must be tempered with the knowledge that one obtains from direct interaction with a physical object experiences that one cannot gain from scrutiny of an electronic representation of the object. The texture of the paper, the look of the print on the page, the weight and heft of the volume, the knowledge that this paper on which one's eyes gaze, that one's hands touch, is the same paper gazed upon and touched by readers long dead—but who somehow live on in the awakened senses of the present-day reader—cannot be duplicated in observation of an electronic image. The words may be present before the reader, but a host of sensations available to the reader of the physical volume will not be there. With the passage of time, more and more readers will have little or no choice but to settle for the image of the thing, not the thing itself. This fact represents a grave cultural and historical loss.

INTRODUCTION

"The railroad, second only to religion, has been the greatest civilizing and en-lightening force in the world." —Frank A. Munsey, 1906.

Given the effects of religion on the planet's happiness, one might suggest that the accomplishment Frank A. Munsey assigns to the railroad falls slightly short of scintillating. Nevertheless, this opening line from his editorial in his new pulp publication, *Railroad Man's Magazine*, is doubtless in reasonable accord with the prevailing sentiments of its time. Pulp magazine publishers like Munsey—a titan among the breed—did not aspire to destroy their opportunities for profit by challenging popular wisdom. They reinforced and exploited that wisdom for money, and, probably more often than not, subscribed to it themselves. Munsey's launching a new pulp aimed at an audience of American railroad workers and anyone else captivated by what was at the time the nation's most influential industry signified the railroad's deep hold on American popular culture. From the outset, *Railroad Man's Magazine* and its successors, *Railroad Stories* and *Railroad Magazine*, for much the better part of a century provided a steady diet of fiction focusing on the railroad and its workers.

Although none was as consistent about it as Munsey's magazine, other popular periodicals had much earlier found the railroad a subject worthy of their space in the form of fiction. Such pillars of the American magazine world as *Scribner's* and *McClure's* had frequently turned in their pages to fictional treatments of the railroad. One could easily locate stories on railroad topics close to the work of the most talented and respected literary artists of their era, and, in some cases, of American literature over the long view, including Mark Twain, Stephen Crane, Edith Wharton, and many others.

Far from occupying the tenement quarter of American publishing, railroad fiction—fiction focusing directly on the railroad—enjoyed life in an artistically respectable habitat well past the turn of the 19th century. The birth of *Railroad Man's Magazine*, however, marked a point of departure in this fiction. The change was gradual, and would have escaped the early notice of most readers of the time, but the frequency of railroad fiction as *railroad* fiction began to decline not long after the 20th century began. Stories in mainstream magazines featuring heroic engineers, brave firemen, young women in distress on runaway trains, and earnest young men determined to carve out careers in rail service appeared with diminishing frequency.

Only in the pulps did the tradition of railroad-focused fiction continue with unabated vigor. In *Railroad Man's Magazine* and its successors, in fact, the focus on the

5

railroad as the subject of fiction became genuinely intense, with an almost obsessive devotion to railroading techniques, equipment, problems, and dangers. Many stories in the genre are so laden with jargon peculiar to the profession that in lengthy stretches they defy the ability of the lay reader to understand what is going on. Writers like E.S. Dellinger, Gilbert A. Lathrop, and James W. Earp were not writing for the general reader: They were writing for railroaders, and for those who followed railroading closely. They seldom felt any obligation to explain the jargon; they simply assumed that their audience already had it in command. Longtime editor Freeman Hubbard assured that his magazine would follow this approach, for his basic rule—one that he rarely broke— was to buy fiction only by writers who had worked on the railroad. This practice led to a high degree of authenticity in the fiction's technical details; it also led sometimes to a certain opacity for naïve readers.

There were, to be sure, authors who sometimes escaped from the domain that pure railroad fiction came to occupy. A handful of writers worked with a desk in both the pulp ghetto and in mainstream popular magazines such as *Collier's* and the *Saturday Evening Post*. The most interesting of these writers was Harry Bedwell.

Bedwell (1888–1955), an Iowa farm boy, hung around the local depot as a youth, learned Morse code, and became a telegrapher, among holding other railroading jobs. He contributed a large number of stories to *Railroad Man's Magazine*, *Railroad Stories*, and *Railroad Magazine*. He wrote clearly and directly, with an occasional inspired line; he seldom lost the reader in a welter of jargon; and, like such railroad fiction colleagues as Frank L. Packard and Frank H. Spearman, he developed a stable of characters that the regular reader could look forward to enjoying

like old friends. (In this respect, early railroad fiction is reminiscent of long-running television series employing characters who do not appear in every episode, but whom the viewer welcomes back upon their return.) In his short but interesting biography of Bedwell, Frank P. Donovan, Jr., calls Bedwell "America's last great writer of railroad short stories."[1]

In addition to his work in the pulps, Bedwell also published a respectable roster of stories in the *Saturday Evening Post*, the majority featuring his most memorable character, and, indeed, the most memorable character of the purely-railroad fiction genre, Eddie Sand. Like Bedwell a telegraph operator, Eddie was a boomer who seldom stayed in one place more than a few months. He seems to have first appeared in a story in 1910 (Entry 53). Following his death in 1955, Bedwell's stories continued to appear in reprinted, sometimes abridged form, in *Railroad Magazine* for many years, a point testifying both to Bedwell's ability and to the relative paucity of new railroad fiction writers able to write on a par with him. According to Freeman Hubbard, *Railroad Magazine* reprinted some of the old fiction in *Railroad Magazine's* last decade because "The oldest pulp issues have turned brown and are crumbling, every time I consult one of them my desk and floor are littered with tiny particles of brown paper."[2] The fact that the older stories were superior to the new work coming in may also have affected Hubbard's reprinting decisions.

We shall return to Eddie Sand in the discussion of some themes of railroad fiction; it is enough for the moment to bear in mind that Eddie Sand is an American archetype, having much in common with characters developed by Mark Twain, Jack London, Jack Kerouac, and other authors who recognized the tensions inherent in "getting civilized" and settling down to a safe, respectable middle-class life.

A Field Ripe for Plowing

Many capable writers have turned their attention to the railroad in America, and have produced a substantial body of literature analyzing the railroad from multiple perspectives. The railroad's role in the industrialization of the country, in its settling, its war-fighting, its uniting, and even in the way it tells time has been explored and debated by historians, economists, and political scientists. Sociologists have studied the roles in the railroad of women, blacks, Chinese, Irish, and other groups who have historically found themselves out of the mainstream of power and authority in American life. The rise and decline of passenger service, the critical place of the railroad in the modern labor movement, political corruption and the railroad, and the unification of the country through the development of the national rail system have received something approaching their due attention by scholars. Indeed, one might wonder what ground remains to till in the vast acreage that the railroad occupies in American life.

One area that those seeking a fresh field should find worth pondering is the subject of this bibliography. One of the most overlooked aspects of the railroad is its place in American fiction. This lack of attention is surprising. The nation's first scheduled steam railroad service began in 1830, on the South Carolina Railroad. In 1831, the DeWitt Clinton ran from Albany to Schenectady; soon, American novelists and short-story writers began to turn to the railroad with regularity, both as a primary focus of their work and as a tool to help them penetrate and illuminate ideas and sensibilities that they found in the broader sphere of the nation's life.

In his influential examination of technology in America, *The Machine in the Garden*, Leo Marx suggests why the railroad almost immediately became a focus of the nation's writers. The railroad joins other manifestations of industrialization as an obvious, readily-grasped symbol of progress:

> The invention of the steamboat had been exciting, but it was nothing compared to the railroad. In the 1830's the locomotive, an iron horse or fire–Titan, is becoming a kind of national obsession. It is the embodiment of the age, an instrument of power, speed, noise, fire, iron, smoke—at once a testament to the will of man rising over natural obstacles, and, yet, confined by its iron rails to a predetermined path, it suggests a new sort of fate…. Stories about railroad projects, railroad accidents, railroad profits, railroad speed fill the press; the fascinating subject is taken up in songs, political speeches, and magazine articles, both factual and fictional.[3]

From the most literary of writers, such as Nathaniel Hawthorne, Willa Cather, and William Faulkner, to the most dedicated boilers of pots in pulp fiction, one finds the railroad and its attendant phenomena—depots, diners, hoboes, boom-towns, ghost towns, strikes, speed, and sundry other matters—in prominent position. Whether the issue is the ugliest face of American racism, the most heroic actions of those who dreamed and accomplished some of the greatest feats of the industrial age, or the manner in which the railroad infiltrated and affected the American experience at almost every level, these writers have embraced the railroad in their work. Through straightforward literal representation and through the most suggestive symbolism, the railroad has gained a place in American literary history that probably surpasses in scope that attained by any other commercial entity.

In spite of the extensive quantity of both literary and popular fiction in which the railroad figures significantly, the reader who seeks commentary and analysis on the railroad in fiction finds relatively little to nourish his or her interest. A tiny handful of hard-to-obtain dissertations and masters' theses, a too-short list of journal articles—commonly focusing on the most obvious candidates for discussion, such as Willa Cather and, of course, mainstream American fiction's most devoted railfan, Thomas Wolfe—whet the interest, and provide some useful and thoughtful insight. After these contributions to serious examination of the subject, one finds very little to savor. Even such an outstanding study as John R. Stilgoe's *Metropolitan Corridor* pays but cursory attention to the railroad in fiction,[4] as does James A. Ward's *Railroads and the Character of America, 1820–1887.*[5]

If American novelists and short-story writers had largely ignored the railroad since its early success, one could easily understand this lack of attention. But American writers have never ignored the railroad. The ways that they use the railroad in their fiction have evolved from the early days, but even today, with the romance of railroading that once captivated so many Americans diluted by such developments as the decline of rail passenger service (abetted by presidential administrations apparently untroubled by massive government subsidies to highways and airports), the demise of the locomotive engineer as an heroic figure, and by the faceless corporate character of railroads sporting such colorless names as "CSX" and "BNSF," creative writers still turn to the railroad for sustenance in their efforts to show and explain the world to their readers.

D.J. Smith is one of the few literary critics who have written at any meaningful length on the fiction of the American railroad. Smith traces the origins of much of the public interest in reading such fiction to the small town and the effects of the railroad upon it—a theme that surfaces often in the works treated in this bibliography.

What man who was a small-town boy in the days of the steam locomotive does not remember all his life the noise and excitement of the local depot, the well-known schedule of trains, the irresistible summons of the whistle ... the exciting people who came and left on the cars; the dreams of one day boarding the train as passenger or, even more breathtaking, as uniformed railway employee?[6]

Although poets, essayists, and historians have all addressed the role of the railroad in American life, Smith contends that "it is the writers of fiction—novels and short stories—who have treated it most convincingly."[7] Smith characterizes the railroad, in the era before automobile travel enabled easy escape to somewhere else for growing numbers of Americans, as a "glamorous" and "mystical" force that represented a route out of the constricting boundaries of rural and small-town life: "The train, although it could be used to represent more sinister forces, was an almost spiritual symbol of life to many fluttering souls caged in the deserts of the great West, the monotonous Midwest, even the small towns of New England."[8]

In a darker vein, Nicholas Daly, in an essay on British railroad fiction, writes that "for the Victorians it [the railroad] stood as both agent and icon of the acceleration of the pace of everyday life; it annihilated an older experience of time and space, and made new demands on the sensorium of the traveler."[9] This observation holds true for Americans of the period, too, as is often evident in both fiction and non-fiction describing railroad travel. The American reaction to the "demands on the sensorium" ranges from dismayed to irritated, with a crusty flippancy and ironic tone often marking the writer's observations. Harriet Beecher Stowe, who moved on from abolition to exhortations to good public health, complains with vigor about passenger trains of the 19th century.

Railroad traveling in America is systematically, and one would think carefully, arranged so as to violate every possible law of health. A red-hot stove heats the upper stratum of air to oppression, while a stream of cold air is constantly circulating about the lower extremities. The most indigestible and unhealthy substances conceivable are generally sold in the cars or at way-stations for the confusion and distress of the stomach. Rarely can a traveller obtain so innocent a thing as a plain good sandwich of bread and meat, while pie, cake, doughnuts, and all other culinary atrocities, are almost forced upon him at every stopping place.[10]

Stowe's complaints are replicated routinely in fiction, with the dissatisfaction extending well beyond freezing and roasting coaches and bad food into indifferent railroad employees, perverse rules, and bureaucratic absurdity.

The only substantial bibliography of railroad fiction of which I am aware is Frank P. Donovan, Jr.'s 1940 compilation, *The Railroad in Literature*.[11] Donovan's bibliography proved indispensable in laying the groundwork for *The Railroad in American Fiction*. As valuable as Donovan's book is, however, it provides scant detail about the works that it lists, and it is only marginally useful as a guide to short fiction. The reasons for this second defect are readily apparent, and easy to excuse. Donovan prepared his bibliography at a time when the print tools available to identify works of short fiction were sorely inadequate. There was no long run of the H.W. Wilson Company's *Short Story Index* for him to consult, and if he turned to the *Readers' Guide to Periodical Literature*, he found that it furnished no subject indexing for most of the works of fiction that it listed, including railroad fiction. Donovan also could not even dream of the advantages afforded by electronic indexing. The present-day researcher revels in such key-word searchable databases as the *Readers' Guide Retrospective*, *Nineteenth Century Masterfile*, *Humanities Abstracts*, *Wright American Fiction*, and other tools that unearth stories that would otherwise likely languish forever in all-but undetectable condition. Thanks to such resources, this bibliography pays considerable and deserved attention to short fiction. In short stories lies some of the most provocative and best-written fiction involving the railroad. In short stories, too, one finds some of the pulpiest of the pulps, including our friend Frank Munsey's magazine.

The Double Track of Railroad Fiction

As I have indicated, a strong track of railroad fiction focuses on the railroad itself, and the railroad's accompanying phenomena; it is, in a real sense, the only genre of fiction that deserves the proper term "railroad" fiction. Since the turn of the 19th century, it has been the property chiefly, but not exclusively, of pulp magazines. Some typical story titles from *Railroad Magazine* suggest the preoccupation with the nuts & bolts of railroading that often characterizes this literature: "The Broken Drawbar"; "The Hotbox Expert"; "Switch-Key"; and "Night Yardmaster."

The other track of railroad fiction carries the mainstream traffic of both "literary" fiction and popular fiction. Here the railroad itself is not, as a rule, the writer's primary concern, even though the railroad may dominate the story regarding locale, action, and imagery. The railroad in this fiction serves multiple purposes. It is a means to facilitate plot development; it allows the writer to use the railroad as a symbol—either positive or negative—of the effects of technological development; it permits exploration of the role of the individual in a massive business enterprise;

it furnishes a ready tool for illustration of important historical events ranging from the settlement of the frontier to the effects of war; and it provides a handy way to bring characters into a setting that encourages their interaction.

The second category of the railroad in American fiction has been active from the industry's outset, and continues to the present day. The first category, with its devotion to the railroad as an entity in itself, has almost completely disappeared. The advent of the automobile struck the first major blow to the public's fascination with the railroad; as the 1920s approached, authors who might have turned to the railroad as the topic of popular fiction turned with growing frequency to the auto. Train tales continued to turn up in mainstream magazines, but with diminishing frequency. The development of air travel and a system of interstate highways further turned public fascination and writers' subject choices away from the railroad, leaving *Railroad Magazine* as a lonely outpost of purely railroad fiction. Even that source, unreplenished by any writer in the genre with a stature approaching Harry Bedwell's, withdrew from the fiction field by the late 1970s, when it merged with *Railfan* to form *Railfan & Railroad*, after gamely carrying on the tradition by reprinting stories by Bedwell and by a few writers who flourished in or near "the Golden Age" of railroad fiction, identified by Frank P. Donovan, Jr., as 1895 to 1915.[12]

In spite of the flagging popularity of railroad fiction, and its general disappearance from popular magazines as the 20th century progressed (or regressed, depending on one's point of view), the railroad itself remained a significant presence in many mainstream and literary novels and stories. The majority of this fiction over the past half century has not focused on railroad workers. Some exceptions occur, such as Anthony Bukoski's "Time Between Trains" (Entry 103), and Tim Gautreaux's "Waiting for the Evening News" (Entry 295). Richard Reinhardt tries to identify reasons for what would seem to be an odd oversight, given the voluminous treatment of nearly every aspect of railroading in works of nonfiction—"But on the subject of the railroad man—practically nothing."[13] He argues that the complexity of railroading, which does not lend itself to easy literary presentation, accounts to some extent for the dearth of such work. More important, in Reinhardt's estimation, is what he considers the essentially closed society of railroad work, with the railroader lacking "the solitary, fatalistic, picaresque code of behavior that gives a heroic dimension to the cowboy.... Isolated in some small town or shabby, brick-paper neighborhood surrounding the divisional terminal, he lived in psychological exile from the general American community, chained to his job, a Babbitt-on-wheels."[14] The difficulty in a writer's penetrating the railroad's industrially insular environment all but assured that memorable works of railroad fiction would be few.

Indeed, Reinhardt dismisses railroad fiction—the stuff of Munsey's magazines and other pulps—as "pseudo-literature."[15] This verdict is unreasonably hard. It subscribes too readily to the unbecoming habit of many who have studied literature formally to turn up their noses at fiction that is less sophisticated than that produced by writers they admire; this is the mentality that divides fiction into "art" and "trash." All fiction is art; all fiction is literature; and it all reveals something of its time, culture, and author. I have myself implied at least a partial endorsement of the art vs. trash fictional dichotomy by referring to "literary" fiction, as opposed to popular fiction. If I may amend, and, I hope, temper that implication a little: Literary fiction possesses a self-consciousness that popular fiction does not; it possesses a sense of importance, of "saying something," rather than of simply "telling a story." Sometimes the effort to "say something" produces results far less satisfactory than the effort to "tell a story." The best writers combine the two objectives more often than not. In any case, fiction is literature, whether the pulp publication of a former brakeman untutored in technique, or the smartly sophisticated issuance of a university English professor in a quarterly journal with 300 subscribers.

By far the most detailed analysis of railroad fiction, and the railroad *in* fiction, that I have found is Patricia Porcello's 1968 doctoral dissertation, "The Railroad in American Literature: Poetry, Folk Song, and the Novel." As her subtitle indicates, Porcello does not treat short stories, but in a 100-page section she provides an in-depth discussion of such novels as Norris's *The Octopus* (Entry 598), May Merrill Miller's *First the Blade* (Entry 559), Zane Grey's *The U.P. Trail* (Entry 314), Edwin M. Lanham's *The Wind Blew West* (Entry 437), and other novels appearing in this bibliography. (Porcello also analyzes a few fictional works not included here.) Porcello is straightforward about the limitations of technique and sensibility evident in popular novels; she points out that it is the more accomplished authors such as Frank Norris and Thomas Wolfe "who demonstrate the physical railroad's potential for providing symbols for the effective literary expression of man's plight in this mortal world and this modern society."[16] Nevertheless, she is much readier than Reinhardt to give popular fiction its due:

> The popular novels frequently lack literary finesse, and their view of historical incidents is often a biased one. Yet they portray actual incidents and characters of railroad history with great conviction, and often with strength and color. At times … the physical landscape which serves as backdrop … is reproduced with vividness and great feeling.[17]

Railroad Themes

To furnish a sense of a given novel or story, the bibliography's annotations tend toward brief plot and character descriptions. I do note occasional subtleties, and make critical observations—especially concerning the most creative work—but generally stay fairly close to the literal events and portraits drawn in the works themselves. Regarding the appearances of the railroad in novels in which the railroad is but incidental to the author's larger purposes, and may appear in only limited passages (in Theodore Dreiser's *Sister Carrie*, for example), the annotations focus on only those passages, and provide little background on the rest of the work, beyond putting the railroad passages into a very general context.

We Americans are a literalistic people. There are reasons for this way of seeing the world; the very act of conquering the vast and forbidding expanse of the American land prevented much in the way of dreamy pondering by those actually doing the work. (Dreamy pondering is especially incompatible with railroading; as one inclined to it, I owe my continued existence to an alert co-worker who yanked me out of the path of an oncoming Detroit, Toledo & Ironton switch engine as I moseyed along a track in a noisy rail yard one July afternoon in 1966.)

Literalism is, however, a bad intellectual habit. We tend to take things at face value, and show a disinclination to penetrate to their hidden hearts. One thinks, for example, of Robert Frost's poem, "Neither Out Far nor In Deep," in which people do not look in either of those directions when they survey the prospect before them. To enjoy and appreciate fiction fully, one must look both out far, and in deep. One cannot take fiction at face value and assume that there is no more to it than what lies on the surface. All fiction, from the most artless to the most accomplished, operates at more than one level. To the extent that the writer is in control of his or her work, the levels below the immediately-observable surface are more deliberate and more purposeful. Ernest Hemingway's story "Big Two-Hearted River" (Entry 345) is a fine and famous example of such work.

Every student of literature is aware of such dynamics, and it is not my aim to point out the obvious to those who know it well. I hope, however, that this bibliography attracts the attention of readers who do not approach it from a background steeped in literary studies, and I want to warn them not to take my annotations as the last, best, or complete word. These readers may be railfans who studied accounting or computer science in college, or whose last experience in an English class came in their junior year in high school—a year most likely spent, like my junior year, with a literature textbook able to induce stupefying boredom with astounding regularity.

Ultimately, no writer can know everything that his or her story reveals, for the writer's unconscious mind is always at work when the writer is at work, and the two often do not communicate candidly with each other. The results of this imperfect communication lead to results that sometimes become apparent only on the reader's prolonged reflection. There is more to see in this fiction than is suggested by the annotations. The only way for the reader to find the greater depth is to read the fiction itself, and to wade into it.

Meanwhile, I would like to dwell, more or less briefly, on a few of the most prominent themes and concerns that emerged in the review of these many novels and stories. There are many other themes to be found in this fiction, of course; readers curious about exploring them should find some useful leads in this bibliography's subject index. The themes below are the ones that caught my attention the most persistently. They are essentially sub themes of those D.J. Smith identifies in her useful essay, "The American Railroad Novel." Smith's scope is much narrower than this bibliography's, limited as it is not only to novels, but also to novels that are arguably centered on the railroad, rather than including short stories, and more broadly-focused work that includes significant appearances of the railroad. Smith finds a handful of basic plots, or themes, in the railroad novel: business manipulation, "human issues" in the railroad business, and mechanical operations.[18]

Company Men and Union Men: Railroad Labor and Loyalty

Both railroad fiction and mainstream fiction that either embodies railroad passages or that makes the railroad a major focus of attention frequently concentrate on railroad workers, up through the first half of the 20th century. To appreciate much of this fiction at any level, some familiarity with the railroad worker's historical background is helpful. Magazine fiction of the 19th and early 20th centuries routinely places railroaders at center stage, presenting their work lives as a mixture of rough but good-natured camaraderie, with constant challenges from nature in the forms of rain and snowstorms, floods, and forest fires. When the railroaders one commonly finds in *Scribner's* or *McClure's* are not risking their lives to battle nature, they put their necks on the line to contend with defective equipment (bad rails, failed couplers, driving rods torn loose, exploding boilers), or with human antagonists, including unhappy Indians, disgruntled coworkers, and unreasonable railroad officials—the last group frequently referred to as "brass collars." Minus the unhappy Indians, much these same matters of the railroader's life persisted in the fiction far into the 20th century.

Popular rail fiction commonly presents its central figure, the railroader—most often the engineer, but also the fireman, the conductor, the brakeman, the switchman, and other personnel—as a man who rises to the occasion to overcome the challenges of the moment, whether natural or man-made. Not infrequently, rising to the challenge entails the railroader's supreme sacrifice: his own death. (Although, contrary to satiric takes on this fiction, this death does not come nearly so often with the grimly set jaw and the hand on the throttle as the locomotive plummets into the abyss).

The loyal railroader of popular fiction, a company man who puts service to the road above his own well being, stands with the noble cowboy as a model of American heroism; it is hardly a coincidence that even to the present day popular fiction often places the railroader in a Wild Western setting. Honest, upright, selfless, the brave railroader found in the work of authors such as Frank L. Packard and Cy Warman provided a moral model for readers ready to put themselves in a set of romantic shoes after their daily duties.

Unfortunately for the railroader in real life, whatever degree of loyalty and devotion he awarded the company did not often return to him in kind from the company itself.

The almost incessantly-revisited issue in popular railroad fiction of the danger of railroad work, and the demands for bravery on the part of those who carried it out, derives from a simple truth: Railroad work through the 19th century and into the 20th was appallingly dangerous. From 1888 through 1893, a total of 14,434 rail-roaders lost their lives on the job, and another 148,708 railroad employees suffered injuries at work. (Over the same period, approximately 1,800 railroad passengers were killed, and slightly over 16,000 sustained injuries.)[19] Writes Richard Reinhardt in his absorbing book, "Early railroading was almost unbearably uncomfortable and dangerous. Death haunted the switchyards, the icy tracks, the slippery car tops, the moving couplers with their lethal link-and-pin clasps. To be crippled, scalded, crushed between the cars—this was the future that waited for the average trainman."[20] As Dee Brown has noted, "During the pioneer days of the transcontinental railroad, more than six times as many railroad men as passengers were killed or injured in accidents, and foremost among the casualties were engineers and firemen."[21] Historian James H. Ducker describes how the deep-seated fear of railroading's dangers penetrated even into men's dreams, sometimes to the distress of their wives:

> In the early 1880s one brakeman striving to stop a nightmare runaway train woke up to find that he was twisting his wife's head instead of the brake wheel, while a Santa Fe engineer woke one night in 1898 with his wife screaming because he was pulling her arm out of its socket trying to reverse his engine.[22]

Is it astonishing, given the working conditions that Reinhardt thus characterizes, that former or present railroaders contributing to *Railroad Man's Magazine* or *Railroad Stories* sought to create a fictional world in which men worked, as a rule, in close harmony, and in which high standards of performance, integrity, and selflessness gave meaning to their labor? How else to bear memories of the carnage that one has witnessed on the job without growing dysfunctionally embittered or cynical?

One of the most dangerous pieces of railroad equipment was the link-and-pin coupler, which required brakemen to place their limbs and bodies in risky proximity to railroad cars in motion as they assembled trains. Railroad historians have pointed out that a good sign of an experienced brakeman was a missing digit or two. The brakeman indulging in a moment's carelessness, or suffering from mere bad luck, was often mutilated or killed. The automatic coupler patented by Eli Janney in 1868 was a far safer device than the link-and-pin for assembling trains, but American railroads showed a characteristic corporate attitude toward its employment, clinging to the link-and-pin system until into the 1890s. It was cheaper and easier to hire a new brakeman to replace one whose hand had been amputated in a coupling accident than to replace all the road's link-and-pin killers with the automatic coupler.

So, too, with the air brake. When George Westinghouse patented and tested the air brake on a train in 1869, the act of stopping a train was an adventure in personal injury. Brakemen had to climb onto the tops of moving cars, regardless of the weather, and wrestle the wheels of handbrakes to bring a train to a halt. The method was inefficient and dangerous; the air brake freed the brakeman from taking his life in his hands in this manner. How did the railroads respond to this life-saving—and, as well, property-saving—innovation? Railroad magnate "Commodore" Cornelius Vanderbilt's reaction when approached by Westinghouse set the tone: "Do you pretend to tell me that you could stop trains with wind? I'll give you to understand, young man, that I am too busy to have any time taken up in talking to a damned fool!"[23]

As with the automatic coupler, railroad officials spurned widespread adoption of the air brake. Why spend money on costly conversion to improved technology with an endless supply of cheap labor eager to replace the trainmen killed and mangled through their use of the existing equipment? In 1873, Michigan was the first state to require by law that railroads use the Westinghouse air brake; Michigan railroads generally responded to this legislation by ignoring it. Railroads raised the specter of the burden of cost and their aversion to government interference in "free enterprise"; state railroad commissions tended to accommodate the railroads.[24] Not until a relentless advocacy campaign by Iowan Lorenzo S. Coffin, who became Iowa's railroad commissioner in 1883, did sufficient pressure come to bear on public policy makers that the automatic coupler and air brake were forced onto reluctant railroad companies. The national Railroad Safety Appliance Act of March 1893 compelled their adoption. Improvements in working conditions for railroaders were prompt and dramatic, with a 60 percent drop in their accident rate.[25]

One can but guess at how many thousands of railroaders would not have died or been maimed on the job in the quarter-century between the invention of these life-saving devices and their forced use had American railroads adopted them promptly. One looks in vain for any suggestion in popular railroad fiction that the railroads were culpable in this needless slaughter. A railroader might be a loyal "company man," and popular fiction might, and did, time and again honor and extol such loyalty, but the company seldom felt any obligation to render to the trainman or other employee the same sort of loyalty it expected from him.

The railroads also showed their "loyalty" to workers by seeking to crush efforts to organize and to obtain fair treatment in wages and working conditions. In the national depression of the 1870s, railroads cut wages aggressively so that they could continue to pay respectable dividends to investors. Railroaders found themselves toiling 15 to 18 hours a day at wages 35 percent less than they had been earning, with desperate jobseekers ready to take their places if they balked at the railroads' practices. The catalyst for the great railroad strike of 1877 was the Baltimore & Ohio's slashing wages to the point that a fireman would make but $1.50 a day, a sum with which it was impossible to support a family. B & O workers walked off the job, and their strike spread across the country. Preaching to his affluent congregation, the prominent New York City minister Henry Ward Beecher mocked railroaders for lacking the gumption to live on a dollar a day; that would, he proclaimed in a true spirit of Christian charity, be sufficient for bread and water.

Although the general public did not share the Rev. Beecher's haughty attitude toward the striking railroaders, the power of the railroads, with their convenient connections in government, enabled them to crush the strike within a fortnight, employing police, federal troops, vigilantes, and strikebreakers.[26]

Seventeen years later, with another financial crisis plaguing the nation, railroad workers again exercised their united strength. The stimulus was the Pullman Company's harsh treatment of the employees who lived in its wholly-owned company town, Pullman, Illinois, a Chicago suburb. Like the railroads in the 1870s, the Pullman Company continued to pay hefty dividends to investors, enabled by deep cuts—close to half—in worker pay, without according reductions in the rent and prices charged workers who lived in Pullman. In 1894, unable to obtain any redress from the company, thousands of Pullman workers went on strike. The American Railway Union, led by Eugene Debs, organized a sympathetic

boycott, refusing to operate trains that hauled Pullman cars. Before long, the nation's rail operations had come to an effective halt. Again, the railroads exploited well-established legal and political allies, and through court injunction and federal troops secured the defeat of the striking workers.[27]

The Pullman Strike of 1894 and the violent labor actions of 1877 have been analyzed in detail by historians. The above synopses barely skim the surface of these critical events in American labor history, but may help the reader keep them in mind when reading popular railroad fiction. With some exceptions, this fiction tends to be plainly skewed in favor of a railroad management view of labor conflict. Strikers are commonly portrayed as easily misled, impulsive, violent, and ungrateful. Among the popular fictional exceptions concerning labor battles worth attention are Cy Warman's *Snow on the Headlight* (Entry 896), in which he struggles to deal fairly with the Burlington strike of 1888; Blanche Mosler's "Railroad Town" (Entry 568), concerning the movement that led to the establishment of the eight-hour workday in 1916; and E.S. Dellinger's "Blacklisted" (Entry 203), his view of the Pullman Strike.

Women and the Railroad

Like blacks, women are infrequent visitors to the pages of pulp railroad fiction. As D.J. Smith wryly remarks of railroad novels, "The presence of young ladies is but a concession to the popular taste; it is also useful for distinguishing railroad novels for men from those intended for boys."[28] When women do appear, it is usually in a romantic capacity. On occasion, they are waitresses in railroad diners—sometimes in so fine an establishment as a Harvey House. In *The Harvey Girls* (Entry 4), Samuel H. Adams offers an entertaining look at this end of the railroad business. E.S. Dellinger tackles the same subject, less capably, in his story "Harvey House Girl" (Entry 205). Infrequently, a woman demonstrates in pulp fiction an ability to perform as a capable railroader, most probably as a telegraph operator. Even more rarely, a woman takes control of the cab of a locomotive and shows that she need not take a back seat to any male engineer (Entry 654). These are exceptional cases, though, and only emphasize the standard role of women as spouses, mothers, and nurturers. These characters include Gilbert A. Lathrop's Ma Flanagan, who mothers the railroaders who live in her boarding house on the Western & Homestead Railway (Entries 441, 444, and 450).

In the train service end of the business, railroading has always been a male world. Before the turn of the 19th century, women were seldom employed in the industry. The Baltimore & Ohio employed one of the first railroad women on record in 1855. The few women rail workers generally performed cleaning tasks; some did clerical work. Not until World War II did a lasting change begin to occur in the kinds of jobs women were able to obtain, including positions in train service and yard work.[29]

During World War I, with heightened labor demands on the industry, tens of thousands of women went to work on American railroads, with most of them hired in 1918. Both during the war and before, women "were clustered in a certain, narrowly delineated, set of jobs. Jobs controlled by the prestigious, train-based railway unions—locomotive engineers, firemen, conductors, and brakemen—were not offered to women."[30] After the war, the numbers of women employed by the railroads fell rapidly as men returned to their jobs.

Railroad fiction now and then does feature women in specifically railroad, as opposed to ancillary railroad, jobs. Women appear with regularity in novels concerning the railroad, and sometimes occupy roles transcending mere romantic interest. None of the leading pulp writers, including Bedwell, manages female characters well. A female telegraph operator turns up in 1899 in Jasper E. Brady's "The Chief Train-despatcher's Story" (Entry 93); the shock to the male reader's system is resolved when the heroine marries the chief dispatcher. This is a typical resolution to a woman railroader story in the pulps: When a woman does demonstrate capable railroading skills, the author undercuts the idea that a woman can do the work by having her fall in love with a male railroader, quit work, and tend the house.

The handful of exceptions to the sex role stereotyping of women (Yes, Virginia, a woman can work on the railroad!) include Cornelia DeWitt Marshall in Taylor Caldwell's *Never Victorious, Never Defeated* (Entry 113); in spite of its title, E.S. Dellinger's young telegrapher in "Railroad Girl" (Entry 208); Lisa Thatcher in William Manchester's "Record Run" (Entry 513); and—one might say "alas"—Dagny Taggart in Ayn Rand's *Atlas Shrugged* (Entry 684). Many stories and novels, of course, feature women in primary roles as passengers or as otherwise involved with the railroad in a non-employee capacity; in these stories, women appear in a full range of perspectives, from the most stereotypical (a nag who cannot fathom her husband's and son's interest in model railroading in Entry 510), to the most fully-realized, including Hamlin Garland's *Rose of Dutcher's Coolly* (Entry 290) and Ellen Glasgow's *Barren Ground* (Entry 298). This bibliography's subject index includes references to entries for these and many other entries under "Women."

Down and Out on the Railroad

A substantial segment of fiction involving the railroad devotes itself not to railroaders, or to railroad customers, but to a forgotten and shunned class of men—almost inevitably, its members are male—the hoboes. (One could call them with sociological and political correctness "transients," but practitioners of the life themselves prefer the term "hobo." The annual Hoboes' Convention has been established for a century; one looks in vain for a "transients' convention.")

No one knows when the first man with an itch or a compelling need to be elsewhere, but no money in his pocket, hopped aboard a freight train and rode gratis—until an officious railroad worker discovered him and excused him, politely or roughly, from that particular trip. No doubt the pioneer knights of the rails began criss-crossing the country on the economy plan soon after train service became a regular event between any two distant points.

As Todd Depastino shows, hoboes rode the rails with varied motivations. Many saw this form of travel as the most efficient way to move from one locale where there was no available work to another where they might find employment. During the national economic crises of the 1870s, the 1890s, and the 1930s, railroad yards and hobo jungles filled with what Depastino calls "refugees from the wage system."[31] In 1932, hundreds of unemployed veterans climbed aboard freight cars in Portland, Oregon, to begin their trip to Washington, D.C., as part of the Bonus March. Few, if any, of these men would have resorted to such a desperate measure had their inability to obtain paying work not driven them to it. Economic upheaval has often tempered railroaders' responses to hoboes' seeking free rides, with railroads acknowledging the hoboes' "right" to ride during tight labor markets. When labor demand was low, however, "railroad detectives and train crews often brutally suppressed trespassing, making job searches all the more difficult and treacherous."[32]

The romantic air that is easy to attach to hoboing—see my above phrase, "knights of the rails"—fogs public perceptions of what is most often not a life chosen through free will, but one to which the occupant is reduced through circumstances beyond his or her control. It is a hard, dangerous, unhealthy life. When Jack London was writing about his experiences riding the rails, "Thousands of hoboes died each year traveling in such fashion, and many more suffered severe injury. Accidents claimed the lives of nearly twenty-five thousand railroad trespassers between 1901 and 1905 alone...."[33] Aside from the risks of bodily dismemberment, the rail-riding hobo faced the ever-present possibility of beatings by railroad personnel, exposure to terrible weather, and the predations of criminals who also traveled the road.

Not every hobo saw himself as a hopeless outcast. Some took pride in their self-determined status as noble wanderers, as men free of the conventional burdens of family, job, mortgage and other paraphernalia of the settled life. Wrote Jack London, who began a hobo's life at the age of 16 in Oakland, California, "I became a tramp—well, because of the life that was in me, of the wanderlust in my blood that would not let me rest."[34] London devotes an entire chapter, "Holding Her Down," in his autobiographical book *The Road*, to the craft of securing and keeping an illicit ride on a train. "Barring accidents, a good hobo, with youth and agility, can hold a train down despite all the efforts of the train-crew to 'ditch' him—given, of course, night-time as an essential condition."[35]

A clear link exists between the hobo, or at least the romanticized notion of the hobo, and that of the railroad boomer, the man who seldom rests owing to his insatiable yearning to see the country, and to steer clear of entangling alliances, whether corporate or domestic. Echoing Jack London, Harry Bedwell's boomer telegraph operator, Eddie Sand—an essentially romantic character with tinges of asceticism, given to quiet reflection upon empty deserts and open skies—on a few occasions voices the inner yearnings that compel him to pack up and move on: Eddie "knew that basically he was alone and some day he'd be hitting the road again.... Wanderlust! The incessant call of the boomer trail!"[36] One cannot doubt that the distance between Eddie Sand's point of view on this subject and that of his creator, Harry Bedwell, is very short, or that Bedwell, Jack London, and Jack Kerouac would have found some pleasure in one another's company.

In the fiction of the railroad, the hobo is a man who has slipped the bonds of society even more thoroughly than the boomer. The boomer, for all his indisposition to establishing lasting ties, except with members of his own fraternity, is more often than not a contributor to the life of conventional society. The boomer sees to it that the material of the nation gets from one place to another, and that passengers can travel where they must to play out their own parts in the national life of getting and spending. The hobo is a man apart, his brotherhood a loose network of others who live without ties, without commitments, without realistic long-range objectives. "The hobo defies society," writes London, "and society's watch-dogs make a living out of him."[37] Latter-day wanderer and railroad brakeman Jack Kerouac reinforces this sentiment: "The hobo is born of pride, having nothing to do with a community but with himself and other hobos and maybe a

dog."[38] Important, if often brief, relationships developed among hoboes: "On the road, men frequently formed partnerships for reasons of safety, frugality, and company."[39] This form of partnership is evident in many of the hobo stories noted in the bibliography.

The hobo-by-choice is sometimes the extreme opposite, in railroad fiction, of the heroic locomotive engineer. He is not the man whom children see as a larger-than-life figure, but as a threatening form who lurks in the shadows of the railroad. He is the figure beneath the overpass, luring young boys to their ruin; he is the ne'er do well occupant of the hobo jungle, squatting with his mates around a campfire by the river. Says Kerouac,

> In America there has always been ... a definite special idea of footwalking freedom going back to the days of Jim Bridger and Johnny Appleseed and carried on today by a vanishing group of hardy old timers.... But today mothers hold tight their children when the hobo passes through town because of what newspapers made the hobo to be—the rapist, the strangler, child-eater.[40]

Authors play the hobo in fiction of the railroad for effects ranging from the comic to the tragic. The frequent sympathy shown the hobo by pulp fiction writers might be a little surprising, considering their general approbation for "the company," and their disinclination to tolerate those who would exploit it. On the other hand, it is worth remembering that many of the pulp fiction writers were railroaders themselves, men who had seen and talked with hoboes, for whom hoboes were real human beings, not vague images conjured from sensational newspaper stories.

Drawing the human connection makes all the difference. One afternoon when I was a small boy in the 1950s, I accompanied my father, then a railroad bridge and building supervisor, on a Sunday afternoon visit to the Ann Arbor Railroad yard. Hoboes had a camp by the river that flowed past the trees and brush behind the B & B shop. When we stopped the car by the shop that afternoon, several of these homeless men approached my father and asked if he might spare them some change. He did so; they thanked him, and went away, maybe to buy some soup for stew, maybe to buy a bottle of cheap wine. When I asked my father why he had given the men money, his answer was succinct: "They don't have anything, and I'd rather give them 50 cents out of my pocket than have them break into the B & B shop looking for something to steal."

There was nothing sentimental in that statement, but it captured a sense of hard reality that the railroad-veteran authors of this fiction surely shared: The hoboes they saw were men with little or nothing in the way of material possessions, but they had human needs, and if it was possible to help them by looking the other way when they hopped a freight in hopes of finding work down the line, or by giving them some food before they moved on, what decent man would not do it, particularly if a moment's generosity was not only humane, but in the road's greater long-term interests?

From time to time, the hobo may be a repository of his fellow citizens' most antisocial impulses, someone who acts out their secret dreams of escape and irresponsibility, and pays for the act with a hardscrabble life that will quite likely terminate in a pauper's grave. The hobo is a Huck Finn of the industrial age, lighting out for the territory in a boxcar when civilization presses too hard on him—and civilization is glad to see him go. His departure serves to emphasize the moral rectitude and admirable responsibility of the majority, even as it allows that same majority an opportunity for safe, vicarious escape from its daily obligations.

Among the leading stories of hoboes noted in the bibliography are Edward Anderson's Depression-era novel, *Hungry Men* (Entry 14), whose title could not have been better-chosen; William R. Burnett's "Along the Tracks" (Entry 106); Jack Conroy's "Anyplace But Here" (Entry 167), which combines a slice of hobo life with racial issues; and any of the remarkable Amado Muro's stories (Entries 572 through 580).

Strangers on a Train

With apologies to novelist Patricia Highsmith, and to director Alfred Hitchcock, whose 1951 film based on her novel kept moviegoers on the edges of their seats, I am appropriating the title of the work they shared for this heading. What other heading would do to describe the phenomenon of chance meetings aboard trains that lead to joyful, terrible, or instructive developments? There is no better place to introduce the principals of a fictional work to one another than on a train. The self-contained world of the passenger train greatly facilitates the writer's need to have people of varying backgrounds, purposes, and characteristics interact with one another. To invoke Hitchcock once more, what would *North by Northwest* have been without Roger O. Thornhill and Eve Kendall sharing a table—and then a compartment—aboard the train? Not as much fun by half.

Whether for an exercise in mystery, melodrama, romance, or existential angst, the enforced proximity of train passengers gives the writer a nearly-ideal world-in-miniature. There is ample opportunity for conversation in the coach, dinner in the diner, drinks in the club car, and whatever happens later in the roomette, from heavy breathing to assassination to psychological insight. The strangers-on-a-train motif can lead to interactions delightful or dreadful. In the second category, few stories are more wrenching than Thomas Wolfe's novella, *I Have a Thing to Tell You* (Entry 941). This 1937 account of a Jewish man attempting to escape Germany by train before the onset of World War II, and his observation by an American writer, is a chilling piece that highlights the common powerlessness of witnesses to terrible events to alter the events' course. "Road-Side Story" (Entry 696), an anonymously-published 1866 work, brings strangers together in a train station in a powerful shared moment of grief over the ruin brought by the Civil War. From explorations of intensely personal experience, such as Jean Toomer's hard-hitting psychological tale, "Love on a Train" (Entry 839), to work that places its characters in the swirl of great historical events—and that sometimes leaves them utterly isolated, surrounded by strangers with whom they simply *cannot* connect— the strangers-on-a-train motif serves diverse authors faithfully and productively.

Black Americans and the Railroad

Discussion of the portrayal of black Americans in this fiction also can benefit from some historical background for context. Black railroaders were effectively barred from all but servile or non-supervisory positions until late in the 20th century. Those who think of the struggle for civil rights today as long and agreeably-settled—if only malcontents and entitlement-seekers would acknowledge the fact—may wish to reflect on the persistent exclusion of blacks from the circles of railroad command. As recently as the 1960s and early 1970s, "all of the industry's top positions requiring authority or involving supervision of other workers—such as conductors and engineers—remained completely closed to all blacks, regardless of their experience, skill, or seniority."[41]

Black laborers, however, had long been numerous in fireman and brakeman positions, in which they tended to work longer hours for lower pay than their white counterparts. Consider, for example, the black fireman who voted the Socialist ticket in 1932 (Entry 101). Black railroaders not only acquired a reputation as efficient, hardworking, and cheap, but as tools useful to management to thwart white organizing. The prospect of being discharged and replaced by black workers willing to do the job for less money could prove an effective deterrent to white trainmen considering a strike.[42] In the 19th century and beyond, white trainmen sabotaged their own economic interests by not setting aside their notions of racial superiority in favor of recognizing their common cause with black workers. The major railroad brotherhoods organized in the 19th century included the Brotherhood of Locomotive Engineers, the Brotherhood of Locomotive Firemen and Enginemen, the Order of Railway Conductors of America, and the Brotherhood of Railroad Trainmen. In their formal membership rules, these organizations denied entry to non-white workers even into the 1960s. Eugene V. Debs's objections notwithstanding, the more left-leaning American Railway Union also denied membership to blacks at its formation in 1893.[43]

Violence against black trainmen was not unknown, nor was physical reprisal against white trainmen who were willing to work with blacks. Today, opponents of affirmative action habitually characterize any organizational target for a number of black employees or students as a "quota," but there was no ambiguity about quotas in American railroading in the first half of the 20th century: White unions secured from management formal limits on the numbers and percentages of black workers who could be hired.[44]

The most prominent railroading position for black workers was that of the Pullman porter. George Pullman's Pullman Palace Car Company built Pullman cars and leased them to American railroads. On a long-distance trip, railroaders transferred occupied Pullman cars from one train to another, so that passengers who could afford the service could make their trips without the inconvenience of changing trains. For close to a century, Pullman porters—sometimes referred to, with patronizing familiarity, as "George," after Pullman himself—worked hard, long hours to assure the railroad's white clientele an agreeable journey. Pullman made sure that his porters performed according to high standards: The company ran a school for porters in a sidetracked car in Chicago.

In his illuminating book, *Miles of Smiles, Years of Struggle*, Jack Santino observes that many black men regarded the Pullman Company as one of their few options for a respectable career; Pullman, meanwhile, "seemed to think that former slaves would more readily perform the often distasteful chores such as cleaning cuspidors, or at least be less likely to balk at them."[45]

Requirements of servility for Pullman porter work squared up neatly with prevailing white perceptions of black workers' natural abilities, if not their natural obligations. Santino interviewed many former porters, including those old enough to have had parents who had been slaves. He contends that the "peculiar institution" underlies everything about the way porters felt about their service: "the tips they earned, the conductors they worked for, and the abuse they took."[46]

By the 1920s, the Pullman Company had more black workers on its payroll than any other private employer in the United States.[47] American blacks wrested a degree of dignity from the life of slavery,

even while they lived in bondage; their innate human resilience also enabled them to make more of the servant's life as a porter than one might expect. Santino's interviews make clear that in spite of the humble nature of the work, the men who performed it approached it, as a rule, with dignity and pride.

In the fiction of the railroad, black characters, aside from their appearance in the work of black writers, are seldom present. When they are present, it is almost always in the background, and they are almost always portrayed as racist caricatures. This treatment is so much the rule that when a writer departs from it, the departure is both bracing and surprising. Such treatment appears in some unexpected places, such as the mystery *Trouble Follows Me*, by Kenneth Millar [Ross Macdonald], in which the porter is reading a copy of the *Atlantic* (Entry 557). Fiction by white writers that recognizes the fundamental humanity of its black characters is the exception well into the 20th century. That a magazine like *Esquire*, with its ambitions to literary respectability, could shamelessly refer to a "nigger" in a story title's subheading in 1934 (Entry 652) is hard to fathom. Could not the editors of a magazine that published Hemingway and Fitzgerald have been alert enough to recognize how out-of-bounds that term was, outside the context of the story itself? Apparently not. It is not without irony that Hemingway himself wrote a story, "The Porter," in which a porter befriends a young boy on a train trip (Entry 347). The boy is, to be sure, not free of racist orientation: He refers to the porter as a "nigger." But the porter's understanding of the world is too deep to let a child's indoctrination dissuade him from a very human relationship with the boy.

Esquire did not lack company in racist bad taste. In Octavus Roy Cohen's collection of stories about the porter Epic Peters

(Entry 164), Peters employs ridiculous, faux-black dialect, replete with "comical" malapropisms. The book's cover bears the caricature of a black man with exaggerated "black" features reminiscent of minstrel show make-up. Black railroaders and other black characters in railroad settings are routinely characterized, in both pulp and mainstream fiction, as slow, dull, lazy, easily frightened, and childlike. These characterizations could have come straight from the pages of antebellum pro-slavery novels. That they are so commonplace in popular fiction, and more common than one would hope in literary fiction, further reminds the reader of the deep entrenchment of racist psychology in the American mind. There is simply no escaping it, on the railroad or anywhere else. Many white writers are, to be sure, well aware of this fact. In Flannery O'Connor's powerful story, "The Artificial Nigger" (Entry 602), for example, a train ride provides the vehicle for a child's tutelage in racist "understanding."

As one might expect, the most interesting fiction concerning black railroad workers, or blacks involved with the railroad, comes from black writers themselves. Of the many fine stories by black writers noted in this bibliography, James A. McPherson's "A Solo Song: For Doc" (Entry 547) is memorable for its portrayal of an aging black dining car waiter; other stories by black writers also achieve excellent effects. Among them, Langston Hughes's "Fine Accommodations" (Entry 392) shows a porter obtaining penetrating insight about an affluent black passenger; Richard Wright's "Big Boy Leaves Home" (Entry 955) juxtaposes the suggestive sound of a distant train whistle with the ghastly aftermath of a swimming outing gone horribly wrong; and in Ralph Ellison's deeply humane "I Did Not Learn Their Names" (Entry 251), a young black drifter interacts in positive ways with white characters also on the tramp.

The above areas are but a few of those worthy of exploration in the fiction of the railroad; this bibliography's subject index will help readers identify others. Among the most promising for investigation are the interactions of children with the railroad; minority groups (not only African-Americans, but Chinese, Irish, Scandinavian, and others); the deep psychological connection between the railroad and death; family relations and the railroad; small-town America and the railroad; and the evolution of passenger experiences on American railroads.

Notes

1. Frank P. Donovan, Jr., *Harry Bedwell: Last of the Great Railroad Storytellers* (Minneapolis, MN: Ross & Haines, 1959), 13.
2. Freeman Hubbard, "The Railroad Heritage: 73 Years of Publishing History: Part Three," *Railfan & Railroad* 3 (July 1980): 24.
3. Leo Marx, *The Machine in the Garden: Technology and the Pastoral Ideal in America* (New York: Oxford University Press, 1964), 191.
4. John R. Stilgoe, *Metropolitan Corridor: Railroads and the American Scene* (New Haven, CT: Yale University Press, 1983).
5. James A. Ward, *Railroads and the Character of America, 1820–1887* (Knoxville: University of Tennessee Press, 1986).
6. D.J. Smith, "The Glamor of the Glittering Rails," *Midwest Quarterly* 11 (Spring 1970): 311.
7. Smith, "Glamor," 311.
8. Smith, "Glamor," 325.
9. Nicholas Daly, "Railway Novels: Sensation Fiction and the Modernization of the Senses," *ELH* 66 (Summer 1999), 463.
10. Harriet Beecher Stowe, *The Chimney-Corner* (1868; reprint, Boston: Houghton, Mifflin, 1884), 149–150.
11. Frank P. Donovan, Jr., *The Railroad in Literature: A Brief Survey of Railroad Fiction, Poetry, Songs, Biography, Essays, Travel and Drama in the English Language.* Boston: Railway & Locomotive Historical Society, Inc., Baker Library, Harvard Business School, 1940.
12. Donovan, *Harry Bedwell*, 87.
13. *Workin' on the Railroad: Reminiscences from the Age of Steam*, edited with commentary by Richard Reinhardt (Palo Alto: American West, 1970), 16.
14. *Workin' on the Railroad*, 16–17.
15. *Workin' on the Railroad*, 18.
16. Patricia Lucille Berger Porcello, "The Railroad

in American Literature: Poetry, Folk Song, and the Novel" (Ph.D. diss., University of Michigan, 1968), 224.

17. Porcello, 224.

18. D.J. Smith, "The American Railroad Novel," *The Markham Review* 3 (Oct. 1972), 61– 62.

19. *Statistical Abstract of the United States, 1906* (Washington: Government Printing Office, 1907), 589.

20. *Workin' on the Railroad*, 19.

21. Dee Brown, *Hear That Lonesome Whistle Blow: Railroads in the West* (New York: Holt, Rinehart & Winston, 1977), 171.

22. James H. Ducker, *Men of the Steel Rails: Workers on the Atchison, Topeka & Santa Fe Railroad, 1869–1900* (Lincoln and London: University of Nebraska Press, 1983), 55.

23. John F. Stover, *American Railroads*, 2d ed. (Chicago & London: University of Chicago Press, 1997), 141.

24. Walter Licht, *Working for the Railroad: The Organization of Work in the Nineteenth Century* (Princeton, NJ: Princeton University Press, 1983), 188.

25. Stover, 142.

26. Milton Meltzer, *Bread—and Roses: The Struggle of American Labor, 1865–1915* (New York: Knopf, 1967), 85–94.

27. Meltzer, 148–159.

28. Smith, "American Railroad Novel," 65.

29. Railroad Museum of Pennsylvania: Women Railroaders. Retrieved Feb. 15, 2005 from *http://www.rrmuseumpa.org/index.shtml*

30. Janet F. Davidson. "Women and the Railroad: The Gendering of Work During the First World War Era, 1917–1920" (Ph.D. diss., University of Delaware, 1999), 23.

31. Todd Depastino, *Citizen Hobo: How a Century of Homelessness Shaped America* (Chicago and London: University of Chicago Press, 2003), 194.

32. Depastino, 66.

33. Depastino, 66.

34. Jack London, *The Road* (1907; reprint, Santa Barbara, CA: Peregrine, 1970), 152.

35. London, 24.

36. Harry Bedwell, "Wanderlust," 1939, reprint, *Railroad Magazine* 100 (June, 1976): 38.

37. London, 197.

38. Jack Kerouac, "The Vanishing American Hobo," in *Lonesome Traveler* (New York, Toronto, and London: McGraw-Hill, 1960), 176.

39 Depastino, 69.

40. Kerouac, 173–174.

41. Eric Arnesen, *Brotherhoods of Color: Black Railroad Workers and the Struggle for Equality* (Cambridge, MA, and London: Harvard University Press, 2001), 40.

42. Arnesen, 25.

43. Arnesen, 28–29.

44. Arnesen, 39.

45. Jack Santino, *Miles of Smiles, Years of Struggle: Stories of Black Pullman Porters* (Urbana and Chicago: University of Illinois Press, 1989), 7.

46. Santino, 9.

47. Santino, 8.

THE BIBLIOGRAPHY

1. Adair, Ward W. *The Lure of the Iron Trail.* New York: Association Press, 1912. 201p.

This short-story collection is a product of the International Committee of Young Men's Christian Associations. In a typical tale, Tom Keenan, a "rough-and-ready, red-blooded young rascal, care-free, indifferent, and absolutely fearless" (17), joins the Morris & Essex Railroad in New Jersey in 1854. He begins work as a wood-passer, handing firewood up to the fireman, and quickly moves into an engineer's seat. Keenan falls prey to the lure of drink, and is expelled on that account from the Brotherhood of Locomotive Engineers. His dissipation ends with his becoming a Christian, "a sort of railroad evangelist," preaching the Gospel along the Lackawanna Railroad, demonstrating "the power of a regenerated and transformed life" (38).

In "The Plain, Heroic Breed," a Christian engineer rescues a child standing on the tracks before the oncoming train—"a steed of iron plunging through the gloom—a little child on the threshold of that mysterious realm we call Eternity" (77). In "Roundhouse Tom," the title character, drunk as usual, stumbles into a mission where prayerful intervention salvages his sinful hide. A fireman with a gambling addiction in "Beating the Wheel" sees the light when he attends a YMCA railroad men's conference in Fort Wayne, Indiana.

2. Adams, Clifton. *Concannon.* Garden City, NY: Doubleday, 1972. 183p.

In this Western, set chiefly in Oklahoma City in the later 19th century, railroad agent Marcus Concannon is on a quest to recover $100,000 stolen from a special Santa Fe Railroad express shipment, and to prove that his friend, Ray Allard, who rode shotgun on the victimized shipment, had nothing to do with the theft. Aside from providing the mechanical underpinnings of the plot, the railroad is not much evident here. The novel is, however, creditably gritty, and Concannon is a serviceable main character.

3. Adams, Moses [George W. Bagby]. *What I Did with My Fifty Millions.* Philadelphia: Lippincott, 1874. 128p.

Available at *Wright American Fiction*: http://www.letrs.indiana.edu/web/w/wright2/

The delusionally-rich purported narrator, Virginian Moses Adams—employed as a hoop-pole splitter in a barrel factory—describes in this funny satire how he plans to invest his imagined loot. Among his projects he considers constructing a public edifice "which should in some faint measure approximate the only really grand, substantial, and tasteful structures of which the city could boast during the last quarter of the nineteenth century. I mean the railroad depots" (52). Although he buys a depot property, he quickly abandons his thoughts of station construction. The typical depot is simply too "unique, stately, and wonderful" (53); furthermore, the railroad track has been removed from his property. He builds a hotel instead. Author Bagby has sometimes been referred to as the Mark Twain of Virginia, and served as Virginia's state librarian from 1870 to 1878.

4. Adams, Samuel H. *The Harvey Girls.* New York: Random House, 1942. 327p.

In this historical novel, three young women of different backgrounds and a common desire to escape them become Harvey

25

Girls. Alma Seelye, Hazel Biggs, and Deborah Rapalje are instructed in the precision service required in Fred Harvey's railroad eateries: "Everything on the tables must be just so: the cutlery set at the precise angle, the plates equidistant from the edge, varying by not so much as a sixteenth of an inch.... All must be perfect; a frayed napkin, spotted cloth, or nicked saucer was anathema, to be visited with dire rebuke, should it be discovered by one of the constantly traveling officials of the company on inspection" (34–35). (Compare this approach with that of the service inspector in James A. McPherson's "A Solo Song: For Doc," Entry 547). With their colleagues, the young women sleep in a Harvey dormitory, and follow strict, convent-like rules of behavior. The quasi-mother superior, Miss Bliss, forbids the girls to go out on the streets after dark. Life as a Harvey Girl is not without its difficulties; Deb, for example, dies nobly—if absurdly—in a cattle stampede. The novel, set in "Mountain Territory" in the town of Sandrock, in the 1890s, is a reasonable effort to place the experiences of the Harvey Girls in an entertaining fictional context. The 1946 Judy Garland film based on the novel (and with the same title) included the song "On the Atchison, Topeka, and the Santa Fe." For an historical treatment, see Judi Morris's *The Harvey Girls: The Women Who Civilized the West* (New York: Walker and Co., 1994).

5. _____. "President and Passenger." *Colliers* 52 (Oct. 11, 1913): 5–6+.

The author presents this story as a compilation of actual occurrences on various railroad lines, which, if they were to occur on a single system, would leave it "cosmic dust." P.D.B. ("Public be Damned") Pitkin, head of The Old Time and Stand Pat Railroad Company, agrees to accompany on a trip of discovery a Mr. Peeples, a man who claims he can show Pitkin why his railroad suffers such a poor reputation among its passengers. Peeples disguises Pitkin, and takes him for a ride on his own railroad, "where everything is up to date except the service" (6).

Pitkin finds, as an ordinary passenger, that his road offers a menu of indolent, sour clerks, crowded cars, absurd rules, careless baggage handlers, and unreasonable schedules. "For three days of short-haul misery they ricocheted over the roller-coaster roadbed of the Original Branch. They waited in ineffably dreary stations for trains almost invariably late. They rode upon coaches which should have been retired in the '80s; and in sleepers without berth lights, or decent sanitation, and with windows hermetically sealed: and once they sat hungry for three hours beyond breakfast time because the dining car superintendent didn't choose to open his car" (27).

Pitkin, like Ebenezer Scrooge, sees the errors of his management ways, and vows nevermore to lose touch with the people—thanks to Peeples.

6. _____. *Success*. Boston, New York: Houghton Mifflin, 1921. 553p.

Errol Banneker is the young agent at the railroad station in the remote Southwestern village of Manzanita. He amuses himself by studying the Sears-Roebuck catalog during quiet stretches on the job. As the novel opens, he gives tobacco and salve to a pair of hoboes, and watches a train roar past the station. He wonders if such a train would "ever bear him away to unknown, undreamed enchantments" (9). Shortly after it passes him, the train suffers a wreck, with multiple fatalities; when Banneker reaches it, bodies lie in grotesque positions alongside the track. Banneker's formal report on the wreck leads to his accepting a newspaper job in New York City. The young station agent, who habitually had sought positions in isolated places, to be alone with his thoughts and his reading (the Sears catalog is not his only literary pastime) leaves the railroad behind, and embarks on a career in the thick of humanity.

7. Alden, William L. "A Ghost Train." *Idler Magazine* 8 (1895–96): 556–562.

The Jericho station-master assures his friend the narrator that "every railroad man knows that ghost trains are liable to be met with almost any night" (556). The station-master relates a suitably spooky story about his boarding such a train one winter night, unaware of its other-worldly nature.

8. _____. "Waiting for the Train." *Idler Magazine* 4 (1893–94): 643–651.

The narrator complains about the haphazard schedules American railroads keep. He describes his irritating wait at the little station of Jericho, Montana. The fat station-master attempts to entertain him, while he waits, with a story of local interest concerning "the row the Baptists had between the preacher and the choir" (644). A mildly amusing tale.

9. Algren, Nelson. "Kewpie Doll." In *The Texas Stories of Nelson Algren*, 31–34. Austin: University of Texas Press, 1995.

Algren describes a 1920 incident in which word reaches the narrator's small town that a coal train will soon come through, and stop for water. The narrator, like the rest of the village boys, exults at the chance to pilfer coal from the train. This is a poor town, and by February, when the incident takes place, families go to bed in the cold after supper from lack of fuel for their stoves. When the Santa Fe Railroad train comes in, pulling two cars of coal, the boys leap aboard and fill their sacks with coal— "almost enough to last us till March" (34). The story's title refers to a Mexican girl's headless doll, which the girl pushes to the scene of the coal theft in a little buggy. The day ends tragically, as the little girl dies attempting to gather coal from the train. "This was all fourteen years ago," concludes the narrator, "but things down here are about the same; rooftops still get white of a morning, and the children still go for coal" (34). The story is an effective portrait of fatalism, in which the railroad is an instrument of both joy and grief, and is altogether indifferent to either of its effects.

10. _____. "Lest the Traplock Click." In *The Texas Stories of Nelson Algren*, 1–14. Austin: University of Texas Press, 1995. First published in the Texas literary magazine *Calithump*.

More an interesting exercise than a successful story, this effort relates the college boy Jonathan's experiences as a vagabond by rail. Following an encounter in a boxcar with a hobo who warns him against becoming trapped in a refrigerator car, Jonathan soon does the obvious, and becomes trapped in a refrigerator car where the cold deranges him.

The story ends on a cozy note, with Jonathan back home in his room, thinking about writing. Algren here has not yet fully developed his literary identification with the down and out; Jonathan's contempt for the hobo in the boxcar is not in keeping with Algren's later sensibilities. Had Algren written the story later in his career, he may have shown a more sympathetic bond between Jonathan and the older hobo, as fellow penniless wanderers, grabbing free rides on a freight. Nevertheless, the business of being caught in a freezing car is persuasive.

11. Allen, Jeffery R. *Rails Under My Back*. New York: Farrar, Straus & Giroux, 2000. 563p.

This hefty, frequently impressionistic saga of African-American life—focusing on brothers John and Lucifer Jones and their wives, Gracie and Sheila—features frequent travels by elevated train, subway, and intercity train, with some good stretches in a railroad vein. Gracie, fresh in Chicago from the Deep South, receives a detailed introduction to the city's complex rail system: "She stared out the green-flying window as a lens, clicking mental photographs at rows of shops and stores exposed to merciless morning sunlight, at streets boiling with life and trouble..." (89). Late in the novel, Lucifer thinks of New York City as "the City of Trains," and develops a tactic to seize a prized seat on entering a subway car, where "you had to box out the other passengers, the same way you boxed out another basketball player to snatch a rebound" (410). The prose is dense and demanding and the plot fragmented, but the book contains abundant imaginative passages, many with rail imagery.

12. Allen, Stephanie. "Passage." In *A Place Between Stations*, 90–105. Columbia, MO, and London: University of Missouri Press, 2003.

"The thing with trains was, one always came eventually" (92). Thelma Stewart finds this thought comforting on the days when she walks from her home to Grand Central Station, where memories of her late husband, Earl, engulf her. Earl was a section gang laborer when the two married; his old coworkers remember him well, and, one day, annoy Mrs. Stewart with their reminiscences when they find her in the station. Earl liked to treat Thelma to solo train rides: He bought her tickets, and she rode, becoming an experienced rail passenger. Thelma thought she would not miss her train rides when Earl left the railroad, but she was wrong.

She decides that the railroad should plant a tree next to the station to commemorate an heroic act that Earl once performed. She persuades the railroad to humor her desire, but even at the moment of its fulfillment, anticipated unhappiness shadows her satisfaction. Mrs. Stewart, one suspects, is succumbing to a fear that the past was not as she would like to believe.

13. _____. "A Place Between Stations." In *A Place Between Stations*, 159–167. Columbia, MO, and London: University of Missouri Press, 2003. *Water-Stone* 1 (Fall 1998): 13–23.

The narrator, an African-American businessman well into middle age, knows that his wife is feeling bereft, and is sick of his daily commute from Grand Central Station to New Haven. He cannot, however, imagine a life without his commute. On the ride in this story, he misplaces his pass; he reflects on the proper way to look out train windows (not steadily, but, when one does it from time to time, openly, to absorb the possibilities of even banal views). His memories stirred by another passenger, he thinks of his grown, distant children. He finds in his briefcase a photo, placed there by his wife, of himself as a boy, just before the train halts at a station he does not recognize.

Everything imaginable is wrong with this man's personal life, except for the fact that he still cares enough about others to try to be nice to them, and to ruminate on lost chances to connect with them. His commute appears to be the only reliable presence in his existence. It is not much to count on, however: It is unaware of him.

14. Anderson, Edward. *Hungry Men*. Garden City, NY: Doubleday, Doran, 1935. 275p.

Hungry Men presents the Depression-era wanderings of men down on their luck, looking for work wherever they can find it. Significant portions of the action take place on freight trains the men ride from town to town—from New York to Chicago to New Orleans—as they pursue rumored work or run from trouble. Always on the lookout for yard bulls and the police, the hungry men form quick, loose alliances with one another as they struggle to survive in a nation that prefers to not recognize their existence.

Anderson describes men like the main character, "Acel Stecker, with lusterless, blood-veined eyes to which the cinders and dirt of freight-train travel still clung" (1, 2). Acel, 25, is a musician who hangs on with gigs ranging from playing trumpet in the street for change to work as a deckhand on a ship.

Acel and a companion talk about young women who wave to them from passing cars, but they know that if they said anything to one of them on the street, she would call the police. "I've thought about it when I was on a freight train," says Acel, "and some girl would wave at you from a Packard. They'll flirt and wave at you like you were somebody they knew as long as there is plenty of distance between you" (57).

No one wants the hoboes around. On the run from trouble in New York City stemming from his involvement in labor activism, Acel drops off a freight train at a depot in a jerkwater town. "Hitch hikers keep hiking," reads a nearby sign. Later a policeman, who has at least enough consideration to give Acel directions to the Salvation Army, complains about "paying taxes every year just to feed birds like you…. You birds don't have any business leaving where you come from" (176).

Acel reflects to himself in bitter irony on the policeman's attitude: "This is fun, runnin' around looking for a place to flop. I don't want to work. Me, want to work? It's too much fun running around from town to town and seeing the country from nice freight trains. It's the bums' fault. A bum shouldn't be running around the country without money" (176).

According to a brief preface, author Anderson himself had spent time on the bum, traveling the country by riding the rails, sleeping in

"Hoover hotels" (abandoned buildings). His experience accounts for the believable details of his account of Acel's travels. At one point, Acel sits in a box car, rain driving against the car. He rewraps a sack of tobacco and matches in waxed bread paper, and places it carefully inside his shirt, then feels over his watch pocket to make sure he still has a quarter he had obtained. When he and two companions get off the train at a town, they debate whether they would be less likely to be harassed by the authorities if they walked on the main street straight through town, or if they skirted the town's perimeter. Acel says that he always walks through a town as though he owned it. These observations belong to a writer who has known the life he describes. So does his later passage depicting Acel climbing onto yet another train, in a pouring rain, facing six hours lying on top of the car in the downpour on the way to New Orleans. "This is pretty tough," thinks Acel, "but it isn't like that train I held down up in Minnesota that February.... This wasn't anything to compare with that" (205–206).

Anderson exhibits a strong sympathy for socialist ideals, but soft-pedals them a bit— perhaps from anxiety that an enthusiastic endorsement for them would lead to bad reviews? In any case, his assurances that America isn't going to "turn Socialist" are not what leave the lingering flavor of *Hungry Men*. That flavor is what comes from seeing destitute, ordinary men struggle for survival in a society that blames them for their own unhappy circumstances.

15. Anderson, Sherwood. "Departure." In *Winesburg, Ohio*, 299–303. 1919. Reprint, New York: Modern Library, 1947.

In the last story in Anderson's timeless depiction of small-town Midwestern life, young George Willard boards the train early one spring morning to go to the city, where his life as an adult will begin. Everyone on the platform shakes his hand and wishes him well. Conductor Tom Little, who knows the people along the railroad intimately, "had seen a thousand George Willards go out of their towns to the city" (302). Aboard the train, George counts his money, and worries about appearing

naïve—although the term that comes to him is "green." He thinks not of the great adventure on which he is embarking, but of small things associated with his hometown. He sits back in his seat, his eyes closed, recalling these details; when he finally looks out the window, Winesburg has disappeared into the distance, and the past.

George, a reporter for the town paper, is a critical character in the stories that compose the book; his connections with the townspeople help Anderson to reveal them. George's departure from Winesburg, as Conductor Little's observations suggest, is emblematic of a fundamental American rite, the deliberately-chosen transition from innocence to experience.

16. _____. "Queer." In *Winesburg, Ohio*, 228–243. 1919. Reprint, New York: Modern Library, 1947. *Seven Arts* 1 (Dec. 1916): 97–108.

This disquieting tale concerns young Elmer Cowley, who works in a Winesburg store that his father runs. Elmer is troubled by the notion, apparently accurate, that he and his family are "queer," misfits in the town. Elmer focuses on George Willard as the embodiment of Winesburg's disdain for the Cowley family's queerness, even though the two men do not know each other. One night Elmer summons George to the train station, planning to lay out the facts—whatever they may be— for George before boarding the train for Cleveland. Elmer fancies that in Cleveland, he will be like everyone else.

George gladly comes to the station, believing that Elmer has some news of interest. When Elmer tries to speak to George on the platform, he can utter nothing but incoherent nonsense. Enraged at his own inarticulateness, Elmer pummels George as the outbound train gets under way. He leaves George half-conscious on the platform, and leaps aboard the train, where he takes refuge on a flat car from which he looks back with pride to see the fallen reporter. "I guess I showed him I ain't so queer," cries Elmer (243).

The pathology of Elmer's departure by train from Winesburg stands in sharp contrast to George's subsequent leaving, described in the entry above.

17. Appel, Benjamin. "Excursion into Dimension." In *Selected Short Stories of Today*, edited by Dorothy Scarborough, 265–278. New York: Farrar & Rinehart, 1935. *The Outlander*, no. 3 (Summer 1933): 1–10.

A group of men brought together by chance jabbers inanely as their train, the Continental Limited, heads west across the Great Plains. A student, a leather merchant, a cement salesman and the rest suddenly enter—what? Another dimension? A parallel world? A vacuum? Their coach seems to be off on its own, disconnected not only from the train, but also from the world as they know it. Anxiety and consternation ensue. The whole experience—"Time and the world loom up out of the annihilations" (278)—recalls the portentous and, one suspects, largely vacuous "light show" experience of the astronaut in Stanley Kubrick's *2001: A Space Odyssey*. At any rate, the travelers do return to the train they apparently left behind. Spectacularly overwrought, the story spares few metaphors for the train, lurid or otherwise: "This bolted Frankenstein, this mighty organism of speed with guts stronger than coal, mocks the passengers" (269). (Yes, the bolts were in the monster, not in Dr. Frankenstein, but why quibble?) "The locomotive tore into time's flank, gobbling up miles; a quaint brute; of the genii; what else'd eat the leagues and hours?" (269).

18. Aurthur, Robert A. "Incident on a Chinese Train." *New Yorker* 24 (April 24, 1948): 28–31.

In pre-revolutionary China, U.S. Marine Lt. John Brock rides a crowded train toward his base in the hills. The train carries a load of food for the Marine camp. A major gives Brock a place to sleep in his car: "Wouldn't want you to ride up with the gooks," says the major (28). The train passes through the hills, where Chinese Communists hide. It is not the Communists, but starving Chinese Nationalists who block the train and demand food. The major intends to resist, but relents and allows the Chinese soldiers to take the food. A shocking denouement to the food heist leads the major, who seemed so callous with his references to "gooks" and "chinks," to reveal his humanity,

and his despair. "We don't give one good God damn," he says in the end (31), and this announcement implies a moral judgment far more sweeping than the immediate incident requires.

19. Baber, Asa. "Last Train to Limbo." In *Tranquility Base, and Other Stories*, 88–94. Canton, NY: Fiction International, 1979.

Avery, an accountant, is riding the train to Penn Station meditating on the aftermath of a political assassination—apparently Robert Kennedy's. Avery is preoccupied with himself, more concerned about his reaction to the shooting than with the shooting itself. As he ponders, the train stops—unaccountably—"hanging in limbo over the New Jersey flatland" (91). As the story closes, the train seems very much in limbo and insulated from the world—rather like Avery.

Bagby, George W. *see* **Adams, Moses**

20. Baldwin, James. *Tell Me How Long the Train's Been Gone*. New York: Dial, 1968. 484p.

Leo Proudhammer discovers subways as a 10-year-old in New York City. He sneaks under the turnstile and pretends to be in the charge of one adult or another; he sits on the train, relishing its speed, watching the other passengers and enjoying the fascinating panoply of black life on the train. He learns quickly the racial demarcations of the city as revealed by the subway population: "I very soon realized that after the train had passed a certain point, going uptown or downtown, all the colored people disappeared," leaving him terrified of what the white passengers might do to him (34). Leo's solitary adventures on the subway, described in a few pages of the novel, are symptomatic of his quest to assert himself, to find direction and objective in his life. When Leo one day becomes lost on the subway, he appeals for help to the first black man he sees; the man treats Leo with respect, and demands that he tell him where he is going. The implication concerns far more than Leo's immediate, prosaic objective of going home to Harlem.

21. Baldwin, William. "The Last Man Aboard." *Ellery Queen's Mystery Magazine* 43 (Feb. 1964): 117–124.

As the electric commuter train from Danton, Conn., to Grand Central Station crosses a highway bridge one morning, a body plummets from the train to the road below. The deceased is a corporate executive, W. John Dunn, often referred to as "the last man aboard the Club Car" (119). The club car is accessible by membership only, and Dunn, the reader learns, had a very jealous rival for membership in that exclusive company.

22. Ballas, Jack. *Iron Horse Warrior.* New York: Berkley, 1996. 280p.

Anyone who despairs that the old-time pulp fictioneer is eternally cursed to wander homeless can take some comfort in mass-market paperbacks like this one, in which Chance Tenery, a West-Point educated engineer, takes a job with the Union Pacific Railroad while hunting his brother's killer. The story is set in the late 1860s in the wide-open end-of-track towns in the West, where the only real law is what the railroad itself enforces. In his supervision of UP bridge and trestle construction, Tenery battles Indians, bad weather, thugs, and crooks—and occasionally his own loyal men. He's the sort of two-fisted boss who wins his men's respect by licking the toughest among them in a bare-knuckle brawl, and then laughing about it with the beaten man afterward.

Ballas has written prolifically in the Western genre, and within the narrow scope of his turf, he is a capable teller of action tales featuring morally upright, hard-nosed heroes. He does enough historical research, including of a railroad sort here, to place his characters in a convincing context. If these characters are basically stereotypes, they are sufficiently well-crafted, and the story moves along at such a pace that—as with the author's pulp magazine progenitors—it is easy to ignore the lack of depth.

23. Bangs, John Kendrick. "The Baron as a Runner." In *Mr. Munchausen: Being a True Account of Some of His Recent Adventures,* 116–128. Boston: Noyes, Platt, 1901.

Baron Munchausen, a man given to embroidery of the truth, arrives late for an appointment one day, and explains his tardiness with a preposterous tale of a runaway locomotive. It seems that the engineer, after starting the train, drifted back to the smoking car to light his pipe. As he tended his tobacco needs, the pin linking the engine with the train broke, and the engine bolted at a furious pace. The fireman couldn't stop it, for "it wouldn't be his place to do it, and these railway fellows are queer about that sort of thing…. The engineers would go out upon a strike if the railroad were to permit a stoker to manage the engine, and besides that the stoker wouldn't undertake to do it at a stoker's wages…" (124). Baron Munchausen saves the day through fantastic exertions.

24. Banks, Russell. "Searching for Survivors (II)." In *Searching for Survivors,* 121–153. Brooklyn: Fiction Collective, 1975.

Narrator Reed describes the effects of his younger brother Allen's death on himself, his mother, their estranged father, and their siblings—the "survivors." Allen, at 17, was a rail fan with an encyclopedic knowledge of railroading. He had hopped a freight to visit a friend in San Francisco; the train was demolished in a mud slide near Santa Barbara. The story concludes with Reed surveying the site of the train wreck after searching cursorily—but with evident success—for signs confirming Allen's presence on the train. "It looked like a place where a war had been lost" (153). At one point in the story, which Reed relates out of chronological order, he drives to Boston's South Station to pick up Allen, who is to arrive on a train. Reed remembers how busy the station was many years earlier; now, in "the cathedral-like interior space of the station" (129) he wonders for a time if it is even operating. A surly ticket agent affirms the station's functional, if debased, status.

25. Banning, Margaret C. "Between Trains." *Ladies' Home Journal* 59 (Sept. 1942): 18–19+.

Subtitled "A man, a girl and a snowstorm—and seven hours to live a lifetime."

Sam Chandler is taking the train to Chicago, where he will have a seven-hour layover before catching his train for the West Coast, to report for naval duty. Aboard the train he meets Griselda, a young woman who, like Sam, is fresh from attending a friend's wedding. At the station, the two join for a day of companionship while a snowstorm rages in the city. This is reasonably standard romantic magazine fare, but the background specter of the war gives it an edge that it would otherwise lack. Saying goodbye at the train station, Sam says, "You'll marry me if I come back?" Griselda answers, "When you come back" (79).

26. Barbara [Wright, Mabel Osgood]. "The Stalled Train." In *The Open Window: Tales of the Months*, 26–66. New York: Macmillan, 1908.

The decaying former factory site of Hattertown breathes new life when the Sky Line Railroad builds a branch line through it and opens a station. Conductor Jim Bradley, who makes regular trips to New York, seems a traveled, worldly man to Miranda Banks, the town's young schoolteacher. All that blocks a budding romance between the two is religion: Bradley is a Catholic, Miranda a Congregationalist. A wreck on the line one February night bridges their conflicting faiths, and serves as a catalyst for the enlightenment of another couple mired in self-centered squabbling.

27. Barr, Robert. "Held Up." *McClure's Magazine* 2 (Feb. 1894): 308–312.

The narrator relates an account told by Tompkins, the railway manager, of a train holdup in a wild part of North Carolina a few days before Christmas. The train included the manager's private, sumptuously-appointed car, and an express car carrying a large sum of cash. In a remote locale, a group of mountain-men stop the train by piling debris on the track. The manager's first assumption is that the men are after the cash; he learns that their real objective is to right a wrong involving a two-dollar bottle of Kentucky whisky.

28. _____. *The Speculations of John Steele*. New York: F.A. Stokes, 1905. 308p.

John Steele, an obscure station master in the hamlet of Hitchens Siding, gamely prevents a train wreck as the novel opens. He wins promotion to assistant in the division superintendent's office in Grand Union Station in Warmington City; the station is "adorned by a massive corner tower holding aloft a great clock that gives the city standard time" (7). Steele rises rapidly in railroading, but loses a fortune in railroad stock in a financial panic. He sojourns in Europe, and on his return to the states resumes his wheeler-dealering—and, at length, shifts "from a career of usefulness into the predatory class" (137). In his commercial predations Steele leaves the railroad behind and moves on to wheat, sugar beets, and further financial debacle.

This wooden tale cloaks an admiration for unfettered dealmaking in the mantle of a cautionary tone.

29. Bartlett, Napier. "The Homeward Journey: A Romance of the Last Days of the War." In *Stories of the Crescent City*, 59–66. New Orleans: Steel & Company's Job Print, 1869.

Available at *Wright American Fiction*: http://www.letrs.indiana.edu/web/w/wright2/

In the last month of the Civil War, two Confederate soldiers, Wheelhanney and Corsely, obtain furloughs to go south. They take a crowded train to Richmond, the Confederate capital, and leave on another train for the deeper South. They become acquainted with a young woman and her invalid mother, and Corsely offers to provide the two women guidance to Georgia.

On the third night out from Richmond, mechanical trouble stops the train in a desolate village. Some of the passengers flock into a decrepit, cold hotel. The rest mill about outside, around a fire built with wood intended for locomotives. During the delay, the old woman dies, after begging Corsely to look after her daughter, Danie. Corsely becomes romantically besotted with Danie as the train chugs through Georgia. By story's end, they have been married—on the train—and Corsely, who has spent his last dollar to assure Danie's safety, discovers that she possesses substantial financial assets. Corsely is thus rewarded for his noble efforts, while his companion, the less noble Wheelhanney, enjoys a less happy fate.

This awkwardly-written story is of interest for its depiction of Southern rail travel in the chaos of the Civil War's end, and for its use of the train as a rolling marriage chapel.

30. Baylor, Frances C. "An Incident of English Railway Travel." In *A Shocking Example, and Other Stories*, 224–239. Philadelphia: Lippincott, 1889.

A young Scotswoman, on an emergency train trip in England, shares a compartment with a man who forces her to cut off his hair, dresses as a cleric, and enlists her aid in eluding his pursuers. Six months later the young woman receives a grateful letter from the fellow, from Plattstown, Colorado. Her kind intervention in the fugitive's flight has set him on course to a good, moral life in the United States.

31. _____. "The Lost Voice." In *A Shocking Example, and Other Stories*, 108–122. Philadelphia: Lippincott, 1889.

Three stout, elderly women arrive at the Slumborough station for the mid-day train, always a major event in the sleepy town's life. One of the three, Miss Roberta, is going to Ohio. With the energetic assistance of their African-American 12-year-old girl carriage driver, they pack off Miss Roberta. She "whirls along at the local rate of speed," which pace "allows the curious traveler to look about him just as if he were walking without the fatigue of that exercise" (112). Miss Roberta, a confirmed stay-at-home, finds the journey exhilarating, although she frets that she will get off at the wrong station, or fall afoul of some worldly evil. The worst that occurs to her is the astonishing incivility of her fellow passengers: typical Ohioans! They refuse to acknowledge her requests and comments, and ignore her so studiously that she begins to fear she has lost her voice. She has not, but there is an explanation for her curious experience. A funny story in which the rudeness Miss Roberta attributes to others is pale compared to her own.

32. Beach, Rex. *The Iron Trail: An Alaskan Romance*. New York: A.L. Burt, 1913. 391p.

Alaskan Murray O'Neill, builder of the famous North Pass & Yukon Railway, is strong, sympathetic, and courageous. He has come to King Phillip Sound ostensibly to pursue coal, in an area where several railroads are under development. Soon O'Neil is in the thick of railroad building in the forbidding northern wilderness, planning to sell his partially-completed road to a competitor. Complications and predictable resolutions follow. This Western potboiler with an Alaskan setting and a love interest spends less time than one might expect on railroads, and offers little in the way of insight, intentional or otherwise. A handful of nice lines turns up, however, such as this one: "He's smarter than us, and if he wasn't handicapped by a total lack of decency, he'd beat us" (282).

33. Beachy, Stephen. "Train." *Chicago Review* 46, no. 1 (2000): 39–46.

Beth, a 12-year-old girl, receives a letter summoning her to see her twin sister, up to this point merely a product of the girl's imagination. She embarks on a fantastic, surrealistic journey, taking a train into the jungle in some foreign land. Her situation takes an unpleasant turn; later, when the family doctor examines Beth, he suggests that on her next trip she should make sure that there is a conductor aboard. The reader may feel free to make of it what he or she will.

34. Beason, Doug. "Determinism and the Martian War, with Relativistic Corrections." In *War of the Worlds: Global Dispatches*, edited by Kevin J. Anderson, 115–132. New York: Bantam, 1996.

A Martian invasion of earth finds young Albert Einstein caught in an Italian train wreck. As he hurtles across the compartment to crash into the wall, Einstein quickly considers the physics of the experience. He awakens a hundred meters from the wreck, smoke rising from the jumbled cars. Einstein's friend, Marcel Grossman, tends him. As the train burns, threatening to ignite a car full of oil, a Martian lurks in the distance, firing a heat ray at the wreck victims. Einstein serves heroically in fending off the alien, and proceeds to an astonishing adventure. Wholly ridiculous, but funny.

35. Beaumont, Charles. "The Train." In *Midnight Specials: An Anthology for Train Buffs and Suspense Aficionados*, edited by Bill Pronzini, 202–212. Indianapolis: Bobbs-Merrill, 1977. Also in Beaumont's *The Hunger, and Other Stories*. New York: Putnam, 1957.

Beaumont, who contributed some fine scripts to the original *Twilight Zone* television series, tells this tale from the point of view of Neely, a 10-year-old boy for whom "the Train" represents far more than an impressive means of getting from one place to another. For Neely, the Train constitutes a separate world, a place where the dreary intrusions and confusions of the adult domain slip away. The story opens with Neely waiting for his mother to reach a sound sleep in their berth, so that he can slide from the berth and explore the train alone, with the wish that this time he will be able to stay in the world of the Train. Neely walks from car to car—and very nearly achieves his wish. "The Train" is an effective glimpse into the imagination and anxieties of a bright, sensitive child for whom the escape from everyday tedium that a passenger train offers becomes a disturbing moment at the doorway of utter loneliness.

36. Beck, Warren. "The Far Whistle." In *The Far Whistle, and Other Stories*, 3–20. Yellow Springs, Ohio: Antioch Press, 1951.

An old, stooped man runs a miniature steam locomotive in an amusement park. The old engineer conducts himself with gravity, although with an attitude that one would not mistake for customer-friendly. The narrator takes his son to the park to celebrate the boy's 11th birthday, with the highlight to be a nighttime ride on the little train. That night, a young, indifferent operator is in the old man's place. In a conversation with the miniature railroad's owner, the narrator learns that the old man was a farmer who always wanted to be a railroad engineer. "He never got over it, neither, wanting to be a railroader.... Seems like ever time he hear a train whistle in the distance, he'd jump like something had touched him sudden on the shoulder ... and he'd turn his head and listen, like a bird dog pointing, if

he could hear the sound of her running" (13, 14). The owner considers firing the old man for his surly manner with customers, but a combination of business sense—the old man takes meticulous care of the engine—and sentiment leads him in another direction. "Ever time I look at the old guy pottering around with that-there oilcan," says the owner, "I say to myself there's one man got it" (19, 20).

37. Bedwell, Harry. "Against Orders." *Railroad Magazine* 65 (Sept. 1954): 16–18+. *Railroad Magazine* 92 (Jan. 1973): 39–45.

Boomer telegraph operator Eddie Sand reunites with his old buddy, trainman Hi Wheeler, when he returns to the Colorado high country and an operator's job in Aspen. Eddie is delighted to learn that the dispatcher is also an old acquaintance, Walt Harmon. All might be well if not for the self-important conductor, "Gallopin'" Gunderson, so-dubbed for his habit of riding roughshod over everyone. Gunderson immediately dislikes Eddie, who refuses to be pushed around. A winter storm traps a special train, under Gunderson's authority, carrying a group of schoolteachers. Wheeler's heroics and Eddie's adept telegraphy rescue the teachers. The best aspect of the story is Bedwell's depiction of the warm camaraderie among Eddie, Wheeler, and Harmon.

38. _____. "Avalanche Warning." *Saturday Evening Post* 229 (May 11, 1957): 30–31+.

When Clinker Ward of the Monte Short Line must report for a physical exam owing to some apparent health problems, the slick and calculating Latimer is appointed temporary trainmaster. A generally unpleasant sort, Latimer bears a special grudge against young brakeman Gene Houghton. Latimer leads a crew out on a plow train, in a gathering mountain blizzard. The hard work grows harder under Latimer's self-important, uninformed direction. At a critical point, Latimer's subordinates turn on him, and assume command of the train, high and snow-bound, and threatened by burial in an avalanche. This was the last of Bedwell's stories for the *Post*; he died in 1955.

39. _____. "Back in Circulation."
Railroad Magazine 28 (Sept. 1940):
88–109.

Recently-married boomer Eddie Sand has
been working at Moss Point, Michigan. He has
grown restless with his routine. When a letter
arrives from an old friend urging him to come
to Los Angeles to work on the Pacific Electric
Railway, Eddie cannot resist, and his wife, Bernice, does not object. On the way to L.A.,
Eddie takes an operator's job at a station in
the Colorado Desert. The lonely position suits
Eddie, who is a compulsive reader who prefers
quiet. The only cloud on the scene forms
around young Madge Slocum, section boss
Gandy Slocum's attractive, and carefully
guarded, daughter. The story narrows its focus
to Eddie's involvement in a romance between
Madge and a young fireman. After a comical,
if not ridiculous, resolution of the young couple's problems, Eddie Sand decides to move on
to Los Angeles, and to send for Bernice: "The
boomer op was back in circulation" (109).

40. _____. *The Boomer: A Story of the
Rails.* New York and Toronto: Farrar &
Rinehart, 1942. 318p.

Boomer telegraph operator Eddie Sand
takes a job at the Cinder Patch, a forsaken
desert station where time got lost, "except as an
item that dealt with train schedules. Otherwise, it stood still and listless in a hot vacuum"
(20).

"The minimum requirement for a boomer
on the drift was a good blue suit, in definite repair and press, ample eating money and a
proper shave and hair cut at all times. Otherwise, you were likely to be shunned as a tramp.
It was a proud craft" (49). Eddie is tempted to
settle down with a sympathetic woman, but
the lure of the road is powerful, however lonely
the life could be with no familiar faces or
friendly greetings. Eddie's only real constants
are his wanderlust and an ever-present book
that he reads at slack times.

Eddie's first crisis at the Patch comes
when the night man cracks up, and deliberately sends a train ahead to pitch off a ruined
bridge. The novel then follows Eddie in
episodic fashion from job to job, from one part
of the country to another. He contends with

men and nature, with an empty emotional spot
that only a woman could fill, and with his own
restless heart. The end contains an effective
passage in which Eddie is on the road again:
"The air from the open window leaned against
his face. He felt good" (316).

The Boomer, Bedwell's only published
book, has its share of melodrama, but the portrait of Eddie Sand as a man loose in the world,
shy of entanglements, fearful of stasis, and very
good at his work, is convincing. Although a
drifter and something of a railroad cowboy,
Eddie is an appealing character, respected by
his peers and his superiors even if they cannot
fathom his disinclination to linger long enough
to put down roots.

41. _____. "Campbell's Wedding
Race." *Railroad Magazine* 70 (June
1959): 54–60. *Railroad Man's Magazine*
10 (Oct. 1909): 10–19.

This story's chief distinction is that it was
Bedwell's first railroad fiction. Locomotive engineer Bruce Campbell is due in Junction City,
100 miles away, at 8 P.M. for his wedding to
Nellie McDonald. The question of the moment: how to get there on time. Campbell
takes an extra freight on a run to Junction City,
and gives his fellow trainmen a hair-raising
ride. Through one delay after another, including a derailment, Campbell reaches Junction
City with minutes to spare.

42. _____. "The Careless Road." *Railroad Magazine* 25 (Feb. 1939): 32–61.
Railroad Magazine 69 (June 1958):
48–61.

Having left Chicago, Eddie Sand has
caught on as an operator at the Auburn station,
somewhere on the plains. The station agent's
daughter, Janet Madden, praises dispatcher
Curt Halman's telegraphy; Eddie considers
Halman inept. While on the job, Eddie helps
Eldon Gilroy, a tyro operator, overcome his
clumsiness and lack of confidence. A crisis involving Halman's work forces Eddie to take
emergency action.

The story's title refers to Eddie's un-
quenchable desire to move on: "It was a powerful pull, when it hit, that desire to drift down
the careless road. It tightened, and you were

miserable till you were on the way again. You weren't fit to live with till that highway was under your feet. But it could be a lonely road, with no familiar faces and no hand raised in greeting" (49–50).

The story offers interesting observations from one who knows the turf on the characteristics of a seasoned telegrapher: "A fine and exciting game it was to keep the traffic rolling" (37). Any reader interested in the psychological details of railroad telegraphy will find this story compelling, once the obligatory romantic subplot gets out of the way. The story could never break into the pages of a mainstream magazine like the *Saturday Evening Post*, owing to its intensely-detailed account of telegraph operations. It is that very detail that helps make the story interesting and perfectly suited to a niche-focused publication like *Railroad Magazine*.

At the same time as the story's technical detail satisfies rail fans, its human appeal—in its passages dealing with Eddie's wanderlust—should strike a resonant chord among general readers. One can readily compare Eddie's point of view with sentiments expressed by Jack London in his nonfiction treatment of the hobo's life in *The Road*, and with Jack Kerouac's notions of the footloose existence in many of his works. In this respect, Bedwell's Eddie Sand stories fit firmly into one important tributary of American literary experience. Bedwell is not a writer without limitations or freedom from inane convention—his forays into romantic matters range from awkward to embarrassing—but when he stays with what he knows, he can be very good at it.

43. _____. "Christmas Comes to the Prairie Central." *Railroad Magazine* 33 (Jan. 1943): 48–72. Reprinted as "Railroaders Don't Celebrate." *Railroad Magazine* 70 (Dec. 1958): 50–63.

Eddie Sand is working on the troubled Prairie Central on Christmas Eve. To a railroader, Christmas "merely means more grief handling people and packages.... Railroaders didn't celebrate. They just fixed it so that everybody else could enjoy themselves" (49). This Christmas is especially glum, with the P.C. anticipating a buy-out by the Big Six

Lines, with widespread layoffs to follow. The railroaders' one hope is that S.A.M. Nickerson, of the Anaconda Short Line, buys the P.C. first, and makes it a connecting link with the A.S.L. On this particular night, the workers are contending with a derailment, a heavy snowstorm, a special train that they fear delaying, and a division superintendent, Donby, whose anxiety obstructs his native good sense. Eddie's cool performance is instrumental in making the holiday a good one for the P.C. crew.

44. _____. "Desert Job." *Railroad Magazine* 37 (May 1945): 90–118; 38 (June 1945): 86–115.

Eddie Sand comes out of retirement to take a desert job near an Army training base, at the station of Gravity. He has been away from the railroad for some time, but has answered the call for experienced manpower "to keep the vast, grim traffic rolling" in the war effort (92). Eddie worked at Gravity as a young man; now the desert seems even larger and more ominous than it did then. The railroad now relies chiefly on orders via telephone, rather than telegraph, and Eddie has trouble adapting to the new approach. His tentative grip on procedures is a nice indication of his humanity: He is bright and capable, but not perfect. His first day on the job yields a succession of awkward actions. At the end of his shift, Eddie realizes that the young Mexican woman who follows him at the desk does the job better than he. In spite of his feelings of superannuation, Eddie shows—when a sandstorm knocks out telephone service—that the techniques of the boomer op's glory days still have their value in railroading.

In one nice passage, the little-used telegraph comes alive, and Eddie listens to all the old-timers on the road, trading stories and jokes in Morse: "It was consoling to the veterans that they could shut themselves into a world of code and converse privately with their own kind in a language those others couldn't follow" (113–114).

45. _____. "The Ham." *Railroad Magazine* 25 (May 1939): 17–24. Reprinted as "Night Operator." *Railroad Magazine* 68 (Aug. 1957): 66–70.

Edgar Foote, a night operator at Woodburn, a small station on the Desert Division, is a "ham," an awkward telegrapher who can barely handle 20 words per minute. Dispatchers dread working with him, but because his mother owns a large portion of the railroad, Edgar is fire-proof: They can't get rid of him. His Woodburn post is so slow that Edgar's major challenge is staying awake through his shift. He meets the challenge poorly, with bad consequences for the esteem in which his superiors hold him. In hopes of persuading Edgar to quit, they assign him to the Sandstorm station, the most desolate, parched, monotonous point on the road. In the climax to this funny tall tale of ineptitude, Edgar precipitates a derailment that sends a sheep-laden freight roaring across the desert sand, straight into the station. Edgar at last finds motivation to seek a new life elsewhere.

46. _____. "Imperial Pass." *Saturday Evening Post* (Jan. 13, 1934):16–17+. *Railroad Magazine* 101 (Feb. 1977): 34–41.

Conductor Cole directs his freight extra on the Anaconda Short Line onto a siding to make way for a passenger train coming up from behind, near Imperial Pass. Up ahead, laborers work to unload a work train before the passenger train arrives. All goes not well: A carelessly-handled flatcar loaded with rails breaks loose, and begins careening downhill. The deadly runaway passes Cole, who watches helplessly as it speeds on toward the oncoming passenger train. In a post-wreck hearing, Cole's courage comes into unjust question, with the assumption broached that Cole could have prevented the wreck had he thought of anything but his own skin. No honest man's reputation can go unredeemed in such a story; Cole's subsequent heroics show that a lack of bravery is not his problem.

47. _____. "In Search of the Sun." *Railroad Magazine* 25 (Jan. 1939): 33–47. *Railroad Magazine* 69 (April 1958): 52–60.

Eddie Sand leaves behind the cold, wet Midwestern spring for the Southwest, where he finds his old pal Hi Wheeler about to get married, and working as a conductor. Both men dislike Hi's new trainmaster, Keeley, who has his job thanks to nepotism, and shows no hint of humanity. Hi invites Eddie to ride on his freight, preparatory to serving as best man at Hi's wedding, but Eddie must ride in the "zulu" car—a car carrying animals. There Eddie reads a book by candlelight. By story's end, Eddie has helped Hi get his train through—with the help of livestock from the zulu car—and in the process they succeed in putting Keeley in his proper place.

48. _____. "Jawbone." *Railroad Magazine* 44 (Nov. 1947): 40–65. Reprinted as "Delay at Mesquite." *Railroad Magazine* 70 (Feb. 1959): 50–59.

Eddie Sand is working at the Gravity station, reading a history of transportation and putting up with a martinet of a trainmaster, Stanley. Stanley was promoted during the war, and feels compelled to show what a fine decision that was. The critical incident here is Eddie's halting the crack passenger train the Silver Arrow at Gravity; he cannot let it proceed until the old engineer Bricks returns with his engine from a water stop up the track. Bricks has made the run for water on verbal ("jawbone"), not written orders—a dubious move—and has been blocked from returning by another train's derailment. The Silver Arrow is packed with influential passengers. Eddie sees that the Silver Arrow moves on, when the time is right, and finds a way to bring humility to Trainmaster Stanley. One character notes Eddie's favorite activity late in the story: "You're always readin' a book.... Ever find out anything from them?" Eddie admits his habit. "Yeah," he says, "you can learn things, and sometimes it comes in handy" (64).

49. _____. "Lantern in His Hand." *Saturday Evening Post* 215 (Jan. 23, 1943): 22–23+. *Railroad Magazine* 101 (Jan. 1977): 20–25.

Boomer brakeman Mel Hatch drifts into the Gloria yard looking for work. The trainmaster dismisses him peremptorily, but Mel's old buddy Bill Lowden, whom he meets in the yard, helps him sign on. The trainmaster has no intention of making life easy for Mel, but a pair of runaway freight cars and an approaching special train, the road's general manager himself at the throttle, give Mel a chance to show his signaling skill with a lantern.

50. _____. "Lassitude and Longitude." *Railroad Magazine* 26 (July 1939): 94–108. Reprinted as "Gods of High Iron." *Railroad Magazine* 69 (Feb. 1958): 52–61.

Eddie Sand almost settles in for the long term as operator in a sleepy Southern town, but the boomer's restless urge strikes again. He comes to rest at a very Western town, Manteca, Texas. There he becomes involved with a bronc-ridin', lasso-throwin' redhead, Calico Kate. Kate informs Eddie that the time has come for him to settle down. At that opinion, Eddie lights out for the Rockies, straight to a job under a difficult superintendent, R.N. Stuben. The railroad gods that Eddie occasionally ponders have an amusing plan for him, involving Stuben, a circus train, and, at the most unlikely moment, Calico Kate.

51. _____. "Mountain Standard Time." *Railroad Magazine* 47 (Jan. 1949): 122–140; 48 (Feb. 1949): 112–129.

Mel Hatch has gone broke investing in a fire extinguisher scheme, and has come to the Rockies to work on the Monte Short Line. He hopes that his old acquaintance, Hank Wheeler, can give him entrée to the boomer fraternity. Nevertheless, he is wary of Hank, who "would take your eye teeth if he needed them—or just for the hell of it" (124). Hank is trying to locate his buddy Eddie Sand, "a rubber-tired pilgrim who moved about like a shadowy myth" (127). In Denver, Hank and Mel spend a long night in a bar, where Mel, his cash gone and his tab rising, pays with his fine railroad watch, receiving $10 and an oversized, ugly pocket watch in change.

With no wandering cash left between them, Mel and Hank must hang on into the winter with the Monte. The work is rugged, and the two see it through a series of adventures, mishaps, and close calls. At one point, Mel's watch serves him in self-defense: He swings it on its chain and strikes a violent hobo in the head, subduing him. The ungainly time-

piece acquires a reputation as bearing the only standard time that exists on the Monte. Alas, the battle with the hobo deranges Mel's watch, and leads to his and Hank's firing. The future looks bleak, but Eddie Sand's arrival late in the story changes the climate for them.

Bedwell's portrait of boomer friendship is enjoyable; the give-and-take among rough but good-natured workingmen is generally believable and entertaining.

52. _____. "Night of Plunder." *Railroad Magazine* 97 (Nov. 1974): 29–36; (Dec. 1974): 38–43. *Saturday Evening Post* 224 (Dec. 22, 1951): 14–15+; (Dec. 29, 1951): 30–31+.

Eddie Sand has been banished to the desert station of Gravity for intemperate remarks to the road's general manager. Nearby, Mexican nationals—illegal immigrants—work on a track construction crew. Bad weather and hoof-and-mouth disease have ruined their farms; "Hungry, hopeless, desperate, some took the long chance, filtering across the border at night.... With a jug of water on a thong, they walked into the terrible blank spaces where death by thirst stalked their dragging steps" (29–30). Eddie is wary of these men, who seem dangerously close to a primitive past. One night the men must work to reinforce a trestle endangered by washout while a luxurious passenger train, the Silver Arrow, waits on one side to cross it, and a freight waits on the other. During the work, a flash flood destroys the trestle and throws several of the freight cars into the torrent. The Mexicans eagerly loot merchandise from shattered cars, while the affluent passengers of the Silver Arrow watch in amusement. The situation deteriorates further, and requires all of Eddie's and his associates' wit and resolve to prevent the night from ending in bloodshed aboard the Silver Arrow.

The story is an interesting example of a writer who seems perplexed about what to make of his subject; it contains a nervous blend of obvious sympathy for the illegal migrants and their desperate condition, with fear and loathing of them at the same time. Several passages contrast the contented self-indulgence of the Silver Arrow passengers with the hopeless poverty of the laborers; as Bedwell puts it, "The

Silver Arrow mocked the slow centuries, the toiling men" (34). (The *Saturday Evening Post* illustrations are not to be missed for their implications of ethnic menace.)

53. _____. "Night Trick at Armadillo." *Railroad Magazine* 70 (April 1959): 60–68. Published as "With His Fingers Crossed." *Railroad Man's Magazine* 11 (March 1910): 237–246.

In this very early Eddie Sand story, the chief dispatcher on the Southwestern learns that operator Sand has been sleeping on duty, from boredom. Rather than firing him, he sends Eddie to a job at Armadillo, a desert mining town. Eddie reaches Armadillo nearly penniless, and hates the place. When a locomotive idles at the station, the crew on a break, Eddie uses a ruse to facilitate absconding with the engine. (Our Eddie, a locomotive thief!) His only ambition is to escape Armadillo. His getaway turns into highly unlikely good fortune for some railroad officials in a bind. This story is short of credible, but the author was young, and Eddie's native wit, so evident in later stories, is on display here. Frank P. Donovan identifies "The Lightning That Was Struck" (*Short Stories*, May 11, 1927) as the first Eddie Sand story, but "Night Trick" antedates that one by nearly 20 years, and probably is the first such story.

54. _____. "Not in the Contract." *Railroad Magazine* 40 (June 1946): 42–65; 40 (July 1946): 110–131. *Railroad Magazine* 93 (May 1973): 44–53; 94 (June 1973): 42–47.

In this story set at the end of World War II, Eddie Sand is working in the busy but dreary desert station, Gravity. Business, including troop trains, has finally abated after a long, intense stretch of work that taxed everyone on the road. Now, in the lull, officials are trying to catch the men in operational rule violations. No one appreciates the effort. Eddie and his dispatcher are at odds over the requirements of his station operator duties. In the story's second installment, a major derailment occurs in the desert, throwing traffic along the road into chaos. The dispatcher orders Eddie to take a motor car out to flag a train. This work is well beyond Eddie's proper assignments—it is "not in the contract"—but the dispatcher appeals astutely to Eddie's pride as a railroader, and Eddie cannot refuse. The story is hampered for lay readers, especially in the first part, by thick railroad jargon.

55. _____. "On the Night Wire." *Railroad Stories* 21 (Jan. 1937): 91–104. *Railroad Magazine* 67 (June 1956): 52–59.

Bill Rudd, a boomer operator cursed by bad luck and mistakes that have cost him several jobs, wanders west to the Anaconda Short Line, high in the mountains, where he takes a job as a night operator. Rumblings of labor trouble are in the area on the ASL, a disorganized, inefficient road, and a saboteur attempts to frame Rudd as an agent of a competing railroad. An incompetent operator, a potential collision, and a fist-fight in the station office blend to change Rudd's luck for the better—professionally and romantically.

56. _____. "Pacific Electric." *Railroad Magazine* 29 (Jan. 1941): 88–113. *Railroad Magazine* 70 (Aug. 1959): 56–64.

Eddie Sand, boomer, hires on with the Pacific Electric Railway in San Bernardino as a relief agent. "San Berdoo" is a busy station; as a relief man, Eddie bounces from station to station—Covina, Glendale, Yorba Linda, Van Nuys, and so on. He finds the electric, or "juice," railroad not much different from the steam roads he knows so well. A spell of ceaseless rain at Christmas knocks out rail service all over the region. Eddie creatively arranges a joint service with the Santa Fe, so that each road can help the other through the bad weather. Things go so well that Eddie passes up a chance to go railroading in British Columbia.

57. _____. "Pass to Seattle." *Saturday Evening Post* 214 (Oct. 4, 1941): 18–19+. *Railroad Magazine* 101 (Nov. 1976): 28–33.

Eddie Sand, second trick operator at the Ledge River station on the Puget Railroad & Navigation Line, annoys "the Old Man"—superintendent O'Conner—with some sound advice on telegraphy. O'Conner sends Sand to

Mammoth Pit, a miserable post, in the first act of a running battle between the easily-provoked O'Conner and the unflappable Sand. In the end, with the customary close calls, Sand convinces O'Conner that his railroading insights are sound, and the super rewards him with a free ride to Seattle.

58. _____. "Priority Special." In *Headlights and Markers: An Anthology of American Railroad Stories*, edited by Frank P. Donovan, Jr., and Robert Selph Henry, 377–406. New York: Creative Age, 1946. Published as a booklet, *Priority Special*. San Francisco: Southern Pacific Co., 1945. *Railroad Magazine* 90 (March 1972): 41–47.

On a train in the U.S. carrying convalescent soldiers wounded in World War II, three especially badly-injured men struggle to bear the jolting and jarring of the coach. Major Laughlin, their commanding officer, finds in Sgt. Ernie Wall a veteran railroader who knows how to help assure a more comfortable trip for the men. Appealing to the concern the railroaders along the line feel for the suffering soldiers leads to the train's designation as a "priority special," with rights to proceed before all other trains, bringing an end to the stop-and-go jolting. Two points stand out in the story: the comical way railroad jargon rolls off Sgt. Wall's tongue, leaving the major baffled; and the effective cooperation of the men and women along miles of railroad, who see that a trip that began roughly for the wounded becomes, if not a pleasure ride, at least not nearly so painful.

59. _____. "Restless Feet." *Railroad Magazine* 32 (Aug. 1942): 52–85. *Railroad Magazine* 69 (Oct. 1958): 50–66.

Eddie, rambling again, reunites with Hiram Wheeler, on the White Water & Central. The job is suitable but for the rigid, suspicious superintendent, J.K. Faber. After Faber foolishly fires veteran engineer Russ Ward, Eddie purchases room and board from Ward and his wife to help the couple. Meanwhile, Hi Wheeler, lovestruck, "borrows" a locomotive to visit a telephone operator, incurring Faber's anger. Eddie's alert actions in a flood enable both Ward and Wheeler to regain their good standing with the railroad, and allow Faber some insight into the necessary flexibility that successful railroading requires.

60. _____. "The Return of Eddie Sand." *Railroad Magazine* 35 (Feb. 1944): 22–43.

In 1941, Eddie has retired from the boomer trail when this story begins, to join his fellow former railroader Walley Sterling on a ranch in the mountains. He and Walley are savoring the serenity of their retreat when the radio brings word of the attack on Pearl Harbor. The next day, Eddie drives into the city and hires on as an operator, with many other old railroaders who have left retirement to help the war effort. Eddie has a Proustian moment when he reports to his new post, the old station at Norwall: "He went inside and met the familiar smells of old dust and musty records that swept him back through the years to the scores of depots he'd served in" (28). Eddie struggles with the pace of war-related business, and with new federal regulations. The major action here involves locating and moving five carloads of cattle feed on Christmas Eve, in a wartime blackout, with the help of an eager but unlikely brakeman.

61. _____. "Screaming Wheels." *Saturday Evening Post* 221 (Feb. 19, 1949): 28–29+. *Railroad Magazine* 101 (March 1977): 27–31.

Early in this story the reader learns the origin of the grudge Latimer bears against young Gene Houghton (see Entry 38). Here the men are running a train pulling a carload of blasting powder just behind another train under Latimer's control. Gene's quiet heroics help prevent a disaster involving sheep and runaway cars.

A passage in this story suggests some of the appeal of this fiction to a certain reader: "Fellows who worked at desks didn't know the feel of night-time in tall country or the delirious smell of hot oil and leaking steam and the shudder of the iron deck as the thundering mogul took hold of the drag and walked it into the grades" (130). They couldn't know it, but, inspired by stories like Bedwell's, they could easily imagine themselves—like James Thurber's Walter Mitty—on that iron deck, running a powerful engine up a mountain grade.

62. _____. "Second-Trick Dispatcher." *Railroad Magazine* 99 (Feb. 1976): 48–55.

A very young Eddie Sand is trying to land a job with the Anaconda Short Line. He feels "deadly" after an accident, but catches on as a second-shift dispatcher. Claire Borden, the strong and competent daughter of an engineer, shows Eddie how to use snowshoes. One day when the two of them come upon a pair of switchmen having a fistfight, the scene moves Eddie to reveal to Claire some of his past. He recounts a near-lethal beating he absorbed from an engineer on the Pennsylvania Railroad, a beating that broke his nerve and sent him to the mountains. Eddie soon acquires a reputation as a coward, but his heady management of a runaway train—with Claire's father in the cab—restores both his self-confidence and his reputation.

63. _____. "Smart Boomer." *Saturday Evening Post* 213 (March 8, 1941): 20–21+. *Railroad Magazine* 90 (Nov. 1971): 58–62. Also in *Short Lines: A Collection of Classic American Railroad Stories*. Edited by Rob Johnson. New York: St. Martin's, 1996.

When Eddie Sand enters the dispatcher's office at Little Grande on the High Desert Division, the chief dispatcher hires him as a telegraph operator. Eddie shows a trait not common to rough and tough railroaders: He reads books. His intolerance of sloth lands him in hot water, and earns him banishment to a remote, forlorn station. There his role in a near-collision leads him to a hearing in the Old Man's office, and to a surprising rapprochement with the railroaders who believed him nothing but a toady to the officials.

Bedwell characterizes his Western railroad men as independent, hostile to authority, but as competent as they feel inclined to be and intensely loyal to each other and to their expertise.

64. _____. "Snow on the High Iron." *Saturday Evening Post* 213 (Dec. 14,

1940): 18–19+. *Railroad Magazine* 101 (Dec. 1976): 34–40.

Engineer Red Kirk worries over doubts expressed about his conduct and courage in a recent accident on Mogul Mountain: "Maybe his nerve wasn't sound. He'd come back to find out" (18). Red is also bedeviled by Annalee, a telegraph operator at the Westwater station: "She seemed too fragile to touch, yet she frequently plagued him into an impulse to spank her" (18). (Really!) A bad snow-slide high up Mogul Mountain catches a hapless train, and Annalee, and gives Red a chance to redeem himself to everyone's satisfaction.

65. _____. "Sun and Silence." *Railroad Magazine* 23 (April 1938): 34–48. *Railroad Magazine* 67 (April 1956): 58–67.

This story serves as the basis for an episode in Bedwell's novel, *The Boomer* (Entry 40). Eddie Sand takes an operator's job at a remote desert station, the Cinder Patch. He finds the other operator at the sun-baked station, Russ Kruger, a bitter man who talks incessantly—mostly to himself. Kruger is long overdue for a transfer from the mind-numbing post, and, his nerves frayed, he attempts a mad act of vengeance on the railroad. Eddie intervenes, prevents catastrophe, and defends Kruger from his boss's anger.

66. _____. "The Third Trick." *Railroad Magazine* 66 (June 1955): 30–31+. *Railroad Magazine* 95 (Nov. 1973): 51–54.

Eddie Sand, working the third shift as dispatcher, "at the pallid end of night when the normal world is abed" (31), has a long night with uncooperative, argumentative engineers, one impatient to complete his run, another who cares little whether he finishes at all. Eddie perseveres in a story not on a par with Bedwell's best.

67. _____. "Thundering Rails." *Saturday Evening Post* 220 (March 27, 1948): 30–31+. *Railroad Magazine* 100 (Sept. 1976): 36–41.

Laid off up north at the end of the harvest season, young Gene Houghton comes to the Gloria yard of the Rocky Mountain Monte Short Line. Within minutes of stepping onto the property, he displays both his brakeman's and his pugilist's skills. The story's title indicates the two-fisted railroading adventure it offers. Although young Gene is a little fella, his shoulders are wide and his heart is strong, and he saves the day. The general manager, "who kept in training by beating up tramps and stray miners" (31), receives his due.

68. _____. "Tower Man." *Railroad Magazine* 29 (May 1941): 92–120. *Railroad Magazine* 70 (Oct. 1959): 54–60.

Eddie Sand is working in Los Angeles on the Pacific Electric Railroad, and growing restive. His nemesis here is Trainmaster Burton, who has a superior attitude and a surplus of ignorance and zeal. Eddie is assigned to the road's interlocking tower in Watts, which handles over 500 trains a day, at a time when the local press is in an uproar over the alleged dangers of the PE's grade crossings. Burton demonstrates abysmal judgment in his dealings with newspaper reporters concerning the grade-crossing issue, and in a crisis Eddie's cool head not only saves the lives of careless motorists, but greatly changes the tone of the PE's press coverage. A highlight of the story, and one that only an experienced electric railroader like Bedwell could present, is an electrical malfunction in Eddie's tower that fries the equipment, and turns its juice on the men who try to quell it. Also of interest is Eddie's relationship with his boss, Supt. O.J. Donaldson, who is unusually candid in his criticism of another railroad official in conversation with his subordinate, Eddie.

69. _____. "Wanderlust." *Railroad Magazine* 100 (June 1976): 34–41. *Railroad Magazine* 68 (April 1957): 56–65. Published as "Official Appreciation." *Railroad Magazine* 26 (Oct. 1939): 52–68.

Eddie Sand has just left the Southwest, and the troublesome redhead Sabrina, for a job in Pennsylvania. He obtains room and board with Cy Irwin, a cheerful fellow operator, and Cy's wife. The couple also work a small farm. The reader senses Eddie's feelings of lack as he observes the young couple in their comfortable home. The Irwins

treated Eddie like a member of the family, but Eddie knew that his wanderlust would call him to the road again. The Irwins' chief problem is Mike Cronin, the impatient dispatcher whose short fuse can cost Cy his job. Eddie intervenes in a crisis to save Cy's position.

The story's conclusion contains perhaps the most complete statement of Eddie's worldview: When asked why a man of his ability doesn't become a company man and climb to a high post, he ponders: "What did he care for climbing? The more you acquired—position, property, babies—the more worries you had. Better move on.... Keep looking for a thing you'll never find.... Eddie Sand, on the boomer trail, was building a mansion for his soul from driftwood scattered along the shores of infinity" (41).

70. _____. "With the Wires Down." *Railroad Magazine* 24 (Oct. 1938): 40–50. *Railroad Magazine* 69 (Dec. 1957): 48–54.

A storm rages at 8,000 feet in the mountains. Eddie Sand is the operator at a station cut off from the rest of the road by downed wires. Unable to know the situation ahead, he refuses to allow a train carrying a group of bankers to proceed. While the train waits out the storm, growing short of food for the passengers and coal to heat the cars, Eddie shows his resourcefulness in preventing the delay from turning into a costly public relations debacle for the railroad.

71. _____. "The Yardmaster's Story." *Railroad Magazine* 26 (Aug. 1939): 82–107. Published as "Yardmaster." *Railroad Magazine* 90 (Jan. 1972): 44–53.

Yardmaster Morgan hires two boomer switchmen, Roach and Sullivan, to work in the demanding Goshen yard, in the mountains. The two men, an oddly matched pair, work hard and well. Another railroader who knew one of them in the past warns Morgan against him, but Morgan ignores the warning, although he senses an inscrutable tension between the two boomers. The story resolves with an explanation of details worthy of the closing pages of a complex mystery. One point worth attention is that of Roach's health: He has TB, and like many others with that disease, came to the mountains hoping that the high altitude, fresh air, and outdoor regimen would relieve his symptoms.

72. Belfer, Lauren. "Trainscapes." In *The Henfield Prize Stories*, edited by John Birmingham, et al., 138–150. New York: Warner, 1992.

Neil, an associate professor of medieval art, has but one true love: his meticulously planned HO railroad layout. The model railroad clearly means more to him than his minimal efforts to go through the motions of trying to secure tenure, or than his hobby of seducing graduate assistants who use him for career advancement. A jarring break in his routine arrives in the form of an ordinary-looking but insightful slide projectionist, apparently the first woman who has ever shown genuine interest in Neil's model railroading.

73. Belland, F.W. *The True Sea: A Novel of the Florida Keys*. New York: Holt, Rinehart & Winston, 1984. 289p.

Set in the Florida Keys, 1909 to 1925, this novel focuses on Arlis, introduced as a 10-year-old. The railroad serves as a partial backdrop for the stories of Arlis and other residents of the island settlement of Doctor's Arm. Arlis believes what he has heard: The coming Miami to Key West Florida East Coast Railroad will be a boon to the community. It starts out with some modest promise: Arlis's father sells liquor to the railroad laborers, a rough bunch of "Yankee trash" (5). The railroad also brings black workers from as far away as New York City. By 1912, when the road is set to make its first 150-mile run across the Keys, everyone in town gathers by the tracks to watch the train get under way: "It was an impossibility that had come true at last" (138). At the festive event, Arlis's father drops dead. The promise of the railroad turns bitter when it refuses to haul the local growers' produce, in favor of more lucrative freight from other sources. The railroad's significance fades as the novel proceeds.

74. Benet, Stephen Vincent. "O'Halloran's Luck." In *Tales Before Midnight*,

51–73. New York and Toronto: Farrar & Rinehart, 1939. Also in Benet's *Twenty-Five Short Stories*. Garden City, NY: Sun Dial Press, 1943.

Tim O'Halloran, like a great many other Irishmen, left his native country to find freedom and easy riches in the United States. What he found was backbreaking labor building the railroads across the West. "And then there was the cholera and the malaria—and the strong man you'd worked on the grade beside, all of a sudden gripping his belly with the fear of death on his face and his shovel falling to the ground" (54). One evening, a drunken O'Halloran saves a leprechaun from the torments of a pair of wolf pups. O'Halloran becomes the leprechaun's protector, and the little man repays him with clever suggestions that help O'Halloran rise quickly in the esteem of his railroad superiors. Thanks to his alliance with Rory the leprechaun, things just get better and better for O'Halloran, and for his family. A light-hearted tale narrated by O'Halloran's grandson.

75. Benson, Ramsey. *Hill Country: The Story of J.J. Hill and the Awakening West*. New York: Frederick A. Stokes, 1928. 356p. *Forum* 79 (March 1928): 351–358, 450–456; (April 1928): 618–631; (May 1928): 776–789; (June 1928): 936–949.

It would be hard to imagine a novel with a title more devoted to a character in which the character is so absent, other than in the effects of his actions. Here James J. Hill's role in "Hill country"—Northern Minnesota—is delineated only through other characters' reactions to and opinions of his enterprises.

The novel opens with a sketch of migrants drawn to the vast plain of Northern Minnesota, partly for the rich land, partly because of the promise of a railroad coming through the area, thanks to James J. Hill. Many of the newcomers—Swedish immigrants—bought land from Hill at low cost, land Hill had acquired indirectly from the government as part of the old St. Paul & Pacific.

Hill makes his influence known in ways both large and small. When a 10-year-old in Gumbo, Minnesota, writes to him pleading for money for her school library, he sends a check for $100. With it he includes a letter praising the Swedes in the region—praise that riles the more settled Yankee residents. He encourages diversified farming; furnishes livestock to the farmers for breeding; but his power inevitably begets suspicion and hostility. Locals blame Hill for high commodity prices and for the apparently exorbitant shipping rates the farmers must pay. Concerns develop over Hill's influence on the legislature, and there is a good deal of to-do about Hill's railroad interests.

Hill is otherwise missing as a character, and, although the author rises (more or less) to the challenging task of portraying Hill without allowing Hill to grace his pages except by implication, the reader may chafe. Waiting for Hill to show up in this novel is like waiting for Godot.

76. Bickham, Jack M. *Dinah, Blow Your Horn*. Garden City, NY: Doubleday, 1979. 201p.

In the late 19th century, Bobby Keller's father, a yardman for the Harristown & Ohio Railroad, lost his right hand in a coupling accident a year before the story opens. At the opening, Bobby and his family are moving to Preacherville. On the same train in which the Kellers reach Preacherville is railroad owner Nathaniel Harris, riding anonymously to evaluate his road's performance. Bobby's mother and father greet Harris with what seems to Bobby an embarrassing display of fawning. Bobby is baffled at his father's gratitude to the railroad for giving him an office job: "It struck me as strange that we should be so almighty thankful to the H & O for keeping my father on the payroll after it had been the H & O that cut off his hand" (10).

Bobby soon learns what it means to be poor, and at the mercy of an organization with little regard for its workers' human rights. Keller joins the Preacherville office during a wildcat strike, and his new boss, Jones, demands servile loyalty to himself and to the road. As Bobby observes the effects of the railroad's decisions, such as raising the prices at its company store, he begins to doubt his father's wisdom in being loyal to the company. As his doubt grows, so does his guilt in the belief that his evolving ideas amount to a betrayal of his father.

Bobby witnesses company thugs attack striking railroaders, clubbing and shooting them, with the cooperation of the Preacherville police. Bobby and his father argue over the battle, his father siding with the railroad's version of events, compliantly related as fact in the local paper; the plot moves on to a satisfying conclusion.

Told entirely from Bobby's point of view, the novel is a compelling story of conflicting and changing allegiances, of corporate villainy and responsibility, and above all of a boy's growing understanding of the complexities of the adult world. It is a succinct, credible, moving, and suspenseful novel.

77. Blackburn, Tom W. "Flatwheel Draws the Line." In *Westerns of the 40's: Classics from the Great Pulps*, edited by Damon Knight, 94–106. New York: Macmillan, 1977. *Dime Western Magazine*, June 1944.

Samuel Smiddy, "president, board of directors, dispatcher, and agent for the one-train, narrow-gauge Fall River line" (95), wants to ship a load of gold bullion to the Denver mint. Flatwheel Clancy, his one engineer aboard the line's engine, *Lucy*, does not want to risk it. A mine cave-in and Flatwheel's heroics in the disaster lead to an amusing climax. Dialog like the following catches well the pulpy tone of the tale: "'You crazy baboon!'" he squawked wildly. 'It ain't enough you've got to try to make this run, but you never covered the tender last night. This wood's wet and won't burn!' Clancy shook his head. 'It ain't me. It's Lucy. She'd burn mush if she wanted. She's miffed. Poor gal, she ain't been treated right!'" (103).

78. _____. "Song of the Steel Rails." In *The Railroaders*, edited by Bill Pronzini and Martin H. Greenberg, 69–80. New York: Fawcett Gold Medal, 1986. *Dime Western Magazine*, 1941 [?].

Longtime engineer Ben Sutton lost a leg in an accident, and has for some time been working as the only operator in an isolated switching tower. On the verge of forced retirement—his nerves are shot—Sutton pulls off an heroic act to save a train and its cargo from a band of robbers. In this pure pulp fiction,

Sutton exemplifies the idealized "pledge of the road" in his determination to see that the train reaches its destination. "It was part of a law by which Ben Sutton had governed his entire life" (76). Sutton's heroism, undertaken with complete disregard for his own safety, further exalts the figure of the old-time railroader as a pillar of courage, integrity, and partaker of derring-do.

79. Blake, Michael. *The Holy Road*. New York: Villard, 2001. 339p.

A sequel to the author's *Dances with Wolves*, this novel concerns the efforts of Plains Indians, especially Comanches, to maintain their way of life in spite of white settlers' and businessmen's relentless advance. The railroad—the white man's "holy road"—stands as a prime symbol of white encroachment on tribal lands. The novel's focus on the railroad is, however, marginal; the chief business is the white effort to drive the Indians onto reservations, and the Indians' efforts to escape regimentation. Chapter 45 does describe a train trip to the East by a dozen Indians, a delegation to Washington, mesmerized and terrified at their first rail journey. They are particularly astounded when the train passes through a mountain tunnel. Historical novels almost always walk an awkward line between didacticism and genuine story-telling; that is true here. When the author tries to enter the worldview of an historical people, the potential pitfalls are numerous. What to make of the Indians' trip to the East? Are their perceptions and reactions to train travel astutely rendered, or are they the not-so-excellent results of a present-day writer whose earnestness exceeds his ability to penetrate the psychology of a vanished culture?

80. Blanchard, G.C. "Ravelwild." In *Metropolitan Tales and Sketches*, 5–22. New York: No publisher, 1873.

Available at *Wright American Fiction*: http://www.letrs.indiana.edu/web/w/wright2/

Ravelwild is a station on the Erie Railroad in a wild and romantic section of New York State. One August day a young usurer, Hardy Cramp, arrives by train and takes a horse from the railroad station to visit Dorrance Cruger. Cramp is about to foreclose on Cruger's farm.

He mocks Cruger, insults his daughter Stella, then hurries back to catch the outbound train. Niger Burse, the station flag-man—who earlier defended Stella from Cramp's advances—watches Cramp leave. Later, Stella observes a group of desperadoes preparing to derail the oncoming express train, to rob the safe it carries. Stella heroically signals the engineer to stop, and on the spot transforms one of the crooks to goodness by her bravery. Stella's valor brings a reward sufficient to fend off the vile Cramp and to save the farm. Sentimental piffle, with the railroad at its center.

81. Bloch, Robert. "That Hell-Bound Train." In *Midnight Specials: An Anthology for Train Buffs and Suspense Aficionados*, edited by Bill Pronzini, 213–230. Indianapolis: Bobbs-Merrill, 1977. Also in *The Fantasy Hall of Fame*. Edited by Robert Silverberg and Martin H. Greenberg. New York: Arbor House, 1983. *Magazine of Fantasy and Science Fiction* 15 (Sept. 1958): 119–130.

Always fond of a clever twist, veteran horror and fantasy writer Bloch delivers a sharp one in this story of Martin, whose father was a railroad man and a drunk. Martin himself is bound for nowhere at the story's outset. His only legacy from his father, aside from a taste for drink, is the old man's favorite tune, "That Hell-Bound Train." Martin meets the conductor of that train, and cuts a deal with him involving a special railroad watch. The deal leads to a very unexpected position for Martin on that Hell-bound train. Although strictly whimsy, the story is entertaining, and won science fiction's Hugo Award in 1959.

82. Blum, Ralph. "On the Night Train to Moscow." *Saturday Evening Post* 237 (May 2, 1964): 38–40.

The American narrator describes the conversation among the passengers in a Russian train compartment on the way from Leningrad to Moscow. The talk turns to deaths suffered in the Great Patriotic War (World War II), particularly the "unaccountable" death of a woman passenger's son. Later, in the corridor, the American and a Russian officer from the compartment smoke and talk as they look out the window. The officer tells the American about the details of the woman's son's death. "When you leave Russia," he says, "you can carry such things with you. There are some feelings, some experiences, it is better to export than to keep at home" (39).

Bodine, Matthias *see* **De Courcy, M.B.**

83. Bond, Nelson. "On Schedule." In *Murder for the Millions*, edited by Frank Owen, 269–272. New York: Frederick Fell, 1946. First published in the *Toronto Star Weekly*, ca. 1939.

Stockbroker Henry Foster plans to murder young Prentiss aboard the club car in the tunnel below the Hudson River on the way into Pennsylvania Station. Prentiss has the goods on Foster's flagrant cooking of the books in the firm. Foster will stab Prentiss in the car's complete darkness, after pulling the switch to extinguish the coach's lights. The result proves a surprise to Foster.

84. Borofka, David. "A Train Heading South." *Gettysburg Review* 10, no.1 (1997): 97–107.

In a story in which objective reality is open to question, pregnant Ariana Lambert boards a train to accompany her mother, who lies in a coffin in the train's last car, to a burial site near Crater Lake. Ariana has never gotten along very well with her mother, and resents having agreed to this journey. That the conductor becomes drunk en route does not improve matters, and all goes to smash when the train crashes and burns two hours south of Eugene. Ariana, hauled from the wreckage, gives birth to a dead daughter in a station wagon near the tracks. That, at least, is how her memory puts it. In her real(?) life, she gives birth to a healthy infant; there has been no train-wreck; and Ariana struggles to understand why she retains the hyper-realistic "memory" of a train ride and disaster that did not occur, with her mother's body incinerated in her coffin in the baggage car. The reader struggles, too, but the food for argument is tasty.

85. Boucher, Anthony. "A Little Honest Stud." In *Masters of Mayhem*, edited by

Edward D. Radin, 202–208. New York: Morrow, 1965. Published as "The Last Hand" in *Ellery Queen's Mystery Magazine* 32 (Sept. 1958): 101–106.

Private eye Fergus O'Breen engages a just-demobilized soldier in conversation aboard the train on the way to Chicago. The soldier, Herb Ellis, is fresh from losing every cent he had in a poker game on the train the previous evening. A shady cardshark named Wentworth fleeced Ellis, but O'Breen promises to win back the young man's money, with a profit besides. In a compartment cramped with gamblers, O'Breen does just that—with a helpful assist from the book of Hoyle.

86. Bowman, Jacob L. *You and Me, or, Sketches for Both of Us.* St. Louis, MO: George Knapp, 1867. 288p.

Available at *Wright American Fiction*: http://www.letrs.indiana.edu/web/w/wright2/

In this miscellany, the chapter "The Railroad 'Ring'" (p. 47–52) is devoted to the "Iron Mountain Railroad Transaction," springing from Missouri's 1866 foreclosure on the Iron Mountain Railroad, and the road's subsequent sale, resale, and reorganization in 1867. The author takes a tongue-in-cheek look at the allegedly easy riches to be had through railroad speculation: "I've struck a good thing and made a pile" (47). "Jumped headlong into the sea of speculation, and came up with a railroad in my mouth" (48). He acknowledges that a pang of conscience strikes occasionally, "But Pshaw! What of that? I am opulent; I am an association—a *Ring*" (49).

87. Boyd, James. "Old Pines." In *Old Pines, and Other Stories*, 3–27. [Chapel Hill]: University of North Carolina Press, 1952. Also in *Short Stories from the Old North State*. Edited by R.G. Walser. [Chapel Hill]: University of North Carolina Press, 1959.

Old Man McDonald, relying on the labor of black workers—black male laborers are "buck niggers" who have "great flat feet" (4)—built a railroad through the Carolina pine forest to the coast, and for many years prospered in the turpentine trade. In time, the turpentine market failed. Dealing with lumbermen, McDonald made his railroad flourish once again by serving companies that leveled the forest. McDonald "failed to see that his fortune was founded on nothing less and nothing more than the ruin of the countryside" (7). With the forest ravaged, the railroad's fortunes sink; nothing remains "except a small traffic in grains and cheap manufactured goods that were carried by a single dingy engine over the crumbling line to the port and the scattered dead hamlets along the way" (9). McDonald now watches a single decrepit train pass his house each day.

The story goes on to show, in a touching manner, the powerful emotional bond McDonald feels for the railroad. In one especially nice passage, he polishes and oils and fires up one of his two old engines, and the link between the man and the machine seems nearly that between two living creatures. The story slips into melodrama in the end, but for its greater part it nicely portrays a true railroader at heart.

88. Boyer, Dennis. *Snow on the Rails: Tales of Heartland Railroading*. Oregon, WI: Badger Books, 2003. 247p.

In this collection, the author aims to portray "the true core of American railroading," "where the urban crossroads of Chicago gives way to the Great Lakes, the Northwoods, and the Great Plains..." (10). Boyer, a former carman with the Milwaukee Road, fashions a well-written group of 14 pieces that, although presented in short-story form, often read like factual, personal narratives. They include such efforts as the title story, "Snow on the Rails," an account of the narrator's life as a yardworker on the Milwaukee Road. The story sets the tone for the book with its gritty but good-natured portrait of the railroaders and their work, and the sudden dangers of a railroad yard. There is nothing sentimental here; the emphasis is on realism, from the nude calendars in the yard shack to the slow decline in the railroad's fortunes during the narrator's tenure.

Other effective pieces include the meditations of a young tower operator ("Tower Time") who prevents an accident, even while a brakeman obscenely excoriates his ability; a Norwegian immigrant responding to an appeal for workers in "North Country Ties," and "Paint Shop Girl," with the narrator the first woman—a socialist organizer—to work in the Milwaukee Road's paint shop. She notes that the shop's old-timers have little use for women, blacks, Mexicans, Indians, or "hippy potheads" (88). "Ice Box" is the story of a black dining car staffer who started work in the 1930s. "The railroads expected more of us in the dining car than any other group of employees. We had to be spotless, in white uniforms, shined shoes, and clean shaven and hair trimmed down to the fuzz" (141).

Boyer clearly listened carefully to the men and women he met while he worked as a railroader; their voices come through authentically and persuasively, and Boyer shows a nice ability to see from perspectives of a variety of people whose backgrounds are very different from his own.

89. Boyle, Kay. "Army of Occupation." In *Nothing Ever Breaks Except the Heart*, 322–338. New York: Doubleday, 1966. Also in Boyle's *Fifty Stories*. New York: Doubleday, 1980. *New Yorker* 23 (June 7, 1947): 29–34.

A young woman war correspondent boards a train in Paris taking American occupation troops back to Germany. She is traveling to rejoin her husband, a newspaperman. The train is rowdy, full of singing, sentimentally inebriated servicemen. The young woman is situated in a compartment with a number of drunken soldiers, who threaten to assault her. At a critical point a young corporal enters the compartment; his arrival prevents the assault, but the story continues with shocking violence. The story's tension is terrible, as is the sense of claustrophobia and danger in the compartment. The various characters, including the young woman, are all suffering from the effects of the war—but some suffer more gracefully than others.

90. Bracker, R. McQ. "The Noon Train." *Woman's Home Companion* 49 (Aug. 1922): 7–8+.

The noon train, a short local, smells of

bananas, chocolate cake, and sheepherders. "Clouds of dust, mingled with generous quantities of coal smoke and cinders, swirled through the coaches and coated the red plush seats with a layer of grime" (7). The noon train leaves heroine Fonnie at the platform in Idaho Center, Idaho. "Damn!" says Fonnie, with the liberated disgust of a 1920s woman. The train has deposited her in a wasteland. Just out of college, Fonnie has come west to teach English. Before long, the noon train also delivers to Idaho Center Fonnie's imperious mother, perturbed by Fonnie's career ambitions, and Fonnie's tedious fiancé, Richard. There is no need to dwell on the resolution, but it involves Fonnie's happy romantic life—and the noon train.

91. Bradbury, Ray. "The Town Where No One Got Off." In *Twice Twenty-Two*, 279–287. Garden City, NY: Doubleday, 1966. Also in Bradbury's *A Medicine for Melancholy*. Garden City, NY: Doubleday, 1959. *Ellery Queen's Mystery Magazine* 32 (Oct. 1958): 108–114.

A salesman taking the train from Chicago to Los Angeles yields to an impulse to get off at a little town, Rampart Junction, Iowa. Convinced that there is something to see in this isolated, unvisited village, he tramps the few streets for hours, seeing nothing. What he finally discovers comes from within himself, in a confrontation with an old man who saw him get off the train. The old man sits in his customary chair tilted against the railroad station wall when the narrator's train leaves town; "He was gazing east along the empty rails where tomorrow or the next day or the day after the day after that, a train, some train, any train, might slow, might stop.... He looked a hundred years old" (287). The old man, it turns out, schemes to kill a stranger who gets off the train; the salesman deterred him with a clever ruse.

92. Bradford, Roark. *John Henry*. New York: Literary Guild, 1931. 225p.

The author no doubt meant well; he obviously *likes* the folk giant John Henry, and intends to present him heroically. Nevertheless, the legendary black laborer deserves better than this painful biography melding a number of Henry stories into a whole. The book does feature some railroad exploits—John Henry helping to build the Yellow Dog Railroad through the Mississippi Delta; singing the blues on the Red Ball freight out of New Orleans; and taking a turn at firing a locomotive—but Roark, a white author from Mississippi, presents his black characters in such a patronizing fashion, in such broad and ultimately racist caricature, that the reader cringes through the book from start to finish.

93. Brady, Jasper E. "The Chief Train-despatcher's Story." *McClure's Magazine* 13, no. 3 (July 1899): 220–224.

The chief dispatcher, Martin N. Bates, relates various tales of his office, involving nepotism with disastrous consequences, dispatchers literally asleep at the switch, a convict operator—and, of most interest, a woman, Miss Ellen Ross, whom Bates hires as his first female employee. Although she is a competent operator, a careless moment on her part forces Bates to discipline her, and more severely than he had disciplined a male operator for a like infraction. Of her punishment, Miss Ross asks, "Are you not doing it just because I am a woman?" (224). Bates relents, and soon Miss Ross is Mrs. Bates.

94. _____. *Tales of the Telegraph: The Story of a Telegrapher's Life and Adventures in Railroad Commercial and Military Work*. New York: Doubleday & McClure, 1899. 272p.

In this apparently autobiographical work residing under a thin veneer of fiction, Brady recognizes that passengers aboard sumptuous trains annihilating space at an astonishing 60 miles an hour have no idea how important telegraphers are to their happy travel experience. Here his narrator, Bates, sets out to remedy the public's ignorance of the profession of the brass key. Bates describes starting work in Kansas City, MO, for less than $40 a month. Although he faces holdups and wrecks, it seems that each disaster leads to his accepting a promotion. He becomes a boomer operator, knocking around the country; has a little dustup with marauding Indians in Arizona; and meets a woman operator, Mary Marsh, who saves a train from catastrophe—although when she realizes her success, "womanlike—she fainted" (32). Bates pictures himself as capable of anything: In a trainmen's strike, he takes out an engine himself—never mind his inexperience as an engineer.

Bates leaves railroad work for an unsatisfying commercial stint, then returns to the rails with ambitions to become a dispatcher. The public may praise the engineer and conductor, "but the brains of the machine ... are all incorporated in the dispatcher on duty" (112). Brady pays close attention to physical details of the dispatcher's office, and to the routines of the dispatcher's workday, including dealing with railroad bureaucracy and personnel management.

Bates abandons the railroad for military service when a good section of the book remains, but the author's portrait of the telegrapher's work of the era, although not fine fiction, is interesting and readable.

95. Braun, Lilian Jackson. *The Cat Who Blew the Whistle.* New York: Putnam, 1995. 240p.

The novel opens with a special excursion run headed by the fully-restored locomotive, Old No. 9, with octogenarian Ozzie Penn at the throttle. The Lumbertown Credit Union is in a spot of bother: The authorities have closed it, following the disappearance of several million dollars, as well as of its president and secretary. The president, Floyd Trevelyan, also owns Old No. 9, and the government will most likely seize it, rendering its initial special run its last special run. An interview with Ozzie Penn, at the Railroad Retirement Center in Mudville, plays a part of some importance late in the book; Penn impresses as a believable character whose pride in his career is not matched by his satisfaction in his personal life. Penn has a surprise up his sleeve for everyone regarding Old No. 9, but an even bigger surprise involving the refurbished locomotive occurs a short time later. The incident is memorialized in a neo-folk tune (lyrics in full on pages 234–236), "The Wreck of Old No. 9." The song isn't bad; neither is the book, which

features Koko the Siamese cat, demonstrating better detection skills than his human companions.

96. Bretherton, Vivien R. *The Rock and the Wind.* New York: E.P. Dutton, 1942. 618p.

Any reader seeking an expansive historical romance and family-cum-industrial saga should enjoy this massive tale of railroad building in the Northwest. The bulk (and bulky it is) of the story concerns Breck Farridon's devotion to railroad construction, beginning with hostilities between his West Willamette Company and villain Jay Suttle's Oregon and California Company. To settle their battle for a land grant, they race to see which outfit can first complete 20 miles of track south from Portland, Oregon. Suttle stops at nothing—not bribery, murder, or sabotage—but his own ruthlessness drives him out of the railroading picture in Oregon. Farridon takes work with Henry Burke, the moving force of the Northern Pacific Railroad; by 1883, Burke oversees the spanning by rail of the nation's northern tier.

Of some interest is the author's portrayal of the Chinese workers who loyally dedicate themselves to Farridon. They are "both cheap and tireless" (305). "Behind the curtains of their eyes their Oriental minds hid thoughts no Occidental could follow. But in their simple dignity they command ... respect" (306). The Chinese fare ill when Suttle hires a gang of toughs to intimidate them.

As much as the novel is an account of railroad building, it is even more the story of Trudy Farridon, Breck's wife, a strong, resilient woman. The perspective is chiefly hers, over the decades. It is she who turns the first shovelful of dirt on the old West Willamette. Cautionary note: The author's determined hewing to the track of high moral tone is suggested in her heroine's most vivid expletive: "Fiddlesticks!"

97. Broder, Bill. "We Have Got Done Praying!" In *The Sacred Hoop: A Cycle of Earth Tales,* 217–228. San Francisco: Sierra Club, 1979.

Hung Jin, a young Chinese, comes to

California in the 19th century to search for the remains of his father, who died in the Sierras while working on the transcontinental railroad. When Hung Jin, a new railroad laborer himself, reaches the place where his father died, he kneels, "taking a handful of crushed ballast in his hands and letting it trickle to the earth. He passed his hand over the ties, the cold metal of the rail, thinking that he could feel his father's touch on these objects" (220). Hung Jin adapts quickly to his work on tunnel no. 6, although the capriciousness of nature appears in an avalanche that kills a dozen of Hung Jin's fellow workers.

Hung Jin does not locate his father's remains, but one day prepares a grave where he buries bones he has gathered to represent his father. It is a moving private rite, later echoed by Hung Jin's attendance at the ceremony in Utah, where the Central Pacific and Union Pacific tracks join.

The author clearly researched the details of this story well, but does not allow mere fact to bind the essential poetry of the tale. Following the story are several photos and other illustrations of work on the transcontinental railroad. (The title refers to a sentence tapped out by the telegrapher at the celebration of the transcontinental's completion.)

98. Browder, Catherine. "The Missing Day." In *Secret Lives*, 124–136. Dallas: Southern Methodist University Press, 2003. *New Letters* 52 (Fall 1985): 21–33.

Elizabeth Burns, an American living in Japan with her family, saves a Japanese woman from suicide one early morning on the platform as the train for Kyoto arrives. She tells no one of her action, not her husband or her children, although the act lodges in her mind like a seed caught between her teeth. Years pass, and still she tells no one; the day itself becomes lost, with the memory of her rescue.

99. Brown, Fredric. "The Last Train." In *Paradox Lost, and Twelve Other Great Science Fiction Stories*, 40–45. New York: Random House, 1973. *Weird Tales* 42 (Jan. 1950): 59–61.

In an effective little weird tale, lawyer Eliot Haig, on a night when an aurora lights the sky, decides that he will finally follow through on his long-harbored plan: He will board the last train out of town, and leave his unhappy, semi-crooked life behind. He bides his time, drinking from bar to bar, while he waits for the last train. His dawdling in the bars takes on a new significance with the information the station agent furnishes him at the story's conclusion.

100. Brown, I.M. *Boomer Bill: His Book.* No place: Von Hoffman Press, 1930. 360p.

I.M. Brown (b. 1889) began railroading in 1909. He served in various positions, and became field editor of the Missouri Pacific Line's magazine. Boomer Bill is Brown's fictional switchman, through whom Brown, as he writes in the book's preface, has "in mind preserving some of the experiences and philosophies of the railroad employe [sic] and demonstrating how his loyalty to his railroad carries him over the rough places of the life he has chosen." Like Brown, Boomer Bill is a company man. In some 70 sketches, Bill expounds (and that is the word: This boomer is a non-stop talker) on Pullman car etiquette, the railroader's duties and Christmas, passenger trains, freight handlers, safety, correspondence schools and railroading, and sundry other topics. Each piece finds Bill in a typical setting—a railroad beanery, a switch shanty, a club car, the yard office—chatting with friends and fellow railroaders about the topic of the moment, always drawing some pertinent lesson, with courteous service his special concern. Much of Bill's "philosophy" is simple good business sense; some of it is 1920s business boosterism; most of it is wordier than necessary. The book recalls John A. Hill's *Jim Skeevers' Object Lessons on Railroading for Railroaders* (Entry 364), but Hill's book is more humorous and better written.

101. Brown, Lloyd L. "The Glory Train." *Masses and Mainstream* 3, no. 12 (Dec. 1950): 22–41.

Growing up early in the 20th century, black Mississippian Isaac Zachary longs to become a locomotive engineer on the local road, the Great Southwestern & Gulf. His neighbors call it, in mockery, the Goin' Straight to

Glory, but to young Zach even this rattletrap railroad is glorious. He first works as a callboy, rounding up crews for their runs, then as a wiper in the roundhouse, where every worker is black. The idea of becoming an engineer seems laughable; as one comrade tells him, in Mississippi "there's three main things Cap'n Charlie won't 'low you to do, and that's mess with his women, vote in the elections or drive a railroad train" (26). Isaac finally moves up to become a fireman, a position he holds for many years, past the time he finally admits to himself that no black man will ever sit in the engineer's seat.

After World War I, black workers suffer large-scale layoffs to protect white workers' jobs. During the Depression, black railroaders face violent attacks from white men who want their positions. As the story slips into reportage instead of fiction, Brown claims that from 1931 to 1934 close to two dozen black firemen and brakemen were killed or wounded or shot at in Mississippi—but the black workers would not quit, knowing that white men would replace them. Zach himself takes a shotgun blast in the back, and nearly dies. When he reports back to work, the Depression has hit bottom. "What could a black fireman do when the great engines, lined up on the rusting rails, stood patient and still like elephants trunk to tails?" (38).

The story, included in Brown's 1951 novel, *Iron City*, closes with Zach elated to see William Z. Foster, a white man and former railroader, running for president on the Communist ticket, with his running mate, the black James W. Ford. To Zach, this is a sure sign that the Glory Train of justice is coming to carry America to the Promised Land. (Maybe. Maybe not. Foster and Ford garnered barely 100,000 votes in the 1932 presidential election.)

102. Buchanan, Rosemary. "Between Trains." *Catholic World* 121 (Sept. 1925): 768–773.

A rural track washout delays a young woman's trip to see her married lover. While waiting for the track repair, she wanders about the little village where the train has stopped; she is full of condescension for the simple rubes who live there. A local woman mending clothes in her yard gives the young woman lemonade and cookies, and good Catholic counsel on her love affair.

103. Bukoski, Anthony. "Time Between Trains." In *Time Between Trains*, 19–30. Dallas: Southern Methodist University Press, 2003. *Louisiana Literature: A Review of Literature and the Humanities* 19, no. 2 (2002): 53–60.

Joe Rubin, a Jewish track inspector ("the Wandering Jew," other railroaders call him), has worked 14 years on the Burlington Northern-Santa Fe in northern Wisconsin. His life has been devoted to the railroad; he lives in an apartment near the yards. He is a solitary man, performing lonely work: He drives his hi-rail truck through endless empty miles, on track and off, through country as desolate as Siberia. His isolated life parallels that of schoolteacher Sofia Stepan, who lives alone, widowed, and, with her third-graders, has less time for introspection than Joe. Joe takes up animal-track observation when he realizes that his devotion to the railroad is excessive. One day Sofia sees him kneeling in the snow, studying tracks, and utters a cryptic remark in Polish. Over the coming months, their most intimate contact is Joe's wave to her, at her house, from a nearby crossroads.

There is much to this tender, moving story that does not enter this brief synopsis. It is well worth reading, both for its presentation of a perhaps uniquely lonesome aspect of railroad work, and for its universal implications of human experience.

104. Bukowski, Charles. "Love It or Leave It." In *Erections, Ejaculations, Exhibitions and General Tales of Ordinary Madness*, 357–363. San Francisco: City Lights, 1972.

The narrator, "Bukowski," describes his trip from Louisiana to California with a group of derelicts and losers rounded up to work on the railroad in Sacramento. Railroad agents herd the men into a filthy old coach to begin the trip, and supply them, for a price, with inedible food. Bukowski's fellow tramps decide that they dislike him, and threaten to brutalize him once they get out on a track job. Bukowski abandons the railroad in Los Angeles, and proceeds to a beating in an auto salvage yard.

The narrator typifies Bukowski's main characters as he stumbles through a world of stupidity and violence. The official who signs him up for the railroad assures him that the railroad "takes care of a lot of guys like you. We help humanity. We're nice folks" (358). Nothing that follows lends credibility to these claims.

105. Bumpus, Jerry. "Selling." In *Things in Place*, 30–36. Brooklyn: Fiction Collective, 1975. *Epoch* 23 (Spring 1974): 227–232.

Traveling salesman Hobart Stull takes the train when he goes to see a prospective client; "the special satisfaction I derived from the train rides" was so remarkable that it was "impossible for me to either understand or accurately describe: I was never so content as when I was riding through the dark" (31). Most of the story concerns a trainride during which a peculiar woman with a photograph album accosts Hobart, followed by a bizarre song-and-dance performance in the aisle of the coach by the woman's daughter. As the light of dawn creeps into the coach, one wonders whether Hobart has been dreaming, or hallucinating. One also suspects that there is less to this story than meets the eye, but there is no doubt that Hobart is a committed train traveler.

106. Burnett, William R. "Along the Tracks." *Scribner's Magazine* 87 (April 1930): 367–373.

In a hobo jungle near Freight Bend, a group of hoboes makes mulligan stew with stolen ingredients. One of them washes in the river his prized silk shirt that he has been wearing daily, and dries it over the campfire. As the men are about to eat, three other 'boes join them—"Mary," an escaped convict; Oregon, a foul-tempered brute with designs on the silk shirt, and Bud, Mary's gunsel. The story, by the author of *Little Caesar*, is a credible, unsentimental look at life among the hoboes. It concludes with most of the men, minus Oregon, huddling together for warmth in a gondola on a fast freight.

107. Busch, Niven. *Duel in the Sun*. Cleveland and New York: World, 1944. 246p.

In the mid–1880s, Texas Sen. Jackson T. McCanles harbors no kind sentiments toward the railroad. It has not yet reached Paradise Flats, and whether it will depends on various points, regardless of the fact that construction has already begun on a depot. The chief point is money, and most of the locals gladly buy railroad bonds. The ranchers look forward to eliminating the 300-mile cattle drive to Dodge City; the wealthier madams and saloon keepers also buy in, with thoughts of railroaders' wages to come. Sen. Jackson sees the railroad's advent as an end to life as he has known it: in charge of area politics. He predicts disaster for the railroad, but its construction is ceaseless. The senator's son, Jesse, works as an attorney for the railroad, and it falls to him to serve the old man with a court order to allow construction to proceed across the senator's land. Family feelings are indisposed; the Texas Rangers get involved, and the railroad comes to Paradise Flats. Its arrival brings true civilization, for better or worse. The changes in the area manifest themselves through the reactions of the characters, who struggle to adapt to, or to deny, the loss of freedom that the Old West made possible. The novel led to a controversial 1946 film of the same title, directed by King Vidor.

108. Butler, Ellis P. "Just Like a Cat." In *Mike Flannery, On Duty and Off*, 3–34. New York: A.L. Burt, 1909.

Interurban express office manager Flannery's new assistant, young Timmy, retrieves a box from the 4:32 train, containing a large, fine Angora cat. The cat's chief defect is that it is dead, and its intended recipient declines to accept it. Ensuing is a farcical, funny misunderstanding with the main office, concerning the cat's proper care and feeding. The story ends on a bizarre and macabre note.

109. _____. "Pigs Is Pigs." *Golden Book Magazine* 19 (Jan. 1934): 96–103. Also in Butler's *Pigs Is Pigs*. New York: McClure, Phillips, 1906.

Mike Flannery, the Westcote agent of the

Interurban Co., speaks with a heavy Irish accent, and engages in a heated argument with customer Mr. Morehouse about the proper shipping rate for a pair of guinea pigs. Mr. Morehouse claims they are pets; Flannery contends that they are pigs. In this comic tale of bureaucratic fumbling and guinea pig multiplication, the time it takes the railroad officials to reach a decision on the case allows the original guinea pigs—doing what they do best—to become the ancestors of "bushel baskets full of guinea pigs" (102–103).

110. Cable, George Washington. *John March, Southerner.* New York: Scribner's, 1894. 513p.

Cable's contribution to the novelistic treatment of the conflict between tradition, especially idealized tradition, and industrial progress features John March, heir to a great tract of Southern property, Widewood. March's father had hoped to secure Northern investment in the land. The chief tension in the novel is that between the notion of pastoral ideal, as embodied in the land, and the busy development of post–Civil War industry. Nothing represents this development better than the railroad, in place when the novel begins, whose right-of-way slashes through the verdant, formerly peaceful land, leaving an ugly scar in its wake, not unlike the way the railroad right-of-way cuts through the land in Faulkner's "Raid" (Entry 261). Here, the completion of the Pulaski City, Suez, and Great South Railroad is a matter of major excitement for the small-town citizens. In the chapter "The Golden Spike," a ceremony marks the railroad's completion in Suez, Georgia; there are many exclamations over the town's lusty growth, capped by the advent of the railroad. Between the lines lie hints of doubt about the unfettered improvements. Nevertheless, a joyous party, including John March, boards the train the day of the ceremony. The president of the railroad, the not-so-coincidentally-surnamed Mr. Gamble, flirts with March's mother on the train, then collars March and urges him to go into a business based on property—specifically, March's family land. Although Gamble irritates March, Gamble's business exhortations take root in March's

mind. March envies the rail tycoon: "A railroad can ask for public aid; but fancy him [March] asking public aid to open and settle up his private lands!" (165). The novel features all-but-impenetrable tracts of Cable's effort to render black dialect as vast as Widewood itself.

111. Cain, James M. "Dead Man." *American Mercury* 37 (March 1936): 326–332. Also in *Midnight Specials: An Anthology for Train Buffs and Suspense Aficionados.* Edited by Bill Pronzini. Indianapolis: Bobbs-Merrill, 1977; and in *The Postman Always Rings Twice; Double Indemnity; Mildred Pierce; and Selected Stories.* New York: Knopf, 2003.

In a story with echoes of Ralph Ellison's "Hymie's Bull" (Entry 250), 19-year-old vagrant Ben Fuller kills a railroad bull who is beating him up after finding him on his train. A reasonable reading of the incident suggests that the killing is a matter of self-defense—the punishment the bull administers goes far beyond tolerable limits—but Ben, who prizes his nickname, "Lucky," is overtaken by guilt and fear of detection. In a stunning conclusion, Ben throws away a perfect opportunity to free himself of suspicion of the crime. Cain, a classic "hard boiled" crime writer best known for *The Postman Always Rings Twice* and *Double Indemnity*, portrays the difficult existence of a homeless man riding the rails through the Great Depression.

112. _____. *Double Indemnity.* 1943. Reprint, New York: Vintage Books, 1983. 115p.

California insurance man Walter Huff conspires with Phyllis Nirdlinger to kill Mr. Nirdlinger to collect on his life insurance. They plan to stage the scene so that Nirdlinger will appear to have died in a fall from a train, since the insurance company will pay double indemnity for a fatality owing to railroad travel. The staging involves Huff's masquerading as Nirdlinger on the 9:45 to San Francisco, and placing the murdered man's body along the right-of-way, as if he had toppled from the observation platform. "There's nothing so dark as a railroad track in the middle of the night," observes Huff (50)—unless, perhaps, it is the heart of a man willing to kill another for money.

The railroad's role in this taut crime novel is brief but critical to the plot's advancement. Like most of Cain's fiction, the story is compelling, as is the classic 1944 film-noir version (Richard Nixon's favorite film, no less) with Fred MacMurray, Edward G. Robinson, and Barbara Stanwyck.

113. Caldwell, Taylor. *Never Victorious, Never Defeated.* New York: McGraw-Hill, 1954. 549p.

This numbingly verbose novel follows the affairs, business and otherwise, of the family behind the great Interstate Railroad Company. The story opens in 1935, the 100th anniversary of the IRC, and quickly backtracks to the road's origins in the post–Civil War boom as the State Railroad Company in Pennsylvania. Caldwell's historical homework shows in her depiction of the evolution of railroading in the period the novel covers, and she features a strong female lead character in Cornelia De-Witt Marshall, "her father's right-hand man [sic]" (511) and a life-long railroader. Caldwell's reputation for a preoccupation with the rich and powerful stands firm in the book; more interesting than this crowd or their personal struggles are Caldwell's occasional remarks on historical developments. Writing of the Panic of 1877, she is hard on the railroads, castigating them for profligacy at the same time as they cut workers' wages; for slipshod construction that endangered passengers; and for paying large dividends as if to mock a nation in economic misery: "Thus quickened the era of men without pride. And as they were men without pride they became the calculated prey of future malefactors in government" (167). Caldwell is equally acerbic when she writes of the Interstate's subsidiary iron and steel company, built in the middle of the community that supplies its labor. The company is a filthy, polluting, "black-smoking dinosaur" (220). Caldwell's approbation for the railroad labor movement does not deter her later attack on communism, or her lamentation over Franklin D. Roosevelt's alleged befuddlement at the specter of this phenomenon.

The novel has some merits, but whatever its firm footing in historical research, or its ability to tell the tale, it is essentially a captains-of-industry soap opera, with too many characters, too much dialog (much of it suggesting that Caldwell seldom listened to real conversation), and far too much superfluous verbal bric-a-brac.

114. Calisher, Hortense. "The Passenger." In *Saratoga, Hot,* 91–131. Garden City, New York: Doubleday, 1985.

"I yearn for trains because of what happened to me on one, fifteen years ago," says the narrator (95). What happened involved a diagnosis of a thyroid problem that had a good chance to involve cancer. Now in her 50s, the narrator—a writer and the mother of a dead child—is taking the train from Chicago to New York. She meets an obnoxious psychiatrist in the club car. He makes leering innuendo; she responds with disdain in an affected English accent. She becomes caught up with her fellow passengers, preoccupied with their stories, told or untold. She wants to help a sweet young couple, but fears being too forward. "Fling me a life, and I remember it," she says, but now she feels overfull of others' lives: "I can't bear this any longer" (113).

The setting aboard the train places the narrator in a context that triggers her obsessive rumination on the past, her habits, her perceptions, and her judgments of others. The narrator is not an appealing character, and the story's prose possesses an arrhythmic, lurching quality, perhaps in keeping with the character herself.

115. Camp, Charles Wadsworth. "The Signal Tower." In *The Best Short Stories of 1920,* edited by Edward J. O'Brien, 66–82. Boston: Small, Maynard, 1921. *The Metropolitan,* May 1920, 32+.

Tolliver, a signal tower operator, has serious concerns about the safe passage, on a dark and stormy night, on the road's single track, of a special Pullman train carrying railroad officials. Competing for his attention is Joe, who alternates tower shifts with him, and who, while boarding with Tolliver, made advances toward Tolliver's wife. Tolliver worries that Joe will bother his wife while Tolliver is occupied in the tower. The story devolves into a mad melodrama, with Tolliver torn between his duty to the railroad and its passengers, and his concern for his wife, at the mercy of the drunken and vengeful Joe.

116. Campbell, Robert. *Red Cent.* New York: Pocket Books, 1989. 221p.

Railroad detective Jake Hatch works for the Burlington Northern out of Omaha, where he lives with his cat in a second-floor flat. When a passenger on the California Zephyr going through Iowa dies from a gunshot, apparently fired from a pickup truck by a passing Indian, Hatch digs into the case. Hatch, part Indian himself, is inclined to give the young Indian men under suspicion the benefit of a little doubt. Consultation with a ballistics expert enlarges the doubt, and sends Hatch off on the trail of the real killer. The railroad figures chiefly as scene-of-the-crime stuff here, but Hatch is an attractive character and the story rolls along on the wheels of no-nonsense prose.

117. Canfield, Dorothy. *The Bent Twig.* 1915. Reprint, New York: Henry Holt, 1922. 480p.

Sylvia Marshall, daughter of a university professor, grows up in this novel. In Chapter 10, "Sylvia's First Glimpse of Modern Civilization," she takes an overnight train trip to Chicago with her mother and sister. Sylvia disappoints her mother by seeming to pay little attention to the details of the train, but she is, in fact, transfixed by the wonder of the experience. Although already a young woman, she is on what is essentially her first real trip; she sits "in a sort of trance of receptivity" (114), taking in every detail of the other passengers, and of the crowds at the stations where the train lingers. While Sylvia's mother gives Sylvia's sister Judith a running instructional commentary on everything they see from the coach window, Sylvia appears to be seeing nothing. But as she stares at her hands in her lap, she imagines her wrists adorned with bracelets—like the wrists of the woman who sits across from her. Sylvia is oblivious to the trackside blast furnaces about which her mother prattles, but Sylvia's imagination is running at white heat behind the façade of her indifference.

118. Canfield, William W. *Along the Way.* New York: Fenno & Co., 1909. 329p.

In this interesting railroading dystopia, Weston, general superintendent of the Denver and Southern Railroad, is on the ship from Europe to the United States when he meets his old employee, Fred Stewart. Stewart has just returned from an engineering job in Russia, and is to visit the U.S. for the first time in a decade. The federal government, in his absence, has taken over railroad operation in the country; the results have been a general disaster, from the destruction of Grand Central Station in New York City to impossible red tape in regulations governing basic railroad business. Bribery is rampant. Weston proposes that private business resume running American railroads at a meeting (dubbed the Boston Conference) of capitalists and former railroad magnates in Boston. The group is up against the Reformers, who advocate federal ownership of everything: banks, railroads, telephones, and utilities. "To follow railroading at present," one veteran railroader tells Fred, "takes out of a man all he ever knew concerning the business" (52).

Present-day air travelers may find a parallel between their experiences and Fred's efforts to find out when the one o'clock train leaves. "Is there no way of finding out when a regular, scheduled train, that is already an hour late, is likely to depart?" he asks a functionary. The latter's answer: "You might try waiting" (75–76).

Neil Raymond, general superintendent of railroads, is "the arch-devil of the whole bunch of grafters" (237). Raymond meets his match in Stewart, who blocks him from assisting the former's legislative stooge, Congressman Barrows, from securing another term in Washington. The Boston Conference issues a statement claiming that the people have unwittingly allowed the creation of a machine that has robbed them of dependable transportation, "and out of the greatest of all public utilities had made a shuttlecock and plaything for political bosses" (263).

Canfield tempers what is essentially a brief for healthy capitalism with a little romance, but it is his vision of a railroad system gone awry under federal control that gives the novel its value. Its strictly literary value is negligible.

119. Capote, Truman. "A Tree of Night." In *A Tree of Night and Other Stories*, 191–209. New York: Random House, 1949. *Harper's Bazaar* 79 (Oct. 1945): 110+.

Kay, a young college student, is taking a Southern train back to school after attending her uncle's funeral. In the crowded train she sits with a short woman with an enormous head and the woman's male companion, a consummately unsettling deaf mute. The odd couple are veteran performers of an itinerant carnival-like act based on the story of Lazarus. The two force themselves on Kay in a terrifying manner. The short, slovenly, big-headed woman—she blows her nose in her undergarment—all but swarms over Kay. "That's what I like about a train," she says, after persuading Kay to talk with her. "Bus people are a closed-mouth buncha dopes. But a train's a place for putting your cards on the table, that's what I always say" (195).

Capote's debt to other writers of Southern Gothic is evident in this early story, but he works the vein for what it is worth, and achieves some highly effective passages. "Strangers on a train" do not come much stranger than the couple at issue here. Capote also nicely details the interior of the shabby coach, with its "stale odor of discarded sandwiches, apple cores, and orange hulls: this garbage, including Lily cups, soda-pop bottles, and mangled newspapers, littered the long aisle" (192). This detritus of travel, apparently unnoticed by the other passengers, helps create an atmosphere suggesting decay fit for the story's tone.

120. Carleton, Will. "The Christmas Car." In *The Old Infant, and Similar Stories*, 137–152. New York: Harper & Bros., 1896.

The Colgrove family children lived in a log house some 60 rods from the Erie and Kalamazoo Railroad in the early days of railroading. The trains passed at an astonishing speed of 25 miles per hour, and almost seemed to fly. The children thought "that the men who could ride on such a glorious creature [as the locomotive], and control it, were themselves something more than human" (138). One day the train stops near the Colgrove house, and leaves a disabled car beside the track. After stoking their courage, the children enter the car. While the car sits, apparently abandoned, over several months, the children turn it into a second home—and prepare to welcome Santa Claus in it on Christmas Day. Railroad officials have not forgotten the car, however, and therein lies a sentimental resolution for the story.

121. Carr, John Dickson. "The Murder in Number Four." In *The Door to Doom, and Other Detections*, edited by Douglas G. Greene, 94–111. New York: Harper & Row, 1980. *The Haverfordian* 48 (June 1928): 3–25.

A murdered man turns up in an otherwise-empty compartment on a mid-December night between Dieppe and Paris run aboard the Blue Arrow. Miss Brunhilde Mertz, "militant feminist, clubwoman and tourist from the United States" (95) figures prominently, although not to her credit, in the tale. In her witness's deposition, Miss Mertz rants about French train travel: "It's a pity you can't ride on a train in this abominable country without getting murdered! And such service! Did you ever hear of the checking system for baggage?" (102). Miss Mertz speaks "with the baffled ferocity of a saint who knows he is right but can convince nobody" (103). In an act of aggressively American self-conviction, she arranges the apprehension and gagging of the man she is sure is the "murderer." Only an American, one suspects, could be as absolutely certain, and as completely mistaken, as Miss Mertz.

122. Carr, Sarah P. *The Iron Way: A Tale of the Builders of the West*. Chicago: McClurg, 1907. 367p.

The author's father, who became assistant general superintendent of the Central Pacific Railroad, was a significant figure in the construction of the transcontinental railroad during her childhood. She relies on information gleaned growing up in this railroader's household to form the basis for this romance of the transcontinental's development. Her hero is

Alfred Vincent, Harvard man, hired by C.P. President Stanford as a troubleshooter in his road's competition with the San Francisco & Washoe Railroad. Of some interest is the tension Carr details between railroad chiefs, such as the C.P.'s Mark Hopkins, and men in the field, who battle daily to carry out instructions from Sacramento that have little connection to down-to-earth realities of the project. Unfortunately, romance—chiefly Vincent's interest in Stella Anthony—eclipses railroading in the novel, which is a disappointing work considering the author's evident closeness to the principals in the history of the "Iron Way," the transcontinental railroad.

123. Carroll, H.G. "Train." *Other Voices* 4, nos. 13–14 (1990–91): 69–72.

A father deals with his high-school son's witnessing a commuter train accident: A passenger on the train fell out an open door to his death. The author's effort to link the train accident to other emotional events in the lives of the father could have been better managed.

124. Carroll, Susan. "Train Woman." *Carolina Quarterly* 46, no. 1 (1993): 50–51.

In this vivid vignette, the narrator, traveling with a companion by train to Chicago, describes a "Goddamn woman" in a skimpy yellow suit who makes life unpleasant for everyone in the crowded car. She tries to smoke; after the conductor quashes that, she repeatedly turns off the car's ventilating system. "Whole damn car's about at ninety degrees and smells like sweat and baby diapers and my skin's sticking to me all over" (51). Like the narrator, everyone but the troublesome woman is warmly dressed; she is freezing, and loud about it. No one offers her a coat or a sweater, and everyone watches her carefully, letting her "know that we weren't going to give in, that there was nothing that we couldn't do" (51).

125. Carter, Emily. "Train Line." In *Glory Goes and Gets Some*, 213–224. Minneapolis: Coffee House Press, 2000. Published, with some variations, as "The Train," *Great River Review* 26 (1997): 67–77.

The female narrator describes how, during World War I, her great grandfather Salvatore, a maintenance man with the Brooklyn Rapid Transit Co., was pressed into service as a brakeman during a strike. The company gave Salvatore some hurried training, and threw him onto a train. Overwhelmed, he forgot his sketchy instructions, and tried to take a dangerous curve at high speed. "It took them four hours to separate the dead from the living, by which time many victims had made the transition" (222). The narrator transmutes this disaster into a thoughtful meditation on her family and her life.

126. Carter, Franklin. *Sierra Passage*. New York: Jove Books, 1995. 262p.

This novel is one in Carter's mass-market paperback Rails West! series; the others are *Rails West!* and *Nebraska Crossing* (both Jove, 1993), and *Wyoming Territory* (Jove, 1994). The book provides a painless, entertaining way to learn about the building of the transcontinental railroad from the Central Pacific side, although only at a surface level. Here Harvard grad and Union Pacific surveyor Glenn Gilchrist, disgusted with the UP's shabby treatment of Irish laborers, finds himself branded a Central Pacific spy by UP management. In 1867, he packs up and heads west to join the Central Pacific.

Rough men, hostile Indians, and actual historical figures populate the story. A good part of the narrative concerns the struggle to blast the Summit Tunnel through Donner Pass. Carter portrays Chinese workers as fearless, risking their lives for pride as much as for money as they dangle in woven baskets from mountain precipices, drilling and blasting. In a sidelight, English chemist James Howden (here called "Bowden") appears, to assist the CP in blasting through the Summit Tunnel with nitroglycerin. The CP abandoned the deadly explosive after completing the tunnel; nitroglycerin had a bad reputation, owing in part to the havoc and death it wrought in a San Francisco accident in 1866.

127. Carter, Nick. (pseud.) "Nick Carter's Enemy." 1902. Reprinted in *Nick Carter, Detective*, edited by Robert Clurman, 246–302. New York: Macmillan, 1963.

As Robert Clurman notes in his introduction to this collection, Nick Carter, a supremely popular turn-of-the-century detective, had much in common with Horatio Alger, Jr.'s plucky boy heroes. He might be—in fact, probably would be—beaten, bound, drugged, or otherwise abused in his efforts to nail the bad guy, but he ever strove, and ever succeeded. Today Carter's adventures come off as stilted and incredible, but, like Alger's equally improbable yarns, they do reflect the popular sentiments of their times, with a devotion to the belief that the morally upright soul will prevail, regardless of vicissitudes.

In the long story "Nick Carter's Enemy," the second chapter, "The Porter's Queer Dream," takes place on a passenger train bound for New York City. Carter is pursuing a murderer, but this night on the train nearly proves his last. It is only thanks to an alert porter's investigation of the odor of ether, which prompts a strange dream, that Carter survives. The porter speaks in a stereotypically heavy black dialect, but is resourceful enough to save Carter's life, and is not portrayed as a "darky" buffoon. When Carter leaves the train, he presses a $100 bill into the porter's hand.

(The Carter stories were the work of many writers, most frequently Frederick Dey. The precise authorship of this story is uncertain.)

128. Carter, Paul A. "The Man Who Rode the Trains." In *Travellers by Night*, edited by August Derleth, 51–68. London: Victor Gollancz, 1968. Sauk City, WI: Arkham House, 1967.

This enjoyable little fantasy covers much ground, both geographical and chronological. It follows the narrator from his train ride from Chicago to Boston as a boy in World War II to his escape from a train attacked in a civil war in an anonymous African nation well into the 21st century. Between these points, the narrator describes several other train trips at various stages in his life. A common feature marks all the trips: the appearance aboard the train of the same inscrutable, shabby, and very old man—a man who seems no older in Africa than he did many decades earlier on the train to Boston. The reader may guess the old man's

identity; in the end, the narrator claims to know, but does not give it away.

The author, an historian, knows enough railroad history to evoke effectively the changing atmosphere of rail travel over the years. His narrator is a dedicated rail fan for whom the trains form a constant in his life, in spite of their evolving (and, in the sense of passenger service, deteriorating) nature. Yet nothing lasts forever, not even "constants," and the author uses the metaphor of train travel and the strange old man to represent that fact.

129. Carver, Ray. "The Compartment." *Antioch Review* 42 (Spring 1983): 133–141. Also in Carver's *Cathedral; Stories*. New York: Knopf, 1983.

In this dreamlike story, a man named Myers has taken a vacation from his engineering firm to meet his estranged son in Strasbourg, France. He has not seen the boy, now a university student, for eight years. He travels toward Strasbourg on a train in which he shares a compartment with a sleeping man. Myers envies the man, because he himself, although weary, cannot sleep.

The initial uncertainty Myers feels about becoming reacquainted with his son erodes with the gathering unpleasantness of his journey. Someone steals from his coat a watch he had planned to give his son; he cannot understand what anyone is saying; and in the sort of absurdity that usually occurs only in bad dreams, he returns from another car on the train to find "his" car, with his belongings, uncoupled from the train and replaced by another car. By this time, Myers's old antipathy toward his son has reasserted itself, and he refuses to get off the train when it reaches Strasbourg.

It is an extremely unsettling story, with the train's ill events feeding Myers's worst feelings about his son. In the end, Myers falls asleep—perhaps to dream—but his waking existence has been a nightmare.

130. _____. "The Train." *Antaeus* 49/50 (Spring-Summer, 1983): 151–157. Also in Carver's *Cathedral*. New York: Knopf, 1983.

In this audacious follow-up to John Cheever's story, "The 5:48" (Entry 146), Miss

Dent waits in the otherwise empty station after releasing Blake with his life. A woman and an older man enter the station; the woman, angry with her companion, breaks into rapid Italian over the issue at hand, whatever it is, while Miss Dent sits clutching her handbag with the revolver in it. The woman finds Miss Dent's silence annoying, and assures her that as she grows older, she will have something to talk about. A commuter train pulls up to the station; the passengers on board look out through the glass at the three people on the platform. They are only slightly curious about the trio boarding the train at this late hour, and, once having sized up the three as recent partakers of a not very good time, they barely give them another thought. The train leaves the station, moving faster until it races through the dark landscape, light from its cars shining out onto the roadbed. Little light shines, however, on the lives of Miss Dent or the odd couple who briefly shared the station with her

131. Castro, Adolph de. "The Electric Executioner." 1970. Reprinted in *The Horror in the Museum, and Other Revisions*, edited by H.P. Lovecraft, 112–133. New York: Carroll & Graf, 1996.

A mining executive pursues a rogue company functionary into Mexico by train in 1889, and recalls the experience 40 years later. Most of the story takes place in a compartment the narrator shares—apparently—with a deranged man who wishes to use his portable electric execution machine on the narrator. The story is suitably weird, in a typical Lovecraftian vein.

132. Cather, Willa. "The Affair at Grover Station." In *Willa Cather's Collected Short Fiction, 1892–1912*. Rev. ed. Edited by Virginia Faulkner, 339–352. Lincoln: University of Nebraska Press, 1970. Also in *Early Stories of Willa Cather*. New York: Dodd, Mead, 1957. *The Library* 1 (June 16, 23, 1900): 3–4; 14–15.

Rodgers, a cashier in a railroad office in Cheyenne, relates the eerie story of the murder of Larry O'Toole, an agent who worked at Grover Station, Wyoming. The story includes some good description of the snow-blown loneliness of remote Grover Station: "The plain was a wide, white ocean of swirling, drifting snow, that beat and broke like the thrash of the waves in the merciless wind that swept, with nothing to break it, from the Rockies to the Missouri" (346). The story's most arresting aspect today is its narrator's forthright racism. The villain is a man, Freymark, revealed to be of Chinese ancestry. The narrator heaps calumny on the Chinese, who are "a race without conscience or sensibilities" (351). Freymark himself is a former railroad man driven from his post by dishonest dealings.

133. _____. "The Bohemian Girl." *McClure's Magazine* 39 (Aug. 1912): 420–424+. Also in *Willa Cather's Collected Short Fiction, 1892–1912*. Rev. ed. Edited by Virginia Faulkner. Lincoln: University of Nebraska Press, 1970.

The train appears here only in the opening of the story, as "the transcontinental express" brings an important character into the action. Today a new character might well drive into the story in a car, but what more logical means of arrival in a remote early 1900s town than by railroad coach?

134. _____. "'A Death in the Desert.'" In *Willa Cather's Collected Short Fiction, 1892–1912*. Rev. ed. Edited by Virginia Faulkner, 199–217. Lincoln: University of Nebraska Press, 1970. Also in Cather's *The Troll Garden*. New York: McClure, Phillips, 1905. *Scribner's Magazine* 33 (Jan. 1903): 109–121.

Everett Hilgarde, a man of worldly connections and sophistication, arrives by train in Cheyenne. There he meets Katharine Gaylord, an accomplished student of his famous composer brother, and an object of infatuation for Everett in his youth. Katharine is dying of a lung disorder, and has come to Cheyenne to wait for the end with her untutored family, including her brother, a former brakeman, and his sister, a telegraph operator. "We're all a pretty common sort," says the brother, "railroaders from away back. My father was a conductor" (203). Katharine is miserable, not only from her illness, but from the cultural barrenness of the West.

Everett finds himself at Katharine's deathbed as she imagines herself aboard a Pullman on her way to New York, returning to her life and work. Before she dies, she mistakes Everett for his brother, Adriance. As Everett waits for the eastbound train, he gazes "again and again up the track, watching for the train" (217). When he boards the train to leave Cheyenne, he is once again mistaken, this time by a German passenger, for his brother.

The train is of prime importance in this story, serving not only as a means of arrival and departure, of beginning and end for the story, but of fevered, delusional release from the pain of death.

135. _____. "Flavia and Her Artists." In *The Troll Garden*, 1–54. New York: McClure, Phillips, 1905. Also in *Willa Cather's Collected Short Fiction, 1892–1912*. Rev. ed. Edited by Virginia Faulkner. Lincoln: University of Nebraska Press, 1970.

Again Cather introduces an important character, Imogen Willard, aboard a passenger train, in the story's opening sentence. (There are no other railroading details.)

136. _____. *A Lost Lady*. New York: Knopf, 1923. 173p.

This novel of loss and change, written with a spare elegance, focuses on Marian Forrester, the wife of Captain Forrester. Forrester is a contractor who has built hundreds of miles of track for the Burlington Railroad. He and Marian live in the prairie town of Sweet Water, Nebraska, a town and region in decline as the 19th century nears its close. In the good days, the Forrester place was a popular stop for visiting railroad officials, but as the economic ties between the city and the railroad wane, the old visitors are not so common, and the up-and-coming locals lack the humanity and virtue of their forebears. At one point, Forrester reminisces: "All our great West has been developed from ... dreams; the homesteader's and the prospector's and the contractor's. We dreamed the railroads across the mountains..." (55).

When Forrester suffers a stroke, Cyrus Dalzell, president of the Colorado & Utah Railroad, comes to see him, and lends him his old porter, Jim, to serve as a valet.

Young Niel Herbert, a frequent guest at the Forresters' since his boyhood, leaves by train at mid-book to study in Boston. Two years later, Niel visits, and Marian says to him, "Every night for weeks, when the lights of the train came swinging in down below the meadows, I've said to myself, 'Niel is coming home; there's that to look forward to'" (111). Marian Forrester's own decline, seen chiefly from Neil's perspective, mirrors that of the general cultural ambiance: The good days have gone, and one's efforts to adapt to their loss by assuming the values and ways of a later, more abrasive, age, are too great a departure from the old ideals to flourish.

137. _____. *My Antonia*. 1918. Reprint, Boston: Houghton, Mifflin, 1954. 372p.

Cather begins this deeply-moving novel of friendship, memory, and life on the turn-of-the-century Great Plains with a railroad setting. Its introduction describes the writer's conversation with old friend Jim Burden as they cross Iowa by train, where they "sat in the observation car, where the woodwork was hot to the touch and red dust lay deep over everything. The dust and heat, the burning wind, reminded us of many things" (i). Reminiscence is the tone of the novel's proper opening, too, as narrator Burden, a railroad attorney, looks back on his experience as a 10-year-old leaving Virginia with his friend Jake, to cross the Great Plains by train. Jim will live with his grandparents in Nebraska. "The only thing very noticeable about Nebraska was that it was still, all day long, Nebraska" (5). A friendly conductor chats with the boys on the train, and tells them of a family of immigrants in another car. He mentions a young girl in the family, and her pretty brown eyes.

When the train stops at the station in Black Hawk, Nebraska, Jim watches the immigrant family huddling on the platform. Soon Jim meets the young immigrant girl, Antonia, and they become the closest of friends. Eventually their lives diverge, but each lives on in the other's memory.

In a railroad moment late in the novel,

the scoundrel Larry Donovan, a conductor, illustrates notions of labor hierarchy. He is "one of those train-crew aristocrats who are always afraid that someone may ask them to put up a car-window, and who, if requested to perform such a menial service, silently point to the button that calls the porter" (304). Donovan also earns the reader's hostility by treating Antonia shamefully. This quiet, beautifully-written novel penetrates the hearts of its characters and the heart of life on the Great Plains; its implications concerning friendship, the passage of time, and memory are timeless.

138. _____. "The Professor's Commencement." In *Willa Cather's Collected Short Fiction, 1892–1912*. Rev. ed. Edited by Virginia Faulkner, 283–291. Lincoln: University of Nebraska Press, 1970. *New England Magazine* 26 (June 1902): 481–488.

In this melancholy story of a professor's retirement, the railroad figures in the landscape of the dreary manufacturing town where he teaches high school. The city has grown bleak, ugly and desolate, its former pleasant features ruined through the offices of industrial avarice. The professor sometimes cannot even conduct his classes properly: "Often, when some lad was reading aloud ... the puffing of the engines in the switch yard at the foot of the hill would drown the verse and the young voice entirely..." (287).

139. _____. *The Professor's House*. 1925. Reprint with notes and other supplementary content in *Later Novels*, 99–271. New York: Library of America, 1990.

The railroad itself is fundamentally absent from this novel, but two primary characters have significant railroading backgrounds. Young Tom Outland, an orphan, meets Professor St. Peter in the professor's garden one morning, and asks for advice on entering the university. Tom worked as a railroad call boy for the Santa Fe. Although fated to die young, Tom proves a successful scholar; the chief portion of the novel devoted to him bears his name. In "Tom Outland's Story" in Book 2, Tom relates details of his life before he met

Professor St. Peter. He had become good friends with locomotive engineer Rodney Blake, and with Blake discovered an ancient, abandoned Indian cliff dwelling on a Western mesa. While Tom tried to interest federal officials in Washington, D.C., in the large cache of artifacts in the city, Blake sold the lot to a visiting German, who spirited them out of the country. Blake's failure to understand the meaning and value of the discovery causes the destruction of his friendship with Tom, a break-up that Cather portrays in a painful passage. The friendship of the engineer, Blake, and Tom Outland recalls the closeness between men found in many railroading stories, but the dissolution of friendship here is atypical and disturbing.

140. _____. "The Sculptor's Funeral." In *Willa Cather's Collected Short Fiction, 1892–1912*. Rev. ed. Edited by Virginia Faulkner, 173–185. Lincoln: University of Nebraska Press, 1970. Also in Cather's *The Troll Garden*. New York: McClure, Phillips, 1905. *McClure's Magazine* 24 (Jan. 1905): 329–336.

Once again Cather's story opening concerns the arrival of a passenger train. This time, the focus is not on a passenger, but on those waiting for it, expectantly, impatiently; the first paragraph captures the scene as "A group of townspeople stood on the station siding of a little Kansas town, awaiting the coming of the night train, which was already twenty minutes overdue" (173). Men in heavy coats shift from foot to foot in the cold, and look in the direction from which the train must come.

When the train whistle blows in the distance, the men spring to life, "and a flash of momentary animation kindled their dull eyes at that cold, vibrant scream, the world-wide call for men" (174). Here on the prairie, the train represents the possibilities of the world, even the end of possibilities, for this night train is bringing an occupied coffin home for burial; a young man's adventures in the wide world have come to a premature end.

141. _____. *The Song of the Lark*. 1915. Reprint, with revisions, Boston and New York: Houghton Mifflin, 1943. 581p.

This novel, substantially revised in 1932, is a realistic story of its heroine's artistic awakening and escape from provincial surroundings to prominence in a sophisticated world. The reader meets Thea Kronborg when she is a young girl in the burg of Moonstone, Colorado, where her father is a Swedish minister. Thea's artistic sensibilities receive minimal encouragement in her little community, but she does make a close friend in railroad conductor Ray Kennedy, who works the Denver run. Ray is 30 when he meets 12-year-old Thea, and decides that he will wait for her to grow up so that he can marry her. Ray is an innocent sort, charming, and holds all women in sentimental esteem. In an engaging passage, he cleans his caboose in preparation for a trip to Denver on which Thea and her mother will join him. He scrubs the car down thoroughly, and carefully removes all the girly-art his trainmates have affixed to the walls. When Thea reaches age 17, Ray is mortally injured when an engine rear-ends his caboose. The wreck leaves the caboose a "pile of splintered wood and twisted iron" (182). In a touching death-bed passage—his "bed" a canvas litter under a cottonwood tree—Ray and Thea have their last conversation.

Ray's earnest concern for Thea outlives him, for she is the beneficiary of his modest life insurance policy. With it, she leaves Moonstone to study music in Chicago. Cather uses the train effectively in Thea's departure from her childhood surroundings. She looks down from her Pullman window at friends and family gathered to bid her goodbye; the image of her looking down as "they all shouted things up at the closed window" (198) reinforces the idea of separation. Thea's crossing of a threshold receives further emphasis when Cather describes her a short time later, in the coach now "speeding" past the country that had been her lifelong home: "Everything that was essential seemed to be right there in the car with her. She lacked nothing..." and she is "surprised that she did not feel a deeper sense of loss at leaving her old life behind her" (199).

142. _____. "A Wagner Matinee." In *Willa Cather's Collected Short Fiction, 1892–1912*. Rev. ed. Edited by Virginia

Faulkner, 235–242. Lincoln: University of Nebraska Press, 1970. Also in Cather's *The Troll Garden*. New York: McClure, Phillips, 1905. *Everybody's Magazine* 10 (Feb. 1904): 325–328.

The discomforts of turn-of-the-century train travel receive brief illumination in this story. A man meets his aunt at the train station in Boston; she has traveled from Nebraska, all the way in a day coach, and "her linen duster had become black with soot and her black bonnet gray with dust during the journey" (235).

143. Chalmers, Stephen. *The Crime in Car 13*. New York: Grosset & Dunlap, 1931. 293p.

In spite of its light tone, this mystery seems far longer than it is. New York newspaper reporter Hamlin Douglas, his bass-fishing gear at his side, is bound for a vacation. On the train to bass country, he observes an argumentative British passenger, Morepath. At night, in the smoking car, he also sees a man with a pitted face, evidently terrified. Douglas puts it all out of his mind, but only briefly; he can barely wet his line before he learns that the Englishman has been murdered in his berth—in the berth that Douglas had originally reserved, only to switch places to accommodate the imminent murder victim.

In unlikely fashion, Douglas is sworn in with the U.S. Secret Service, and is instrumental in solving a case with grave international ramifications. Considerable running back and forth by train to and from New York City takes place, but the train action is unengaging. Chalmers refers to an African-American porter as "George," and has Douglas address him as such—because "all porters are 'George,' of course..." (10)—presumably after the inventor of the sleeping car, George Pullman.

144. Chambers, Robert. *Whistling Cat*. New York: Appleton, 1932. 379p.

In the form of the reminiscences of a veteran telegrapher, Juan Maddox, this novel concerns his adventures as an operator with the Union Army during the Civil War, including railroad activities. Substantial research supports the book, which features a number of historical characters, but the narrative plods, and railroading is not a primary concern.

145. Chaput, W. J. *The Man on the Train.* New York: St. Martin's, 1986. 247p.

It is December, 1941, in this fast-moving mystery thriller. The Central Vermont Railroad runs through Richmond, Vermont; on Dec. 16, station master Whitley Raymond prepares for the Washingtonian, coming south from Montreal. Whitley receives a mighty shock when the train roars past—a body flies from an open train door, smashes into obstacles on the platform, and crashes into a cabinet in Whitley's office. Is it a suicide? A drunken blunder? It all has to do with Winston Churchill's forthcoming visit to the United States, his planned railroad trip to Ottawa, and a scheme to "poison a whole goddamn Pullman full of innocent people" (197)—not to mention Churchill himself—by spiking the water supply serving the coach.

146. Cheever, John. "The Five-Forty-Eight." In *The Stories of John Cheever*, 236–247. New York: Knopf, 1978. *New Yorker* 30 (April 10, 1954): 28–34.

Blake, "an insignificant man" by his own reckoning, also habitually takes advantage of the weak. After sexually exploiting his new secretary, Miss Dent, he has her fired. Miss Dent shows up one evening to trail Blake home from work. They both board the 5:48 commuter train, where Miss Dent seats herself next to him and places a gun to his belly. Her agenda is Blake's abasement.

This fine story contains several memorable railroad moments. Blake settles himself in his seat in a coach that "was old and smelled oddly like a bomb shelter in which whole families had spent the night.... The filth on the window glass was streaked with rain from some other journey, and clouds of rank pipe and cigarette smoke had begun to rise from behind each newspaper.... The train traveled up from the underground into the weak daylight..." (241), not unlike a vehicle emerging from the lower depths of Hell.

Another nice passage describes the gradual absorption of commuters in the train station parking lot as various family members come to meet them. Blake, of course, has another destiny, on this trip. He meets it near the railroad freight house, where he watches "a rat take its head out of a paper bag and regard him" (246). In the end, he lies with his face pressed to the coal littering the surface of the railroad yard. It is a suitable posture for a man with no regard for others. (See also Entry 130.)

147. Cherry, Kelly. "The Train: A Story." *Commentary* 86 (Nov. 1988): 52–54.

A woman is taking her flinty 75-year-old mother to an English train station after a visit. She wants her to stay. On the way to the station, the old woman expresses regret over not having lived up to her own mother's religious standards. At the station, mother and daughter speak of life and death, until the train arrives, "a zipper pulling into the station on the seams of the track" (54). The old woman boards; from the platform, the daughter sees her mother by a window: "I run to the window and stand on tiptoe and knock on the pane. She turns to me and smiles distantly and turns back, staring ahead" (54). The train pulls out, leaving the daughter all alone on the platform, reflecting on the bravery of people, "alone and dying, now and forever alone, brave beyond belief" (54). The train's departure is clearly the old woman's death. The daughter notes that the old woman took nothing with her, not even the butt of her last cigarette.

148. Chesnutt, Charles W. "The Exception." In *The Short Fiction of Charles W. Chesnutt*, edited by Sylvia L. Render, 353–356. Washington, D.C.: Howard University Press, 1974. (First publication; written after 1901.)

Chesnutt was an African-American writer. In this lightly ironic tale, a small theater company is stranded on a winter day at a train station in a little Michigan town. Its members lack money for tickets to travel to Kalamazoo, where they have sold out their next show. A foppish acquaintance of the company manager, also waiting at the station, refuses to pay a small debt to the manager—an amount that would cover the cost of the tickets—and makes it impossible for the ticket agent to arrange a deal with the manager, a regular customer, for a lower fare. The manager enlists the aid of the local law officer, who helps the company overcome its plight.

149. _____. "Stryker's Waterloo." In *The Short Fiction of Charles W. Chesnutt*, edited by Sylvia L. Render, 365–373. Washington, D.C.: Howard University Press, 1974. (First publication; written between 1888 and 1899.)

Longtime failure Napoleon Stryker is badly injured in a railroad accident in 1884. Edgar Hall, the railroad's ostensibly genial claims agent, solicitously looks after Stryker in the aftermath, chiefly in hopes that Stryker will accept a modest settlement. Stryker disappoints Hall when he decides to sue the road for $100,000. "It's a durned, mean, low-lived sneaking piece of business for Stryker to sue us," laments Hall (367). During protracted court wrangling, Hall shadows Stryker everywhere, convinced that if he can obtain evidence of Stryker's recovery, the court will award him peanuts. Hall conceives a ploy which, when carried out, leaves Stryker up a tree—literally—and with his case lost.

This story features a curiously benign, if not sanguine, attitude toward the railroad. Stryker was truly injured in the wreck; was, in fact, near death. Yet Chesnutt treats Stryker's corporate opponent, Hall, as very nearly a hero for helping the railroad weasel out of a fair settlement with Stryker.

150. Chester, George Randolph. "The Strike Breaker." *McClure's Magazine* 25 (Sept. 1905): 450–468.

Lanigan, a locomotive engineer and an ardent unionist, has given up on the union during a strike and is desperate for work; he plans to return to the railroad. He admits to his wife that he is a traitor, but he believes he has no other choice, with his young son ill. Strikers discover Lanigan's intentions, and beat him. Lanigan then has a fist-fight with the inept "engineer" who has abused his old locomotive, and is reluctant to return it to Lanigan's care. Lanigan's old fireman, Red Coleman, also returns to work, with vocal condemnations of the union. Lanigan soon comes under suspicion of sabotage, but Coleman proves to be the culprit.

Winter drags on, and the strike disintegrates. All that prevents a settlement is the union's insistence that Lanigan be discharged.

Lanigan sacrifices himself for the good of the brotherhood, and Coleman carries out a final act of cowardly vengeance. "The union is right," says the dying Lanigan, "first, last, and all the time. Tell the boys I said that, won't you?" (468)

The story is a tear-jerker, to be sure, but it avoids simple-minded choosing-up sides. The reader admires Lanigan, who struggles to act honorably when torn by conflicting, intense loyalties.

151. _____. "The Tin Railroad, Incorporated." *Saturday Evening Post* 177 (Oct. 8, 1904): 5–8+.

The Overland Flyer has come to a halt, blocked by snowdrifts in Eagle Pass. The passengers react with attitudes ranging from annoyance to acceptance. The "Tin Railroad" emerges from the belongings of one of the passengers, who takes the toy train, complete with track, from his baggage to amuse a small boy on the coach. He lays out the little wind-up railroad in the aisle, where it runs to everyone's enjoyment. Before long, the Tin Railroad evolves into a seriously-played game of business, with incorporation and selling of stock—and bartering of stock for sandwiches from the porter's supply when hunger strikes the stalled train. Acrimony, argument, and injured feelings follow, although all ends happily, with a romantic overtone. This story could have amounted to more than passing entertainment, but it is an interesting look at the ready enthusiasm with which the public, from one writer's view, regarded railroading at the time.

152. Childs, Marquis W. *Washington Calling!* New York: William Morrow, 1937. 280p.

Its title is uninspired, but this novel is a fairly decent treatment of political and legal maneuvering in the nation's capital, with believable characters and a degree of suspense. The issue at hand concerns the receivership of the Green Valley and Pacific Railroad, controlled by the Esterbrook brothers, and their efforts to assure that the proceedings go their way through the appointment of a pliable federal judge. The Esterbrooks' chief ambition is to rob their stockholders via exploitation of willing political figures.

Although far from steel rails, steaming locomotives, and the sweat of section hands, the novel convincingly depicts an aspect of the business that affects everyone connected with the railroad. (Ignore the limp romantic subplot: It only interferes with the story that matters.)

153. Chin, Frank. *Donald Duk; A Novel.* Minneapolis: Coffee House Press, 1991. 173p.

Donald Duk, a young Chinese-American boy, lives with his family in San Francisco. An unprepossessing youth, he carries himself with a "please beat on me" posture. His father tells him to stand up straight, look people in the eye, and expect them to nod a greeting or step aside. Self-assertion is a hard skill for Donald to master, but as the novel unfolds, he finds an awakening strength in his Chinese identity. The strength develops in large part through a series of vivid dreams in which Donald sees himself as a member of the Chinese work force laying track eastward on the Central Pacific Railroad's route to meet the Union Pacific at Promontory Point, Utah. In Donald's dreams the Chinese workers are a hard-driving, serious lot, determined to better the performance of the Irish laborers also engaged in building the transcontinental railroad.

Donald does extensive research in the library to learn about the true roles of the Chinese railroad builders, and is outraged to see how popular accounts of the meeting at Promontory Point ignore them: "We made history," he notes. "Twelve hundred Chinese. And they don't even put the name of our foreman in the books about the railroad" (122). Instead, the picture presented the public implies that the transcontinental railroad is naught but the result of white men dreaming "white dreams. White brains and white brawn" (131).

The book's real conclusion occurs when Donald sets his teacher straight during a schoolroom lecture that advances all the racist clichés about the "passive, non-competitive" Chinese: "We did the blasting through Summit Tunnel," says Donald. "We worked through two hard winters in the high Sierras .... We set the world's record for miles of track

layed [sic] in one day. We set our last crosstie at Promontory..." (151).

Donald Duk is both an amusing and a sharply-pointed reminder of the way the powerful demean and then forget the contributions of the minorities on whom they depend.

154. _____. "The Eat and Run Midnight People." In *The Chinaman Pacific & Frisco R.R. Co.*, 8–23. Minneapolis: Coffee House Press, 1988.

In an impressionistic piece, the narrator, "the first Chinaman to brake on the Southern Pacific line" (15), describes making love on the beach, and going into work in the yards in the early morning, at a time when "all railyards come to this moment of peculiar quiet, of muttering dark iron, locomotives going nowhere at all. All dark. Iron. Painted steel. Shadows. All the same blackness" (16). The narrator's friend, a thumbless former brakeman, tells him a story involving his assistance with an embalming job. An engineer who disdains using the electric toilet in the locomotive urinates out the door as the train whips along at 60 mph. Meanwhile, the aggressive intimacy continues on the beach. This story is not the easiest to assimilate, and the FCC would not countenance its reading on the air, but it has numerous good lines, some funny ones among them.

155. _____. "Railroad Standard Time." In *The Chinaman Pacific & Frisco R.R. Co.*, 1–7. Minneapolis: Coffee House Press, 1988. Also in *Growing Up Asian American: An Anthology.* Edited by Maria Hong. New York: William Morrow, 1993. *City Lights Journal*, 1978[?].

The Chinese-American narrator opens this meditation and reminiscence of growing up with an account of acquiring his grandfather's best railroad watch as an early adolescent. The narrator never knew his grandfather, not even his name, but "I like to think he was tough, had a few laughs and ran off with his pockets full of engraved watches" (5). He keeps the watch with him for many years, through his own service as a Southern Pacific brakeman. The watch disappears from view in a relatively free-associating story, but the reader assumes that with its 19-jewel mechanism, it kept reliable time of the narrator's life.

156. Churchill, Edward. *Steel Horizon.* 1950. Reprint, New York: Avalon Books, 1970. 253p.

Just after the Civil War, the U.S. Congress has demanded that the Cree City and Northwestern, General Worthington's railroad, finance a line from Cree City to the Dakota line, all the way across Nebraska Territory, to qualify for land grants for further extension. The initial construction must meet a congressional deadline. Worthington hires Harp Blayne to work undercover security for him; many interests stand in the railroad's way, including those invested in riverboats and overland wagons. The story offers standard B-Western fare: Indian attacks, bad guys, ornery cattle ranchers, revenge, and a love interest. Competent; forgettable.

157. Churchill, Winston. *Coniston.* New York: Macmillan, 1906. 543p.

In this political novel spanning events from the 1830s into the 1880s, set in a state readily identifiable as New Hampshire, Churchill fashions his lead character, Jethro Bass, after the real-life political machinist Ruel Durkee. Bass, inspired by a biography of Napoleon, parlays his wealth from a tannery business to build political power before the Civil War. After the war, his influence extends over the entire state legislature. The chief railroad interest in the novel involves Bass's contest with Isaac D. Worthington, a philanthropist for show and a conniving businessman for riches. Worthington has put his fortune into railroads—"the greatest modern factor in prosperity" (143)—and aims to consolidate the state's western roads. Bass, who has no interest in relinquishing power to a railroad combine, is determined to block Worthington's scheme. The novel has been characterized as a treatment of the evolution of American politics from the era of the all-powerful "boss" to that of the corporate entity controlling public policy. Although immediately popular with a readership unhappy with perceived abuses by railroads, the novel's sentimental love-story subplot, slow pace, and contrived (and unbelievable) happy ending will not endear it to most 21st century readers.

158. _____. *Mr. Crewe's Career.* 1908. Reprint, New York: Macmillan, 1919. 498p.

Hilary Vane, a man of wealth and discretion, is a 65-year-old railroad attorney who believes deeply in the railroad's right to have its way. Vane's vexation is his son, Austen, a "wild" Harvard graduate whose taste runs to the semi-wild West. Austen has no interest in taking over as the railroad's chief counsel without proving himself legally capable. His first big case is representing a farmer who nearly died when a train slammed into his wagon. The railroad wants to pay off the farmer to avoid the bad publicity of a jury trial.

Vane subscribes to social Darwinism: "Life," he tells his son, "is a survival of the fittest" (57). Austen does more than survive the farmer's case: He wins it. Rich businessman Humphrey Crewe also solicits Austen's counsel in a contest with the railroad. Crewe is soon elected a state legislator. One legislator's standing joke, with the first-person singular referring to the United Northeastern Railroads: "For bills may come, and bills may go, but I go on forever" (147). The railroad has the legislature in its back pocket. The state's Republican Party leaders are, in effect, the chief lobbyists for the railroad. Urged on by those who resent the railroad's manipulation of state politics, Mr. Crewe goes on the offensive to reclaim the government for the people.

The story plods along, burdened with excess dialog, but it is a good example of fiction aimed at serving high ideals, as well as at selling books. The novel is dedicated "To the men who in every state of the Union are engaged in the struggle for purer politics." Like *Coniston*, *Mr. Crewe's Career* opens a window on its time, and for that reason remains useful, but it is unsatisfying today for much the same reasons that the earlier novel is unsatisfying.

159. Ciresi, Rita. "Orphan Train." *Southern Humanities Review* 30, no. 1 (1996): 57–67.

The narrator lives with her Italian family in New Haven. Her father is a soda company delivery man; her mother obsesses over sweepstakes scams, and, when the children annoy her, tries to silence them with talk of the "orphan trains" that during the influenza pandemic transported the children of flu victims to new homes around the country. The tactic fails; the children relish the idea of a train trip: "Little did Mama realize how the lowly chug of that train sounded like great and glorious music to our ears" (60).

160. Clark, Alexander. *The Old Log School House.* Philadelphia: Leary, Getz & Co., 1861. 288p.

Available at *Wright American Fiction*: http://www.letrs.indiana.edu/web/w/wright2/

Following a story of the schoolteacher's life, the narrator presents a section of "Life Musings" in a vein founded on fact but filtered through a fictional sensibility. The musings focus frequently on his railroad travels. He rides the Louisville and Nashville to Mammoth Cave; en route, "Evening closed over us as we sped along our iron way ... while the distant thunder and the sobbing of the rain storm were blended with the roaring of the train" (153). He travels to Kentucky aboard the Pennsylvania Central, and from there takes the Fort Wayne and Chicago extension through Ohio. In May of 1860, he rides the Philadelphia, Wilmington, and Baltimore to Washington, D.C., a trip that inspires him to poetic rhapsody. His travels continue on the comfortable cars of the Philadelphia and Reading; at last he is homeward bound on the Louisville, New Albany, and Chicago, whose superintendent he "shall ever remember for his many kindnesses" (277).

Clark offers not a hint that railroad travel circa 1860 was anything less than pleasant, civilized, or gracious. There are no sweltering or freezing coaches, or cinders in the eye, or cantankerous fellow passengers in his experience. One can imagine that his recitation of the exotic-sounding railroad names must have titillated the contemporary reader whose own travels were more circumscribed, usually involving no more picturesque scenes than the south end of the family horse.

161. Clingerman, Mildred. "Mr. Sakrison's Halt." In *Best from Fantasy and Science Fiction: 6th Series,* edited by Anthony Boucher, 37–44. New York: Ace Books, 1957. Also in Clingerman's *A Cupful of Space.* New York: Ballantine, 1961. *The Magazine of Fantasy & Science Fiction* 10 (Jan. 1956): 122–127.

The narrator as a child frequently rode the Katy (the Missouri, Kansas, & Texas Railroad) to Chapel Grove to visit her grandparents, and shared the trip with Miss Mattie Compton, an odd little woman in her 50s. Reaching Chapel Grove, Miss Mattie stays in the train, waiting to return. It is only the traveling back and forth that matters to her—that, and her preoccupation with Mr. Sakrison. She and Mr. Sakrison were one day taking the Katy to their wedding; at a station—"the dearest little halt!" (41)—he got off the train. From the window, Miss Mattie saw him exchange greetings with "a colored gentleman" near a sign on the station: "Waiting Room: One and All" (42). Mr. Sakrison did not reboard the train, and Miss Mattie has never seen him again. With the narrator's sympathetic aid, Miss Mattie searches for the mysterious station where Mr. Sakrison disappeared. This story is a gentle piece in which the railroad serves as a means to elusive racial harmony, for Miss Mattie, if not for the narrator.

162. Cobb, Irvin S. "Faith, Hope and Charity." In *Midnight Specials: An Anthology for Train Buffs and Suspense Aficionados,* edited by Bill Pronzini, 81–102. Indianapolis and New York: Bobbs-Merrill, 1977. Also in *Thrillers and More Thrillers.* Edited by Robert Arthur. New York: Random House, 1968. *Cosmopolitan* 88 (April 1930): 30+.

Three criminals—a Spaniard, an Italian, and a Frenchman—are being transported across the Southwest. They overpower a guard and escape from the train during a stop. All three ride trains farther from the scene, and all three meet ironic fates in perfect tune with the judgments previously levied upon them for their crimes.

163. Cohen, Octavus Roy. "Common Stock." *Saturday Evening Post* 195 (July 22, 1922): 14–15+. Also in Cohen's *Jim*

Hanvey, Detective. New York: Dodd, Mead, 1923.

Gerald Corwin has been assigned to carry a proxy vote from Los Angeles to a stockholders' meeting in New York City that will prevent the takeover of the K.R. & P. Railroad by a gang of rascals. Corwin is under the wing of Detective Jim Hanvey, who expects one of the rascals, Billy Scanlon, to try to steal the proxy on the train trip to New York. Corwin, Hanvey, and Scanlon ride east on the California Limited. During the trip, Hanvey demonstrates curious methods of protecting Corwin and the proxy, including a remarkably chummy relationship with Scanlon. Hanvey and Scanlon match wits as the train steams on, in a pleasing little crime and suspense story.

164. _____. *Epic Peters, Pullman Porter.* New York and London: Appleton, 1930. 299p.

Epic Peters, "one of the star porters on the Southern system" (2), works the run from Birmingham to New York City. The book is a collection of tales featuring Peters in central roles, frequently as a solver of mysteries. Cohen draws Peters as a good-humored, well-meaning sort. Although he is a capable porter, he is no mental athlete. For him, excessive thinking is an unnatural act, and leaves him with a headache. Nevertheless, he has a certain naïve aptitude for solving problems in such tales as "Traveling Suspenses," "The Trained Flee [sic]," and "A Toot for a Toot." Peters speaks in stereotypical dialect prone to the comical malaprop: "He's a regular Sherlock Hones" (179). Other sample dialect: "How much tips I is gwine git this trip wouldn't buy a crease fo' one pants leg. Gosh, Pullman porterin' ain't what it used to be.... Ise thinkin' of resignin' away fum the service" (133); and when Epic Peters dines, he is "Gittin' my eatments" (145). Cohen's condescending treatment interferes with any credible sense of Peters as a complete character: His portrayal is thin and two-dimensional, missing both intellectual and emotional substance. He is not a man, but a caricature of a stereotype.

165. Condon, Phil. "Seven." In *River Street: A Novella and Stories*, 13–28.

Southern Methodist University Press, 1994. *Prairie Schooner* 67 (Spring 1993): 88–99.

A badly-married couple, Madeline and Mitchell, occupy a roomette on the Lake Shore Limited on their way back to Chicago. They have had an unpleasant vacation out East. Madeline, who has undergone a double mastectomy, must fight off the advances of a stranger in the vestibule of the coach. Mitchell, drunk, bellows over the inability of anyone in the coach to remember the uniform number of his favorite baseball player, Mickey Mantle (hence the story's title). Mitchell loses his wallet; Madeline tucks him in the roomette and comforts him with her recitation of Mantle's number; she sees three snow geese flying near the train, from the roomette's window. A strong sense of foreboding runs through the story, as if everything that matters to Madeline will soon crumble and vanish. The three geese seem to be an ominous sign.

166. Connolly, James B. "Quilten." In *Head Winds*, 51–79. New York: Scribner's, 1916.

The narrator, Hare, reminisces about his old college acquaintance Quilten. Following college, the two once met in a ticket line for the train from Paris to Havre. The train was not up to third-class standards, but was a rolling hovel for emigrants, dirty, reeking and hot. Enraged by coach windows that would not open as designed, Quilten smashed one after another with his boot heel, to the emigrants' joyous relief. This action only suggests the changes in Quilten since his restrained college days; a murder aboard the train reveals others.

167. Conroy, Jack. "Anyplace But Here." In *The Weed King & Other Stories*, edited by Douglas C. Wixson, 179–181. Westport, CT: Lawrence Hill, 1985.

Conroy (b. 1899) was a significant figure in the literary end of the American labor movement. Among other work, he wrote *The Disinherited* (Covici, Friede, 1933), one of the landmark fictional treatments of the movement. In this story, set during the Depression, white and black adolescents ride the rails together to Detroit, looking for work. A railroad bull surprises them at their camp one day; he marches the black youths off at gunpoint, and warns the white boys not to try to ride the Red Ball manifest. The bull forces the black youths to shovel a carload of hot cinders in their street shoes; they escape at an opportune moment and stumble back to the camp, their feet badly blistered by the heat of the coals. The white boys cover for their companions, who hide when the bull returns, furious. "Promise me you won't never travel with or 'sociate with no damned niggers," he says to the boys (180).

The black youth ignore the bull's warning about the Red Ball, and catch it on its way out of Detroit. "We don't give a damn *where* it goes," one shouts to his white companions, "just so it goes away from *here*. Any place but *here*!" (181).

168. _____. "The Boomer Fireman's Fast Sooner Hound." In *The Weed King & Other Stories*, edited by Douglas C. Wixson, 41–44. Westport, CT: Lawrence Hill, 1985.

In this tall tale of an itinerant fireman and his hound dog who loves to run, the dog runs so well that he can keep up with a train—and on a bet, the fireman sets him out to race the road's fastest train, the Cannon Ball. The dog succeeds, and shows his superiority to the machine by urinating on its wheels as it steams down the track. "A boomer fireman is never long for any one road," the story opens. "Last year he may have worked for the Frisco, and this year he's heaving black diamonds for the Katy or the Wabash" (41).

169. _____. "Bull Market." In Conroy's *The Weed King & Other Stories*, edited by Douglas C. Wixson, 213–228. Westport, CT: Lawrence Hill, 1985. *The Outlander*, no. 3 (Summer, 1933): 17–28.

Railroad detail figures in the opening portion of this story, set in the 1920s, during the great Bull Market. Some folk are not enjoying the benefits of the market. The narrator and three other men in a boxcar bound for Detroit have a close call one night with a railroad detective, and now wait by the track for another freight. An occasional passenger train roars by,

and the men look into the lighted coaches as they pass. "A diner with suave colored waiters in attendance and complacent swells wielding silver cutlery and dabbing at their mouths with linen napkins reminded us that we had not eaten since noon, twelve hours before" (215).

As they ride between cars on another freight, the narrator nods off and nearly falls; his friend Ed saves him from "being ground to hamburger" (216). The men finally reach Detroit, where they swing off the freight at an outer depot and join the anonymous crowds.

170. _____. "Greedy-Gut Gus, the Car Toad." In *The Weed King & Other Stories*, edited by Douglas C. Wixson, 70–73. Westport, CT: Lawrence Hill, 1985.

A "car toad" repairs railroad cars suffering the effects of age or accident. In another of Conroy's tall tales, Greedy-Gut Gus, a confirmed slacker and corner-cutter, is crushed into oblivion by a car he raises with a faulty jack—being too lazy to find a good one. Gus's new assignment: The devil makes him "king of all the car toads in hell.... You're signed up for me from now on," says the devil (72). Alas, Gus proves too lazy even for Old Nick's purposes.

171. Cook, Will. *Iron Man, Iron Horse*. 1960. Reprint, Thorndike, ME: G.K. Hall, 2000. 216p.

Ben Holliday, only 32, is chairman of the board of the Midland-Pacific Railroad. His sole purpose is to pull the line out of the red. Headquarters is in a dreary little Texas town. It won't be easy to put the road on the right track: The area citizens are reluctant to ship on the railroad, for fear of aggravating the Indians, who see the railroad as a threat to their way of life. Holliday's father, the road's founder, reports that an anonymous party is interested in buying it. Cattle-baron Murray Singer, among others, is after the road, and intends to pay bottom dollar for it. Holliday can return to his father's affluent domain in Chicago; the poor old MPRR's fate doesn't hold the cards for his own, except as Ben is determined to prove his mettle as an independent businessman. This is standard railroad-Western, with Indians, locomotives, ranchers, and virile business all around.

172. Cooke, Rose Terry. "Lost on a Railway." In *Sphinx's Children, and Other People's*, 79–107. 1886. Reprint, New York: Garrett Press, 1969.

The story opens at Moosop Station, Conn., with the elderly Mrs. Dodd anxious about her forthcoming train journey behind "that incarnation of Young America,—a locomotive" (79). Her anxiety proves justified. At an early stop she gets off the train and makes the wrong connection, boarding a train headed for Boston. She makes one misstep, and one missed connection, after another, and realizes at length that she is not only on the wrong train, but is traveling to the wrong state. A series of rude fellow passengers and impatient trainmen provide no help, but a gentleman— "that rarest of modern curiosities" (106)— eventually sees to her interests. The sentimental resolution involving the gentleman's kind aid undercuts a story that is otherwise a sympathy-evoking comedy of errors in a none-too-considerate world.

173. Cooper, Courtney R. *End of Steel*. New York: Farrar & Rinehart, 1931. 281p.

Kirk Devore, ticket-taker of the Grand United Circus, has been looking for an old partner who swindled him in a business deal. At the northern Canadian town of The Pas, he narrowly misses collaring his man, then takes up as a partner with railroader Scotty McPherson.

Cooper describes early, ineffective efforts to build a railroad to Hudson's Bay; the construction, left to the powers of nature, had rotted away over the years, leaving only the Mounted Police and the Cree Indians to find the forlorn roadbed useful as a trail, but in time the Muskeg Limited has been built into the far north. Devore rides a colonists' train on the Muskeg, until it reaches the end of the track, the "end of steel." He and Scotty join other laborers in the back-breaking work of pushing the steel farther; Devore becomes a work-gang boss. The novel's look at pioneer railroading in the Canadian wilds is far more interesting than the ho-hum manhunt that holds the plot together; conditions in the northern wilds receive realistic treatment, as "the mosquitoes and blackflies crowded about them; sand gnats whined" (110). "Dog tired men dragged their way bunkwards with darkness; labor was incessant" (122). The men fight brushfires, "blazing sun and lashing storm, slime, muck, flies, and solitude in this battle against the North" (145).

174. _____. "Silk Train." *American Magazine* 114 (July 1932): 24–27+.

Young engineer Jack Hailey receives a disciplinary layoff after being held responsible for a collision with a silk-hauling train. The action places Jack on the cusp of losing his job in the middle of the Great Depression. Abandoning hope of reinstatement after his layoff, Hailey drifts west, to Colorado and Wyoming, "merely one of thousands driven into momentum by the swinging pendulum of hard times.... Depression had all but suffocated the railways" (26, 27). Cooper's description of the Depression-battered rail industry is succinct and vivid: "Engine dead lines had become crowded, stacks covered, movable parts grease-coated, side rods removed. Storage yards were congested with surplus rolling stock. Smoke had ceased to rise from shop stacks" (27).

Hailey works on a paving gang, but, as business picks up a bit, returns to the railroad as a guard aboard a silk train racing east across Canada. Redeeming himself, he assumes the engineer's position in an emergency.

In spite of the contrived happy ending, the story presents a convincingly detailed picture of railroading. Noteworthy is a passage in which Hailey reflects on the vast organization that works to deliver a train to its destination: "No longer did he feel that the man in the cab was alone; there were hundreds, thousands behind him, bracing him with the precaution and precision of ceaseless workers, in yards, in offices, on track, at telephones and telegraph keys, in roundhouses and shops" (121).

175. _____, and Leo F. Creagan. "Martin Garrity Finally Pulls a Bone." *American Magazine* 91 (April 1921): 28–31+.

Section boss Martin Garrity and his men were honored to receive distinction as the best section on the O.R. & T. Railroad. Thanks to the pleas of the general manager's daughter, Martin is promoted to trainmaster. Soon he makes division superintendent, with a private car and "an imported Jap" cook (30). Garrity is known as a lucky man, but most of his fellow railroaders expect his luck to run out one day. An absurd misunderstanding in which Garrity confuses the death of a dog with the imagined death of the general manager's daughter would seem to confirm their expectations, but Garrity's luck holds, as an unlikely coincidence turns Garrity's blunder to his superior's advantage.

176. _____. "Martin Garrity Gets Even." In *Best American Short Stories, 1919–1924*, edited by Blanche C. Williams. Vol. 1, Book 3, 113–126. Garden City, N.Y.: Doubleday, 1926. Also in *O. Henry Memorial Award Prize Stories of 1921*. Garden City, N.Y.: Doubleday, 1921. *American Magazine* 92 (July 1921): 20–23.

Martin Garrity is superintendent of the Blue Ribbon Division of the O.R. & T. Railroad. He receives a curt telegram from Chicago requesting his resignation; he will be supplanted, under the road's new management, by another man. He and his wife, Jewel, are stricken: "Now, all they had worked for, lived for, longed for, and enjoyed together had been taken away, without warning, without reason, and given to another!" (115).

Garrity's deposed boss, Barstow, secures a post with the decrepit Ozark Central, and hires Garrity to help him knock the flea-bag road into proper shape. Barstow is determined to wrest the St. Louis–Kansas City mail contract away from the O.R. & T. In spite of his hard-nosed reputation, Garrity makes an evident blunder, buying a fleet of rotary snowplows for the Ozark, even though the road has never had a problem with snow. Garrity is a laughingstock over the error. Inevitably, the snowplows play a vital part not simply in winning the mail contract, but in the merger of the two railroads, with Barstow and Garrity assuming control.

177. Coover, Robert. "Great Train Robbery." *Playboy* 45 (Oct. 1998): 84–86+.

A band of outlaws waits to waylay a train while their orange-haired bandit queen, Belle, sings to them of their exploits. The outlaws have followed the elusive rails thanks to their fine-cinder spoor; at one point, the track apparently dead-ended in a water hole. As they wait for the train, the outlaws argue about whether they have the right location. "Mebbe these're jest more false tracks that consarned train has laid down t'throw us offn its trail," says one desperado (86).

The train is much like an animal quarry in this funny, surrealistic spoof; the train tries to hide in a mine-shaft—and, "Judas train" that it is, plays a nasty trick on the gang.

178. _____. "In a Train Station." In *Pricksongs & Descants*, 98–104. New York: Dutton, 1969.

Commuter Alfred, a man in his early 50s, is trapped in a loop of time and action in which he must reenact endlessly the same ghastly scene in the train station waiting room: the banal conversation with "the Stationmaster" about the weather, his sack lunch, his bluegill fishing and the health of his tomatoes—and the absurd murder of a drunk who stumbles into the waiting room and vomits on a bench. Alfred yearns to escape the loop, but the Stationmaster sternly reminds him of his duty to play his part.

179. Cottrell, Dorothy. "Tiddlywinks and the Train Wrecker." *Ladies' Home Journal* 48 (May 1931): 11+.

This "women's magazine" fiction raises sentimentality to a high pitch. Little Mary and her pipsqueak terrier, Tiddlywinks, surprise the local Bolshevik as he attempts to set the stage for a derailment near Big Hill. With poor Mary knocked unconscious by the commie, brave Tiddlywinks races for help—then, on seeing the express train approaching, sits down on the track and howls. "The engine driver had a schedule, but he had once possessed a dog of his own, a small dog whose death had left his world very bleak and empty" (134). The engineer stops the train, and all is well.

180. Coulson, G.J.A. [Alcibiades Jones]. "Mrs. Spriggins, the Neutral." In *To Live and Die: Collected Stories of the Civil War, 1861–1876*, edited by Kathleen Diffley, 280–283. Durham and London: Duke University Press, 2002. *Southern Magazine*, Feb. 1871.

The narrator describes an incident on a train in 1864. A tall woman on crutches enters his coach; not a man in the crowded car moves to help her until the narrator does so. She proves to be a nurse, with the Union, a Mrs. Spriggins. As the train rolls along, she relates volubly her experiences in the hospital tending the battle wounded; she is unaware, as is the reader, that the narrator's sympathies lie with the Confederacy. At the trip's end, when he reveals to Mrs. Spriggins his political allegiance, she tells him that although she does not believe "any of them Rebs can ever git to heaven at any price," that does not stop her from nursing them. "Sometimes they are our boys, and sometimes Rebs, but in the horspittle I'm always *nootral!*" (283)

181. Cousins, Margaret. "Uncle Edgar and the Reluctant Saint." *Good Housekeeping* 119 (Dec. 1944): 20–21+. Also in *21 Texas Short Stories*. Edited by W.W. Perry. Austin: University of Texas Press, 1954.

The narrator recalls the time she had to take a four-hour train trip as a child, alone, on Christmas Eve. Sissy Grant boarded the train, relying on the old conductor to look after her. She found herself in a car full of men, and not one woman or other child. A sheriff in the next seat realizes that she is Charlie Grant's daughter, and torments her with mean jokes; he suggests that her father will forget to pick her up at the station. Just as Sissy is about to cry, her beloved Uncle Edgar enters the car. When he learns that the sheriff has snuffed out Sissy's belief in Santa Claus, he thrashes the man, to the approval of the other passengers. Immediately afterward, word comes that the train will be marooned all night owing to a bridge emergency. Sissy weeps in despair, but as she sleeps that night, her uncle and the other men in the car prepare an astonishing surprise for her: "All

these sad, homeless men, who never would have been on the Brazos Valley & Central passenger train on Christmas Eve if they really had any place to go (they were probably all going up to Wichita to get drunk) embraced the Christmas spirit and were children together" (186)—including even the sheriff, in a most unlikely role. Although sentimental, this sweet and charming story accurately depicts a child's sensibilities.

182. Crane, Stephen. "The Bride Comes to Yellow Sky." In *The University Edition of the Works of Stephen Crane*. Vol. 5, *Tales of Adventure*, edited by Fredson Bowers, 109–120. Charlottesville: University Press of Virginia, 1970. *McClure's Magazine* 10 (Feb. 1898): 377–384.

Naïve newlyweds Jack Potter and his wife delight in the splendid appointments of the coach in which they ride through Texas to Yellow Sky. In their estimation, the surroundings reflect the glory of their wedding that morning in San Antonio. The other passengers, however, find the couple's gauche innocence amusing, and the black porter entertains himself by insulting them without their realizing it. Potter, the marshal of Yellow Sky, anticipates that the town's brass band will greet him and his wife at the station. When they arrive, only the station agent is on the platform. As Mr. and Mrs. Potter enter town, they find themselves confronted by Potter's old, and thoroughly drunken, nemesis, Scratchy Wilson. Wilson threatens them while Potter has a vision of the luxurious Pullman on which he and his wife recently rode. Wilson's discovery that he is standing before Potter's new wife deflates his violent ambitions.

This brilliant story of psychological tension, irony, and erroneous perceptions opens with a memorable and original railroad image: As the train bearing the Potters rolls west, everything it passes—plains, houses, trees, "all were sweeping into the east, sweeping over the horizon, a precipice" (109), as if dropping off the edge of the world.

183. _____. "An Excursion Ticket." In *The University Edition of the Works of*

Stephen Crane. Vol. 8, *Tales, Sketches, and Reports*, edited by Fredson Bowers, 58–65. Charlottesville: University Press of Virginia, 1973. Also in Crane's *Prose and Poetry.* New York: Library of America, 1984. First published in the *New York Press,* May 20, 1894, part iv, p. 3, under the title "Billie Atkins Went to Omaha."

Billie Atkins, a penniless tramp, has been on the road for 16 years. Billie "has seen the cold blue gleam of the Northern lakes, the tangled green thickets of Florida and the white peaks of the Rockies" in his life on the road (58).

One day in Denver a sudden desire to visit Omaha seizes him. The story follows him on a series of trains, and a series of abuses by trainmen who catch him riding illicitly. Billie is thrown off the train, stomped on, and doused with freezing water as he clings to the end of a car. When he reaches Omaha, he pleads for a place to sleep in the city jail.

Crane portrays Billie as a good-natured simpleton who, once he has satisfied his urge to see Omaha, convinces himself that he must start for Denver in the morning. The story features themes of adventure and class conflict: The trainmen, hardly well-off themselves, demand money from Billie. When he cannot provide it, they exercise their authority forcefully.

184. _____. "A Freight Car Incident." In *The University Edition of the Works of Stephen Crane.* Vol. 8, *Tales, Sketches, and Reports*, edited by Fredson Bowers, 105–109. Charlottesville: University Press of Virginia, 1973. Also in Crane's *Prose and Poetry.* New York: Library of America, 1984. First published April 12, 1896, as a syndicated piece in the *Nebraska State Journal* and other newspapers.

Although brief, this story shows Crane's sense of absurd irony. The narrator—"The Major"—describes the time at an auction when he stepped into a nearby freight car to obtain some ice. Someone slammed the door shut behind him, and he spent a terrifying few minutes trapped in the dark interior with a heavily-armed man trying to escape the vengeance of some locals. Much hinges on whether the Major will, at the low-life's order, slide back the car door and likely expose himself to gunfire.

Creagan, Leo F. *see* **Cooper, Courtney R., and Leo F. Creagan**

185. Crichton, Kyle S. "Working on the Railroad." *Collier's* 109 (Jan. 3, 1942): 13. Also in *The Best Short Short Stories from Collier's.* Edited by Barthold Fles. Cleveland: World Publishing, 1948.

Albert Halley, a freshly-retired conductor on the Pawhasket—New York Division of the Midlands Railroad, spent his entire career loathing commuters. On his first trip as a pass-wielding commuter himself, Halley receives a quick introduction to life on the other side of the fence, and finds it not so sweet.

186. Croft, Jesse Taylor. *The Railroad War: The Trainmasters, Book II.* New York: Popular Library, 1989. 405p.

The heart of this historical romance consists of Confederate Major Noah Ballard's efforts in 1863 to transport a large number of locomotives from Mississippi to Atlanta. Southern railroad bosses have hidden scores of their best locomotives, hoping to keep them out of service until war's end, with plans to use them in their postwar business. Confederate General Johnston learns of the hidden locomotives, and orders them exhumed, put in order, and set to military use. As Ballard prepares the engines for shipment, Union General Sherman learns of the plan, and assigns master spy Sam Houston Hawken to help thwart it. Hawken and Ballard are old friends, now in different uniforms, therein residing much of the tale's tension. A number of historical figures play important parts in the story, including Sherman, Johnston, and Gen. Grenville Dodge. A romantic subplot does little but interfere with the novel's progress, and a bit too much present-day sensibility creeps into the story from time to time. It is, nevertheless, an entertaining vacation book.

187. Cullen, E. J. "The Second Law of Thermodynamics." In *Our War and How We Won It*, 28–31. New York: Viking, 1987.

"The man is in a train somewhere" (28) in this brief reflection on disintegrating lives—or a life, specifically, his own. The man, a father, feels like a failure in that capacity, and, as he watches the passing landscape from his train window, wonders if he has anything to give his children that is worth having. In spite of references to concrete locales—Nice, France, for example—there may be some question whether a physical train is involved at all in this story.

Cunningham, A.B. *see* **Hale, Garth**

Cunningham, Albert B. *see* **Hale, Garth**

188. Currey, Richard. "Waiting for Trains." *North American Review* 272, no. 3 (1987): 18–21. Also in *The Best American Short Stories, 1988*. Edited by Mark Helprin and Shannon Ravenel. Boston: Houghton Mifflin, 1988.

The narrator, back from a hitch with the Marines in Vietnam, takes a job as a gas station attendant in San Francisco. He makes friends with Shirl, a waitress in a diner. One night they drive by an old rail depot in Oakland, triggering memories of the narrator's boyhood, when he and his late brother enjoyed what they thought of as a secret place near a railroad trestle. There they threw stones at boxcars, and set pennies on the track for the trains to flatten. Shirl and the narrator loiter about the station while the janitor sweeps the floor. Events slide downhill fast from this point.

189. Currier, Isabel. "I've Been Working on the Railroad." *American Mercury* 54 (March 1942): 337–344.

In this pathetic story of a man whose life consists of nothing but his job, Henry Elmann, a 40-year fast-freight engineer for the railroad, is about to retire, following his last run, the 5:40 to Montreal from Vermont. Friends and family see Henry off at the yard. In the crowd is his old pal Craig, a capable engineer who, in only a year of retirement, has turned into a drunken shell of his former self. As Henry leaves the yard, his engine pulls a motley lot of cars: "Great Northern, Chicago, Milwaukee & St. Paul.... Relics of railroads long lost in their mergers followed Henry Elmann, locomotive engineer, retiring, out of his terminal for the last time" (342).

Owing to railroad rules, Elmann cannot serve as engineer on the return trip, since on the day of return he will be 65. He deadheads back to Vermont aboard the caboose. On his arrival at his old familiar yards, a welcoming party greets him, but Henry steps off the caboose, turns his back on the train and the party, and runs awkwardly away. "The people on the platform called to him at first, then they let him go. "The Legion Band played 'Casey Jones,' but nobody listened" (344).

Dannay, Frederic *see* **Queen, Ellery**

190. Davenport, Guy. "The Haile Selassie Funeral Train." In *Da Vinci's Bicycle; Ten Stories*, 108–113. Baltimore: Johns Hopkins University Press, 1979. *Mulch* 3 (Fall 1975): 40–41, 43–46.

An American reminisces about riding Ethiopian emperor Haile Selassie's funeral train in 1936. Aboard the train are such literary luminaries as Apollinaire and James Joyce. Joyce, in particular, has a good deal to say, some of it comprehensible. In the midst of the exotica, the narrator has a flash of home: "I thought of the engineer Elrod Singbell, who used to take the mile-long descending curve of Stump House Mountain in the Blue Ridge playing *Amazing Grace* [sic] on the whistle" (113).

191. Davis, Clyde Brion. *Nebraska Coast*. New York and Toronto: Farrar & Rinehart, 1939. 423p.

The story begins in 1860 in upstate New York. Eleven-year-old narrator Clint MacDougall and his family sell their canal boat and head out on the train for Nebraska Territory to make a new life, "clear out to the Nebrasky coast," says Clint's father (67). When the glistening engine and its brightly-painted coaches pull into the station where the family waits, it creates a sensation among the station loungers.

Aboard the train, Clint's Aunt Christine is so overcome by the immensity of it all that she requires a whiff of smelling salts from the bottle in her reticule. Going downhill, the train reaches the breathtaking speed of 40 miles per hour.

The family changes trains at Buffalo, and crosses Canada into Michigan. Their excitement at their first train journey would be easy to mock, but Davis treats it with a gentle good humor. They reach Chicago at night, and soon steam off for Hannibal, Missouri. There they meet a man who ridicules the notion of a transcontinental railroad. The skeptic, Major Brown, has a scheme to steal the railroad's thunder by instituting "steam wagon" traffic on the territorial roads, relying on steam-driven vehicles that will halt any congressional urge to subsidize railroad development in the West. While Major Brown is off fighting Indians, and a prototype steam wagon stands rusting and useless, the Union Pacific starts laying track for the transcontinental route. As history would have it, the railroads prevail, and the Macdougalls, hitching their business interests to the local road—the Midland Pacific—prosper.

Although it suffers from the drawbacks that plague historical novels as a genre, the book is genial and readable, and a painless way to absorb some history.

192. Davis, Elmer H. "Mr. Peters Makes His Train." *Collier's* 87 (April 18, 1931): 7–8+.

Twenty-nine-year-old Howard Peters is the director of the Gosler Foundation for Social Justice, and makes a handsome $25,000 a year despite the Depression. He is riding the train to a conference at Lake Wiskonka to give an address. In a gallant effort to assist what he believes to be a young widow and her small boy in the crowded dining car, Davis runs afoul of the Gosler family, traveling on the same train, and is sacked on the spot. From this point, Peters finds himself in a situation worthy of a Hitchcock plot: false identity, bootleggers, dope smugglers—which ends with Peters appointed by the governor to head the state crime commission. Escapism for the Depression-bound.

193. Davis, Harold L. "Extra Gang." In *Team Bells Woke Me, and Other Stories*, 240–259. New York: Morrow, 1953. *American Mercury* 24 (Oct. 1931): 161–170.

When one of the young black extra gang members suffers serious injury in an accident, the timekeeper (who narrates the story) helps load him onto a handcar to take him to the nearest town for treatment. The response there is unenthusiastic: "One of them niggers. Cure him up, and what you got?" (251). The town doctor sews up the wounded man, who takes the operation bravely, but when the timekeeper tries to secure a room at the hotel, the door is closed. The woman who runs it is "fitty about colored men" (254). The timekeeper, the only white man in company with a half-dozen African-Americans, experiences something of a racial awakening thanks to the courage of the injured man and the racist behavior of the townspeople who refuse the party a place to sleep. The rail workers bed down in a patch of grass by the river. "We were all broke and bedeviled, and we were, therefore, all better than the people who bedeviled us. I wouldn't have traded that patch of grass ... for the station-agent's bed, or all the beds those townspeople had ever slept in or hid under" (256). The story shuns easy good feeling, and closes on a dispirited, somber note—a note that renders the timekeeper's insights all the more convincing.

194. _____. "The Flying Switch." In *Team Bells Woke Me, and Other Stories*, 192–214. New York: Morrow, 1953. *Collier's* 86 (Aug. 2, 1930): 14–15+.

A tale in the "rollicking yarn" category, "The Flying Switch" features a runaway section gang car, occupied by seven men. One of the seven is the notorious old crank, Stub Johnson, long-time foreman and pain in the hindquarters. The runaway, which is not without its tragic aspect—including a man dying when he leaps off the speeding car—nevertheless furnishes some funny moments, and achieves predictable satisfaction in the failure of old Stub to soften his ways, even after looking death in the face. "Ain't he an old catamount, though?" asks one of Stub's crew. "God," says another, "if I don't believe he's worse'n he ever was!" (214)

195. _____. "Railroad Beef." *Collier's* 96 (Oct. 19, 1935): 29+.

The foreman of an extra gang wants to send some of his trusted old hands off to a nearby town to buy two sides of beef for their meals. Tom Steele, a cattle rancher, leaps to the conclusion that the railroad gang, a group of 40 men, provided the market for the cattle recently stolen from him, and threatens violence against the foreman. The railroaders help Steele, whose livelihood hangs in the balance, recover his lost investment, and solve the rustling caper. This Depression story depicts Steele and his family on the verge of losing everything, and the railroaders as heroes. They even develop a fondness for Steele's little boy, and buy him a new set of clothes.

196. _____. *Winds of Morning.* New York: William Morrow, 1952. 344p.

The events of this novel—part Western, part mystery, part history—take place in the late 1920s in the Columbia River area. Attention to railroading is generally slim, but in one substantial passage (160–173), narrator Amos G. Clarke describes a Greek track gang. "Greek track workers always argued loudest and most passionately over some totally abstract quibble..." (160). Argumentative the Greeks may be, "but they never allowed any body, no matter of what race, creed, color or condition, to get past one of their outfit trains without being hauled in and fed... (161). The foreman of the gang cordially allows Clarke to examine railroad payroll records for clues about the man he is trying to find.

197. Davis, Keith. "Railroad or Ramble." *Railroad Magazine* 80 (Dec. 1966): 40–43.

A trainmaster's clerk at the Yucca yards tells this story. A new man, C. Steele, hires on as yardmaster in the busy harvest season. Steele clamps down on the yardmen, telling them to "railroad or ramble" (42). He makes things move, but his dictatorial style sticks in everyone's craw. No one would suspect that Steele has a human side, but he shows it one day when

he discovers and assists a poor family living in a boxcar. This act flies in the face of railroad rules, leaving Steele to follow his own dictum: He rambles.

198. Davison, Charles S. "How I Sent My Aunt to Baltimore." *Scribner's Magazine* 12 (Aug. 1892): 249–252.

The narrator's elderly aunt is determined to travel to Baltimore, from her New England home. He accepts the task of seeing her safely off in a drawing-room car. All is haste and confusion; in New Jersey, a functionary recites, "in unintelligible tones, the names of most of the railroad stations of the United States" (250). The narrator escorts his aunt aboard the train, then must leap from the car when the train leaves the station early. He takes with him his aunt's purse, and all her money. He realizes also that he has sent his aunt to the wrong city. He pleads for help from railroad officials, who, rather than invoke bureaucratic rules and regulations, go out of their way to make the old lady's trip a happy one. Marvels the narrator, "I came away with the general stunned feeling which we all experience when we run up against an approximately perfect system, working without hitch or delay" (252). The narrator assures the reader that this is not a story, but a true account. To present-day readers, the narrative is too incredible to take as anything but fiction.

199. Day, Dianne. *Death Train to Boston.* New York: Bantam, 2000. 257p.

This detective thriller set in 1908 opens in the aftermath of an explosion aboard a train bound for Boston from San Francisco. Heroine Fremont Jones, badly injured, has been rescued by a Mormon polygamist who aims to make her his next wife. Her partner, Michael Kossoff, is also injured, and has no idea of Jones's whereabouts. The railroad hired Jones and Kossoff to investigate a string of "accidents"; whether the explosion is another accident, or something more sinister, is an open question. The book is diverting, fluffy entertainment, with well-drawn characters and numerous passages set aboard trains.

200. Dealey, Ted. "Blackstone Does His Stuff." *Saturday Evening Post* 200 (Dec.

17, 1927): 32+. Also in *Best Short Stories from the Southwest.* Edited by Hilton R. Greer. Dallas: Southwest Press, 1928.

The Sulphur Bottom and Northeastern Railroad's fast freight plows through a half dozen of Charley Webb's heifers one night, leaving hamburger on the tracks. Webb sues. Attorney Guy Oates takes the case, his first. Oates is up against old Col. Botts, a disdainful counselor. Botts meets his match in the clever Oates, and finds himself not only on the short end of the law, but a figure of public ridicule as the young lawyer helps the poor farmer get the goods on the railroad's high-handed lawyer. (The "Blackstone" of the title refers to Oates's professional inspiration, Sir William Blackstone.)

201. De Courcy, M.B. [Matthias Bodine]. *Sons of the Red Rose: A Story of the Rail in the Early '80s.* Washington, D.C.: J.W. Cannon, 1905. 234p.

In the preface, the author describes this semi-autobiographical novel as "the reminiscences of a brakeman, switchman, conductor, and freight and passenger engineer." The hero is one John Gray, a Virginia lad who falls in with mentor Frank Howe. Howe shows him the "how to" of the railroad. As they go deeper into the life of the rails, Howe asks Gray how he likes it. "I'm just beginning to live," says Gray (28). The chapter titles tell it all: "How John Gray Passed through His First Wreck, and Learns How Men Face Death"; "Tells How Alcohol Burns Men's Souls As Well As Stomachs"; "Tells How a Boiler Head, Scoop and Firebox, Looks to a 'Green' Fireman," and so on. Although the book is fairly artless as fiction, the author's knowledge of railroading informs it with credible period detail. When not occupied with railroading, the novel is a sentimental tale of goodness and earnestness triumphant.

The author wrote this book after a harrowing rail career, during which he lost fingers, toes, and his right foot; was struck by lightning and electrocuted. He finally died of a heart attack while sitting on a railroad bridge abutment in Pennsylvania.

202. Delbanco, Nicholas. "The Writer's Trade." *Paris Review,* no. 112 (Winter 1989): 160–176. Also in Delbanco's *The Writer's Trade & Other Stories.* New York: Morrow, 1990.

Twenty-two-year-old Mark's first novel receives glowing reviews, and he becomes taken with the notion of living the writer's life, expecting, for example, that a passenger aboard the train he is riding will recognize him from his picture in *Saturday Review.* Rather than stoking his writerly ego, the train ride from Grand Central Station jolts Mark out of his wallowing in youthful success: The train stops after rolling over a young woman lying on the tracks. It is not clear whether the event is suicide or murder, but for Mark, "his blithe assumption of the primacy of art was made to seem ridiculous by fact" (176).

203. Dellinger, E.S. "Blacklisted." *Railroad Magazine* 100 (May 1976): 40–53.

In 1892, the Ozark Central presses into service a number of engines so ill-maintained that they endanger their crews. Fireman Ted Sharon and his father, Engineer Bill Sharon, are struggling with the old No. 343 when the boiler explodes, killing the older man. In a trumped-up "investigation," the railroad holds Ted culpable, and fires him. When Ted's union fails to support him, he alienates union officials, and is blacklisted. The next year, eating lunch at a railroad diner in the West, Ted complains to an engineer: "How'n the devil can a fellow get a job when every official in the country turns him down because one son of a bitch fired him for something he didn't do; and a weak-kneed Brotherhood didn't have the guts to see he got justice?" (45).

Ted's personal story intersects with the efforts of locomotive fireman Eugene V. Debs and the American Railway Union to organize the railroad brotherhoods into a single powerful organization. Ted, hired without a reference check by the Pacific Coast Line, joins the ARU and works to win more converts. In 1894, the Pacific Coast Line union men join railroaders across the country in the Pullman Strike. Ted and his pal, engineer "Monkey" Morgan, weather both the railroad's perfidy and the strike, which the federal government crushes. Ted finally escapes the blacklist.

Dellinger, born in 1886, began his railroading career as a brakeman on the Missouri Pacific. He plainly sympathizes with the union in this interesting story, and devotes a large part of it to description of the tactics the railroads and the government used to break the strike and destroy the ARU. Concludes Dellinger, "The real fight for better working conditions on the railroads had only just begun" (53).

204. _____. "Branch-Line Operator." *Railroad Magazine* 32 (Nov. 1942):48–58.

Matt Jacobs, for over 30 years a telegrapher at an isolated mountain depot, receives word in 1940 that he must move to main-line service with the Copper Mountain Railroad. The road plans to abandon the cut-off line on which Jacobs works. He is convinced that with the coming war, the railroad will need every mile of track it owns in operation. His belief gains support when the Pentagon opens a new Army base near the line, assuring that life will go on as before at the out-of-the-way depot—only much busier.

205. _____. "Harvey House Girl." *Railroad Stories* 16 (March 1935): 54–77.

Dellinger begins this semi-historical tale on January 17, 1884, the date of a fire that destroyed the Montezuma resort in Las Vegas, New Mexico. Among those driven from the blaze are the invalid wife and child of yard conductor Jim Hartley. Mary Carson, a Harvey House girl, tries to comfort Hartley and his young daughter, Helen, when Mrs. Hartley dies of pneumonia in the fire's aftermath. Mary has for some time served Hartley meals at Las Vegas's Depot Hotel (an actual Harvey establishment) without charging him; almost everything that he earned had gone into sustaining his family at the Montezuma. By 1899, Hartley has died in a railroad accident, and his daughter Helen returns to the West, where she works in a Harvey House, the newly-built Casteneda in Las Vegas. There she meets Mary Carson, who is now widely considered a blessed figure among railroaders. The story goes on to relate the romantic doings of Helen

and assorted railroaders and local cowboys who frequent the Harvey House. Although it does sketch some details of the Harvey House system, the story fails to follow through on its promise to present a good historical portrait of the life and work of Harvey girls.

206. _____. "The Hobo's Secret." *Railroad Stories* 20 (Oct. 1936): 98–127.

Kiamichi Bill and Blackie Burns are "blanket stiffs," carrying blanket rolls as they wander, and sleeping where the night finds them. They have traveled together for six years. Bill, the younger hobo, stops a runaway string of cars, saving the lives of two young women on the caboose platform, and rail officials offer him a job. Bill takes the job, splitting up with Blackie. Bill works as a student brakeman under Conductor Charlie Ross, who gives the young man a fierce "rawhiding": a harsh, abusive introduction to the railroad. Years later, Bill has become a capable brakeman, and finds himself back on a train under the hobo-hating Ross. Complicating the story, and in the end explaining the "secret," is a family relationship involving Ross, his wife and daughter, and old Blackie Burns. This better-than-usual Dellinger story offers some genuine tension and excitement, but its main strength comes from its focus on human relations rather than on railroad hardware and procedures.

207. _____. "The Middle Order." *Railroad Magazine* 94 (Sept. 1973): 33–35. *Railroad Magazine*, April 1939.

The author describes the middle order as a reminder order concerning distant engine meetings issued train crews on a mountain division. An engineer's failure to read a middle order in a timely way nearly leads to disaster in this story; thanks to the responsible conduct of a young brakeman, the outcome is less severe. Aside from the matter of the order, the story is another example of true railroaders overcoming personal differences and mistrust in their service to the road.

208. _____. "Railroad Girl." *Railroad Magazine* 24 (June 1938): 28–54. Reprinted as "Brass-Pounding Girl." *Railroad Magazine* 102 (Aug. 1977): 34–47.

Twenty-year-old Nellie Ames arrives in the Kansas & Arizona yards one day during World War I to report for her new job as a telegraph operator. The men on the scene joke among themselves about the young woman in the threadbare clothes; they are convinced that railroading is men's work, and theirs alone. They are unaware that Nellie is the daughter of an old K & A conductor. Nellie's first night on the job seems to bear out the railroaders' pessimism. Everything goes wrong for Nellie, and several workers question her intelligence. One brakeman, Jimmie Dean, saves Nellie from being struck by an engine in a careless moment; she repays him by teaching him telegraphy, and he instructs her in fine points of railroading. In a story thick with train-order details, Nellie and Jimmie together salvage her career, and head off a wreck in the making. The superintendent praises her as a "railroad girl," and she is elated. (Does it go without saying that no male railroader ever finds delight in being identified as a "railroad boy"?)

209. _____. "Skeleton Crew." *Railroad Magazine* 60 (Feb. 1953): 94–104. *Railroad Magazine* 88 (April 1971): 57–61.

Brothers Harry, Dave, and Jack Wardlow are taking a new electric locomotive on a test run over a Rocky Mountain route with a short crew. Harry is the engineer, with his twin Dave spelling him at the controls; kid brother Jack is the brakeman. They worry about a suspect air brake line, but haven't time to check it before proceeding with orders. In this story Dellinger writes the railroad story equivalent of "hard" science fiction: The real emphasis is on the technology, with a parallel focus on the dangers created by railroad management—the "brass collars"—trying to operate on the cheap. In an unusual complication, Harry Wardlow, recently elected to the state legislature, is being excoriated by other trainmen, including his own father, for failing to shepherd a full-crew bill to a successful vote.

210. Dempsey, Al. *Path of the Sun*. New York: Tor, 1993. 320p.

Set in 1888, this novel describes railroad magnate James J. Hill's interests in seeking statehood for the territory of the Northwest.

The leading character, young Zachary Horton, is something of an 1880s Zelig or Forest Gump, called upon by Hill to assist him in his efforts to bring statehood to the areas so critical to his grand railroad-building ambitions. Zack has family background in railroading: His grandfather built the Dakota and Western, a feeder line on which Hill has his eye. Zack goes west from his New York City turf to join Hill; once in Hill's domain, he meets an astounding number of the era's important people, from President Grover Cleveland to an up-and-coming Teddy Roosevelt and President-elect Benjamin Harrison. Other historical characters surfacing in the plot include Hill's competitor, Henry Villard, and labor leader Samuel Gompers.

Like so many historical novelists, Dempsey here wanders away from the story to passages of straightforward didacticism on such topics as the Credit Mobilier scandal. These passages can be enlightening, but do not serve the ends of good fiction. Nevertheless, the story moves along at a good pace and in a good humor.

211. Depew, Herbert. "Pickup on the Train." *Saturday Evening Post* 226 (Oct. 10, 1953): 34–35+.

Young women whom one meets on trains in 20th century popular magazine fiction are almost always "girls." On the commuter train here, George Hunt is determined to win the interest of a "girl" whose efforts to create an underwear advertisement have dead-ended. In spite of her coolness, George and the other boys in his commuter bridge foursome help the ad woman out with some snappy copy. One thing leads to another, romantically speaking.

212. Derby, George H. "Great Railroad Project!" In *The Squibob Papers*, 223–226. New York: Carleton, 1865.

Available at *Wright American Fiction*: http://www.letrs.indiana.edu/web/w/wright2/

Subtitled "The Belvidere and Behring's Straits Union Railroad," this tongue-in-cheek piece mocks the national railroad building mania by describing plans for a railroad that will run from the town of Belvidere, Illinois, to Behring's Straits, with a branch line to the

North Pole, "to secure the ice trade" (223). Another branch will run underground to the Dead Sea, and will "be built under the supervision of eminent Ohio engineers, they having had much experience in works of that character" (224). The stupendous project is to fling railroad tracks over most of the planet.

Derby, a little-remembered California humorist of not inconsiderable talent, wrote under the pseudonyms Squibob and John Phoenix; he was also an officer in the Corps of Topographic Engineers, a background that gives his absurd railroad scheme some extra bite.

Derleth, August *see* **Grendon, Steven.**

213. Derleth, August. "The Adventure of the Lost Locomotive." In *The Memoirs of Solar Pons*, 156–175. Sauk City, WI: Mycroft & Moran, 1951.

In this story set in England, Derleth's "private enquiry agent," Solar Pons, receives a request for help from the director of the Great Northern Railway: "One of our locomotives has vanished," he says (157). Pons—Derleth's homage to Sherlock Holmes—cleverly solves the case, which reveals unscrupulous shenanigans among business executives.

214. _____. *The Adventure of the Orient Express*. New York: Candlelight Press, 1965. 60p. Also in Derleth's *The Solar Pons Omnibus*. Vol. 2. Sauk City, WI: Arkham House, 1982.

On the Orient Express, returning from a medical conference in Prague in 1938, Dr. Lyndon Parker passes time playing chess with a German who speaks excellent English. Soon the two of them are heaving a dead body through their open compartment window, confronting a beautiful girl who claims that the Gestapo is chasing her, search for microfilm concerning the forthcoming invasion of Poland—and, at last, arrives Solar Pons himself. This little novella is an amusing burlesque of the mystery-on-a-train theme.

215. _____. "The Battle Over the Teacups." In *World's Great Spy Stories*, edited by Vincent Starrett, 419–423.

Cleveland: Forum Books, 1944. First published in *Oriental Stories* magazine, 1933.

Shaw, the narrator, describes a baffling poisoning aboard a train traveling through Japanese-controlled China.

216. _____. *The House on the Mound*. New York: Duell, Sloan and Pearce, 1958. 335p.

Hercules Dousman, an actual historical figure, is the lead character in this novel spanning 1848 to 1868. Dousman is eager to see the Milwaukee & Mississippi finish its line to Madison, Wisconsin, but the railroad is strapped for money. Dousman pulls what financial strings he can, and invests heavily. When the road finally reaches Madison, and then Prairie du Chien, Dousman wonders if its arrival will cause as many changes in the area's life as did the arrival of the first steamboat. When the first train arrives in Prairie du Chien, hundreds of residents shout and cheer, and an artillery company greets the train with a 200-gun salute.

Although the book pays homage to Dousman's dedication to business as well as to his integrity and interest in helping others, its constant undertone concerns not money, or railroading, but Dousman's inability to build a successful relationship with his son, George. This is the gnawing absence in Dousman's heart, and his business interests, including the railroad, seem in large measure efforts to compensate for this one great frustration.

This slow-moving sequel to *Bright Journey* (1940) is one of Derleth's Wisconsin Saga novels. The house of the title, known as the Villa Louis in real life, is Dousman's mansion at Prairie du Chien.

217. _____. "Man in the Dark." In *Dwellers in Darkness*, 150–158. Sauk City, WI: Arkham House, 1976. *Strange Stories* 1 (June 1939): 77–80, 87.

In this taut, effective ghost story set in England, the narrator waits out a train delay at a remote, dreary station in the country. The narrator, preoccupied with doubts about his impending marriage, is surprised when an elderly man speaks to him, and gives him some uncannily apropos marital advice. The old man is disturbed; at one point he nervously opens his kit bag, to reveal an astonishing sight within. The old man vanishes, but when the narrator looks back at the station as the train pulls out, he sees one more mind-wrenching sight. Derleth takes a back seat to few in the realm of concise horror tales.

218. _____. "The Man on B-17." In *Midnight Specials: An Anthology for Train Buffs and Suspense Aficionados*, edited by Bill Pronzini, 139–146. Indianapolis and New York: Bobbs-Merrill, 1977. Also in Stephen Grendon's [pseud. for Derleth] *Mr. George and Other Odd Persons*. Sauk City, WI: Arkham House, 1963. *Weird Tales* 42 (May, 1950): 82–85.

A locomotive engineer gives a deposition on strange events of a winter night, as he steamed across trestle B-17 in rural Wisconsin. This tidy little ghost story features a touching rapport between the engineer and his locomotive—"the old girl"—and the atmosphere of night, snow, and ice is evocative.

219. _____. "McCrary's Wife." *Good Housekeeping* 119 (Aug. 1944): 36–37+. Also in Derleth's *Sac Prairie People*. Sauk City, WI: Arkham House, 1948.

In a story that goes deeper than the usual train romance, Bill McCrary accompanies his friend Norman's wife, Christine, and her young daughter, on the train from Chicago to New York. The conductor mistakes Bill and Christine for a married couple, and they encourage the error. Bill finds Christine attractive, and wonders how his life, "the essential loneliness of it pushing through layer after layer of superficial business" (122), might have been different if he had met Christine before Norman did.

On their return from the dining car, at night, "he watched Christine next to him, thinking that the dim light made her fine-featured face of even greater beauty than before ... just as, beyond the window, the mystery of the night, its luminous darkness, made magic of the commonplace" (122).

Coming back from New York, alone, Bill is in the same coach he shared with Christine, and chooses the seat in which he had sat with her. He reflects on how odd it is that she lives in Sac Prairie, the little Wisconsin village that he has left far behind. The same conductor they had met earlier inquires about his "wife," and Bill takes a strange delight in hearing her referred to as such. On many subsequent trips, Bill seeks out John, the old conductor, whose questions about Bill's "family" somehow allow him to feel that he is a family man. Bill grows close to John, and when John announces his retirement, Bill is devastated. The imaginary life he has spun out for the old railroader will fall apart. John asks Bill to write to him, from time to time, of his family's life—and Bill eagerly grasps the chance to maintain in this manner the world he has invented for himself.

"McCrary's Wife" is a profoundly sad story; Bill's loneliness is terrible, and his refuge in fantasy pitiful.

220. _____. "The Mouse on the Train." In *Wisconsin in Their Bones*, 148–158. New York: Duell, Sloan, and Pearce, 1961.

Nineteen-year-old Cassandra Howard is leaving school teaching in Sac Prairie to start a career, she hopes, in Chicago. The train to Chicago is delayed in a winter storm at a rural stop. Cassandra fears that the delay might encourage the young man next to her to speak to her. Her dear grandmother has warned her about such men. As the train sits, the passengers "began to talk with other people who had likewise been riding alone in towers of silence and preoccupation with the secret problems which haunted the unknown avenues of their mysterious lives" (150). As Cassandra frets about the young man at her side, a mouse runs through the car, causing a sensation. Women cry out, and men affect attitudes of bravery. The mouse's presence further stimulates Cassandra's wild (and, one suspects, wishful) misinterpretation of the young man's "intentions."

221. _____. "Pacific 421." In *Journey into Fear and other Great Stories of Horror on the Railways*, edited by Richard Peyton, 73–82. New York: Wings Books, 1991. (Originally published as

The Ghost Now Standing on Platform One: Phantoms of the Railways in Fact and Fiction. London: Souvenir Press, 1990.) Also in Derleth's *Something Near.* Sauk City, WI: Arkham House, 1945. *Weird Tales* 38 (Sept. 1944): 52–57.

Albert Colley has just bought the old Parth place a couple of miles outside a Missouri town. The real estate agent has cautioned Colley not to spend too much time in the evening at the far end of the property, where a stretch of the Pacific railroad line cuts across the land. Colley promptly ignores the warning, and one evening witnesses the phantom wreck of the Pacific 421 on that section of track. Colley, a scoundrel, conceives of using the ghost train as a means of hastening the death of his rich stepfather, whose only heir is Colley. The old man's demise is duly accelerated, but not with the consequences that Colley anticipates.

222. _____. *The Wind Leans West.* New York: Candlelight Press, 1969. 323p.

In the mid–1840s, Alex Mitchell—an actual historical figure—is pressured into becoming a director of a proposed railroad from Milwaukee to the Mississippi. He distrusts the initiative's point man, Kilbourn, for his impetuosity. Kilbourn has already failed at a Wisconsin canal project, but touts the railroad as the shipping choice of the future. Kilbourn becomes mayor of Milwaukee, and at the same time succeeds in embarking on the railroad project, dubbed the Milwaukee & Waukesha Railroad Company (later the Milwaukee & Mississippi). Construction begins in 1849, and the company, short of cash, pays its workers in stock. Many of the laborers are farmers, "so anxious for a road of iron," says Kilbourn, "they'll make any sacrifice" (257). The company does not yet have enough cash to buy rails, although Kilbourn has ordered a locomotive. The novel's chief business, however, is not railroading, but banking, and the Milwaukee & Waukesha disappears from view as suddenly as it appears two-thirds of the way through the novel. This is the last book in Derleth's Wisconsin Saga, following *Bright Journey, The*

House on the Mound, The Hills Stand Watch, and *The Shadow in the Glass.*

223. Detzer, Karl W. "The Wreck Job." In *O. Henry Memorial Award Prize Stories of 1926*, edited by Blanche C. Williams, 69–90. Garden City, NY: Doubleday, Page, 1927. Also in *Recent Stories for Enjoyment.* Edited by Howard F. Seely and Margaret Rolling. New York and Boston: Silver, Burdett, 1937. *Short Stories*, Sept. 10, 1926.

Detzer sketches Michael Ahearn's sudden commitment to the railroader's life on the Atlantic Western Railway at the age of 20: "He yielded to the lure of the rails, to the resistless witchery of tracks and ties, to the seductive song of iron wheels" (71). The closely-observed detail in the story leads the reader to suspect that Detzer himself at some point felt the same lure as his main character. Ahearn makes his mark with a performance on Valentine's Day, 1909, following a collision between a passenger train and a freight. The account of preparations for the wreck job includes a fine picture of the relief train that pulls out of the yards to tend the wreck and its victims.

Years later, Ahearn has risen to a railroad management post, but cannot abide the influx of college men in the road's hierarchy. They are soft but officious men who have never felt the sting of sleet on their faces as they cleared a wreck, or who have smelled creosote rising from fresh ties on a July afternoon. Furious over his new college-boy superior's insistence on efficiency reports, Ahearn quits the railroad for a job he hates, in a stone quarry. One day he witnesses a wreck on his old railroad and leaps in to do what is in his blood, even if not in his present job description. Although somewhat sentimental, the story is exciting, with credible detail, and a believable conflict between the old-time railroader's way and the new approach dominated by bureaucratic efficiency experts.

224. Deutermann, P.T. *Train Man.* New York: St. Martin's, 1999. 354p.

This effective thriller opens with a riveting description of a high bridge being blown apart with explosives as a train crosses the span across the Mississippi River linking Missouri and Illinois. The bomber strikes again in St. Louis, blowing a bridge as a coal train crosses. The bomber's motive is revenge: His wife and children died at a rail crossing wreck, their car and lives obliterated by a train. His objective now is nothing less than "to stop the trains, stop up the entire national railway system. Bring the country to standstill if he had to" (110).

As tends to be the case in such lone-psycho melodramas, the reader soon perversely cheers on the bomber as he tallies one railroad bridge after another. The author did enough background research to be persuasive in his railroading details, and the story moves right along, with the ante steadily rising until it involves weapons of mass destruction. Given today's anxieties about terrorism, *Train Man* possesses an unsettling ring of plausibility.

225. Deutsch, A.J. "A Subway Named Mobius." *Astounding Science Fiction* 46 (Dec. 1950): 72–86. Also in *Where Do We Go from Here?* Edited by Isaac Asimov. Garden City, NY: Doubleday, 1971.

In an elaborate future subway system in the Northeast, 227 trains carry over a million passengers a day. Some of those passengers vanish with their entire train, on the Cambridge-Dorchester run. Dr. Tupelo, a Harvard math professor, contends that the train has hit "a node"—"a singularity. A pole of high order" (75). Seeking answers, he rides the system himself, and observes astonishing incongruities in his fellow passengers' reading matter. The tale bears thematic similarities to the old *Twilight Zone* episode, "The Odyssey of Flight 33."

226. Dillard, Annie. "Hugh on the Train." In *Elvis in Oz: New Stories and Poems from the Hollins Creative Writing Program*, edited by Mary Flinn and George Garrett, 397–400. Charlottesville and London: University Press of Virginia, 1992.

In this short story plucked from Dillard's novel *The Living* (HarperCollins, 1992), 17-year-old Hugh Honer crosses the country on the Union Pacific, going west in 1893. He sits in the smoker, while his mother and younger brothers are ahead in a Pullman. Hugh observes his fellow passengers, listening to them brag about their accomplishments. Later, he enjoys—at first—an apparently friendly card game with a young fellow who claims to be a college man. As the game begins to go badly for Hugh, the conductor hands him a telegram. The telegram is from the Union Pacific Railroad itself, and casts a new light on the "college man" and the game of cards.

227. Dixon, Stephen. "Training to Magna." In *Friends: More Will and Magna Stories*, 62–72. Santa Maria, Calif.: Asylum Arts, 1990. First published in *Telescope*.

Mr. Taub, a college English teacher who lives near Baltimore, regularly takes the train to see a friend in New York City. He wants to be alone and rest on the trip, after a long, tough week at work, but on the crowded train chatterbox fellow passengers make it impossible for him to achieve this objective. Ed, a student from his college, recognizes him and badgers him about doing an interview with the school radio station, and tells him that he is "an incredibly nice smart guy" (70). At last Taub finds a free seat, to his great relief next to a passenger who does not speak English. Taub feigns sleep to avoid further conversation with other passengers who have pestered him.

There is nothing like being trapped in a small space with someone who will simply not be quiet, and in this funny story poor Taub must contend with several blabbermouths. (Compare to Entry 440.)

228. Dorris, Michael. "The Dark Snake." *The Georgia Review* 42 (Winter 1988): 773–781. Also in Dorris's *Working Men; Stories*. New York: Holt, 1993.

A mother tells this story of her son Andrew, who, at 15 in the year 1900, lies to the local railroad officials about his age and hires on as a fireman. He has been drawn to the job by his admiration for his older brother, also a railroad worker. Andrew dies in a derailment his first day on the job. Enraged, the mother sues the railroad, seeking not money, but vengeance: She wants to ruin the road. She obtains both money and retribution, and seems indifferent that her vendetta against the railroad costs her surviving son his job. The snake of the title refers to the woman's luxuriantly long hair, but alludes to the serpent of self-absorption that coils around the human heart.

229. Dorsey, Tim. *The Stingray Shuffle*. New York: William Morrow, 2003. 303p.

Serial killer Serge Storms has a deep preoccupation with Florida railroading, with a very material focus on $5 million stolen from Amtrak's New York-Miami express, the Silver Stingray. "I've decided to completely dedicate my life to the stuff of trains and things that look like trains," says Serge (71). *The Stingray Shuffle*, though, as described in the novel, is a paperback book by one Ralph Krunkleton. The book has come back from oblivion, and Krunkleton is faced with a publicity tour aboard a mystery train, with dramatic renderings. This is violent and ridiculous but funny pop froth, absent any aspirations to durable readability, and provides amusement while it lasts. It includes scenes set aboard the Silver Stingray.

230. *Down and Back: A Railroad Story*. Boston: Privately printed; McGrath-Sherrill Press, 1917. 50p.

Dedicated to those who have built and run the railroads, this is an odd little book in which the anonymous author, evidently from personal experience, offers tips to shippers in a semi-fictional form. "Old Bob Shaw" and the narrator started an express business in the Boston area employing trucks. Most of the book consists of a folksy meditation on the business, interspersed with quotations on pertinent topics from period railroading magazines. It includes commentary on railroad freight handlers' alleged "license to steal" (36), and on the "cat and dog feelin'" developing between express and railway companies: "They are quarrelin' all the time" (42).

231. Downing, Todd. *Vultures in the Sky*. Garden City, NY: Doubleday, Doran, 1935. 321p.

In this not-bad mystery set in Mexico, a Pullman carload of diverse characters wonders who among them is a murderer. Their curiosity and anxiety owe to the discovery of the body on the car of Eduardo Torner, on the way to Mexico City. At a time of labor unrest among Mexican railroaders, suspicions surface that Torner may have been involved in a plot to blow up the train. Hugh Rennert, a U.S. Treasury agent on board the train, works with Mexican officials to unravel the mystery. The unraveling does not come quickly enough to prevent further murders performed in fiendish and clever style. At one point, the engine breaks down, leaving passengers and crew stranded in the desert. Before it resumes its journey, diabolical hands uncouple the Pullman, leaving Rennert and company abandoned—and soon to discover the porter, freshly killed, in an upper berth.

Drago, Harry S. *see* **Ermine, Will**

232. Drake, Albert. "Odyssey: Corinthos to Patras, by Train." In *In the Time of Surveys & Other Stories of Americans Abroad*, 41–55. Adelphi, MD: White Ewe Press, 1978. First published in *Aate*.

The narrator, Alfred, an American laborer, has married a fleshy woman determined to educate him up to her art-loving social class. They are riding the train out of Greece, after a long ordeal of self-improvement. "She has brought me into Europe to get cultured," says Alfred (47). The two argue about pudding Alfred buys from a boy on the train, and about his treatment of an old man who cannot find a seat. Sudden clarity propels Alfred to a taste of freedom, although it seems likely that these two mismatched souls will go on hating each other interminably.

233. Drake, Robert. "Connections." In *The Picture Frame and Other Stories*, 157–164. Macon, GA: Mercer University Press, 2000. 157–164.

The narrator has believed since childhood that the purpose of the railroad "was finally making connections, bringing people and their wares together at their common destination ... all of it on time, nothing left to chance, all predictable" (159). He describes the Illinois Central Railroad, which runs through his little town halfway between Chicago and New Orleans, and its trains, *The City of New Orleans* and *The Panama Limited*. The story is the narrator's reminiscence of travel in the days of the steam locomotive, especially on his "old friend," the IC. "Trains had a glamor then, no doubt about it. But ... it was on trains that dead bodies were shipped home from big city hospitals, transports which brought back disasters from the battlefield and the ominous news brought by newspapers and telegrams—none of it pleasant" (161).

234. _____. "Mr. Marcus and the Overhead Bridge." In *Amazing Grace*, 141–146. Philadelphia: Chilton Books, 1965.

The L. & N. railroad (presumably the Illinois Central) runs straight through the heart of the Southern town of Woodville in a deep cut. Some hundred feet above the track, a bridge links one side of the town with the other. The bridge is a popular choice for local suicides, ranging from prominent citizens to "several Negroes" (142). The narrator likens Marcus Bascombe, one of the town's favored sons, to the poet Rupert Brooke and the poetic character, Richard Cory. Bascombe, a World War I veteran, a world traveler, admirably schooled in every grace, comes home to Woodville one night and jumps off the bridge. A section gang finds his body on the tracks in the morning. The narrator wonders whether "Mr. Marcus had known all along that, when he finally ran out of places to go, Woodville—and the overhead bridge—would be right there waiting for him" (146).

235. Dreiser, Theodore. *The Financier.* New York: A.L. Burt, 1912. 779p.

In pre–Civil War Philadelphia, young Frank Cowperwood is making his way in the banking and finance industry. He is also interested in the railroad, and learns that a new line of streetcars, incorporated by the North Pennsylvania Railway Company, is on the verge of development in the city. Cowperwood invests heavily in the street railways, and begins to dream of controlling a line. Edward Butler,

risen from humble circumstances to become politically powerful, also seeks hefty profits in street railway stock, and takes on Cowperwood to help him acquire it. Soon Cowperwood is working in shady deals with city treasurer George Stener—"borrowing" from the treasury—to finance speculation. He uses "peculiar" (i.e., marginally crooked) means to gain a majority share of stock in one line for himself and Stener. Inevitably, its collapse hastened by the economic effects of the Great Chicago Fire, the financial scheme that Cowperwood and Stener create disintegrates. Cowperwood goes to prison, but on parole reestablishes his capitalist success.

The railroad is present here as something spoken of, not experienced; for most practical purposes, it could have been supplanted by livestock, wheat, ore, or other elements of economic interest. Dreiser's purpose is to show men at work who care fundamentally about nothing but making money. (Dreiser used as a model for Cowperwood the real-life railroad financier, Charles T. Yerkes.)

236. _____. *Jennie Gerhardt.* New York: Boni and Liveright, 1911. 431p.

Only one major passage in this novel features the railroad in a critical way, but this passage comes at the book's conclusion, and is one of the most memorable in the fiction of the railroad.

Jennie Gerhardt, born to humble circumstances, becomes the mistress of Lester Kane, a well-to-do manufacturer whose family disapproves of Jennie. The novel follows her up-and-down life, building sympathy for her as she weathers the effects of forces beyond her control. In the end, Lester, whose family has pressured him into leaving Jennie—whom he genuinely loves—suffers a heart attack, and soon dies. After Lester's funeral, his body is taken on Thanksgiving Eve to the train station in Chicago, from which it will go to Cincinnati for burial. Jennie is at the station, waiting for a glimpse of her beloved's coffin; all around her people looking forward to the holiday are in a festive mood. "Throughout the great railroad station there was a hum of anticipation, that curious ebullition of fancy which springs from the thought of pleasures to come" (429).

Jennie hears with an aching heart a station official call out a route that she and Lester had sometimes taken. She sees the coffin coming, pushed along on a cart by a porter oblivious to the loss that the coffin represents. A long, red train pulls into the station, and a train-hand calls out, "Hey, Jack! Give us a hand here. There's a stiff outside!" Jennie watches the men load the coffin onto the train. "The fireman, conscious of the heavy load behind, flung open a flaming furnace door to throw in coal." Jennie watches the train leave the station, "until the last glimmer of the red lamp on the receding sleeper disappeared in the maze of smoke and haze..." (430).

Dreiser has taken more than his share of criticism for his occasionally awkward writing. He does produce an ungainly sentence or paragraph with some regularity, but few American writers can match the powerful effects he achieves when his vision and his prose meet in harmony. One of those meetings occurs when Dreiser describes Jennie's farewell to Lester at the Chicago station. The portrait of Jennie, watching the train bearing her dead beloved disappear in the distance as she looks ahead to a future of bleak loneliness, is hard to bear, and speaks directly to universal truths about loss and human helplessness.

237. _____. *Sister Carrie*. 1900. Reprint, Cleveland and New York: World, 1927. 557p.

The railroad plays a significant part in this story of a young woman's ascent and unhappiness. *Sister Carrie* opens with 18-year-old Caroline Meeber boarding the afternoon train in her Wisconsin hometown to go to Chicago. Her possessions are scant: a little trunk, a cheap satchel, a box lunch, a purse, and four dollars. Dreiser describes her as "bright, timid, and full of the illusions of ignorance and youth" (1). She will board the train to make a new life; the train is her vehicle of escape from the constraints of her adolescence: "Whatever touch of regret at parting characterized her thoughts, it was certainly not for advantages now being given up" (1). Aboard the train she meets Charles Drouet, who furnishes the first step in the erosion of Carrie's innocence.

Dreiser describes the rail approach to the great city of Chicago as "a wonderful thing" for "the child, the genius with imagination, or the wholly untravelled" (9). Carrie occupies two of those categories. She looks out the window at the passing cityscape, her heart "troubled by a kind of terror. The fact that she was alone, away from home, rushing into a great sea of life and endeavor, began to tell" (10). (Readers familiar with Edward Hopper's moody and threatening 1946 painting, "Approaching a City," may be reminded of it by this passage.)

Through Drouet, Carrie meets G.W. Hurstwood, who falls in love with Carrie. Later, now a thief and running from the law, Hurstwood hustles Carrie on a ruse aboard a train to Detroit, from which they will proceed to Montreal. In effect, he abducts her. Carrie objects, insisting that she will get off at the next stop, but Hurstwood sweet-talks her into accompanying him on his flight. By the time they are on their way to Montreal, Carrie has made a remarkable adjustment to her condition, thinking that, as she looks at the scenery flying past, "Her life had just begun.... Possibly she would come out of bondage into freedom—who knows. Perhaps she would be happy" (305). That is not how things work in Dreiser's world.

238. _____. *The Titan*. 1914. Reprint, Cleveland and New York: World Publishing, 1951. 552p.

Here Frank Cowperwood finishes the prison time he earned in *The Financier*, and is released in the 1870s. He takes the train to Chicago, where he soon resumes his intense devotion to business, with a commitment to sexual liberty on the side. As Cowperwood comes into Chicago on the train, he senses "something dynamic in the very air which appealed to his fancy" (4). He carries over his earlier interest in street-car lines as his "natural vocation" (5), and the novel dwells in major part on his cornering the horse-drawn, and then cable, street railway business in the city. Dreiser also attends to the development of something much closer to a real railroad than horse-drawn or cable cars: the Chicago elevated system. Cowperwood realizes deep into the story that he must convert his entire system to electric operation.

Through most of the novel, the street railway system is in the background. Occupying the foreground are Cowperwood's strategies and tactics, both financial and political, that enable him to build his empire. In this respect, as in *The Financier*, it scarcely matters whether Cowperwood is dealing in public transportation, sausage, or munitions: The real issue is his method of manipulating others to achieve his ends. Achieve them he does, for the most part. Late in the novel Dreiser describes the vast extent of Cowperwood's street railway holdings, and laments the limitations of the common soul: "Pity the poor groveling hack at the bottom who has not the brain-power either to understand or to control that which his very presence and necessities create" (473). Cowperwood himself finally comes up short of controlling the creature of his creation: In spite of slipping back into underhanded means, in the end, near the turn of the century, he cannot carry off the grandest of his schemes.

Dresser, Davis *see* Halliday, Brett

239. Dromgoole, Will Allen. "Engineer Connor's Son." *McClure's Magazine* 8 (Feb. 1897): 355–360.

Nashville and Chattanooga engineer Jack Connor buys a cottage on a hill in the village of Antioch, overlooking the railroad, next door to the "cripple," Jerry Crane. Jack is confident that Jerry's wife will keep an eye on his own wife when he is off on a run. In Antioch, "the train was about the biggest thing around" (355).

One day Jack stands at his post in a bad wreck, in spite of the crew's exhortations to jump. "You forget I'm the engineer," he reminds them (357), and stays at the throttle, to his considerable detriment. On his deathbed, Jack adjures his son, Little Jack, to remember that the engineer must stick to his post, no matter what. Later young Jack receives a ride in the engineer's seat on old No. 6; he worries about leaving his dear mother alone for a whole day. He need not have worried, but on another day his mother fails to return from a brief train trip. "He never knew the terrible story, how in stepping from the train her foot slipped and she fell beneath the

wheels, which passed over her body" (360).

Years pass, and Jack, following his father's dying counsel, goes each day to meet his dead mother on the train, announcing his presence as the train pulls in. Only the lad's own death brings an end to this bathetic ordeal. Today's reader will snicker at this tale's unabashedly morbid sentimentality, but it presumably struck a responsive chord in the minds of readers of the time.

Duncan, Actea *see* Thomas, Carolyn

240. Duranty, Walter. "The Gold Train." *Collier's* 91 (Jan. 28, 1933): 15+. Also in Duranty's *Babies without Tails: Stories*. New York: Modern Age Books, 1937.

An American reporter "travelling hard" in Siberia meets a young woman whose father was a prosperous Kulak, a farmer. She regales him with the story of how she witnessed the robbery of a gold train, and how she was able to salvage enough gold coins from the attack on the train to pay her way into marriage with a soldier of the Red Army. The story bears an obvious admiration for the laborers of the Revolution. One of the coins the young woman acquires is a $20 American gold piece that she wears on a chain around her neck.

241. Earp, James W. *Boomer Jones*. Kansas City, MO: Burton Pub. Co., 1921. 96p.

This little book offers 14 episodes in the life of Boomer Jones, "the boomeriest of boomers a nomad of the glistening rail who had never lingered long enough on any one job to get more than a speaking acquaintance with his fellow workers..." (3). Jones relates among others his adventures with bears in Colorado, the acquisition of nick-names, and the time he did a female-impersonation act. Jones is an amiable blowhard and tale monger who cannot resist bending the ears of his fellow railroaders with the stories of his exploits. That he is a boomer is all to his benefit; if he stayed in one place very long, his dubious claims would catch up with him—but possibly not before his listeners found a way to keep him quiet. This is a crudely-designed book, although it includes a few fairly good cartoons. One can imagine it proving of interest to railroaders of the era who might have enjoyed seeing a liar lampooned.

242. Edgerton, Wild. *Railroad Life in America.* Chicago: Birney Hand, 1870. 279p.

Available at *Wright American Fiction*: http://www.letrs.indiana.edu/web/w/wright2/

Edgerton distills what he refers to as 20 years' experience and observation into a fictionalized treatment purporting to show life and work behind the scenes among the nation's railroads and their workers. "The wonders they accomplish are patent to all," he declares; he claims to be the first to look "into the lives of those who achieve the miracles over which men marvel" (8).

Edward (Ned) Livingston, fresh and eager from college, arrives at the railroad town of Pickatonic to begin his new life. Pickatonic is a temporary town, erected only as a base for railroaders while construction occurs on a nearby bridge. Ned takes a job as secretary to Superintendent Wynworth. Ned is relieved to learn that his classical studies in college did not incapacitate him for a job in the practical world, and he finds that railroad life possesses a "deep charm" (31). His role as a cog in the grand industrial scheme pleases him, and he revels in the camaraderie of railroaders. Their talk concerns but one thing: not women, as one might suspect, but railroading, and it is of the "heroic" aspect of railroading that they speak.

Edgerton's vision of railroading and railroaders is fanciful. "The boys" all enjoy dressing up for church on Sunday (nary a hangover in the lot, apparently). After church, they hang about the office, chatting "with the quiet enjoyment of children" (51). There is just enough in the way of human orneriness in the book to provide salt for anecdotes. Engineer Jim Hook, for example, is an obnoxious fellow who rankles Ned. Yet even Hook has an ounce of gold in his base character; indeed, the railroaders "are all noble fellows," as one character puts it, who practice "manliness, honesty, integrity and fidelity" (69).

Ned becomes a substitute conductor in his climb up the railroad ladder, and struggles with a variety of difficulties in that capacity. When Ned is badly hurt, Jim Hook's kindness awakens Ned to his underestimation of the engineer.

As unintentionally mirthful as the book may be, from time to time, its portrait of railroaders as a kind of industrial nobility speaks to popular sentiments of the era.

243 Edwards, Charlotte. "Fast Train to New York." *McCall's* 83 (April 1956): 40–41+.

Annie Dean is a writer traveling from California on the Super Chief to see her New York agent. She was not initially eager for the trip. When she looks out the window of her roomette at the station, she sees her husband Bruce and her best friends. "There was a strange light on their faces, eerie and remote" (134). With the train under way, she turns away from the window, suddenly aware that she is glad to turn her back on her friends and family.

Annie finds an unsigned note in the observation car. She reads it in her roomette; it claims that its author is going to commit suicide. From that point, each person she meets on the train causes her to wonder if that could be the one who wrote the note. In the end, a sudden insight awakens her to an overlooked love in her own life, and she sets out to write the story of her discovery in a piece titled "Fast Train to New York."

The story rests on an interesting idea, although Edwards does not execute it with complete success. The piece's ultimate reinforcement of convention is too pat; even so, Edwards's dwelling on what she comes close to declaring a universal rumination on suicide is a brave departure from the norm in popular magazine fiction.

244. Eggleston, Edward. *The Mystery of Metropolisville.* 1873. Reprint, New York: Orange Judd & Co., 1890. 320p.

Eggleston's Western boomtown of Metropolisville, alive with speculation and grand dreams in the mid–1850s, suffers the fate of so many towns whose ambition exceeded their means. The railroad receives only brief mention in the novel, but its role is nevertheless telling in its absence. Early in the story, a "fat gentleman" notes his intention "to buy some lots in this place. It'll be the county seat and a railroad junction, as sure as you're alive" (35). In the end, Metropolisville "is only a memory now. The collapse of the land-bubble and the opening of railroads destroyed it. Most of the buildings were removed to a neighboring railway station" (320). The plight of Metropolisville—bypassed by the railroad and left in the lurch of commercial development—represents every 19th-century boomtown's worst fears, with its main street "now a country road where the dog-fennel blooms almost undisturbed ... the lot once sacredly set apart (on the map) as 'Depot Ground' is now nothing but a potato-patch...." (12).

245. Ehle, John. *The Road.* 1967. Reprint, Knoxville: University of Tennessee Press, 1998. 401p.

This much better than average historical novel begins in 1876, when Weatherby Wright—president, superintendent, and chief engineer of the Western North Carolina Railroad Company—prepares to start a two-year project to build a railroad up Sow Mountain, North Carolina, to Swannanoa Gap. The state-sanctioned project entails the labor of some 40 men hired by the railroad, and 600 prisoners detailed by the state. The workers include women prisoners who prepare the meals that the male prisoner-laborers shovel into their mouths. The women also wash the workers' clothing and dishes. Trusted convicts, both men and women, earn opportunities for occasional sexual entertainment, a firmly-segregated practice in which black and white prisoners repair to different sides of the woods. At one point, another group of 150 convicts arrives; the boxcars that carried them "smelled of human excrement." Wright is furious, over both the cruel treatment of the prisoners and the abuse of the boxcars: "We'll never get the odor out of those cars" (87).

The story includes considerable careful detail on the development of the line, from the correct size of gravel for ballast to surveying matters. Ehle provides an entertaining, well-researched, and realistic portrayal of the natural enemies of 19th-century railroad building, including bad weather, mud, landslides, disease,

and, above all, the arduous labor. Ehle's treatment of the prisoner laborers is notably sympathetic.

246. Ellin, Stanley. "Broker's Special." In *Quiet Horror: A Collection of Mystery Stories,* 180–194. New York: Dell, 1959. Also in *Great Tales of Mystery and Terror.* Pleasantville, NY: Reader's Digest, 1982.

Cornelius, a Wall Street broker, learns of his wife's involvement with another man. He uses his commute on a train other than his usual, the Broker's Special, to help cover his homicidal plan for his wife's lover. His plan is effective, but he does not reckon on his wife's reaction, or at the role the Broker's Special will play in the outcome.

247. Ellison, Harlan. "Riding the Dark Train Out." In *Love Ain't Nothing but Sex Misspelled,* 99–108. 1968. Reprint, with a new introduction by the author, New York: Ace Books, 1983. First published circa 1961 in *Rogue Magazine.*

In this early story, Ellison, who went on to prominence in science fiction, follows down-and-out jazz musician Ernie Cargill on an eventful trip aboard a boxcar. When a young couple jumps into the car, Ernie plans to rob them and have his way with the girl. Another hobo soon joins them, and Ernie behaves selflessly to save the young couple from tragedy.

248. Ellison, Ralph. "Boy on a Train." In *Flying Home, and Other Stories,* 12–21. New York: Random House, 1996. *New Yorker* 72 (April 29–May 6, 1996): 110–113.

In 1924, on a train from the South to Oklahoma City with his widowed mother and baby brother, young James Weaver begins to incorporate an understanding of the African-American's burden in a racist world. James and his family are the only occupants of the coach seats "reserved for colored." They share the dirty coach with a body in a coffin, and with white passengers' baggage. At one point, a white man aboard tries to grope Mrs. Weaver. Her weeping interrupts James's engrossed observation of the passing scenery. She reflects on her trip on the same railroad line 14 years earlier: "We traveled far, looking for a better world, where things wouldn't be so hard like they were down South.... Now your father's gone from us, and you're the man" (18). James feels a growing anger at whatever it is that has hurt his mother, and vows to himself that he will destroy it. Although the story ends with James looking out the window, wondering if there will be boys to play football in the town where they are going, no one can doubt that the most important part of this trip is his flash of insight into his mother's grief.

249. _____. "A Hard Time Keeping Up." In *Flying Home, and Other Stories*, 97–109. New York: Random House, 1996.

Two black trainmen, the narrator and his friend Joe, get off their train at 4 A.M. and hurry through the fast-falling snow to the city's black section to find a room. Joe takes long strides; the narrator finds it hard to keep up with him. The narrator gives a bag of sandwiches to a white beggar; then he and Joe enter Tom's place, a black bar. Sensing trouble ahead, they leave quickly. The trouble proves not nearly as serious as they fear in this story with a comic ending—but the comedy turns on rational expectations of bloody violence.

250. _____. "Hymie's Bull." In *Flying Home, and Other Stories*, 82–88. New York: Random House, 1996.

In this short, effective story, the narrator, a young man looking for work in 1934, rides the rails with his fellow drifters. He refers to the railroad bulls as "pretty bad people to meet if you're a bum.... They have head-whipping down to a science and they're always ready to go into action" (83). The Chicago yard bulls are especially tough on black bums.

The main portion of the story relates what "an ofay bum named Hymie from Brooklyn" (83) does to a bull who catches him asleep on top of a boxcar. To put it succinctly, the bull ends up dead alongside the track, his throat slashed. No one turns in Hymie; "sometimes the bulls get the worst of it" (83).

Ellison provides some good observations

of the illicit life aboard the freights. In one passage, the men play blackjack for cigarette butts until it becomes too dark in the boxcar to read the cards; in another, the narrator's voice is swallowed by the wind and the noise on top of a boxcar.

251. _____. "I Did Not Learn Their Names." In *Flying Home, and Other Stories*, 89–96. New York: Random House, 1996. *New Yorker* 72 (April 29-May 6, 1996): 113–115.

A young black music student who left home to earn money for his school tuition is riding the rails. He is lucky to be alive: Morrie, a white man and fellow tramp, saved him from falling between two cars. The young man has had some bad experiences with white folk, but this incident suggests to him that he should soften his protective cloak of hostility. On his way to Alabama, he meets an elderly white couple, also riding in a boxcar. The white couple treat the young man kindly as they share their sandwiches with him. They are on their way to visit their son on his release from a Missouri jail; they are eager to see the young fellow.

The story, which takes its title from the fact that the young black traveler does not learn the old couple's names, evokes a sense of shared humanity among the outcasts on the rails. "I had learned that on the road you really had no place; you were all the same," notes the young man—"though some of them did not understand that" (93). Both Morrie and the old couple did understand that. The young man ends up in jail himself at story's end when yard bulls apprehend him in Decatur. Beyond its literal origin, the story's title suggests that names may not be important when people's hardships are similar.

252. Elston, Allan V. "Drawing Room B." In *The Best American Mystery Stories*, edited by Carolyn Wells, 481–505. No place: Albert & Charles Boni, 1931. *Adventure* magazine, April 15, 1930.

Minturn has apparently murdered a man in his train compartment, and assumes the man's identity to assure the conductor's help in evading detection. The dead man goes out the compartment window, Minturn makes a clever escape, and a twist at the end suggests that all is not what it seemed.

253. Erdman, Loula. *Many a Voyage*. New York: Dodd, Mead, 1960. 309p.

This engaging, if uncritical, historical novel focuses on the life and career of Edmund G. Ross, who was vital to Andrew Johnson's narrow escape from conviction upon his impeachment. When the novel opens, Ross, a Kansas farmer and journalist just before the Civil War, believes that the region must have railroad service. While opposing interests battle for the state's entry into the Union as slave or free, Ross campaigns for a railroad via newspaper articles and editorials. He and his associates propose various routes to Congress, and choose a name for the non-existent road. The war delays the railroad, but on the close of hostilities Ross goes to Washington as a U.S. senator, the railroad at the top of his agenda. He becomes caught up in the impeachment proceedings against Andrew Johnson, and his involvement in the railroad again occupies a back seat. Even so, he wins the honor of turning the first shovelful of dirt to begin construction of the Atchison, Topeka, and Santa Fe Railroad.

254. Ermine, Will [Harry S. Drago]. *Barbed-Wire Empire*. New York: Green Circle Books, 1937. 256p.

Rusty Maxwell, owner of a vast ranch, hates the South Western Pacific Railroad. His fury stems from the railroad's right-of-way condemnation proceedings, endorsed by the state's governor, which threaten to cut Maxwell's ranch into two awkward halves. Maxwell vows that the railroad will never cross his ranch. The novel is customary Western fare with a plot fashioned around the inexorable advance of the railroad. It is of some interest to see the author borrow from Frank Norris's imagery when he writes that the South Western, approaching Maxwell's ranch, is an "octopus" that "extended its slow, remorseless tentacle" (66). For the most part, the novel concerns the stereotypical conflicts of Western development, with the leading edge of commerce—in this case the railroad—threatening established practices.

255. Ester, Mary Ellen. *The Boxcar Brigade: A Novel*. Mansfield, Ohio: M.E. Ester, 1993. 311p.

The story begins around the turn of the 19th century. Seventeen-year-old Johnny Lansuer takes the train from Pennsylvania to Oklahoma, to mend his health in the dry climate. On his attempted return, a con man swindles Johnny of his small supply of cash, then "helps" the boy onto the wrong train. Johnny does some ranch work, and then lands a job with the Baltimore & Ohio. A solicitous railroader, Davey, gets Johnny squared away at a railroad boarding house; in a funny passage (105–106), Johnny listens to a bewildering torrent of railroaders' slang at breakfast.

Johnny—soon called Jack—starts as a menial roundhouse helper. He works up to fireman, and barely escapes mortal injury in a wreck in which his engineer dies. While healing, Jack receives a promotion to engineer, not only because he qualifies for the job, but because the B & O is now short one engineer. Davey, who refers to the railroad as "the boxcar brigade," bluntly tells Jack to face the hard reality: When a railroader dies, the brigade moves on, "and the sooner ya learn it the better" (140).

This self-published book could have benefited from the help of a thoughtful editor. Presented as fiction, it is clearly family history, a fact made obvious by the jarring inclusion mid-book of photographs of family members, including Jack. Whatever its many rough spots, the story is believable and tolerably written, told from the heart and from personal experience as it follows Jack through his career and to his death. It possesses a candor that more polished railroad pulp fiction seldom attains; the graphic description of Davey's horrible death by scalding in a wreck puts to shame the melodramatic but sanitary deaths of railroaders in most pulp fiction disasters.

The book might have been much more than it is. The material is here, as are the writer's honesty and good intentions, but sound fictional technique is absent.

256. Everett, Percival L. "Hear That Long Train Moan." In *The Weather and Women Treat Me Fair; Stories*, 51–56. Little Rock: August House, 1987.

In this fine story of obsession, retired dentist Virgil Boyd has turned both his house and yard into the site of an elaborately-detailed HO train layout. The layout includes models of cities—Detroit, and Ashland, Kentucky—and a computerized command center in Boyd's basement. Boyd's friend, Morrison Long, stops to visit, and begins to suspect that there is something seriously wrong with Boyd, for whom the line between the model world and the real world seems to have eroded dangerously. In the story's climax, the men wait for "a terrible thing" to happen on a trestle above a backyard pond. Long recommends obvious practical action, such as shutting off the power, but Boyd dismisses his friend's ideas. "There is only so much I can do," says Boyd. "It's hard enough just to make this shit. You know what I mean, don't you, Morrison?" (56)

Boyd's consumption by what was once a hobby recalls that of the title character in Robert Coover's novel, *The Universal Baseball Association, Inc., J. Henry Waugh, Prop.* (Random House, 1968).

257. Fairchild, June. "Joy Ride." In *Writers for Tomorrow*, edited by Baxter Hathaway, 10–15. Ithaca, NY: Cornell University Press, 1948.

Marilyn, a young woman on a crowded train to Ithaca, New York, is trapped next to Tim, a retired railroad worker. Tim requires no provocation to regale Marilyn with a free-associating series of banalities about his personal and family life. Marilyn yearns to escape him; ironically, Tim persuades the conductor to secure a berth for her, on the pretext that she is his daughter. Marilyn tries to tip the conductor for his help, but he angrily rejects the money. In the end, Marilyn, an educated woman, appears to be reevaluating her impressions of the garrulous, inarticulate retired laborer.

258. Farrell, James T. "On a Train to Rome." In *Judith and Other Stories*, 97–104. Garden City, NY: Doubleday, 1973.

The American narrator shares a crowded compartment on a train bound for Rome. The compartment is hot, the passengers restless.

"To put myself to sleep, I tried to think about baseball, and all the players who had been in all the World Series games I could remember" (101). The narrator finds irritation in the presence of a loquacious, little fat boy in a red sweater who dominates the compartment with his chatter. The narrator realizes that America is part of the boy's conversation, but he does not speak Italian, and gathers nothing else of the boy's speech. The reader begins to share the narrator's aversion to the boy until the story's last few paragraphs, which undergo a surprising shift in tone and focus.

259. Fast, Howard. "The Little Folk from the Hills." In *The Howard Fast Reader*, 355–361. New York: Crown, 1960. Also in Fast's *Departure: And Other Stories*. Boston: Little, Brown, 1949. *Masses & Mainstream* 1 (Dec. 1948): 19–25.

The narrator is traveling aboard a mail train, plodding its way across India during World War II. Accompanying the narrator are two U.S. Army sergeants, and a British colonel and his young subaltern. Everywhere the train goes, the men see starvation and disease. At one stop, a hundred or so short, naked tribal people, obviously starving to death, make a half-hearted effort to board the train. After the authorities drive them off, the narrator joins the other men in handing out their meager food supplies to the tribespeople.

The heart of this powerful and disturbing story concerns the different reactions of the men to the misery they have witnessed. The British acknowledge it, but with a civilized fatalism, almost of good cheer. The Americans become quietly enraged, by turns with the suffering they cannot soothe, with the attitude of the British, and with each other.

260. Faulkner, William. "Pennsylvania Station." In *Collected Stories*, 609–625. New York: Random House, 1950. *American Mercury* 31 (Feb. 1934): 166–174.

A group of homeless men seek shelter in New York City's Penn Station on a cold winter night. When they enter the station, "They seemed to bring with them the smell of the snow falling in Seventh Avenue" (609). Their clothes are Salvation Army issue, their shoes sometimes mismatched. They sit on the benches "in attitudes of thought or repose and looking as transient as scarecrows blown by a departed wind..." (610). As the men, young and old, kill time in the station, an elder among them—he may be 60, or he may be an old-looking 48—tells a long story about his sister's purchase of her coffin.

A uniformed railroad employee enters the waiting room and rousts the vagrants from their benches. At the story's end, as the waiting room empties of its sad crowd, the old man relates the business of his sister's death. He and a young man ponder moving to Grand Central Station, where, with luck, they will be able to loiter until 5 A.M. before railroad officials evict them. "Then it will be only two hours more till daylight," says the old man (625).

Faulkner's use of the story within the story—the account of the old man's sister and her coffin embedded in the larger picture of a group of down-and-out men trying to find refuge from the cold—works well. So does the troubling yet understated role of the railroad authority, acting to make sure that people with no place to go have to keep moving.

261. _____. "Raid." In *The Unvanquished*. 1938. Reprinted in *Novels, 1936–1940*, 371–399. New York: Library of America, 1990. *Saturday Evening Post* 207 (Nov. 3, 1934): 18–19+.

"Raid," one of several short stories Faulkner wrote featuring Bayard Sartoris and Bayard's slave and close friend Ringo, received some reworking for inclusion as a chapter in *The Unvanquished*. Here Bayard recalls how in childhood during the Civil War he had an advantage over his brighter friend, Ringo: Bayard had seen a railroad and a locomotive, but Ringo had not. Nevertheless, the railroad and the locomotive symbolized for Ringo "the motion, the impulse to move which had already seethed to a head among his people," an impulse that would lead them they knew not where, "empty handed, blind to everything but a hope and a doom" (374). Bayard also describes his first sight of the railroad, "the straightest thing I ever saw, running straight and empty and quiet through a long empty

gash cut through the trees ... and the light shining on the rails like on two spider threads..." (378). What Bayard and Ringo see together, however, is the railroad ruined, its track torn up by Union troops, the rails twisted into "Sherman's bowties" around nearby trees, the material of the track already being reabsorbed by nature.

The railroad is also significant in the chapter in *The Unvanquished* concerning Bayard's cousin Drusilla's relation of a locomotive chase between engines operated by Union and Confederate troops. For Bayard, this thrilling contest represents the sort of emotional engagement he hopes to find in the war.

262. Ferber, Edna. "Our Very Best People." In *One Basket: Thirty-One Short Stories*, 251–268. New York: Simon & Schuster, 1947. *Cosmopolitan* 76 (March 1924): 30–35+.

On the Santa Fe branch-line, San Querto is a "little bare railroad town where caste lines were drawn as definitely as in Mayfair. Brakemen's wives were beneath freight-train conductors' wives in the social scale. Stationmasters' wives patronized conductors' wives. The wife of a division superintendent queened it over the wives of both stationmasters and passenger-train conductors" (264). Substitute brakeman Dan Yard rises quickly, and becomes division superintendent at 33, and at 46 the general manager of the Santa Fe.

As Ferber says in her foreword, the story "is an example of book-length material wasted in a short story" (251). Indeed, the tale of Dan and his wife Hannah often reads like an outline for a novel. Hannah goes West to work as a Harvey Girl after her father drops dead in Kansas City's Union Station. On the job she meets the Irish-American Dan. The narrative includes some interesting details of the Harvey Girl's tasks. Hannah learns the ropes of waitressing quickly: "She learned to remember six orders taken at one time in the rush of a crowd just off a waiting train" (262). Hannah shows her stuff at railroading, too, becoming a telegrapher after her marriage. An enjoyable novel of Western railroading—never to be written, alas—lurks in this story that covers too much ground in too few pages.

263. _____. *Saratoga Trunk*. New York: Grosset & Dunlap, 1941. 352p.

Ferber tends to the career of 89-year-old Clinton Maroon—prototypical railroad magnate, art collector, opera stockholder, and a continuing preoccupation of the press, which refuses to believe him when he claims that he robbed and killed to build his fortune. The Saratoga Trunk is a 100-mile stretch of railroad between Albany and Binghamton, and is worth millions because it links the new Pennsylvania coal fields with New England. Competing interests, including those of Jay Gould and J.P. Morgan, are contending for the plum trunkline in ways legal and otherwise.

The novel is nine parts limp "society" romance to one part industrial history, but Ferber does give a few arresting lines to old Maroon that testify to his late disgust for his part in the ravage and rapine indulged in by some 19th-century tycoons. Late in the book, he unburdens himself to a crowd of doubtful reporters: "They've clamped down on fellows like me who damn near ruined this country.... Another quarter century of grabbers like us and there wouldn't have been a decent stretch of forest or soil or waterway that hadn't been divided among us.... The time's coming when there'll be no such thing as a multi-millionaire in America, and no such thing as a pauper. You'll live to see it, but I won't. That'll be a real democracy" (350–351).

Maroon—and Ferber—were wrong on all these speculative counts. One can only wonder what the two of them would have made of the latter-day robber barons who ran WorldCom, Enron, and other pillars of marked cards in a more refined era, when the thugs did their violence via spreadsheet, sustained no bloody knuckles in the process, and made a more grotesque mockery of democracy than Gould, Morgan, and their ilk ever envisioned.

264. _____. "Trees Die at the Top." In *One Basket: Thirty-One Short Stories*, 423–456. New York: Simon & Schuster, 1947. *Cosmopolitan* 102 (April 1937):22–25+.

Frances Content books space on the San Francisco Streamliner out of Chicago, summoned by her husband Jay's dying, rich grandfather in San Francisco. She, her husband, their children, and two servants are all aboard. The story alternates between passages showing the pampered, soft Content family (the surname is not an accident) on the train with those describing the wagon train trip across the country that old Jared Content made as a boy in 1849, on nearly the same route the train takes. Ferber contrasts a day on the streamliner with a month on the wagon trail, the air of spoiled entitlement of the 20th century Contents with the hard lives of their forebears. Modern "hardship" entails waiting two hours to have one's suit pressed. "God, what kind of a train is this!" shouts the wrinkly Jay in disgust (447). Frances joins Jay in her petty, whining self-indulgence aboard the train.

The contrast between historical eras is clever and effective, and, with the Great Depression still chugging along at the time of the story's first publication, contemporary readers suffering that debacle's effects would have had no trouble working up a good two-minute hate for the too-comfortable Contents.

265. Fergusson, Harvey. *In Those Days*. 1929. Reprint, Boston: Gregg Press, 1978. 267p.

Using main character Robert Jayson as a tool to set up situations illustrating his views, Fergusson offers a lively version of Southwest history, from horse-and-wagon to horseless carriage days. Between those two eras, and overlapping both, comes the railroad. "In those days men believed in liberty as they believed in God. Progress was salvation and work was a holy cause.... The rails went west on a wave of faith and energy nothing could check" (129). Even before the rails arrived, railroad money could transform a town, as it does Jayson's adopted home, a little adobe village beside the Rio Grande. The economy booms; prices soar. Time seems to speed up: Sooner than seems possible, Jayson becomes "an old codger that came before the railroad. A whole generation had grown up and moved in to which the building of the railroad was a remote historical event.... And now he found himself unaccountably sitting half-idle among a litter of relics" (231–232). The book is a nice historical portrait of a Western boom-town, with good character development saving it from mere recitation. Its third section, "Railroad," contains most of the pertinent detail on the middle portion of the period covered.

266. Ferrier, Ian. "Blue Train." *Review—Latin American Literature and Arts*, no. 66 (Spring 2003): 23–24.

The narrator, a Northerner, describes in quasi-poetic imagery the way he became "infected" with the blues, a condition he stumbled upon when he hopped what he thought was a routine freight car in the Badlands one night—"but of course it wasn't a freight" (23). In effective equation of the emotional state of the blues with a mysterious train ride with a woman who shares his uncertain life, the narrator does the only thing he can do in the grip of the blues: "I get up from my seat, and I do a crazy shuffle, and I start to sing" (24).

267. Field, Eugene. "Humin Natu' on the Han'bul 'nd St Jo." In *Second Book of Tales*, 1–12. New York: Scribner's, 1896.

The narrator pays his two dollars to ride the Hannibal & St. Joseph Railroad in the spring of 1867, on his way to Kansas. Colonel Gates, "the richest man in Marion County 'nd a director uv the Han'bul 'nd St. Jo to boot," is riding in the same sleeper (5). A young woman with a crying baby disturbs the sleep of all the passengers, and Col. Gates pleads with her to quiet the infant. His ire is transformed when he learns the story behind the baby's presence on the train. Twenty years later, the narrator notes that everything has changed—"everythink except humin nature" (12). As suggested by the quotes, Field relies extensively on sight dialect in his effort to evoke local color in this story, which, though first published here, he wrote in 1888.

268. Finney, Jack. "The Third Level." In *About Time; Twelve Stories*, 11–16. New York: Simon & Schuster, 1986. *Collier's* 126 (Oct. 7, 1950): 36+. Also in Finney's *The Third Level*. New York: Dell, 1959.

Among Finney's numerous enjoyable stories of time travel is this delightful little gem.

Charley, a harried New Yorker, one day stumbles upon a lower level of Grand Central Station, where the ticket agent wears a green eyeshade and black sleeve protectors, women wear ankle-length dresses, and a little funnel-stacked locomotive looks like something from a Currier & Ives print. A newspaper nearby shows that the date is June 11, 1894. Charley hopes to return with his wife, and make a permanent home in the 19th century, but he can never again find the corridor that led him to the third level. A letter from his old friend Sam later shows that where Charley failed, Sam succeeded.

269. Fisher, Clay. "For Want of a Horse." In *The Railroaders*, edited by Bill Pronzini and Martin H. Greenberg, 100–115. New York: Fawcett Gold Medal, 1986. Also in Fisher's *Nine Lives West*. Toronto and New York: Bantam, 1978.

The James Gang, led by Frank and Jesse, outwits the officials of the Missouri & Western Railroad as they pull a train robbery in Hatpin, Kansas. Strictly from the pulp mill, the story romanticizes the outlaws who strike against the M & W.

270. Fitzgerald, F. Scott. "The Night Before Chancellorsville." In *A Treasury of Civil War Stories*, edited by Martin Greenberg and Bill Pronzini, 19–25. New York: Bonanza, 1991. *Esquire* 3 (Feb. 1935): 24+. Also in Fitzgerald's *Taps at Reveille* (as "The Night of Chancellorsville"). New York: Scribner's, 1935.

Nora, a self-absorbed and not overly intelligent young woman, describes a train ride during the Civil War. She and a friend have heard that "a good clean-looking girl" (21) can live profitably in Virginia, tending the recreational interests of Northern soldiers. On the trip, the train goes through part of the Battle of Chancellorsville, and Union soldiers commandeer the car ahead of the one Nora and her friend occupy for use as a field hospital. Rather than aching for the men butchered in battle, Nora bemoans her own inconvenience aboard the train: "I never been treated like that in my life.... And in the papers next day they never said anything about how our train got attacked or about us girls at all! Can you beat it?" (25).

271. _____. "A Short Trip Home." In *Journey into Fear, and Other Great Stories of Horror on the Railways*, edited by Richard Peyton, 289–308. New York: Wings Books, 1991. (Originally published as *The Ghost Now Standing on Platform One*. London: Souvenir Press, 1990). *Saturday Evening Post* 200 (Dec. 17, 1927): 6–7+. Also in *The Short Stories of F. Scott Fitzgerald: A New Collection*. Edited by Matthew J. Bruccoli. New York: Scribner's, 1989.

Eddie Stinson, the narrator, is a Yale sophomore visiting friends in St. Paul, Minnesota, at the Christmas holiday. His friend Joe's girlfriend, Ellen, for whom Eddie has strong feelings, unaccountably declines to accompany them to a party. Ellen has met "a hard-looking-customer" (293) on the train, who seems to exert a hold over her. Later that week, Ellen takes the Burlington from St. Paul to Chicago; Eddie follows on another train, and apprehends Ellen at the telegraph counter in the Chicago station. She is there to meet a man—we believe we know who he is—and tells Eddie to leave her alone. Eddie senses a "contagion of evil in the air" (301). He insists on joining her to take an evening train for the East. In her compartment, Eddie tells Ellen he loves her, and begs her to tell the truth about the strange man. The story evolves into a good ghost tale, with Joe confronting the man aboard that very train, and witnessing some remarkable effects.

272. Flanagan, Michael. *Stations: An Imagined Journey*. New York: Pantheon, 1994. 104p.

Lucius Caton, former journalist and now farmer, is the narrator here. His photographer cousin, Russell McKay, was a devoted railroad fan. After compiling a book, *Stations*, on the places and histories of two railroads—the Buffalo & Shenandoah, and the Powhatan—McKay took a job as a brakeman with the B & O. Two years later, he died in a grade-crossing accident caused by a drunken truck driver. In this beautifully-produced book, Caton presents an ostensibly-salvaged copy of his cousin's book, some 40 weather-beaten, often torn and wrinkled black & white railroad photos, exquisitely colored by Caton's sister, Anna, an artist who was in love with McKay. Caton's narrative, accompanying McKay's "book," takes the reader and viewer on a guided trip into the American past, and into the personal pasts of the people whose lives intersect as a result of McKay's obsession with railroads. Original and provocative, *Stations* is a wonderfully imaginative marriage of fine art and fiction. (The illustrations as well as the text are by Flanagan.)

273. Fontaine, Robert L. "Girl on the Train." *Woman's Home Companion* 78 (Sept. 1951): 42–43+.

Gentle, good-humored Norman has found his marriage a trifle stale. On his daily commuter train ride to New York City, Vera, an attractive young woman, sits next to him, and "Norman felt a warm glow of adventure" (84). They share the ride into the city for the next two months, with growing intimacy. Vera is an out-of-work actress. On the day that she boards the train to tell Norman she has found a part in a play, "the entire train senses that something wonderful had happened" (87). All ends happily in this pat little tale of renewed domestic bliss.

274. Foote, Mary H. "On a Side-Track." *Century Illustrated Monthly Magazine* 28 (June 1895): 271–283. Also in Foote's *The Cup of Trembling, and Other Stories*. Boston and New York: Houghton, Mifflin, 1895.

Two Quakers—a young woman and her father—and two men are the only passengers in the Portland car leaving Omaha one February day. The young woman, Phebe, observes the younger man's air of sadness. She is solicitous toward her semi-invalid father, and the sad young man admires her beauty and character. Her father thrills to discover that the young man, Charles Ludovic, is the grandson of Phebe's grandfather's business partner. The reader learns that Ludovic's companion, Burke, is his guard; Ludovic is under escort to what will likely be a long prison term for murder. As the train waits on a siding for the track ahead to clear, Phebe and Ludovic are drawn to each other; he eventually confesses his situation to her. The story resolves happily, if not realistically, amid heavy sentiment. Nevertheless, when Phebe tells the anguished Ludovic, "I am thy sister," it is a moving moment.

275. Ford, Corey, and Alastair MacBain. "Snow Train." *American Magazine* 125 (Jan. 1938): 20–22.

Unmitigated escapist fluff: A specially-chartered train, the J.J. Fracker Winter Sports Special, hauls a cargo of New Yorkers off on a skiing weekend in New England. Romantic rivalry, a pretty girl with a broken ankle, and the wrong train station all play their parts.

276. Ford, Paul L. *The Great K & A Train Robbery.* New York: Dodd, Mead, 1897. 200p. *Lippincott's Monthly Magazine* 58 (Aug. 1896): 147–207.

Narrator Dick Gordon, a former Yale football player, seeks to set the record straight about the not-so-great K & A train robbery. A superintendent on the Kansas & Arizona Railroad in 1890, Gordon was called upon to facilitate the visit to Colorado of a Missouri Western vice president, a Mr. Cullen, coming in his private car. Soon enough the Cullen party and Gordon became caught up in a train robbery. Several in the party foiled the bandits, but curious elements about the event disturbed Gordon.

This railroad Western involves shady business concerning a stock takeover attempt, a staged robbery, and Dick Gordon's continued rise in the railroad game, thanks in part to pluck and brains, and in part to his convenient descent into love with Vice President Cullen's daughter. The ho-hum mystery-romance offers unconvincing railroad details. Black trainmen receive the standard condescension of the time: The narrator "will tell the darkies to bolt the front door" (30).

277. Ford, Richard. "Optimists." In *Rock Springs: Stories*, 171–191. New York: Atlantic Monthly, 1987. *New Yorker* 63 (March 30, 1987): 28–36.

Frank, the narrator, relates events of his 15th year, 1959, when his father, Roy, a locomotive fireman on the Great Northern Railway in Montana, killed a man and went to prison. Roy is worried about keeping a job with the railroad, with the superfluous position of fireman on a Diesel engine and widespread complaints about featherbedding undermining his security. Roy comes home wild-eyed one night, having seen a hobo cut to pieces under a train. A visitor who scarcely knows Roy drunkenly accuses him of failing to act properly in the accident, and of being a worthless featherbedder. Roy kills the man with a single blow to his heart. Roy spends a few months in prison; when he comes home, the family falls apart and scatters, with Frank—who used to lie in his bed at night listening to the locomotives humming nearby—lying about his age to join the Army. Frank thinks that both his parents were optimists, but neither of them could foresee the consequences of their actions well enough to justify any optimism. Many readers will find this a story of crushing despair and emptiness, in spite of a slight gloss of resolution at the end.

278. Fox, Norman A. "The Brass Pounder." In *They Rode the Shining Hills*, 90–106. New York: Dodd, Mead, 1968. First published as "Boothill Returns a Telegrapher," 1943[?].

Britt Rutledge, veteran telegraph operator ("brass pounder") on the Montana-Idaho Railroad, foils a gang of train robbers and demonstrates once again his value to the road. This is the sort of pulp Western in which people are "hogtied" and the lead flies freely.

279. Fox, William P. "Have You Ever Rode the Southern?" *Saturday Evening Post* 236 (July 13, 1963): 38–41+. Also in Fox's *Southern Fried Plus Six.* Philadelphia: Lippincott, 1968.

The narrator recalls his experience as a World War II airman, a lieutenant, as he traveled by train from California to South Carolina. The trip goes well until he changes to the Southern Railway somewhere before Atlanta. The lieutenant has not slept for two days, and finds no respite about the Southern coach. A guitar-strumming rube insists on entertaining him, to the delight of a loud-mouthed whiskey drinker across the aisle. An unpleasant vendor wakes him up, lies to him about where the train is, and sells him scalding coffee. Says the vendor, after pouring the coffee: "You better make haste and drink that. Them cups melt fast and you can't hold 'em long" (40). The coffee, of course, ends up on the lieutenant's boots. A band composed of 10-year-olds boards the coach at 2 A.M., and sets to work raising a racket. The lieutenant plans to propose to his beloved when she meets him at the station in Columbia, South Carolina, but that plan falls through to put the coup de grace on this train ride from the nether realm. A comical story whose credibility any veteran train rider could endorse.

280. Frank, Larry. "Train Stops in Your Mind." In *Train Stops: Short Stories*, 18–23. Santa Fe: Sunstone Press, 2003.

Courtney Morehead rides the train through the countryside, on her way to join her new lover, leaving her estranged husband behind. The train passes a series of small towns, "one after another, with no separate identity" (21). Courtney ponders the two men in her life, and finds her intentions surprisingly derailed by the actions of one of them.

281. Frank, N.E. "Chauffeur Extraordinary." In *The Best Stories of Heroism I Know*, edited by John C. Minot, 79–93. Chicago: Wilcox & Follett, 1946.

Young Tom Husey, an ambulance driver in World War I, slips back into life in his hometown of Millersville in anonymous fashion. He describes himself as a chauffeur, and works at his father's mill. No one expects anything notable from him. One day, however, he rushes to help at the site of an horrific train wreck, and quickly puts into play all the emergency medical skills he learned on the battlefield in France. The president of the Central & Western Railway is on the scene; impressed by Tom's ability, he offers him a job as his personal assistant. Virtue, modesty, and ability triumph.

The story's theme of ability overlooked and good work rewarded is hackneyed, but the author draws interesting connections between battlefield carnage and the very similar injuries occurring in a train wreck. Tom Husey also, it seems, suffers a degree of post-traumatic stress disorder: "In France the horrors of war had not kept him awake; in Millersville they did. He had only to close his eyes to have them pass before him in review..." (82).

282. Fraser, James W. "The Trick at Eagle's Nest." *Railroad Stories* 19 (May 1936): 110–116. *Railroad Magazine* 72 (June 1961): 40–44.

Boomer telegrapher Bob Nelan is stuck in a blizzard in his shack in the High Sierras. Not only is his food supply nearly gone; he has run out of coal for his pot-bellied stove. When he tears apart the coal shed for wood, a gust of wind picks up the shed and dumps most of it down a canyon. Working in the gale and freezing cold is all but impossible. Nelan remains in telegraphic touch with the dispatcher's office as he exhausts his food and fuel. As Nelan's condition deteriorates, the dispatcher hounds him with insulting messages—which, as Nelan later realizes, were intended only to keep him awake and moving until help could reach him. The author, himself a boomer telegrapher and dispatcher, writes with persuasive authority of the forlorn Nelan's plight.

283. Frym, Gloria. "Columbus Day." In *Distance No Object: Stories*, 71–75. San Francisco: City Lights, 1999.

On Columbus Day, a crowded commuter train heads into San Francisco while a mentally disturbed passenger shouts insults at the other passengers on his coach. Everyone tries to ignore him, until a muscular Native American in sunglasses administers some direct physical attention. The story ends on a note of ominous ambiguity. Frym suggests the fragile veneer of civility that, when things go tolerably, governs strangers crowded into a small space.

284. Gabriel, Daniel. "The Man on the Train: A Border Story." *Four Quarters* 32, no. 3 (1983): 19–28.

Ryder, an American traveling by train through Yugoslavia, meets a countryman, William McGee. Ryder, it grows clear, is engaged in surreptitious human rights work; McGee is a chatterbox eager to relate his adventures. As the train goes on through the night, McGee tells a harrowing story of his experiences with Bulgarian border officials. After his tale, McGee ventures to the dining car for cigarettes. Ryder falls asleep, and awakens at dawn to find McGee gone—and a foil package of contraband drugs from the pack he had left behind also gone. What is happening here is not exactly clear, but it is clearly bad, and the reader's uneasiness at the end echoes that of Ryder.

285. Gardner, Carol. "On a Red Line Train." *Potomac Review* 4, no. 4 (1997): 36–40.

The narrator, a woman, is riding a commuter train and finds herself the seatmate of a woman who is plainly half-mad, and who begins to divulge every detail of a medical procedure she has just undergone. The narrator wishes that she could disappear as other riders turn to stare at her and at her talkative companion. When the woman gets off the train, guilt sweeps over the narrator, who believes that she should have done something to try to help the poor stranger.

286. Gardner, Erle Stanley. "Death Rides a Boxcar." *American Magazine* 139 (Jan. 1945): 141–160. Also in *The Case of the Murderer's Bride and Other Stories.* Edited by Ellery Queen. 1969. Reprint, New York: Davis, 1974.

A lost purse containing thousands of dollars and some cryptic notes leads investigator Jayson Burr and his colleague, Gaby Hilman, to an examination of switching procedures in the Los Angeles rail yards. A dead body and a beautiful girl heighten the stakes. As the plot develops, the two investigators find themselves beaten senseless with brake clubs; they come to in a boxcar. The immediate outlook is not promising, but Burr and Hilman are up to the challenge.

287. _____. "Only by Running: Flight into Disaster." In *The Case of the Murderer's Bride and Other Stories*, edited by Ellery Queen, 28–42. New York: Davis, 1974. *This Week*, May 11, 1952.

A woman on a fast transcontinental train is in a panic. She realizes that while she was at dinner, a man searched her compartment. Seated in the club car, every man in sight is suspect. The woman is so certain that evil agents want the item she has concealed in her shoe that she leaps off the train at a flag stop in Wyoming—the same stop where the one man on the train she trusts also gets off. Good guys, bad guys, and FBI agents follow.

288. Garland, Hamlin. "Mrs. Ripley's Trip." In *Main-Travelled Roads*, 171–183. 1891. Reprint, with additional stories and front matter, New York: Harper & Bros., 1956. *Harper's Weekly* 32 (Nov. 24, 1888): 894–895.

Although the railroad never appears in this simple, moving story, it is central to the action. Mrs. Ripley, who lives with her husband Ethan in a shanty on a farm on the Iowa prairie, has not had a day to herself in 23 years. She has, however, been able to save enough money—a dime and a quarter at a time—to take the train back to New York to see her family. Ethan is astonished and annoyed at his wife's plans, but after fuming, he sells some livestock so that he can buy her a railroad ticket (before he learns of the money she has saved).

Most of the story concerns Mrs. Ripley's determined preparations for the trip. "I ain't goin' on no sleeper," she says; "I'm going on the old-fashioned cars, where they ain't no half-dressed men runnin' around" (179). On the big day, Ethan takes her, with their grandson, to the train station, "a frightful little den" (180). Mrs. Ripley is so flustered over the trip that she forgets to kiss Ethan and her grandson goodbye. The story concludes with Mrs. Ripley's return to the farm. "Her trip was a fact now.... She took up her burden again, never more thinking to lay it down" (183).

The resoluteness of the Ripleys, their clear commitment to each other, and the heartbreaking relentlessness of their work to survive on their pitiful farm—coupled with the only moment of freedom Mrs. Ripley may experience until she dies—give the story powerful emotional impact.

289. _____. "The Return of a Private." In *Main-Travelled Roads*, 112–129. 1891.

Reprint, with additional stories and front matter, New York: Harper & Bros., 1956. *Arena* 2 (Dec. 1890): 97–113.

A group of weary, demobilized Union soldiers ride the train to their Wisconsin homes after the Civil War. When they stop at one station or another and a few of the men get off, they find no cheerful greeting or cries of acclaim, and "while the train stood at the station, the loafers looked at them indifferently" (112). The train reaches La Crosse at 2 A.M., and the last few soldiers, all local farmers, get off. The station is deserted and dark, and, although it is an August night, chilly. All but one of the men, disinclined to spend two dollars for hotel rooms, sleep on the hard chairs or benches in the dingy station. The next morning they look at the hills around the station and, before moving on, find a restaurant where they buy bad coffee to wash down their breakfast of hardtack.

The joyless return from the war is a fit beginning of the men's resumption of their running battles with nature and quotidian injustice.

290. _____. *The Rose of Dutcher's Coolly*. 1895. Reprint, New York: AMS Press, 1969. 354p.

This novel follows Wisconsin farm-girl Rose Dutcher from the farm to college to a big city career, and back again. The railroad figures prominently in several important passages. The first comes when Rose takes the train to Madison, Wisconsin, to start school at the university. Naïve and anxious, she is miserable all the way to the station: "Home and peace and comfort were all behind her" (75). Aboard the train, she sits terrified and rigid. "The speed of the train, which seemed to her very great, aided her to realize how swiftly she was getting into the world" (76). Soon Rose, an attractive young woman, becomes the sport of both the brakeman and the conductor, who recognize her vulnerability, and pester her without cease. A considerate woman intervenes, and saves Rose from further embarrassment, but even this woman leaves Rose acutely uncomfortable with her admonitions about men and marriage.

Madison is to Rose a great art and literary center, but its cultural appeal scarcely mitigates her initial distress at leaving the familiar behind. When she gets off the train at the busy Madison station, she is "white and tremulous with fear" (82).

Rose's next big train trip is far different. In Chapter 15, "Chicago," she leaves her university days behind to pursue a literary life in Chicago. Approaching the city on the train, she thinks of the pastoral scenes of her childhood, but she feels tremendous excitement and anticipation at the prospect of the city. She is "a fresh, young, and powerful soul rushing to a great city.... On every train at that same hour, from every direction, others, like her, were entering on the same search, to the same end" (156). The closer the train comes to the station, the more appalling and chaotic the city looks, but every possibility beckons: "She was at the gate of the city, and life with all its terrors and triumphs seemed just before her" (157).

In the novel's penultimate chapter, Rose's future husband, Mason, arrives by train for a critical meeting with her. He sees her waiting for him in a carriage at the platform, and a thought lights in his mind: "There sits my wife!" (341).

291. _____. "Up the Coolly." In *Main-Travelled Roads*, 45–87. 1891. Reprint, with additional stories and front matter, New York: Harper & Bros., 1956.

Howard McLane returns home for the first time in a decade to the little Midwestern town he had left for his successful career in New York City. As he rides through Wisconsin by train, he leans back in a reclining chair, savoring the landscape, "a panorama of delight" (45), thinking of all the vigorous, productive farming taking place in his privileged view. In the evening, the train pulls into a "grimy little station," and Howard steps out onto "the broiling-hot, splintery planks" (46). The train station idlers seem to be the same fellows Howard left behind 10 years earlier, only grayer and more bent. The surrounding town is decrepit and wretched. Before he reveals himself, the loiterers speculate with dull humor on Howard's identity.

Howard goes to visit his mother and

brother at their farm. He finds himself hard-pressed to square up the squalor of their lives with the success of his own. In the end, he grasps it: As he tells his brother, "Luck made me and cheated you. It ain't right" (86).

The image of Howard grandly traveling through the land on a luxurious train, with fanciful notions of farm life playing in his mind as he looks out the window, considerably sharpens the sting of the poverty and despair that he learns is his neglected family's lot.

292. Garrett, Garet. *The Driver.* New York: Dutton, 1922. 294p. *Saturday Evening Post* 194 (Dec. 24, 1921): 3+; (Dec. 31, 1921): 17+; (Jan. 7, 1922): 14+; (Jan. 14, 1922): 17+; (Jan. 21, 1922): 20+; (Jan. 28, 1922): 20+.

The Driver, an all but completely forgotten business novel, remains an interesting work in the genre owing to its author's ability to champion his ideas about capitalism without neglecting to tell his story, and while creating a more than usually compelling central character.

That character, speculator and railroad tycoon Henry M. Galt, is the guiding force—"the Driver," as he calls himself—behind the fortunes of the Great Midwestern Railroad. Galt is an unrelenting master of financial machinations; his Great Midwestern Railroad stumbles, fails, and goes into receivership, but thanks to Galt's efforts is reborn to ever-increasing grandeur. Galt may be "a solitary worker in the money vineyards" (63), but he possesses tremendous force of will, operational genius, and political shrewdness. Galt, who began buying Great Midwestern stock when it was next to worthless, parlays his hand to control some 15 other railroad properties. His success arouses his enemies' jealousy and unified opposition, and leads to federal investigation of Galt's business. Galt beats back the challenge to his industrial empire, but not without paying a steep personal price.

One can sympathize readily with the pugnacious, determined Galt, to the extent that one forgets the social and economic drawbacks associated with business trusts. Garrett's prolific pro-business articles routinely appeared in the *Saturday Evening Post, Colliers,* and other magazines; his own sympathies lie clearly with the noble entrepreneur, his antipathy directed to government meddling and the pestiferous attacks of Galt's competitive inferiors.

Some readers of *The Driver* see it as the source of Ayn Rand's less capable, and far better known, novel, *Atlas Shrugged* (Entry 684). In "A Reviewer's Notebook: The Businessman in American Literature" (*The Freeman*, March 1983), John Chamberlain contends that *The Driver* is based on the life of the Union Pacific's E.H. Harriman. Regardless of its own derivation, or its role in Rand's conception of her novel, *The Driver* is a useful and generally readable book that illuminates an ideal of the American businessman in the 1920s. (Readers can slip over the obligatory love interest in the novel without missing very much.)

293. Garth, David. *Fire on the Wind.* New York: Putnam's, 1951. 378p.

In 1865 Minnesota, Wayne Preston spurns a job with the Union Pacific Railroad because he believes that the future lies in lumbering and iron mining. He is determined to build a railroad to handle iron shipments from Duluth across northern Wisconsin to Green Bay, south of Escanaba—the Northern Empire Route. In 1868, he treks through Wisconsin and Michigan's western Upper Peninsula to reconnoiter his long dreamed-of rail route. Late in the novel work finally begins on the right-of-way, with Preston leading a crew through the wild land, clearing timber and preparing the roadbed. One of the devils of the forest—a raging, wind-driven fire—destroys the railroad before it can get properly under way, leaving twisted, melted steel in its path. The same fire nearly obliterates the Preston timber interests, but patriarch Rufus Preston, probably the best-developed character in the story, sees another side of the disaster: "Great speed, and sweep, and power. So you look on the other side of the coin—and instead of gettin' a blast of hot destruction comin' like a diving hawk, you get a country building big and fast—that's the real fire on the wind—" (365). Garth's picture of the industrial development of the region in question is readable and interesting.

294. Gautreaux, Tim. "Perfect Strangers on a Train." *Oxford American* 32 (April 2000): 26–36.

The narrator, a teacher, boards the Amtrak train, the Crescent, in New Orleans for the long trip to Washington, D.C. He has a reservation on a sleeping car. At breakfast in the dining car, he sits across the table from a college student who is surprisingly candid about his uncertain prospects. In the lounge car, he plays cards with a construction worker. The game ends, and the college boy takes the construction man's place. "The kid was talking to me as if I were his roommate" (30). Later a husband and wife from Massachusetts grumble about their property taxes, in tedious voices. Generally, the narrator observes, watching "how people can get along in their small trapped world on the train" (32). The train passes little towns reminiscent of poverty-stricken Third-World villages—and then goes through the back ends of cities in even worse condition. In this story of things seen and heard, Gautreaux is a careful, thoughtful observer of humanity and nature.

295. _____. "Waiting for the Evening News." In *Same Place, Same Things*, 19–36. New York: St. Martin's, 1996. *Story*, 42, no. 3 (1994): 104–117.

Louisiana engineer Jesse McNeil celebrates his 50th birthday by slugging down half a pint of whiskey shortly before climbing into the cab of a chemical train, known by some railroaders as the "rolling bomb." All goes well, and McNeil feels fine, until a derailment tears the train apart as it speeds through some no-name village. McNeil flees the flaming scene. On a motel television on the road to New Orleans, Jesse sees helicopter coverage of the wreck, which has, evidently, destroyed much of the town, and learns that the police are seeking him. He hangs out at the motel, waiting for the evening news, hoping to hear that everything is, somehow, all right. The news only grows worse, referring to "a growing scene of destruction and pollution perhaps unequaled in American railroad history" (28).

This is an absorbing and expertly-written story of a man who thinks of himself as an invisible nobody being turned into a national villain. McNeil seems on one level to represent every man brought to ruin by a whim of fate; he feels "as empty-handed and innocent as every man on earth" (35). The story's religious dimensions, including McNeil's conversations with a Catholic priest, and a reference to a drunken Noah, lend further fuel to its substance.

296. Gellhorn, Martha E. "Slow Train from Garmisch." In *The Heart of Another*, 178–185. New York: Scribner's, 1941.

American author Gellhorn succinctly shows the effects of a young woman's romantic disappointment on a number of passengers aboard a train to Munich. An old couple, a young couple, a group of bankers on holiday, all react strongly, if privately, to the young woman's obvious grief as her former boyfriend leaves her—forever—on the train.

297. Gilman, Charlotte Perkins. "The Girl in the Pink Hat." In *The Charlotte Perkins Gilman Reader*, edited by Ann J. Lane, 39–46. New York: Pantheon, 1980. *The Forerunner*, Feb. 1916, 29–33.

The narrator, a self-described "spinsterish" woman, and her sister are taking the train to New York City. The narrator overhears a young couple arguing over their wedding plans in the seats ahead of her. The young woman, put off by her fiance's refusal to humor her wishes, decides to get off the train. He asserts his "authority" as her future husband, and attempts to force her to remain with him. The narrator and her sister intervene with a clever ruse, and free the young woman from the clutches of a suitor who proves to be a criminal. The train in this story serves as a kind of mobile prison for the young woman, until the narrator comes to her rescue.

298. Glasgow, Ellen. *Barren Ground.* Garden City, New York: Doubleday, Page, 1925. 511p.

This affecting novel of endurance and struggle focuses on Dorinda Oakley, daughter of a poor Virginia farmer. The family's home, Old Farm, lies near the bleak little settlement of Pedlar's Mill and its train station. Early in the novel, Dorinda looks through falling snow at "the bare station," "the gleaming track," and at the old freight car where Butcher lives, "the lame negro who pumped water into the engines" (11). Young Dorinda works at the local store, where she listens daily for the sound of approaching trains, for they represent to her "a part of that expected miracle, the something different in the future" (11). In the receding smoke from a passing train, Dorinda sees glamor and the promise of escape; she fantasizes about someone on a train seeing her from the train window, and returning to take her away, by train, to a different life.

Dorinda becomes pregnant, and, rejected by the father, turns to that gleaming track in hopes of a new life: "I'll go on the first train, the one that whistles at sunrise" (181). It makes no real difference to her, she thinks, where the train goes; she will ride it as far as she can, as far as her money will take her. On the rainy, dismal morning when she sets out to leave, a neighbor asks her destination. She tells him she is going to New York; it is the most distant place she can bring to mind. Waiting at the station, Dorinda is cold and miserable. Even so, hope stirs in her. As the engine rushes toward her, her knees tremble. When the train leaves, with Dorinda aboard, "The figures at the station wavered, receded, and melted at last into the transparent screen of the distance" (193).

Although Dorinda loses her unborn baby as a result of a street accident in New York, the two years she spends there as an assistant to a physician significantly enlarge her confidence. She returns to Pedlar's Mill and the farm, by train, in the wake of her father's stroke. As the train approaches, the old station looks small, and "stranded like a wrecked ship" in its barren setting (250). Dorinda sees the station's untidiness, "the shabbiness and crudeness of the country people meeting the train," and the "disreputable rags" of Butcher (250). Everything she sees from the train looks mean and trivial and ugly after her two years in New York City. The conductor who helps her with her bags is the same one who helped her board the train the morning she left home. "He did not recognize her, and for some obscure reason, she felt flattered because he had forgotten her" (251).

Dorinda remains in Pedlar's Mill, taking over the family farm, and, with a certain grim will, forcing the place to flourish as it never had. As the years pass, she falls into predictable habits. She is not unaware of "the arid monotony of her life" (394), and the "something different" she imagined as a girl fades into oblivion. The railroad furnishes one last significant moment in the novel: Nathan Pedlar, the storekeeper whom Dorinda eventually married, dies in the aftermath of a train wreck, trying to free other passengers from a burning car. Like so much else, his death seems to Dorinda the result of insignificant, if not random, choices and chance. Dorinda, never a conventionally happy character—this is not the sort of novel that rests on the assumption that happiness is something to which one reasonably aspires—does achieve a measure of satisfaction through her achievements, with her ability to subdue the hard land to her will. In the end, her adolescent railroad dreams of escape, or rescue from her arid monotony by a stranger on a train, have long since been replaced by an adult acceptance of the realistic options that life has presented her.

299. _____. *The Romance of a Plain Man.* New York: Macmillan, 1909. 464p.

This is the saga of Benjamin Starr, who rises from humble origins to become a power in the railroad industry, then in banking, only to see his fortunes collapse. With his wife at his side, he rebuilds from nothing, and, on the verge of achieving his boyhood dream—a railroad presidency—disavows it for the sake of his marriage.

General Bolingbroke, president of the Great South Midland & Atlantic Railroad, is an important secondary character throughout the novel. When Ben is a young boy, he meets Bolingbroke; years later, Bolingbroke helps him get started in his career. Ben profits from Bolingbroke's financial advice, and before long works for him—and very nearly worships him as a model businessman and exemplary human being.

By mid-book, Ben has moved from railroading to financial speculation and banking. Bolingbroke continues to give him avuncular marital and financial support, and warns him against approving loans to the shaky Cumberland and Tidewater Railroad. Meanwhile, in spite of widespread financial panic, the South Midland grows rapidly, "swallowing up everything that comes in its way, like a boa constrictor," says Bolingbroke (294). Ben's bank fails, and he starts anew, with Bolingbroke's aid, on a subsidiary of the South Midland. Speaking of money, Ben's wife, Sally, wonders, "Is there a spot on earth ... where in this age they worship another God?" (438).

The novel reads well, but Starr's renunciation of his dream of railroading grandeur when it lies within his grasp is dubiously credible.

300. Godey, John. *The Taking of Pelham One Two Three*. New York: Putnam's, 1973. 316p.

Commuter Train 123 Conductor Bud Carmody enjoys his job, doesn't mind "dumb questions," and likes to speculate on his passengers' lives. Motorman Denny Doyle calculates the gross weight of his passengers and the train, making a private game of it. When the train is hijacked on the way to Grand Central Station, the bad guys hold the passengers for ransom. Caz Dolowicz, veteran train master, pitches a profane fit when he realizes the problem with 123, and thinks of Mrs. Jenkins, nearby in the control tower. "Christ," thinks Dolowicz, "if I have to watch my language, I'm going to pack it in. Did they ever think of that when they opened up towerman classification to women? How the hell could you run a railroad without swearing?" (54). That is probably the best line in this tense thriller. Dolowicz's own opportunities for good lines are limited, for his involvement in the event ends quickly and unpleasantly when he demands to board the hijacked train. The novel makes excellent use of the claustrophobic environment of a subway train motionless in a tunnel. Perhaps not so curiously, the reader tends to line up on the side of the hijackers, who are more engaging characters than are the representatives of legal and corporate authority who contend against them. Joseph Sargent directed a good 1974 movie version, with the same title.

301. Going, Charles B. "Off the Track." *Scribner's Magazine* 41 (June 1907): 754–762.

In this business adventure, a seasoned veteran helps a talented but inexperienced up-and-comer grasp the rules of the road. Westerton Clifford has just resigned as division engineer on the W.&N. Railroad to take a job with the Dos Bocas Development Commission overseeing a massive excavation in the tropics. The company chief tries to impress upon Clifford the urgency of following through on the job systematically, but when the work goes badly—with routine derailments of freight cars and ghastly weather—Clifford halts the work. The chief's wise counsel allows Clifford to see that focusing on temporary economies may prove costly in the long run.

302. Gold, Michael. "Faster, America, Faster." In *120 Million*, 135–144. New York: International Publishers, 1929.

A private train carrying the Big Boss speeds through the night, bound for Hollywood. While rich Hollywood types cavort in their private car, the train crewmen, from the engineer and fireman to the African-American porters, work hard to assure their passengers a happy, comfortable trip. As the partying troupe revels, the fireman snaps, seizes control of the engine, and wrecks the train, leaving bloody residue. "America is a private train crashing over the slippery rails of History," writes the disapproving Gold: "Faster, faster, America!" (135–136).

303. _____. "On a Section Gang." In *120 Million*, 115–122. New York: International Publishers, 1929.

Sunburned section hands receive their pay envelopes as this story opens. Many of the men have suffered from boils brought on by skin contact with the creosote that soaks the new ties they install. The two dozen men on Section Gang 10 speak six languages. "There were five Wops, three Hunyaks, a Swede, a Jew, an Irishman (there's always one apiece for every kind of excitement in the world), three Mexicans, two Poles, and a bunch of Yank hundred-percenters. There was also a Negro named Harry" (116). They all hate each other; they

especially hate Rich, the foreman. One excruciating, hot July day, after one of the men
passes out in the sun, the rest sit down under
a tree and refuse to work. "It was a kind
of strike" (119). The section hands—gandy
dancers—"are the lowest in the scale of migra-
tory workers" (120).

Less a story than a slice of section gang
life, the piece gives some sense of what this
backbreaking work was like at the time.

304. Gonzalez, Ray. "Train Station." In
*The Ghost of John Wayne, and Other Sto-
ries*, 81–85. Tucson: University of Arizona Press, 2001.

A man waits for his grandfather, whom he
has not seen in many years, to arrive by train
at the old station in El Paso. His mother has
assured him that his grandfather will be on this
train. The train arrives, but the old man is not
aboard. The man sees his grandfather in a photograph of a long-ago railroad crew on display
in the station, and assumes that he can detect
aspects of his grandfather's character in the
image. An inquiry at a downtown hotel where
his grandfather once stayed produces astonishing results.

305. Gordon, A.C. "Flandroe's Mogul."
In *Stories of the Railway*, 149–195. New
York: Scribner's, 1893. Also in Gordon's
*Envion and Other Tales of Old and New
Virginia*. London, New York, and
Chicago: F. Tennyson Neely, 1899.

James Flandroe is suing the Southern
Railroad Company over the loss of his right
arm. Flandroe, with 36 years in the road's service, receives some succinct counsel from an acquaintance: "A po' man don't stan' no mo'
chance a-lawin' of a railroad-compn'y than a
bumble-bee stan's in a tar-bucket" (168). Indeed, the Southern treats Flandroe con-
temptibly: "He had served this company a lifetime, and now that it had maimed him and
destroyed his usefulness, it proposed to turn
him to die like a dog in a ditch" (170). The tale
takes a strange turn from the theme of ordinary
man against the corporation and becomes a
ghost story. Either theme standing alone might
have turned out well; forced together, neither
does.

306. Gordon, Mildred, and Gordon Gordon. *Campaign Train*. Garden City,
NY: Doubleday, 1952. 188p.

Governor Wallace X. Martin is running
for president when someone takes a shot at him
as his cross-country campaign train rolls along
one night through the Midwest. Jackie Moxas,
a 19-year-old stenographer in Martin's retinue,
chafes under his authority and thinks she
wishes him dead. She seems to have nastiness
in mind for many of those around her. When
a waiter greets her pleasantly in the dining car,
she thinks that he should drop dead. A cheerful lass! The train goes through Illinois, Missouri, and Michigan. When it comes to light
that Jackie is a reform school graduate, some
are shocked. Jackie nearly becomes an accomplice in Martin's murder, but instead becomes
an accidental (and cynical) heroine, somewhat
clumsily developed. Details of campaign train
activities, though, are convincing.

307. Graham, Margaret. *Swing Shift*.
New York: Citadel, 1951. 493p.

In this pro-labor tract novel, Joseph Ed-
mond McCaffrey—Mac—the chief character,
handles a railroad swing shift position filling in
on relief jobs when other workers are ill, hurt,
or on vacation. Born and raised in a coal mining town, he left the miner's life at 16 and signed
up with the railroad. One of his first acts on the
job is joining the Order of Railroad Telegraphers; this involvement in the union movement
marks his career. When he moves on, he goes
to James J. Hill's Great Northern in 1916, "a
good union road, broke in by Debs and his ARU
way back in ninety-four" (32). The novel is ultimately more a sympathetic history, if not a
propaganda screed, concerning the 20th century labor movement, with an emphasis on railroads, than a work of fiction. The author's dedication to the movement is so pronounced that
she has Mac go for a sojourn in Revolutionary
Russia, where he helps establish an up-to-date
train dispatching system. Back in the U.S., Mac
continues his organizing, to serve "the dream of
united action between engineers and firemen,
conductors, brakemen and switchmen, shop
crafts and maintenance crews..." (489). In addition to Russia, settings include Kentucky, Colorado, Minnesota, and Florida.

308. Grant, Douglas [Isabel E. Ostrander]. *The Single Track*. New York: Grosset & Dunlap, 1919. 290p.

In this sentimental romantic melodrama, the Gildersleeve Copper Company faces financial ruin unless it can build a railroad to carry ore 30 miles from a new Alaskan mine to a seaport. It must compete for the only available right-of-way with another mining company, the unscrupulous Unatika outfit. Spoiled but plucky young Janetta Gildersleeve vows to go to Alaska to keep an eye on the family's interests in the matter. She appears on the scene under an assumed name, and takes a humble job in the company store to facilitate her surveillance. There is not much railroading here, in spite of the novel's title, but in a boffo climax Janetta fires a locomotive racing to a pitched battle at a trestle between guys good and bad, where her true love is in danger. The title has a double meaning, referring to a proper marriage as well as to the railroad.

309. Grant, Richard. "Drode's Equations." In *The Ascent of Wonder: The Evolution of Hard SF*. Edited by D.G. Hartwell and K. Cramer, 278–287. New York: Doherty, 1994. First published in *New Dimensions 12*. Edited by Robert Silverberg and Marta Randall. New York: Pocket Books, 1981.

The narrator, a railway official on a long train trip, examines a set of mathematical equations—Drode's—that he unearthed in the family library. The equations concern time; the train trip, through a landscape marked by the colors and decay of late fall, also suggests the action of time. The narrator observes the passing autumnal display from his window, and admires it; an elderly fellow passenger disagrees with the official about the pleasure of the season, and regards fall as a time of sadness and endings. As the official sips a cup of tea, with the autumn evening gathering around the train, a feeling of serene understanding descends upon him, and the mystery of Drode's equations yields. An evocative story in which the narrator, through the aid of his train ride, slips the surly bonds of time, if only momentarily.

310. Grant, William. *The Trackwalker*. New York: Lynx, 1989. 211p.

Jared Macalester is, to all appearances, a trackwalker for the Union Pacific. His first notable action in this entertaining Western potboiler is to throw a boorish cowboy off a train, while the train is in motion. The cowboy had been pestering a woman newspaper editor. Before Macalester can show his face in the tale, bandits rob a UP train of its money shipment, and kill an agent. Macalester has, in fact, been assigned by the Faraday Security Agency to solve the robbery case, and uses the trackwalker position as a cover. His assignment evolves to cleaning up the railroad town of Ironsprings, and is complicated by the corrupt local lawmen and various roughnecks.

311. Greeley, Andrew M. *The Bishop and the Missing L Train: A Blackie Ryan Mystery*. New York: Forge, 2000. 285p.

One of Chicago's elevated trains, bearing Auxiliary Bishop Gus "Idiot" Quill, has gone missing. The disappearance hints "of monumental evil, something huge, twisted, and depraved" (34). Bishop Blackie Ryan, assigned by the archbishop of Chicago to retrieve his none-too-bright colleague, learns that the train consisted of a single car, with Quill the solitary passenger. The L train driver surfaces, mostly unconscious, in an alley. The train disappears in more ways than one from this complexly-plotted mystery, but Greeley uses it to good effect to give the story a flying start.

312. Grendon, Steven. [August Derleth.] "The Extra Passenger." In *Mr. George and Other Odd Persons*, 152–162. Sauk City, WI: Arkham House, 1963. Also in *The Night-Side: Masterpieces of the Strange and Terrible*. Edited by August Derleth. New York and Toronto: Rinehart & Co., 1947. *Weird Tales* 39 (Jan. 1947): 33–37.

Mr. Arodias acts on his clever plan to kill his uncle; his getaway involves a surreptitious debarking and reboarding of the night train for Aberdeen from London. All goes well, but for the extra passenger he finds in his compartment on reboarding the train after his evil deed. The identity of the extra passenger proves greatly unsettling for Mr. Arodias.

313. _____. "The Night Train to Lost Valley." In *Mr. George and Other Odd Persons*, 192–209. Sauk City, WI: Arkham House, 1963. *Weird Tales* 40 (Jan. 1948): 57–65.

Mr. Wilson, the narrator, reminisces about his days as a traveling leather goods salesman near the turn of the century. He often rode an old, short train—locomotive, coal car, coach, and baggage car—on his New Hampshire route to Lost Valley and back. He took the night train through "dark, brooding country" (192). He was often the only passenger, and frequently chatted with train crewmen. On Mr. Wilson's last trip before his assignment to office work, Conductor Jem Watkins tries to talk him out of the journey. The crewmen are unaccountably distant, and the familiar residents of Lost Valley are dismayed to see Mr. Wilson. That night he rises from a troubled sleep to look out the window of his room. He sees a crowd at the railroad station, where the engine stands, steam up, and goes down to join them on a trip into the wilderness. The story is reminiscent of Hawthorne's "Young Goodman Brown."

314. Grey, Zane. *The U.P. Trail*. 1918. Reprint, Mattituck, NY: Amereon House, 198[?]. 409p.

"The building of the U.P. will be hell!" (26). Thus observes a character early in this novel after exploration of the route for the intended transcontinental railroad. The novel follows men surveying the future right-of-way for the Union Pacific through the mountains. Hell arrives in the form of Indian attacks and brutal weather. One of the party, Service, freezes to death in his shelter. Warren Neale, one of the central characters, laments Service's loss, observing that the train will eventually pass the place where he lies buried: "Thousands of people—going, coming, busy, happy at their own affairs, full of their own lives, will pass by poor Service's grave and never know it's there!" Responds the trapper, Slingerland, at Neale's side: "Wal, son, if people must hev railroads, they must kill men to build them" (97).

Slingerland hates the railroad; he sees it as a provocation for government theft of Indian land, broken treaties, and the industrial befouling of the wilderness.

Neale rises in the ranks of the UP. Considering the laborers who built the tracks, he "divined that these men were all alike. They all toiled, swore, fought, drank, gambled. Hundreds of them went to nameless graves. But the work went on—the great, driving, united heart beat on" (383). Grey closes with a brief, sympathetic chapter from the perspective of an aging Sioux chief, who one evening watches a train steam across the plain far below, and ponders the inevitable loss of his people's way of life.

Grey gums up the novel with a superfluous love story, and no one will mistake the good parts for great literature, but the story possesses enough sense of the complex meaning that lies below the surface of the railroad's advance that it is more than a mere romance.

315. Grimes, Martha. *The Train Now Departing*. In *The Train Now Departing: Two Novellas*, 1–116. New York: Viking, 2000.

In this gently and gracefully written psychological tale, the female lead character has trains in her past. She remembers going to meet the train with her mother; she likes the anonymity of a train ride: "It's eerie. As if the self were in some kind of limbo" (11). She eats a piece of pie in the café of the old station in her home town, and thinks of the station refreshment room in David Lean's 1945 film, *Brief Encounter*. Although trains evoke sad feelings for her, she is drawn to them, and to the old station. Her unappealing male friend, a travel writer, thinks that she devotes too much time to her railway impulses. He likes to take her to pretentious restaurants, when all she wants is a grilled cheese sandwich at the railroad station café. She haunts the station, watching trains come and go; she sees the passengers through the coach windows, and wonders "if the ones who looked out thought the same as she did, that she inhabited a world from which they were excluded" (36).

She realizes that she has lived her life without room for accident, carefully and cautiously.

Late in the story, she imagines herself going on a train trip, boarding a train departing for La Paz. "She would be one of the faces on the other side of the windows, staring out at the platform and the empty air she had recently occupied" (103). The story ends sadly, but not hopelessly, for the woman whose life has been so circumscribed understands in her unexpected grief a dimension of her existence she had not previously grasped.

316. Grimsley, Jim. "Jesus Is Sending You This Message." In *New Stories from the South: The Year's Best, 2001*, edited by Shannon Ravenel, 194–205. Chapel Hill: Algonquin Books, 2001. *Ontario Review*, no. 52 (Spring/Summer 2000): 141–150.

The narrator, a white man who works in an Atlanta hospital, takes the commuter train to work daily. One day a neatly-dressed black woman delivers a statement, allegedly at the inspiration of Jesus, to the passengers in general. She warns them that "woeful days are coming," and that time is running out for her listeners to get right with the Savior. "That's what Jesus told me to tell the people" (195). The narrator finds the same woman on his train nearly every trip; she makes the same apocalyptical announcement on every commute. Annoyed, then angry, the narrator tells her to be quiet. His forwardness earns him the woman's scorn, and the contempt of the other passengers. He alters his daily routine, then, in dread of being trapped again with this self-appointed messenger from Jesus. It is easy to sympathize with the narrator.

317. Gulick, Bill. "Big Olaf Paints for War." In *Rawhide Men*, edited by Kenneth Fowler, 157–175. Garden City, NY: Doubleday, 1965. Published as "The Madness of Big Olaf." *Dime Western Magazine*, May 1948.

Jeff Holt, assistant engineer in charge of a track-laying crew, rides up the mountain trail into the woods to see why the fresh-cut ties have not been sent floating downstream. The villainous saloon owner Walt Riley, who covets the lumbering contract, is keeping the crew of Swedes supplied with women and liquor to distract them from their jobs. "You know

Swedes," says their boss, Pop Barden (162). "Those damned Swedes like whiskey and they like their women," Pop warns Holt; "They'd tear you limb from limb" if Holt spoiled their fun (164). Olaf Jensen, one of the hands at the camp, is instrumental—in his own befogged way—in helping Holt abruptly dispense with Riley, his saloon, and the crew's slovenly performance. Through the story, the Swedish laborers are portrayed as dim-witted lummoxes.

318. Haines, William W. *High Tension*. Boston: Little, Brown, 1938. 299p.

In the Depression, out-of-work electrical linemen are relieved to learn that a railroad plans to electrify 150 miles of its route. The project will mean work for thousands of men who have been living on hope and the occasional railroad make-work job. The narrator, Jig, and his buddy Beckett are assigned to Grassland Junction, a backwater where "They wasn't no movie, they wasn't no pool hall, they wasn't no saloon, and the filling station closed at nine o'clock evey [sic] night" (9). No matter: "We stayed right there and worked sixteen and eighteen hours a day and was glad to have it. There's nothing like having enough work ahead so that you can't even see your way out of it" (11). Grassland Junction soon hosts a camp with hundreds of railroad laborers, and like the boom towns of the Old West, its morals are obscured in the influx of money. A little bordello opens near the camp, and, although the local minister condemns it, the pecuniary advantages of the place persuade the townsfolk to tolerate it.

Haines writes with nearly perfect pitch for the language a bright but unschooled working man like Jig might use in such a narrative. His treatment is realistic and unsentimental, with engaging characters, humor, and a believable romantic interest. If the story settles a little too far into melodrama, it is good melodrama, with a conclusion at the scene of a train wreck that justifies the book's title.

319. _____. "Remarks: None." *Atlantic* 154 (Aug. 1934): 143–155. Also in *The Best Short Stories of 1935*, edited by Edward J. O'Brien. New York: Houghton-Mifflin, 1935.

Scarfe, a railway electrician, persuades his supervisor, Jig, to hire as a railroad lineman an old friend, Regan, who has had problems with women and gambling. Jig warns Regan about the dangers of working with the high-voltage lines in the railroad yard: "If you fool around ... you'll find yourself about half cooked before you ever get to hell" (145). Jig sums up the nature of the job: "In railroad work you always got to wait till you can get the use of the track. And in a hot yard you got to wait till track and power clearance synchronize. And then you got to get your train moved in to where you want it, your towers pulled up to the right level, your deck lights set, and your men to work. And you got to do it fast" (145–146).

Regan proves a fine worker, but his personal life haunts him, and begins to interfere with his performance. The story ends with a tragic act, and the complicity of Jig and Scarfe in concealing the truth about it in the official report, which concludes, "Remarks: None" (155). Haines nicely foreshadows the story's terrible end. The story's realistic dialog and the depiction of men at work in a dangerous job—and an informed look at an aspect of railroad life that receives little observation elsewhere—also help make it worthwhile.

320. _____. *Slim*. Boston: Little, Brown, 1934. 414p.

Haines, although only 25 when he wrote this novel, was already a veteran electrical lineman. His hero, Slim Kincaid, becomes a journeyman lineman. In Part Six (pp. 333–414), he goes into railroad work. The chapter opens with Slim's first day in the rail yard, where he eyes with relief familiar components from his previous work, and with some dismay the unusually complex array of electrical infrastructure on which the railroad relies. The reader learns details of railroad work along with Slim, who makes no pretense of knowing more than he does. He adjusts with difficulty to the fact that line work in the yards is of its nature an array of jobs set aside in progress, to be resumed when conditions allow.

Haines gives considerable attention to the interaction and professionalism of the wire train crew, led by the Duke. The crew members mix serious, focused work with off-the-job pranks.

The danger of working within inches of hot wires is always on Slim's mind, the more so when he is responsible for other men's safety. He "considered it a boss's moral duty to stand whenever possible in the narrow space between the men and the live wires" (389). In spite of the danger, "it was thrilling, too. There was a fresh keen excitement about it each time they went to work" (395).

The Depression has its effects in layoffs and shorter hours even as Slim takes on supervisory duties. The Depression finally knocks Slim out of his job, in spite of Duke's dedicated efforts to retain him. Being out of work tortures Slim.

Haines's intimate knowledge of the work gives this novel an air of authority in both its technical details and in its portrait of relations among the railroad electrical workers. Including a credible love story, *Slim* is a most impressive accomplishment by a very young writer.

321. Hale, Edward Everett. "The Brick Moon." In *His Level Best, and Other Stories*, 30–124. Boston: James R. Osgood, 1873. Also in *Masterpieces of Science Fiction*. Edited by Sam Moskowitz. Cleveland: World Publishing, 1967. *Atlantic Monthly* 24 (Oct. 1869): 451–461; (Nov. 1869): 603–611; (Dec. 1869): 679–689.

Available at *Wright American Fiction*: http://www.letrs.indiana.edu/web/w/wright2/

Captain Fred Ingham, the narrator, reminisces about how he and his college mates speculated on launching a new satellite, made of bricks, into orbit around the earth. It was chiefly want of funding that left the project existing only in fancy and in a portfolio of working drawings. Seventeen years later, Fred's old friend George Orcutt appears; he has made a fortune in railroading, chiefly through the astonishing fact of being "a railroad manager caring for the comfort of his passengers!" (45). This approach contrasts with that passengers obtain in the standard passenger coach, "in which the backs should be straight, the heads of passengers unsupported, the feet entangled in a vice [sic], the elbows always knocked by the passing conductor" (45–46). With Orcutt's initial financial backing, the brick moon project succeeds. Sales of railroad stock further support the scheme. Thus, the great transportation mode of the 19th century helps launch a form of travel that would not become a reality for nearly another century. This story may present the first description of an artificial, earth-orbiting satellite. (Hale, for several years chaplain of the U.S. Senate, is best known as the author of the 1865 exercise in patriotic sentimentality, "A Man Without a Country.")

322. _____. *G.T.T.; Or the Wonderful Adventures of a Pullman.* Boston: Roberts Bros., 1877. 221p.

The title abbreviation means "Gone to Texas," according to Hale an old term for a disreputable character's farewell inscribed on a door when he finds the local scene inhospitable. Hale's long-term interest in Texas inspired this story, which focuses on Hester Sutphen and her friend, Euphemia, who board a Pullman in New Jersey for the first leg of their trip to San Antonio, where they plan to open a school for young women. The train disappears, for the most part, fairly early in this stilted romantic quasi-travelogue, but does resurface late in the book. As the main characters ride along, Hale observes of the scene they view from the coach windows:

"There is something almost weird and uncanny in this sailing through oceans of green, only broken by pretty copses of wood or gentle swells of land, without a fence, a house, a barn, a road beside that you travel on, without cow or horse or sheep. Only an unused fertile world waiting for men!" (213).

The vastness and fallow emptiness of the American landscape are much more readily noted from a train than from an airplane. The last, somewhat unsettling, sentence in the above quote suggests that nature had better look out for men eager to "use" her.

323. Hale, Garth [Albert B. Cunningham]. *Legacy for Our Sons.* New York: Dutton, 1952. 319p.

Hale portrays the true American railroad as an enterprise where favoritism is non-existent:

All that counts is one's ability to do a job (as long as one was not a Negro, one might add, or a woman, or Chinese, or a Jew, or perhaps the division engineer's nephew). So it was on Hale's fictional railroad, the Median and Southern, where the workers "were willing to go beyond the limits of their specific tasks in order to insure the smooth operation of the road. There was a pleasant esprit de corps, with everyone willing to do all he could..." (35). Discussing the ideal reality of the railroad with his father, young Harrison Day exults: "Why ... it's the system that's put America where she is today! Men can work and get the reward they deserve" (56).

Hale engages in wide-eyed capitalist bromides. Before the 1930s, he contends that the individual was his own man, his achievement limited only by his own choice or ability. Indeed: Mere circumstances of chance had no effect. What ruined this wonderful world, in Hale's opinion? "Regulation and government spending" (121). Hale rants against the "staggering taxation" of the late 1940s (123).

Harrison Day, the book's much-oppressed hero, finds himself in a near-future America in which the rich have vanished, soaked by taxes to fund the indolent. He "understood that forces inimical to the American Way might be termiting the economic order" (207). His worthless son Barny wants to go into railroad work as a telegrapher, since he judges that the position most likely to allow him to be laid off, and idle away on the largesse of unemployment compensation. In the novel's crisis, Barny—his shallow mind corrupted by totalitarian enemies of the American Way—blows up a railroad bridge. As the story ends, the federal government is on the verge of complete takeover of the railroads. Socialism is on the march and Harrison Day, with quaint ideas about individual responsibility, gets sacked from his job.

Naïve, simplistic, paranoid, mindlessly anti-union—and begging mockery at every turn—the novel appeals to widespread ideas boiled down from complex abstractions to the tarry goo of popular wisdom. To grasp the American mindset, or at least an influential part of it, of the 1950s (a mindset that flourishes yet in some influential quarters), one cannot ignore such popular fiction, or its more "philosophically" developed siblings, such as

Ayn Rand's *Atlas Shrugged*. These are books one could reasonably expect to find on any hard-right ideologue's shelf, next to copies of Herbert Philbrick's *I Led Three Lives* and Fred Schwartz's classic, much favored by Goldwater Republicans of the early 1960s, *You Can Always Trust the Communists ... to be Communists*. (The last title, unfortunately, is almost impossible to locate today.)

A black character does appear in the novel, by the way: as a porter, chef, and general factotum for the new division superintendent, Guild. Guild is awarded a private car with his post, and "a Negro went with the car" (63), along with the upholstery and lamps, apparently.

324. _____ [A. B. Cunningham]. *This Pounding Wheel*. New York: Dutton, 1947. 314p.

Barber's son and lightly-educated but determined Clinton Ball is the C&O division superintendent; John Gaunt is the trainmaster, and Luke Eddington is the engineer on Number 1, the pride of the C&O stable in the 1890s. Ball is having an affair with Beverly, Luke's wife. Ball thinks of the Chesapeake and Ohio as "a swashbuckling giant" distinguished by its workers: "In origin they were a cross-section of America. But in *esprit de corps* they were a proud and a swaggering and a rip-roaring aggregation" (56–57).

The novel offers some good characterizations, such as that of Trainmaster Gaunt, whose name fits his build. Gaunt learns of the affair between Ball and Beverly, and nasty complications follow. A resolution to the mess occurs, but not without a serious wreck. Ball's superior excoriates himself for letting his anger over private behavior interfere with his professional judgment: "I pulled out the best railroader we have west of Newport News. And why? Because you got tangled up with a woman! What the hell did that have to do with running a railroad?" (313). Railroad details in the story are convincing, but they have nothing innately to do with the love triangle with which the plot is concerned.

325. Halliday, Bret. [Davis Dresser]. "Human Interest Stuff." In *Rogue's Gallery*, edited by Walter Gibson,

51–64. Garden City, NY: Doubleday, 1969. Also in *Hard-Boiled: An Anthology of American Crime Stories*. Edited by Bill Pronzini and Jack Adrian. Oxford and New York: Oxford University Press, 1995.

The narrator drifts into a construction camp of the St. Louis, Mexico, & Asiatic Railroad, somewhere south of the U.S.-Mexican border. He hires on as a construction supervisor while the regular man is out sick. He claims that his Mexican workers "take lots of bossing. The one thing they haven't got is initiative" (53). With relief he hires another American drifter, Sam, to run a level for setting grade stakes. It becomes apparent that Sam is wanted for murder back in the States. A twist in the tale's end does not play fair with the reader, but for those who do not object to being manipulated, the effect is not unpleasant.

326. Hamblen, Herbert. "Dumb Luck." *Saturday Evening Post* 173 (June 1, 1901): 6–8.

Engineer Tom Davis is out of sorts over a troublesome locomotive, the 333, that has been the bane of every man assigned to it. Now, he must operate the recalcitrant machine. Initially his trip goes well; the 333 is thriving with a special grade of coal. Tom receives a train order that puts him on collision course with a special train carrying the railroad's president. In a case of divine intervention, a herd of hogs on the track in Tom's path forces him to come to a halt, although not without porcine casualties. "The moon's fair face was scarred with packing-house products, there was a boarding-house air of broiling chops, and the stilly night was rent with blood-curdling squealings..." (8). Thus the pigs were sacrificed to save the railroad's bacon.

327. Hardin, J. D. *The Northwest Railroad War*. New York: Berkley, 1988. 185p.

Under the oversight of Andrew Onderdonk, a New York builder and engineer, laborers are at work on the British Columbia section of the new Canadian Pacific transcontinental railroad. Bad business is afoot: Saboteurs are targeting the railroad, and someone has been spreading rumors among Onderdonk's many Chinese workers (who receive a dollar a day, in contrast to white laborers' two dollars) that the railroad will not live up to its wage agreement with them. Onderdonk brings in the prime Pinkerton operative, Raider, to take things in hand. Mounties, Inuits, polar bears, and plenty of he-man outdoor action mark this railroad (north)Western. No one can doubt that Raider—with a name like that, how could he fail?—will smoke out what the jacket copy refers to as the "low-down murdering varmints" obstructing the railroad.

328. Harding, Allison V. [Milligan, Jean]. "Take the Z Train." In *Journey into Fear, and Other Great Stories of Horror on the Railways*, edited by Richard Peyton, 175–182. New York: Wings Books, 1991. (Originally published as *The Ghost Now Standing on Platform One*. London: Souvenir Press, 1990).

As usual, Junior Assistant Supervisor of Transportation Henry Abernathy leaves the office a little after 5 P.M. and walks to the subway station. He always catches the A or B train; not until after he boards this evening does he realize that he has stepped into the Z train—a train he has never heard of. As the train speeds along, Henry sees that all the passengers in the car are people from his past life, including himself as a young man. The story, an atmospheric, technophobe's nightmare, penetrates the heart of Henry's carefully-measured, dull life.

329. Harrar, George. "The 5:22." In *The Best American Short Stories, 1999*, edited by Amy Tan and Katrina Kenison, 120–128. New York: Houghton Mifflin, 1999. *Story* 46 (Autumn, 1998): 47–54.

Walter Mason has nodded at a woman for over a year at 5:22 when the Western Local pulls into Lincoln Station. One day, when a gust of wind dislodges her scarf, he sees that her right ear is missing. He is embarrassed for staring at her. Following the revelation of the ear, 47-year-old bachelor Walter grows preoccupied with the woman, and with her absence from the station. Not only does the one-eared woman vanish: So does reliable old Mel,

Walter's favorite conductor, replaced by a fellow lacking all warmth. Vanishing as well is Walter's longtime stop at Lincoln: Abruptly, the train now stops a good two miles from Lincoln.

It would spoil the reader's pleasure to say too much about the story's resolution, but Walter's concluding line, "I'm going farther today" (128), suggests that the life he has measured out in coffee spoons may yet yield something rich.

330. Harrington, Joseph. "Subway Fire." *Saturday Evening Post* 211 (Jan. 21, 1939): 10–11+. Also in *Saturday Evening Post Stories, 1939*. Edited by Wesley W. Stout. New York: Random House, 1940.

Stenographer Millicent Kitter is routinely accompanied on her subway ride to Manhattan by the immigrant Joe Winoslaski. Joe has poor English skills and a serious crush on Millicent. She considers him a pest, crude and embarrassing. One day on their ride into Manhattan, the train stalls, losing power below the East River. A fire has broken out, and smoke starts to fill the train. Harrington presents a convincing picture of the passengers' transition from uneasiness in the crowded darkness to outright fear and flight: "Queer, it was so silent. Everybody sat as though frozen" (51). The train's position under the river adds to Millicent's anxiety: "She'd always thought how horrible it would be if the water came pouring in, filling the train" (53).

The conventions of popular fiction receive their due in this story (Joe and Millicent wed), but the passengers' reactions to the crisis are credible, and the denouement, featuring heroism falsely claimed and true heroics unrecognized, is also effective.

331. Harris, James C. "A Greenhorn Wins His Spurs." In *Tales of the Rails*, edited by Veronica Hutchinson, 242–251. Cleveland and New York: World Publishing, 1952. *Railroad Magazine* 41 (Dec. 1946): 40–46.

Photography buff Bo Bronson is a new signal maintainer on the Pacific & Western Railway. His first day on the job goes badly, and a veteran engineer, Gussie McMore, upbraids him for his ineptitude. The railroad has just installed new electric signals, and everyone has trouble adjusting to them, but several engineers have found a way to cheat the company and blame the signals—and Bronson. Bronson turns to his photo skills to upset the tables on the dishonest engineers.

332. Harshbarger, Karl. "Train to Chinko." *Ploughshares* 29, no. 2–3 (Fall 2003): 43–66.

Peterson, an American traveling in an unnamed country—apparently part of the former Soviet Bloc—finds it difficult to let the train station operatives know that he wants to go to the town of Chinko. He finally boards what he hopes is the correct train, and is astonished to hear a Dixieland band playing "Sweet Georgia Brown" as part of a celebration on a nearby platform.

When the train makes an emergency stop, the crewmen herd the passengers out. Peterson, clueless, follows a small group to a highway. His post-train trek takes him "to where he had always wanted to go" (66). Where that is, is a topic for conjecture. The story's sense of Peterson's helplessness, its religious imagery, the necessity of faith in strangers, and other details make it much more than a narrative of a man's trouble with foreign geography and language.

333. Harte, Bret. "A Sleeping Car Experience." In *Women and Things: America's Best Funny Stories*, 31–40. New York and London: Harper & Bros., 1906. Also in Harte's *Drift from Two Shores*. Boston: Houghton, Osgood, 1878.

The passengers' long night in a Pullman berth is relieved by the conversations of two men bound for Joliet. Their gossip about a recently deceased acquaintance, and the sensitive manner in which the undertaker laid him out for viewing by the mourners, earns the engrossed attention of all the passengers within earshot. Just as the story reaches a climax, the train arrives at Joliet, the men get off, and the unfortunate eavesdroppers are not favored with the end of the tale.

334. Hastings, Dorothy. *Death at the Depot.* New York and London: Harper & Bros., 1944. 241p.

In September, 1941, Dr. Peter Hamilton is recuperating in a remote Vermont village—Crawford's Bend—from a fever contracted in West Africa. The village is so isolated that the developing world war hardly seems real. Hamilton eats at Mrs. Barnard's boarding house, where the conversation limits itself to the doings of the locals. Through Hamilton, the reader meets the various other principals. In spite of the mystery's title, the real action, such as it is, consists of the boardinghouse palaver, and what it reveals about the village characters. The dramatic exception is one character's death at the train station from what appears at first to be an unfortunate close encounter with the midnight fast freight. Facts prove otherwise.

335. Hawthorne, Nathaniel. "The Celestial Railroad." In *The Writings of Nathaniel Hawthorne.* Vol. 4, *Mosses from an Old Manse*, vol. 1, 259–288. Boston and New York: Houghton Mifflin, 1900. *United States Magazine and Democratic Review* 12 (May 1843): 515–523.

The narrator relates his dream journey by railroad from the City of Destruction to the Celestial City, or nearly so. The glib Mr. Smooth-it-away accompanies the narrator; he is also a director of the railroad and one of its largest stockholders. In the 19th century's brave new age of pilgrimage, the inconveniences of the past have vanished. "Our enormous burdens, instead of being carried on our shoulders as had been the custom of old, were all snugly deposited in the baggage car..." (263). The Celestial Railroad greatly eases the strain of the trip; no longer must the pilgrim struggle over the Hill Difficulty, or slog through the Valley of Humiliation. The railroad's cuts, fills, and tunnels ease the way wonderfully. Even the Valley of Death has been illuminated by natural gas, although the narrator glimpses disturbing sights in the region's shadows.

The minions of Beelzebub now work as functionaries at the railroad station. The engine, driven by Apollyon, Christian's antagonist in John Bunyan's *Pilgrim's Progress*, looks like a "mechanical demon that would hurry us to the infernal regions," rather than the Celestial City (256). At a long stop-over in Vanity Fair, the narrator nearly abandons his plan of reaching the Celestial City; a pair of old-fashioned pilgrims, roundly ridiculed by the modern sort, assure him that the railroad will never reach its promised destination. Indeed, the journey does not go as flawlessly as Mr. Smooth-it-away promised, and the narrator is greatly relieved to awaken in the end.

Hawthorne's moral earnestness and pointed, amusing satire make this story a pleasure. That infernal device, the steam engine, is just the vehicle to pull a trainload of pilgrims bound for a destination somewhat warmer than the Celestial City.

336. _____. *The House of the Seven Gables*. Boston: Ticknor, Reed, & Fields, 1851. 344p.

Eclipsed only by *The Scarlet Letter* as Hawthorne's best-known work, this gothic tale of family curse, greed, miscarried justice, and all-around evildoing in Salem, Massachusetts, concentrates in major portion on the fates of two characters, the spinster Hepzibah Pyncheon and her delicately-balanced brother, Clifford. In Chapter 17, "The Flight of Two Owls," Hepzibah and Clifford symbolically escape the burden of the past represented by their ancestral home, the house noted in the novel's title. Their method of flight is the railroad, which Hawthorne presents far more positively here than in "The Celestial Railroad." When the pair flee the gloomy and accursed house, they find the train waiting for them at the station, with the locomotive "fretting and fuming, like a steed impatient for a headlong rush" (274). With Hepzibah and Clifford aboard, the train departs, and as the world races past them outside the window, they alternate between a suspicion on her part that the experience is but a dream, and his certainty that he has "never been awake before!" (274). Hawthorne effectively describes the details of the situation aboard the train as they might be witnessed by two people long-accustomed to isolation from the wider world. The activity of passengers, of snack vendors, and the speed

and racket of the train tax the aging pair's senses. When the conductor asks for their tickets, Clifford hands over a bank-note, and in response to the conductor's question about "how far?" replies, "As far as that will carry us" (277). Later, in conversation with another passenger, Clifford waxes ecstatic: "These railroads ... are positively the greatest blessing that the ages have wrought out for us. They give us wings; they annihilate the toil and dust of pilgrimage; they spiritualize travel!" (279).

Clifford's jubilation subsides when he and Hepzibah get off the train, but no matter: They have slipped the shackles of the Pyncheon curse, and from this point their lives improve.

337. Haycox, Ernest. *Trouble Shooter.* 1937. Reprint, Boston: G.K. Hall, 1981. 471p.

In 1868, Frank Peace rides a Union Pacific train hauling five cars full of laborers to the end of the track beyond Cheyenne. There work will resume on the transcontinental railroad, and these men will join thousands at the job. Cheyenne is a boom town, "steeped in sin and proud of it" (23). The UP is desperate to reach Salt Lake City ahead of the Central Pacific; otherwise, it will likely lose control of the entire road from San Francisco to Omaha. Peace is the man assigned by Gen. Grenville Dodge to make sure that the road's progress does not falter. Peace battles marauding Indians, outlaws, and Nature, and forms a special enmity with tent-saloon entrepreneur Sid Campeaux. Campeaux's enterprise depends on erecting a makeshift saloon in a tent at the site of every succeeding end-of-track town, to separate railroaders from their wages as efficiently as possible.

There is no question of the novel's endorsement of the transcontinental effort, but its approval is tempered by such voices as that of the veteran mountain man, Mormon Charley. Charley tells Peace that the advancing railroad, and white civilization in general, have spoiled the region. "I never was no good livin' white style," he says. "I can remember when this was a pretty land" (85). He acknowledges that the Indians are difficult, but the "white men have pushed 'em from one place to another," driving them to a more aggressive stance (84). Haycox, a highly-regarded Western writer, moves the story along at a good pace, and appears to have done his research carefully.

338. Hayes, A. A. "The Denver Express." In *Short Story Classics; American.* Vol. 2, edited by William Patten, 559–592. New York: P.F. Collier, 1905. *Belgravia*, Jan. 1884.

The Denver Fast Express is ready to pull out for the Northwest. The passengers are a mixed lot—miners, cowboys, laborers, Irish, German, Welsh, Russians, Chinese—and in the Pullman sleepers, other diverse, more well-to-do nationalities. Hayes depicts the train's night-time travel through the wilderness as "almost weird ... as if a bit of civilization, a family or community, its belongings and surroundings complete, were flying through regions barbarous and inhospitable" (561–562).

On one of the Pullmans is Henry Sinclair, a rising assistant engineer with the railroad, his wife, and Cyrus Foster. In a flashback on Sinclair's career, Hayes describes Western railroad boom towns, "uncanny aggregations of squalor and vice" (566). In one of the lawless towns, Sinclair saved the life of young Foster by facing down a gang of toughs. "You *know* that if you lay your finger on a railroad man, it's all up with you," he told them, alluding to the hundreds of men at the railroad construction camp nearby (570). Back in the present, Foster aids Sinclair when, aboard the Fast Express, they learn that a notorious gang plans to derail and rob the train.

339. Hayes, William E. "Big Engine." *Saturday Evening Post* 204 (Feb. 13, 1932): 6–7+. Also in *Great Railroad Stories of the World.* Edited by Samuel Moskowitz. New York: McBride, 1954.

A rip-snorting tale of a veteran engineer rising to meet a deadline challenge. Can he haul the trainload of apples over the Montana Division in time to land the big contract? You bet! Considerable technical railroading detail and good humor elevate the story beyond run-of-the-pulp-mill.

340. _____. "Tank Cars Rolling." In *Tales of the Rails*, edited by Veronica Hutchinson, 145–180. Cleveland and New York: World Publishing, 1952. *Railroad Magazine* 31 (March 1942): 88–106.

Although engineer Jerry McAleer's hot temper has plagued him, he has a reputation for fast, careful work on the Midwest Trunk System. With World War II making its demands, Jerry has been busy night and day. Here he works as the engineer on a special run to test the route's ability to deliver oil to the East Liberty yards near St. Louis, and to pick up a load of gasoline for the East Coast. East Liberty is an unappealing place, "Between the main stem of the Midwest Trunk System and the refinery yard tracks with the settlement of company houses where the workers lived in the awful stink—long monotonous rows of frame houses built to look alike" (156). McAleer is disciplined for exceeding speed limits on the oil-hauling leg of the assignment, but later redeems himself, and saves the railroad's oil contract, through heroic action in a freight-yard conflagration.

341. Heinemann, Arthur. "Subway to Brooklyn." *Collier's* 123 (March 5, 1949): 30+.

A young schoolteacher comes to New York City to tell her fiancé, Mike, a musician, that she has decided not to marry him. A long subway trip, alone, gives her a chance to reevaluate her true feelings, and to reverse her decision in Mike's favor.

342. Helprin, Mark. "Katherine Comes to Yellow Sky." In *A Dove of the East, and Other Stories*, 86–93. New York: Knopf, 1975.

Katherine, a dreamer from the gray East who "believed incessantly in what she imagined" (87), is taking the train to the West she has long fancied. She is bound for Yellow Sky. "The train's exact and faithful forward motion led her to expect something ahead at all moments..." (90). The conductor must tell Katherine that the little mountain village they have reached is Yellow Sky, and she is all but transported by the ineffability of it all. She might do well to lie down and calm herself, but the story is yet another example of the railroad as a means to a new life—perhaps. The story begs by its title for comparison with Stephen Crane's "The Bride Comes to Yellow Sky" (Entry 182).

343. _____. "Waiting for the 20th Century." *Esquire* 106 (Nov. 1986): 239–241.

The narrator reminisces about his childhood, when he and his friends played on New York Central property, indulged by tolerant switching tower workers. One evening the railroaders, in exchange for the boys' running off to a diner to buy them a bag of hamburgers, agree to have the 20th Century Limited crawl past the tower when it arrives. The train, it was said, carried movie stars, and if a boy was lucky, he might see from the tower a movie star changing her clothes for dinner on the train. The boys do see a beautiful woman changing her clothes, but the mood changes rapidly from one of excited voyeurism to concern for the privacy of the woman in her compartment. It is a nice manipulation of reader expectations. Also nice is the description of the famous train coming into view in the yards, "its bright headlight swaying from side to side as if it were looking for something to eat..." (241).

344. Hemingway, Ernest. "The Battler." In *In Our Time*, 63–79. 1925. Reprint, New York: Scribner's, 1955.

When the story opens, Nick Adams, having stolen a ride on a freight, has just been knocked off the train by the brakeman a few miles from Mancelona, Michigan. The brakeman fooled Nick, and, having won his confidence, punched him in the eye and knocked him off onto the roadbed, alongside a swamp. Nick walks along the track until he comes upon a campfire where he meets two tramps, the has-been boxer Ad Francis and Ad's companion, a black man named Bugs. After a confrontation with Ad, from which Bugs rescues Nick, Nick continues walking along the railroad track toward Mancelona. The tension of this story matches its economy.

345. _____. "Big Two-Hearted River." In *In Our Time*, 175–212. 1925. Reprint, New York: Scribner's, 1955. *This Quarter* 1 (Spring 1925): 110–128.

In this story's first sentence, the train is disappearing up the track around a hill of burned timber, immediately after it has dropped off young Nick Adams at what used to be the town of Seney, in Michigan's Upper Peninsula. Nick sits down on his bundle that the baggage man tossed from the baggage car and looks around at the scant remains of the town, recently burned to the ground in a forest fire. Nick walks down the track to the railroad bridge, and from there watches trout in the river below. He then returns for his pack, slings it onto his back, and sets out into the scorched country to find a good place to camp and fish.

On the surface, this *is* a story about camping and fishing, and it works fine at that level. Below the surface, it is a story of a man scourged by his experiences in World War I trying to retain his sanity by carefully following a set of rituals that he knows well, from a more innocent time. The train's passage through the burned-out landscape, and its deposit of Nick at the center of the destruction, recalls the devastation that Nick has seen in the war. This is one of the great American short stories of the 20th century.

346. _____. "Canary for One." In *The Complete Short Stories of Ernest Hemingway*, 258–261. New York: Scribner's, 1987. *Scribner's Magazine* 81 (April 1927): 358–360.

An American couple traveling to Paris meet another American, a woman, on the train. The woman, an affluent, middle-aged New Yorker with a canary, is a chatterbox whose banal stream of patter also reveals her as a provincial, self-centered bore. The narrator and his wife respond just enough to the woman's yapping to encourage her to continue. At last the train reaches the station, and the three Americans separate. Separation is the issue of the moment, since the reader learns at story's end that the couple is coming back to Paris to establish separate residences.

347. _____. "The Porter." In *The Complete Short Stories of Ernest Hemingway*, 571–578. New York: Scribner's, 1987. (First publication.)

This story, like "A Train Trip" (below), is drawn from an unfinished novel. Jimmy and his father ride a Pullman into Canada, via the Detroit-Windsor crossing. Jimmy's father is drinking heavily, and keeping to himself in an upper berth. A black porter befriends Jimmy, and gets him breakfast from his pal, the chef. The porter, a "nigger," in Jimmy's term, demonstrates for Jimmy how to use a straight razor in a fight—but cautions, "The razor's a delusion.... The razor's no defense" (576). The porter, under the influence of liquor that Jimmy's father has given him, reveals probably more than he means to about his sorrowful view of life. He asks Jimmy what his father does when he wakes up punchy from drinking. "He exercises," says Jimmy. "Well," says the porter, "I got twenty-four berths to make up. Maybe that's the solution" (577).

When he and the porter are not exchanging observations, Jimmy spends a lot of time looking out the train windows at the autumn land, as the train goes "through fine country that looked like Michigan only with higher hills and the trees were all turning" (572). The interaction between Jimmy and the porter makes this story a pleasure to read.

348. _____. "A Train Trip." In *The Complete Short Stories of Ernest Hemingway*, 557–570. New York: Scribner's, 1987. *Esquire* 108 (Dec. 1987): 162–164+.

Young Jimmy and his father leave their cabin in the Michigan woods and at the nearby station catch a train bound for Chicago. Jimmy watches the woods and hills passing from the train window, and feels uncomfortable about all the unfamiliar sights, even if these woods and hills look like the ones he knows. In the smoking car, Jimmy and his father sit near two men accused of murder. Each man is handcuffed to a guard. The men are flippant and disrespectful with their guards and with Jimmy and his father. At a lunchroom in Cadillac, Jimmy's father sees one of the prisoners pocket a table knife—the same knife the prisoner later uses to stab his guard in the coach bathroom before escaping out the bathroom window. Jimmy's father often asks him how he feels; he is solicitous of his son's perceptions. The

stabbing allows him to pass on to Jimmy some truths about what "you run up against when you lead an active life" (570).

349. Hemley, Robin. "Installations." In *All You Can Eat; Stories*, 150–180. New York: Atlantic Monthly Press, 1988. *Another Chicago Magazine*, no. 19 (1989): 83–104.

Rick, the narrator, is a Chicago El conductor who lives in a "sty" of an apartment near Wrigley Field. He keeps his tickets for upcoming Cubs games in his refrigerator, hoping that, should fire take the place, something of value will remain. He tries to be friendly with the deranged passengers he meets on the train: They give variety to the work. One day he meets a young woman, Ivy, on board. Ivy is a performance artist who, unbidden, moves in with him. She accompanies Rick to work, and through her eyes he sees his stale surroundings in a new way, as art. "The commuters at rush hour are art, too. They way they crane their heads over the platform to see the train coming.... Up and down the line they wait, sticking their necks out. Ivy says they look like a bunch of pigeons jostling for breadcrumbs" (168–169). Rick begins to assist Ivy in her performances—her "installations"—including one on the El train involving raw liver and chicken gizzards. The story ends with Rick experiencing an epiphany. A funny piece, with sober undertones.

350. Hempel, Amy. "Tom-rock through the Eels." In *At the Gates of the Animal Kingdom; Stories*, 117–127. New York: Penguin, 1991. First published in *Taxi*.

A young, or youngish, woman on a solo train trip from California to the Midwest does what is so easy to do when traveling a long distance alone: She reflects on her life. She mulls over her late mother, and the friends and friends' mothers of her childhood. (The rail passenger's absence of responsibility—one simply sits and rides—promotes meditation on long journeys.) She makes some accurate observations about such travel. After pointing out that the trip from California to the Midwest takes 48 hours by train, she describes some of the people one will inevitably meet: "...the extroverted youth with guitar who takes over the club car for spontaneous hootenannies. You will stand in line for snacks behind good clothes on bad bodies, behind the man who is so drunk he has lost his shoes, and so belligerent no one will help him find them" (122).

In a variation on the common train-travel theme of looking out the coach window, or trying to look out but seeing only inwardly, the woman says that "I see my face reflected in the window and face the sad truth—that I happen to look my best when there is no one there to see" (123).

351. Henry, O. "Hearts and Hands." In *The Complete Works of O. Henry*, 1666–1667. Garden City, NY: Doubleday, 1953. Also in Henry's *Waifs and Strays*. Garden City, NY: Doubleday, Page, 1919.

A U.S. marshal and his prisoner, handcuffed together, sit down in a crowded passenger coach at Denver across from a pretty young woman, who recognizes one of the pair. Any alert reader will see the O. Henry twist coming well ahead of its delivery in this little vignette, but, even foreseen, it still satisfies.

352. _____. "Holding Up a Train." In *The Complete Works of O. Henry*, 831–839. Garden City, NY: Doubleday, 1953. *McClure's Magazine* 22 (April 1904): 611–619. Also in Henry's *Sixes and Sevens*. Garden City, NY: Doubleday, Page, 1911.

A fellow purportedly an experienced train robber cogitates on his career on the rails. "My advice to you, if you should ever be in a hold-up, is to line up with the cowards and save your bravery for an occasion when it may be of some benefit to you" (838). Mostly tongue-in-cheek, the story succeeds in casting an event fraught with terror and sudden death in a comic mold. The narrator's description of his first train heist, when he and his sidekicks shook down the passengers after appropriating the contents of the train's safe, is especially good. A certain solemnity creeps into the closing paragraphs, when the narrator speaks of the inevitable rough end awaiting the train robber. This "is one of the reasons why the train-robbing profession is not so pleasant a one as either of its collateral branches—politics or cornering the market" (839).

353. _____. "The Passing of Black Eagle." In *The Complete Works of O. Henry*, 429–438. Garden City, NY: Doubleday, 1953. Also in Henry's *Roads of Destiny*. Garden City, NY: Doubleday, Page, 1913.

Chicken Ruggles, a hobo, swindles a child of 90 cents, and hops a southbound freight in St. Louis. Chicken reclines in his private cattle car with a quart of bad whisky, a bag of bread, and some cheese. He eventually comes upon a sheepherder's hut, and helps himself, in the herdsman's absence, to clothing, weaponry, and sundry. It all fits into Chicken's absurd transformation into "Black Eagle," who, with a band of thieves, terrorizes the Texas-Mexico border country. Chicken's life reverts to normal when he and the boys are about to stage their first train robbery. Farcical and funny, the story portrays bandits and train robbers as ordinary lads, "simple, artless" folk who lead modest lives, aside from the occasional "shooting of such of their acquaintances as ventured to interfere" (436).

354. _____. "The Roads We Take." In *The Complete Works of O. Henry*, 1174–1177. Garden City, NY: Doubleday, 1953. Also in Henry's *Whirligigs*. New York: Doubleday, Page, 1910.

"It ain't the roads we take; it's what's inside of us that makes us turn out the way we do," utters Bob Tidball, in a somewhat inelegant variation on Shakespeare (1176). Tidball ought to know: He's a train robber, fresh from a big job on the Sunset Express near Tucson. Bob learns the truth of his homespun philosophy when his partner, Shark Dodson, finds a solution to the problem of Bob's injured horse. The story shifts gears suddenly, and, like James Thurber's Walter Mitty aroused from one of his fantasies, Mr. Dodson, a Wall Street broker, leaves his dream of the Wild West behind to show the road he has taken as a businessman. That road proves to be as low and dirty as the one his alter ego, Shark, followed to terrorize the crew and passengers of the Sunset Express.

355. Herrick, Robert. *Together*. New York: Macmillan, 1908. 595p.

John Lane works for the Atlantic and Pacific Railroad, and takes his bride Isabelle on their honeymoon via train. Lane has a "persistent force,—patient, quiet, sure" (31), but Isabelle feels no passion for him. He began as a clerk for the A&P in its St. Louis traffic department. Within a few years, he rose to superintendent in Indiana. Nevertheless, in this long-winded domestic drama, the railroad recedes to a nearly invisible point. Late passages concern corrupt railroad practices, and Lane, who becomes a vice president of the A&P, is indicted by a federal grand jury. Questioned about his role in the matter, John is an unrepentant capitalist: "Business has to be done according to its own rules, not as idealists or reformers would have it done. The railroad has done nothing more than every big business is compelled to do to live,—has made a profit where there was one to make... [ellipsis in original] This would be a poor sort of country, even for the reformers and agitators, if the men who have the power to make money should be bound hand and foot by visionaries and talkers" (56). Isabelle is dubious about Lane's self-serving rationalizations. So is the jury: It finds Lane guilty as charged. The A&P had favored its secret partners at the expense of their competitors, and Lane is correctly branded a grafter.

356. Hershey, Lenore. "The Winter Train." *McCall's* 86 (Nov. 1958): 48–49+.

A winter storm has disrupted traffic on the East Coast. In Washington, Sen. Barton Tyson doubts that he will reach his scheduled New York meeting on time. At Union Station, northbound trains are going nowhere. He has confided in no one about the purpose of his trip—to see a specialist for his newly-diagnosed Parkinson's disease. Tyson finally persuades a conductor to admit him to an already-crowded train; he must share a drawing room with two women. Shortly after the train gets under way, it pulls into a siding and stops. "Inside the compartment the niggardly light seemed to pinpoint all the frustrations and discouragement that had led them to this bleak cell in a becalmed railroad car. They were

three human beings, so close they could touch one another by lifting a hand. Yet they knew they were isolated strangers" (91). The three share a drink from a bottle Barton has brought, and think about their respective personal problems. As the train stands idle, the three passengers grow closer, and the older of the two women helps Sen. Barton and the younger woman see their own crises in a more rational and mature light. A nicely written, not overly sentimental story.

357. Hibbard, George A. "As the Sparks Fly Upward." *Scribner's Magazine* 8 (Dec. 1890): 721–734. Also in Hibbard's *The Governor, and Other Stories*. New York: Scribner's, 1892; and in *Stories of the Railway*. New York: Scribner's, 1893.

The express train is ready for its Christmas Eve run, but Spurlock, the fireman, has disappeared. Spurlock runs up at the last moment, and the train departs. Irby, the engineer, had rescued Spurlock from drunken oblivion nearly a year earlier. In the engine cab this Christmas Eve, these two men without families—with only each other's regular companionship—share confidences about the past. The sharing provokes a startling act of violence, later explained in detail. What might have been a fine story succumbs to contrivance and sentimentality. Even so, Hibbard very nicely describes a large, busy station at the holiday: "People swarmed everywhere—passengers and employe's [sic], baggage-men, brakemen, and express-men. Heavy trunks, overloaded with luggage, were wildly trundled through the place; small iron carriages, piled high with mail-bags, were recklessly rolled past; and in and out darted the bearers of flaming torches that cast a wild glare about them ... who, with long-handled hammers tested the car-wheels with ringing blows" (722).

358. Highsmith, Patricia. *Strangers on a Train*. 1949. Reprint, London: Heinemann, 1966. 307p.

Many readers of this novel have seen Alfred Hitchcock's fine 1951 film based on it. The story begins aboard a train on which Guy Haines, a young architect, meets another young man, Charles Anthony Bruno, an apparently feckless scion of a rich family. In a drunken conversation in Bruno's squalid compartment, Bruno seeks to enlist Guy in a demented murder-by-proxy scheme: Bruno will kill Guy's wife if Guy kills Bruno's oppressive father. Guy initially dismisses the notion as the babble of an intoxicated, and perhaps not altogether sane, man; Bruno, however, takes the plan seriously. Highsmith describes how the train bearing these two fated men "tore along with an angry, irregular rhythm"—not unlike the rhythm of Bruno's bizarre fantasies—and how "it would wait impatiently for a moment, then attack the prairie again" (1).

359. Hill, Ashbel F. *John Smith's Funny Adventures on a Crutch: Or, the Remarkable Peregrinations of a One-Legged Soldier after the War.* Philadelphia: J.E. Potter, 1869. 374p.

Available at *Wright American Fiction*: http://www.letrs.indiana.edu/web/w/wright2/

The eyebrow-raising title indicates author Hill's wry perspective in this lightly-fictionalized memoir. Hill, a soldier in a Pennsylvania infantry unit, lost a leg in the Battle of Antietam—the same fate that befalls his hero here, John Smith, who has occasional adventures by rail as he travels around the country. He rides the New York Central Railroad from Albany to Rochester. Aiming to overcome the smoke and cinders that assail the eyes of the passengers in a coach with open windows, he wears a pair of goggles throughout the trip. The goggles protect his eyes, but do nothing for his lungs; he complains of being afflicted with a deadly cough. Several passengers inquire about his eyes, and Smith reflects that he must have been a disconcerting sight: "A good-looking young man like myself, on a crutch, with such an immense round patch on either side of his nose, must have been a marvel to look at" (116). Later, when he tries to secure a room at a hotel, the desk clerk ignores him, no doubt, Smith realizes, because his traveling clothes are filthy with the smoke and dust of his railroad journey.

Elsewhere, Smith refuses to surrender his window seat on the train when a man accompanying a woman requests it. Smith prefers this seat, not only because of the view, but because that location gives a man a chance to "jump out headforemost, if he sees another train coming from the opposite direction on the same track" (154). Smith observes that a man is naturally selfish, "and nowhere is his selfishness brought out in so strong a light as on a railroad car" (157).

Smith's subsequent railroading adventures include a near-catastrophic wreck; cleverly avoiding the scheme of a confidence man in Indiana; complaining about the tedium of night travel; and becoming trapped in an irritating conversation with a railroader about his absent leg. Of the con man, Smith counsels: "Reader, in your travels, beware of friendly strangers. John Smith always bewares of 'em, and it pays" (263).

Hill's prose retains a freshness and readability that exceeds that of much popular literature of the period, and his observations on train travel are both informative and funny.

360. Hill, Edwin C. *The Iron Horse.* New York: Grosset & Dunlap, 1924. 329p.

Hill, a newspaperman, provides a novelization of director John Ford's 1924 silent film classic, *The Iron Horse.* (Ford reportedly employed some 3,000 railroad workers to help give the film an authentic look.) The story is the usual blend of Western pot-boiling action and romance, but succeeds in part at evoking the expansive spirit behind the transcontinental railroad. It opens in Illinois in 1853. Dave Brandon tries to persuade his townsmen that a railroad spanning the country is a good idea; they consider him addled. He and his young son Dave go west to pursue their railroad dreams; they find a pass that will accommodate a right-of-way through the Rockies, but an Indian band murders Brandon. Young Dave is rescued and grows up in California, never abandoning his railroad hopes. Years later, the Union Pacific begins to advance across the land, "a shining rapier thrusting at a sullen frontier" (127). After a long absence from the book, Dave reappears, and helps the railroad relocate the pass he and his father had discovered. The novel concludes with an account of the meeting of the Union Pacific and Central Pacific in Utah.

361. Hill, Grace L. *The Red Signal.* 1919. Reprint, Mattituck, New York: American Reprint Co., no date. 198p.

Hilda Lessing, a young woman, is rescued by a stranger as she is about to blunder into the path of a train in a rail yard. She is on her way to a job at Platt's Crossing, to furnish domestic help on a German truck farm. Her rescuer is Dan Stevens, a locomotive engineer. Hilda later reflects on what a courageous, admirable specimen Stevens is. Life on the farm proves hard, but Dan signals Hilda with his engine whistle whenever he passes, giving her inspiration. The farm family consists of loyal Germans, on the Kaiser's side in the war, led by the patriarch Schwarz, who is cooperating in a railroad bridge sabotage scheme to hinder the U.S. war effort. Hilda is instrumental in thwarting the spies and saboteurs; in her brave, patriotic efforts, she takes a train to Washington, D.C., to notify federal officials of the Platt's Crossing cell. Engineer Stevens goes to war and is gassed and captured; having escaped, he goes home on a furlough, and during this break saves Hilda from disaster at the hands of the evil ones.

The story is patently preposterous, but of some interest in its illumination of domestic anti-German anxiety during World War I. Religious overtones—Hilda is much concerned with God's role in the nonsense—run throughout the book.

362. Hill, John A. "The Clean Man and the Dirty Angels." In *Stories of the Railroad*, 27–44. New York: Doubleday & McClure, 1899.

Jack Alexander meets the veteran engineer Elijah ('Lige) Clark early in his railroad career. 'Lige is an upright, honest man whom the other men trust to represent their interests to management. 'Lige leads the men on a strike in 1877 (a year marked by great upheaval in the American labor movement), then heads west to find work, where he prospers in a boomtown. 'Lige is deeply involved in charity work, but believes that prostitutes—who were plentiful in such towns—deserve no sympathy or help. An accident on the railroad leads him to reexamine his beliefs on this point.

363. _____. "An Engineer's Christmas Story." In *Stories of the Railroad*, 7–26. New York: Doubleday & McClure, 1899. Also in *Stories from McClure's: The Railroad* (attributed to James A. Hill). New York: McClure, Phillips, 1901.

Jack Alexander, the narrator, was a young and, for practical purposes, homeless fireman for engineer James Dillon in the early 1860s. Dillon and his wife take Jack on as a boarder, and treat him like a son. A misunderstanding over some money Dillon's wife has been saving to allow her husband to buy a farm leads Dillon to leave his family and enlist in the Union Army. Hill ladles out a heavy cream of sentiment in the story's happy resolution.

364. _____. *Jim Skeevers' Object Lessons on Railroading for Railroaders.* New York: American Machinist Press, 1899. 157p.

This enjoyable book collects Hill's sketches from the periodical *Locomotive Engineering*. There he wrote under the name John Alexander, contributing instructive little pieces in the guise of fiction "to teach some things to locomotive engineers, firemen, master mechanics, etc.," as he writes in the preface, about the craft of railroading. These tutorials feature engineer Jim Skeevers, a dedicated and clever railroader who knows the business thoroughly and imparts the lessons he has learned over the years with humor and wit. Of the 21 selections in the book, many are no more than two or three pages long. Whether helping a group of veteran engineers understand that they have not been keeping up-to-date on procedures, or showing a fireman that doing the job right makes for the lightest work in the long run, James "Skinny" Skeevers presents his "object lessons" with good will. He does not limit his pedagogy to subordinates or peers. In one of the book's relatively long pieces, "Sixty-nine Years of Useless Work on a Clinker Pit," he enlightens General Manager Wider on a range of issues, from proper pay for master mechanics to effective disposal of clinkers (the hard waste left from burning coal). When Skeevers demonstrates that the road has "paid a man's wages for sixty-nine years" because it has been too short-sighted to invest $200 in technical improvements, his object lesson is, in the G.M.'s opinion, "a devilish good one" (91).

Jim Skeevers' object lessons combine to make an early version of American management theory—but the total quality he advocates comes in a much more down-to-earth and entertaining package than any business school textbook.

365. _____. "Jim Wainwright's Kid; A Railroad Story." *McClure's Magazine* 11 (Oct. 1898): 529–538. Also in Hill's *Stories of the Railroad*. New York: Doubleday & McClure, 1899.

John Alexander runs into an old engineer colleague, Jim Wainwright. Their reminiscences soon turn to "the kid," Reynolds, who used to fire for, and worship, Wainwright. Wainwright tells the story of his long partnership with the Kid, and reveals a surprising aspect of the Kid's nature. The Kid, it turns out, was a woman masquerading as a man; she and Wainwright eventually married, and she died in a train wreck.

366. _____. "A Midsummer Night's Trip." *McClure's Magazine* 11 (Aug. 1898): 365–371. Also in Hill's *Stories of the Railroad*. New York: Doubleday & McClure, 1899.

In August, 1877, the narrator is running a Baldwin locomotive in the Southwest when he sees an approaching storm. Following the storm, the engineer and his fireman see a woman standing between the rails ahead of the train. She warns them about a storm-damaged bridge ahead. The woman, daughter of a rich Spanish Don, had become lost in the storm, and threatened by wolves. For rescuing her, the woman's father rewards the trainmen with a hunting trip on his ranch. Billy the fireman becomes enamored of the young woman, and asks the engineer his "opinion about white men marrying with that mongrel race" (370). The story ends on a humorously ironic note.

367. _____. "Mormon Joe, the Robber." *Everybody's Magazine* 1 (Sept. 1899): 31+. Also in Hill's *Stories of the Railroad*. New York: Doubleday & McClure, 1899.

Joe Hogg—"Mormon Joe"—is a Western engineer with time on the Santa Fe and the Utah Central. Though a moral man, he is arrested as an accomplice in a gold mine robbery. Years later, Joe tells John Alexander the curious true story of the mine robbery.

368. _____. "My Lady of the Eyes." In *Stories of the Railroad*, 97–150. New York: Doubleday & McClure, 1899.

Alexander, down on his luck, takes an engineer's job with a Rocky Mountain road. His assignment is Engine III, which has a troubled history. A yard man lends Alexander a clock for the engine cab; on the face of the clock is a partial portrait of a woman's face, with haunting eyes. The eyes seem to speak to the engineer with their expressiveness, and somehow alert him to a series of dangers. The clock belongs to another engineer, Scarface Hopkins, and the portrait is that of his wife, Madalene, who has not spoken a word in 10 years. The story proceeds to an account of romantic rivalry, disfigurement, and death—with a passing case of scarlet fever added for flavoring. This is a strange story, with its romantic theme, laced with morbidity and violence, and cruel physical torment of the heroine: Hopkins accidentally scalded his beloved's face with live steam that he meant to direct onto his rival. She and Hopkins marry, and she spends the rest of her life with a veil covering the scarred portion of her face.

369. _____. "A Peg-Legged Romance." *McClure's Magazine* 11 (Sept. 1898): 469–475. Also in Hill's *Stories of the Railroad*. New York: Doubleday & McClure, 1899.

Alexander, who functions as a sort of freelance counselor for his fellow railroaders, tends to the perplexities of engineer Miles Diston, who is much taken with sweet Marie Venot. Marie, however, wants to marry a hero, a status Miles does not enjoy. Not at first, anyhow; he joins the ranks of the heroic just in time to win Marie, with Alexander's help.

370. _____. "Some Freaks of Fate." In *Stories of the Railroad*. New York: Doubleday & McClure, 1899. 151–190.

The selfless engineer Oscar Gunderson

tells his life story to John Alexander. It involves a dance hall proprietress with a heart of gold, her illegitimate daughter, Gunderson's noble commitment to care for the child, and a nun who figures prominently and sentimentally.

371. Hitchens, Bert, and Dolores Hitchens. *End of the Line*. Garden City, New York: Doubleday, 1957. 224p.

Railroad detective Farrel, a heavy-drinking veteran on the job, and his young, uncertain partner, Saunders, try to track down the former conductor Parmenter. Parmenter, fresh from a Mexican prison, may be implicated in blackmailing survivors of a train wrecked in a tunnel several years earlier. Parmenter was the conductor on the train. The survivors played loose with the truth to collect generous post-wreck settlements. The railroad background, although not abundant, is convincing, and the characters and plot, with as much scurrilous business in the present as in the past, are satisfyingly complex. In the end, Peg Parmenter, the conductor's daughter, proves a person of greater interest than her father.

372. _____. *F.O.B. Murder*. 1955. Reprint, New York: Permabooks, 1956. 183p.

The colorful cover of this novel's paperback edition depicts a disheveled blonde in a barely-there dress attempting to crawl off a railroad track and out of the path of an oncoming train. We know what jumps off the wire rack at the drugstore! This first cooperative literary effort of the Hitchens team opens with Los Angeles railroad detective Collins discovering a terrified Mexican on a refrigerator car where he has lain injured for several days. McKechnie is another railroad dick who grew up wanting to be an engineer, but is now glad to know that trains are part of his life, even if he doesn't run one. Collins and McKechnie work to solve matters of murder, a missing fortune in diamonds, and other criminal issues. Like other entries in the Hitchens line-up, the writing is crisp, the settings—including railroad scenes—persuasive, and the characterizations satisfying.

373. _____. *The Grudge*. Garden City, NY: Doubleday, 1963. 185p.

Tommy Collins—named after the drink—is on the lam, and enjoys blowing things up with dynamite. Railroads are his favorite targets. His unhappy employment history with the railroad has a bearing on that: He has a grudge. Collins attempts to extort money from the railroad in exchange for not sabotaging it. Special Agent Farrel of the Los Angeles railroad police has his hands full bringing the homicidal wretch to justice in this serviceable mystery set chiefly in L.A. Attention to actual railroading, however, is slim.

374. _____. *The Man Who Followed Women*. Garden City, NY: Doubleday, 1959. 192p.

When a series of perplexing rail freight robberies takes place out in the desert, Agent Farrel joins the young Korean War vet Michael Kernehan in pursuing the solution. Their efforts entail the preoccupation of the decidedly peculiar Leonard Howery, a Los Angeles tile salesman who habitually follows women. One night he begins to follow a woman who haunts railroad yards by night, watching freights pass. Howery stumbles into the custody of Kernehan, setting the plot in motion. At about the same time, dead dogs—poisoned—begin turning up in the yards, and a former switchman is found flattened at the bottom of a hopper car full of gravel. The Hitchenses tie the threads together neatly, relying on colorful characters, effective railroading details, and few wasted words.

375. _____. *One-Way Ticket*. Garden City, NY: Doubleday, 1956. 224p.

Railroad Chief Special Agent Ryerson (Los Angeles division) takes on a forgery case, with the help of his young assistant, Vic Moine. The case soon proves more sinister, and more lethal, than mere forgery. The novel is a very capable procedural mystery, with nicely-developed characters, an interesting plot, and credible settings, including the L.A. railroad yards. The credibility presumably owes in large part to co-author Bert Hitchens's experience as a railroad detective. The chief character of concern is Moine, new to the railroad and unsure of himself and of his career choice.

Hitchens, Dolores *see* **Hitchens, Bert, and Dolores Hitchens**

376. Hoch, Edward D. "The Problem of the Locked Caboose." In *Midnight Specials: An Anthology for Train Buffs and Suspense Aficionados*, edited by Bill Pronzini, 48–69. Indianapolis and New York: Bobbs-Merrill, 1977. *Ellery Queen's Mystery Magazine* 67 (May 1976): 141–159.

This witty "locked room" mystery occurs on a train, with the locked room the caboose. The story features a female villain with a violent streak, and the author's series character, retired New England physician Dr. Sam Hawthorne. Almost all the story's action occurs aboard the train.

377. Hoffman, Malcolm A. "Fraternity." In *Novel and Story*, edited by Ellery Sedgwick and H.A. Domincovich, 44–46. Boston: Little, Brown, 1939. *Story Magazine* 13 (July-Aug. 1938): 24–25.

In this very short story, the train serves as a means of escape from political oppression. The narrator and his friend Groggin, both American journalists, are traveling from Germany to Switzerland. The German oppression of the Jews is well under way. The journalists observe a lone Jew in the coach, in obvious anxiety, apparently trying to flee Germany. When the Jewish traveler loses control of his emotions, the journalists engage in a spontaneous ploy to protect him from the officials aboard. For a work in a similar vein, see Entry 941.

378. Hoffman, Robert F. *Mark Enderby, Engineer.* Chicago: A.C. McClurg, 1910. 373p.

The 23 chapters composing this novel of mountain railroading in the Southwest purport to attain a unity as a story, but the book's origin in separately-published pieces (in such periodicals as *Scribner's Magazine* and *Railroad Man's Magazine*) remains clear. Continuing characters and settings do not obscure the manner in which the episodic chapters succeed each other in link-and-pin-coupled fashion. Locomotive engineer Mark Enderby is the chief recurring character, but even he is of little or no importance in several essentially self-contained chapters. The content is typical of turn-of-the-century pulp railroad fiction. There is the melodrama; in "Against the Mountain," a train hurtles down a mountainside, its fireman dead, the engineer grimly possessed; there are colorful characters (hogger Rock-a-By Johnson, and Braintree, a railroader apparently gifted with ESP); and there is a brave, anthropomorphized locomotive: "Rejoicing in her strength, laughing, whispering, booming forth her deep-voiced defiance to the winds... (223).

Perhaps the best effort in the book is the amusing "A Tangle in Red Tape," a satire on bureaucracy in which a master mechanic's request for a canister of soap emulsion causes official reaction absurdly out of proportion to its importance. Hoffman seems in command of technical railroading matters, but as a whole the work is not up to the standards of such writers as Frank L. Packard or Frank H. Spearman; the writing is too florid and the characters not well developed.

379. Hogan, Kay. "The El Train." *Descant* (Texas) 26, no. 4 (1982): 19–23. Also in *Bless Me, Father: Stories of Catholic Childhood*. Edited by Amber C. Sumrall and Patrice Vecchione. New York: Plume, 1994.

Eight-year-old Kathleen loves to ride the elevated train, even though her mother embarrasses her by lying about Kathleen's age to obtain a reduced fare. "What fun, riding past people's lives, peering in windows and whizzing by," thinks Kathleen (19). On the trip one day, Kathleen's pleasure is tempered by her realization that her mother is taking her to the hospital, yet again, to have her club foot treated. Author Hogan does well at capturing a young child's sensibilities.

380. Holland, Cecilia. *Railroad Schemes.* New York: Doherty Associates, 1997. 271p.

The title suggests a focus that is ultimately

secondary in this nicely-written novel set in 1850s Southern California. In spite of considerable attention to the machinations involving the Southern Pacific Railroad's plans for Los Angeles, the story's most interesting and most engaging feature is the developing—and finally tragic—relationship between 15-year-old Lily Vining and robber King Callahan. Callahan possesses a naturally-acquired hatred of railroads in general, owing to the abuse he absorbed while working on the Pennsylvania Railroad as a new Irish immigrant. He had worked on a track-laying crew, and the bosses "had ordered him around, starved him, beaten him up, cheated him of his pay, worked him almost to death ... everything he had seen since convinced him that this was every railroad's going practice, not just toward skinny ignorant helpless Irish boys but toward all working men. He always looked for ways to take shots at the Railroad" (81). Callahan's chief antagonist is the one-armed railroad agent Brand, whose loyalty to the railroad for giving him a decent job is powerful. Holland's depiction of the region is engaging, and her account of her characters' emotional lives is more affecting that what one finds in most historical novels.

381. Horgan, Paul. *Main Line West*. 1936. Reprinted in *Mountain Standard Time*, 7–199. New York: Farrar, Straus and Cudahy, 1962.

Danny Milford's mother, Irma, deserted by her husband, works in a café in a small California town. Danny likes to hang around the local railroad yards. An old brakeman warns Danny and his friend Tom to shun the yards, since bad men there—hoboes—cannot be trusted. The brakeman's warnings encourage the boys to investigate the hobo jungle, and one day they stumble upon a pair of hoboes. The young one, Oscar, is a sadist who steals their lunches and torments them, and forces Danny to steal money for him—from his mother. Irma is at first convinced that Danny has become a bad boy, but he at last tells her why he took the money.

Later in the novel, Danny and his mother, who now works as an evangelist, live at a cheap railroad hotel in southern Colorado. Danny is filled with excitement as he watches new

soldiers come through town on troop trains, on their way to the front in the world war. "Danny watched them with longing and envy" (128). Irma is not so taken with the appeal of blood and death. In the novel's climactic passage, a patriotic mob assaults her and Danny owing to her preaching against the war. The mob stones the pair; a skulking man in a trainman's uniform hurls a piece of concrete that strikes Irma in the head, badly injuring her. They escape, and flee on the next westbound train, to return to California. Aboard the train, Danny recognizes the conductor as the trainman who injured his mother. Danny realizes that the conductor is a coward who merely impersonated a patriot. The conductor confronts Irma, who is in severe pain and barely conscious, demanding to know what she—a "German spy"—is doing on "his" train (178). He conceives a plan to turn in this dangerous woman to the authorities.

Irma dies on the train, probably from her head wound. The only people on board who treat Danny kindly are the members of a Mexican family. When the Mexican father intercedes in Danny's behalf, the conductor, "thin-souled and thick-skinned," claims that "there is no provision on the train to take care of the dead" (187).

Danny is put off the train in an Arizona town with his dead mother. An undertaker and his wife decide to take Danny in, but, in his rage and grief, Danny wants only to move on; any place at all would be better than this place. The novel ends with Danny, his mother's financial legacy of $16 in cash rolled up in his handkerchief, hopping a freight. "The wheels began to roll and when they pulled him along in the half-empty box car, they tore no roots from under him" (199).

Main Line West is a short, gripping novel; the mob scene, a horrifying melange of deracinated patriotism and warped religiosity, is based on one Horgan witnessed as a boy.

382. _____. "The Surgeon and the Nun." In *The Peach Stone; Stories from Four Decades*, 259–280. New York: Farrar, Straus, & Giroux, 1967. Also in *The Best Short Stories of 1937*. Edited by Edward J. O'Brien. Boston: Houghton

Mifflin, 1937. *Harper's Bazaar* 70 (Dec. 1936): 98–99+.

The narrator, a doctor, describes events of 30 years past, in 1905, when he left Chicago and took the train to New Mexico to start a new life. In the Southwest, the coach is an oven. The doctor sees a nun in conventional habit sitting nearby; he wonders how she can bear the heat in her heavy clothing. At a stop, he examines a fallen Mexican section gang laborer whose foreman accuses him of malingering. The man proves to be malingering with appendicitis. The nun helps the doctor operate on the laborer in a stinking, tin-roofed shed. While they work, the train leaves. They load the post-op section hand onto an outgoing train the next day, and accompany him to New Mexico. Throughout, the section gang foreman exhibits consummate obnoxiousness: He refuses to help; he objects to the operation taking place; and he hides from responsibility by invoking his lack of "authority." The surgeon—a spectacularly profane sort—and the nun, however, make a fine team.

383. Houston, Noel. "The Toonerville Trolley." *New Yorker* 20 (Nov. 25, 1944): 28–29. Also in *North, East, South, West; A Regional Anthology of American Writing.* Edited by Charles Lee. New York: Howell, Soskin, 1945.

Businessman Harry Everett, 51, boards a Diesel-powered passenger train composed of stainless-steel coaches. He hates train travel, but must reach New York from Raleigh, North Carolina. The one car in the train not of the streamlined variety is Harry's coach, an old green sleeper. While waiting for the porter to prepare his upper berth—a lodging Harry much detests—he sees a shabby young Negro man he had earlier bumped into at the station. The obviously impecunious young man is inexplicably waiting for the lower berth to be made up, for him.

In the smoking compartment, Harry again meets the poor young man. "Where you headed, boy?" he asks. The "boy" is on his way to report for Coast Guard service. In response to the young man's naïve remark about his joy at riding a streamliner, courtesy of the Coast Guard, Harry rips the old green coach as "this

damned ancient Toonerville trolley." The young man's former good cheer evaporates, and Harry chastises himself for deflating the fellow's youthful pleasure. Harry is so disgusted with himself that he abandons his ambition to persuade the young man to trade berths with him.

384. Howells, William Dean. *A Hazard of New Fortunes.* 1889. Reprint, with an introduction by Everett Carter and textual apparatus, Bloomington and London: Indiana University Press, 1976. 558p.

One of the author's most notable works, this novel concerns the career of Basil March as a magazine editor in New York City. His publisher is young Conrad Dryfoos. Railroad action in the novel is limited, but a street railway strike in the city plays a vital part in the plot. The strike is massive. When scabs from Philadelphia try to operate the cars, violence breaks out; the railway companies involved refuse to negotiate. Conrad Dryfoos defends the strikers to his father, who considers them all lazy ingrates and liars. The elder Dryfoos is so enraged over his son's defense of the strikers that he hits Conrad in the face, drawing blood. Soon thereafter, Conrad stumbles onto the scene of police clubbing strikers in the street; Conrad dies from a stray gunshot fired during the melee. The elder Dryfoos's grief and shame are profound.

385. _____. "Incident." In *Selected Short Stories of William Dean Howells,* edited by Ruth Bardon, 30–32. Athens: Ohio University Press, 1997. First published in the occasional Boston newspaper, the *Pellet* 2 (April 17, 1872): 4.

In this story that is barely more than a vignette, American realist Howells depicts a nameless young couple on a train ride. They are "alone together in a whole car full of strangers" (30). The chief function of the railroad car is to place the young couple alone in a crowd, surrounded by but isolated from their fellow passengers—at least from appreciating them as human beings. They do amuse themselves by observing others, particularly a house painter who boards the train at a station stop. The painter meets a tragic fate, but the nameless couple is barely affected. Howells includes some sharply-observed details of period railroading, such as cinders from the locomotive ticking like "small, bitter rain" against the coach's windows, and the description of the country station, with "the girl operator ... bending over her telegraph ribbon, the station master coming out of the door with a despatch in his hand; the recumbent dog with his tongue out; the man in his shirt-sleeves getting a drink of water at the bucket in the waiting room" (30).

386. _____. *The Rise of Silas Lapham.* 1885. Reprint, New York: Modern Library, 1951. 324p.

It seems ironic that a novel culminating in an affluent industrialist's financial ruin would refer in its title to his "rise," but this story's concern is moral enlightenment, not the questionable satisfactions of avarice. The railroad is the catalyst for New England paint tycoon Silas Lapham's redemption from a life of too much money, and too much preoccupation with money's trappings. Lapham's one-time business partner, Milton K. Rogers, has secured a loan from Lapham with property containing various mills. A local railroad, the P.Y.&X., serves the mills, but the Great Lacustrine & Polar Railroad has taken a long-term lease on the smaller road, and plans to develop its properties further. The big railroad is sufficiently powerful to dictate terms of sale of the mill property. Lapham runs into serious financial trouble and hopes to cushion the hardship by selling it. Rogers lines up apparently gullible potential buyers; as Lapham learns, the buyers represent a consortium of investors who will suffer the brunt of the loss if the G.L.&P. exercises its power. He refuses to sell to these buyers, unwilling to take advantage of them when he knows that the G.L.&P. will likely fleece them. The railroad's ability to control the proceedings infuriates Lapham. "He set his teeth in helpless rage when he thought of that property out on the G.L.&P., that ought to be worth so much, and was worth so little if the Road chose to say so" (283). Before Lapham can sell the mill property at any price, fair or foul, the G.L.&P. acts, with an offer Lapham

cannot refuse. He is ruined financially, yet feels morally improved, and believes that he would behave in the same honorable way if given another chance.

387. _____. *Their Wedding Journey.* Bloomington and London: Indiana University Press, 1968. 240p. Boston: J.R. Osgood, 1871. *Atlantic Monthly* 28 (July 1871): 29–40; (Aug. 1871): 162–176; (Sept. 1871): 345–357; (Oct. 1871): 442–460; (Nov. 1871): 605–624; (Dec. 1871): 721–741.

Howells based this fictional travelogue, his first novel, on a trip he and his wife took in 1870. It follows Basel and Isabel March through New York State and Quebec and back. Much of the journey depends on trains. Although the tone of the book is generally light (the market for gloomy travel books is understandably slim), Howells is too careful an observer and too good a writer to let the reader escape without some pointed passages. He remarks on gaping drawbridges, weak rails, boulders that threaten to tumble down onto the passing train, and on the passenger's sense of pure helplessness to do anything about such dangers. Yet this feeling is so complete "that it begets a sense of irresponsibility, almost of security; and as you drowse upon the pallet of the sleeping-car, and feel yourself hurled forward through the obscurity, you are almost thankful that you can do nothing, for it is upon this condition only that you can endure it.... You think hazily of the folk in their beds in the town left behind, who stir uneasily at the sound of your train's departing whistle; and so all is a blank vigil or a blank slumber" (13–14).

388. Hrebik, Dale. "Train Tracks." *Xavier Review* 23, no. 1 (2003): 35–40.

Fifteen-year-old Colby likes to sneak out of her bedroom window at night to wander along the railroad tracks by the Mississippi. One night she sees another girl, about her age, lying across the track, her head propped on a rail. The African-American girl tells Colby that she is waiting for the train. Colby pleads and argues with her to get off the track, the girl first tells her to leave her alone, then slugs Colby in the stomach and pushes her down the track embankment before resuming her position on the track. Colby, bruised and rattled, flees.

389. Hubbard, L. Ron. "Mr. Luck." In *Lives You Wished to Lead, but Never Dared: A Series of Stories*, 35–55. Clearwater, FL: Theta Books, 1979.

Engineer James Kelly, so far frustrated in his ambition to build a rail spur in Colombia, becomes partners, of sorts, with a plucky young orphan whom he dubs "Mr. Luck." The boy cleverly helps Kelly raise the money he requires to pay the laborers working for him so that they can complete the spur. Pure pulp from the founder of Scientology.

390. Hubly, Erlene. "The Woman Who Lived in Grand Central Station." *Colorado Quarterly* 18 (Summer 1969): 41–49.

Most of this story concerns the dissolution of Jonathan's and Lila's never-very-satisfactory marriage; eventually, Lila moves out. In time, Jonathan tracks her down in New York City's Grand Central Station, where she watches the trains come and go. She does not recognize him as he disappears from view on a departing train. The story's quasi-surrealism is not appealing, nor is either of the two main characters.

391. Hughes, Dorothy B. *Dread Journey*. New York: Duell, Sloan & Pearce, 1945. 180p.

The Chief is on its way from California to New York, bearing a number of show business types in Porter James Cobbett's car. The show people include Kitten Agnew and her lover, movie producer Viv Spender. Spender is a notorious womanizer, and Kitten is convinced that he has murdered a past lover—and that she is the next in line for the same treatment. Spender has his eye set on the beautiful young librarian, Gratia Shawn, whom he plans to mold into a star. The most interesting character aboard the car, however, is Porter James Cobbett himself. Cobbett conducts himself with dignity and restraint. No patronizer of the rich and powerful in hopes of a big tip, he goes about his business giving due respect to his passengers, but no more than that.

"Cobbett had pride in himself, he didn't consider a man equal to him unless he were equal in dignity and pride" (83). This portrayal of a porter is a novel departure from the racist stereotypes characteristic of most fictional treatments of porters up to this time. Cobbett, a sensitive man, sees the evil that surrounds Spender. Hughes's use of Cobbett is consistent with her frequent focus in her mystery fiction on loners or outsiders; Cobbett is the ultimate outsider, a black servant in a white world.

392. Hughes, Langston. "Fine Accommodations." In *Short Stories*, edited by A.S. Harper, 239–243. New York: Hill & Wang, 1996. Also in Hughes's *Something in Common, and Other Stories*. New York: Hill & Wang, 1963.

Porter Peter Johnson helps passengers board the New York Limited in Atlanta, and feels a surge of pride when "two members of his own race" whom he thinks of as "rich colored folks" board the train and take an expensive drawing room (239). One of the pair is an older, distinguished-looking man, the other his secretary, a young man not long out of college. When Johnson has a chance to talk with the younger man alone, he learns that the older is the head of a black college in the South, and that he is preserving his own narrow interests by selling out those of ordinary black workers. That the young man's father was also a porter whom Johnson once knew encourages him to spill the ugly truth about his boss. "The last Negro passenger I had in that drawing room was a pimp from Birmingham," thinks Johnson. "Now I got a professor. I guess both of them have to have ways of paying for such fine accommodations" (243).

393. Hull, Jessie H. "Pullman Car Wooing." *Overland Monthly* 17, 2d Series (March 1891): 288–291.

Nineteen-year-old Gladys's father takes her to the Oakland train station, from which she leaves for Omaha aboard a Pullman to take part in a wedding. "Gladys felt a little frightened at ... her first long journey alone, and kept her face turned toward the fast-flying but unnoticed landscape..." (288). She is surprised to see her persistent suitor, Jack Hollis, enter the

Pullman from the smoking car. Gladys resists Jack's beseeching proposal of marriage, but the closed world of the cross-country train assures their continued interaction, and Gladys's eventual succumbing to Jack's pleas.

394. Hull, Raymond. "Pickaninnies and Pills." *Railroad Magazine* 41 (Nov. 1946): 80–94.

Representations of African-Americans in railroad pulp fiction are almost non-existent, save for the occasional black character, usually an obsequious porter, in the background. Black characters are prominent in this story, but their portrayal is as stereotyped as usual. Pullman conductor Bert Lardner is working as an agent for the summer on Cape Haddock, where he has his hands full with the young children of Sampson Gypson, a black car cleaner. Gypson's wife has left him for another of her flings, and, while he works, Gypson leaves his two children under Lardner's oversight on a day when a railroad superintendent is visiting for an inspection. This same day, Lardner must deal with a theft from a Pullman passenger—with a witness implicating Porter Jud Potter. Lardner discounts the charge, because "that Negro was one of the best" (83). While Lardner struggles with Gypson's unruly children, Gypson passes out from sleeping pills that he mistook for aspirin. The children create chaos for Lardner; at one point, their behavior puts the visiting superintendent on the verge of incarceration. This slapstick story itself is on the verge of being funny, but its racial stereotyping spoils the humor.

395. _____. "Rules and the Redhead." *Railroad Magazine* 49 (Sept. 1949): 103–125. Reprinted as "The Ball of Fire." *Railroad Magazine* 89 (July 1971): 56–60.

Conductor Bucky Shaw is having trouble with his red-headed wife. Early one morning inspector Bert Lardner boards Shaw's train on Cape Haddock, and finds it a mess. Shaw is sleeping off a drunk, having crawled into an empty berth, overcome not only by drink but also by the wreck of his marriage. His wife, Molly, is a newspaper reporter. Lardner intercedes in the dispute. The battling couple reach accord, if only temporarily, on their own, aboard train. Molly first runs amuck on the trip—"But when a red-headed girl developed a full head of steam, she had little respect for the rules. You had to allow for things like that in railroading" (125). And in pulp fiction, too.

This story is an oddly-conflicted compilation of romantic stereotype, sexual suggestiveness (in a scene worthy of adolescent fantasy, Shaw helps a passenger, dressed only in a flimsy nightie, down from her upper berth), and implied approval of female independence, as long as it is tempered by domesticity.

396. Hungerford, Edward. *Little Corky.* Chicago: A.C. McClurg, 1912. 406p.

In this pedestrian business romance, "Little Corky"—James Corkingham—is a trolley magnate in the Midwestern town of Tremont. The novel contains two passages of railroad interest. In the first, heroine Genevieve endures an excruciating ride to Tremont aboard a hot, stuffy, slow train. The hours drag by, and, with nightfall, Genevieve can no longer enjoy looking outside: "She tried to look from the car window but it was light within and dark without, so that the glass only mirrored the inside of the car" (88). In the second passage, Corkingham invokes his status and his connections with the Tremont and Southwestern Railroad's general manager to force a trainmaster to provide him a special train, without notice, for a run to Chicago, in an effort to overtake a train bearing his romantic interest, Genevieve. Corkingham then appeals to the engineer's vanity, hoping to goad him into making the run in record-setting time, even in a dangerous fog. The engineer's feat becomes legendary on the railroad.

397. Hurston, Zora Neale. *Jonah's Gourd Vine.* 1934. Reprint, New York: Harper-Perennial, 1990. 229p.

Hurston, a major black American writer who lapsed into obscurity before a revival beginning in the mid–1970s, details in this novel the story of John Pearson's life and career. The railroad plays a substantial part in the conclusion of Pearson's existence. A preacher, he delivers a sermon late in the novel laden with some potent imagery regarding the "damnation train." In the book's conclusion, Pearson dies when a train strikes his car following the revelation that he has been involved in a tawdry affair. The connection between the sermon and his death is unavoidable. Hurston foreshadows Pearson's later involvement with the train in an early passage in which, as a 16-year-old, he first sees a locomotive, "a fiery-lunged monster" (16) that frightens but also intrigues him.

398. Husband, Joseph. "Semaphore." In *Twenty-Two Short Stories of America*, edited by Edith Mirrielees, 257–263. 1915. Reprint, Boston and New York: Heath, 1937.

In this impressionistic account of a ride in the cab of a locomotive pulling a train to Cleveland, Husband anthropomorphizes the engine: It has a "hoarse" whistle, "steel lungs panting heavily," and oil "sweats" from its sides. In vivid language, he relates the sense of mechanical racket and thunder of the speeding engine, and wonders at the faith its crew places in the trackside signals (hence the title) that indicate a clear way ahead. The engine crew may seem to function in a world of its own, but "Far off in the great city the chief dispatcher was following our flight...." The crew and passengers owe their safety to the dispatcher and others: "In the green star [of the signal] they trusted" (262, 263).

399. Hyman, Vernon T. *Seven Days to Petrograd; A Novel.* New York: Viking, 1988.

Alienated American intelligence agent Harry Bauer is called by Winston Churchill to find a way to stop V.I. Lenin's secret trip by train from Switzerland to Petrograd (St. Petersburg) in 1917. Bauer is just the man for the job—a former professional baseball player, and the son of a railroader who "hung around the yards a lot" (65) when he was a kid. He knows trains, and he knows how to handle the high, hard one. This is enjoyable foolishness, with numerous real-life historical characters and train action adequate to satisfy the rail fan.

400. Idell, Albert E. *Centennial Summer.* New York: Holt, 1943. 426p.

Set chiefly in 1876, the centennial year of the United States, this family saga features railroader Jesse Rogers, a Philadelphia Quaker, his wife, children, and assorted relatives and acquaintances. In the teetering economy of the time, the Philadelphia & Reading Railroad demotes Rogers to night yard superintendent in a retrenchment program. A visiting priest warns Rogers that severe labor trouble is coming, and "One place it will hit hardest is with the railroads—take my word for it" (101). Rogers opposes the union movement, rails against the Republican Party, President Grant, and railroad tycoons. The priest's ominous predictions seem to lay the ground for Rogers' involvement in the labor violence that marked 1876, but the novel rarely rises above dull family matters, and the priest's prescience is for naught, as far as the plot is concerned. *Stephen Hayne* (below) is a better work from every angle.

401. _____. *Stephen Hayne.* New York: William Sloane, 1951. 422p.

This story of coal mining and railroading in Eastern Pennsylvania features complex characters, a suspenseful story, nicely interweaving plot lines, and strong sense of identity with those who struggle under the weight of corporate greed and state collaboration in that greed.

In the 1870s, Stephen Hayne returns from the West to work the family farm in Pennsylvania Dutch territory. He vows that if he cannot make the farm profitable, he'll enter railroading. His path to the railroad begins with labor in a colliery's rail yard; he wins promotion, and at one point meets the president of the Philadelphia & Reading, Franklin Gowen, "the man who bought up railroads and canals, coal lands and collieries, as though there were no end to his wealth or that of his company" (130).

Hayne leaves the farm to live in a company shack at the colliery, and helps the miners through hard times. The P&R angles to corner the coal shipping market, and, buying on margin, Hayne makes a big profit on the railroad stock and leaves the colliery behind. He takes the train to Philadelphia; he admires the big locomotive, which confirms his "faith in his own good judgment in picking out as his means of attaining wealth, the company that could design and use such a glorious machine" (183). He sinks almost all his resources into the P&R, again on margin, believing that when the present coal strike is settled, the stock will soar. (The railroads, including the P&R, had hoarded coal to help them weather a long strike, and, in fact, helped provoke the strike.)

Hayne's rise as a capitalist contrasts with the struggles of his old friend, collier Terry Shannon, who long held out in the strike, only to succumb to the power of the railroad. Terry is a union man, an official, and suspected by the public and press as being a Molly Maguire. He believes that the P&R is spreading stories to undermine the union.

Hayne helps turn the P&R into the dominant force in the Eastern Pennsylvania coal fields—"a monster designed to suck the blood of trade" from the region (271). Yet his concern for Terry, his family, and the men still working the mines never evaporates, and when railroad police arrest Terry on trumped-up charges, Hayne comes to his aid, and turns on Gowen.

402. Ing, Dean. *The Big Lifters*. New York: Doherty Associates, 1988. 243p.

Industrialist Wes Peel has lost a bid on a contract to develop a magnetic levitation passenger train for the Santa Fe's superspeed railway. Now he and his company are working on a "maglev" track maintenance vehicle. The maglev principle entails rails, but the train does not touch them: "Its magnets repel the rails and other magnets accelerate the train" (44). Sounds logical! So is the Big Lifter: an aircraft, of sorts—a dirigible—that can unload a railroad flatcar literally on the fly. Santa Fe brass are interested, their appetites excited at the prospect of grabbing a logistical edge over truck shipping. Railroad presence is fairly thin in this science fiction treatment of heavy-duty hauling in the future. It's good to know, however, that some visionaries see the railroad as having a place there. The major plot line, other than Peel's development of the Big Lifter, involves a crooked trucking lobby working in cahoots with an Arab terrorist bunch.

403. Jackson, Shirley. "Journey with a Lady." In *Just an Ordinary Day*, 284–

293. New York: Bantam, 1996. *Harper's* 206 (July 1952): 75–81. Also in *Ellery Queen's Lost Ladies* (as "This Is the Life"). New York: Dial Press/Davis, 1983.

Nine-year old Joe is going off on his first solo trip by train to visit his grandparents. His mother, anxious over his safety, hovers at the platform, reminding Joe to do one thing and another. She maintains her nervous chatter even after Joe is aboard the train: She stands outside his window, giving instructions to him that he cannot hear. As the train pulls out of the station, Joe meets a young woman who makes his trip even more memorable than he would have expected. She is a fugitive from the law. Joe cooperates in masquerading as her son as she tries to fool a police officer searching the train for her. The two have a pleasant lunch together in the dining car.

This is lightweight popular fiction, but cleverly written. It is also one story of many that presents the world aboard the train as self-contained, barely tied to the banality of a stationary existence. Joe's adventure is not in his arrival, but in his traveling.

404. _____. "The Witch." In *The Lottery*, 63–67. New York: Farrar, Straus, 1949. Also in *The Short Story: Fiction in Transition*. Edited by J.C. Taylor. New York: Scribner's, 1969.

In this very short story, both funny and horrible, Johnny, a four-year-old boy, his mother, and his baby sister are riding in a nearly-empty coach. Johnny studies the passing scenery, and points out items that catch his attention: a river, a cow—and a witch that Johnny claims to have chased away. A man enters the coach and engages Johnny in an appalling conversation. Johnny concludes that he was probably a witch.

Author Jackson economically evokes the sudden weirdness that can arise aboard a public conveyance, as well as the unfettered perceptions of which a young child is capable.

405. Jackson, Thomas W. *On a Fast Train from New York to 'Frisco*. Chicago: Thomas W. Jackson, 1905. 96p.

Following the approach he uses in *On a*

Slow Train through Arkansaw (below), Jackson packages a hit-or-miss collection of jokes and anecdotes; the take-off point for this outing is New York City, and the basic gag rests not on the train's sluggish progress, but its speed. "I said, 'Porter, does this train stop at Rochester?' He said, 'Boss, it doesn't even hesitate'" (5). Jackson fires off the usual anti–Semitic jibes, mildly risqué bits, Dutch jokes, Mormon jokes, Irish jokes, "Chinaman" jokes, and "darky" jokes until the train reaches San Francisco on the book's last page. As in *On a Slow Train*, numerous cartoons augment the text.

406. _____. *On a Slow Train through Arkansaw: Funny Railroad Stories, Sayings of the Southern Darkies, All the Latest and Best Minstrel Jokes of the Day.* Chicago: Thomas W. Jackson, 1903. 96p.

In rapid-fire delivery, Jackson belts out one joke after another, starting with a focus on the plodding pace of the train he took through Arkansas—or "Arkansaw"—and moving on to varied topics, including many of a railroading nature. The jokes range from funny to flat to racist and anti-Semitic. Numerous illustrations enhance the book's appeal for the popular audience of the period.

407. Jakes, John. "Hell on the High Iron." In *The Railroaders*, edited by Bill Pronzini and Martin H. Greenberg, 172–212. New York: Fawcett, 1986. Published as "The High-Iron Killer," *Big-Book Western Magazine*, March 1953.

Kansas & Western troubleshooter Mark Rome returns to his hometown of Warknife, Kansas, where some landowners are refusing to sell right-of-way to the railroad. A stagecoach outfit sees the railroad as a business threat, and will use any means to prevent its completion. Competent but standard railroad-Western melodrama; the story does convey some sense of the tension between the interests of expanding railroads and those of established businesses and communities.

408. James, Marquis. "The Stolen Railroad Train." In *Great Railroad Stories of the World*, edited by Samuel Moskowitz, 23–47. New York: McBride, 1954. Also in James's *They Had Their Hour*. Indianapolis: Bobbs-Merrill, 1934.

Pulitzer Prize-winner James turns in a lightly fictionalized, straightforward account of the Civil War's most famous railroading exploit, the 1862 effort by a group of Union spies to wreak havoc on a critical Southern rail line. The spies, led by J.J. Andrews, met initial success as they seized a Southern locomotive, the *General*, at Big Shanty, Georgia. Their plan to leave a succession of burned bridges in their wake fell apart as determined Confederate forces chased them with another engine, the *Texas*. This incident evokes the valor and intrepidness that marked the conduct, at its best, of those on both sides in the war. The excitement of the pursuit, coupled with national and regional sympathies aroused by the circumstances, have given the Andrews Raid durable appeal for storytellers. The popular draw of the tale was highlighted by the event's treatment in the 1956 Disney film, *The Great Locomotive Chase.*

409. January, Jason. "Express Stop." *Manhunt* 5 (April 1957): 48–51.

Only a few passengers are on a commuter train car when five adolescent punks in black leather jackets climb aboard. They begin harassing a young woman traveling alone. Red, the punk leader, paws the girl as his friends form a semi-circle around them. The other passengers are passive, until, inspired by a workman who cannot bear to witness the abuse, they converge on the punks and beat them senseless. An old woman kills Red by stabbing him with her umbrella. Gruesomely violent, the story exploits the popular panic over hoodlums in black leather jackets that was commonplace in the 1950s.

410. Jewett, Sarah Orne. "Going to Shrewsbury." In *Novels and Stories*, 700–709. New York: Library of America, 1994. *Atlantic Monthly* 64 (July 1889): 18–24.

The narrator meets the aging village fixture Mrs. Peet aboard a train bound for a connection that will take her to the town of Shrewsbury. Mrs. Peet has been cheated of her house and farm, and is now going to rely on the kindness of relatives. She has never before ridden a train; the brakeman courteously helps her with her baggage. Mrs. Peet discourses on her distress for some time, but becomes absorbed in her surroundings: "She was simply a traveler for the time being..." (705). She pays close attention to her fellow passengers, wondering where they might be going. When she leaves the train to make her connection, the narrator watches her: "The sight of that worn, thin figure adventuring alone across the platform gave my heart a sharp pang as the train carried me away" (707). Here, as in so many stories, the train is a vehicle marking a major transition in a character's life.

411. _____. "A Way Station." In *The Uncollected Short Stories of Sarah Orne Jewett*, edited by Richard Cary, 168–170. Waterville, ME: Colby College Press, 1971. First published in the New York *Globe and Commercial Advertiser* Christmas supplement, Dec. 17, 1890.

Set on Christmas Eve, at a wooden station on a branch line railway. A solitary old woman joins the festive passengers waiting for the next train; when the train leaves, full of holiday revelers, the old woman turns and walks back to her house. The station master informs the narrator that the old woman has regularly met this train since her son was once due on it, but did not arrive, owing to a fatal accident. "The figure that came and went has kinship with all lonely figures whose hearts cannot help seeking the love and care that they never find" (170).

412. Johnson, Denis. "Train Dreams." *Paris Review*, no. 162 (Summer 2002): 250–312. Also in *The O. Henry Prize Stories*, 2003. Edited by Laura Furman. New York: Anchor Books, 2003.

In 1917, Robert Granier helps fellow workers try to throw a Chinese man off a railroad bridge they have been building, in retribution for a supposed crime on the man's part. The fellow escapes, but not before cursing the would-be executioners. In the following years,

Granier works on massive lumbering and construction jobs, often for the railroad. He lives into his 80s, and in his old age finds himself reviewing memories, including the time he almost saw Elvis Presley as Presley's private train went through Montana. "He'd started his life story on a train ride he couldn't remember, and ended up standing around outside a train with Elvis Presley on it" (262). The ride he couldn't remember occurred when he was a small boy, shipped on the Great Northern to live with relatives in Idaho.

The story shifts back and forth between phases of Granier's hard life. Its title derives from a passage in which he often dreams of a train, in a succession of scenes apparently from his childhood. This examination of a solitary man, told in the manner of memory's randomness, develops the reader's feelings for Granier in a subtle progression, so that by the end, after one wonders what kind of man would help hurl another from a railroad bridge, one wonders how Granier could endure the grief of his life and remain sane.

413. Johnson, Gerald W. *Number Thirty-Six*. New York: Minton, Balch, 1933. 315p.

The reader meets the Thirty-six, the crack train of the Southern railway, as it roars into the little town of Rogersville, North Carolina, one day shortly after the turn of the century. Don Watson, a boy who dotes on the train, watches it stop to discharge three passengers from the Jim Crow coach. "Having to stop Thirty-six for niggers!" Don thinks, amused at how this affront must have annoyed Conductor Fogg (7).

In school, Don watches the tops of Pullman cars pass the fence that separates the world he loves—the railroad—from the one he hates: school. His chief ambition is to become a railroad engineer. Don is a voracious reader, but the apparent impracticality of schoolwork grates on him. At 14, he gets "saved" at a revival. He watches his sister Martha take the Thirty-six off to college; the train "bore Martha off into a new world..." (110). Don thinks of the "great cities, the wide seas, the glamour and adventure that lay beyond the curve around which the observation car at the end of Thirty-six daily disappeared" (114).

After college, Don becomes a newspaper managing editor, and he takes the Thirty-six to New York before serving in World War I. On his return, he takes the Thirty-six on his honeymoon. The train slips into the background for most of the book's last half, but returns in symbolic fashion at the end, after Don has struggled gravely with his responsibilities as a journalist in reporting the details of a violent strike at a Rogersville cotton mill.

The novel is a chronologically straightforward treatment of Don's life, with the train appearing at times to signify watershed points in his moral and intellectual development. Aside from its dogged adherence to a linear depiction of events, the book is a worthwhile treatment of a man's growth.

414. Johnston, Calvin. "Messengers." In *Best Short Stories of 1919*, edited by Edward J. O'Brien, 237–268. Boston: Small, Maynard, 1920. *Saturday Evening Post* 191 (May 1919): 42+.

Dan Regan, an unprincipled man, has clawed his way up the administrative ranks of railroading. He is merciless and friendless—and his fortunes are about to intersect with those of the young vagrant, Tim Cannon. Tim observes Regan from a distance, and seeks to model himself on the flinty, take-no-prisoners industrialist. The raw material of a good story lurks here, but the treatment is so awkward in both structure and diction that it is all but unreadable. The story's inclusion in a "best of" anthology defies comprehension.

415. _____. "Sampan O'Connor." *Sunset* (Central West Edition) 26 (March 1911): 297–311.

Told by the freight conductor to the yard crew in an annoying attempt at Irish dialect, this tale concerns the only Chinese railroader who ever worked the old P&T—the Poverty & Trouble Railroad. Known "humorously" as O'Lung, he lived in a shack he built himself in an abandoned brickyard. One night, O'Connor, the disreputable night switchman, stops by to ask O'Lung how he lives on so little while he himself struggles. In anger, he strikes the Chinese man's idol to the floor. O'Lung tells O'Connor that he was a sampan man in China;

O'Connor, unfamiliar with the term, suspects that it has a sinister meaning. Sharing heroic action in a flood draws the two men together as friends. It is almost worth the effort required to locate this story to see a Chinese accent rendered in a forced Irish dialect. One would not have thought it possible.

Jones, Alcibiades *see* **Coulson, G.J.A.**

416. Jones, Joseph S. *Life of Jefferson S. Batkins, Member from Cranberry Centre.* Boston: A.K. Loring, 1871. 496p.

Available at *Wright American Fiction*: http://www.letrs.indiana.edu/web/w/wright2/

Batkins, an "American statesman," is ostensibly the author of this tongue-in-cheek purported autobiography. "No one will deny that I have been a distinguished individual," claims Batkins, quickly establishing his tone in the opening sentence (7). The main railroad business here comes in Chapter 5, "The Indignation Meeting." Here Jones offers a very funny account of a proposal to run a railroad through the village of Cranberry Centre, Massachusetts. The railroad corporation aims to place its right-of-way straight through the town cemetery, "and to remove the dead, free of all expense to the survivors, to the new location upon a hill, where it was not probable that any railroad would interfere with their repose at least for a century to come" (28). Jeff Batkins's father Jethro, outraged at the intended corporate sacrilege, calls a town meeting to address the matter. The villagers are in an uproar, but during the meeting a railroad agent suggests sotto voce to Batkins that Batkins stands to profit nicely should the railroad press on through the graveyard. A thrifty sort, the elder Batkins—with young Jeff witnessing—does not let the presence of his deceased wife in the graveyard interfere with his newfound esteem for commerce.

417. Joolen, Bernadette Maria. "The Night Train." *Crab Creek Review* 16, no. 1 (2002): 30–34.

A poor immigrant family rides the train across the desert toward Los Angeles. The father reads to his children from an old book about the marvels of L.A. As the train progresses, the children watch the passing sights, and ask naïve questions. In Los Angeles, they all stumble out of the world of the train, saying good-bye to the people they have met. "They fan across the railyard like drunken sleepy vagabonds" (34). The father believes that they are "home." One wonders.

418. Kantor, MacKinlay. "The Second Challenge." In *The Fantastic Pulps*, edited by Peter Haining, 196–208. New York: St. Martin's, 1975. Also in Kantor's *Author's Choice: 40 Stories*. New York: Coward-McCann, 1944. *Real Detective Tales and Mystery Stories*, Feb. 1929.

The Little Owl café, where Illinois Central special agent Chuck Noel likes to pass the time with his German shepherd, Kaiser Wilhelm, is hard by the C.&N.W. yards. One night Noel and the dog are checking on the yards when the night operator relays a wire alerting Noel to a fugitive who may be headed toward Chicago. A Pullman train arrives, stops, and leaves—and Noel sees a man jump off the last car and disappear. A chase through the yards ensues.

419. Kase, Elizabeth Parker. "One Time on the Santa Fe Super Chief." In *The Extra Wife, and Other Stories*, 99–106. Santa Barbara, CA: Fithian Press, 1994.

In 1939, the narrator and her infant son travel by train from Chicago to Pasadena. Nothing happens aboard the train that is arguably dramatic, mysterious, humorous, or threatening. A minor celebrity from the 21 Club in New York City gives the narrator some miniature bottles of liquor after overhearing her ask for a drink at dinner as the train passed through the teetotaling state of Kansas. He inquires as to whether she might have a laxative for his constipated dog. This story is proof, if anyone requires it, that a cross-country train trip can be as banal as staying home and rearranging one's closets.

420. Keillor, Garrison. "My North Dakota Railroad Days," *New Yorker* 51 (Dec. 1, 1975): 46–51. Also in Keillor's *Happy to Be Here*. New York: Atheneum, 1982.

The narrator, a retired railroader, opens with a lament about the woebegone condition of the Brotherhood of North Dakota State Railroad Employees—"broke, flat busted, beat down" (46)—and slides into a reminiscence about Teddy Roosevelt's 1912 visit to his hometown of Lakota. Or, rather, TR's passing through. The brief presence of the president, albeit in his sleep, inspires the young boy, and by 1930 he has become a conductor. His train, the Prairie Queen, is beautifully appointed, "the Jewel of the Plains," as the road's general manager, Houtek, dubs it. "Houtek was king, and when you rode his train, you felt like a Prince of the Realm..." (48). The Prairie Queen also "killed more people in her twelve years than floods and blizzards put together," owing to the unguarded crossings on the road. G.M. Houtek proves to be a complete crook, and his financial ventures doom the Prairie Queen to a blazing death. As for the Brotherhood, "We sit in our shack, we old Railroad Boys, and now and then remember him [Houtek] to the extent of wishing him safely in Hell" (51).

This story is vivid and funny, and nicely captures the wounded bitterness of an old railroader who cared too much about his train.

421. Kelland, Clarence B. *Gold*. New York: Harper & Bros., 1931. 360p.

Banker, financier, and hot-head Anneke Van Horn is the central character in this novel of 19th century business. The action occurs from 1845 to 1882, and features some attention to railroad scheming and dealing representative of the era. Many historical characters appear in the story, including Commodore Vanderbilt, portrayed with an appealing crustiness. He and Anneke Van Horn collaborate in taking over the Harlem Railroad, partly to make money, partly so Anneke can crush her enemies. Her head for business is not on a par with her head for human relations; as one character says, "In business she is a genius. In her personal life she is a fool" (193). At times, Anneka's unhinged intensity recalls Gloria Swanson's performance in *Sunset Boulevard*.

422. _____. "The Mountain Comes to Scattergood." *Saturday Evening Post* 190 (Nov. 24, 1917): 26+. Also in Kelland's

Scattergood Baines. New York and London: Harper & Bros., 1921. 54–80.

Kelland was long a prolific contributor to popular American magazines. One of his regular characters, Scattergood Baines, is a clever fellow easily mistaken—at first—for a rube. When he hoofed into the valley town of Coldriver, he was nearly broke, but announced his intentions of going into business. The locals were skeptical, but the crafty Baines soon developed a variety of thriving commercial interests in the valley. In this story, Baines exhibits marvelous chutzpah: When he learns that an established railroad, the G&B, might seek to take some of his land via eminent domain, he follows the same tactic—against the G&B. Baines also manipulates the legislature expertly to push through bills that will improve his position in his scheme to build his own railroad in the valley. The story is an amusing account of how a certain stock character of American fiction, the shrewd schemer in disguise as an innocent, outfoxes railroad executives, legislators, and wraps public opinion around his finger to obtain his objectives.

423. Kemmerer, John. "The Roundhouse." In *Selected Short Stories of Today*, edited by Dorothy Scarborough, 349–357. New York: Farrar & Rinehart, 1935. *Hound & Horn* 4 (April-June 1931): 372–381.

Al is a roundhouse man on the night shift. He lives with his parents. His mother makes him breakfast in the evening, when he stumbles out of bed; he sits around the house until he leaves for work. He makes his way through the yards and waits with his friend, the old turntable operator, for engines to service. As Al labors, he watches a train pass, and sees the passengers in the lighted windows of "the palatial observation car ... business men in cool expensive suits sat smoking cigars, and girls in white and immodest frocks leaned back in armchairs languidly" (355). The effect here is of a man who lives for nothing but his job, even though his job immerses him nightly in sweat, smoke, coal dust, and grease—and leaves him too exhausted for anything but going home to fall into bed. The glimpse of the passengers in the observation car suggests a world that Al

will never know except as it passes him by while he toils, brutelike, in the yards.

424. Kerouac, Jack. *The Dharma Bums*. 1958. Reprint, Cutchogue, NY: Buccaneer Books, 1986. 192p.

Ray Smith, the Kerouacian narrator of this novel of wandering and spiritual discovery, begins his account with a description of grabbing a ride on a freight train out of Los Angeles in September, 1955. He climbs into a gondola where he meets a thin old bum. The two of them struggle to stay warm. At a stop, Ray sprints to a store and buys wine, bread, and other victuals, and shares them with the old man, who then pulls out a slip of paper with a prayer on it. The prayer, attributed to Saint Teresa, promises that she will shower the earth with heavenly roses. The old man had found the prayer years earlier. "And you squat in boxcars and read it?" asks Ray. "Most every day," says the old man.

When the train resumes its trip, Ray and the old man again try "everything in our power and will power not to freeze and chatterteeth too much" (7). They part at a crossing. Ray makes a little camp on a beach, where he cooks hot dogs and beans, "and exulted in one of the most pleasant nights of my life" (8).

425. _____. "The Railroad Earth." In *Lonesome Traveler*, 37–83. New York: McGraw-Hill, 1960. *Evergreen Review* Part 1: "October in the Railroad Earth." 1, no. 2 (1957): 119–136; Part 2: "Conclusion of the Railroad Earth." 4, no. 11 (Jan.-Feb. 1960): 37–59.

Kerouac capitalizes on his experience as a railroad brakeman in this fast-flowing, pretty-much stream-of-consciousness detailing of one "Kerroway's" railroad life in San Francisco in the early 1950s. Kerroway is earning $600 a month from the railroad and living on less than $17 a week. He is too intent on saving money for a sojourn in Mexico even to buy a pair of decent gloves, relying instead on sad lost & found mismatched gloves from different railyard sites. He eats in dumpy diners and lives in a skidrow room. There is a very nice passage here in which Kerroway gets up early before work and prepares his breakfast, frying his eggs in his "little skidrow frying pan" (48), and, all fed, "I'm already picking up my brakeman's lantern from where it's been hanging on the door handle and my tattered timetable's long been in my backpocket folded and ready to go, everything tight, keys, timetable, lantern, knife, handkerchief, wallet, comb, railroad keys, change and myself" (49). In another good passage Kerroway is late for his train and must run for it as it leaves the station on a Sunday morning. He calls it "a social embarrassment to be caught sprinting like a maniac after a train..." (52). He refers, too, to the dangers of the brakeman's job, recalling how Conductor Ray Miles, who showed him the basics on his student trips, said, "When those wheels go over your leg, they don't care about you" (57). No, they don't, as many railroaders have learned to their regret.

A reader in the mood will find this free-wheeling railroad trip just the ticket; one not in the mood may decide to drop off before reaching the station. Suggestion: Hang on and go the route.

426. Kerr, Alvah M. *The Diamond Key, and How the Railroad Heroes Won It.* Boston: Lothrop, Lee, & Shepard, 1907. 376p.

Compiled in part from stories published in *McClure's, Collier's Weekly,* and other popular magazines of the period, this novel dwells on the building of the mountain railroad, the Western Central, running southwest from Denver into Arizona, where it connects to a transcontinental line. Kerr tells the tales of the winners of the Diamond Key, an award given by the W.C. to those who perform heroic service. Among the heroes are "Dreamy" Meadows, a telegraph operator who helps road officials overcome the efforts of strike organizers—"regular reds" led by a canny Italian (28); Jimmy "Freckle" Hogan, an operator from Chicago who saves dozens of men from death when a runaway car of blasting powder explodes in a tunnel; Ruth Patten, a telegraph operator and daughter of a station-master, who captures an extortionist who has been terrorizing the railroad; and Clark Sanborn, the railroad president's son. When he tells his father that he wants to be a railroader, the old man

makes Clark start at the bottom as a section hand. Clark proves his mettle in an heroic race against the schedule and a deadly cyclone after his promotion to fireman.

The underlying theme of this loosely-rigged novel's episodes is very much of the Horatio Alger, Jr., strive and succeed sort: Good character, earnest application, selfless courage, and determination will win the day, every time. The book could have served a dual audience, youth or adult. Its homiletic qualities are inherent in every seam and stitch. An earlier Kerr book—*Young Heroes of Wire and Rail*—advertised in *The Diamond Key* received praise from such sources as the *Episcopal Recorder* and the *Christian Register.* The *Boston Herald* called the earlier book "healthful and inspiring," and the *New York Times* celebrated its ability to teach "bravery, unselfishness, and forethought." Kerr is up to the same thing here.

427. _____. "The Luck of the Northern Mail: The Story of a Runaway Boy and a Runaway Train." *McClure's Magazine* 14 (Jan. 1900): 230–235.

Saul Banks, a youth fleeing a wrongful accusation of theft, stops at an old woman's house near the railroad tracks and pleads for food. Saul was kicked off a train at the nearby village, where tramps were unwelcome. He trudges along the tracks after the old woman feeds him, and slips onto a flat car on a passing train. The train climbs the Rockies during the night, and at dawn begins its descent. On the way down, a freak accident leaves Saul the only person on the train, now a runaway. Saul saves himself by a timely leap, but when he recovers his senses, he sees that, on the track far down the mountain, an oncoming passenger train, the Northern Mail, is squarely in the runaway's path. Showing selfless heroism, Saul saves the threatened train, and far from being thought a thief, "Today he holds an enviable position in the employ of the great railway system in whose interest he displayed such masterly courage..." (235).

428. Kerr, Orpheus C. [Robert H. Newell]. *Smoked Glass.* New York: G.W. Carleton, 1868. 277p.

Available at *Wright American Fiction*: http://www.letrs.indiana.edu/web/w/wright2/

This author's humorous concoctions have lost most of their effervescence with time's passage, but in the ostensible "letters" composing *Smoked Glass*, he gives a sense of the average passenger's feelings about train travel after the Civil War. In one letter, he laments the Grand Southern Trunk Railroad's postwar deterioration, noting that "until the President of the company can make enough money by his present occupation of apple-peddling to purchase a hammer and a few nails, the track will not be entirely safe for a high rate of speed" (110). He and his companion wear padded-rubber suits to protect themselves on the lurching, bumping coach, to save themselves "from the usual fate of American railroad-excursionists" (112). In a later letter, the author suggests that travel on American trains is an effective means to an attenuated life. He amplifies his anxiety with a facetious description of a train wreck, in which the locomotive's exploding boiler deposits passengers in tree-tops, and the conductor "impaled upon a lightning-rod surmounting a lofty flag-staff, and striking feebly out with his hands and feet, after the manner of a fly on a pin" (159). The author's pseudonym—Orpheus C. Kerr—can be read as "Office Seeker."

429. Kester, Vaughan. *The Manager of the B&A*. New York: Grosset & Dunlap, 1901. 275p.

This novel opens with Dan Oakley, young manager of the Buckhorn and Antioch Railroad, learning that his long-estranged father has been pardoned from prison in Massacusetts. His personal circumstances are not the greatest of his concerns; the unprofitable B&A faces possible sale, which would likely wipe out the town of Antioch. Oakley persuades the brass to let him do his best to turn a profit and save the town. With a free hand, he embarks on a program of wage cuts and layoffs. He regrets the pain his moves cause, but knows that the alternative is Antioch's economic collapse.

Oakley's father, Roger, finds Dan, and takes great pride in his son's achievements. Oakley hires the old man to work in the carshops. Dan runs afoul of Ryder, the local newspaper editor, for failing to support Ryder's political interests; in turn, the editor lambastes Dan in print over the railroad cost-cutting measures. The elder Oakley's criminal past also becomes a catalyst for further trouble, thanks to Ryder's tale bearing.

B&A workers go on strike. Kester portrays them as tools of cynical men, oblivious to their own self-interest as they allow themselves to be manipulated by the press and politicians, who use the strike to posture sympathetically on behalf of the workers. The railroad's vice president argues for replacing the striking workers with foreigners—"Americans are too independent," he claims (170)—but Oakley opposes that scheme.

Difficulties are exacerbated when the elder Oakley accidentally kills Ryder. Ryder's death inspires Kester to an acidic irony worthy of Twain or Lardner. Even those who did not know Ryder feel that they have lost a champion in the sleazy editor; "Indeed, the mere fact that he had been murdered would have been sufficient to make him popular at any time. He had supplied Antioch with a glorious sensation" (184).

In the novel's conclusion, itself calculated for maximum sensation, Dan and Roger Oakley risk their lives to bring a relief train to Antioch, which is threatened by a forest fire. Their heroics, and a predictable resolution to the story's romantic subplot, make a somewhat disappointing finish for a story whose complications were developing well.

430. King, Frank. *Take the "D" Train*. New York: Dutton/Plume, 1990. 167p.

When the novel opens, narrator Sally Tepper is carrying a large pot of oatmeal to the homeless who live on the abandoned Penn Central tracks in New York City. When she returns to her apartment, she finds that she has been evicted. In spite of her personal troubles, she becomes caught up in a spate of murders of derelicts in the subway. The victims include two of her friends. Pursuing the case, she realizes that most of the killings have taken place along the route of the "D" train, and her investigation takes her on foot, down into the subway tunnels, where part of the mystery resides in food and medicine stored in vaults in the 1950s for use by survivors of nuclear attack.

Action in the subway is a relatively minor part of the novel.

431. King, Woodie, Jr. "The Train, the Funeral, and the Boy." *Negro History Bulletin* 26 (Oct. 1962): 58–59+.

One rainy April day, the narrator enters a decrepit one-room railroad station in Benville, Alabama. He has come to attend his grandmother's funeral. The agent looks like a prisoner behind the bars of his window. The agent calls the narrator a nigger, and tells him to get out. The narrator complies, and stands outside on the platform. A small boy waving at a departing train triggers memories of the narrator's childhood in Benville. After the funeral, the narrator ponders the charred remnants of the cabin where his grandmother died in a fire; finally, he boards the northbound train, and looks for a long time at the sign on the little station: "I knew I would never see it again" (66).

432. Kline, Burton. "In the Open Code." In *Best Short Stories of 1918*, edited by Edward J. O'Brien, 149–153. Boston: Small, Maynard, 1918. *The Stratford Journal*, Feb. 1918, 1+.

Workmen restoring an old Virginia manor house realize that the engine of the freight train that regularly passes in a nearby valley plays the notes of the last two bars of "Annie Laurie" with its whistle. They learn in the local village that the engineer whistles the snatch of song as a signal to his sweetheart. The workmen come to count on the whistle, but in the end it plays a much different role than it did initially. This story is both maudlin and morbid: The engineer marries his sweetheart; she dies, and he signals her every day when he passes her grave.

433. Kyne, Peter B. *The Valley of the Giants*. Garden City, New York: Doubleday, Page, 1918. 388p.

Col. Seth Pennington, a lumberman from Detroit, wants to establish a railroad right-of-way through California land belonging to John Cardigan—land where Cardigan's prized giant sequoias stand. Cardigan's son Bryce performs some heroics in saving Pennington's daughter from death aboard a runaway lumber train. "Oh, Shirley, my love! God help you!" cries Bryce. God's help is not required with a stalwart chap like Bryce at hand. This plodding romance is redeemed only by its foreshadowing future conflict between industrial developers and environmental protectionists.

434. Laing, Dilys. "Train in the Wood." *The Yale Review* 37, no. 3 (1948): 428–433.

Bill and Jean, an approximately middle-aged married couple, quarrel over Bill's interest in listening to the departing train at a little station in a wood. Jean is furious with her husband, considering his fixation on the train infantile. For him, the train evokes something deep and elusive: "The noise of the train going off in the hills reminds me of something—takes me somewhere—I want to find out where—what it is—that's all" (430). One night, in something like a waking dream, the associations with the train in Bill's unconscious mind become clear to him, if only briefly. Jean fails to encourage him to make whole in consciousness his insight about the train in the wood, and when he returns to bed, "a door had swung shut against him and would not open again" (433). The train in the wood, in fact, recalls a train that frightened Bill when he was on an outing as a small boy with his parents, and there is likely a good deal more to Bill's epiphany than he is able to discern.

435. Lamson, David. "Never Marry a Railroad Man." *Saturday Evening Post* 216 (Jan. 22, 1944): 14+.

Told from the point of view of a boy, this routine sentimental story concerns a young woman's uncertainty about whom she should marry: a straight-arrow locomotive engineer, or a dudish cowboy. The one striking passage in the story describes the boy's paean to the engine that hauls the train carrying the story's principals: "A locomotive satisfies the soul.... The real locomotive has weight and mass to match its power; it lives and breathes and speaks, and all its parts move visibly.... There is no magic like a locomotive. To stand within hand's reach of one is glory for a boy" (71–72). Although attributed to the young narrator, this is the diction of an adult, and it reveals sentiments that the author shares with a great many rail fans.

436. _____. "A Wife for Mr. Meecham." *Saturday Evening Post* 212 (Sept. 30, 1939): 12–13+. Also in Lamson's *Once in My Saddle*. New York: Scribner's, 1940.

A woman and her son are crossing the wintry Canadian prairie by train. She loses her cash, and cannot pay for sleeping accommodations. A trainman allows her and the boy to spend the night in the "colonist car," a Spartan coach with unupholstered seats and uncurtained berths. "During the summer months whole trains of these cars rolled across the prairies, bringing homesteaders to the new land..." (13). Lamson describes the immigrant occupants of the colonist car, most of them women and children, Finnish and Russian, "their future ... as blank to them as the mysterious white void outside the car windows" (43). During a long, snowbound delay, Mother helps the immigrants round up a communal breakfast. As the snow piles up, the colonist car becomes a haven for passengers from the other cars, and for the train crew, too. The story features a thrilling rescue and some adroit matchmaking (hence the title), but its most interesting aspect is its portrayal of life aboard the colonist car.

437. Lanham, Edwin M. *The Wind Blew West*. New York: Longmans, Green, 1935. 481p.

With the promise of a railroad in the offing, the town officials of Rutherford, Texas, lure settlers from other states. Everything hinges on the town's future as a "railroad center of Texas and the industrial center of the whole Southwest" (326). The work of grading the Texas and Pacific line from Fort Worth to Rutherford begins in 1879: "At last Rutherford's hopes are to be fulfilled...." (335).

The train trip from Fort Worth to Rutherford takes 90 minutes, in contrast to five hours by stagecoach. Soon after the line reaches the town, however, new directors of the railroad, with Jay Gould prompting them, decide to build immediately toward the coast, depriving Rutherford of its cherished status as a terminus and, thus, trade center. Town officials stupidly antagonize the railroad by enforcing a Sunday no-work regulation, fining the railroad for going about repairs on the Sabbath, and provoking it to pull most of its operations out of Rutherford. The town's dreams of commercial success are dashed. In a coda, the author writes that the "locomotive blew its whistle from steam-filled lungs, heralding the new decade [the 1880s] of booming cattle prices, of new cities with gas and water works, chambers of commerce and boards of trade and red-light districts; cities without history, sprung not from the land but from the railroad" (479).

Unfortunate Rutherford is modeled loosely on Weatherford, Texas, once a larger city than Fort Worth.

438. Lansdale, Joe R. "Trains Not Taken." In *Westeryear; Stories About the West, Past and Present*, edited by Edward Gorman, 240–259. Boston: G.K. Hall, 1990. Also in Lansdale's *High Cotton: Selected Stories*. Urbana, IL: Golden Gryphon, 2000. *RE:AL*, Spring, 1987.

In an alternative past, clerk James Butler Hickok and his wife travel by train across the West. He looks out the Pullman window at the famous Japanese cherry trees that cover the plains. He observes a beautiful young woman walking down the aisle, and imagines himself enjoying her favors free of his alcoholic, bitter spouse. In this past, set at the time of George Custer's massacre, Sam Clemens writes dime novels and Walt Whitman cheap popular verse, and trains run on electricity across the Plains. Hickok compares himself and his wife to "Trains on a different track going opposite directions, passing fast in the night, going nowhere really" (255–256). At a scheduled middle-of-nowhere stop, the young woman Hickok has admired gets off the train. Dismissing both convention and his drunken wife, so does Hickok.

439. Lardner, Ring W. "Travelogue." In *Round Up*, 305–316. New York: Scribner's, 1929. Also in *The Best Short Stories* *of 1926*. Edited by Edward J. O'Brien. New York: Dodd, Mead, 1924. *Cosmopolitan* 80 (May 1926): 36–39+.

Three travelers—Dan Chapman and the friends Mildred Orr and Hazel Dignan—meet on the westbound limited out of Chicago. They exchange surpassingly inane chit-chat, dominated by Hazel. "My friends always say they envy me my teeth," says Hazel, in a highlight (309). Hazel babbles ceaselessly, and every statement she utters is a stupefying banality. She talks so determinedly that poor Dan can barely tell the story of his own tooth extraction, much less make a move on Mildred, who interests him far more than Hazel. This is vintage Lardner; most long-distance travelers will not have escaped a companion like Hazel at some point in their journeys.

440. _____. "What of It?" In *The Ring Lardner Reader*, edited by Maxwell Geismar, 655–661. New York: Scribner's, 1963. Also in Lardner's *What of It?* New York: Scribner's, 1925. *Liberty* 1 (June 7, 1924): 6–7+.

Sooner or later, anyone who rides public conveyances ends up in the company of a stranger who proves to be a jabbering bore. Here Dexter Cosset, a neophyte playwright, is on his way home to South Bend by train, trying hard to think of a title for his new play. His train of thought derails thanks to the nonstop chatter of a fellow passenger, a fellow in "the elevator game." The chatterbox, Ben Lacey, runs on without pause, inflicting pricelessly pointless information on Cossett, including such tidbits as his detail about his brother-in-law: "They was a couple of his front teeth was discolored. But after you got used to him, you didn't notice it so much" (658).

Mr. Quolt, a witness to Cossett's distress, demonstrates an effective way to hush the chatter in the coach washroom. This is not a substantial story, but it is very funny—and the reader may be tempted to try Mr. Quolt's "treatment" when next overwhelmed by a bore.

441. Lathrop, Gilbert A. "Division Mother." *Railroad Magazine* 28 (Aug. 1940): 92–115.

Ma Flanagan runs the railroad boarding house at the Echo City division point on the Western & Homestead Railway. Her care, feeding, and counsel of the railroaders has made her something of the saint of the division. The orphan Myrtle Thompson helps Ma around the boarding house. One day Ma agrees to advance hobo Alec Moore room and board until he starts work on a promised job as a fireman. Alec's first run is with the ill-tempered engineer, Blackie Denton. Denton makes Alec's introduction to firing a painful one. Back at the boarding house, Ma Flanagan and Myrtle doctor Alec's left wrist, burned from the heat of the firebox because he had no gloves. Denton continues to tyrannize Alec, and Ma looks after the young man. Myrtle mothers him at every chance. In the climax, Ma Flanagan, "mother to the railroad men" (115), takes the railroaders in hand and gets to the bottom of the trouble between Alec and Denton.

442. _____. "Green Timber." *Railroad Stories* 21 (June 1937): 98–112.

In 1916, the town of Gilson on the Narrow Gage & Western line is enjoying a war boom, and business on the railroad is about to double with a new coal-hauling job, with a consequent need for additional labor. Railroad officials argue about the relative costs of hiring experienced boomers, or training "green timber": new men without a railroad background. The story focuses on young Clem Warren, a new man on the job for whom things go badly. He falls off a train and hurts his leg, passes out on the job, and generally shows no indications of being a railroader in the bud. Clem shows his stuff, though, when a lazy boomer's work endangers men and trains in a snow removal operation.

443. _____. "Iron Mike." *Railroad Stories* 18 (Oct. 1935): 55–62.

Narrow Gage & Western engineer Iron Mike loves his old engine, the 216, even though it is long past its prime and barely fit for service on the steep mountain grades. Mike is the butt of kidding for his sentiments about the 216, but wins everyone's admiration when he and the engine save three of his youngest tormentors from a burning snowshed. (A snowshed is a structure that protects a track from being buried in snow.) At the story's close, Mike's devotion to the 216, now an incinerated wreck, is so complete that he quits his job rather than take over a new engine.

444. _____. "A Man's Job." *Railroad Magazine* 38 (July 1945): 127–137. *Railroad Magazine* 88 (Nov. 1970): 45–52.

Young Henrietta Newcomb is the new operator at the Waterfill station on the Alberta & Pacific. Lanky Hanks is skeptical of her ability to handle the work at this difficult section of track. Back at Ma Flanagan's boarding house (Entry 441), Ma defends the new op, and complains that women haven't been fairly tested in railroad service. When an avalanche knocks engineer Blackie Denton's locomotive from the tracks, Henrietta is the first to arrive on the scene, in spite of the personal danger she faces. Blackie congratulates her on being able to do "a man's job" (137).

445. _____. "Master Mechanic's Blood." *Railroad Stories* 18 (Nov. 1935): 120–128.

On the Narrow Gage & Western, business is just beginning to rebound after the panic of 1907, but railroad brass are tight-fisted with supplies as they try to control costs. The valves of the road's engines require large doses of oil made of animal fats. The oil costs $1.30 a gallon, a price that has earned it the nickname "master mechanic's blood." Officials suspect engineer Harry Dobbet of stealing valve oil from company stock to use on his locomotive. Indeed, Harry has caches of valve oil stashed all along the line. Caught in the act of helping himself to the oil, Harry is fired on the spot—but when the brass call him back to make an emergency trip to deliver cash to a bank besieged by a run, Harry's ideas about valve oil hold water. An apropos Depression-era tale.

446. _____. "Night Yardmaster." *Railroad Magazine* 32 (Nov. 1942): 108–129. *Railroad Magazine* 104 (July 1978): 40–51.

In 1915, Lanky Hanks is the night yardmaster at Craghead in the Canadian Rockies, on the Alberta & Pacific Railway. The new yards are large and complex, and Hanks is short of able workers. Under pressure, he hires two men he does not fully trust: Bill Breen and Hard-Hat Flavin. Breen, in particular, bears an old grudge against Hanks.

Lathrop, who worked as a switchman with the Western Pacific, writes convincingly of Hanks's evaluation of his men: "Funny how a fellow could spot the real carhands, those who were desirous of getting somewhere on the job. Mixed among them were the usual tramps and loafers, dissipation written on their coarse features. A couple of them were phonies.... They were clumsy and awkward on their feet..." (118).

This story is unusual in rail pulp fiction in its focus on human relationships rather than hardware and the dangers of the road, with the chief concern Lanky's memories and his gradually shifting perceptions of the men he fears he cannot trust. A nice story, within the limitations of the genre.

447. _____. "Overtime." *Railroad Magazine* 87 (May 1970): 42–48.

Lang Bolton, a cattle baron and bank president, has always worked his hired hands to the maximum, and has never paid them overtime. He likes to rant about organized labor's "stranglehold" on American industry. Railroaders he finds especially culpable. His estimation of this working class does a 180-degree turn when he rides along in the caboose as a Southwestern Railway train ships a load of his steers through the Rockies. He sees for the first time the men's diligence, teamwork, and skill. In the end, he puts all his available funds into railroad stock. The story's undertone is that of a writer aggrieved over hearing too many complaints about "overpaid" and "underworked" railroaders.

448. _____. "Railroad Crazy." *Railroad Magazine* 86 (April 1970): 44–46+.

Young Bill Gillis, a roundhouse hand on the Narrow Gage & Western, wants to be a locomotive engineer. One day, driven by his desires, he attempts to move an engine he has been cleaning up just a few feet. He sends it nose-first into the turntable pit, and is fired on the spot. His hero, engineer Tom Layden, holds Bill in contempt for the accident, but

Bill—railroad crazy—finds a way to win Layden's respect, and a job as a real railroader.

449. _____. "Railroad Man." *Railroad Magazine* 36 (Oct. 1944): 34–42. *Railroad Magazine* 96 (July 1974): 20–23.

Tom Lawson is a new brakeman on the Pacific & Alberta. His career begins with a string of mistakes, and Conductor Lanky Hanks doubts that Tom will ever make a competent railroader. After Tom makes an especially costly error, Hanks risks his own job by urging the brass to give Tom one more chance. Tom seizes it when he saves a runaway cut of cars on a mountain grade. Author Lathrop's railroad knowledge informs the story's technical details.

450. _____. "Throttle Artist." *Railroad Magazine* 34 (Sept. 1943): 44–63.

In 1917, Blackie Denton is working on the Alberta & Pacific, hauling war munitions and materials. He has been plagued by a secret fear of losing control of a train on a downgrade, since being involved in a runaway in the early 1900s. His fear grows when he loses an A&P train with brake failure in a wreck that hospitalizes him. "He'd had the fear before, but never like now. The very thought of climbing into an engine cab caused him to break out in a cold sweat" (48). Owing to wartime pressures, Blackie agrees to return to engine service, well before he is emotionally prepared. He overcomes his fear, as the reader knows he will, and pilots a troop train to its destination on time, thanks to heroic action on his part. Back at the boarding house, Mrs. Flanagan tells him how proud of him she is. Blackie, not one to suffer praise easily, glowers. "Lot of damn foolishness!" he says (63).

451. _____. "Tony's Tin God." *Railroad Magazine* 87 (Aug. 1970): 41–44+.

The Albanian section-gang boss, Tony Spinozzi, has been with the railroad 15 years. He idolizes engineer Skyrocket Bill, but Bill reveals himself as a graceless sort, unfairly blaming Tony for a minor derailment. Tony is crushed. When the roadmaster fires Tony based on Bill's report of the accident, Tony realizes that Bill was nothing but a "tin god" (43). In spite of his dismissal, Tony performs

selflessly, saving Bill and his engine from a burned-out bridge—and Bill shows that he is not composed entirely of tin.

452. _____. *Whispering Rails.* Chicago: Goldsmith, 1936. 212p. Also in *Rail Fiction Classics.* Denver: Intermountain Chapter, National Railway Historical Society, 1974.

Jerry Twyman works as a fireman on the B & L Railroad, the same Western road on which his engineer father died on a runaway train. An older fireman, Tom Bender, looks after him. "Bender was a typical railroader. Carefree, happy-go-lucky, big hearted, staunch in his friendships" (29). General Manager John Mason has hired Jerry in hopes that Jerry will be able to learn behind-the-scenes details of cargo theft—"boxcar pilfering"—running epidemic on the road. The story features accidents, floods, homicide, plenty of technical railroading detail, and courageous railroaders rooting out the bad guys in their midst. Women are basically absent from the pages, other than rooming house operator Ma Kennedy, "one of them motherin' souls who think every roomer is under her personal care" (28). Chapter titles such as "Wrecked!"; "The Gang Show Their Teeth"; and "Creeping Death" suggest the melodramatic tone of the tale.

453. Lawrence, Albert E. "Somewhere Within that Sea of Fire; A Railroad Story." *National Magazine: An Illustrated Monthly* 9 (Jan. 1899): 379–386.

Locomotive engineer Wirt Bathrick of the Detroit & Lake Huron is having a spat provoked by acute jealousy with lovely Marie La Tour. Marie pulls off the ring he gave her; "I'll send the rest of your presents to your boardin' house in Saginaw," she says (380). Their squabble comes at a time when the Michigan pine woods are tinder waiting for a spark. Bathrick worries about Marie and her father in their house near the woods. When the woods in the La Tour neighborhood go ablaze, Bathrick madly, bravely, charges through the inferno in his uncoupled engine to save his beloved. Bathrick does not succeed easily, but no reader could question the certainty of his prevailing.

454. Lee, Jennette. *Simeon Tetlow's Shadow*. London: Hodder & Stoughton, 1909. 316p.

Simeon Tetlow is a railroad president with a crisis: his right-hand man, young John Bennett, resigns to care for his sick mother. Grudgingly, Tetlow arranges a position for John in the Bridgewater freight office, but eventually lures him back to his own office. Although the farmers in the region have ill regard for Tetlow and the railroad, "he had watched the great system stretching out—not to drain the wealth of the country, not the huge monster that battened on its strength, but a vital necessity—a thing of veins and arteries ... without which life itself must cease altogether or run feeble and clogged" (73–74).

The novel is a sentimental story characterized by a reverence for motherhood, honest entrepreneurialism, fealty to parent and superior, and other conventional virtues.

Lee, Manfred B. *see* **Queen, Ellery**

455. LeForge, P.V. "Railroad Days." In *The Principle of Interchange, and Other Stories*, 21–37. Tallahassee: Paperback Rack, 1990. First published in *Sun Dog: The Southeast Review*.

The railroad serves in this story, as it often does, as a symbol of change, departure, and loss. On the verge of moving from the Tallahassee house he has lived in since a child, the narrator reminisces in a melancholy mood about his old best friend, Jerry. Jerry as a youth became addicted to riding the rails; he would hop the freights in the yard near the narrator's house. A more cautious sort, the narrator could not bring himself to accompany his friend, and the two found their lives diverging. The narrator tells the story 10 years after last seeing Jerry, stepping onto a train to go—somewhere. At the time, the two promised to reunite, but they did not: "I've been waiting for Jerry for ten years," the narrator says, "but Jerry didn't come and I'm trapped alone with myself" (37)—and with the memories of his railroad days.

456. LeGuin, Ursula K. "Two Delays on the Northern Line." *New Yorker* 55 (Nov. 12, 1979): 50–57. Also in LeGuin's *The Compass Rose; Short Stories*. New York: Harper & Row, 1982.

Eduard Orte studies his reflection in the coach window as the train moves on through a black, rainy night. He is on his way to see his sick mother, having received a "come at once" message from his brother, Nikolas. When Orte gets off the train, and finds "in the wet commotion of the platform and the glare and echoes of North Station nobody to meet him, he felt let down, betrayed" (50). By the time Orte reaches his brother's house, his mother is dead, and her body removed. She died while he was on the train, beyond contact, held up by flooded tracks.

In the second part of the story, Eduard Russe has inherited a house from a great-uncle. On the way to deal with the house, he takes a train that derails when it hits a hay truck, but "nobody was hurt, except for the truck driver, who had been killed" (56).

The train journeys by the two main characters represent great transitions in their lives, and their coming to an understanding of themselves.

457. Lewis, Sinclair. "The Cat of the Stars." In *Selected Short Stories*, 141–158. New York: Literary Guild, 1935. *Saturday Evening Post* 191 (April 19, 1919): 5+.

Nearly every reader knows of the old rhyme "For Want of a Nail," concerning the terrible consequences flowing from a lost horse-shoe nail during a battle. Here Sinclair takes an event even more innocuous—a small child's petting the family kitten—and extrapolates the effects into widespread catastrophe leading to the deaths of thousands. In this deliberately absurd tale, young Palmer McGee, assistant to the president of the M&D Railroad, is central to the plot. He suffers the consequences of the kitten's stroking, fumbles his interview for a higher position, and settles for a dead-end job in another railroad's purchasing department. The sorry McGee appears to be heading down the road of alcoholism before the story ends.

458. _____. *Elmer Gantry*. 1927. Reprinted in *Arrowsmith, Elmer Gantry,*

Dodsworth, 473–914. New York: Library of America, 2002.

Elmer Gantry is a vinegary attack on religious hypocrisy, a quality fully embodied in the evangelist title character (inevitably imagined as looking like Burt Lancaster by any reader who has seen the 1960 film version). Gantry is a perpetually on-the-make con artist who believes, fundamentally, in nothing. He lies, cheats, steals, and breaks most of the Ten Commandments without a qualm. The novel contains two points of transition in Elmer's life, facilitated by the railroad. In the first, Elmer is on the train to the city of Monarch for his first promising ministerial assignment, on Easter Sunday. While Elmer makes sermon notes on the back of an envelope ("slam atheists etc."), he meets a salesman on the coach. After denying his religious profession, Elmer shares a bottle of liquor that the salesman produces—"and they drank together, reverently" (624). Upon reaching Monarch, Elmer goes out for drinks and fun with the salesman and some of his pals. The chance meeting on the train throws Elmer off the preaching track, and he spends the next two years as a farm implement salesman.

Much later, after his affair with the ill-fated revivalist Sharon Falconer, Elmer accepts a position at the humble Methodist Church in Banjo Crossing, to which he travels by a train consisting of "two seedy day-coaches and a baggage car" (740). After inflicting his pious interventions on unwilling fellow passengers, Elmer, having "satisfied the day's lust for humanitarianism" (740), puts his feet up on the seat across from him and relaxes in delight with his holiness. Elmer anticipates an enthusiastic reception at the Banjo Crossing station; what he gets is an empty platform, and a station agent amused by Elmer's airs. From this point, the route is onward and upward for Elmer's lust and avarice.

459. _____. *Main Street: The Story of Carol Kennicott*. 1920. Reprinted in *Main Street & Babbitt*, 1–486. New York: Library of America, 1992.

Probably Lewis's best novel—better than *Babbitt* or *Elmer Gantry*, for example, because of the main character's complexity, and because

Lewis does not exhibit contempt for her—*Main Street* describes librarian Carol Kennicott's struggle to find a satisfying life in the provincial town of Gopher Prairie, Minnesota. The novel opens with a memorable description of Carol's first trip to Gopher Prairie with her new husband, Dr. Will Kennicott. Gopher Prairie is Sinclair's representative of every small town in the United States, where, according to a brief preface, "Our railway station is the final aspiration of architecture," and what the locals do not know is either not worth knowing, or worse.

Carol, fresh from library school in culturally-rich Chicago, grows increasingly apprehensive as the train nears Gopher Prairie. The coach is full of the "sharp scent of oranges cutting the soggy smell of unbathed people and ancient baggage." The passengers are cramped, thirsty, and dirty; they struggle to sleep in contorted positions (no well-appointed Pullman on this run!). The passengers "do not read; apparently they do not think. They wait" (24). Their stolidity disturbs Carol; the ugliness of the passing towns does likewise. At one dreary stop, the station is a one-room box, flanked by a cattle pen and a grain elevator. The air on the train is nauseating. "With the loneliness which comes most depressingly in the midst of many people she [Carol] tried to forget problems, and look at the prairie objectively" from the coach window (29). When Carol finally sees Gopher Prairie, her heart sinks. It looks like all the other faceless towns the train has passed, if slightly larger. She finds the platform at the train station crowded with "unadventurous people with dead eyes" (31). Carol joins her husband in greeting the people who welcome them at the station, "but she clung a second to the sleeve of the brakeman who helped her down before she had the courage to dive into the cataract of hand-shaking people, people whom she could not tell apart" (32).

In spite of her efforts to bring "culture" to the town in the form of a literary group, and drama performances, Carol finds life in Gopher Prairie stultifying. One of the few things that buoys her is the passing trains, on which she depends "for assurance that there remained a world beyond" (255). For Gopher Prairie, "the tracks were eternal verities, and boards of railroad directors an omnipotence" (255). Aside from the mysteries of mass at the Catholic Church, the railroad provides the only departure from dull routine. Two conductors live in town, and are figures of romance. The telegraph operator is a man of melodrama, often imagined the imminent victim of robbery. The engineers, "inscrutable, self-contained, pilots of the prairie sea—they were heroism, they were to Carol the daring of the quest in a world of groceries and sermons" (257). At night, Carol lies in bed, listening to the express whistling in the distance, the sound of "the world going by" (257).

On a rare outing, Carol exults in riding in a caboose on a freight train. Will plays cards with the conductor and two brakemen; Carol admires the trainmen's "air of friendly independence" (325). Her exultation evaporates when they reach their destination, at a station indistinguishable from the one in Gopher Prairie.

460. Lieberman, Herbert. *The Green Train.* New York: Putnam's, 1986. 334p.

A train going from Leningrad to Helsinki carrying a diverse group of international passengers—some of them Americans—is detained by the Russians, allegedly on the grounds that there may be spies aboard the train, but actually because the Russians intend to hold the train as leverage after a Russian submarine has been caught in Swedish waters. Predictable behavior, good and bad, ensues among the passengers. This thriller is a bit on the dated side, owing to political changes since its publication, but Lieberman is a capable creator of characters. Bring a magnifying glass to this one: The print is tiny.

461. Lincoln, Joseph C. *The Depot Master.* New York: A.L. Burt, 1910. 379p.

The male citizens of the Cape Cod village of East Harniss gather at the depot to await the train and the mail it carries, regardless of whether they know anyone on board or expect any mail. The train's arrival at the depot precipitates general excitement. The depot master is Captain Solomon Berry, a retired mariner. In spite of the title, this sentimental and nostalgic novel's focus is not at all on railroading, and the appearance of the occasional train is barely incidental to the story.

462. Little, Peggy. "Commodities." In *Out of Dallas; 14 Stories*, edited by Jane R. Wood, et al., 147–154. Denton, TX: University of North Texas Press, 1989.

In this less than riveting story, an American woman, traveling by train across Europe, is "liberated for a month from house, husband, and child" (153). Her trip has focused in part—in large part, one suspects—on reawakening "the passion of her adolescent dreams" (148). She meets a man on the train to Geneva, and appears to be about to spend the night with him, but does not.

463. "Little Sunbeam." *Harper's Weekly* 15 (May 27, 1871): 478–479.

In this anonymous tale, a sweet but poor 12-year-old girl, Milly Floyd, sells wintergreens on a New York Central train for a penny a bunch. Business goes badly as affluent passengers ignore her, but a young man, Tom Granger, buys all of her stock for a dollar. He calls to her from his coach window as she stands on a station platform, promising to see her again. Milly is astounded. She returns to the shabby house where she lives with her grandfather, disabled from wounds suffered in the Mexican War. He calls her Sunbeam. There she is doubly astounded, for the folded bill Granger gave her proves to be two dollars, not one. Others also show kindness to Milly: Brakeman Jim Matthews takes the berries she picks and sells them for her in the city; New York Central firemen drop coal at trackside for Milly to pick up in her little wagon.

Tom Granger returns by train, and visits Milly's grandfather. In a coincidence that Charles Dickens would have savored, Granger proves to be the son of the man whom Milly's grandfather saved in battle long ago. Granger's family arranges for a better pension for the old man so that Milly can cease hawking on the train. Years later, Milly and Granger marry.

464. Lloyd, John U. *The Right Side of the Car.* Boston: Richard G. Badger, 1897. 59p.

The narrator, accompanying an excursion party of physicians on the Northern Pacific

Railway, is the only man in the party not a doctor. He is also the man designated to serve as the "special attendant" of a young woman, Myrtle, traveling to her home on the West Coast. Myrtle is strangely withdrawn and quiet. When the narrator suggests that she join him sitting in the shade, she insists that the sunny side is the right side of the car for her. The train traverses Minnesota and the Badlands, and enters the Yellowstone Valley. The narrator at last draws forth from Myrtle the information that she is going home, to Mount Tacoma. "Mount Ranier, you mean," says the narrator. She corrects him. "I look for Tacoma. That is the real name..." (46).

She does see Mount Tacoma, from "the right side of the car," and when she lays eyes on it expires in joy and peace on the narrator's shoulder. He wishes that he himself might be on "the right side" when he sees his own Mount Tacoma.

This is a marvelously sentimental, maudlin story that wallows unashamedly in romantic death-mystery.

465. Lockwood, Scammon. "An Arrival at Carthage." In *The Best Short Stories of 1932*, edited by Edward O'Brien, 152–164. New York: Dodd, Mead, 1932. *The Frontier* 12 (Nov. 1931): 15+.

Two arrivals and one departure mark this story. On a bitter cold January day in 1881, an ancient locomotive pulls a short mixed train across the Iowa prairie. Only seven passengers are aboard. The train crewmen, afraid of becoming snowbound on the prairie, decide to stop at the next town, Carthage. When they reach the small station, they find it empty, dark, and cold. The station agent lies dead on his bed. One of the passengers is about to give birth. The conductor takes the lead in tending to the delivery, in the men's waiting room, site of the station's only stove.

466. Loomis, Noel. "Tough Hombre." In Loomis's *Heading West; Western Stories*, edited by Bill Pronzini, 53–65. Unity, ME: Five Star, 1999. *Adventure*, Dec. 1949.

"Big Blue" Buckley, a tough, no-nonsense rail boss, leads a crew laying track through Mexico's Sonoran desert in 1880. In his crew are a number of men on the run from U.S. law, including Wade Gholson, who bears Buckley a grudge over the death of his brother. The two settle their hash one day by squaring off with spike mauls. Blows that would fell a normal man do not deter "tough hombre" Buckley in this manly man's world of sweat, alkali dust, and the ringing of steel on steel.

467. Lopez, Robert. "Man on Train with Flowers." *New Orleans Review* 28, no. 2 (2002): 134–135.

A man sits on a train holding flowers for a woman, thinking about his "situation." The woman he sits next to on the train is better looking than the one for whom he buys flowers. "The flowers I hold directly over my situation so no one can see but there is nowhere to hide neither" (135). Situations are like that, sometimes.

468. Lumley, Brian. "What Dark God?" In *Nameless Places*, edited by Gerald W. Page, 129–136. Sauk City, WI: Arkham House, 1975.

The narrator boards a crowded British train. He and a boorish fellow passenger force their way into a closed compartment occupied by four travelers. The quartet somehow place the new arrivals into a sleep-like trance while they perform an arcane and ghastly religious rite.

469. Lutz, Giles A. *The Great Railroad War*. Garden City, NY: Doubleday, 1981. 183p.

This Western set in the town of Enid in late 1880s Oklahoma opens in an unusual way, with several saloon women sweating their way through a steamy summer night, complaining that whatever business the Rock Island Railroad has brought the area fails to compensate them for living in a "hellhole" where they "fry in the summer and freeze in the winter" (3). Their frustration and anger boil over when they attack and pummel a railroad official, John Kevan, who has abused one of them. Railroaders are generally low on the town of Enid's hero list; the Rock Island has been using underhanded means to gain control of land adjacent its depots, hoping to cash in on boom-town development. Kevan is vice president of the Rock Island, thanks to marrying President Cable's daughter. When Cable hears Kevan's heavily-edited version concerning the "toughs" who jumped him in Enid, Cable, infuriated, gives him free rein to take vengeance on both Enid and neighboring Pond Creek. The railroad war begins. Thanks to Kevan's infatuation with saloon women, the townsfolk win the war and the railroad's proper services. Passable fare for railroad station waiting room reading; the saloon sisterhood offers an entertaining departure from the typical Western heroine.

470. _____. "Westward Rails." In *The Railroaders*, edited by Bill Pronzini and Martin H. Greenberg, 146–163. New York: Fawcett, 1986. Also in Western Writers of America. *Silver Anniversary Anthology.* New York: Ace Books, 1977.

Although it declines into a standard Western melodrama, this story does contain some persuasive passages describing the traveling conditions of emigrants moving west by rail. They occupy coaches of barren appointments, and share the space with household furniture, farm implements, horses, cows, dogs and cats. "The reek of unwashed human bodies was becoming overpowering" in the California desert heat, "and when the smell of hot animal flesh and the rich, ripe aroma of manure rose, a man gagged on it" (147).

471. Lutz, John. "The Midnight Train." In *Love Kills*, edited by Ed Gorman and Martin H. Greenberg, 92–98. New York: Carroll & Graf, 1997. *Alfred Hitchcock's Mystery Magazine*, March 1968.

Ulman, a seasoned hobo, drops off a freight at midnight, somewhere in the sticks. He hopes to barter for bed and breakfast at a farmhouse before hopping the next morning's train to continue his journey. An accommodating widow offers him bed and breakfast, and a bit more besides. Standard, if modestly amusing, pulp.

472. _____. "The Shooting of Curly Dan." In *Midnight Specials: An Anthology for Train Buffs and Suspense Aficiona-*

dos, edited by Bill Pronzini, 18–25. Indianapolis and New York: Bobbs-Merrill, 1977. *Ellery Queen's Mystery Magazine* 62 (Aug. 1973): 109–115.

Although introduced by Ollie Robinson's great-great-grandson, the real narrator of this neat little murder mystery is old man Robinson himself. He tells of the hot summer day when a crewman on a gandy dancer team shot to death one of his fellow laborers. The mystery element is reasonably clever, but from a railroading point of view the most interesting aspect of the story is its evocation of the rugged, indeed, backbreaking, work carried out by gandy dancers as they shift out-of-true rail back in line, to the calls of their line boss: "the job, it be all rhythm" (23).

473. Lynde, Francis. "An Assisted Destiny." *Scribner's Magazine* 18 (July 1895): 92–100.

The crew in the Colorado & Grand River Railway dispatcher's office talks about the problems of personal finance; when Fergus MacDonald leaves, chief clerk Reddick excoriates him for pretending poverty, when he has money in the bank. MacDonald did say that he had a rich aunt in Canada. Reddick sends a forged letter to MacDonald announcing the old woman's death and his new prosperity as chief beneficiary of her will. The fall-out from Reddick's practical joke nearly ruins MacDonald's career, to say nothing of costing him his sweetheart, the railroad superintendent's daughter. All resolves neatly and happily.

474. _____. "The Brake-Beamer." *McClure's Magazine* 32 (April 1909): 671–680.

Trainmen haul a hobo from the wreckage of a train catastrophe on the Dolomite and Utah Pacific. Track-walker Mart Duggan and his daughter take in the battered 'bo, and summon a doctor. After a long recovery, the hobo takes a job in a roundhouse on the D and UP, claiming to be "Jim Smith." Smith's history is blighted by crime, but he works hard to repay the Duggans. Smith's selfless heroics in saving a passenger train from tumbling off a ruined bridge seal the railroad's determination to protect him from paying for yesterday's crime.

475. _____. "By Special Invitation." *Scribner's Magazine* 16 (Dec. 1894): 746–754.

Railroad President Mayhugh is coming on his private car, the Argyle, to inspect the new line near Mountain Junction on the Colorado & Grand River Railway. Newlywed Chief Clerk Burwell falls for a practical joke perpetrated by one of his station hands to the effect that Mayhugh has invited Burwell and his bride to join him aboard the Argyle. The crusty Mayhugh's irritation at finding Burwell & bride aboard the Argyle dissolves when he learns that Burwell, an accomplished stenographer, can help him execute a backlog of correspondence. This is an interesting little glimpse into a time when a "man's job" could entail in significant part assignments that later came to be known as "woman's work."

476. _____. "Clagett." *Scribner's Magazine* 41 (Jan. 1907): 95–105.

Kate Shannon presides over the lunch counter at the railroad station in the remote mountain mining town of Chrysolite, where Dan Clagett is the station agent. The railroad established the lunch counter to help Kate, after a train killed her section-foreman father. Clagett is in love with Kate, whose worthless brother is a burden to her. One winter night, the railroad auditor discovers that Clagett's accounts are $540 short. At the moment of Clagett's embarrassment and accusations of theft, he leaps to heroics when the Fast Mail train runs through a frozen signal. "Little Millions" Upham rewards Clagett with a posting to a station in a more pleasant climate—where he and Kate can raise fruit trees. (The feckless brother pilfered the $540.)

477. _____. "The Cloud Bursters." In *Scientific Sprague*, 253–327. New York: Scribner's, 1912. Also in *The American Rivals of Sherlock Holmes*. New York: Penguin, 1978. *Popular Magazine*, 25, no. 4 (Sept. 1, 1912) and 25, no. 5 (Sept. 15, 1912).

Calvin "Scientific" Sprague, a "government chemist," is the hero in this Wild Western with a railroad dressing. Sprague helps Dick Maxwell, chief field officer on the local

railroad, the Short Line, with various problems. Here, Sprague suspects that an irrigation company's dam-building project conceals untoward motives. Sprague deduces, in fact, that the earthen dam has been designed to lead to the wash-out of over 30 miles of Short Line track. Sprague and companions struggle to save the railroad, in spite of general approbation for the dam by the vicinity's snookered populace.

478. _____. *David Vallory*. New York: Scribner's, 1919. 402p.

Young and idealistic David Vallory has been called home from his engineering job in Florida to the town of Middleboro. On the train, he meets an older man, also an engineer, who tries to relieve David of some of his idealism. David trained as a railroad builder, but has been doing government work on rivers and harbors. He learns that his father, a banker, has been unable to manage his bank's assets effectively; it is on the verge of collapse, saved only by the intervention of Eben Grillage.

Back in Florida, David works on a great concrete railroad bridge for Grillage's engineering firm. The railroad inspectors who examine the bridge are exacting. David's boss enlists him in a ruse to use low-grade cement for the project. His shock at learning that he has been used by his employer to cheat the railroad soon transmutes to an idea that he has "grown" in his understanding of business: "The transition from loyalty to an ideal to loyalty to a cause is not so violent as it may seem" (86).

David becomes so much the company man that his judgment of others' rational behavior is sometimes clouded when that behavior does not serve company interests. "The company's business is my business," he says, "and I haven't any other" (101). From the bridge job, David takes a promotion to oversee a railway realignment project in the mountains, on the Nevada Short Line. He works near the settlement of Powder Can, a little boom town replicating end-of-track towns of the old days, with plenty of workers' money to turn the wheels of vice and dissipation.

Grillage's daughter Virginia chastises her father for assigning David to the Short Line job, where he will be expected to cut corners and cheat the railroad. "As a people we had forgotten that there was such a thing as an American conscience," she tells her father; "Some of us are remembering now" (122).

Without David's knowledge, Grillage men cut and cheat at every chance, including actions that cause dangerous defects in railroad structures. David begins to accommodate his company's myriad dishonesties, and is slow to see through to the manner in which his accommodation has corrupted him.

The novel's ethical theme gives the book its strongest qualities. Its too-easy resolution of David's errors and a routine romantic subplot pull it down a few notches, and Lynde telegraphs too much of David's fate too soon. Even so, the conflict between railroad interests and contractors will be credible to anyone who has worked on or studied a large construction project, and David's gradual absorption by a corrupt company is persuasive. The novel is one of Lynde's best efforts.

479. _____. "The Electrocution of Tunnel Number Three." In *Scientific Sprague*, 120–192. New York: Scribner's, 1912.

Tunnel 3 on the Nevada Short Line is being wired to operate an electric locomotive in an effort to trim several miles from the route. Sprague becomes caught up in shady business on the railroad. Stribling, the young electrical engineer overseeing the tunnel project, has been engaged by the Short Line's nefarious competition to destroy the tunnel with explosives. Stribling, in Sprague's opinion, represents the nadir of American life: a good boy gone bad, fatally bad, from a misplaced loyalty to corporate crooks.

480. _____. *Empire Builders*. Indianapolis: Bobbs-Merrill, 1907. 377p.

In Colorado, young Stuart Ford is "superintendent and general autocrat of the Plug Mountain branch of the Pacific Southwestern" (2). The branch is the road's perennial financial headache; Ford is determined to make it turn a profit. This "master of men," as the first chapter's title puts it—one looked up to by all honest laboring railroaders—will surely succeed. His plans call for extending the Pacific Southwestern, via the Plug Mountain, to Salt Lake City, a development that would enable the road to compete on an even footing with other, larger railroads. The novel is far from Lynde's best. Whatever Ford's struggles, he is a "determined young pacesetter" (369) and a "golden youth" (63), and his rise to a vice president's and general manager's position is both predictable and inevitable.

481. _____. *The Fight on Standing Stone*. New York: A.L. Burt, 1925. 248p.

The novel begins at the G.L.&P.'s end-of-track mountain construction camp on the Standing Stone River. Claiborne Stannard is "the stalwart young chief of construction" (4). The railroad is competing with the Overland Northern to reach Standing Stone Canyon first. A demand by a road boss who wants to bring a hunting party to the camp throws work off-kilter. So does a strike by rock dynamiters. More critical for the long term is Stannard's success in track-building to allow hauling construction materials to a tunnel before winter. Failing this, the future of the railroad will be in doubt. Stannard solves the labor trouble, but the tunnel threatens to collapse. No reader could doubt Stannard's ultimate success, for this is the sort of novel in which clean-living, hard-working, upright men must prevail. It has, in other words, only a marginal connection to life as most know it.

482. _____. "The Floating of the 'Utah Extension.'" *Scribner's Magazine* 39 (March 1906): 318–327.

Construction engineer Brice is leading a survey through the Rockies for the Utah Pacific, hoping to establish a western extension before the rival Overland Central. The U.P.'s tactics are a closely-held secret, but in a careless moment Brice reveals them to a woman whom he trusts. Soon the Overland takes legal action to thwart the U.P.'s plans, and Brice is convinced that the woman he found romantically appealing is little more than a company spy for the other road.

483. _____. *A Fool for Love*. Indianapolis: Bobbs-Merrill, 1905. 204p. *Lippincott's Monthly Magazine* 75 (April 1905): 385–460.

Railroad right-of-way battle meets love

story in this Lynde outing. Morton Adams and construction engineer John Winton wait at Kansas City's Union Station for the Transcontinental Express to take them to Denver. In the West, they will try to help the Utah Short Line establish a right-of-way that will allow the road to evade the monopolistic ambitions of the Colorado & Grand River. The C.&G.R. has notified the Short Line that it will cancel its agreement to lease track rights to the Short Line; Adams and Winton will have but a few months to build a track to the Short Line in time for it to maintain business.

Before Winton and Adams board the train, they see a woman on the observation platform of a private car. Virginia Carteret, with intimate family ties to the C.&G.R. administration, becomes Winton's love interest.

The C.&G.R. uses every means available, from petty legal harassment to armed mercenaries to sabotage, to thwart Winton and the Short Line. Ironically (and so romantically) Virginia Carteret provides the inspired idea that allows the Short Line to save its day, and its business. All ends happily, if not altogether credibly, with the railroading antagonists treating each other as gentlemen.

484. _____. "Gavin, of Broken Arrow." *Scribner's Magazine* 43 (June 1908): 728–739.

Broken Arrow telegraph operator Gavin narrowly saves a group of foolhardy young people, led by budding reprobates Harry Driscoll and Fred Faulkner, from disaster after they hitch a small push-car to the back of a caboose. Railroad officials discuss a promotion for Gavin, but there is suspicion of his involvement with ore theft from company shipments. His career, as well as his romantic interests, appear finished when he cooperates with robbers taking gold from the railroad safe. The outcome is far different from what Gavin, or the reader, anticipate.

485. _____. *The Grafters*. Indianapolis: Bobbs-Merrill, 1904. 408p.

David Kent is the local attorney for the Western Pacific Railroad in the boom-to-bust burg of Gaston. The townsfolk hate the railroad for reducing it to a whistle-stop and for exploiting its position as the only railroad in the area. Early in the novel, the interestingly-named Bucks, an anti-railroad demagog, is elected governor of the state. Railroad officials conspire to bribe Bucks to veto anti-railroad legislation. Kent loses several cases for the road: "Justice for the railroad company, under present, agrarian conditions, was not to be had in the lower courts..." (59). Kent rises, however, to more important legal functions with the railroad.

This novel is a bit stilted, trying too hard to be literary, and in the process achieving only marginal readability. The action focuses on politics, business, and romance. The bad guys receive their comeuppance, Kent prospers not only as a railroad attorney but also as a politician, and love triumphs. The book contains a significant quantity of railroad action, but its stiff composition interferes with the pleasure it might otherwise offer.

486. _____. "High Finance in Cromarty Gulch." In *Scientific Sprague*, 57–119. New York: Scribner's, 1912. *Popular Magazine*, July 15, 1912.

Calvin Sprague is traveling on the Nevada Short Line's Flying Plainsman. At a remote station, the train stops to pick up an apparently-occupied coffin. Later, Sprague learns that the Plainsman has been held up by bandits at Cromarty Gulch, with the chief objective of the bandits the occupant of the coffin. Sprague sees through it all, in a case involving an attempted stock takeover of the Short Line and a gold bullion heist.

487. _____. "The High Kibosh." In *Scientific Sprague*, 328–406. New York: Scribner's, 1912. *Popular Magazine* 25 (Oct. 1, 1912): 155+; 26 (Oct. 15, 1912): 178+.

The story opens with Sprague playing golf with Short Line lawyer Stillings. The Short Line is in the cross-hairs of a New York company that wants the road to help it establish a short cut to the southern coast. Further shenanigans are afoot—the New Yorkers' local outfit, the Transcontinental, is laying track and about to encroach on Short Line right-of-way, but Sprague demurs when Superintendent

Maxwell begs his assistance. The Transcontinental has hundreds of armed men in its track-laying crew. With a court's help, it takes over the Short Line. Sprague convinces the Short Line crew that the only hope is to show that the judge accepted a bribe. The indefatigable Sprague again carries the day, and puts his own high kibosh on the crooks.

488. _____. "The Hold-up on Split Mountain." *Munsey's Magazine* 30 (Dec. 1903): 414–419.

Four men of different backgrounds gather one night in a Pullman smoking room aboard the Denver Flier. At the encouragement of the rest of the group, which holds credible whoppers in high esteem, a young man in their number tells the story of a train hold-up, entailing an appropriated packet of legal documents, false accusation, intrigue, and discovery. He leaves the other men, who find his story too unlikely to believe, with a final astounding revelation.

489. _____. *The Honorable Senator Sage-Brush.* New York: Scribner's, 1913. 411p.

Born on a Western ranch, Evan Blount is a recent Boston law school graduate. His father is David Blount, a former senator from the "Sage-Brush State." Evan has lost touch with his father, who, some say, purchased his office. The elder Blount now is the main cog in the Sage-Brush State's political machine. He is sympathetic to forces that would retain rate regulations that officials of the Transcontinental Railroad consider punitive. These officials try to bribe Blount to help them put their own man into the governor's office, and seem to succeed in turning son against father when they hire Evan as legal counsel. The railroad is a nest of the corrupt: "When the court comes to investigate," says one character, "it will find that every crooked deal in this campaign has had a railroad man or a corporation man at the back of it" (397). All ends well, with Evan and his father. Good triumphs as the evil railroaders are driven from the political life of the Sage-Brush State.

The novel is plodding and predictable, but it helps illuminate one aspect of the railroad in American life: its occasional position in popular opinion as the devil made flesh.

490. _____. "The Kidnapping of Cassandra." *McClure's Magazine* 30 (April 1908): 759–766.

Bartley Hungerford, chief engineer of the Red Mountain extension, invites his beloved—but betrothed to another—Cassandra Wainwright on a final prenuptial ride aboard a private car. The trip turns into Hungerford's attempt to keep Cassie from marrying her intended, and to persuade her to choose him, instead. Romantic railroad piffle.

491. _____. *The King of Arcadia.* New York: Scribner's, 1909. 354p.

Breckinridge Ballard, a construction engineer, is summoned to Colorado by the Arcadia Irrigation Company to build railroads, dams, and what-not. Railroading detail is relatively sparse, but Chapter 10, "Hoskins's Ghost," relates the way a superstitious engineer causes a railroad wreck.

492. _____. "Little Millions." *Scribner's Magazine* 40 (July 1906): 110–121.

Railroad general manager Dickie Brice urges Gebhart Upham to stay on the D. & U.P. road after finishing his supervision of the Elk Pass Tunnel project. Upham agrees, but the railroaders in general do not trust him, since he comes from a rich family. "Little Millions," they call him, and carry on a campaign of un-cooperativeness and contention that threatens Upham's authority and the road's welfare. Brice counsels Upham on the need to approach the men in a down-to-earth manner, to lose his patrician air. In a series of incidents, Upham reveals himself as ready to get down in the dirt, literally, with the laborers. "Mebbe there's a man inside o' them store-clothes o' his'n yet," says one (115). When Upham risks his life to save an injured engineer, the rank and file are ready to stand firmly behind him forever.

493. _____. "M'Graw." *Century Illustrated Monthly Magazine* 27 (Nov. 1894): 136–139.

One morning a tall, gaunt man—M'Graw—appears in Mr. Harold's St. Paul, Minnesota office, seeking railroad work in

Colorado. His scheme is to arrange for a gang of workmen to ride at half-fare from St. Paul to Colorado, the remaining portion of their fare to be paid by the labor-starved Colorado Overland. M'Graw rounds up nearly 60 men, and Harold, M'Graw, and the new recruits steam out of St. Paul for the West. M'Graw talks to Harold in the smoker; Harold judges him boastful and ineffectual. His estimation changes completely when, after a derailment and fire on the way to Colorado, M'Graw sacrifices his own life to save Harold's. As happens so often in popular railroad fiction, the man of crude surface qualities demonstrates noble inner character.

494. _____. "Minshew Makes Good." *Scribner's Magazine* 60 (July 1916): 54–64.

Few believe that the timid relief operator John Minshew will ever make a real railroader. Kate Gallagher, who tends the station lunch counter, tells him he simply needs something to live up to. On a company picnic, Minshew more-or-less rescues a young woman from drowning. His heroics, however inadvertent, cause a sensation, and lead to his more confident manner, and a promotion. In spite of his success, Kate spurns his marriage proposal, until the aftermath of the day her half-addled father absconds on an impromptu run with a locomotive. Modesty, selflessness, responsibility, and conscientiousness are the values the story endorses.

495. _____. "The Mystery of the Black Blight." In *Scientific Sprague*, 193–252. New York: Scribner's, 1912.

Three trainmen and a mail clerk have been killed in a wreck on the Short Line. It is the road's third wreck in a week. Superintendent Dick Maxwell is convinced that the Short Line's troubles owe to a creeping psychological malaise among its employees, leading to a general decline in performance and alertness. Calvin Sprague determines that a sharp increase in alcohol use among the railroaders is at the heart of the problem. "Your railroad is practically an inebriate asylum in the making," he tells Maxwell (220). Who is behind the workers' sudden devotion to liquor? Hewing

to his customary "scientific" observation, Sprague penetrates the mystery, which includes not only dipsomania, but clever sabotage of locomotives.

496. _____. "The Nerve of the Upjohns." *Scribner's Magazine* 31 (Feb. 1902): 243–250.

Amos Upjohn runs a locomotive on the Wind River Division. His son Mark is his fireman. Neither man qualifies well in boldness, and Mark, distressed by a pair of close calls on the road, leaves his post to work as a machinist in a railroad shop. Mark's lack of nerve dismays his sweetheart, Kate Bryan. An ugly strike, with acts of lethal sabotage, gives both Upjohns a chance to quash their reputation for timidity. With narrator Jack Perkins, the train-master, they take out a passenger train, braving dynamiters who flee in horror from the approaching engine. The reason for their flight becomes clear at story's end, and, although bizarre, the image of a wild Irish lass in a white party dress riding through the freezing night on the front of a locomotive has a certain thrilling appeal.

497. _____. "Pasquale." *Lippincott's Monthly Magazine* 71 (May 1903): 726–731.

An ill-tempered passenger agent must employ the Italian Pasquale to help arrange travel for Pasquale's fellow Italian railroad laborers. The passenger agent "had no love for Italians" (726). Pasquale is worried about accommodations for his countrymen; lately the railroad has been transporting them in boxcars, in freezing weather. Pasquale speaks little English; the passenger agent speaks no Italian—and the agent errs in thinking that Pasquale is an agitator when in fact he is trying to protect the agent from his angry co-workers. All ends well, with Pasquale awarded a fruit-stand in front of the agent's Denver office.

498. _____. *A Private Chivalry*. New York: Appleton, 1900. 332p.

George Brant, college graduate and draftsman, flees a blighted past by catching a train to Denver. On the train, he meets the comely Miss Dorothy Langford. At a dining stop, Brant embarrasses himself before Dorothy with his rough temper; he punishes himself by hiding in the smoking car, out of her sight, when the train resumes its journey. A minor derailment sends Brant rushing from his self-imposed isolation to Miss Langford's aid, and he vows to look after her until they reach Denver.

This romantic relationship sustains through the novel, which wraps Brant's efforts toward self-redemption in mystery and melodrama, frequently with a railroading backdrop. Murder, handcar chases, and railway derring-do feature prominently. The railroader's scourge, alcohol, turns up in the chapter "The Demoniac," in which a telegraph operator, already besotted by unrequited love, enters "the drunkard's paradise" while on the job, "that exalted frame of mind in which the most abstruse problems seem to solve themselves of their own motions" (161). Seem to, but do not: The operator bungles orders for a special train carrying the railroad's general manager and his party.

499. _____. *The Quickening*. Indianapolis: Bobbs-Merrill, 1906. 407p.

Old Major Dabney of Paradise Valley is hostile toward the idea of yielding any of his land for a right-of-way for the Great Southwestern Railway. Railroad functionaries threaten the use of eminent domain. Major Dabney prevails, and the railroad skirts around Paradise Valley through the surrounding hills. Even in a novel whose chief focus is far from railroading, Lynde cannot resist bringing the railroad into the scene, if only in a glancing way.

500. _____. *The Real Man*. New York: Scribner's, 1915. 450p.

Montague Smith, bank cashier, a young man of conservative values, good behavior, and tasteful haberdashery, leaves for dead his bank's president in a confrontation over a bad loan. Smith flees, and in a chapter of considerable tension, "The Hobo," hops a westbound freight. He quickly transforms to the life of a man on the run, and "could feel the shacklings of the reputable yesterdays slipping from him" (44). In the Colorado hills, Smith takes a situation in a quarry, with the Timayani Ditch Company. He quickly rises to acting financial secretary with the concern, which is struggling to overcome evil antagonists. The "real man" of the title is that of Smith's inner character emerging in his quest to assist the forces of goodness. The novel is a conventional tale, but can still hold the reader's attention. The best portion, and the only part with a critical railroad presence, is that concerning Smith's flight west and his temporary transformation into a hobo. Lynde includes some nicely-observed details, such as Smith's hungry devouring of a ham sandwich and a cup of bad coffee after his long flight to freedom in a boxcar.

501. _____. *A Romance in Transit*. New York: Scribner's, 1897. 227p.

A mixed group of passengers travels on the Colorado and Utah Railway's Flying Kestrel across the Great Plains. Among them is railroader Fred Brockway, and, on a special car at the train's rear, his romantic interest, the railroad president's daughter, Gertrude. The president is unenthused about Brockway's regard for his daughter, but she has eyes for young Fred—and not the calculating eyes of her father. She regards Fred with "the steady gaze of clean-hearted guilelessness" (21). Brockway shows his resourcefulness by repairing the cookstove in the president's car. He escorts Gertrude to the engine for a ride in the cab: "It is quite possible for two persons to converse in the cab of a flying locomotive, but the factor of distance must be eliminated. Wherefore he bent over her till his mustache brushed the pink ear" (58–59). Goodness!

In a chapter headed "Chiefly Scenic," the couple stand on the rear platform of the train as it reels through the stupendous mountain scenery. Brockway points out the natural wonders the train passes. At the next stop, Brockway helps Gertrude in her descent from the sublime to share some pie with him.

Predictable complications and obstacles dog the young couple, but—as if the reader could have the slightest suspicion of any other outcome—all ends well.

502. _____. *The Taming of Red Butte Western*. New York: Scribner's, 1910. 410p.

The Red Butte Western—"the most hopelessly demoralized three hundred miles of railroad west of the Rockies" (4)—is a division of the Pacific Southwestern. Howard Lidgerwood is called on by Stuart Ford, Pacific Southwestern vice president, to restore the Red Butte, a valuable line in the PS's overall strategy. Lidgerwood hesitates, owing to his deep doubts about his own courage and ability to manage difficult men. He swallows his fear, and signs on as Red Butte's general superintendent. Some of the first Red Butte railroaders who meet Lidgerwood believe that the road's rougher characters will "eat him alive, just for the fun of it" (51). Lidgerwood has to deal with truculent, two-faced railroaders, organized criminals, attempted murder, drunken engineers, thieving conductors, and assorted nasty characters in his quest to bring the recalcitrant road to peace and efficiency.

The novel shows Lynde doing what he does well: blending a little Wild West, a little romantic subplotting, and a railroading theme in a smoothly-written story with enough plot maneuvers and enjoyable characters to keep the reader awake. The novel doesn't pass within several blocks of the neighborhood of fine literature, but its workmanlike execution deserves credit—and consider this point: How many popular entertainments of the 21st century would dare mention, as Lynde does, Goethe's *Mephistopholes*?

503. _____. *The Tenderfoots.* New York: Scribner's, 1926. 334p.

In 1879, railroad clerk Philip Trask is on his way to a new job in Denver, hearing hopes of finding his father, who disappeared under mysterious circumstances. He rides a train crowded with men drawn to Colorado by the discovery of silver. On the train the reserved New Englander Philip meets a startlingly candid young Mississippian, Jean Dabney, who is going to Denver with his family. They come close to arguing about the Civil War, but instead step out on the platform to enjoy their first look at the Rockies. In Denver, Philip rooms with another railroad clerk, Middleton, who advises him to shed his tenderfoot ways.

Philip works for a narrow-gauge railroad that runs to Leadville, site of a silver strike. With riches calling from the hills, Philip leaves his railroad job and sets out with Bromley, an amusing and equally naïve tenderfoot, as his partner, to strike it rich. Before long Philip has also abandoned his strait-laced worldview for one more in keeping with the moral ambiguities of the Western life.

There is only occasional railroad business in the story once Philip heads for the hills, but one late passage deserves note: Philip returns to Denver after his life has changed profoundly, and in an exchange with the railroad passenger agent at Union Depot learns that the railroad has turned a willfully blind eye to its use in a scheme involving white slavery. "You may not know it," says the agent, "but women—of a certain sort—are shipped into this over-manned town like so much freight—prepaid freight, at that" (270). Philip buys a young woman her freedom from a brothel, and sends her back, by train, to her family.

Overall, this is an engaging and more than usually thoughtful Lynde novel; humor now and then lightens the tone.

504. _____. *Waters of Strife.* New York: Scribner's, 1930. 323p.

Robert Armstrong, former draftsman for the Pacific Railways, is to head an irrigation project in an arid Western region that has come to life with the new railroad, an extension of the Grass Valley and Pacific, that serves it. Armstrong's friend, Burdick, is the general manager of the G.V.&P. Armstrong's chief trait is an intense devotion to accomplishment. Burdick provides some support as Armstrong contends with forces hostile to the irrigation job, but the influence of the railroad appears chiefly in the two men's characters; some railroading activity takes place in the book, but it is as background to the story's primary concerns. In this novel, Lynde's last, the virtues he touts are as always courage, honesty, steadfastness, and decency.

505. _____. "The Wire-Devil." In *Scientific Sprague*, 3–56. New York: Scribner's, 1912.

Calvin Sprague turns up at the dispatcher's office on the Short Line just as word arrives by wire that the Apache Limited has derailed and caught fire. Sprague joins the men on the wrecking train racing to the site, only to discover that the Limited is secure, on the track—and the subject in the latest of a series of bogus wire transmissions. The railroaders call the sender of these fake messages the "wire-devil." Sprague works on the case, and moves along quickly through the red herrings to a clever solution. Sherlock Holmes would not be awed, but the story is good fun.

506. _____. *The Wreckers.* New York: Scribner's, 1920. 377p.

The male stenographer to railroad boss Mr. Norcross narrates this tale, which opens with a comical error: Graham Norcross, stenographer Jimmie Dodds, and two young women slip off the last car of a train at a water stop, and are left behind when the train moves on. While waiting for help, they witness the hijacking of a special train.

The novel focuses on the Pioneer Short Line, a railroad being bled dry by its owners, Wall Street speculators interested only in driving up the road's stock price so they can dump it at a high profit. They care nothing for the road's workers or for the towns it serves. Norcross assumes the general manager's job on the PSL; his assignment: Clean up the mess. A vintage John Wayne belongs somewhere in this rootin' tootin' railroad Western.

507. _____. *Young Blood.* New York: Scribner's, 1929. 323p.

Frederic J. Burdick, 28, works in the Pacific Railway's Detroit office. When the road closes the Detroit operation, it installs Burdick as general manager on a small feeder line out West, the G.V.&P. Burdick's sub rosa assignment is to show that the G.V.&P. will be better off if it abandons its semi-independence and leased lines from the Pacific, and lets the larger road call the management shots completely. The G.V.&P. has been systematically slighted by the Pacific, with shoddy equipment and structures: "The picking of the bones had been thorough. There were cross-ties dry-rotting and bridges that were none too safe; every material pile on the road had been carefully and painstakingly culled of its best; the rolling stock, cars as well as locomotives, tallied up with the inventories as to quantity but were woefully deficient as to quality" (44). Coupled with such abuse are the extortionary long-term contracts the Pacific has negotiated

with local shippers who might otherwise use the G.V.&P.

This readable melodrama follows Burdick through many ups and downs as he shows the fire in his "young blood" by doing what conventional wisdom deems impossible: saving the G.V.&P.'s independence in an age of consolidation. The story's effects are dimmed, however, by the reader's certainty that Burdick will succeed, regardless of the obstacles in his way.

MacBain, Alastair *see* **Ford, Corey, and Alastair MacBain**

508. MacDonald, John D. "Noose for a Tigress." In *The Good Old Stuff; 13 Early Stories,* 257–287. New York: Harper & Row, 1982. Published as "Trap for a Tigress." *Dime Detective* 67 (Aug. 1952): 12–27; 111.

On a cross-country train bound for New York, Simon Pell—returned from combat against the Vietnamese communists—awakens from a dream that he is back in 'Nam. In the club car, his ex-wife Marj and her lawyer nag him about their divorce settlement. Marj, in big trouble, needs money fast. Soon her trouble grows: Someone kills her lawyer on the train, and makes it look like her work. Much of the action in this crime tale—one boiled about as hard as they come—occurs on the train, including the mugging of a conductor in a restroom. (MacDonald updated this story for the anthology publication, adding references to Amtrak and the Vietnam War.)

Macdonald, Ross *see* **Millar, Kenneth**

509. MacDonald, William C. *Thunderbird Trail.* Garden City, NY: Doubleday, 1946. 215p.

An investigator for the Texas Northern & Arizona Southern Railroad, Gregory Quist, looks into a train wreck. He suspects that freight robbers were involved. Quist cleaned out a nest of freight thieves in Oklahoma, so he knows his business. The wreck killed several train crewmen, and the cargo was looted. Quist is a no-nonsense operator: As he adjusts his sidearm, he tells Division Superintendent

Fletcher why he doesn't wear a cartridge belt: "Any man that can't finish the job he's got to do with what's in the gun and a extra fistful hasn't any business carrying a gun" (22). Murder, gunplay, lead poisoning (the rifles "bark"), and chapter titles like "Damned Loyal," "Knockout," and "Man Hunt" mark this as a hard-boiled Western. The railroading, although fundamental to the story, is seldom front-and-center.

510. MacMurragh, Jack. "My Boy's a Railroad Man." *Collier's* 109 (Jan. 10, 1942): 27.

This one-page story, with much of the page consumed by a cute illustration of a little boy in switchman's garb, shows how a father and his son reinforce their mutual love of railroading, and each other, in spite of maternal interference. Little Danny's language, during an imaginary train operation, comes too close to blunt railroading vernacular for his mother's ears, and she insists that his father, a railroader himself, punish the child. He does so, but the two find a way to rise above the petty moral concerns that plague Mom. Centimeters below the surface, the story reinforces popular notions of rough, manly friendship and female prissiness.

511. Madden, David. "Burning the Railroad Bridges on the Grand Trunk Line in the Great Valley of East Tennessee." *Gettysburg Review* 2, no. 3 (1989): 396–412.

In 1861, Reverend William B. Carter of Tennessee conceived a plan to burn all nine bridges of the Confederate-controlled Grand Trunk line through East Tennessee, on the same night in November. Union Army invasion was to follow on the heels of the bridge-burning. The Lincoln administration supported Carter's plan. The bridge attack went surprisingly well; the rest of the operation failed miserably, and the bridge burners suffered a ruthless, swift response from the Confederates. This story, presented as a document found among the papers of a fictional Confederate sharpshooter, relates in detail the planning and execution of the bridge raid. "We are the fire that goes before the army of

deliverance," says Rev. Carter (401). Unfortunately for the railroad raiders, the army of deliverance did not arrive in a timely manner, a fact on whose unpleasant details the author does not dwell.

512. Malzberg, Barry N. "The Man Who Loved the Midnight Lady." In *Midnight Specials: An Anthology for Train Buffs and Suspense Aficionados,* edited by Bill Pronzini, 252–260. Indianapolis and New York: Bobbs-Merrill, 1977. Also in Malzberg's *The Man Who Loved the Midnight Lady; A Collection.* Garden City, NY: Doubleday, 1980.

An eerie and unsettling original work of science fiction set in the year 2112, this story concerns the narrator's vetting for membership in the Bureau of Historical Reconstruction. In his bureau assignments, he rides various trains—from a New York commuter to the Orient Express—and experiences time as it was. The Midnight Lady figures tragically in one of the narrator's reconstructions. The narrator is comforted in knowing that, through his work and that of his colleagues, the great trains will endure forever.

513. Manchester, William. "Record Run." *Saturday Evening Post* 229 (April 13, 1957): 40–41+. Also in *Where Speed Is King: Stories of Racing Adventure.* Edited by Phyllis R. Fenner. New York: Morrow, 1972.

Sam Lacy has recently leased an old Connecticut depot and turned it into a railroad museum. His business collapses when the local railroad, the Great Eastern, abandons the town, taking with it all the tourist traffic. Coming to Sam's rescue are the pride of the museum, an 1856 locomotive, and Lisa Thatcher, a pretty and knowledgeable rail fan who happens to be the daughter of the Great Eastern's president. The most notable departure from the norm in this story is that the lead female character is not simply a fluffy accessory in a man's world, but is herself a capable railroader.

514. Marshall, Bruce. "Immodest Maiden." *Saturday Evening Post* 224 (July 21, 1951): 20–21+. Also in *Saturday Evening*

Post Stories, 1951. New York: Random House, 1951.

The narrator is riding a rundown express from Barcelona to Madrid. He becomes spellbound by a beautiful young woman who is traveling with another man. An old woman observes his silent jealousy, and tells him that "a fellow traveler on a long train journey whom one will never see again is like a priest in the confessional: you can speak to him without fear of what he is going to think about you afterward" (21). Over lunch on the train, she relates a long, personal story of her youth—a story in which the old woman, by confessing her life's sad history, seeks to help the narrator see his own life more clearly.

515. Marshall, Lenore. "Christmas Eve." In *The Confrontation, and Other Stories,* 108–113. New York: Norton, 1972.

On Christmas Eve on a Rock Island Line train going west from Chicago, a widow and a retired couple carry on dull conversations as the train passes cheerless, desolate small towns. The anonymous narrator speculates on the emptiness of the land seen from the train, and on the paucity of cultural resources. "The train flew by [the occasional human being] so quickly that questions could scarcely form" about what people did, or how they lived (111). The conversation reveals the pathos, if not the outright desperation, of the widow, who has sold her house and is on her way to move in with her son and his wife, without first notifying them of her intent.

The last paragraph is especially effective. It describes the widow looking out her window, "seeming to try to push through it to the other side, of little lighted cottages within which the illusion of human goodness shone bright, the miracle of human love must surely be taking place for someone ... despite all the sorrows in the world" (113). For someone, perhaps; not for her.

516. Martin, Dave. "Signal Tower Girl." *Railroad Magazine* 28 (June 1940): 103–112.

Annie Mahoney is a beautiful day operator at the W.&P. signal tower at its grade crossing with the T.&A.C. One morning in 1938, a brakeman kicks hobo Wabash Whitey off a train as it passes the tower. Annie sees Whitey hit the ground, and, a compassionate sort, she encourages him to see her father, who bosses a section gang, for a job. Whitey flourishes under Mahoney's regimen, and becomes friends with Annie.

The story's central issue concerns the T.&A.C. crossing. The financially-strapped T.&A.C. is legally obligated to maintain it, and the W.&P., with a grudge against the smaller, weaker road, beats the daylights out of the crossing with 20 heavy trains a day. Annie, alas, is in love with a T.&A.C. section hand, Terry Finnegan. Because of the sour rivalry of the two railroads, their families are not speaking to each other. Whitey uses his wits, and his fists, to help mend the breach between the Mahoneys and the Finnegans, and facilitates Annie's marriage to Terry Finnegan.

In one passage of interest, Annie asks Whitey if he was ever married or had a sweetheart. Whitey scoffs. "There's no place for a skirt in my business," he says. "Hittin' the road; home in a boxcar; side-tracked meals; missin' sleep; dodgin' dicks. What t'ell dame wants that sort of dish served up to her?" (108).

517. Martin, David. "Louise on the Train." *Amelia* 6, no. 1 (1990): 78–82.

Louise awakens early in the morning in her seat on an Amtrak coach rolling through Ohio. She does not know what town the train is passing through, but she knows where she is going: home, for the first time in over a decade. Anxiety is having its way with her as she anticipates her homecoming. An obnoxious woman in the seat ahead accuses Louise of talking to herself. When the train reaches the station, Louise sees her mother on the other side of her window, "as if she had known exactly what car and seat Louise would be sitting in" (82). Louise craves, at one level, to stay on the train, all the way to Chicago, but she joins her mother on the platform, and breaks into weeping. The reader believes that Louise needs to come home, and hopes that the visit will soothe her troubled heart.

518. Martin, Valerie. "The Way of the World." In Martin's *The Consolation of*

Nature, and Other Stories, 21–30. New York: Vintage, 1989.

A woman in her 40s looks back on her first train ride by herself, at the age of 11, while she waits at a station for her young daughter to arrive aboard an Amtrak train. It is an interesting juxtaposition, and the narrator's memory of sharing her lunch aboard the coach with a harried, exhausted young woman is well conceived. The story does not work as smoothly as it might; the vocabulary and perceptions the narrator attributes to her 11-year-old self are too mature to be fully credible.

519. Mason, David J. "The Man on the Back of the Train." *North Dakota Quarterly* 54 (Fall 1986): 248–257.

In this powerfully sad story of loss and the indifference of time, a mother and her two children, Sue and Robby, live with the children's grandmother. They are excited to see a freight train passing nearby. Sue wonders who "the man who waves" is at the end of the train. The passing train is close enough that it rattles the windows of the house. One June day the train stops nearby, and Sue and Robby see two trainmen on the caboose. One of them is Al Hammond, the man who waves; he gives the children a brief tour of the caboose, and wishes them well in their search for their father, who is missing in action in Vietnam.

On another day, when the children's mother is preparing for a date, Sue mentions Al Hammond. Her mother wants nothing to do with him. "There's two kinds of men, Susy," she says. "One kind has ambition and the other kind works on the railroad" (523).

In the fall, Sue goes back to school, and before long, Mr. Hammond is gone, the railroad line closed, the track torn up, and, by the time Sue is 16, the roadbed is nearly overgrown with vegetation. Sue's father never returns; her mother marries another man—and Sue asks her boyfriend to park near the old railroad right of way, where Mr. Hammond used to wave to her from the caboose.

520. Masterson, Whit. *The Gravy Train.* New York: Dodd, Mead, 1971. 219p.

Anthony Heaston is an escapee from a Colombian prison and former Army star turned mercenary—and the FBI wants him. Here he's out to rob a train; on the Tres Muertos ranch, he and his cronies practice for the job, using an old wood burning train that they run around in circles, and a helicopter with which they intend to haul off the loot. A shipment from the Denver Mint at first looks like the probable target, but a load of Bruegel paintings by the 15th century Flemish artist looms as a larger objective as the plot progresses. Even that proves a mistaken end, however: Heaston is planning a heist much more bizarre, decidedly ghoulish—but original and amusing. Most of the novel's railroad action occurs in the last 70 or so pages, where the plot accelerates.

521. Matozzo, Francis J. "Railroad Pegasus." *Pulpsmith* 3 (Summer 1983): 60–63.

One summer day a group of trackmen watches one of their number, Half-A-Deck, tear open the door of a shack in the woods near the tracks. Half-A-Deck emerges from the shack leading a great, white winged horse. The district engineer, Armstrong, appears, and threatens to fire Half-A-Deck if he refuses to return to work. Half-A-Deck has better things to do in this pleasant little fantasy.

522. Matthews, Brander. *In the Vestibule Limited.* New York: Harper, 1892. 93p.

In this quaintly tiny book, the reader meets Hallett Larcom traveling west aboard the New York and Chicago Limited, despairing over the lover's quarrel that has apparently ruined his wedding plans. As coincidence would have it, he learns that his beloved, Anita Vernon, is also aboard the train. The entire story takes place on the train, and focuses on the young couple's joyous reunion. They even succeed in getting married aboard train after rounding up a clergyman among the passengers. They say their vows "while the New York and Chicago Limited was rushing onward through the gathering night at a speed of nearly fifty miles an hour" (93). The book includes several illustrations of the interiors of passenger cars, rendered in a manner conveying the author's notions of the luxury and elegance afforded those fortunate enough to travel so grandly.

523. Matthews, Jack. "Toward a Distant Train." *Southwest Review* 49 (Summer 1964): 274–281.

A six-year-old boy lives with his ill-tempered, vindictive grandmother. The old woman poisons the boy's thinking about his evidently-dead mother, who put on lipstick and perfume, packed her bag, and went to the train station one night. According to Grandma, the conductor "had fangs like a wolf and the eyes of a serpent. And the engineer was dressed in a frock coat and had the tail of a dog" (277). The train, she claims, took the boy's mother to "the bad place," because she was a bad woman. The same train still passes, in the distance, and the boy can hear its whistle. Grandma threatens to put him on that train. The story moves to a wrenching concluding paragraph in which the boy flees his grandmother's house to run to the train on which his mother vanished, convinced that she is still aboard, and that she will smell like flowers. The story achieves an effect of sickening psychological horror that one would expect from a writer like Peter Straub or Ramsey Campbell.

524. Maund, Alfred. *The Big Boxcar*. London and New York: Longmans, Green, 1959. 177p.

Sam, an African American, jumps a slow, northbound freight in rural Mississippi. The boxcar he hops has several others aboard—a total of one white man and five black—and, as the rest discover during a craps game on the floor of the car, one woman. As the train rolls through the night, each of the riders tells a story of Southern life. They take turns until they reach Birmingham, where city and railroad police search the train. They kill Spook, one of the boxcar riders, and are on the verge of gang-raping the woman when a white yardman comes up to the group and intervenes. Sam and the woman save their remaining companions in a creative fashion, and at novel's end they are married, living by the train tracks. "The trains go by and shake the walls and rattle the dishes, and they laugh.... And their joke together is that maybe on their next freight ride they'll get as far as Atlanta" (177). The train north is here both a literal means of escape from racial oppression, and a symbol of freedom.

525. Maxwell, William. "The Old Man at the Railroad Crossing." In *All the Days and Nights*, 405–407. New York: Knopf, 1995. Also in Maxwell's *The Old Man at the Railroad Crossing and Other Tales*. New York: Knopf, 1968.

An old railroad crossing guard cryptically tells each passerby to "rejoice." Everyone either ignores him or mocks him, but for one middle-aged woman who tells him he has given her something to think about. Shortly afterward, the old man falls weak, and loses his job to a younger man. The woman visits the old man on his death bed, and says "what he used to say at the railroad crossing, to every person who came that way" (407). This story is open to various interpretations, and something could be made of the relationship between the old man's service as a crossing guard and his own preparation to cross the track between life and death.

526. McAulay, Sara. "Engine, Rider, Engineer." *California Quarterly* 26 (1985): 55–67.

In a somewhat disjointed story, McAulay relates a woman's meditations and memories of her father, who died when she was a young girl. The woman's thoughts weave together images of her father, a highway engineer whom she long thought was a locomotive engineer, with those from a vivid dream of death in which she prostrates herself on a railroad track and waits for the next train, only to have her "death" somehow appropriated by a "passenger." The railroad death dream evidently owes to the countless rail disaster songs the woman's father sang to her when she was a child. The story's end resolves the tensions, for the most part, that drive the woman's deathly railroad dreams.

527. McCague, James. *The Big Ivy*. New York: Crown, 1955. 312p.

The Indiana Valley Line—the Ivy—runs from Chicago to New York City at the turn of the century. The novel proper opens with young Jem Gandee dropping out of school after punching his teacher, and taking off on the Ivy. Jem starts with a year in the roundhouse, after lying about his age, and progresses to fireman. "I figgered I'd have t'git onta yer ass about them jobs, like with most greenhorns," an old hand tells Jem (24). Jem's initial trip as a fireman is an embarrassment, but he survives and flourishes as a railroader. *Big Ivy* flourishes as a novel of the railroad, combining an informed understanding of the technology with an unsentimental sensibility. McCague's railroaders talk like real railroaders: They swear enthusiastically. Had Frank L. Packard and Frank H. Spearman been in their prime in the 1950s, it is conceivable that they may have written in the vein McCague mines here. The novel features believable, well-drawn characters, and contentious passages about such topics as company loyalty. Some set-pieces, such as Jem's beating of the notorious rail-yard bully Bad Bill, are well written and exciting. In all, *The Big Ivy* is an engaging, entertaining novel of the days, as the dedication puts it, when "railroading was not so much an occupation as a whole way of life to a breed that is all but gone today." McCague's grip on railroading reality no doubt owes in considerable measure to his father's having served as an engineer on the Twentieth Century Limited.

528. McCarthy, Mary. "Artists in Uniform." *Harper's* 206 (March 1953): 41–49. Also in McCarthy's *On the Contrary*. New York: Farrar, Straus, Cudahy, 1961; and in *Modern Short Stories: The Uses of Imagination*. Edited by Arthur Mizener. Rev. ed. New York: Norton, 1967.

The narrator, a young woman traveling across the country, meets an Air Force colonel ("in procurement") in the club car. She assumes that the colonel and other men in the area have mistaken her for a "Bohemian." She is, after all, reading a book. She stumbles into an argument with the colonel and the others about an alleged Communist on the faculty of a university. "They're all Reds, Colonel," claims one passenger. "They teach it in the classroom" (43). The colonel disparages Jews—infuriating the narrator, who, though named McCarthy, has Jewish ancestors. The argument continues in a bar during a rest between trains; the narrator boards her departing train, apparently having made no dent in the colonel's anti-Semitic hide.

529. _____. "The Man in the Brooks Brothers Shirt." In *Story; An Introduction to Prose Fiction*, edited by Arthur Foff and Daniel Knapp, 103–132. Belmont, CA: Wadsworth, 1964. Also in McCarthy's *The Company She Keeps*. New York: Harcourt, Brace, 1942. *Partisan Review* 8 (July-Aug. 1941): 279–288; 324–343.

A young woman on a westbound train considers the world outside as the train crosses the plains: "the drought and the cow bones strewn over the Dust Bowl seemed as remote as a surrealist painting" (112). She finds herself drawn to a steel executive in a green Brooks Brothers shirt. Although she thinks of herself as drawing him out, in fact the great majority of the revelations in their conversation come from her. Nearly compulsively, she informs him of her failed marriage and her series of lovers, all of whom also failed for one reason or another. Their conversation precedes a night of drunken and violent lust in the man's compartment. He wants to marry her; she is aghast. The train provides a secure and separate place for the young woman to reflect intensely (and, for the reader, a touch wearyingly) on her personal situation, her reflection and insight triggered by her brief affair with the businessman. In this story, McCarthy ignores the maxim that in fiction it is better to show than tell. Here she tells—and tells. Nevertheless, the story's ahead-of-its-time sexual candor and theme of female independence earned it considerable notoriety.

530. McClary, Tom. "Commuter." *Railroad Stories* 20 (Sept. 1936): 28–31.

Most stories of passenger treatment focus on the railroad's alleged indifference, or worse, to customer comfort. This story provides a nice reversal of the routine. Businessman John Nason grouses about everything connected to his daily train commute, from the steps up to the car to the window shade by his seat. His perceived abuse drives him to write angry letters to editors, creating trouble for the railroad. Like many, Nason is a man who refuses to be pleased. When the railroad places new, updated cars into service, their very perfection provokes Nason's ire, and further letters to the editor.

531. McClintock, Harry K. "Railroaders Are Tough." *Railroad Magazine* 78 (Dec. 1965): 41–44.

Prairie City, a former end-of-track boom town, is getting worse as it ages; reputedly, the only decent citizens in town live north of the railroad tracks. The rest of this Wild West town is full of dance halls, gin mills, crooked gambling dens, and red-light houses. Brakeman Tom Hardy aims to organize the railroaders to run the city as well as the railroad. Soon the railroaders themselves are pitted against the company in a strike, and against the rowdy cowboys who make Prairie City a hell-hole for righteous folk. The railroaders settle the strike, and the cowpokes' hash, in manly fashion.

532. McConnaughey, James P. "Hattie's Railroad." *American Magazine* 118 (Aug. 1934): 44–47+.

Tycoon John Cleve assigns his indolent, golf-loving nephew Tommy Cleve to run a down-at-the-heels railroad whose ownership he shares with his former fiancée, Hattie Whalen. Tommy, in fact, has just met Joan Whalen, Hattie's mother, on the golf course. The only railroading action in this story involves Tommy's astute negotiation of a profitable sale of the railroad. Slightly below the plot's surface, the *American Magazine* invokes great wealth, beautiful, devil-may-care "society" types, and breezy financial wheeler-dealing in a way that would allow Depression-hobbled readers a few minutes of escapism in a fantasy of "the rich life."

533. McElroy, Colleen J. "A Brief Spell by the River." In *Jesus and Fat Tuesday, and Other Short Stories*, 1–16. Berkeley, CA: Creative Arts, 1987. Also in *The African American West*. Edited by B.A. Glasrud and Laurie Champion. Boulder: University Press of Colorado, 2000.

Cressy Pruitt, a 15-year-old rural black girl in 1880s Missouri, witnesses a train robbery on her hike to a neighbor's house. Later, the head of the bandits rapes her when he finds her alone in the fields. What begins in violence turns to an unlikely love affair between the two. The story ends several years later with Cressy's outlaw lover waving his manacled hand to her from a train as they see each other for, presumably, the last time.

534. McGinnies, William. "The Belated Christmas Train." *Ladies' Home Journal* 22 (Dec. 1904): 16.

In this story complete on one page, a train plods its way east across the Southwest the day before Christmas. The passengers are ornery at the train's tardiness, annoyed at the likelihood of missing connections that would take them to their homes and families for Christmas. The mood changes when the train halts for an obstruction on the track. Several of the passengers get off the train, and discover a burial service taking place in a nearby clump of trees. The deceased is a small child, and her parents are distraught. The pathetic scene unites the previously cantankerous passengers in a bond of Christian sympathy with the bereaved couple. (There is nothing like a dear little dead girl clutching a battered doll to bring strangers on a train to their religious sensibilities.)

535. McGivern, William P. "The Sound of Murder." In *My Favorite Mystery Stories*, edited by Maureen Daly, 70–85. New York: Dodd, Mead, 1966. Also in *Alfred Hitchcock Presents Stories to Be Read with the Door Locked*. New York: Random House, 1975. *Bluebook* 95 (Oct. 1952): 90+.

American foreign correspondent Adam James, riding the Orient Express, submits to the usual customs inspection at the Yugoslav border, then listens again, uncomprehending, to the angry argument between the man and the woman in the next compartment. The conductor tells Adam that he is not like most Americans, whom he finds impatient and excitable. Adam maintains his coolness when he deduces the guilty party in the murder of the woman in the adjoining compartment. (His deduction depends on a stereotype about women's communication habits, a stereotype that the conductor endorses.)

536. McHugh, Maureen F. "The Lincoln Train." In *The Best from Fantasy & Science Fiction: The Fiftieth Anniversary Anthology*, edited by Edward L. Ferman and G. Van Gelder, 329–343. New York: Tor, 1999. *Fantasy & Science Fiction* 88 (April 1995): 11–23.

In this alternate history, Abraham Lincoln has been gravely wounded but not killed by John Wilkes Booth. After the shooting, Union forces round up former slaveholders and send them by rail to exile in the Oklahoma territories. The story's narrator, young Clara Corbett, sees her mother trampled to death at the station before the forced boarding. The train trip is a nightmare of crowded chaos and confusion. Clara pounds on the train window, trying to attract the attention of someone outside who will give her the valise she dropped on the platform: "One of them glances up at me, frowning, but then he ignores me" (335). Quakers who have established a new underground railroad rescue Clara.

537. McHugh, Vincent. "Green River Train." *Atlantic Monthly* 177 (June 1946): 116–118. Also in *Short Story Craft: An Introduction to Short Story Writing*. Edited by Lillian B. Gilkes. New York: Macmillan, 1949.

Sometimes when two trains pass, passengers on one can look out their windows and see the faces of those going in the opposite direction, looking out their own windows. In this story, two trains, one a troop train, one carrying civilians, meet in the night and stop abreast of each other in a remote Utah town. The soldiers have left the European Theater and are on their way to fight in the Pacific. Some of the eastbound passengers, including a war correspondent and his wife, get off their train and stretch their legs in the space between the trains. The correspondent, who has spent time in the Pacific, observes the soldiers and listens to their aimless talk and minor bickering. He watches a solder make a gentle gesture toward a young woman whose husband is missing in action. Soon the trains continue their journeys. The sense of lives passing each other in a fleeting, insensible manner is mitigated by the contact between the passengers, by the soldier's kindness to the bereaved woman, by the correspondent's meditation—and by a soldier's tune—"Green River"—on his guitar. There is more here than anonymous faces flashing past in the glass.

538. McKay, Claude. "Truant." In *Calling the Wind: Twentieth Century African-American Short Stories*, edited by Clarence Major, 39–49. New York: HarperCollins, 1993. Also in *American Negro Short Stories*. Edited by John H. Clarke. New York: Hill & Wang, 1966. First published in McKay's *Gingertown*. New York and London: Harper & Bros., 1932.

Barclay, a West Indian Harlem resident, is 36, university-educated, and a railroad waiter who feels like nothing but a servant boy. He lives with his wife, Rhoda, and their four-year-old in a small apartment; they rent one of their three rooms to a railroad porter.

Barclay reports to work at Penn Station at 6 A.M., "A dutiful black boy among proud and sure white men, so that he could himself be a man in Harlem with purchasing power for wife, child, flat, movie, food, liquor..." (41). Petty thievery among waiters and cooks distresses Barclay. He worries about his daughter's education. And what would she do with it? "Perhaps marry a railroad waiter ... and raise up children to carry on the great tradition of black servitude" (42).

Barclay had always been honest and reliable, but on one ugly run from New York to Washington, D.C., he grows disgusted with his own regular ways, and fails to report for the train's departure from D.C. The railroad suspends him for 10 days—his first break from work in three years. One evening while Rhoda is out, Barclay reflects on his arrival in the city, his attendance at a Negro university, and his work with the railroad, which he had never given serious thought. Considering it deeply for the first time, he realizes that the railroad called to his youthful energy. "There was a rude poetry in the roar and rush and rattle of trains, the sharp whistle of engines and racing landscapes, the charm of a desolate mining town and glimpses of offices lost as soon as seen" (48). Barclay achieves an epiphany regarding his marriage, his "social position," and the "eternal inquietude" that might constitute his true life. His insight leads him to a dramatic action.

539. McLarn, Jack. "Beanery Queen." *Railroad Magazine* 66 (Oct. 1955): 66–71. *Railroad Magazine* 99 (March 1976): 37–40.

Matt Hale, engine house clerk, has two things on his mind: the 20 pounds he must gain to qualify for a fireman's job, and Sally Norton, the dreamy counter worker at a popular railroaders' eatery. He has just stood up Sally for a date as a result of overtime work, and now he has another off-the-clock job to do for Trainmaster Bert Carney. Carney exploits Hale's desire to advance, but shows no inclination to reward his hard work—put off, apparently, by Hale's obsequiousness. When Hale stands up to Carney in an argument over what action to take in a flash flood that devastates the yards, he proves himself worthy of advancement—and of Sally Norton.

540. _____. "Dangerous Crossing." In *Tales of the Rails*, edited by Veronica Hutchinson, 190–210. Cleveland and New York: World Publishing, 1952. *Argosy*, Feb. 1949.

When the Valley Division's beloved superintendent dies, the company brings in a new man, Kenneth Disman, with a frosty attitude and a by-the-book mentality. MacQuillan, the trainmaster, anticipates unpleasantness. It comes quickly: "Hard, rigid, unaccustomed discipline settled down over the Valley Division like an evil fog" (195). Disman improves efficiency, but at a notable human cost. He orders MacQuillan to fire Pop Matthews, the road's oldest engineer, and an opponent of the new Diesel engines. Things look bleak, but valiant assistance to a little girl with polio forms the centerpiece of Disman's initiation into the human side of railroading. The story features a fistfight in an engine cab that in real life would probably leave both participants hospitalized, if not dead. In this man's world, it simply leaves them sore but emotionally bonded.

The story is representative of an underlying theme in this genre of railroad fiction calling for workers to be free to tend their jobs with latitude for their own judgment, rather than serving as automatons.

541. _____. "Trackside Grave." In *Great Railroad Stories of the World*, edited by Sam Moskowitz, 115–128. New York: McBride, 1954. *Railroad Magazine* 30 (Sept. 1941): 30–53. *Railroad Magazine* 65 (Nov. 1954): 22–24+.

Brandt Duncan, a trainman implicated for carelessness in the deaths of an engineer and fireman, is recalled from layoff during a burst of business. His fellow workers, although contemptuous of him, fought successfully to clear him, "because Duncan was then a brother trainman. You went to bat for a brother, right or wrong" (121). Duncan had apparently engaged in worse than carelessness: At one point, he had been involved in criminal enterprise. Railroading fiction offers a man, sometimes, a second chance. Duncan takes his, and gains legendary status through an act of self-sacrifice at the scene of a wreck. He dies in the act, and is buried in a place of honor alongside the track. Well-crafted genre fiction, the story makes a case for the popular belief that honor and redemption are available to the lowliest, if only they seize their opportunities when they arise.

542. _____. "Wreck Call—Emergency!" *Saturday Evening Post* 223 (April 7, 1951): 37+.

Narrator Willie Harrison thought he was a hotshot telegraph operator back at Grimes Junction, but his new post at Two Rivers gives him all he can handle, and then some. One night an old operator, Sealey, visits the office, does Willie a favor, and collapses. Willie takes him to his own boarding house to care for him. Recuperated, Sealey takes the dispatcher's job that Willie craves, until Sealey's past comes to light and Willie supplants him. Willie is a little awed by his new job. Studying his reports, he finds "the little black numbers" turning into "living, crawling things. There were people in them. People in the steel boxes on wheels.... And they put their trust in me, in

Willie Harrison, a kid dispatcher in a dingy little office" (134).

Willie commits a major dispatching blunder on Christmas morning, sending orders that will bring two trains together head-on. This is effective melodrama, with Sealey a self-sacrificing hero, apparently, and young Willie learning that confidence must be earned, not assumed.

543. _____. "Yardmaster." In *Great Railroad Stories of the World*, edited by Samuel Moskowitz, 229–248. New York: McBride, 1954. *Railroad Magazine* 63 (May 1954): 36–45.

A young woman assigned as a clerk to the yardmaster at the Morgan Yard quickly shows her management skill, to the chagrin of her know-it-all boss. The story threatens to break out of the mold of popular stereotype, but it is not hard to see what is coming: the businesslike young woman assuming her proper place in the sex role game. By story's end, she has fallen for the yardmaster. "Gosh, I wish I could be home cooking a steak for him," she says. Thus, the story's feint at upsetting convention folds into the heroine in the kitchen and the hero in the control tower, running the show.

544. McLaughlin, Robert. "A Short Wait between Trains." *New Yorker* 20 (June 17, 1944): 27–29. Also in *A Short Wait between Trains: An Anthology of War Short Stories*. Edited by Robert Bernard. New York: Delacorte, 1991.

Four black soldiers are passengers aboard a train pulling into a dreary textile mill town somewhere in the South. At the station, they see a group of German POWs, who do not appear much different from anyone else. Hungry, the soldiers ask a baggage handler if they can find a place to eat nearby. No luck: "Maybe you can get a handout someplace, but they sure no place for colored around here" (28). The four men obtain permission to eat in the station kitchen, provided they go outside and enter by the back door. While they wait for the black cook to prepare their food, they see the POWs, "relaxed and easy" in the station lunchroom, "lighting cigarettes, drinking water, taking rolls from baskets on their tables..." (29). One

of the soldiers, furious at the situation, stalks out of the kitchen without eating. Says the cook, "All the white folks around here is talking about all the nigger killing they going to do after the war. That boy, he sure to be one of them" (29). This simple story, well told, still delivers a blow to the reader 60 years after its first publication.

545. McMurtry, Larry. *Streets of Laredo*. New York: Simon & Schuster, 1993. 589p.

In this absorbing, if slow-moving, sequel to *Lonesome Dove*, Amarillo railroad accountant Brookshire has been assigned to hire a bandit killer. An effete Easterner, he has something like a panic attack at the dreary little train station when he and his newly-hired gun, former Texas Ranger Captain Woodrow Call, board the train for San Antonio. Everything about this passage, from Brookshire struggling with his hat in the wind to Call's understated kindness in rendering assistance, emphasizes the gulf in frontier know-how that separates the two men. Call's task is to eliminate the notorious bandit Joey Garza, who has been terrorizing trains in remote parts of the Southwest. Joey is a vicious, sociopathic killer who murders trainmen with no more provocation than a desire to try out his new rifle. His first train robbery is merely incidental to this rifle testing, but it inspires him to further, grander jobs. Eventually, Garza meets a fate that suits his nature. The railroad is for the most part in the background, but it serves as the basis for Garza's life of crime.

546. McPherson, James A. "On Trains." In *Hue and Cry*, 31–40. Boston: Little, Brown, 1969. Also in *Black American Short Stories: One Hundred Years of the Best*. Edited by John H. Clarke. New York: Hill & Wang, 1993.

The action in this story occurs entirely aboard a passenger train that has left Chicago, heading west across the plains. The focus rests on the crew members—the Pullman porter, the conductor, the bartender, and others who serve the passengers as they have so often before. Of special concern is the Pullman porter, a black man who has been working at his job for over

40 years. The moment of crisis comes when a female passenger objects to the porter's occupying the car while she and the other passengers sleep. Pressed for the source of her antipathy, she cries, "He's black! He's black!" (39). The woman finally decides to sit up in a coach all night, and the porter sleeps as always in the back of the Pullman, "his ear next to the buzzer in case someone should ring" (40). The story is a credible behind-the-scenes look at the black trainmen who display patient and polite endurance of their clients' stupidity and racism.

547. _____. "A Solo Song: For Doc." In *Hue and Cry*, 41–73. Boston: Little, Brown, 1969. Also in *The Workshop: Seven Decades of the Iowa Writers' Workshop*. Edited by Tom Grimes. New York: Hyperion, 1999.

Some people identify so strongly with their jobs that when their jobs disappear, so do they. This story of a dining car waiter—"a Waiter's Waiter"—draws an engrossing portrait of what it means to provide exemplary service aboard the train. It also shows how hard it is for those whose jobs are their lives to find a way to live when they retire.

The narrator, an old-line waiter in his 60s, tells a young summer temp about Doc Craft, a legendary Waiter's Waiter whose only real satisfaction comes from exercising his mastery of his position, including an encyclopedic knowledge of the railroad's rule book for waiters. The narrative illustrates the way the black waiters see themselves in relation to their mostly-white clientele, and presents a convincing insiders' view of the black trainmen's give-and-take, complaint, and sly machinations that passengers never recognize.

The ways of Doc and his fellow old-timers are doomed, and they know it. Following World War II, the railroads began to lose passengers to the airlines, and their officials regarded passenger service as a growing burden. Although urged to retire, Doc could not consider it. "I have to go out [on the train]," says Doc. "Going out is my whole life ... I ain't never missed a trip, and I don't mean to" (59). Doc is still working at 73, giving good service.

The story's climax concerns Doc's luncheon service to a surprise inspector determined to catch Doc in a slip-up the railroad can use as a pretext for demanding his retirement. McPherson achieves an astonishing tension in his description of Doc's serving the inspector an iced tea, a sandwich, and a bowl of soup. The story ends tragically, as any reader would know it must. "A Solo Song" addresses multiple themes, from race relations to the dignity of work well performed, from the problems of the aging worker to the decline of rail passenger service, and does it all with subtlety and deep insight. A fine, fine story.

548. Mealand, Richard L. "Girl on the Train." *Saturday Evening Post* 220 (Dec. 13, 1947): 29.

Jeff, a construction engineer, takes a fancy to a young woman he regularly sees on his New York commuter train. The story features typical train romance complications, including the hero's taking the 5:02 instead of the 5:31 to maximize chances of seeing the young woman; trying to save a seat for her in a crowded coach, and so on.

549. Means, David. "The Grip." In *Assorted Fire Events*, 69–80. New York: Context Books, 2000. *Antioch Review* 57 (Fall, 1999): 463–470.

"His intention, his sole intention, was to live through the night, to hold on" (73). Holding on is not an easy task: Young Jim is clinging to a precarious hold on the exterior of a freight bound for Santa Fe. The time is the Great Depression; "There were plenty of dead in that time of wandering" (80). Jim, exhausted and numb from holding onto the car as the train travels across the desert, is on the verge of letting go when a vision of his dead mother rescues him, and gives him the strength to endure the ride. A kind brakeman helps him when the train finally stops. The vision that saves Jim could easily have given the story a mawkish tone, but here it is credible and affecting.

550. _____. "Railroad Incident, August 1995." *Harper's* 295 (July 1997): 76–81. Also in Means's *Assorted Fire Events*. New York: Context Books, 2000.

In this grim story with suggestions of homosexual rape, a "dainty," neatly-dressed man leaves his car idling by the road and walks for miles along a railroad track near the Hudson River. After removing and setting aside his shoes, he cuts his heel badly on a shard of glass. Business and marital disasters hound him. Down the track he stumbles upon a quartet of young punks, who beat him savagely. "The spot where they hung out, just before the tracks carved a dark hole in the overflowing Cliffside, was strewn with old railroad debris, rails and tie plates and gobs of black tar and broken bottles..." (77–78). When the punks finish with their victim, they throw his unconscious body across the tracks, "an afterthought, a coda, a grand finish that would stand out as one of their great moves" (80).

The story has two endings, the second the credible one: A New York Central engineer sees the body on the tracks, and cannot avoid running over it with his train. The engineer carries the weight of the man's death around with him, unaware that the man died before the train sliced his remains into sections. In the end, the engineer toughs it out: "It was a good job, even if things weren't going the way they should in the world. It was a good, good job," he concludes (81), with a curious echo of the assertion in Jerome Bixby's story adapted for the *Twilight Zone*, "It's a *Good* Life."

551. Meekins, Lynn R. "Two Booms." *Harper's Weekly* 33 (Feb. 16, 1889): 130–131. Also in Meekins' *The Robb's Island Wreck, and Other Stories*. Chicago and Cambridge: Stone & Kimball, 1894.

Anthony Hoddle, a prosperous grocery merchant, comes to Salem City and invests heavily in local properties, having learned that the town is to become the terminus of the Prairie and Deep Water Railroad. "We shall become wealthy, famous, happy" (130), he tells his family, sounding a bit like Col. Sellers in *The Gilded Age* (Entry 847). Unlike Sellers, Hoddle shows a genius for speculation, and soon, thanks in large part to his work, Salem is a boom town. The locals bestow the sobriquet of "Colonel" upon him, and he runs his real es-

tate game with a free hand as the railroad approaches the city.

When a well-dressed stranger, J. Maximilian Ross, arrives on the scene, Col. Hoddle sizes him up as an easy mark, and engages him in a series of land purchases that the Colonel is sure are to his advantage. He discovers, however, that Ross is a far sharper man than he imagined; as an agent of the railroad, Ross creates a false boom in a neighboring town—sowing the impression that the railroad is changing its route—deflates the value of Salem property, snaps it up for the railroad—and persuades the Colonel's daughter to marry him. The con man is conned, and the greedy citizens of Salem get their railroad, as well as a little financial tutorial. A comical story quite likely inspired by *The Gilded Age*.

552. Meigs, Cornelia L. *Railroad West*. Boston: Little, Brown, 1937. 326p.

Philip Fox trudges through the northern Minnesota wilds to his first job, in 1870, on a survey party for the Northern Pacific Railroad, backed by financier Jay Cooke. Almost the first thing he sees when he reaches the construction site is an entire work train, with engine, disappearing into the black mud of a Minnesota swamp, leaving only the smokestack visible above the surface of the muck. Surveying proceeds with painful slowness, making it seem impossible that the job could reach across the continent, one stake at a time. The construction engineers, including Fox, work long hours trying to find ways to overcome the awesome obstacles of nature and the impatience of the money backing the railroad.

The story follows Fox and the other railroaders across the country, from Minnesota to North Dakota, through crises of weather and business, men straight and crooked, and Indian attacks—and on to the Rockies and the coast. This readable and believable historical novel includes actual historical figures among the purely fictional. (Fox sees Gen. George A. Custer, flush with victory following a battle with the Sioux, a few years before Custer's defeat at the Little Big Horn.) The Sioux, who make such difficulty for the railroad builders, receive more equitable treatment than one might expect in a celebration of railroading and Manifest Destiny. The emphasis on surveying rather than on locomotive hardware is an agreeable change-of-pace, and the sensibility of the time and place credibly drawn: Out in the wild, "This untrammeled space seemed utterly remote from all the despair and disillusionment, all the venomous differences of Reconstruction, all the political fraud and corruption which seemed to swarm so inevitably after the heels of a war. Room, room and to spare for the bold spirit of a new era" (69).

553. Merwin, Samuel. *The Road Builders*. New York: Macmillan, 1905. 313p.

Circa 1875, the S.&W. Railroad is officially the Sherman and Western, but is better known as the "Shaky and Windy." With its scant 35-pound rails and its wobbling finances, its nickname is apt. Construction engineer Paul Carhart has been engaged to complete the line to Red Hills, where it can connect with Eastern roads. Like a military officer, Carhart commands 1,000 men. In the haste to complete the work, "If the existing track was sketchy, the new track would be worse. Everything was to be sacrificed to speed" (33).

The story evokes the days of fierce competition among railroads for right-of-way. Carhart struggles with supplies (notably water, in the desert), and labor unrest: The men find their $1.50 per day pay unsatisfactory. Rather than being portrayed as noble laborers, the men under Carhart are very much normal working men in their up-and-down nature. An entire chapter goes to the crew's desperate search for water, with a persuasive scene of success as men and mules alike wallow in a pool in utter relief. Trouble with Apaches, horse thieves, and other staples of the genre peg this effort as a fairly routine railroad Western. It offers the occasional nugget of condescending racial and ethnic "insight": "It takes an Irishman, a nigger, and a mule to build a railroad.... The mule will do the work ... the nigger will drive the mule, and the Irishman'll boss 'em both" (37).

554. _____, and Henry K. Webster. *Calumet K*. 1901. Reprint, New York: Grosset & Dunlap, 1912. 345p. *Saturday Evening Post*: 173 (May 25, 1901): 1–3+; (June 1, 1901): 9–11; (June 8, 1901): 9–11; (June 15, 1901): 9–11+; (June 22, 1901): 10–11+; (June 29, 1901): 6–7; 174 (July 6, 1901): 6–7; (July 13, 1901): 8–9; (July 20, 1901): 8–9; (July 27, 1901): 8–9+; (Aug. 3, 1901): 8–9; (Aug. 10, 1901): 6–7; (Aug. 17, 1901): 12–13.

Materials for a huge grain elevator in Calumet, Illinois, to be delivered on cars owned by the G.&M. Railroad, have been languishing in a storage yard. Charlie Bannon deduces that the delay is deliberate, part of a complex scheme by a clique of speculators to corner the wheat market. Bannon has the material hauled by boat to the construction site; the local railroad, the C.&S.C., is balky about allowing construction workers to cross its tracks, adjacent the site. The railroad does not play a major part in the action; chiefly it hovers in the background with its uncooperative attitude. Bannon, representing a Minneapolis company, has more trouble with a corrupt labor organizer than with the railroad.

Calumet K was one of Ayn Rand's favorite books; she wrote an introduction for a 1967 edition. One can easily see why. The portrayals of a union man as a conniving weasel, laborers as tractable sheep waiting to be led by their noses, and a capitalist agent as heroic savior fit her worldview well.

555. _____. *The Short-Line War*. 1899. Reprint, Ridgewood, N.J.: Gregg Press, 1967. 334p.

Rescued from oblivion by Gregg Press as a selection in its Americans in Fiction Series, *The Short-Line War* remains a reasonably entertaining story of political intrigue, legal manipulation, and no-holds-barred turn-of-the-century capitalist confrontation.

The line in question is the Manchester and Truesdale Railroad, a single-track road of 200 miles between the cities in its name. The profitable coal mines along the route make it an attractive takeover target. Principals in the contest for the M.&T. are its president, Civil War veteran and Chicago-headquartered Jim Weeks, and his chief antagonist, William C. Porter, a competing road's vice president. Porter and his allies are gunning for the M.&T. Weeks receives loyal and faithful support from Harvey West, his personal secretary. Harvey,

26, "had yet to learn that in [railroad] dealing with a municipality or with a legislature, the law of success has but two prime factors, money and speed" (32). Harvey learns this lesson well by the novel's end.

Porter and company are trying to seize stock control of the M.&T. Their tactics range from the above-board to the under-handed and violent. Dirty work is a stranger to neither side in the battle, and includes the employment of a pliable judiciary; hired thugs; Pinkerton guards; a state senator with a penchant for revenge; kidnapping; and sundry other elements of bare-knuckle business brawling.

Stretches of vivid railroad action and trainman heroics leaven the novel's backroom and private-parlor intrigue. Supporting character Jawn Donahue, a nice example of the engineer hero, is of interest as he makes more than one critical appearance in the cab. Here, in one emergency, he takes off with Jim Weeks aboard Engine 11: "He knew old 'eleven,' every foot of her, every tube, bolt, and strap.... Old Jawn, perched upon his high seat, never shifted his eyes from the track ahead. His face wore the usual scowl, but betrayed no emotion.... He knew that he was the best engineer on the road..." (56–57).

After delivering Weeks to his destination, Donahue turns to the railroad president and addresses him plainly: "I brung ye a hundred and three mile in eighty-one minutes. There ain't another man on the line could 'a' done it" (58).

Also of interest is Porter's daughter, Katherine, a surprisingly strong character who refuses to submit to the notion that railroading and its peripherals are strictly a man's business. Katharine is a complicating romantic interest for young West, but insists on being treated like something other than a household decoration. "Why is it," she asks, demanding information about the details of the M.&T. deal, "that a man never credits a woman with common sense? I am not blind" (162). Nor do Merwin and Webster portray her as if she were.

556. Merz, Charles. "Millie Turner." In *Centerville, U.S.A.*, 175–192 New York: Century, 1924. Published as "Millie

Turner Waits for Jim." *Collier's* 74 (Aug. 30, 1924): 22+.

The depot lunchroom waitress at a small-town railroad stop falls in love with a yellow-haired engineer, but rejects him years later. Millie Turner is close to marrying Jim Holden when she learns of his long-vanished first wife. Holden goes west to resolve the obstacle, but years pass before he again sets foot in Millie's lunchroom. In the meantime, the old depot staff and hangers-on move on, but Millie remains, gaining age, weight, and bitter wisdom.

557. Millar, Kenneth [Ross Macdonald]. *Trouble Follows Me.* New York: Dodd, Mead, 1946. 206p. Also published as *Night Train.* New York: Lion Books, 1955.

In the long middle passage in this mystery, several principals, including chief character Ensign Sam Drake, travel by train from Chicago to California. The trip entails some dedicated alcohol consumption, a substantial amount of flirting, and the exchange of uninspired conversation among strangers pressed together on the crowded train as it crawls across the continent. The journey also features murder and attempted murder. The train passes through one undistinguished city after another, "cities that one saw for the first time with remembering [sic] boredom, and left immediately with relief.... I felt very sorry for all Topekans, whose city was a poor gathering of feeble lights in the immense darkness of the hemisphere" (98–99).

Drake's companion, Mary, does not share his cynicism; she reflects on how the passengers she saw on trains in the Depression "were like kings and queens on thrones" behind their lighted windows; "It gives me a feeling of power to ride across the country and leave the rest of the world sitting" (99).

Drake, for good reason, becomes convinced that a killer is on the train—a killer who intends to include him among his victims. An interesting racial angle develops as Drake enlists the porter Edwards in obtaining information about a subversive black organization in Detroit. Drake first approaches Edwards to find him closely reading a copy of the *Atlantic Monthly*. Edwards initially plays an Amos &

Andy stereotype, but when he realizes that Drake takes him seriously, his "darky" accent vanishes, and he assists Drake capably. Their conversation over, Drake watches Edwards return to work, and sees him change his demeanor from that of the intelligent, literate man he is to one fit for the prejudiced assumptions of the white passengers: "His personality shrank to fit the smooth black shell which white opinion has hopefully constructed for Negroes to live in" (126).

Later, Mary says, "A train journey has a funny effect on me.... I feel cut off from the real world, isolated and irresponsible. The time I spend on a train is like an interlude from real life" (136). When the train reaches Los Angeles, Drake gets out, feeling that he is "climbing out of a tight little hell into an unpredictable chaos" (144).

558. Miller, Heather Ross. "Depot Street." *Crescent Review* 10, no. 2 (1992): 70–76.

This reflective story of a woman's relationship with her mother shifts perspectives and times, from the 1940s to the present, and from the narrator, Laramie, as a young girl to Laramie as a 50-year-old woman. In her childhood, her mother instructed her to avoid Depot Street, site of the long-closed and dilapidated local railroad station. Of course, then, Laramie felt obligated to sneak over to Depot Street to watch the freight trains pass. In a ruined garden near the station, where travelers used to rest, she cleaned out an old birdbath so that it could fill with rain, and had imaginary conversations with the "mean men" her mother had warned her against. At the end, her mother having succumbed to a heart attack, Laramie imagines returning to the garden with her mother.

559. Miller, May M. *First the Blade*. New York: Knopf, 1938. 631p.

This long historical novel follows the lives of California settlers in the second half of the 19th century, chiefly from the point of view of Amelie McNeil, of an Irish immigrant family. Most of the novel lacks a railroading focus, but the author compensates for this lack in the book's final quarter, whose climactic action concerns the abuse of Amelie's family and their fellow California settlers by the El Dorado

Pacific Railroad. Miller appears to lean heavily on events in Frank Norris's *The Octopus* (Entry 598). The railroad reneges on contracts with the settlers concerning improvements they make on railroad-owned land that they have been farming, with the understanding that they could purchase the land at an original per-acre price, regardless of improvements. The railroad's faithless conduct results in the settlers' inability to buy the land to which they had committed themselves.

"This great El Dorado Pacific, so wealthy, owning more power than any company in the nation had ever owned ... this imperial force..." (422) treats the settlers with contempt, charging them sometimes as much as ten times more for the land than the contracts stipulated. When the settlers cannot pay, the railroad dispossesses them: "Then they just began to move things out, furniture, beds, everything. They carried out the stove with the fire in it" (501).

Miller chooses up sides in this conflict without reservation. One can practically hear the cruel laughter of mustache-twirling railroad functionaries as they wreak havoc upon the poor settlers: "...talk about Ireland being oppressed by landlords," says one victim; "they have many, many landlords, while we have only one. The El Dorado Pacific is that landlord.... they cast their helpless victims—women and children and babes—out into the road without warning" (509).

The action devolves into a gunfight between a federal marshal and his men, acting on behalf of the railroad, and a group of settlers. A number of settlers die, and others are convicted for their efforts to make an end run around a legal system that will provide them no relief. The settlers' best efforts to enlist the law in their quest for justice come to naught; as one of the Scandinavian-descended victims says, "You yust can't buck a railroad" (548). Or, as Norris puts it in *The Octopus*, "You can't buck against the Railroad."

560. Millett, Larry. *Sherlock Holmes and the Red Demon*. 1996. Reprint, New York: Penguin, 2001. 334p.

This must for Sherlock Holmes fans is purportedly the text of a lost manuscript by Dr. John Watson, discovered by an electrician while working in the library of the James J. Hill mansion in St. Paul, Minnesota, in 1994. The manuscript reveals the astonishing visit to Minnesota, a hundred years earlier, of the great detective Holmes and his companion, Dr. Watson. They came at the call of railroad magnate Hill, whose rail empire was being threatened by a diabolical villain. Responding to the summons from Hill—and the promise of a very large fee—Holmes and Watson cross the Atlantic, and take the train to Minnesota. The culprit is an arsonist, aiming to torch the pine forests so crucial to the welfare of Hill's freight operations.

In this fast-reading tale, the climax comes with Holmes and Watson caught in the great Hinckley fire of 1894, a conflagration in which some 400 people died, and which, for the novel's purposes, was the work of Hill's antagonist, the Red Demon. The rescue-by-train of the fortunate among Hinckley's citizens is a high point in the book. Numerous endnotes heighten the sense of historical scholarship and the conceit of the "lost manuscript," as does the inclusion of such historical figures as Joseph G. Pyle, James J. Hill, Angus Hay, and William Best, the heroic engineer who saved as many Hinckley residents as he could.

Milligan, Jean *see* **Harding, Allison V.**

561. Mills, John Paul. "Vanishing Tail Lights." In *Tales of the Rails*, edited by Veronica Hutchinson, 301–311. Cleveland and New York: World Publishing, 1952. *Railroad Magazine* 35 (March 1944): 116–120.

This compact story compresses into its few pages two railroad careers, those of telegraph operator Sam Gilmartin, and eventual division superintendent Thomas Hardwicke. It opens in 1919, with Gilmartin instructing his first assistant, then 18-year-old Hardwicke, a raw and apprehensive lad. Twenty years later, Gilmartin is about to retire, and he dwells on a note of appreciation he has received from Hardwicke. The story offers a good portrait of the effects of time and compassion bestowed on a neophyte. (The lights referred to in the title belong to the first train for which Hardwicke

issues orders—in writing so cramped by anxiety that it is barely legible.)

562. Mitchell, Edmund. "Tantalus of Thirty-Seven." *Sunset* (Central West Edition) 29 (Oct. 1912): 415–429.

In November, the hobo fraternity is heading for California, "a mendicant swarm twenty thousand strong" (416). The hoboes are battling the railroads, and orders have gone out to crack down on illicit riders. The hoboes survive on wit, stealth, and the occasional bribe, "But the conductor as a rule is the flint-hearted and implacable foe of the stealer of free transportation" (416). Yuma subdivision conductor Tim Flannigan expresses a special hobo loathing, one that his engineer, Teddy Blake, dismisses as not truly felt. Nevertheless, Flannigan has been the scourge of hoboes riding No. 37, the 8 A.M. freight out of Gila. One hot December day on the Colorado desert, Flannigan runs into a defiant little hobo who makes a fool of him. Through the run, the acrobatic fellow eludes Flannigan, much to the amusement of other trainmen. Flannigan loses a standing wager as a result of not apprehending the hobo, but is secretly glad that the hobo eluded him, and is "not lying out cold and hungry and thirsty under the gleam of the desert stars" (429).

The story possesses a two-reeler chase-comedy quality that relieves its sentimentality to beneficial effect.

563. Monteleone, Thomas F. *Night Train.* New York: Pocket Books, 1984. 337p.

This horror-mystery-thriller hinges on an engaging premise: that a New York City subway train disappeared somewhere below the city in 1915, and, with its dozen passengers and motorman, was never heard from again. The reader deduces quickly that Something Nasty lurks down there, deep in the bowels of the city. Does it have anything to do with the "Subway Slasher," a serial killer now stalking the system? Lya Marsden, a television news reporter, begins to poke around in the subway's management and history. An interview with an old conductor confirms her suspicions of unnatural events in the tunnels. There are, indeed, evil things down in the subway, things that would have felt comfortable slithering from the pen of H.P. Lovecraft. Even if the novel sometimes lapses into the sort of prose that announces important developments with the alarm, "Then it happened!" it is enjoyable escapist fare. Subway riders may not wish to read it while on the train.

564. Morley, Christopher D. *Human Being*. Garden City, NY: Doubleday, Doran, 1934. 350p.

This life story of the late publisher Richard Roe includes a chapter titled "The Railway Guide," describing Roe's fascination at the start of his career in the early 1900s with a directory, *The Official Guide of the Railways and Steam Navigation Lines of the United States, Canada, Mexico and Cuba*. The chapter is little more than a recitation of colorful railroad names, exotic (to the New York City-bound Roe) towns, and train designations. "And after passing through Scandinavia, Plover, Independence, Arcadia, you would be in Winona ... even more thrilling, see the dotted line across Lake Michigan, the 'car ferry' (magic sound) to Ludington. That would lead on toward White Cloud, Owosso, Saginaw, Ann Arbor. Names read in newspapers or seen in the office files or overheard in salesmen's talk became suddenly real" (99). Roe's fascination with the directory helps reveal his calling as a born salesman, a life that, although well-rooted in New York City, covers a wide swath of the nation.

565. _____. "Omnia Vincit Amor." In *Hostages to Fortune*, 23–25. Haverford, PA: Haverfordian, 1925.

Buck Hoskins, telegraph operator at Pewee Junction, New Mexico, reads Balzac in slack times. One hot day a boy rolls into the junction on a hand-car and collapses on the platform. Soon after Hoskins has splashed water in the boy's face he must rescue a young woman from assault by a hobo, and then from angry reprisal from her father, who also shows up at the junction on a hand-car. The story's locus in the author's undergraduate work is evident in its loopy silliness, but the matter of the hobo in the refrigerator car is an agreeably absurd touch.

566. Morris, Wright. *The Huge Season*. 1954. Reprint, Lincoln: University of Nebraska Press, 1975. 306p.

In this complex book with twin narrative lines, Latin professor Peter Foley struggles with the vacuity of life, the death of a friend, with his memories of coming of age in the 1920s (the "huge season" of the title), and with the specter of the hearings being conducted by Sen. Joe McCarthy. Feeling ground down by the emptiness of it all, Foley ponders suicide, and with that thought in mind, at Penn Station carries a gun onto a train in his trench coat. His meditations aboard the train lead him to step out onto the rear platform, where he tosses the gun over the railing into the river below. Earlier in the book Morris describes Foley approaching Penn Station on the train though a hellish landscape; he looks at his reflection in the coach window and sees "the Devil's horned profile and his leering smile of good fellowship" (77).

567. Morrison, Toni. *Sula*. 1974. Reprint, New York: Knopf, 1999. 174p.

In this novel's second chapter, set in 1920, Helene Wright and her daughter Nel take the train south to visit Helene's ill grandmother. They board in Medallion, Ohio, accidentally entering a whites-only car. Helene, a proud woman, rather than stepping off the car leads her daughter the white car's length. The conductor apprehends them as they enter the "Colored Only" car. "What you think you doin,' gal?" he demands (20). The demeaning word "gal" triggers deep feelings of shame in Helene, owing to details of her past, and she all but grovels before the sour conductor. She apologizes, slips into slovenly English, and then, to Nel's embarrassment and the disgust of the nearby black passengers who witness her action, Helene gives the conductor a blatantly flirtatious grin, as though appealing to him with sexual submissiveness. Nel vows that she will ever be on her guard so that she is not trapped into such humiliating behavior. When Helene and Nel take their seats in the Colored Only car, not a man moves to help Helene with her baggage, so off-putting did they all find her obsequious posturing before the conductor.

568. Mosler, Blanche Yvonne. "Railroad Town." *Railroad Magazine* 25 (March

1939): 24–32. *Railroad Magazine* 80 (Jan. 1967): 32–36.

The year is 1916. Cedar City's constant dark pall of smoke marks it as a railroad town. Railroader or not, nearly everyone's living in town depends on the railroad. Life is better for railroaders than in the old days, but many of the younger ones have forgotten the sacrifices their predecessors made, through strikes and hardship, to win better pay and working conditions. In 1916, the Brotherhood is still pressing for an eight-hour day; the threat of a strike clouds the town, and the nation. A young locomotive fireman and his girlfriend agonize over what will happen to them if a strike hits. The story draws on actual events, culminating in Woodrow Wilson's successful pressure on Congress to pass the Adamson Act in 1916. The act headed off a potentially crippling railroad strike by establishing the eight-hour day for trainmen, a work period that became generally accepted.

569. Mott, Frank Luther. "The Freight Whistles In." In *Five Stories*, 61–83. Iowa City, IA: Prairie Press, 1962. First published in *The Midland*.

Mrs. Shultz visits her neighbor, the widow Mrs. Baines, one spring day. The railroad tracks are visible through Mrs. Baines's open front door, at the end of her yard. Mrs. Baines likes living by the railroad, and freely feeds the hungry tramps who stop by her house. That is what prompts Mrs. Shultz's mission: At the behest of the Ladies Aid, she seeks to persuade Mrs. Baines to desist offering food to the tramps. While the busybody Mrs. Shultz sputters, a tramp comes to the door, filthy with the grit of riding the rails. Mrs. Baines welcomes him, convinced that the tramp is her own wandering son, Tommy, whom she has not seen in years. She is correct, and what ensues is a conversation in which mother and son discuss "Tommy" with the pretense that they are speaking of a third, absent person.

Sentimental beyond reasonable belief, the story nevertheless achieves an undeniable emotional effect, thanks to the author's manipulation of a timeless archetype: the return of the prodigal (or, at least, the lost) son.

570. Muheim, Harry. "The Train to Trouble." *Colorado Quarterly* 2 (Summer 1954): 368–383.

A man may think himself safely isolated from the world, but the train brings the world to him, and returns him to it. On the North California Railroad, there is only one train, McNally's, headed by a stubby, old engine. It makes regular stops at the Bell Springs station—which amounts to little more than a platform—where Sam Patterson serves as station master. Sam has foregone the demands of an executive career in San Francisco, and is happy at Bell Springs, able to let the world alone. The world intrudes one day when McNally drops off a water pump part for Sam; in the downstate newspaper in which the part is wrapped, Sam sees a disturbing article about an old acquaintance he had thought dead, and whose undeniable existence forces Sam to risky action.

571. Mulford, Clarence E. "The Holdup." In *The Railroaders*, edited by Bill Pronzini and Martin H. Greenberg, 19–37. New York: Fawcett Gold Medal, 1986.

The author created one of the most famous fictional cowboys in American popular culture, Hopalong Cassidy. In this story published in 1913, Hoppy and the boys from the Bar-20 ranch are taking a train home after escorting a herd of cattle to the city. They play cards, joke, and grumble about the train's rough ride, and listen to a trainman's account of a recent holdup. The boys scoff at the railroaders' feeble defense of the train—and soon find themselves merrily engaged in fighting off a gang of bandits. A jolly bonhomie marks the style of Hoppy and his six-shootin' pals; their struggle against robbery and murder suggests that the Wild West was good, clean fun. As Hoppy concludes after leaving the train, "Won't th' fellers home on th' ranch be a whole lot sore when they hears about the good time they missed!" (37)

572. Muro, Amado [Seltzer, Chester]. "Blue." In *The Collected Stories of Amado Muro*, 113–117. Austin, TX: Thorp Springs Press, 1979. *Arizona Quarterly* 27 (Spring 1971): 74–78.

Amado Muro, whose sensitive stories of Mexican life earned widespread respect as faithful depictions of the people and their sensibilities, was in reality Chester Seltzer, son of a Cleveland newspaper editor. His masquerade was, in a sense, only on the surface, for he lived the life he depicted in his stories, marrying a Mexican woman and riding the rails of the Southwest until his death in 1971. For more details on Muro, see Lou Rodenberger's essay, "The Southern Border," at http://www2.tcu.edu/depts/prs/amwest/html/wl0622.html

In this story, the narrator meets another hobo in a Mississippi town that shows no warmth toward drifters: "The towners are clannish and they don't cater to freight train stiffs," says the other man (113). He limps, and has a dog named Blue. Blue keeps watch when the man sleeps in boxcars. The men build a fire and sit beneath an oak tree in a hobo jungle while they wait for a train to hop to go to Louisiana. The man with the dog is hungry; when the narrator offers to buy him food, he declines. "I'd be uncommonly grateful if you was to get some dog food for Blue, though," he says (117).

573. _____. "The Gray-Haired Man." In *The Collected Stories of Amado Muro*, 156–160. Austin, TX: Thorp Springs Press, 1979.

A gray-haired man with one arm shows the narrator the way to the railroad yards. Both are hoboes. The one-armed man describes his lack of skill at begging, and discusses the prospects for catching a train. At length, he tells the story of his missing arm: In Seattle, he fell between the cars, and the train ran over him. "I saw a car knocker and a brakeman turn their faces away when the wheels went over it, but I didn't moan or cry out" (16). Later, he did.

574. _____. "Hobo Jungle." In *The Collected Stories of Amado Muro*, 107–112. Austin, TX: Thorp Springs Press, 1979. *Arizona Quarterly* 26 (Summer 1970): 158–163.

The narrator jumps off a freight on a cold winter day with a companion nicknamed Rails, owing to his once having worked on the railroad. They stop in a hobo jungle where an old black man is cooking lima beans. Soon the cook's friend, Big Snead, steps into view from the brush; he took cover fearing that the new arrivals were railroad bulls. The men talk quietly around the fire. A train stops nearby and changes crews. When the beans are done, Big Snead tells the visitors to help themselves, because "color don't matter" (112), and he splits a loaf of bread four ways.

575. _____. "Hobo Sketches." In *The Collected Stories of Amado Muro*, 91–96. Austin, TX: Thorp Springs Press, 1979. *Arizona Quarterly* 20 (Winter 1964): 355–360.

Muro presents several quick slices of hobo life. A Mexican porter in San Antonio gives the narrator money for food; the narrator rides in a gondola out of the Southern Pacific yards at Lordsburg : "Scorching air, bugs, and cinders lashed our faces" (92); he chats with an old black drifter in a jungle; he scores a free meal at a Mexican woman's shack; he eats beans and hot peppers at a Skid Row mission; he sleeps in a car in Los Angeles; he hangs out under a viaduct with a bearded hobo who smokes wrapping paper; and he listens in Fresno to a work gang boss blather about what "a good Christian" a vineyard owner is (96). The fast changes of scene go past like little film clips, like the steady-rolling life of the man on the road.

576. _____. "Homeless Man." In *The Collected Stories of Amado Muro*, 150–155. Austin, TX: Thorp Springs Press, 1979.

The narrator jumps off a Texas and Pacific boxcar. Another, tall hobo follows him along the tracks toward Odessa. The tall hobo offers to get the narrator some coffee, who reciprocates by offering the tall man the blanket he found in a boxcar. They go to the tall man's campfire, near an overgrown spur track, and share a pot of boiled coffee. The tall man, 65 years old, speaks of his hopes of going home to Missouri in the summer, and qualifying for a state pension that will allow him to "live so I don't have to jump from my own shadow" (155).

577. _____. "Hungry Men." *Arizona Quarterly* 23 (Spring 1967): 34–38. Also in *The Collected Stories of Amado Muro*. Austin, TX: Thorp Springs Press, 1979.

Two hoboes wait for a Southern Pacific freight; one of them last ate three days earlier at a Bakersfield mission. "The Bible guys give you two bowls of soup there if you swallow the first one in a hurry," he says (34). In the story's next vignette, the narrator comes into Cleveland on a boxcar on a brutal, cold night. He meets a one-armed hobo boiling coffee in a jungle. A passenger train goes by; they see men smoking in a club car. The one-armed man describes his earlier life, when he was a hard worker, not a beggar, before losing his arm. He lost the arm when he fell between two trains; the railroad gave him $600 when he left the hospital. "I never had six hundred dollars before," he says (38)—and it is unlikely that he will ever see that much at one time again. Like Muro's other hobo stories, this one is a stark picture of men only slightly on this side of the line between survival and death.

578. _____. "Night Train to Fort Worth." *Arizona Quarterly* 23 (Autumn 1967): 250–254. Also in *The Collected Stories of Amado Muro*. Austin, TX: Thorp Springs Press, 1979.

Two hoboes ride a Texas and Pacific freight through a snowy night, on their way to Fort Worth. The ride is rough. One of the men, Sticks, has one leg and a set of crutches. He describes selling blood plasma, and what a good deal that is. Sticks speaks matter-of-factly about his hard life. "I been on the rail all my life," he says. "I got to hear that train rolling and the wheels clicking" (251). The reader gathers some true sense of the narrow dimensions of Sticks's life. He closes the story with thoughts of Sioux City: "They pay twenty dollars a pint for O-positive blood there" (254). One suspects that there is a less draining way to raise meal money, but imagining so seems beyond Sticks.

579. _____. "Road Buddy." *Arizona Quarterly* 22 (Autumn 1966): 269–273. Also in *The Collected Stories of Amado Muro*. Austin, TX: Thorp Springs Press, 1979.

The narrator climbs aboard a fast-moving Southern Pacific flatcar in Arizona. A burly hobo already on the car helps him up. The narrator—whom the big hobo dubs Pancho—is sick with hunger, and feverish. The big fellow gives him water and advice, and when the train stops in Casa Grande he scrounges up deposit bottles to raise money for food for Pancho. Pancho asks him why he takes such good care of him. "Pancho, a stiff ain't himself when he's hungry—he's liable to steal.... And I wouldn't want to see a young field tramp do that when I could make a hustle to help him" (273). The story is realistic and unsentimental, but touching in its depiction of two down-and-outers.

580. _____. "Something About Two Hoboes." In *The Collected Stories of Amado Muro*, 97–101. Austin, TX: Thorp Springs Press, 1979. *Arizona Quarterly* 25 (Summer 1969): 120–124.

The narrator relates two vignettes. In the first, he meets an arthritic old hobo on a boxcar. As the train rolls, the old man describes his struggles to survive. "I'll tough it out, and see what God says," he mumbles (100). In the next piece, in a jungle near the Southern Pacific yards, an old hobo with a bum arm shares mulligan stew with the narrator and praises his blind buddy, the Dutchman. "I'm the luckiest man in all the world to have a friend like the Dutchman," he says (101), even though most would find it hard to identify any "luck" in his Spartan, uncertain life.

581. Murray, Albert. *Train Whistle Guitar*. 1974. Reprint, Boston: Northeastern University Press, 1989. 183p.

Gambling, playing guitar, and riding the rails were the only habits anyone knew Luzanna Cholly possessed. Folks in Gasoline Point, Alabama, also said Cholly was crazy, although not in the out-of-his-mind mode. The narrator, Scooter, who has always had Cholly in his thoughts, believes they mean a "polite madness" (14). One day Scooter and his pal Little Buddy hop a northbound freight, eager to emulate their mythic hero, Cholly. Cholly intercepts the boys a few miles up the line, and embarrasses them by picking them up bodily and setting them on a southbound back to Gasoline Point. He rides with the boys, and gives them some wisdom before he snags another train and says goodbye. The railroad then falls from focus as the novel moves on to show Scooter's family life and maturation, but in the background is always Luze Cholly, a prototypical wandering bluesman who wants to see his young admirers grow up well and prosper.

582. Murray, W.H.H. "A Ride with a Mad Horse in a Freight Car." In *Short Story Classics; American.* Vol. 1, edited by William Patten, 283–304. New York: P.F. Collier, 1905.

The narrator was a major in a Massachusetts infantry unit in the Civil War. At the battle of Malvern Hill, a beautiful riderless horse stood above him after he was wounded. He named her Gulnare, and took her with him when he went to recover in a Washington hospital. The horse stayed with him throughout the war. The narrator hired a boxcar to ship Gulnare to his home at war's end, and shared the car with her on the trip. On the journey, Gulnare was afflicted with some dreadful ailment—brain inflammation, diagnosed the major—and went berserk in the boxcar. The major feared for his life as the great horse flailed and dashed about in the car.

There is some genuine pathos in this story, as well as sympathetic fear at the idea of being trapped in a confined space, with one's life threatened by a trusted creature.

583. "My Pickpocket." *Harper's Weekly* 10 (June 2, 1866): 350.

Miss Howard, about to embark on a train journey, receives pointed counsel from her friend Miss Borey about the prevalence of pickpockets who prey on naïve travelers. "They positively swarm on the lines of railroad," she says; "Why, every station-house on every road in the land has its sign up, Beware of Pickpockets ... and *they* know what they are about, those railroad men." Polite, genteel, and handsome young men are especially dangerous. Miss Howard boards the train the next morning in agitation, and to her dismay sees a sign blurting a warning against pickpockets. Miss

Borey was right! A handsome young man sits down next to her in the crowded coach, and Miss Howard makes the predictable assumption about his intentions. When the train enters a long, dark tunnel, Miss Howard panics and makes a fool of herself. Fortunately, the young man understands, and a trainboard romance blooms. The anonymously-written story is funny and entertaining enough that one can shrug off the sentimental conclusion.

584. Mygatt, Gerald. "Seat in the Subway." *American Magazine* 108 (Dec. 1929): 18–19+.

Alicia, a former librarian, has come to New York City to get a job, not to get married, but men are on her mind. She works in a large store's book department; she rides the subway to and from work, and hates it: The train is stuffy, crowded, and smells bad. Capitalizing on subway riders' penchant for yielding seats to the handicapped, Alicia and a coworker pretend to be deaf mutes. The deceit works, and the other riders pity them enough to give them seats. The scam collapses when the young women are confronted by a handsome man who knows sign language. The train in this story serves as a convenient vehicle for the author to cook up a little romantic dish seasoned with a tidy moral.

585. Naparsteck, Martin. "The 9:13." In *The Deadliest Games: Tales of Psychological Suspense from Ellery Queen's Mystery Magazine,* edited by Janet Hutchings, 185–202. New York: Carroll & Graf, 1993. *Ellery Queen's Mystery Magazine* 99 (Feb. 1992): 68–83.

During the Gulf War, one snowy night two men wait for the 9:13 Amtrak at the Rochester, Wyoming, station. One of the men is an apparent escapee from a hospital for the criminally insane, but the reader cannot be sure which man the escapee is. Both exhibit odd behavior. One is anxious and awkward; the other is aggressive and demanding. They board the train when it arrives, over an hour late. The anxious man, Joe, is convinced that the other fellow, Eddie, is dangerous. Eddie is definitely dangerous, in ways that neither Joe nor the reader anticipates. Almost all the action in this taut little thriller occurs on an all-but empty Amtrak coach.

586. Nebel, Frederick. *Sleepers East*. Boston: Little, Brown, 1933. 282p.

Everett Jason, an auto dealer, is waiting for the train one winter night. His hovering mother pesters him about his teeth, his shoes, his socks, and his smoking habit. Jason is sanguine, however, for in his Gladstone bag he has $20,000 in cash to assist him in a flight from his mother, his job, his wife, and his life. On the train, free of his wife and mother, he indulges himself with whiskey in his compartment and an expensive meal in the dining car. Slightly intoxicated, he chatters foolishly to an attorney at his table. This is the beginning of "a strange flight among the stars" (281) for Jason, and a readable, noir soap opera aboard the train. Nebel peoples the novel with a wide range of characters, from Magowan, the engineer, who is making his last run before retirement, to a U.S. representative, a woman journalist, and an imperturbable and circumspect porter who has seen every variety of human behavior aboard the train. Murder, intrigue, accident, hard men, fast women, and some aggrieved railroaders keep the story moving toward Jason's late realization that on this train ride he has gone somewhere that he never expected to visit.

587. Neidig, William J. "Alibi." *Saturday Evening Post* 202 (April 12, 1930): 24–25+. Also in *The Best American Mystery Stories*. Edited by Carolyn Wells. New York: Albert & Charles Boni, 1931.

Insurance company jewel expert Donovan is taking an upper berth on the train from Chicago to Fort Wayne. When he learns that a notorious crook is also on board, and that a diamond robbery has just occurred, he enlists the aid of Conductor Garrick in solving the case. Not a gem of a story.

588. Nelson, Kent. "The Train through Dominguez Canyon." *Virginia Quarterly Review* 66, no. 3 (1990): 426–437.

The author leaves much unsaid in this account of a man, Mead, who has had a falling-out with his girlfriend, and is recovering from some of the effects of his own drunken stupidity. Mead's father was not a model of domestic reliability. A railroader, he taught Mead fly fishing, sometimes took him out inspecting tracks—and one day deserted his wife and son. Mead drinks too much. He retreats to the mountain wilds, hoping to escape his own thinking. One night, as he camps, he feels the faint vibrations of an approaching train. Eventually its headlight appears around a bend in a gorge; the train seems to be coming straight at him. He curls into himself, "shielding his head with his arms and his body" (437). It won't work: Even in the mountains, there is nowhere to hide from the train of one's own history.

589. Nelson, Victoria. "Main Train Station." *AGNI* 41 (1995): 108.

A tidy impressionistic piece posits a single main train station in a universal city, to which everyone who leaves must return. One can go anywhere from the main station, "but you always come back. There is no way except the way through main train station," and regardless of the length of your trip, "you'll soon be back" (108). If the traveler's fate here sounds rather like that of the visitor to the Hotel California in the Eagles' song of that title, it is probably intentional.

590. Nevins, Frank J. *A Yankee Dared*. Chicago: O'Sullivan, 1933. 405p.

This historical novel's opening section describes the DeWitt Clinton's inaugural run. Apprehensiveness is rampant, with fears abroad that the infernal machine will explode, and send to glory a number of prominent citizens. Balancing the anxiety are boosterish visions of the railroad opening up "our wonderful West to the homesteaders that are only hesitating here in the East" (43). Indeed, all does not go well as the pioneer locomotive gets under way: Particles of burning pine, flung from the engine's stack, fall onto the passengers and ignite their clothing. It is but a momentary lapse in the great march of Progress. This work formed the basis for the 1950 film, *The Rock Island Trail*. It explores railroad planning and building in the Midwest, with rail competition with riverboats perhaps its most interesting aspect. Nevertheless, the book displays some of the worst attributes of the historical novel, including a tendency for characters to make speeches about the shape of things to come as though they possess great insight— "Railroads are destined to become the warp and woof of our nation" (215)—when what they actually possess is nothing but the author's knowledge of historical events. The writing is also of the sort in which people "ejaculate" their statements, rather than merely saying them.

591. Newbury, Penny. "Joan on the Train." *Descant* (Texas) 34, no. 1 (1994): 12–15.

The narrator's mother, Joan, annually took her two daughters and a high-school drama class to see an off-Broadway play in New York. They went by train, because Joan knew trains, loved Union Station, and could get everyone to the city and back successfully. Joan liked to talk to strangers on the train. In time, Joan began having mental difficulties; she would take off on a train to an undisclosed location, and return with exclamations about her wonderful "adventure." "That's what you're supposed to do: just get on a train and go," she said (15). The narrator closes with a remark on how she would rush to the station, now, if her mother called her for a ride home. Indications are that this is a call that will not come.

592. Newell, David M. "The Tollivers & David Does It." In *The Trouble of It Is*, 168–173. New York: Knopf, 1978.

This story, a chapter in the saga of the Driggers, of Withalacoochee, North Carolina, is an amusing version of the rube dealing with the stuff of civilization. The Driggers are a Carolina hill country clan. Billy Driggers narrates the book in a convincing local dialect. Here, young David Driggers visits the Tollivers in Rocky Mount. A good part of the story involves seeing David off on the train to Rocky Mount. Complaints surface about the distance to the sleeping car as the train waits at the station, fellow passengers and their annoying habits. David gives an account, on his return home, of his romantic escapade aboard train with a college dropout. "I'll tell you now," he says, "if you ain't done it in one of them sleepin' cars, you ain't done it!" (73).

Newell, Robert H. *see* Kerr, Orpheus C.

593. Newell, William V. "Railway Law." *Sunset* (Central West Edition) 52 (June 1924): 48–50.

An old Indian woman sells "authentic" Navajo and Hopi artifacts, most of them manufactured back East, to the passengers at a railroad platform. The railroad news agent cheats her of her rightful price for a true Indian ware—a woven basket. Some hilarity follows as the train pulls out, leaving the old woman in a fury on the platform. It happens that Tom Adams, the son of the local Indian agent, is on the train, and steps in to assert justice: "I'm not going to see these people robbed by any greasy train-butcher," he says (49). Adams makes good on this assertion, and so impresses the railroad's general attorney that he wins a job in that official's office.

594. Newmark-Shpancer, Brittany. "Lost Train." *Gettysburg Review* 3, no. 4 (1990): 728–735.

The narrator, an American elementary school teacher, reflects on her deceased grandmother, who appears to her as a ghost in her kitchen. The old woman was a survivor of the Holocaust; the narrator relates her grandmother's account of being hauled away by train from Warsaw with a crowd of Jews—bound, perhaps, for the concentration camp of Maidanek or Auschwitz. The old woman tells a fantastic story of the train's becoming "lost," and its occupants settling in a forest, at the end of the track, for the war's duration. It is evident that the old woman's imagination was the chief tool of her survival.

595. Noble, Hollister. *One Way to Eldorado*. Garden City, NY: Doubleday, 1954. 286p.

Howard Bierce, road foreman of engineers on the Mountain Division of the Great Western Railroad, is also an accomplished painter of railroad scenes. His wife's initial failure to grasp his artistic ambitions leads him to a solo sojourn in a jerkwater burg in the Sierras. A tolerable adventure ensues, with a diverse cast of characters, both railroaders and otherwise.

The story combines mystery, romance, robbery, thrilling railroad action in winter storms, and other steam to keep the pages turning. Noble pays significant attention to the details of railroading in the high country, and presents them in a convincing manner. Nevertheless, the novel functions at the surface of human affairs, rather than negotiating their depths.

596. Nolan, William F. "Lonely Train a'-Comin." In *Journey into Fear and other Great Stories of Horror on the Railways*, edited by Richard Peyton, 310–321. New York: Wings Books, 1991 (Originally published as *The Ghost Now Standing on Platform One*. London: Souvenir Press, 1990). Also in Nolan's *Dark Universe*. New York: Leisure Books, 2003.

Rancher Paul Ventry waits on a bench at a Montana station, icy wind blowing down his collar. He waits for a train whose arrival at the closed station is uncertain; as he waits, he tortures himself with thoughts of his recently-deceased sister, Amy. She had vanished aboard a train on her way to a new job; her bones turned up near an abandoned spur track. The railroad denies that Amy could have been riding the steam train she described in a postcard to Ventry: It no longer ran steam. The truth behind the mysterious train lies in a climax of marvelous pulp horror fiction, gloriously improbable and overwritten, but fun.

597. Nordan, Lewis. "Train, Train, Coming Round the Bend." *Southern Review* 26 (Autumn 1990): 844–855.

The narrator, a young boy, routinely hangs onto the ladder of a boxcar of the "snail-slow freight train ... that dragged its back legs through town each morning like a sorry dog," stopped briefly, then continued on to the Mississippi (844). Ordinarily, he gets off in town, but one day he rides the train out of town, his "insides alive with anxiety and joy" (845). The sights from the train, which travels all of five miles, thrill him. When his people see him, "no one noticed that I had been transformed by imagination and the possibility of distances" (847). The story, by turns hilarious, bitter, tragic, and horrible, moves on from here. One fears that the narrator's train ride is the last true joy of his life.

The title alludes through its quotation of a snatch of its lyric to Elvis Presley's great early song, "Mystery Train." There is, indeed, something of the same spirit and eerie dread of the song in the story. The story's chilling last line—"What is the source of all my terrible rage?" (855)—shares with Presley's "long black train" the scent of Southern doom.

598. Norris, Frank. *The Octopus.* 1901. Reprint, Garden City, NY: Doubleday, 1954. 635p.

The Octopus is one of the great works of American literary naturalism. Its basic plot concerns the struggles of California ranchers with the railroad. The P.&S.W. railroad not only determines the rates the ranchers must pay to ship their goods; it owns the land they farm, and refuses to sell it to them at the previously agreed-upon price of $2.50 an acre, aiming instead to sell the land to a third party to benefit from improvements the farmers have made in it. The railroad's legal sharks regrade the land's improved value to $27 an acre, far beyond the farmers' reach. The courts provide the ranchers no remedy; the U.S. Supreme Court douses the ranchers' last hopes when it rejects their claim upon "their" land. The railroad buys the law, the press, and the government.

The railroad generally treats its own with little more consideration than it treats the ranchers. Dyke, an old engineer fired by the road, tries to start a new life raising hops. After telling him it would ship his hops at two cents a pound, the railroad grossly hikes the rate, eating all of Dyke's gains. When Dyke demands to know the rationale for the railroad's rate setting, railroad official S. Behrman—the book's chief figure of villainy—tells him: "All—the traffic—will—bear" (Book 2, 64). "You can roar till you're black in the face," says one character, "but you can't buck against the Railroad. There's nothing to be done" (Book 2, 68). Driven half mad, Dyke robs a train; the law chases him across the countryside; with his pursuers minutes behind, he steals a locomotive, and in a gripping passage makes a desperate effort to gain his freedom.

The ranchers unite in the San Joaquin League; their stand against the railroad leads to a ferocious gun battle, leaving both ranchers and railroad forces with casualties. In the aftermath of the gunfight, the opponents set aside their conflict, briefly, as they try to help the wounded. Even S. Behrman for once acts like a man of some compassion and assists in the lifesaving effort.

Norris's manipulation of the reader's sentiments in *The Octopus* is skilled and effective. He creates great sympathy for the ranchers and their families; only a reader with a heart of ice could witness the destruction of these people by the railroad and its minions without feeling some of their rage and grief. By the time the ruined rancher's wife Mrs. Hooven dies of starvation as her little girl attempts to aid her, the pathos is heavy—too heavy—but Norris has prepared the reader well, and what one might otherwise dismiss as sentimental excess passes as tragedy.

In a revealing exchange with the railroad's President Shelgrim late in the novel, one of the ranchers, Presley, is compelled to see a different view of the matter than he has previously entertained. He is disoriented to find the magnate in the middle of an humane act toward a former employee. He is further discommoded when Shelgrim, the issue of the ranchers' ruin on the table, disavows Presley's claim that he "controls" the railroad. Shelgrim describes the railroad as but one element in a conflux of agents beyond anyone's power to control: "You are dealing with forces ... not with men," he says (Book 2, 285).

Is the railroad a kind of natural force, like the wheat it carries? Thinking of the railroad as a sort of organic response to the law of supply and demand, or, perhaps, to the insatiable appetites of humanity, might allow the reader to assign the adjective "natural" to the railroad with some equanimity. It is, at any rate, a conceivable idea, and once conceived lends Norris's ideas of the railroad as belonging to those natural forces of colossal indifference that drive the affairs of humanity more substance than the control-craving individual might wish to acknowledge.

This commentary does faint justice to a book that raises points for argument throughout, and which contains many unforgettable passages of dramatic and symbolic content. No one with an interest in the railroad in American history or fiction can ignore it.

599. Nugent, Beth. "Riding into Day." In *City of Boys; Stories*, 74–95. New York: Knopf, 1992.

Twelve-year-old Alice and her parents are traveling from Ohio to Arizona for a wedding. Alice's father said that train travel would be a good way for her to see country, "but so far everything they pass looks like everything else they have already passed" (76). Her father carefully monitors the train's progress on a map. Alice monitors her parents' low-keyed bickering; signs of serious marital trouble reside in their testy dialogue. Alice's mother is bored with the trip. As the atmosphere grows more suffocating thanks to her parents' antagonism, Alice looks out the coach window at a car waiting at a crossing; she imagines that she has made eye contact with a boy in the car, and even imagines herself in the car itself, on her way to swimming practice, or shopping. The boy and his mother in the car "know nothing of what it is to be on this train" (91). "Arkansas ... Oklahoma," says her father. "What's the difference? It's all the same. And it goes on forever and ever" (93).

This story is an excellent, if terrifically depressing, portrait of familial despair, with the train a test-tube in which the ingredients of that despair have been measured and shaken, with the acrid product of the concoction manifesting itself in Alice's vision of her future in the train restroom.

600. Oates, Joyce Carol. "The Crossing." In *The Collector of Hearts; New Tales of the Grotesque*, 260–279. New York: Plume, 1999. First published in *Ruby Slippers, Golden Tears*. Edited by Ellen Datlow and Terri Windling. New York: Morrow, 1995.

In this train-as-vehicle-for-the-dead story, a dying woman, Martha, revisits in her imagination the house in upstate New York where her Aunt Alma lives. There she hears the whistle of the Chautaqua and Buffalo train on its nearby tracks, as she did so often as a girl. Martha lives essentially the same day endlessly, early each morning watching a train emerge from a tunnel and disappear to a point in the distant West. The red-haired engineer waves to her, but no one else in town seems to see her. Of course not: The people in this town are all dead, and simply functioning in the theater of the dying woman's mind. In the end, the engineer beckons her aboard.

601. Ockside, Knight Russ, M.D., and Q.K. Philander Doesticks, P.B. [Edward F. Underhill]. *The History and Records of the Elephants Club; Compiled from Authentic Documents Now in Possession of the Zoological Society.* New York: Livermore & Rudd, 1857. 321p.

A group of men in Gotham form a social club bound by nonsensical rules, for the sake of their general amusement. They meet occasionally to regale one another with absurd stories. The unnumbered chapter, "First Evening with the Club," presents a lengthy account of a difficult railroad trip. A member describes this train journey across Michigan. The people aboard the train were dust-covered and uncomfortable. The conductor deliberately disturbed them: "And this conductor, in common with conductors in general, deserves notice for the diabolical ingenuity which he displayed in forcing from his helpless victims the greatest number of growls in a limited space of time" (99).

After the train leaves the prettily-named burg of Scraggville, a group of passengers strikes up a sing-along, which goes awry when the train derails, leaving the engine looking "like an insane cooking stove turned out-doors for misbehavior" (109). A relief engine enables the train to continue its trip.

602. O'Connor, Flannery. "The Artificial Nigger." In *Flannery O'Connor: Collected Works*, edited by Sally Fitzgerald, 210–231. New York: Library of America, 1988. Also in O'Connor's *A Good Man Is Hard to Find, and Other Stories.* New York: Harcourt, Brace, 1955. *Kenyon Review* 17 (Spring 1955): 169–192.

Mr. Head, 10-year-old Nelson's grandfather and sole guardian, has arranged for a special stop of the Atlanta-bound train at a nearby junction. He plans to take Nelson to the big city, to disabuse him of the notion that the city is a pleasant place. They board the crowded train before sunrise, and find two empty seats. There they look at their reflections in the dark window glass. One of the old man's objectives is to instill in Nelson a suitable hatred for "niggers." Nelson has never seen a black person, but on the train his grandfather points out one to him. "That's his first nigger," the old man tells another passenger (216). He then insults— wittily, he believes—a black dining car attendant.

Much of their visit to the city consists of a nightmarish search for the train station, from which they'll be able to return home. During their wandering, the old man displays a shocking disloyalty to the boy, and finally wallows in a repentance so exaggerated as to be self-congratulatory. They finally locate the train, their foul relationship temporarily repaired through mutual wonder over a plaster figurine, the "artificial nigger" of the title.

In this tale of psychological indoctrination and brute sensibility, the train provides the medium of movement from tawdry innocence to debased experience.

603. _____. "The Train." In *Flannery O'Connor: Collected Works*, edited by Sally Fitzgerald, 753–762. New York: Library of America, 1988. Also in O'Connor's *The Complete Stories.* New York: Noonday Press, 1973. *Sewanee Review* 56 (April-June 1948): 261–271.

Nineteen-year-old Hazel Wickers, whose mental acuity matches his nickname, "Haze," is riding the train from (presumably) an Army camp to Taulkinham. The porter tells Haze that his (the porter's) father "was a railroad man." Haze laughs at the idea of "a nigger being a railroad 'man'" (759). Painfully naïve, shy, and dull, Haze makes errant assumptions about the black porter's family, reflects on how his mother used to talk to nearly everyone on any train she rode, and suffers an excruciating visit to the dining car, where he orders and bolts the first thing on the menu, and does not look at the people at his table. When the porter prepares his upper berth, Haze is dismayed to find that it lacks a window. He lies in the coffin-like berth, thinking about his dead mother's burial.

With Haze reminding one of the mentally deficient Vardaman in William Faulkner's *As I Lay Dying*, the story is a disturbing sojourn in the mind of a young man haunted by death and disabled by his own stupidity.

604. Ogden, George W. *The Cow Jerry*. New York: Grosset & Dunlap, 1925. 328p.

"Jerry" is an old term for a railroad section-gang worker. In this novel set in the Kansas cattle town of McPacken, Tom Laylander is a Texas cowman reduced to rocky circumstances as a cowboy section hand—hence, the "cow jerry"—on the railroad. As a section hand, Laylander is at the bottom of the railroad social hierarchy, the distance between him and other railroaders as great "as between white men and black" (89). The other section men, though, like Tom, and help him learn the ropes. Ogden describes the jerries as "a careless, spendthrift, hardy set of rovers, veterans of the army that pushed the rails across desert and mountains," most of them Irish. They are often illiterate, and "so accustomed to hardship that the word scarcely had any meaning to them" (102). They are resigned to their humble status, without ambition or pretense to higher positions.

The railroad's advent in McPacken gives the town a progressive air, and brings many new jobs. Some tensions exist between railroaders and range workers, but in general, both being critical components of the cattle economy, they get along peacefully. Cordiality suffers when Laylander acts against his nemesis, the underhanded cattleman Col. Cal Withers. The showdown comes in the chapter "Range and Railroad Meet," when the railroaders back Laylander against Withers. This good-natured Western has just enough of Ogden's reflections on railroad workers' lives, especially those of the section gang, to raise it above run-of-the-mill horse operatics.

605. _____. *The Ghost Road*. New York: Dodd, Mead, 1936. 264p.

The county of Clearwater has for 50 years staggered under a bond debt incurred when its residents trusted an unscrupulous gang of railroad promoters. The promoters left the county in the lurch with nothing to show for its "railroad" but an embankment. A sad-sack little railroad serves the area, but it has no connection with the infamous, non-existent Palestine & Gulf, now referred to as the "ghost road." The county's chief town, Vinland, is a decrepit sight, and the locals, crushed beneath a debt that they can never repay, have no hope or expectation but utter ruin. Into town one day comes Tom Calvert, successor to the con artists who left the county such a dreary case. Calvert has the bonds with him, and aims to settle matters equitably. The immediate reaction to Calvert's announcement that he is the bondholder is the belief that he has come to complete the pillaging his predecessors began.

The railroad is rarely more than a specter in this book, but even lacking objective reality, it holds evil sway over the county's life. Calvert heroically changes that situation. Apart from railroad issues, the reader may find one character of special interest: the mentally and physically deformed, ape-like Rex, whose tragic lot plays a role of some importance in the story.

606. _____. *Sooner Land*. New York: Grosset & Dunlap, 1929. 329p.

In this novel of the 1893 opening of the Cherokee Strip to settlement, several thousand people wait to travel by train into the newly-opening territory. The train is "packed to the last inch of standing-room and, in spite of the trainmen's orders and threats, men were climbing to the tops of the cars" (3). The people awaiting the rush are "vigorous and eager ... honest man and villain alike, in the sweating, dust-powdered army of the disinherited" (5). The story revolves around two men aboard the train, Oliver Howard and Jake Zickafoos. The train run into the strip and the deboarding are chaotic, but the railroad largely evaporates from the novel after this opening section.

607. _____. *West of Dodge*. New York: Dodd, Mead, 1926. 305p.

Andrew Hall, from Topeka, comes to Damascus, Kansas, west of Dodge City, as the new railroad doctor. Shortly after arriving, he receives misplaced credit for killing Sandiver, one of the town's most thuggish residents. Hall has his hands full, with Sandiver's vengeful brother and with Old Doc Ross, the town's established quack, who sees Hall as a rival.

Hall's office is a dingy freight car set on a bank of cinders near the main track. The car is partitioned in two sections: the office proper, and Hall's sleeping quarters. The around-the-clock nature of railroad mishaps demands that Hall be available any time of day or night. A boarding train stands on a siding across from Hall's office; here railroad men live, their dining needs tended by Mrs. Charles and her large daughters. "I'm feedin' between sixty and seventy men every day," says Mrs. Charles. "It takes a lot of grub to fill up that many railroaders" (70). She awards Hall a place at the private table she shares with her daughters.

Hall perseveres through the local roughnecks, jokers, and all-around characters to establish himself. *West of Dodge* is a good-humored and readable book, but Ogden's reminiscence, *There Were No Heroes: A Personal Record of a Man's Beginning* (New York: Dodd, Mead, 1940), may be a better place to see the railroad life from Ogden's perspective. That book is a well-written, unsentimental account, with considerable railroad detail.

608. O'Hara, John. "Drawing Room B." In *Collected Stories of John O'Hara*, 91–97. New York: Random House, 1984. *New Yorker* 23 (April 19, 1947): 25–28. Also in O'Hara's *Hellbox*. New York: Random House, 1947.

The fading and none-too-happy-about-it movie star Leda Pentleigh goes to Penn Station, accompanied by a publicity flunky, to catch a train for the West Coast. To her obvious distress, no one in the station "bothers" her. She sits in her coach drawing room with the door open, watching other passengers go by; they all have "that beaten look of people trying to find their space..." (92). She meets a minor, if well-dressed actor, Kenyon Littlejohn. When he asks her for business advice, she goes on a rude tirade over East Coast actors trying to make their way in Hollywood. After Littlejohn withdraws, she downs a few drinks and reconsiders her treatment of him. Her plans for a new approach sound no more promising than her initial attack.

609. _____. "The Ride from Mauch Chunk." *Saturday Evening Post* 236 (April 13, 1963): 38–41. Also in O'Hara's *The Hat on the Bed*. New York: Random House, 1963.

A young man—a law student—and a young woman board the train at Mauch Chunk, New York, bound for New York City. The law student attempts to pick up the young woman, relying on what he believes to be his gift for clever patter. He makes a racist joke about the crew in the dining car: "They give you black looks if you sit here and don't order something—no pun intended" (40). The future lawyer's pick-up effort falls flat, and, in a little coda, the reader learns that the failure was to the young woman's advantage.

610. _____. "The Windowpane Check." In *The Hat on the Bed*, 346–354. New York: Random House, 1963.

Phillips, standing in line at a New York City train gate, sees a shabby man ahead of him in line. The man wears one of Phillips's old jackets, fashioned of a windowpane check material. Phillips gave the jacket to charity after his wife's death to escape the memories it evoked of her. On the way to Philadelphia, the man in Phillips's old jacket reveals that he knew Phillips's late wife, in Paris, in the 1920s. The shabby man, Jack Roebuck, is an artist. What begins as a troubling reminder of Phillips's wife progresses to an irritating conversation, but a turn in the talk brings Phillips and Roebuck onto common ground.

611. Oliver, Chad. "Transformer." In *Another Kind; Science Fiction Stories*, 92–107. New York: Ballantine, 1955. *Magazine of Fantasy & Science Fiction* 7 (Nov. 1954): 70–81.

The narrator, a cranky old woman, lives in a "town"—Elm Point—that forms part of the background for a model railroad: "So my world is on a big plywood table in an attic" (94). Her husband works in the tin switchman's shanty up the tracks. Everyone able to do so rushes about madly when the current is on, and everyone in town hates Willy Roberts, the 13-year-old owner-operator, to the extent that Elm Point's citizens have decided to kill Willy via electrocution. Willy, a budding psychopath, deliberately stages train wrecks. This whimsical, witty, and funny story succeeds in chafing the reader's feelings over the disappointments of a toy.

612. "On a Slow Train." In *On a Slow Train: The Original Story.* Baltimore: I&M Ottenheimer, 1905. 5–8.

In a story that reads like the vaudeville routine on which it is undoubtedly based, the narrator laments the sluggishness of the train he must take. The one-liners come thick, fast, and corny: "I told the conductor about the slowness of the train and he told me if I didn't like it I had better get out and walk. I said: 'I would, but my folks don't expect me until the train gets there'" (5).

The rest of the jokes struggle to equal the standard that one sets. The book in which the story appears bills itself as the best work of vaudeville and minstrel show jokers; of the many pieces that concern railroading, this is the most substantial. It bears a striking resemblance to the opening pages of Thomas W. Jackson's *On a Slow Train through Arkansaw* (Entry 406).

Ostrander, Isabel E. *see* **Grant, Douglas**

613. Otto, Lon. "Waiting for the Freedom Train." In *A Nest of Hooks,* 45–48. Iowa City, IA: University of Iowa Press, 1978.

In the Bicentennial summer of 1976, excitement grips a little Illinois town as the residents anticipate the passage of the Freedom Train along the old Illinois Central line. The train will not stop; the town is too small for such attention. Nevertheless, everyone wants to see it. The train is due at 5:30 P.M., and most of the town turns out to watch it pass. It is at first a little late, then quite late, then very late. Most of the locals wait, afraid that they will miss the spectacle. The train arrives at last, at 10:30 P.M. In less than a minute, it is gone. "After a few minutes of gazing down the empty track, the people of the town gathered up still half-asleep and sleeping children, and said good night to each other in quiet voices, and went home" (48).

614. Oursler, Fulton. *The Great Jasper.* New York: Covici, Friede, 1930. 296p.

Streetcar motorman Jasper Horn works in an anonymous Southern city. Jasper is a good-time fellow who does not let personal loss, including his daughter's death, spoil his enjoyment of life. The first dramatic event in the novel involves Jasper's promise to his boss to take out a streetcar, in defiance of the line's striking workers. Jasper's company loyalty wins him a promotion to division boss—of the very men who threatened to kill him for strike-breaking. Jasper's company loyalty does not prevent him from having an affair with his boss's wife, and, in a rage of gratitude and hatred, his boss, McGowd, fires him, and gives him land in California and a large check, demanding that he never show his face around McGowd again. Jasper becomes the Great Jasper, an Atlantic City fortune teller. He flourishes at sooth-saying, and the railway life is history. The Great Jasper's last words, for what they are worth: "I think I see Jesus" (296). He would prefer, however, to be riding a train to attend his son's wedding.

615. Overholser, Wayne D. "Steel to the West." In *The Railroaders,* edited by Bill Pronzini and Martin H. Greenberg, 116–125. New York: Fawcett Gold Medal, 1986. Also in *The Best Western Stories of Wayne D. Overholser.* Athens, Ohio: Swallow Press/Ohio University Press, 1989.

Every town wants the railroad for the prosperity it brings, but prosperity can have a dark side, as well. Here the action focuses on the arrival in Cheyenne of the Union Pacific track-laying crew. Narrator Jim Glenn describes the event from a first-hand perspective: "I was amazed at the proficiency and speed with which the job was done" (117). Glenn, a local businessman, worries about the effects of the railroad's presence on the town's ability to maintain a law-abiding atmosphere, with the trains bringing in a motley lot of railroaders, mule skinners, hunters, whores, pimps, gamblers and con men. He yields to the encouragement of a townsman to become an officer in a vigilante group organized to keep peace in the new rail town.

616. Owen, George W. *The Leech Club, or, The Mysteries of the Catskills.* Boston: Lee & Shepard, 1874. 298p.

Available at *Wright American Fiction*: http://www.letrs.indiana.edu/web/w/wright2/

One is assured in this socio-political satire that "Railroad and other powerful corporations are in fact the real Government of the country. If a man wants to be elected to the legislature, he has need of the aid of any railroad corporation that may be in his district.... I tell you, sir, the railroads are the ruling power in the country, and we might as well admit it first as last" (23). This from the noble statesman Mr. Swellup, whom the narrator condemns as emblematic of the prevailing venality and corruption, comfortable with "the most outrageous acts of public robbery" (24), or, perhaps, what George Washington Plunkett of Tammany Hall would have referred to with an untroubled mind as "honest graft." Owen later condemns the railroad operators who fleece the public by the thousand with daily overcharges, and who are "spoken of as the Hon. Mr. So-and-So," while the petty thief does hard time. "Thus the greater crimes, and infinitely the greater amount of robberies, are committed by those who are soon looked up to as among the most honored members of the community..." (139).

617. Packard, Frank L. "The Age Limit." In *The Night Operator*, 169–203. New York: A.L. Burt, 1919. *Railroad Magazine* 79 (July 1966): 58–63.

Packard, an American born in Canada in 1877, is probably best remembered for his mystery stories. His background in railroading—he worked for the Canadian Pacific—gives his railroad stories technical credibility. Here, engineer Dan MacCaffery is one of the Hill Division's old-time heroes. Everyone in the rough town of Big Cloud likes him, and all adore his wife. The two of them are scrimping along, paying over time a debt incurred by their late, ne'er do well son. Eastern interests buy out the Hill Division, and the new officials come out to look over the acquisition. The visit is a disaster for the railroaders at Big Cloud—especially for MacCaffery, who, at 62, is two years' past the new owners' mandatory termination age. The story ends with MacCaffery's apparent willing death in an accident on his last run. This is an unusually grim story in the Packard canon; the Eastern interlopers pay no price for their callousness, but the men of the Hill Division are left with no illusions about the dubious humanity of their new bosses.

618. _____. "The Apotheosis of Sammy Durgan." In *The Night Operator*, 76–111. New York: A.L. Burt, 1919.

Sammy Durgan is a perpetual foul-up on the Hill Division, fired from nearly any position one could name, yet always turning up in another. He is convinced that if given a chance to rise to meet a real emergency, he could show everyone what a fine railroader he is. He mistakes a movie crew and actors for an actual gang of train robbers, and makes a fool of himself in "stopping" the hold-up they are staging, and for which they have paid the railroad a large sum for its cooperation. Sammy disappears after his blunder, but resurfaces in an absurd bit of accidental heroism as he flees a flaming runaway tank car on a handcar. Packard writes with a sense of the ridiculous here that is not common in railroad pulp fiction.

619. _____. "The Blood of Kings." In *Running Special*, 281–304. New York: George H. Doran, 1925. Also in Packard's *On the Iron at Big Cloud*. New York: Crowell, 1911. *Popular Magazine* 19, no. 2, Feb. 1, 1911.

"King" Gilleen, a red-headed Irish engineer, acquired his nickname as an ironic sobriquet applied by his boss, master mechanic Regan, who cannot resist provoking Gilleen. One provocation proves too much. Gilleen and Regan come to blows, and Regan fires him. Another official takes Gilleen on as a night switchman in the yards. One night a calamitous fire in the shops leads Gilleen and Regan to repair their breech—and to Gilleen's rightful claim to the nickname that had previously mocked him.

620. _____. "The Builder." In *Running Special*, 9–36. New York: George H. Doran, 1925. Also in Packard's *On the*

Iron at Big Cloud. New York: Crowell, 1911.

The Hill Division, a rough-and-ready outfit, had seen few rougher than construction boss Spirlaw. Spirlaw forms an unlikely friendship with Keating, a shy, quiet type, but a hard worker, with a keen ambition to be an engineer, a builder. A nasty strike breaks out; Spirlaw sends Keating off to headquarters, ostensibly to gather information, in fact to protect him from violence at the construction site. Keating returns to report devastation in the Big Cloud yards wrought by strikers, with a dozen men left dead. Soon the violence hits the construction camp, as a mob of Spirlaw's workers—"Polacks"—attacks Spirlaw and Keating. Failing to kill the two men with dynamite, the mob, stoked on liquor, gives chase, and "the cries of the maddened Polacks" fill the night; the strikers are like "wild beasts" (33). Ethnic stereotype and slander and outrageous melodrama do not enhance this story.

621. _____. "Corrigan's Best." In Packard's *Running Special*, 65–94. New York: George H. Doran, 1925. *Popular Magazine*, Feb. 1, 1913.

Corrigan, an Eastern railroader with a wooden leg, joined the Hill Division and made a name for himself as a crack switch engine operator. He is also a wild storyteller, sometimes at his own expense: "He was an awe-inspiring, breath-taking liar, nothing else" (85). Here Corrigan runs afoul of a local lawman, performs an heroic act of self-sacrifice, and tells his best lie of all.

622. _____. "The Devil and All His Works." In *The Night Operator*, 204–233. New York: A.L. Burt, 1919. *Popular Magazine* 30, no. 1, Oct. 15, 1913.

Noodles, son of the old boiler washer Bill Maguire, starts work for the Hill Division at the age of 12 as a call boy, running messages to train crews. He has an irritating taste for practical jokes. Master mechanic Regan is the boy's godfather, but not even that can save Noodles from the axe when his jokes go too far. Furious at Noodles, Regan renounces his responsibilities as godfather, and Maguire—a religious sort—goes apoplectic and quits. Noodles,

intoxicated on nickel thrillers, concocts a farcical plan for vengeance on Regan, and ends up saving his life, and his father's job. (As a note apropos of not much, Bill Maguire pronounces "boy" as "b'hoy," precisely like W.C. Fields in Fields's great short comedy, *The Fatal Glass of Beer*.)

623. _____. "The Guardian of the Devil's Slide." In *Running Special*, 37–64. New York: George H. Doran, 1925. Also in Packard's *On the Iron at Big Cloud*. New York: Crowell, 1911. *Popular Magazine*, Jan. 1, 1911.

The Devil's Slide is the worst stretch of track on the Hill Division, if not in North America: "It twisted, it turned, it slid, it slithered, and it dove around projecting mountainsides at scandalous angles and with indecent abruptness" (39). Engineer Chick Coogan is a popular railroader; when his wife and baby die, every man on the road shares his grief. Packard describes these railroaders: "...poor men and rough they were, nothing of veneer, nothing of polish, grimy overalled, horny-fisted toilers, their hearts were big if their purses weren't" (58).

On the anniversary of his marriage, Coogan barely cheats death in a wreck on the Devil's Slide, and emerges befuddled from his hospital bed. Coogan's only ambition is to guard the Devil's Slide, and to see that no equipment failure will lead to another wreck. His story ends sadly, but the story—sentimental but effective—ends with a neatly-conceived revisionist version of the wreck that night on the Devil's Slide.

624. _____. "The Hobo." In *Running Special*, 95–125. New York: George H. Doran, 1925. *Popular Magazine*, Feb. 7, 1915, 99+. *Railroad Stories* 17 (Sept. 1935): 96–108. Reprinted as "The Spotter." *Railroad Magazine* 79 (Sept. 1966): 40–46.

Budd Masters, a Hill Division engineer, has 11 children. He is a generous, considerate man, a great contrast to Joe Scharff, the nasty-tempered, thuggish conductor who works with Masters on the Fast Mail train. One cold night Masters helps a young hobo whom Scharff is manhandling. When Masters later is off work with a broken leg, the hobo, Prouty, takes a job as an engine wiper and gives his pay to the Masters family. The truth about Prouty eventually comes out, as does his heroism. The story is as sentimental as a cheap greeting card, but is slickly told.

625. _____. "It Doesn't Matter." In *Running Special*, 182–221. New York: George H. Doran, 1925. *People's Favorite Magazine*, Sept. 1919.

"Spud" MacGallaghan is the son of a wiper in Big Cloud; he himself starts railroad work at 13, indifferent about his assignment. "It doesn't matter," he says (187). That sums up Spud's attitude toward everything, except for his favorite pastime, gambling. He sets up a gambling den on company property, and exploits the local Indians. Spud pursues a series of blunders born of indifference until he falls under the spell of young Fred Blainey, a night dispatcher. Their friendship spurs Spud to valor in a near-disaster, and to the knowledge that it *does* matter. The story follows the typical Packard formula of the wastrel's redemption.

626. _____. "The Little Super." *Century Illustrated Monthly Magazine* 75 (March 1908): 715–722. Also in Packard's *On the Iron at Big Cloud*. New York: Crowell, 1911.

Engineer MacLeod's small boy, Bunty, is inclined to make a pest of himself around the Hill Division yards, so much so that he's banned from the premises. The only place he can enter, he finds, is the engine shops, where the men call him "the little Super." Years pass, and Bunty becomes a fixture among the railroaders. One winter, when the men struggle to keep up with intense business, Bunty learns of the importance of the railroad's president and directors. When he asks his father who those people are, MacLeod is succinct: "Fools, mostly," he says. "Bunty nodded gravely, and his education as a railroad man was almost complete" (718). His life as a "railroad man" takes a new turn when he performs heroically, if incredibly, at a wreck scene—and McLeod learns that the railroad president is not the fool he previously believed.

627. _____. "The Man Who Confessed." In *Great Railroad Stories of the World*, edited by Sam Moskowitz, 59–91. New York: McBride, 1954. Also in Packard's *Running Special*. New York: George H. Doran, 1925.

Barty McClung, rescued from a train wreck, is taken on as a fireman on a local freight run. McClung quickly earns everyone's good will, except for that of Johnnie Dawes, an engine wiper who hates him for usurping the post that Dawes believes he deserves by virtue of seniority. Soon McClung and his engineer, Steve Patch, are promoted to a new engine on a fast passenger run. The story features a convincingly-rendered train wreck and heroic rescue. A question concerning McClung's past honesty in railroad service raises a signal issue for the company man, for whom "discipline and authority come first over every other consideration" (86).

628. _____. "The Man Who Squealed." In *The Night Operator*, 134–168. New York: A.L. Burt, 1919.

One P. Walton appears in Big Cloud one day, in the Hill Division's early years, looking for railroad work. Walton is a man with bad lungs who hopes that the mountain air will restore his health. Superintendent Carleton hires him to help with bookkeeping, and lends him $10 to get settled. The consensus among the men is that Walton has come out West to die. Death—brave and selfless—figures in the story, and Walton proves to have a more complicated past than anyone would have imagined.

629. _____. "Marley." In *Running Special*, 157–181. New York: George H. Doran, 1925. Also in Packard's *On the Iron at Big Cloud*. New York: Crowell, 1911.

Marley is a general factotum on the Hill Division, having arrived half dead as a hobo in a refrigerator car. Many attribute his taciturn style to innate surliness, but a few believe it shyness stemming from Marley's homely appearance. Marley soon demonstrates two qualities: immense strength, and a hair-trigger temper when teased over his looks. In an astonishing act of selflessness, Marley repays the Widow Coogan, who nursed him back to health after his rescue from the reefer.

630. _____. "McQueen's Hobby." Retrieved January 28, 2005, from http://www.virtualrailroader.com/library.html Also in Packard's *On the Iron at Big Cloud*. New York: Thomas Y. Crowell, 1911.

McQueen's "hobby" is coal. An engineer on the Hill Division, he obsesses over the stuff that brings his locomotive to life. McQueen is also a company man, and stands in the way of fellow engineer Noonan's ambition to foment a strike. Noonan exploits McQueen's dissatisfaction with the quality of the railroad's coal to win his endorsement of, or at least acquiescence in, a strike that proves violent. When McQueen discovers the truth about the way Noonan manipulated him, he is the catalyst for the strike's end—and soon finds himself in a position with the Hill Division that suits his coal preoccupation.

631. _____. "Munford: A Story of Railroad Life." *Outing* 54 (April 1909): 61–70. Also in Packard's *On the Iron at Big Cloud*. New York: Crowell, 1911.

Munford, a bridge gang laborer, worked on the Hill Division from its beginning, back when Big Cloud was a boomtown, full of gambling dives and saloons. A brawny man with a sense of outrage, Munford leads fellow railroaders in an effective action to force the town's most crooked establishments out of business. The other workers are proud of Munford for cleaning out the riff-raff, but rumor has it that one of the bunch has vengeance in mind. Munford and his bridge gang pals would gladly oblige, but their supervisor, Burton, is more concerned about working than brawling. The men suspect that Burton has sold out to the gambling interests, until he shows his good faith toward Munford and the rest of the gang.

632. _____. "The Night Operator." In *The Night Operator*, 13–45. New York:

A.L. Burt, 1919. *Railroad Magazine* 24 (Aug. 1938): 98–112.

An unusually short newsboy, meanly dubbed "Toddles" by the conductor on the train where he works, longs to be a true railroader. Conductor Reynolds and Toddles fight aboard the train; in the aftermath, dispatcher Donkin encourages Toddles to take up telegraphy, which poses no size requirements. Toddles, short of stature but large of heart, seizes the chance to show that he truly is fit material for a railroader.

633. _____. "On the Night Wire." In *The Night Operator*, 234–260. New York: A.L. Burt, 1919. *Popular Magazine* 30, no. 4, Dec. 1, 1913. Reprinted as "The Circus Special." *Railroad Stories* 20 (Nov. 1936): 112–124.

Dan McGrew is a fine telegraph operator, when sober. To enhance his opportunities for sobriety, Superintendent Carleton sends him to the remote post at Angel Forks, where no one could find a bottle of alcohol. Charlie Keene—"The Kid"—soon joins McGrew at the station. He knows unpleasant secrets of McGrew's past, and, after McGrew's alcoholism reasserts itself, the reader learns how Keene came to be so intimate with McGrew's story.

634. _____. "The Other Fellow's Job." In *The Night Operator*, 261–287. New York: A.L. Burt, 1919. *Popular Magazine*, Feb. 15, 1913.

Jimmy Beezer is a talented fitter in the Big Cloud roundhouse, but suffers from a common "disease": envy of the other fellow's job, regardless of how little he knows about its demands. Beezer's special envy is the engineer's job; he begins to study the position with a pilfered copy of the rule book. Mrs. Beezer has no enthusiasm for her husband's ambition. A runaway train gives Beezer his chance to show his engineer's stuff, and show it he does, with unexpected results.

635. _____. "Owsley and the 1601." In *The Night Operator*, 46–75. New York: A.L. Burt, 1919. *Railroad Magazine* 79 (Oct. 1966): 42–50.

Old-time engineer Jake Owsley joins the Hill Division, bringing with him "a love for his engine that was like the love of a man for a woman" (47). Although reluctant to surrender his old engine for a new one, he comes to love his new 1601. One night he plows the 1601 into a freight train; observers say he ran a red signal, but Owsley swears the light was white, for "proceed." The wreck leaves both Owsley and the engine unfit for regular service. On a dark and stormy night, Owsley—slightly deranged but still in love with the 1601—takes his beloved for one last run. In the process, he coincidentally saves a passenger train from disaster at a washed-out bridge, and fulfills his promise: "When I go out, I'm going out with my hand on the throttle.... And me and the old 1601, we're going out together..." (64).

636. _____. "Rafferty's Rule." Retrieved January 28, 2005, from http://home.mindspring.com/~railroadstories/index.htm. Also in Packard's *On the Iron at Big Cloud.* New York: Thomas Y. Crowell, 1911.

This story could stand as the prototype for its genre. In it, the new man on the job, a young fellow named Dick Holman, overcomes the better judgment of a veteran railroader to win the challenging job of locomotive foreman with the Hill Division. His success depends on his ability to gain the allegiance of the bullying shop foreman, Rafferty. When Rafferty decides that Holman is a baby-faced impostor, the outlook is bad. Holman and Rafferty come to blows, through which Holman earns some respect, but not until a crisis arises in the form of a wrecked passenger train, giving the two antagonists a chance to show their loyalty to their fellow railroader, does Holman break through Rafferty's opposition. Although formulaic, the story is well-written and exciting, and effectively invokes primitive archetypes of courage, virtue, and loyalty.

637. _____. "The Rat River Special." In *The Night Operator,* 288–320. New York: A.L. Burt, 1919. *Popular Magazine* 31, no. 6, April 1, 1914.

Martin Bradley, a fireman on the Hill Division, was a quiet fellow, back in the day when Big Cloud was still a roughneck frontier town. Bradley boarded at the MacQuigan place, and

formed a special liking for young Reddy Mac-Quigan, a wiper. Bradley can't stop the boy from turning to drink, but Reddy sobers up after his father dies in a barroom brawl. Soon afterward, Bradley learns that his daughter, whom he supported in a school in the East, has died in an accident. Bradley himself resorts to the bottle, and one day his boss, Regan, catches him drunk on the job. "Other men might drink and play the fool and be forgiven and trusted again ... but a man in the cab of an engine, never. Reasons, excuses, contributory causes, counted not at all—they were not asked for—they did not exist" (308). Regan fires Bradley. The melodrama mounts, with a conclusion featuring an homicidal Italian maniac and Bradley's spectacular heroics.

638. _____. "Shanley's Luck." In *Running Special,* 127–156. New York: George H. Doran, 1925. Also in Packard's *On the Iron at Big Cloud.* New York: Crowell, 1911.

Shanley, a passenger from out East, distinguishes himself heroically in a train wreck, and seeks a job on the Hill Division. Immediately on his hiring, he goes on a drunken binge. Rather than firing him, the boss sends him to a far-off construction camp where can help boss "a jabbering Italian labor gang" (140) building a switchback. The Italians "are simple, demonstrative, and their capacity for adoration—of both men and things—is very great" (144). Left in temporary charge of the camp, Shanley gets drunk on Chianti supplied by the Italians. The story's title suggests the ironic effects that Shanley's intoxication has on the railroad and his career.

639. _____. "Spitzer." In *Running Special,* 222–245. New York: George H. Doran, 1925. Also in Packard's *On the Iron at Big Cloud.* New York: Crowell, 1911.

Spitzer is a diffident sweeper and wiper in the Big Cloud roundhouse, with no apparent ambition. He has to summon all his will to ask for a 10-cent raise after six years on the job. Somehow, his success at obtaining the pathetic raise fires his latent thirst for upward mobility, and the men of the Hill Division are amazed to learn that Spitzer is human. His objectives include not only a job firing in a locomotive, but also the heart of sweet Merla Swenson, a local lunch counter worker. When a regular fireman falls ill, Spitzer gets a chance to prove himself in the cab. His performance during a critical equipment failure is more than anyone would have thought possible of the reticent, retiring Spitzer.

640. _____. *The Wire Devils*. New York: A.L. Burt, 1918. 318p.

Harry Maul, also known as "The Hawk," a notorious and freshly-escaped train robber and "gentleman crook," enters the story early in a dramatic appearance at an out-of-the-way depot. MacVightie, pugnacious head of the railroad detective force, is the Hawk's would-be nemesis. The Hawk is an expert telegraph operator, as are the "Wire Devils" who use this basic tool against the railroad. This Packard work is basically pulp Western adventure fiction, with two-fisted action, secret codes, double agents, a surprise ending, and not much in the way of redeeming social or literary value.

641. _____. "The Wrecking Boss." In *The Night Operator*, 112–133. New York: A.L. Burt, 1919. Reprinted as "The Wrecking Master." *Railroad Stories* 16 (March 1935): 122–133; *Railroad Magazine* 76 (March 1965): 40–44.

Flannagan is the wrecking boss on the Hill Division. He's a big, hard man, who goes sweet on a circus performer, Daisy MacQueen, and persuades her to marry him. The marriage founders on Flannagan's foolish jealousy; Daisy departs, Flannagan retreats to liquor, and Superintendent Carleton fires him. Flannagan returns to himself when Daisy and the couple's infant are trapped in a dreadful wreck. One of the last images in the story gives away the climax, but it is too wonderfully lugubrious to ignore here. When his fellow wrecking crew members find Flannagan in the wreck, he is "dandling a tiny infant in his arms, crooning a lullaby through cracked lips ... to a little one long hushed in its last sleep" (133). A Victorian sentiment of death couples with the heart-rending picture of a hard-living railroader reduced to the most pitiful tenderness.

642. Page, Thomas Nelson. "How the Captain Made Christmas." *Scribner's Magazine* 14 (Dec. 1893): 779–786. Also in Page's *Burial of the Guns*. New York: Scribner's, 1894.

A few days before Christmas, a group of clubmen reminisce about Christmases past. One, Lesponts, describes a memorable rail journey from Washington, D.C., to New Orleans aboard a crowded train. While the train waited for a wreck to be cleared from the track ahead, the conductor—dubbed "Captain" by Lesponts—proved a most congenial host. He even escorted the passengers on a tour of a nearby Civil War battlefield. The Captain's chief aide is a porter, whom the Captain calls "a very good boy" (as Lesponts notes, this African-American "boy" is 55 years old) (783). The Captain had formerly employed a mulatto porter, but threw him off the train; he didn't know his place. "The black is a capital servant," says the Captain, "when he has sense, far better than the mulatto" (783). By the time the train resumed its progress, the Captain was friends with everyone on it—at least, presumably, every white person.

643. _____. "The New Agent." In *Under the Crust*, 39–97. New York: Scribner's, 1907.

Young Joe Shannon is the new railway agent in the town of Lebanon. He works not only as the station agent, but as the telegraph operator and depot hand in the one-man station. He is in love with Elizabeth Fostyn. Local stuffed-shirt Deacon Grantham's son also aspires to Elizabeth's favor, and the deacon promises to make life hard for Joe. Nevertheless, the station becomes a magnet for the local young folk, drawn by Joe's good nature. When someone tampers with a switch, causing an accident that mars Joe's record, he suspects Grantham. One rough winter night Joe valiantly rides a horse to another town to summon a relief train to rescue a passenger train trapped in the storm; his heroism wins the town's admiration.

644. _____. "Run to Seed." *Scribner's Magazine* 10 (Sept. 1891): 367–376. Also in Page's *Elsket, and Other Stories*. New York: Scribner's, 1891.

Jim Upton's father died at Gettysburg; the Uptons are the poorest people in a poor neighborhood. The Upton family has, as one cruel neighbor says, "clean run to seed" (370). Jim, who stutters badly, beseeches the president of a Virginia railroad for a job. He asked the right man, for Jim's father was in the railroad executive's command at Gettysburg. He starts Jim as a brakeman. Jim's piety—he goes to church, shuns strong language, and is silent at coarse stories—does not endear him to his hard-bitten fellow railroaders. Dick Rail, the engineer, is especially hard on poor Jim. Jim soldiers on, and sends his money home. In this two-hankie weeper, Jim comes to a tragic but heroic end, and even Dick Rail sings the boy's praises, when it is too late. This is sentimental hokum cranked a notch or two higher than standard.

645. Palmer, Stuart, and Craig Rice. "Once Upon a Train." In *Detective Duos*, edited by Marcia Muller and Bill Pronzini, 220–239. New York: Oxford University Press, 1997. Also in Palmer's and Rice's *People Vs. Withers and Malone: Six Inner Sanctum Mystery Novelettes*. New York: Simon & Schuster, 1963.

Stephen Larsen, a Chicago politico whom John J. Malone has just gotten off the hook for embezzlement, is fleeing town by train for New York, stiffing Malone on the three grand he owes him. Malone races to catch the same train, and bribes the Pullman conductor to give him a compartment next to that of a striking redhead. Malone meets his partner-to-be, Miss Hildegarde Withers, on the train, and Larsen turns up dead in her compartment. A light-hearted whodunit and how come, the story features a crabby cat named Precious in a supporting role.

646. Parkman, Francis. *Vassall Morton*. Boston: Phillips, Sampson, 1856. 414p. Available at *Wright American Fiction*: http://www.letrs.indiana.edu/web/w/wright2/

This sentimental novel features an early example of attempted terrorism acted out on a railroad. In Chapter 19, hero Vassall Morton learns that a bridge has been sabotaged on the nearby railroad. With its supporting timbers nearly severed, the bridge will collapse beneath the weight of an oncoming train, sending passengers and crew to their doom. Morton heroically plants himself in the middle of the track and waves down the train, which halts but a few yards from disaster. The grateful passengers try to reward Morton, but he spurns mere money—to the relief of some who had their purses open. The culprit proves to be an Irish mechanic formerly with the railroad, seeking revenge for being dismissed from his job over an infraction.

647. Parson, Kirk. *On the Mountain Division*. New York: Eaton & Mains, 1903. 255p.

In a well-written and credible story, Parson presents the life of a boy—an orphan—who begins working as an indentured servant on a farm at the age of eight. He labors hard for several years, then, at 13, runs away from the farm. When he is about 16, he finds work as a wiper on the C.O.&B. Railroad at Bryson, the terminus of the road's Eastern and Mountain Divisions. The boy is all eyes and ears when he begins railroad work. "The roundhouse became my home; the railroaders my companions. At first they all appeared about the same to me, gruff, hurrying, reckless, jolly, swearing, and selfish fellows. But a week's time not only revealed to me many good-natured 'boys,' but also many a true, clean heart beneath the greasy, blue blouses" (86). Soon he becomes a brakeman, not unaware of that job's frequent risks; he cites figures showing the carnage associated with railroads, with nearly 26,000 railroaders killed on the job from 1888 to 1899. He himself barely averts death in a wreck.

The book is an episodic, and autobiographical, account of life on the railroad, through strikes, management changes, long hours, and assorted dangers. Its light veneer of fictional style qualifies it for entry here.

648. Parsons, Elizabeth. "At the Station." In *An Afternoon*, 185–188. New York: Viking, 1946.

In this good little story, a young woman senses the possibility of escaping the predictable patterns of her life, but lets it pass without acting. Deborah and Hugh sit on the yard at a seaside train station, waiting for her parents to arrive on the afternoon train, to take her home. Another train stands at the station platform, ready to leave. "Suppose we jumped on that train—what would become of us?" thinks Deborah. If Hugh asked her, "she would go, forsaking everything she knew, in the one sure act of her life" (187). Hugh does not ask, and the train leaves. Deborah listens to its whistle, "falling and dying away as the train went off along the valley to the unknown, impossible world" (188).

649. _____. "The Candy Box." In *An Afternoon*, 157–168. New York: Viking, 1946.

Alison boarded the train at Grand Central Station, on her way to somewhere in Connecticut. She sits next to a fat woman who offers her chocolates from a box. Alison declines, and looks at her reflection in the dark glass of the window beside her. Her "image floated on the windowpane, smeared by the rain.... I look positively dead, thought Alison..." (158). In the crowded dining car she shares a table with a slightly drunk but agreeable man, Howard Fuller. Fuller really is the decent sort he seems to be, and offers Alison a helpful reassurance about herself, helpful enough that she takes on a different attitude toward the fat woman and her candy box.

650. Patrick, Q. "Who Killed the Mermaid?" *Ellery Queen's Mystery Magazine* 17 (Feb. 1951): 114–117.

New York City cop Lt. Timothy Trant (Homicide) is riding a Pullman on the Flier, with a true-crime magazine for company. He realizes that the man across the aisle is observing him, with a poor attempt at discretion. The fellow wears a hideous chartreuse tie depicting a mermaid brandishing a cocktail glass. When Lt. Trant returns from the dining car, he finds the man across the aisle dead—strangled with his own necktie. Lt. Trant solves the case with aplomb.

651. Patton, Frances G. "Loving Hands at Home." *New Yorker* 24 (Jan. 29, 1949): 21–26. Also in Patton's *Twenty-Eight Stories*. New York: Dodd, Mead, 1969.

Agatha Debnam rides the train from Georgia to her home in a Philadelphia suburb. It seems to be the very train she rode north to school 25 years earlier, right down to the skinny black porter, "who acted as if he owned the railroad and despised its passengers" (21). During the trip, Agatha reflects on her emotional distance from her Southern relatives and on her satisfaction with her Northern home. At one point, several newly-enlisted soldiers board the train. One of them addresses the black porter: "Hey, Sambo!" he says. "Where do we eat?" (22). The soldiers provoke Agatha's worry over her own draft-age son. On reaching home, she learns that her son has, in fact, enlisted in the Army, and is gone. While she composes a "beautiful" letter to him, she recalls a letter her father wrote to her immediately after she left home for college. She retrieves the letter from an old box, and reads it for the first time in many years. The letter opens her own past to her in ways she thought impossible. The letter, which focuses on her father's association of the train's long-ago departure, is a simple, powerful account of a man losing his daughter to adulthood. Its reference to the train cars going over a bridge—"When the last one was over, I knew that you were gone" (25)—evokes his close ties with his daughter drawn and obscured by time and distance. The story is all the more affecting because of Agatha's late awakening to her own truth.

652. Paul, Louis. "No More Trouble for Jedwick." In *O. Henry Memorial Award Prize Stories of 1934*, edited by Harry Hansen, 3–15. Garden City, New York: Doubleday, Doran, 1934. *Esquire* 1 (March 1934): 58–59+.

Jedwick, an escaped black chain-gang prisoner, walks the railroad track on a blazing hot Virginia day. He hopes to hop a freight up the line and make good his getaway. He kills a man in a shack along the tracks for trying to report him to the police, and continues loping along the tracks toward Alexandria. In the Alexandria yards he briefly joins a white hobo from the North, then hides alone in an empty freight car. Jedwick and a railroad bull carry on a running game of hide-and-seek on the way north; the game ends badly for the bull.

Jedwick is presented as a man who seeks only peace and freedom, but when circumstance dictates—in his own view of himself, at any rate—he resorts to violence. The story benefits from a better-than-usual effort to capture Southern black dialect, and from believable dialog between Jedwick and the people who cross his path. Readers who turn to the story in *Esquire* will see a jarring subheading on its first page: "Account of a chain-gang nigger's effort to make his way from the far South to a haven in Harlem." Editor Arnold Gingrich apparently did not find this use of the word "nigger" troubling.

653. Peake, Elmore Elliott. *The Darlingtons.* New York: McClure, Phillips, 1900. 416p.

The High Point, Rankelman, Ashboro, and Southern Railroad is a 102-mile "system," presided over by C.A. Darlington. He has served in nearly every railroading capacity: fireman, brakeman, station agent, and telegraph operator among the rest. His son is the road's traffic manager; his daughter the auditor and comptroller. Headquarters are in Ashboro, North Carolina. C.A. opens the book at a dedication ceremony for a plush new station in Ashboro; he has bullied stockholders into approving it. He professes—and follows his word—concern for his customers' convenience.

The story's first major conflict involves C.A.'s refusal to provide a pension to the mother of a worker killed while intoxicated on duty. A local minister, Kaltenborn, makes a persuasive pitch for the pension, but C.A. will not yield until much later. Carol Darlington, the auditor, is a strong character, but young Bert Darlington is a binge drinker, going months between bouts, and infuriating C.A. when he falls off the wagon.

Kaltenborn assumes increasing importance for Carol, and much of the novel focuses on their relationship. Passages of pure railroading do appear; in one, C.A. and the roundhouse gang admire a new locomotive: "There were engineers and firemen standing there who regarded a locomotive as little less than human," and Peake expands to describe the intimacy the railroaders feel with the great, insensate object of iron and steel (234). Not to

be missed, either, is Bert in a drunken, axe-swinging fit in the chapter "The New Engine's Mettle," commandeering the new engine on its maiden run and giving the passengers a trip they would not soon forget.

The novel evolves (or declines, depending on one's viewpoint) into an earnest study of Minister Kaltenborn's perceived religious obligations, and Carol's equally earnest determination to go whither he shall goest. The story is much more fun when wild-eyed Bert is wielding his axe.

654. _____. "The Night Run of the 'Overland.'" *McClure's Magazine* 15 (June 1900): 143–149. Also in *The Railroad: Stories from McClure's.* New York: McClure, Phillips, 1901.

Sylvia Fox, a woman born to prosperity, now nurses her sick engineer husband in a hovel near the tracks. Sylvia has disappointed her powerful father with her humble marriage. One winter night, they hear the Overland whistling in the distance; the woman assures her bed-ridden mate that one day "you will hold the throttle of that engine, and I shall be the proudest girl in the land" (144). The Overland stops nearby, and a knock at the door brings with it a plea from the road superintendent: The engineer is suffering a fit of apoplexy. Could not Fox take over? Fox cannot lift his head from his pillow, but volunteers Sylvia for the task, with assurances that she knows an engine as well he does himself. "The superintendent, staggered at this amazing proposition, gasped, and stared at the young woman" (144).

In a story that today is unintentionally hilarious, Sylvia seizes control. What a woman! What a ride! Railroad brass in their private car sip wine and puff on Havana cigars as Sylvia makes up for lost time, hitting 120 miles per hour on the trip. She gives the ride of his life to her own father, railroad President Staniford. "Oh, papa, call me your dear little red-head once more!" she sobs.

655. Pearson, Ridley. *Parallel Lies.* New York: Hyperion, 2001. 356p.

Former homicide cop Peter Tyler investigates unpleasantness on the Northern Union

Railroad, including murder and derailments. The case leads to a threat to the New York City to Washington, D.C. bullet train, the ultimate objective in the revenge scheme of Umberto Alvarez. Alvarez blames the railroad for the deaths of his wife and daughters when an N.U.R. train struck their car. For Alvarez, "nothing short of destroying the huge Northern Union Railroad would do" (6). As is the usual case in such thrillers, the villain is more interesting than his opponents, although Alvarez would be a more entertaining villain if a trifle madder, rather than merely determinedly angry. The novel packs in substantial railroad action, both on and around trains, and picks up speed as it progresses.

656. Pei, Mario. "The Roomette." In *Tales of the Natural and Supernatural*, 143–153. Old Greenwich, CT: Devin-Adair, 1971.

Jim, the narrator, describes events aboard a New York to Chicago train one January. He goes to sleep comfortably in his roomette, but awakens to find a strange woman beside him. When she turns to face him, he recognizes Ann, with whom he had a chaste affair, and whom he has not seen in nearly a decade. The reunion is passionate and joyous; apparently Ann had the roomette across from Jim's, and slipped into his owing to its defective latch. In the morning, Ann is gone, and it takes Jim a month to learn the truth about her ghostly visit.

657. Percy, Walker. *The Moviegoer.* 1961. Reprint, New York: Knopf, 1977. 242p.

Alienated narrator John "Binx" Bolling, searching unsuccessfully for meaning in America—primarily through movies—is a Southern stockbroker. Late in the novel, he and his romantic interest, Kate Cutter, go on a train trip from Louisiana to Chicago for business purposes. It is Bolling's first train trip in a decade. He remarks how trains have changed, with upper and lower berths and other appointments gone. All that seems the same is the disagreeable porter. "Our roomettes turn out to be little coffins for a single person" (184). From the observation car, Bolling watches passing cemeteries that look like cities. He sits next to

a man who neatly underlines passages in a newspaper as the tone of civility in the car deteriorates. Bolling and Kate repair to their roomette, where they sit knee-to-knee and argue about their prospective future. "You remind me of a prisoner in the deathhouse," she says (193).

An interval in a vestibule, fueled by whiskey from Bolling's flask, improves the tenor between them, but when they return to the roomette, the way is again unhappy. When they reach Chicago, Bolling feels like a stranger, overwhelmed by the train station. He and Kate return to Louisiana by bus.

658. _____. "Sieur Iberville." In *Something in Common: Contemporary Louisiana Stories*, edited by Ann B. Dobie, 99–113. Baton Rouge and London: Louisiana State University Press, 1991.

This extract from *The Moviegoer* focuses on the train trip to Chicago described in the preceding entry.

659. Perry, Dick. *The Roundhouse, Paradise, and Mr. Pickering.* Garden City, NY: Doubleday, 1966. 208p.

This enjoyably sentimental, touching, and amusing novel concerns the relationship of the title character, an eccentric Ohio railroad machinist, with young George, the narrator. Mr. Pickering dies shortly before the novel begins when, apparently drunk (a common condition for him), he is struck by a train as he walks along the track. From this point, George looks back on his experiences with Mr. Pickering.

George's father, a longtime New York Central railroader, dies two days after George finishes high school. Setting aside his dreams of going to college and becoming a writer, George hires on at the local roundhouse to help keep the household afloat financially. His first job, running the turntable on the night shift, brings him into contact with Mr. Pickering, who crawls out of the firebox of a locomotive under repair. There he had been sleeping, according to his custom. Mr. Pickering proves to be a selfless soul who feeds baby sparrows in the roundhouse, takes to heart George's future, and aches for the children of a railroader caught stealing company property.

"God is mad at railroads for some reason," he says. "There's got to be a way to get God looking out for the New York Central" (56).

Mr. Pickering hatches a plan to have the roundhouse blessed; he takes kind care of a drunken, delusional woman; in a dreamy fugue, he runs a passenger locomotive through the roundhouse wall; and he plans to make bootleg whiskey with locomotive boilers. The episodic plot is marginal: The real story is the relationship between George and Mr. Pickering. Mr. Pickering's wisest observation: "All the next times is now" (193). The story concludes, delightfully, with an imagined interview in Heaven between God and Mr. Pickering. It is a Heaven few believers would imagine or endorse, but for Mr. Pickering, it sounds just right.

660. Petesch, Natalie L.M. "The Immigrant Train." In *The Immigrant Train and Other Stories*, 41–59. Swallow Press/ Ohio University Press, 1996.

Stasio has boarded a three-car immigrant train bound from Philadelphia to Minnesota. Rumors suggest that the journey may take as long as three weeks. The train takes forever to leave. Impatient, Stasio gets off and enters the station, where he sees "a great round clock on the wall with its red second hands turning slowly and endlessly, like some eternal warning signal" (47). In the station Stasio falls into an engrossing, if mostly incomprehensible, conversation with a news boy, and becomes so rapt in it that he misses his train when it leaves. It is a fateful moment that changes Stasio's life utterly. Some time—apparently years—later, he returns to Philadelphia from Michigan by train. While on the train, he has a dream, or a vision, of his old home in Poland. The dream recurs through the rest of his life, and always ends with him standing on the platform at an empty railroad station, the train gone.

The closing passage of this compassionate and deeply-felt story, suggesting Stasio's loss of his homeland, and the great loneliness implicit in the empty train station, is very moving and expertly composed.

661. _____. "The Orphan Train." In *The Immigrant Train and Other Stories*, 23–39. Swallow Press/Ohio University Press, 1996.

The narrator, Marriek Wesoloski, a New York City orphan, describes growing up in the streets. One day he and his friend Antiosek succumb to the pitch of an orphan train shill. The shill promises them happy new lives in the West if they will join other boys on a train to Michigan. They have a good time on the train, but when they reach northern Michigan, the farmers waiting for them at the station pick the boys like livestock to go home with them. No one wants the pint-sized Marriek, who ends up back on the train, going farther west, without his friend. "As the train speeded up, everything moved past my window like a river—trees, farms, lakes, buildings, towns, churches" (31). Marriek laments his losses— his parents, his friends—as much because they seemed not to regret losing him as because he can no longer associate with them, making him "feel that the rest of my life was going to be like this train: stopping here and there, being sized up, being refused..." (32). Marriek comes to the end of the line in a non-entity of a town in northern Minnesota. There he goes to work for a farmer.

In this grim, humorless story, the railroad is an agent of alienation, separating Marriek from everything and everyone he has cared about.

662. Phelps, Elizabeth Stuart. "Calico." In *Men, Women, and Ghosts*, 265–308. Boston: Fields, Osgood, 1869.
Available at *Wright American Fiction*: http://www.letrs.indiana.edu/web/w/wright2/

Eighteen-year-old Charlotte, better known as Sharley, lives on a farm. She eagerly looks forward to the arrival of the four o'clock train, which will deliver her friend Halcombe Dike. She dresses in fresh calico and lace for his arrival. "Sharley drew her breath when the sudden four o'clock whistle smote the air, and a faint, far trail of smoke puffed through the woods..." (268). Sharley fails to intercept Hal at the station, and soon he leaves, taking the train away, Sharley's ill-focused dreams crumbling with his departure on the train. Time passes, and Sharley mopes, convinced that hers will be a spinster's life. One cold, stormy afternoon she goes out walking on the tracks, and conceives of a solution to her pain. As snow falls and the shriek of an oncoming locomotive rises above the roar of the wind, Sharley lies down by the track and places her neck upon the rail. Her resolve is brief, however, and she tumbles down the embankment and crouches in a snowdrift "till the hideous tempting thing shot by" (299).

In this story of simple "Christian" values, Sharley's resignation to her burden helps lead to her deliverance—into the arms of Halcombe Dike. The three critical appearances of the train—Hal's arrival, his departure, and Sharley's flirtation with suicide—lend the story interest.

663. _____. "Little Tommy Tucker." In *Men, Women, and Ghosts*, 161–172. Boston: Fields, Osgood, 1869.

Available at *Wright American Fiction*: http://www.letrs.indiana.edu/web/w/wright2/ Jack Harmon, a ne'er do well businessman, aims to desert his faithful wife and five children. He buys a ticket for Colorado, and boards the westbound train. He sits in the corner of the car, his hat over his eyes, as the train pulls out. A boy with a fiddle enters the car, seeking to amuse the passengers, and to collect tips, by playing his repertoire of sentimental tunes. Harmon, overcome by thoughts of hearth and family that the boy's playing evokes, renounces his runaway intentions, and returns home. Well within the tradition of American domestic morality fiction, the story is an outing in sentimental piety.

664. Poe, Edgar Allan. "Mellonta Tauta." In *The Collected Tales and Poems of Edgar Allan Poe*, 384–394. New York: Modern Library, 1992. *Godey's Lady's Book* 38 (Feb. 1849): 133–138.

Most of this satirical futuristic tale, purportedly with composition beginning on April Fool's Day, 2848, concerns the narrator Pundita's observations in a series of letters to a friend about balloon travel, and about evident defects in the society of the day. Pundita is off on a grand but not especially agreeable air trip with some 200 other travelers, and complains about the slow pace—not more than 100 miles per hour. In Pundita's letter of April 4, he reminds his friend of another means of travel of the era: "*Do* you remember our flight on the railroad across the Kanadaw continent?—fully three hundred miles the hour—*that* was traveling. Nothing to be seen though—nothing to be done but flirt, feast and dance in the magnificent saloons" (389). Pundita goes on to complain about not being able to see anything from this fast-moving train, and says that he prefers the "slow train" that travels but 100 miles per hour: At least from that train one can look out the window at the passing countryside. Poe may have enjoyed seeing a bullet train in action; on the other hand, it might have seemed to him confirmation of his pessimistic expectations.

665. Poole, Ernest. *The Nancy Flyer*. New York: Thomas Crowell, 1949. 232p.

Beneath the surface of this agreeable historical novel of the New England stagecoach business lurks the shadow of the railroad. The shadow breaks the surface some two-thirds of the way through the story. In Chapter 21, the railroad's threat to the old transport business turns imminent. Local boosters clamor for a railroad, and in 1852 track-laying begins. By December, "the first little locomotive came yowling up the valley ... and at the depot in Littleton, when that infernal engine came spitting fire around the bend at fifteen miles an hour, the fool crowds yelled their lungs out... (168).

Although the horse-drawn coach whose name gives the novel its title defeats the train in a five-mile race, the victory is hollow, for the unstoppable character of the railroad will clearly have its way in the long run. Stagecoaching in the West draws out the string a little further, but the transcontinental railroad tolls the last bell for this romantic way of life. The character focus in the novel is generally on the Nancy's driver, Bob Gale, whom the story follows from his prime in the coach business to his bravely inspired but foolhardy finale in the 1870s.

666. Powell, Lawrence C. *The Blue Train*. Santa Barbara: Capra Press, 1977. 128p.

In Part 1 of this short work, Jack Burgoyne, the American narrator and a student in

Dijon during the Depression, describes boarding and getting situated on a French train
going to Switzerland. There he will meet a
young woman, Nancy Clary, he knows only
from correspondence. They commence an
affair, and Jack takes the train back to Paris.

In Part 2, Jack has a rendezvous aboard a
train with Erda, another young woman. They
go to an hotel; she must eventually leave, again
by train: "and through a smother of steam I
saw its two ruby lights, like the eyes of a beast"
(56).

In Part 3, Jack meets Joyce Davies. They
go to the station together to watch the Blue
Train, the deluxe passenger train bound for
Marseilles. One thing leads to another. "I don't
know which has gone most to my head," says
Joyce, "you, the brandy, or the trains..." (66).
The end is inevitable, and Joyce slips away one
night on the Blue Train, leaving Jack bereft,
but not too bereft for sophisticated chatting
with a sympathetic waiter.

In Part 4, Jack finishes school, and with
a modest sum from his mother's estate feels
well-off. Before taking the train to Nice, he
dines in the station, with a boundless sense
of well-being. He slips into a new affair with
Madeleine Montrechet, one that also ends
with his love vanishing, in a mood of sweet
melancholy, on the Blue Train. Jack is not
done yet: In the concluding chapter,
"Martha," his latest romance evaporates in
the smoke of a train departing Waterloo Station. "Martha put down the window and
reached her hand to me.... The train began to
move. I walked along [the platform] still
holding her hand, until we were pulled apart"
(121).

Poor Jack! Women are always leaving
him behind as they go off on trains. But the
bitterness is sweet, for as Henry Miller observes in the afterword, each of Jack's little
loves features a blossoming, a ripening, and
a death. A reader with a taste for romantic
love unsullied by conventional moral qualms
or the tedious exigencies of the world should
find *Blue Train* a rewarding novel. And, as
Miller observes, there are always the trains.
(Librarians may be happy to know that the
author was the chief librarian at UCLA from
1944 to 1961.)

667. Powell, Richard. *I Take This Land.*
New York: Scribner's, 1963. 437p.

Spanning the years 1895 to 1945, this historical romance concerns the development of
Southwest Florida. A good part of the action
involves hero Ward Campion's efforts to bring
railroad service to the region. Campion, a college man and former locomotive fireman, wins
a railroad charter in a card game. The Fort
Taylor and Southern exists in name only, with
the charter to expire in a year if its terms
go unmet. Campion, who works for railroad
magnate Henry B. Plant (an actual historical
figure) receives little encouragement from his
boss, but perseveres through one setback after
another. A little romance, a little ordinary lust,
too many characters, and a general lack of focus
mark the novel. Fort Taylor is modeled, more
or less, on Fort Myers, Florida.

668. Price, Reynolds. *The Surface of the
Earth.* 1975. Reprint, New York: Scribner Paperback Fiction, 1995. 491p.

One of the main characters here,
Grainger, dreams that he is once again a boy,
traveling by himself on a train through a
springtime countryside. At one point the
white-haired conductor takes Grainger to a car
with only one seat, and tells him to sit there.
An incomprehensible "message" is supposedly
in Grainger's possession. Grainger is miserable
until the dream shifts its tone, and he finds
himself in the presence of a man who will care
for him.

669. Pronzini, Bill. "The Desert Limited." In *Detective Duos*, edited by Marcia Muller and Bill Pronzini, 383–396.
New York and Oxford: Oxford University Press, 1997. *Louis L'Amour Western
Magazine* 2 (Nov. 1995): 39+.

Detectives John Quincannon and Sabina
Carpenter are aboard a passenger train, the
Desert Limited, traversing the California
desert sometime in the 1890s. They tail the
wily criminal, Evan Gaunt. Gaunt eludes them
by crawling out of a bathroom window and
from there atop the fast-moving train—and
then seems to disappear. Gaunt's ruse is clever,
but not clever enough to fool this detective
duo.

670. _____. *Firewind.* New York: M. Evans, 1989. 171p.

"To the yards! Run for the yards!" (68). It is a reasonable command when a wildfire threatens to incinerate the Northern California town of Big Tree; the only hope of escaping the fire lies with the railroad (compare with the Hinckley fire in Entry 560). It sounds like a good plan, but what the would-be escapees do not know is that a pair of boxcars in the train contain ordnance, notably a load of black powder, that had been hoarded by lumber baron Austin Trace. Pronzini races through this fiery melodrama with sure-footed skill. There is nothing serious about the book, but it furnishes excitement, heroes, and villains more than sufficient to its length.

671. _____. "Night Freight." In *Love Kills*, edited by Edward Gorman and Martin H. Greenberg, 74–82. New York: Carroll & Graf, 1997. *Mike Shayne Mystery Magazine*, March 1967.

A man hops a northbound freight somewhere in the California citrus belt, four days after the court granted his wife a divorce. He sits in an empty boxcar with his suitcase, a cold wind coming in the open door, blaming himself for the marriage's failure. Two vagrants also climb aboard the boxcar, and, after demanding cigarettes from the mournful traveler, take his suitcase from him in hopes of finding a sweater or a blanket. The suitcase's contents exceed their expectations, but not agreeably so.

672. _____. "Sweet Fever." In *Midnight Specials: An Anthology for Train Buffs and Suspense Aficionados*, edited by Bill Pronzini, 245–251. Indianapolis: Bobbs-Merrill, 1977. *Ellery Queen's Mystery Magazine* 68 (Dec. 1976): 16–20.

The "sweet fever" is, at first impression, a hankering for the life of a railroader. Here an old man reflects on how his own life was intimately tied to the railroad as he and his grandson wait for a train to emerge from a tunnel. They are surprised to see a man jump from an open boxcar as the train passes. The story quickly changes pace, and the "fever" proves something far more sinister than an occupational craving.

673. Propper, Milton. *The Ticker-Tape Murder.* New York and London: Harper & Bros., 1930. 332p.

This mystery begins with a New Jersey train schedule. The first chapter, "The Body on the Tracks," concerns a run to the seashore, interrupted by the apparent suicide of a man who lay down on the tracks in front of the train. The "suicide," as passenger Detective Daniel Gilmore discerns, is actually a murder; the balance of the novel is devoted to bringing the facts to light, and separating the innocent from the guilty.

674. Pugsley, Edmund E. "Corn in Egypt." *Railroad Magazine* 54 (May 1951): 106–117.

Solomon John, an honest, hard-working track foreman, has no use for the suggestion of his roadmaster, Soapy Bob Waters, that he grab some graft from "the little Japs" (108) Waters is assigning him for a job. "White man, black man, yellow man, brown man all same," Says John. "Same pay, same grub, same work" (109). John, in fact, persuades Waters to let him take on one of the Japanese workers as an assistant foreman; he also helps an injured Japanese worker win compensation from the railroad. John's persistence and creativity finally lead even Bob Waters to acknowledge his merit. (The story's title owes to Waters's interpretation of a Bible story involving an Egyptian with a talent for making a profit.)

675. Putnam, Clay. "The Wounded." In *Twenty Years of Stanford Short Stories*, edited by Wallace Stegner and Richard Scowcroft, 86–99. Stanford, CA: Stanford University Press, 1966. *Tomorrow* 8, no. 11, July 1949.

American soldiers accompany Italian civilians on a train into Italy, where the Italians will return to their homes after the war. At one stop, a pastry cook tries to board the train after it is under way; he falls, and the train runs over and kills him. One morning, well into Italy, the train crew abandons the train. A drunken wake, of sorts, takes place on the train for the dead cook, and Lt. Evander Colum, the chief American character, retrieves a new train crew from a nearby village as the wake proceeds. Colum's antagonist is an American captain with no sense of the gravity of the situation, and who rearranges the bunks in the car to help illustrate strategic points in a past battle.

676. Quad, M. "The Legend of a Baggage Smasher." In *Quad's Odds*, 277–280. Detroit: R.D.S. Taylor, 1875.

Available at *Wright American Fiction*: http://www.letrs.indiana.edu/web/w/wright2/ "Bumps" was a local character whose uncle used his influence to secure the boy a position as a railroad baggage man. "He went on the railroad a pure young man" (277). Bumps realizes early in the game that the only way to retain his post is to treat passengers' luggage as roughly and indifferently as possible; that is the railroad's standard! One day Bumps fails to ruin a piece of luggage, and expires from shame. The railroad tries to find his like, and locates some men who could do serious damage to passengers' belongings, "but they couldn't stand up with that sweet smile on their faces and apologize to passengers in a way to make people feel ashamed that they hadn't brought along more trunks to be demolished" (280).

677. Queen, Ellery. [Frederic Dannay and Manfred B. Lee.] "The Black Ledger." *Ellery Queen's Mystery Magazine* 26 (Dec. 1955): 100–106. Also in *Queen's Bureau of Investigation*. Boston: Little, Brown, 1954.

Ellery Queen has agreed with federal agents to transport a ledger with the names of figures involved in a nation-wide narcotics ring from New York to Washington, D.C., via the Capitol Limited. The Dope King apprehends Queen on the way to Pennsylvania Station, and in Queen's train compartment searches Queen for the ledger—thoroughly. This is an amusing little story of yet another Queenly bit of cleverness.

678. _____. "Snowball in July." In *Midnight Specials: An Anthology for Train Buffs and Suspense Aficionados*, edited by Bill Pronzini, 165–174. Indianapolis: Bobbs-Merrill, 1977. *Ellery*

Queen's Mystery Magazine 28 (July 1956): 123–129.

Inspector Queen sets out to track down a missing train in this semi-digestible mystery, redeemed only by some smart lines.

Queen, Ellery *see also* Ross, Barnaby

679. Quertermous, Max. "Night Train to Memphis." *University Review* 35 (Winter 1968): 106–112.

The narrator is taking the train to Memphis on a rainy night. A young woman, perhaps 25, sits next to him, and begins to describe a ghastly compulsion that came to her in a dream. She talks until the train reaches Memphis, and leaves the narrator thoroughly unsettled. The sense of powerlessness at witnessing a passing embodiment of imminent horror is potent.

680. Quick, Herbert. *Aladdin & Co.: A Romance of Yankee Magic*. New York: Henry Holt, 1904. 337p.

Quick takes financial speculation to task in this novel of a Western boomtown, Lattimore, and the men who puff it up—and see it collapse. Albert Barslow, the narrator, is the friend and partner of James Elkins, the prime mover—the magician—in Lattimore's adventure. Elkins is an insurance agent looking for greater prosperity, and turns to Lattimore as a laboratory to test his ideas. When Barslow and his wife arrive from the Midwest in Lattimore, they find that it lacks rail service. After assorted financial shenanigans, the railroad comes to town, to the huzzahs of the locals. Not everyone sees the commercial developments afoot as evidence of forthcoming perpetual prosperity. Old General Lattimore, with perceptions honed by time and experience, warns that those who "buy to-day and sell to-morrow," eventually, "having, in their greed, grasped more than they can keep ... [find that] all at once the thing stops, and the dervish-dance ends in coma, in cold forms and still hands, in misery and extinction!" (160–161).

Lattimore's boosters ignore this prophecy. Typical is the reaction of syndicate member J. Bedford Cornish: "Of course ... we must keep boosting ... whooping it up for Lattimore"

(207). In time, Lattimore's house of cards begins to teeter. The climax comes in a mad train run through blizzard and flood, in hopes of saving the day; unlike the results in scores of popular railroading stories, the day is not saved: Failure strikes. It is not total failure; as the denouement shows, Lattimore climbs out of the pit its blinkered boosters have dug for it—but it climbs slowly, to emerge with perhaps a wiser collective consciousness than prevailed in its boomtown days.

681. Raine, William M. *Roads of Doubt.* New York: Grosset & Dunlap, 1925. 327p. *Woman's Home Companion* 52 (Feb. 1925): 15+; (March 1925): 23+; (April 1925): 29+.

Jarvis Elliott is trying to build a railroad through a section of the Rocky Mountains thought impassable by rail, in hopes of cutting 200 miles from the transcontinental route. He "dreams, and translates his dreams into reality.... He's an empire builder" (53). Actual railroading, however, plays a relatively minor part in the story. The chief matter is Elliott's daughter Joyce's standing in for her father when he is badly injured in an accident. Joyce is a modern woman fond of country clubs, cars, and the cad Ordway. Her assumption of responsibility for her father's work helps her realize how little she cares for his handsome but villainous rival, Winthrop Ordway, a man "notoriously ready to take all a woman would give" (5). Heavens! Joyce acquires a conscience, and sees that the upright construction engineer Bob Hallack is a more suitable suitor than Ordway. Railroading here means little except as a handy tool to jump-start a conventional romance.

682. _____. *Roaring River.* New York: Grosset & Dunlap, 1934. 297p.

Jim Grey, son of New York railroad magnate Aldous Grey, has frittered away much of his young life at shallow amusements. The elder Grey sends Jim out West to remove him from the temptations posed by his "chorus girl" girlfriend. Banished to Wyoming, Jim, under the alias Tom Green, works at the roughest jobs, eventually pulling fresh ties on a sled in winter, and goes on to a critical role in his

father's efforts to build a connecting link between his Denver Central and the Pacific & Utah Railroads. Fistfights (the dust jacket shows two handsome, manly men gracefully clobbering each other), log jams, forest fires, and true love are prominent ingredients in this romantic potboiler. Its "bound to rise" theme has much in common with the Horatio Alger, Jr., books, but is pitched at an older (if only slightly more sophisticated) audience than the one that inhaled the Alger stories.

683. _____. "The Winning of the Transcontinental." *McClure's Magazine* 14 (April 1900): 573–578. Also in *The Railroad: Stories from McClure's.* New York: McClure, Phillips, 1901.

Jim Messiter of Willapa Bend doggedly advocated the West Coast town as the best terminus for the Trans-Continental Railroad. Willapa Bend, a booming but raw and bleak place, is clearly a second choice to the better-established town of Inverness. When the railroad president comes to look over the prospects, Messiter wins his favor, and the railroad, with modest good taste, tasty home cooking, and a cordial game of whist. The mayor of Inverness blows his chance with over-aggressive salesmanship and insensitivity. The railroad's arrival means everything to the town, and Messiter promises everything: a bridge over the river, convenient right of way, a good site for an ocean wharf, and plenty of room for rail yards and shops. The feeling is that Messiter would hand over his shoes and socks to the railroad if it would sway the decision toward Willapa Bend. Present-day readers may wish to compare the generosity of Willapa Bend with that of cities giving huge tax breaks to companies that promise to build new plants, or simply to stay in town.

684. Rand, Ayn. *Atlas Shrugged.* New York: Random House, 1957. 1,168p.

This would-be doorstop is perhaps the worst novel that anyone ever took seriously. Rand's enthusiasts take it seriously, indeed; many consider it her best book. It is not; *The Fountainhead* is better, if only because it is shorter. Set in the near future, this exposition of Rand's ideas features a brainy, self-possessed heroine, Dagny Taggart, official of the Taggart Transcontinental Railroad. Her ambition is to run the railroad in a businesslike, aggressive way, in the face of a national economy going to hell on a very fast handcart, owing to simpering notions of socialism and such that have left American industry enfeebled and passive. As Dagny struggles nobly, more and more of the nation's most creative individuals are dropping from sight, leaving the country at the whim of government flunkies who excel only at incompetence. The novel's major character is not Taggart, but John Galt, whose presence is felt only by implication and reference until relatively late in the story. The book's first line, "Who is John Galt?" (eventual answer: a pompous windbag), has become a catch-phrase in this dreary society to indicate general despair. Galt is the brilliant antagonist of the forces of federal evil and economic blight who lies behind the disappearances of the gifted.

Fundamentally a tract for the advancement of Rand's "philosophy," the novel goes on as if it will never cease, with its cast of paperboard characters and its shallow, sour grasp of being human. The reader who can hold out until trudging the full length of Galt's late harangue to the nation ("This Is John Galt Speaking," Part 3, Chapter 7—in which Galt bloviates without pause for an incredible 60 pages) deserves either commendation or sympathy, or both. Readers who would like to absorb much of the message of *Atlas Shrugged* in a more readable, shorter book may wish to turn to Garet Garrett's *The Driver* (Entry 292), which may or may not deserve its reputation among some readers as the inspiration, or blame, for Rand's novel.

685. Rawlings, Marjorie Kinnan. "The Provider." In *Short Stories*, 326–337. Gainesville: University Press of Florida, 1994. *Woman's Home Companion* 68 (June 1941): 20–21.

As in some other railroad stories, here the main character constructs an elaborate "understanding" of the life of strangers, in this case of strangers observed from the cab of an engine. The fantasist is Joe, a fireman. Joe is a man without a family, but with a great desire for one. In a pitiful manner he adopts a poor family who live in a shack on his regular run through the Georgia countryside. He regularly tosses them a shovelful of coal to help heat their house. He also dreams of providing them other material comforts, and studies catalogs, pondering clothes for the two small children who live in the shack. Joe eventually gets sacked for giving away the coal, but losing his job makes it easier for him to concentrate on his ersatz family. When he finally comes to knock at the shack's door, he finds the place abandoned; an envelope with a return address he finds in the deserted shack stirs his hopes of finding the former occupants. "A man's thoughts, a man's dreams—Why they were thoughts and dreams," reflects Joe, "and there was a long bridge between them and the world of fact" (337). A nice story, insightful and sad; compare with Thomas Wolfe's "The Far and the Near" (Entry 940).

686. Reamer, Charles W. "John Hammel, Railroad Conductor." *National Magazine; An Illustrated Monthly* 10 (June 1899): 310–315.

"I'm taking this train to hell, and you're going with it" (315). Thus warns the demented locomotive engineer in this story, addressing the principal character, a nameless tramp. The tramp has begged to ride the train to Rockford, where he hopes to find work, and Conductor Hammel finally relented, reminded by the tramp of his own son, vanished these many years. The tale leaps to a high niche on the sentimentality scale when the truth about the tramp—revealed only after his heroic death in the confrontation with the engineer—becomes known.

687. Reed, John. "The Thing to Do." In *Adventures of a Young Man; Short Stories from Life*, 83–88. 1966. Reprint, San Francisco: City Lights, 1975.

Reed is the author of *Ten Days That Shook the World*, on the Russian Revolution. In this story, written in 1916, the narrator describes his trip from the Pacific Coast to Chicago aboard the Lucullus Limited, " a train which loses an immense sum of money every trip it makes. For it provides all the comforts of a hotel and a club ... and tea in the observation car" (83). The chief part of the story concerns the narrator's efforts to engage an English passenger in discussion of the war in Europe. The Englishman, on his way to join the fighting because it is "the thing to do," takes a disdainful tone toward the narrator, who suggests that even in England the war may prompt class conflict.

688. Reeve, Alice M. "The Train Stepped Aside." *Good Housekeeping* 102 (Jan. 1936): 88–91+.

Although it settles into a cozy endorsement of true love, this story initially flirts with ideas more provocative. Reta Fleming and her mother are aboard the Gold Coast Limited, and Reta, although excited at the trip, is a little nervous, "aware of something final, of something almost terrifying, in the way this train thundered down the tracks like a monster that rushed her inevitably away from everything familiar into the dark unknown" (88). On the train, Reta—herself heading for her wedding—meets her old friend Gerrie Parr, also on the way to his wedding. At a station stop, Reta watches from her window as a young woman exits the train, straight into the embrace of a young man on the platform.

Reeve likens the train to "A comet hurtling through space. Tiny people going on tiny missions, on and on into the night..." (103). At a stop in Ogden, Utah, Reta and Gerrie take a walk in the snowy streets, until the train's whistle summons them: "Because you couldn't escape from it. Nobody, anywhere, could ever escape from the train" (103–104)— that is, the inexorable requirements of convention and propriety. When the Gold Coast Limited leaves the station without them, Reta and Gerrie act decisively to address their mutual interest.

689. Reeve, Arthur B. "The Treasure-Train." In *The Treasure-Train*, 1–25. New York: Grosset & Dunlap, 1917.

Professor Craig Kennedy, "scientific detective," contends with a modern-day tactic in a train robbery: a chlorine gas assault on the train. The nefarious scheme entails not only robbery, but manipulation of the Continental Express Company's stock price. Prof. Kennedy,

who might feel in good company with Francis Lynde's Scientific Sprague, is up to the task.

690. Reilly, Helen. *Compartment K.* 1955. Reprint, New York: Macfadden-Bartell, 1971. 239p.

In this serviceable murder mystery, the train fulfills its most reliable function for mysterious purposes: packing a quantity of characters, including suspects, into a conveniently sealed environment for a protracted time. As Detective Todhunter, the prime sleuth, observes, "a big overland train was an excellent scene for a successful killing" (39). The action begins with a gruesome homicide in New York City, and quickly moves on to a crowded Canadian Pacific train heading from Montreal across the continent toward the Rockies. One of the passengers is the killer, and not long into the journey, a male passenger turns up shot to death in Compartment K. It is not the last death in the tale. In a sense, the train could have been a desert island, a cruise ship, or an Antarctic camp: The only point (aside from exploiting the innate romance of train travel) is to isolate the principals.

691. Rettock, C.M. "A Railroad Tragedy." *National Magazine; An Illustrated Monthly* 9 (Feb. 1899): 458–462.

Put this one in the bathos pile. On Christmas Eve, big-hearted engineer Bill Edwards will not tolerate brakeman Reddy's appropriation of his Mexican wood-passer's blanket when they bed down on the floor of a freight car on their stalled train. Edwards and Reddy struggle; the matter seems resolved, to Reddy's embarrassment, but as Edwards drops off to sleep, Reddy shoots him, wounding him mortally. Reddy himself comes to a ghastly end. In the conclusion, Edwards expires in the arms of one of his trainmen, gamely insisting with his last breath that "I shall spend Christmas—at—ho—" (462).

692. Rhodes, Eugene Manlove. "Consider the Lizard." In *The Best Novels and Stories of Eugene Manlove Rhodes*, edited by Frank V. Dearing, 401–426. Boston: Houghton Mifflin, 1949. *Saturday Evening Post* 185 (June 28, 1913): 3–5+.

Rhodes describes a train hold-up in New

Mexico. The brigands clean out the goods of train and passengers. There is nothing unusual in the basic situation, but Rhodes approaches it with a skewed perspective. His robbers are good-humored and genteel, and Rhodes reports their doings with a comic undertone that lends a degree of mirth to the proceedings. The robbery causes a great sensation in the town of Oasis, where the sheriff rounds up a posse to apprehend the crooks. Two locals, Johnny and Todd, exercise their wits, more adeptly than the sheriff, in an amusing turning-of-the-tables. The story's title alludes to seeing all that there is to see when one looks at something, whether a lizard or a train robbery. Rhodes, who was a genuine cowboy, writes with authenticity of men on horseback, and informs his story with a clever wit and sense of justice.

Rice, Craig *see* Palmer, Stuart, and Craig Rice

693. Richter, Conrad. "Smoke Over the Prairie." In *Early Americana, and Other Stories*, 38–83. New York: Knopf, 1936. *Saturday Evening Post* 207 (June 1, 1935): 5–7+.

Frank Gant, of the town of Capitan, manages mule and bull train wagoneers on their cross-desert treks. He considers plans for a railroad to span the southwestern desert naught but a scheme to wrest bond money from desert towns. The railroad will come to nothing, he thinks, after soaking the citizens for millions. This attitude augurs ill for his daughter Juliana's suitor, the railroad's chief engineer, Vance Rutherford. The couple elopes; Rutherford later offers Gant a chance to buy stock in the forthcoming railroad, but Gant rudely dismisses him.

Soon the smoke of the locomotives on the approaching railroad rises from the prairie beyond Capitan. The story's narrator, Gant's son, considers his mother's equation of the railroad's arrival with that of civilization: "I could tell ... that in this thing my mother called civilization there was no quarter, no compromise, no pity." This was, in fact, something "of another and newer age" (66–67).

When Gant refuses to sell land for the railroad right of way, the road threatens legal action. The story ends with a fatal crash involving Gant's own buggy and a train. Gant's son, injured in the wreck, looks from the train through the crowd including his sister, who had planned to celebrate the 4th of July in Capitan. "All I could see," he says, "between tailored trousers and gaily flounced dresses were the iron bands of the railroad running triumphantly westward and glinting like mottled silver in the sun" (83). The story nicely evokes the relentless advance of the railroad and the inexorable disappearance of an earlier way of life that lies in its path.

694. Rinehart, Mary Roberts. *The Man in Lower Ten.* Indianapolis: Bobbs-Merrill, 1909.

When the narrator, Blakely, enters a Pullman, he comments on the "dingy" curtains and the sweating porter, "trying to be in six places at once: somebody has said that Pullman porters are black so they won't show the dirt, but they certainly show the heat" (24). Contemporary readers will not be much inclined to this novel, except for the unintentional sociological insight it offers. The plot concerns a mystery involving the occupant of a lower berth on a Pullman crossing Pennsylvania. The egregious racism embodied in the quote above is not the book's unique example. When the "darky" porter discovers a murdered man on the train, he loses his composure and rolls his eyes. The reader visualizes Stepin Fetchit at his most embarrassing.

695. Roach, C.A. "Boomers Eastbound." In *Tales of the Rails*, edited by Veronica Hutchinson, 252–268. Cleveland and New York: World Publishing, 1952. *Railroad Magazine* 56 (Dec. 1951): 92–100.

Boomer Roach and his buddy, Hungry John, reverse Greeley's exhortation, and in 1895 head east looking for work. Pickings are poor, but Roach finally lands a brakeman's job in Danville, North Carolina. Working on a run where men have not often lasted long, he finds that someone has been tampering with brake mechanisms, and suspects that a derailment was sabotage. Most of the trainmen attribute the problems to "spooks." Roach dismisses the notion of spiritual intervention in railroad business, and soon discovers that the line's bad fortune owes to a deranged railroader and to a farmer with a grudge over a cow killed on the tracks. Although a capable sleuth, Roach has his fill of railroading east of Chicago or Cincinnati: "There're too many odd occurrences way back in the hills of North Carolina," he concludes (268).

696. "Road-Side Story." In *To Live and Die: Collected Stories of the Civil War, 1861–1876,* edited by Kathleen Diffley, 321–330. Durham, NC, and London: Duke University Press, 2002. Originally published in *Land We Love,* Aug. 1866.

A man in a train station waiting room invites an old woman to sit nearer the fire. The old woman and the boy with her are obviously poor, to judge by their clothes. Sometime later a well-dressed young woman enters. As the group awaits the train, the old woman relates a wrenching account of the hardship, hunger, and loss that she and her family endured during the Civil War. At the end of the story, "we three bowed our heads and wept together" (330). They are strangers in the station, but a spontaneous unity of feeling overcomes them.

697. Robinson, Arthur. "The Boy on the Train." *New Yorker* 64 (April 11, 1988): 36–43. Also in *The Best American Short Stories, 1989.* Edited by Margaret E. Atwood and Shannon Ravenel. Boston: Houghton Mifflin, 1989.

The chance discovery that old Lewis Barber Fletcher rode the New York Central, alone, from Florida to Camden, New York, at the age of five in 1891 causes a minor family uproar. The old man had forgotten the trip until reminded of it by a newspaper clipping. Son Edward tries to imagine his father being led to the train by his own father, "so dumb with misery and fright that he couldn't cry, knowing only that he was going somewhere out there into unknown space" (37). The railroad disappears from the story after its second page, but it serves its purpose of setting the story in

motion, and providing an important point of departure for familial insights.

698. Robinson, Barbara. "Last Train to Elm Grove." *McCall's* 100 (May 1973): 72–73+.

A high-school senior accompanies her grandfather on a one-car train trip from Scioto Station, Ohio, to Elm Grove. Her grandfather is "an old railroad man, forced to retire before what he considered his prime" (128). Aboard the train, the old man meets a long-ago friend, Billy Wilson, who has come all the way from Detroit to make a farewell ride on the route. The trip turns into a 30-mile tour of the past, with Grandpa, Billy, and other old passengers recalling and debating every feature that had marked the way in years gone by. The young woman finds the recollection a little hard to endure, but discovers that she herself is aroused to examine her memories when the train returns to her home town of Scioto. From her train window, she sees passing buildings and other landmarks that prompt thoughts of her disappearing childhood—and her grandfather's excited engagement with the past no longer seems so much the behavior of an old man without a future.

699. Robinson, Kim Stanley. "A Transect." In *Remaking History,* 224–235. New York: Doherty, 1991. *Magazine of Fantasy and Science Fiction* 70 (May 1986): 61–70.

The story moves back and forth from a salesman traveling to the U.S. by train from Montreal to a black bricklayer traveling by train in South Africa under apartheid in a coach full of immigrants. The story's title suggests the coming together of two very different lives. If the story is not completely successful, it is nevertheless original and interesting.

700. Rodney, George B. *The Vanishing Frontier.* New York: Grosset & Dunlap, 1935. 247p.

The year is 1868, and the Union Pacific Railroad is pushing west across the continent. As the rails advance, the laborers are "cursed by their contractors, man-handled by their section bosses [and] they also lived in daily fear of the Indians who realized all too late what that twin line of steel meant to them and to their hunting grounds" (3). U.S. Cavalry officer Barry Newton helps keep order in the wild and booming territory; important business takes place at the Golden Spike saloon— named in anticipation of the transcontinental road's completion ceremony. "Cavalry! Indians! Buffalo!" shouts the dust jacket, and that about sums up the book, although this is the sort of Western in which Indians tend to be "Injuns." The railroad's chief function here, as in many books in the genre, is to provide an excuse for wild Western action.

701. Rohde, William L. "Conductorette." *Railroad Magazine* 84 (Jan. 1969): 28–30. *Railroad Magazine* 37 (Jan. 1945): 96–101.

Conductor Tim O'Brien (Zip O'Brien in the 1945 version) is skeptical when Phyllis Quinn, whose father was a mountain division trainmaster, joins him as brakewoman on his train. O'Brien calls her a "conductorette." "Train service is no job for females," he thinks (28), but Phyllis, well-trained by her father, handles all her responsibilities. On Christmas Eve, she exceeds all male expectations by saving her train from being rear-ended by a freight. Her reward: O'Brien marries her. "You don't often see a conductor kissing a brakeman," says one character (30). Probably not; and in pulp railroad fiction, one seldom sees a woman railroader spurn romance won as a result of doing her job.

702. Roosevelt, Robert B. *Five Acres Too Much: A Truthful Elucidation of the Attractions of the Country.* New York: Harper & Bros., 1869. 296p.

Available at *Wright American Fiction*: http://www.letrs.indiana.edu/web/w/wright2/

In a satirical treatment of getting away from the city to savor the good life in the country, Roosevelt includes a funny chapter, "The Country—How to Get There." One of the chief ways to get there, of course, is by railroad. Roosevelt ridicules the railroad's comfort, safety, and ability to follow its schedule: "There is an unreasonable prejudice in the public mind against being killed on a railroad. There are many worse deaths: there is hanging,

for instance..." (79). The narrator deliberately chooses the most unprotected seat on the train, so that "if I am to be killed, have it done out of hand and without prolonged inconvenience" (80). He describes waiting on a platform "not more than two feet wide, and, unmoved, let[ting] one train whiz past in one direction and another whiz past in the contrary, without allowing dress or person to be caught or struck.... Of course, a few 'go under' in learning how, but the mass of the traveling public is vastly improved by the experience" (81). (The author was Theodore Roosevelt's uncle.)

703. Rose, Meredith. "On the Train—Off the Train." *Chiron Review* 50 (1997): 30.

A woman—a lesbian reading Allen Ginsberg's poetry to pass the time—has just acquired a very short haircut before boarding the California Zephyr in Chicago. A man sits down next to her. Talking to someone on his cellphone, he says that he is "sitting next to this fella.... From Massachusetts." The woman, mortified, feels compelled to pretend to be the "man" for whom she has been mistaken. She retreats to the first deck of the car, where another man also mistakes her for a man. Not until she reaches California and is reunited with her girlfriend does she feel relieved of the confusion and anger her appearance has precipitated.

704. Rosenfeld, Isaac. "The Railroad." In *Preserving the Hunger; An Isaac Rosenfeld Reader*, edited by Mark Shechner, 287–298. Detroit: Wayne State University Press, 1988. *Kenyon Review* 9, no. 2 (Spring, 1947): 235–247.

The narrator, now an itinerant telegraph operator, describes his years spent in the railroad control tower as the very best of his life. The post was not so much a mere job; "It was rather a work of inwardness, as when we say a life's work or a work of love" (287). A tragic accident near his tower, although not his fault, drove him away from control tower work. The story is full of closely-observed details; for example, the narrator turned up the kerosene heater in the tower when he took over from the day man on winter nights, and long afterward "the odor of kerosene is to me the odor of solitude and peace" (288). In another passage he speaks of the collective humanity behind the railroad's operation, invoking the need for faith in such functionaries as the engineer, the ticket sellers, freight agents, stevedores, gatemen, track inspectors, stationmasters, and others who work toward the same end. He calls the railroad "an intimate thing to the men it embraces, and we are all content to have it so" (291).

The narrator's true wife is not the woman to whom he is married, and from whom he is separated months at a time, but the railroad. He has a mistress in Salt Lake City, a waitress at the railroad station lunch counter. The railroad allows its workers to learn many things, so "that in the end we become the fools of our own wisdom and give ourselves anew to each experience in the hope that our knowledge will at last bear fruit" (295).

The story possesses considerable depth, in both the narrator's reflections on his life and work, and beyond that to implications about personal identity, the meaning of work, and the connections (or lack thereof) among people.

705. Ross, Barnaby [Ellery Queen]. *The Tragedy of X.* New York: Viking, 1932. 373p.

The railroad's presence in this whodunit is slight, but vital: A broker is cleverly murdered aboard a New York City street railway car. Suspicion turns to conductor Charles Wood, who himself is soon hauled up dead from the river. The mystery is one of those unfortunate productions that, rather than revealing the truth along the way, relies on a long-winded concluding explanation of who, what, where, when, and why.

706. Ruffin, Paul. "Trains." *Southern Humanities Review* 31, no. 3 (Summer 1997): 231–236.

With his father away at war, the narrator stays with his mother at his grandparents' house, two blocks from the tracks in Millport, Alabama. He loves the trains, "chuffing, blaring, clacking trains" (231). His grandfather, too, pays special attention to every train arrival.

The boy reveres the big steam engines: "Even sitting still it throbbed with energy, straining to be on its way again, like some colossal black beast happy with its lot, glad to pull for the men who fed it" (232). The train represents to him the world that he has not seen, one of great cities, beautiful women, and powerful men. The engineer, admired then like an airline pilot in a later era, was "a man of gravity and dignity" (234). The narrator describes in fine detail the train and its cars at a station, the train crew, and the activity at the depot. He remembers one conductor especially, a tall, well-built black man who gave the impression of aristocratic imperiousness: "His was a different language from that of the local blacks, curt and crisp, his teeth flashing boldly when he spoke, though he never smiled" (235). (Given the rigid barriers to African-Americans serving as conductors anywhere until at least the late 1960s, one must doubt the accuracy of this memory.)

Very much in the form of a childhood memoir, this story presents a marvelously precise picture of a four-year-old's perceptions, filtered through a grown man's understanding.

707. "Run for Life: A Railroad Adventure." *Harper's Weekly* 5 (Oct. 5, 1861): 639.

This story combines father-son conflict, survivor guilt, the hazards of alcohol, and slam-bang action, all in one page. Charley, the narrator, describes how he spent his early life among the shops and men of the railroad, where his father worked. His ambition was to become a locomotive engineer, like his friend Mark Hibberd's father. Hibberd's father was a fine engineer, but given to drink. One evening in the 1840s, when 15-year-old Charley and Mark were lounging about the engine house, they expanded on a modest bit of assistance to a shopworker and took the engine he was working on out onto the main line, planning a run of a few minutes' duration before returning. The outing proved a disaster when Mark's drunken father came flying up behind the boys' engine on another engine. The elder Hibberd, beyond reason or influence, precipitated "the great accident to the night express," with lethal results.

708. Runkel, William M. *Wontus, or, The Corps of Observation*. Philadelphia: Lippincott, 1874. 363p.

Available at *Wright American Fiction*: http://www.letrs.indiana.edu/web/w/wright2/
New Yorker Olympus Wontus, disturbed by the Civil War's early stages, decides that he will organize a "corps of observation" (he pronounces it "corpse"), and visit the conflict to use his personal fortune to assist the troops. It is difficult to imagine anyone reading this novel for pleasure today, in part because of its jarring vacillations between a comical tone and seriousness. Nevertheless, its occasional references to the railroad help illuminate its place in the war. Runkel describes the scene at the Washington depot, overrun with "Grief-stricken mothers in search of wounded sons; disheartened wives in search of missing husbands; bereaved sisters prepared to follow a loved soldier-brother to a premature grave; men seeking office; politicians seeking jobs; statesmen, soldiers, seamen, and men of every cast, condition, and complexion..." and, in Mr. Wontus's view, all acting in "supreme selfishness" (95–96).

Wontus and his companions travel by rail to follow the Army, and render aid to the injured and dying. Their efforts are not without risk: On a train run to Washington to obtain mess supplies, they come under attack by Confederate raiders: "I saw about three hundred ranged along the railroad, firing away at us as if it was a glorious piece of fun..." (312).

709. Rushmore, Robert. "The Stopping Train." In *A Life in the Closet, and Stories*, 104–117. Indianapolis: Bobbs-Merrill, 1973.

A young psychiatrist struggles to help William Sanderson, a former GI who lives in England, understand why he had sought to grasp a young woman's breast aboard a crowded train. The doctor is convinced that the key to Sanderson's uncharacteristic impetuosity lies in a past rejection by a woman with whom he enjoyed trainboard trysts as a young man. The doctor is correct about the answer lying in the past; he is wrong about what the answer is.

710. Russell, John. "McKeon's Graft." *Golden Book Magazine* 5 (March 1927): 350–354. Also in Russell's *In Dark Places*. New York: Knopf, 1923.

Latin American station agent McKeon also fills the roles of shipping clerk, postmaster, freight handler, conductor, brakeman, and express messenger. The story opens with him looking over his customers of the day. He is disappointed to see "an undue preponderance of lighter skins. That meant, naturally, more passengers who could not be bluffed with safety into paying twice the legal fare, more difficulty in fixing arbitrary freight rates, and less reward for a hard-working functionary like himself" (350). McKeon cheats both customers and the railroad in his campaign of modest graft. His point of view changes when a group of bandits attempts to seize control of the train. A company official happens to be on board, in disguise, and witnesses McKeon's brave struggle with the felons. "They wanted to rob the company!" says McKeon. (354).

711. Ryan, Alan. "Hear the Whistle Blowing." In *The Bones Wizard*, 116–132. New York: Doubleday, 1988. Also in *After Midnight*. Edited by Charles L. Grant. New York: Doherty, 1986.

Wayne, an engineer, is thoroughly rattled by the wreck he recently experienced on the Chicago-Champaign run. His brakeman alerted him to the red van racing toward the crossing ahead of the fast-moving freight; the train nailed the van, full of teenagers, dead center. None of Wayne's fellow trainmen can grasp his feelings, not even Dickie Clinton, who once plowed through a van carrying eight retarded adults. Wayne feels anger, remorse, sadness, disgust—and something else. The something else is a ghastly, barely-suppressed ambition to go on hitting vehicles with his train, to increase the death toll. When Wayne meets a mysterious drifter, Ford Spellman, Ford gives Wayne the insight he requires to go on, in a most unnerving fashion.

712. Saroyan, William. "Old Country Advice to the American Traveler." In *My Name Is Aram*, 185–191. New York: Harcourt, Brace, 1940.

Before Uncle Melik travels by train from Fresno to New York, his old Uncle Garro visits him and plumps him full of nonsensical exhortations about maintaining his personal safety aboard the train. Uncle Melik listens closely, does the opposite of what Uncle Garro advises, and has a very enjoyable trip. A modestly funny little piece.

713. _____. "Train Going." In *Great Railroad Stories of the World*, edited by Samuel Moskowitz, 157–160. New York: McBride, 1954. Also in Saroyan's *The Saroyan Special*. New York: Harcourt, Brace, 1948.

In this brief, emotionally intense story—less a story than a vision reduced to words—Saroyan speaks of "What hearts break at railway stations, and how the tears fall" (157). The two principal moments of heartbreak are the partings of lovers and the separation of mothers from their sons as the sons board trains to go to war: "The mothers of life stand in the railway stations of the world and weep. And they know, as the lover knows, that it shall ever be so" (159). Here the train represents not simply departure, but grievous, irreparable, and unavoidable loss.

714. Schaefer, Jack. "Raid on the Railroad." *Saturday Evening Post* 232 (April 30, 1960): 34–35+.

When a Santa Fe railroad engineer startles several dozen horses just rounded up with considerable trouble by a band of tired cowboys into a stampede, the cowboys vent their rage on the railroad and the trainmen. The foolishness extends to one cowboy lassoing the smokestack of the engine and breaking it loose. Boys will be boys in the Old West, evidently, and the code of frontier behavior absorbs the "raid" in stride.

715. Schoenfeld, Howard. "All of God's Children Got Shoes." In *Midnight Specials: An Anthology for Train Buffs and Suspense Aficionados*, edited by Bill Pronzini, 175–184. Indianapolis: Bobbs-Merrill, 1977. *Ellery Queen's Mystery Magazine* 22 (Aug. 1953): 120–125.

In this good, economically-told tale of subtle menace, the narrator and his buddy Carl, two vagrant, petty thieves, are riding the rails through the South. Carl's pal wants a new pair of shoes, and obtains one after frightening a naïve reporter out of his wits. These two "gentlemen of the open road" meet several other hoboes, either professional or occasional, on their route, and treat all of them with a chilling contempt. The undertone of imminent violence recalls the effect Ernest Hemingway achieves in "The Battler" (Entry 344). A streak of humor, although humor of a decidedly warped sort, makes the story's unsettling undercurrents all the more potent.

716. Schramm, Wilbur L. "Dan Peters and Casey Jones." *Saturday Evening Post* 215 (Jan. 9, 1943): 9–11+. Also in Schramm's *Windwagon Smith, and Other Yarns*. New York: Harcourt, Brace, 1947.

Mild and dependable engineer Dan Peters, whose chief quirk is that he talks to his engine, "Casey Jones," has disappeared with his train somewhere on his usual Ohio milk run. Stories surface of a train running about the countryside, but not on the tracks. Hallucinatory train sightings pepper the Midwest, and truck drivers report being run off the road—by a locomotive. An enjoyable fantasy rooted in fears about what happens to men whose machines become their masters, rather than their servants in labor.

717. Schuyler, Charles H. *"Jim": A Railroad Novel.* Omaha: Henry Gibson, 1892. 386p.

Jim, a young engine wiper, opens this novel by freeing an engineer trapped in a wrecked locomotive, with a fire approaching—by cutting off his leg with an axe. Jim's heroics save the poor fellow from death by fire; he bleeds to death, instead. Schuyler follows this melodramatic absurdity with a passage of surpassing bathos: He pictures the situation at the dead engineer's home, where his bereft wife and mother swoon, and his uncomprehending small children wonder why their father is late, even as the chaplain of the Brotherhood of Locomotive Engineers comes to the door.

Jim soon becomes a telegraph operator with the road. Schuyler provides footnotes in several places that explain the terms and codes Jim sends and receives. Jim's new job is complicated by Percy Ravenwood, the man he replaced. Ravenwood was stealing from the railroad, and bears Jim a grudge. Soon Jim becomes the depot office manager. Ravenwood continues to bother Jim, who moves on to become an operator with a telegraph company in New York City. He takes the train to Colorado to assist in the apprehension of Ravenwood; while Jim and some railroad colleagues pursue him, Ravenwood takes up train robbery.

The novel concludes with a paean to railroad unionization, and with Jim in California as a passenger train conductor. He addresses a convention of conductors, extolling the benefits of the union. The book is undecided about whether it aims to be a Western adventure, a "bound to rise" saga of personal heroics, a pro-union exercise, or a sentimental romance. It tries to hit all these targets. The results are peculiar, but also curiously engaging.

718. Schwartz, Jason. "Ox." In *German Picturesque*, 55–60. New York: Knopf, 1988.

In this impressionistic and marginally comprehensible piece a cross-country train trip's details slide into and out of focus, courtesy of the vivid and elliptical perceptions of a child traveling with his family. Not far from the domain of prose-poem land.

719. Scott, William D. "Willy's First Trip." In *Tales of the Rails*, edited by Veronica Hutchinson, 211–241. Cleveland and New York: World Publishing, 1952. *Railroad Magazine* 40 (Aug. 1946): 100–119.

Young Willy Anderson exhibits the standard heroics of the dedicated railroader in the pulp fiction universe. Willy, a fireman who has just passed an examination to qualify for engineer, receives a surprise call one night to make his first run. It proves a rough trip, with the inexperienced Willy struggling to maintain the locomotive and his own nerves. It doesn't help that his brakeman tries to take covert slugs from a liquor bottle hidden in his overalls. Willy gets through the trip, "fourteen hours of hell," as he puts it (238), having saved his

brakeman's life, performed first-class work with the engine, and impressed a railroad official traveling incognito as a fireman.

Seltzer, Chester *see* Muro, Amado

720. Serling, Rod. "The Ghost Train." In *Journey Into Fear and Other Great Stories of Horror on the Railways*, edited by Richard Peyton, 26–50. New York: Wings Books, 1991 (Originally published as *The Ghost Now Standing on Platform One*. London: Souvenir Press, 1990). Also in *Rod Serling's Twilight Zone*. New York: Bonanza Books, 1983.

On a trip to a skiing contest, friends Pete Dunning and Bert Carey, in a blizzard, nearly drive into the path of an inexplicably antique steam locomotive and its dozen passenger cars. All the cars are white. Pete soon stops to pick up a young woman begging a ride, and drops her off near her house. Bert sleeps through the whole business, and later cannot confirm Pete's account of the strange train. Pete lingers on assignment in the area, determined to penetrate the mystery of the white train and the young woman. The train proves instrumental in her tragic story. The story is not among Serling's best, with a surfeit of explanation and too many exclamation marks.

721. _____. "A Stop at Willoughby." In *The Twilight Zone: Complete Stories*, 234–251. New York: TV Books, 1990. Also in *Stories from the Twilight Zone*. New York: Bantam, 1986.

Adman Gart Williams rides the New Haven Railroad commuter train home after an especially hideous day at the agency. Williams looks out the window at "the bare, lifeless trees ... the patches of dirty, early snow, the dull gray-black of rolling hillocks, stripped of color" (240). Williams nods off, and dreams that he awakens as the train stops in the serene 1880s village of Willoughby. The conductor, a gentle fellow, advises Williams to spend some time there, where he could "live his life full measure" (241). On another day, Williams again dreams that he is aboard an old coach, with velvet trim and gas lanterns, lingering at the

Willoughby station. Determined to escape the constrictions of his life, he vows to get off the train in Willoughby—and does. One of the television series' *Twilight Zone's* most memorable episodes, this story speaks to a nearly universal wish to return to an idealized past of peace and contentment, and it is, of course, the train that serves as the vehicle that makes the return possible—in a sense—for Gart Williams.

722. Sharpe, John. *Railroad Renegades.* New York: NAL, 1991. 170p.

This entry in the author's Canyon O'Grady series ("With a smile or a six-gun, Canyon O'Grady became a name feared by some and welcomed by others, but remembered by all," the flyleaf copy assures). This one opens in 1861, with President James Buchanan traveling by train across Pennsylvania, and Special Agent O'Grady seeking to foil a presidential assassination scheme at the Bixby station, only the latest in a series of possible trouble spots on the trip. A nefarious band led by a woman is tracking Buchanan's special train, and is devoted to killing him—by pistol, rifle, or bomb planted on the tracks. The motive is vengeance. With a little shootin',' a little sex, and men who are men and women who are glad of it, the book is pure potboiling latter-day pulp.

723. Shepard, Lucius. "Bound for Glory." *Fantasy & Science Fiction* 77 (Oct. 1989): 162–192.

The narrator, a failure and a wreck, and his female companion Tracy are taking a train trip through the Bad Patch, with Glory their destination. It is only desperation that drives them to this trip; the Patch is a place "where things out of nightmares appeared, where time and possibility converged" (168). Cole, the train chief, expects the worst: "Now, last time things was this bad, I lost me nine passengers" (171). The passage through the Patch is indeed a nightmare, but the narrator reaches Glory, and transformation.

724. Shepard, Sam. "Southwest Chief." In *Cruising Paradise; Tales,* 151–154. New York: Knopf, 1996.

The narrator, who has recently been working with Los Angeles police detectives,

describes the people around him on board the Southwest Chief. "Zombies" stare at the televisions in the non-smoking lounge. In the smoker, young women sporting tattoos laugh and talk and smoke up a storm; a "huge" woman sits down across from the narrator and, unbidden, spills out details of her personal life. She has eyes "that look beat up by booze and endless nights" (153). "A black guy" bellows about some "Italian bitch" he means to take up with once again. Through it all, the narrator, "flying by train" (154), maintains a discrete demeanor and watches the proceedings like a detective. He is glad to be alone, and watching. The story rings true in its evocation of the way a quiet observer in a closed environment learns about others simply by watching and listening.

725. Shepherd, Jean. "The Marathon Run of Lonesome Ernie, Arkansas Traveler." In *A Fistful of Fig Newtons,* 95–129. Garden City, NY: Doubleday, 1981.

An Army company of radar operators is summarily led off to a troop train, destination unknown and probably unpleasant. Rumor is that the men are headed for Fort Benning, Georgia. The narrator and two other men, including Ernie, draw KP detail on the train, where they have a dreadful time dishing out food to an apparently endless line of hungry soldiers. When the train stops briefly in Arkansas, the men spy a nearby store advertising "BEER." Ernie jumps off the train to buy some, and the train proceeds without him. The story is funny and convincing; the reader can almost feel the heat and smell the odors in the troop train mess car, and the specter of poor Ernie, chasing the train, wearing only his GI underwear, a sack of beer bottles clanking at his side, arouses fear and pity—and laughter.

726. Shreve, Susan R. *The Train Home.* New York: Doubleday, 1993. 262p.

The opening and closing passages of this compact novel are the critical bits, both for the story and for the train presence within it. In the opening, Annie Blakemore, an opera singer, observes an attractive priest on a Washington, D.C., subway. Something about the priest rivets her, and she begins to follow him. The "priest," Will Huston, is not a priest, but an impostor, with a motive Annie could not imagine. In the closing passage, the two meet on the train from Washington to New York City, and the truth envelops both of them: Annie senses that something has happened between them, and "on the train hurtling east ... she had the sense of going home" (262). The novel is a worthwhile variation on the strangers-on-a-train theme.

727. Shulman, Max. "The Trouble with the Railroad." *Saturday Evening Post* 217 (June 9, 1945): 18. Also in *The Saturday Evening Post Stories 1942–1945.* New York: Random House, 1946.

Sam Lamb, an Army accountant, regularly takes the train from his base in Washington, D.C., to New York City, where he attends plays. The expense forces him to a meticulous budgeting of his meager Army pay. In this comical wartime story, Lamb becomes tied in financial knots over train ticket prices, following his encounter with a four-foot-tall ticket agent who refers to Lamb as "little man."

728. Slavitt, David R. "The Long Island Train." In *Short Stories Are Not Real Life; Short Fiction,* 58–62. Baton Rouge and London: Louisiana State University Press, 1991.

The narrator relates a story his father used to tell about a woman who has been given instructions on reaching the Bronx on the Third Avenue El. The story illustrates the way people misunderstand others' intentions. It closes with another of the train tales from the narrator's father, showing another peculiar human habit, that of holding others responsible for satisfying expectations they do not realize exist.

729. Smith, Alicia. "Cornfield with Lights." In *Stories and Poems from Close to Home,* edited by Floyd Salas, 339–350. Berkeley, CA: Ortalda & Associates, 1986.

Sometime in the steam era—during the Depression, perhaps—a young woman who calls herself Andy masquerades as a boy and rides the rails with her partner, Elmo. One day she and Elmo climb into a Union Pacific boxcar, where Andy has a frightening encounter with another hobo. The reader can feel the tension building well before the confrontation turns ugly.

730. Smith, Francis Hopkinson. "Compartment Number Four—Cologne to Paris." In *The Under Dog,* 215–238. New York: Scribner's, 1911.

An American landscape painter traveling from Cologne to Paris bribes the ticket agent to obtain the last berth on the train, then becomes annoyed at the petty bribery a man he takes to be a circus manager uses to gain favor from the agent. Aboard the coach, he finds that the "full" car is all but deserted. He intervenes in a young mother's dispute with train officials over her family's accommodations; she is, after all, "a pretty woman, an Anglo-Saxon—my own race" (227). This matter squared away, he returns to his compartment, where his fellow occupant, a Russian, treats him with deference. The narrator assumes that the man "had recognized instantly, from my speech and bearing ... that dominating vital force, that breezy independence which envelops most Americans, and which makes them so popular the world over" (231). That, perhaps, or the fact that the fellow has mistaken the American for a financial magnate.

This gentle satire on American self-satisfaction, and habitual leaping to conclusions about people of other nationalities, ends with a special surprise for the narrator.

731. _____. "John Sanders, Laborer." *Harper's New Monthly Magazine* 90 (Feb. 1895): 344–349. Also in Smith's *Gentleman Vagabond, and Some Others.* Boston and Cambridge: Houghton, Mifflin, 1895.

John Sanders, railroad laborer, resides in a shanty with his sickly daughter near his work. Smith draws a bathetic picture of Sanders and his pitiful child, living in a world of grime, railroad noise, smoke, rain, and dust. Their only relief lies in their Sunday visits to a secluded pond a mile or so from their hovel. The two adopt a forlorn stray dog, dubbed

"Rags" by Sanders's fellow railroaders. Sanders sacrifices his life to save the poor dog in an incident in the train yard.

732. _____. "Knight of the Legion of Honor." In *The Novels, Stories and Sketches of F. Hopkinson Smith*. Vol. 1, *LaGuerre's and Well-Worn Roads*, 101–130. New York: Scribner's, 1908. *Century Illustrated Monthly Magazine* 45 (Dec. 1892): 223–229.

The narrator, an American painter in Venice, forms an acquaintance with a fellow ship passenger, Bosk, also an American. Bosk tells the story of his involvement, aboard a train bound for Vienna, with a young Polish woman of considerable social standing, but with an air of great sadness. Bosk treats the woman, whose tale proves one of intrigue, injustice, and European decadence, as any American gentleman would: He assures her, "There is not a man the length and breadth of my land who would not feel for you now as I do, and there is not a woman who would misunderstand him" (112). The train trip gives the good-hearted American an opportunity to show the innate nobility of American manhood.

733. _____. "A Night Out." In *The Novels, Stories and Sketches of F. Hopkinson Smith*. Vol. 11, *At Close Range*, 3–33. New York: Scribner's, 1905. *Scribner's Magazine* 34 (Sept. 1903): 307–319.

The narrator, upon leaving the stage of the Opera House in Marshall, Michigan, one winter night, receives a telegram summoning him to speak in Toledo, Ohio, the next afternoon. His hotel clerk helps him plan a complicated, frequently-stopped, and train-changed route to Toledo. He boards an unheated coach in the middle of the night for his first stop, Battle Creek. There he is left alone in the cozy station while a storm blows, with a fireplace and an armful of fresh wood, to wait for his connection. "The only sounds were the creaking of the depot signs swaying in the wind and the crackle of the logs on my hearth—*mine* now in the isolation, as was everything about me" (14). A few of the locals drift in and join him at the fire before his train arrives. On it, he sits among a raucous group at one end of the

car: "I began to realize now why the other passengers were packed together in the far end of the car" (21).

The story proceeds in amiable fashion, describing the ups and downs of the trip to Toledo. It is an engaging story, even though in the conclusion the narrator gibes the considerate and alert "darky" porter aboard the train on the last leg of his trip.

734. _____. "Sammy." In *The Under Dog*, 239–263. New York: Scribner's, 1911.

The narrator has a lower berth on the Night Express out of Louisville, bound for points south. While the porter prepares his berth, he sits across from a man behind a newspaper, and speculates about the man's nature. With an oath, the man lowers his paper and says angrily, "I say it is a shame, sir ... the way they are lynching the negroes around here.... It's an infernal outrage, sir!" (244). He blames the lynchings on the way abolition deprived slaves of their homes in bondage. "The negro is infinitely worse off than in slave days. We never had to hang any one of them to make the others behave themselves" (246). The narrator subtly urges the man to continue, hoping for a glimpse into his character. He obtains it when the man reminisces about a slave with whom he was friends as a boy, when he was known as Sammy. Now an aging Confederate veteran, Sammy tells a maudlin tale about Aleck the slave; the narrator swallows it whole.

735. Smith, Stephe R. *Romance and Humor of the Road: A Book for Railway Men and Travelers*. Chicago: Horton and Leonard, 1871. 219p.

Available at *Wright American Fiction*: http://www.letrs.indiana.edu/web/w/wright2/

In a folksy manner, Smith relates anecdotes and tales and an occasional sentimental poem about the Chicago, Burlington, and Quincy Railroad. Smith's approach ranges from the fictional to straight narrative; the "gossip" sections give his impression of good cheer and camaraderie prevailing among railroaders of the period, or at least the railroaders of the C.B.&Q. Chapter titles include such as "Engineer's Gossip," "No One to Blame," "The Side-Track," and "Dead—And No Name."

736. Smolens, John. "Night Train to Chicago." In *My One and Only Bomb Shelter*, 109–123. Pittsburgh: Carnegie-Mellon University Press, 2000. Published as "Train to Chicago." *William and Mary Review* 37 (Spring, 1999): 68–77.

Richard, the narrator, is looking at his reflection in the train window as the train pulls out of the East Lansing, Michigan, station. "I might have been looking at a grainy black and white photograph, a composite of shadows" (111). The old woman in the seat behind him also looks out her window, while talking to herself. Richard, trembling from stress or an incipient physiological ailment, bumps into Laura, a woman in her 30s, and the two establish a quick rapport. She claims that she is being stalked by Paul, a man in the same coach. When Paul speaks briefly to the narrator in the dining car, he tells him that Laura is "crazy." "She does this more and more frequently," he says, "running off to Chicago" (115). Richard and Laura hide from Paul in one of the coach's restrooms. The train stops and the lights go out, and Laura and Richard embrace and kiss in the dark, small space while Paul pleads for her to come out.

The story concludes in unhappy fashion for Richard, who (altogether idiotically) finds himself left behind beside the tracks when the train resumes its journey after a brief stop. He looks through the windows into the now-lighted coaches, and sees Laura and Paul drinking coffee at the snack bar, and the old woman who talked to herself looking out blindly into the night. No one can see him in the dark; no one can hear him cry out as the train moves on toward Chicago.

737. Snyder, Ralph A. "Ready in Five Minutes." *Railroad Magazine* 77 (July 1965): 39–40.

Boomer dispatcher Bill Stevens is ready to pound his desk over the sluggish progress of eastbound Extra 135, which has been holding up train traffic far longer than the "five minutes" its crew promised it would take them to

get moving. Stevens is so steamed at the boomer trainmen on the 135, and at the general irritating excuse for railroading on this outfit, that he plans to head west, to Denver, and pick up a job there. An ironic development changes his plans.

738. Somerville, A. W. "Authorized by Time-Table." *Saturday Evening Post* 200 (Nov. 26, 1927): 16–17+.

Somerville was born in 1900, near St. Louis, Missouri. He began his railroading career as a machinist with the Texas and Pacific. As is the case with so many other writers of popular railroad fiction, the practical experience of the railroader's life gives Somerville's stories an undeniable air of authenticity. It is obvious that Somerville delights in the mechanical stuff of the railroad, and it is in that area where his strength as an author lies.

According to this story's narrator, this tale of a wreck is "really the saga of one man, a negro railroad porter by the name of Charlie. A humble person, this Charlie, a respecter of the Jim Crow car, a believer in the dominance and superiority of the white race" (16). The wreck is set in motion when a "negro" bum attacks with a knife a conductor on a boxcar one night. The conductor flings the attacker from the top of the car. The bum, badly injured, survives to jimmy a switch days later, setting the stage for a collision. Charlie is a skilled railroader: "If he had been white he would have made an exceptionally good conductor" (17). The bum succeeds in causing the wreck in which Charlie dies; the bum receives vigilante justice when a conductor and brakeman beat him to death—with the narrator's evident approval. This unusually grim popular-market story concludes with a bit of dark irony.

739. _____. "Counterbalance." *Saturday Evening Post* 200 (Dec. 10, 1927): 24–25+. Also in *Headlights and Markers: An Anthology of American Railroad Stories*. Edited by Frank P. Donovan, Jr., and Robert Selph Henry. New York: Creative Age, 1946.

Master Mechanic T.P. Patchbolt is on the outs with Deekman, the general foreman, who in Patchbolt's opinion wields entirely too much influence over locomotive issues better left to Patchbolt. Completely absorbed in his work, Patchbolt lives in a railroaders' hotel 20 feet from the tracks, and does not hesitate to crawl under a locomotive to check a mechanical problem in his brand-new suit. T.P.'s genius receives a test from Engine 359, a locomotive noted for derailing and killing engineers. The story centers on an unusually interesting case of mechanical detection, one that satisfies Patchbolt's pride, as well as his annoyance with Deekman. Somerville is at his best with the nuts and bolts, and he does not stray far from them here.

740. _____. "Foundation Job." *Saturday Evening Post* 203 (June 20, 1931): 37+.

Neophyte construction entrepreneurs Peter Pendleton and John Jay Herd take on the Foundation Extension of the Latigo and Arkansas Railroad. Pendleton falls for Muriel Buckner, daughter of a top L&A official, H.H. Buckner, whom Somerville portrays as a hard-nosed, tight-fisted empire builder. Buckner aims to wrest maximum work from the young builders, but they are up to it, as are the laborers in their enterprise: "The mule skinners, the grubbers, the shovel stiffs, the bridgemen? They stuck. Belly deep in the swamp, wrestling with the muck.... And on poor pay.... they liked to work on a job that any fool could tell was going down into history" (54). The obligatory romantic angle is merely a tangent here; the real story concerns hard work, loyalty, honesty, and wit combining to make men prosper in this Depression-era tale designed to inspire as well as to entertain.

741. _____. "Green Rags." *Saturday Evening Post* 200 (Feb. 25, 1928): 8–9+.

Somerville explains that green rags, or flags, properly placed on a locomotive signify that this train is the first section of a first-class, scheduled train. The story's main character, Old Man McIntosh, is a cantankerous engineer: "If pressed, he would grunt a greeting at some brother engineer, but that was the sum and the total of his social activities" (8). Uncharacteristically, upon retirement he adopts the orphaned daughter of a fellow railroader, and she becomes the light of his life. Fortunately

so, for otherwise McIntosh is lost without the railroad. No number of railroaders stopping by his house for free meals and rail chit-chat makes up for the absence of work on the daily service. An accident that threatens the girl's life leads to some exciting action featuring employment of the green flags.

742. _____. "High-Class Security." *Saturday Evening Post* 200 (June 30, 1928): 18–19+.

The railroad has ordered 5,000 automobile cars, and, to ensure that the builder meets specifications, has assigned its own men to inspect the car plant. A brouhaha erupts over the cars' axles when a young inspector with a ready micrometer finds them not up to specs. The inspector has his way, as he does in other facets of construction. A winter wreck involving the carefully-built cars later demonstrates the economic sense of taking extra pains at the manufacturing end. This story's soul focus on hardware, and on the efforts of railroaders to see that the goods are delivered per contract, is worth some attention. That the story, bereft of any romantic tinge save that of conscientious industrialism, fits in a magazine on a page facing an ad for "Hosiery Colors for Summer's Varied Moods" suggests a good deal about the national mindset of the late 1920s.

743. _____. "High Water." *Saturday Evening Post* 201 (July 14, 1928): 12–13+. Also in *Best Short Stories from the Southwest*. Edited by Hilton R. Greer. Dallas: Southwest Press, 1928.

Two telegraph men, Allbright and Carter, go to the business car on the train to alert the Old Man to the downed wires between Adelaide and Cloudy Bend. One of them mocks the black porter's speech when the porter, Dudley, is reluctant to awaken the Old Man. One character calls Dudley "a black scoundrel" (12), even though Dudley has done nothing but his job. Later in the story, another black character, "a very scared darky" (96) takes some sarcastic abuse when he expresses reservations about the wisdom of the plan being engineered by T.P. Patchbolt. Aside from its unintended sociological interest, the story concerns heroics in a flood involving restoration of telegraph service and the rescue of unfortunates adrift on a raft.

744. _____. "Highball!" *Saturday Evening Post* 201 (Sept. 22, 1928): 14–15+.

Master mechanic Fred Deekman must forego taking his fiancée to a dance in favor of running a special engine, the 1465, to Washington, D.C. The engine is to leave Washington with a press train, carrying to hungry newspapers photos of the wedding of the U.S. president's daughter. When the engineer assigned to the newspaper run pulls up sick, Deekman takes over. Somerville loves mechanical detail; he spends two long paragraphs describing the way an engine scoops up water from a trough between the rails, and he has a taste for the odd metaphor: "The 1465 was a high-wheeled, short-coupled Atlantic with a twenty-six-inch stroke and she ate up the miles as a starving wolf would sample a lollipop" (15). The run north from Washington is a wild one, fraught with near calamity. When Deekman learns in Philadelphia the true cargo the special carried, one could excuse him for feeling a little sick himself. The romantic subplot concerning the president's daughter is beside the point except as an excuse to pull off some railroading pyrotechnics, Somerville's forte.

745. _____. "Lost Locomotive." *Railroad Magazine* 50 (Oct. 1949): 90–101. *Railroad Magazine* 88 (March 1971): 52–55.

In frigid winter weather, the railroad has run short of coal, both to fire locomotives and to heat its buildings. Master Mechanic T.P. Patchbolt's office is freezing, and one of his engines, the old 201, has apparently vanished. Hoping to obtain some clues to its fate, Patchbolt sequesters himself with the engine's voluminous paper trail, beginning with documents of its construction, and its attaining a speed of over 116 mph in 1904. Rebuilt multiple times, the 201 was reduced to a plodding yard engine. Patchbolt finds the engine, and its discovery is the catalyst for the railroad's acquiring 50 new Diesel locomotives—as well as coal to heat its offices.

746. _____. "No Brakes." *Saturday Evening Post* 201 (Dec. 8, 1928): 20–21+.

Dude Hardy, "a thick-shouldered Irishman" (20) and Dusty Edwards are boomer brakemen, longtime partners. They dump a dull job with an Indiana road and head west, where they catch on with a road near the Pacific. They are astounded to learn that their timekeeper is a woman. "Women have no place on the operating end of a railroad and even less in a construction camp. They don't fit" (20). But this woman, one Pinkie Lee, is different: She grew up around the railroad, and is no powder puff. She would, however, in Dude's opinion, "make somebody a warm little squaw" (130). The two boomers both go sweet on Pinkie, and both propose to her, hoping to solve "their female problem" (135). A runaway car on a dangerous mountain pass, with Dude and Dusty aboard, gives Pinkie a chance to engage in heroics, but her efforts fail to please the boomer twins: "It just goes to show you that they ain't no women fit to railroad," says Dusty. "They jus' ain't got the judgment" (137).

747. _____. "On One Side." *Saturday Evening Post* 203 (Feb. 28, 1931): 36+.

In the first years of World War I, the railroad is staggering under the increase in business, and presses into regular service engines fit only for the salvage yard. T.P. Patchbolt, division master mechanic, receives orders to rescue a stranded artillery train in a blizzard. Somerville's close attention to railroading detail carries this story of a trainman's exceptional efforts.

748. _____. "Over the Hump." *Saturday Evening Post* 200 (April 21, 1928): 20–21+.

Boomer switchman and all-around railroad roughneck James Mulligan O'Cluskey hopes to settle down, at the advanced age of 29, in the town of Harbor, where he has taken a job in the yard, and fallen for pretty Maybelle Delaney, a local lass much favored by the rail workers. O'Cluskey has a bit o' brawlin' to do with some robbers operating in the yard before he can win Maybelle's hand. (The story explains at length the function of the hump, an elevated portion of the yard used to facilitate sorting freight cars.)

749. _____. "Sand—and Gravel." *Saturday Evening Post* 200 (Dec. 31, 1927): 12–13.

"Uncle" Pete Pendleton, industrial magnate of Pendleton, Herd & Co., has built railroads in the Deep South, Central America, and elsewhere. Pete is a two-fisted type, but here he lets two railroad officials pressure him into a bad business deal involving a gravel-dredging project; all ends well, with heroics aplenty.

750. _____. "A Tale of the Old Main Line." In *Great Railroad Stories of the World*, edited by Samuel Moskowitz, 3–19. New York: McBride, 1954. *Saturday Evening Post* 202 (Dec. 14, 1929): 20–21+.

Somerville offers another popular tale of the relationship between railroading and domesticity. Told from a perspective some years after the event, the story concerns the spectacular 1903 wreck of the engine Luella Maddox, which engineer Robert Maddux named after his wife. Maddux proves to be far more devoted to his faithful engine than to his faithless wife, although the latter's fate seems a little out of proportion to her failings. The story achieves a considerable tension as Luella Maddox (the engine, not the woman) races to her demise.

751. _____. "That Big-Rock Candy Mountain." *Saturday Evening Post* 201 (Nov. 24, 1928): 6–7+.

The narrator, an engineer on the Denver run, describes his boomer machinist, Bill, repairing leaks in the fire door while singing "That Big Rock-Candy Mountain." Bill is an old-timer, "known from the U.P. Trail to Gould's right of way through the Louisiana swamps, and from the four-track arteries of the East to the roundhouses in the California valleys" (6). The story relates Bill's history, accomplishments, and beliefs. Among other principles, Bill holds the formally educated class in some disdain, given their soft hands and tender hams: "I ain't arguin' against clerks, I ain't arguin' against the guy with all the money.... But ... I'd like to see every young buck what some day will be sittin' in a swivel chair

do somethin' besides sneer every time he sees a pair of overalls" (146). Bill expounds on everything from working on the Yucatan Central to the ever-perplexing problem of women. Somerville presents him as an admirable, hardworking, upright man, a railroad hero, even if he performed his heroics in the matter of routine, conscientious duty, rather than in sensational events. Somerville's admiration for the down-to-earth, sweat-of-his-brow workman is common among popular railroad writers.

752. _____. "Tin Train." *Saturday Evening Post* 211 (Oct. 8, 1938): 10–11+.

Mr. Patchbolt responds to the introduction of a Diesel-powered streamliner—a "tin train"—on the railroad. "I guess there ain't nothin' like progress," he says (68). When Patchbolt sees the new train, his skepticism diminishes. The streamliner has comfortable chairs, nice washrooms, a coffee bar, a sun room, and many other fine appointments. Patchbolt catches the streamlining bug, and at story's end is hatching design schemes taking advantage of the new materials and systems. The old locos were a way of life, but progress is so very American!

753. _____. "Transportation." *Saturday Evening Post* 200 (Sept. 3, 1927): 15+.

Deekman, the night roundhouse foreman, receives an urgent call from the division superintendent ordering him to get an engine onto a line of refrigerator cars. Deekman goes out in the yard looking for someone to fire up an engine. The first person he sees is a black worker. "Where you been, you black ape?" says Deekman, and orders the man to the engine.

"Yes, suh, boss," says the worker: "The darky knew better than to argue" (15). The available engine is an old job, potent in her day, but now underpowered and touchy. There can be no question of the trip's success; on the way, Somerville packs in an astonishing quantity of technical detail on the care and handling of the old engine.

754. _____. "Valhalla." *Saturday Evening Post* 201 (Jan. 12, 1929): 42+.

The narrator credits freight conductor Johnny Griswold for filling him in on the details of this story; Johnny remembers everything about everyone connected with the railroad. The details concern Prairie Division Superintendent Old Man Knuckles, "the toughest guy on the railroad, tempered like tool steel...." The virtues consistent with a certain type of manhood—the kind of hard-headed, hard-fisted manhood that put this country on the map—these virtues he had in abundance" (42). Knuckles cleaned up the slipshod work in the rail yard at the oil boomtown of Valhalla, with the help of his loyal dog, Bum. When a competing railroad threatens to put in a right of way that crosses Knuckles' line, legally but unethically, Knuckles and Bum show their mettle. This is a violent Somerville tale, but, as usual, it reinforces the ideal of the hard-jawed, two-fisted railroader. The story's only sentimentality involves the bond between Knuckles and Bum. (There are no women here.)

755. _____. "Wide-open Throttle." In *Short Lines: A Collection of Classic American Railroad Stories*, edited by Rob Johnson, 203–220. New York: St. Martin's, 1996. *Saturday Evening Post* 202 (Feb. 8, 1930): 52+. *Railroad Magazine* 91 (Oct. 1972): 30–34.

On a run to the East Coast, freight conductor Johnny Griswold relates the story of Oil-Can Tommy Wilkins and High-Wheeled Mike Cassidy, longtime engineer rivals on the railroad. When the road wanted to reduce the time required to haul fresh produce east, it pitted the two against each other in a race. The race ended in death, disaster—and, in sentimental fashion, reconciliation between the two mortally wounded engineers. "Th' railroads in them days, you see, was man-killers," says Griswold. "If you didn't want to take th' chances, you didn't have no right bein' in th' game" (219). The story ends on a somewhat unlikely note, with Griswold questioning the value of the expense of money and life for the sake of moving an orange from California to New York 30 minutes faster than before.

756. Spearman, Frank H. "As the Despatcher Saw It." *Outlook* 71 (June 14, 1902): 461–462.

Frank Spearman (1859–1937) first became acquainted with railroaders when he hung out with Burlington Route workers in McCook, Nebraska. In this vivid, raw slice of turn-of-the-century railroad life, the dispatcher narrates the events during a terrific blizzard that hit the River Division one March night. Clearing the line preoccupied him, until news arrived that a man had been hurt. The victim had been trapped under the forward truck of a tender, and was in bad shape. The dispatcher and other railroaders struggled to free the injured man, but their effort was futile. A priest gave the dying man last rites while he lay beneath the tender, his leg crushed by a wheel. "I have forgotten the man's name," says the dispatcher. "I have never seen the old priest, before or since. But, some time, a painter will turn to the railroad life. When he does, I may see from his hand such a picture as I saw at that moment—the night, the storm, the scant hair of the priest blown in the gale, the men ... about him; the hush of the death moment, the wrinkled hand raised in last benediction" (462). It is a far different image of railroad life than one sees in the romantic, idealized paintings of such present-day artists as Paul Detlefsen.

757. _____. "A Black Rapids Love Story." *Cosmopolitan* 29 (June 1900): 201–206.

George Blake arrives in Black Rapids with little more than a good sense of humor; he has come to manage the Blanchard paper plants. George has a beneficial effect on Margaret Murray, whose father's business has failed. One spring a new group of Easterners comes to town; they "drank mineral water and spoke their English in a foreign tongue." They include General Stagert, new vice-president of the railroad that serves Black Rapids; "with his breadth and magnificence he fairly captured Black Rapids" (15). George courts Stagert's daughter, Louise, and abandons interest in Margaret. Eventually the Stagert fortunes, including the railroad, go bust, and George must humble himself to obtain help from Margaret. Railroading details in this financial-romantic melodrama are sketchy. The story concludes with a scene reminiscent of the revelation about Mrs. Bates's true nature in Hitchcock's *Psycho*.

758. _____. "Bucks: A Story from the Train-Despatcher's Office." *McClure's Magazine* 14 (Dec. 1899): 147–153. Also in Spearman's *The Nerve of Foley*. New York and London: Harper & Bros., 1900.

Back in the old days of railroading on the West End—according to an old-timer's reminiscence—"Bucks was assistant superintendent and master mechanic and train master and chief despatcher and storekeeper—and a bully good fellow" (148). The story is set on Christmas Eve, when a wild windstorm triggers a runaway freight that heads straight for an oncoming passenger train. Only the quick thinking of Bucks and the ready assistance of two young dispatchers avert disaster. This exciting story features a patently sentimental twist: Bucks's dear old mother is aboard the passenger train. Bucks, who appears often in Spearman's stories, is characteristic of the idealized railroader of the era: bright, noble, honest, hardworking, brave, and so on.

759. _____. "The Christmas Special." *Saturday Evening Post* 176 (Dec. 5, 1903): 12–13+.

Engineer Jack Santry and his new wife live in a boxcar in a tent-and-raw-lumber end-of-rail settlement on "the front" of the railroad-in-progress. Santry is a reliable engineer, but one Christmas he seems to go berserk, hooking his house-car to an engine and rampaging against orders, off to Blue Hill, site of the only doctor in the region. The "Christmas Special" proves to be a delivery that simply will not recognize train orders.

760. _____. "Conductor Pat Francis: How the Yellowstone Excursion Escaped Its Pursuer." *McClure's Magazine* 15 (Aug. 1900): 330–338. Also in *Stories from McClure's: The Railroad*. New York: McClure, Phillips, 1901.

Pat Francis, a veteran conductor on the Mountain Division, hopes to help deliver a trainload of excursionists to Yellowstone in a timely manner. With his position jeopardized by an oversight in collecting a fare, Francis risks his life in an heroic leap from the train to throw a switch to head off a wreck. Heroism holds the fort, and Conductor Francis, though pounded mercilessly by his leap from the train, retains his job.

761. _____. "The Cough in Lower Seven." *New England Magazine*, n.s., 29 (Dec. 1903): 415–421.

In this odd blend of humor and pathos, talk in the Pullman smoking room on the way to Los Angeles has turned to "kickers"—whiners and grousers, in general. A "travelling man" tells the story of his last trip west, when someone started coughing after midnight in the berth below (no. 7). In the morning, the cougher, a young man, berated a fellow passenger who railed over his disturbing everyone's sleep. The young fellow was ill, and his medicine satchel misplaced. When he saw the satchel near the man who complained so loudly, he questioned the porter's efforts to locate it during the night. "The darkey shuffled darkey fashion" (417). The porter informed the young man that the complaining fellow had refused to let him search near him. The young man criticized the older, in harsh language for which he later apologized to the traveling man. The ill man leaves the train, but the nights do not grow any quieter on this trip.

762. _____. *The Daughter of a Magnate*. New York: Scribner's, 1903. 273p.

Many of Spearman's favorite characters from the Mountain Division—Bucks (now a vice president of the railroad), Foley, Callahan, and others—turn up in this mostly entertaining novel of the division's reorganization and resuscitation. The story's hero, Abner Glover, has left his cushy job as chief engineer out East at the request of Bucks to take on the less lofty post of construction engineer on the Mountain Division. Glover is convinced that the heart of the entire system is the Mountain Division, and that he can make it profitable. Spearman is at his best when he dwells on his beloved railroad action, and on the challenges facing railroaders of the period, including weather, terrain, and equipment. He knows these issues well, and presents them in a lively, convincing way. His forte as a short-story writer asserts itself in the novel's episodic form. Some portions could be plucked whole from the book and easily stand on their own.

The novel's most unfortunate aspect is suggested by its title. Spearman devotes far too much space to a romance between Glover and the daughter of the railroad's president. He is simply not very good at this sort of thing; his real romance lies in driving wheels, snow-storms, and locomotive cabs. Even so, the chapter "An Error at Headquarters" is an amusing account of Glover's mistaking the magnate's daughter for the new stenographer the railroad has assigned him.

763. _____. "The Despatcher's Story: The Last Order." In *Held for Orders*, 141–179. Garden City, NY: Doubleday, Page, 1912.

Night dispatcher Blackburn is a quiet sort with a grief-ridden past; he seems made for night work. Young Fred Norman takes over at 4 A.M. Fred, from Detroit, has come to the mountains in hopes of curing his consumption, but is a first-rate dispatcher. Blackburn comes to Fred's aid when the young dispatcher is on the spot for an accident that occurred on his shift. One night Blackburn himself blunders, and gives orders that send two trains racing to a head-on collision. "Others may blunder; others may forget; others may fall and stand again: not the despatcher; a single mistake damns him. When he falls he falls forever" (166). The story ends with notes of supernatural intervention and religious morbidity as Blackburn prays that no wreck occur—and then dies, as if sacrificing himself for those on board the two trains.

764. _____. *Flambeau Jim*. New York: Scribner's, 1927. 334p.

The story begins in the Rockies, on a train drawn by the engine known as Soda-Water Sal. Chick Callahan, railroad superintendent, boards the train, having caught up to it on a handcar. In the caboose, he chats with temporary conductor Bill Pardaloe; soon, he comes to the aid of a young woman, Pickie, being accosted by thugs, and delivers her to her veterinarian father northwest of the town of Sleepy Cat. Given the book's publication date, a paragraph describing the railroad headquarters in Sleepy Cat could stand as an elegy for the Golden Age of railroad fiction: "What it has

seen, what its cracked and battered walls could tell of early-day men, early-day violence, and early-day heroism in the railroad story of the Rocky Mountains, no one cares to hear from it now; the gray hairs of its declining years find it the victim of complete neglect" (34). And, indeed, reviewers almost completely ignored this novel.

The story focuses to a considerable degree on the romance between Pickie and the character Flambeau Jim; as usual, Spearman is at his best when his subject is the railroad itself. Subplots concern the search for a pay-car murder gang and railroad construction through Flambeau Canyon.

765. _____. "From the Cab Window." *The Outlook* 65 (June 2, 1900): 253–260.

On a westbound coach, narrator Frank Hamilton, a railroader, fires back at a man from Chicago who calls him a slave to his superintendent. Hamilton points out the Chicago man's own lack of freedom in his desk-manacled office job. Hamilton, on his way to a post as master mechanic with the West End, refreshes himself with a ride in the cab, from which he obtains an intimate view of the mountain scenery. His first assignment on the job is to ride as an observer on a new engine, the Empress. This journey gives Spearman a chance to further describe the view from the cab. He furnishes several nice passages, including one about a thunderstorm. The rage of nature dwarfs the mighty engine and her occupants, leaving "her crew shrunk to the complexion of boys playing with a teakettle" (258). When Hamilton sees a great many Chinese section gangs in solitary stretches of the road, his inquiry about them prompts the fireman's quick reply: "How could a white man stand it [the solitude]?" (260).

This story avoids melodrama, in spite of a section concerning a wreck and its aftermath; Spearman is writing from the heart, here, a heart both knowledgeable and under artistic control.

766. _____. "The Ghost at Point of Rocks." *Scribner's Magazine* 42 (Aug. 1907): 159–172.

Point of Rocks is the most godforsaken station on the Mountain Division, "the dread of all operators" (159), and 20-year-old Hughie Morrison's new assignment. Aside from the day man, and the section gang in quarters a half-mile away, there are no people within miles. One evening Morrison explores a ruined house near the station, one abandoned long ago by a failed rancher. There he finds a broken ivory miniature of a little girl, presumably a former occupant of the house. That same evening, the old shepherd who told Morrison about the house dies when struck by a train. The engineer leaves the body with Morrison. Later, as Morrison writes an official report on the man's death, he hears a voice behind him. He turns to see a ghostly figure, with the face of the girl in the ivory miniature.

This might have been a satisfying ghost story, but Spearman is too determined to explain it in a material, if unconvincing, fashion.

767. _____. "How McGrath Got an Engine: The Wiper's Flying Trip on Extra No. 240." *McClure's Magazine* 15 (Sept. 1900): 443–449. Also in Spearman's *Held for Orders*. Garden City, NY: Doubleday, Page, 1912.

The reader meets Aloysis McGrath, a roundhouse sweeper on the West End. He wins promotion to wiper, and aspires to become a fireman, but three years pass; "Nobody got killed; nobody quit; nobody died" (444), and the economy did not justify adding further crews. A runaway train on a 20-mile downgrade, the rails slick with October frost, gives McGrath his big chance, and he doesn't muff it. Division Superintendent Bucks rewards McGrath's courage and skill with a position beyond the one he sought: engineer.

768. _____. "The Kid Engineer." In *The Nerve of Foley*, 47–61. New York and London: Harcourt & Brace, 1900.

When the big strike hits, fireman Dad Hamilton is the only man of 180 engineers and firemen who refuses to walk out. His loyalty to division master mechanic Neighbor is too strong. Hamilton is miffed when paired with the green engineer Georgie McNeal, who takes a beating from some strikers. Not even that

event persuades Dad to warm to the boy. A terrifying accident in which Georgie plays the hero, although badly hurt, convinces Dad that the young fellow is a true railroader.

769. _____. "The Master Mechanic's Story: Delaroo." In *Held for Orders*, 209–245. Garden City, NY: Doubleday, Page, 1912.

Maje Sampson is a 270-pound windbag on the West End; his run is a dull little trip to Silver River and back on the tired old 264. Delaroo, an Indian and a born listener, is the only man on the railroad who can tolerate Sampson's jawboning. When Delaroo contracts smallpox, Sampson takes him home to his family—all but one of whom had previously been infected—and nurses him to health. Delaroo becomes Sampson's fireman on the 264, and Sampson tries to interest him in his favorite pastime, secret societies. In the aftermath of a collision, Delaroo cannot be located—for a time. The story emphasizes Delaroo's devotion to Sampson and his wife, and reinforces Spearman's portrait of the honest railroader as a man with few moral peers.

770. _____. "The McWilliams Special." In *The Nerve of Foley*, 109–135. New York and London: Harcourt & Brace, 1900.

Chicago banker Peter McWilliams calls in an IOU from the railroad he saved financially some years earlier: He demands that a special run take him to Denver by 10 A.M. the next day. The outlandish order throws the whole railroad into a tizzy, nowhere more so than on the West End, which has seven hours to haul McWilliams 400 miles. Not even a harrowing passage across a burning bridge can stop the McWilliams Special, or the railroaders who operate her. Thanks to their courage and good American hardware, McWilliams heads off a bank panic in Denver.

771. _____. *Merrilie Dawes*. New York: Scribner's, 1913. 382p.

Far from Spearman's best, this novel, once it stumbles through a wearisome "high society" opening, details the creation of a financial panic. The characters, including Merrilie Dawes, are either rich, or filthy rich. Among them is industrialist Amos Hamersley, who combines a family vacation in old haunts in New England with inspection of various railroad lines in which he has interests. He and his wife travel north from Florida aboard two private railroad cars. The chief character, aside from Merrilie, is John Adrane, consulting engineer, railroad builder, and steel entrepreneur. There is not much of the railroad in the novel, which consists chiefly of Spearman manipulating characters who do not come to life, in scenes that lack persuasiveness, with dialog hewn of wood.

772. _____. "The Million-Dollar Freight Train: The Story of a Young Engineer on His First Run." *McClure's Magazine* 14 (Feb. 1900): 380–386. Also in Spearman's *The Nerve of Foley.* New York and London: Harcourt & Brace, 1900.

During a violent strike, the West End Railroad assumes responsibility for a large shipment of silk. Finding an engine is a challenge; the few available are committed to passenger service, because "In order to win a strike, you must have public opinion on your side" (381). Road officials believe that if they can move the silk, they will break the strike. Eighteen-year-old Bartholomew Mullen, an engine wiper, receives the charge to take a silk train to Zanesville. The narrator, the trainmaster, accompanies Mullen, with the load disguised as a cargo of oranges, in fear of strikers' sabotage. The plan does not go smoothly, but success, and thwarting of the evil strikers, occurs in the end. Spearman's emphasis is on independent thinking and action, as exemplified in Mullen's alert mastery of a potential disaster, versus the craven saboteurs among the strikers who try to wreck the silk train.

773. _____. *The Mountain Divide.* New York: Scribner's, 1912. 319p.

Bucks has just arrived on the scene at Medicine Bend, an earnest and innocent 17-year-old telegraph operator. A few years his senior, lineman Bill Dancing tries to bring Bucks up to speed on frontier life. Bucks needs help, for his inexperience nearly proves fatal — twice — his first day on duty. The boom town of Medicine Bend is a street consisting of "a long assemblage of saloons, restaurants, boarding-houses, gambling-houses, dance-halls, and shops" (35). The street is alive with sundry characters: trappers, settlers, soldiers, and railroaders. The story proceeds to an account of grading and track-laying out in the wild, but the emphasis is generally at least as much on Indian fighting as on railroading. When the Indians are not harassing the railroaders, outlaws—chiefly, the Medicine Bend Gang—fill in for them. In a climactic confrontation, railroaders and other honest men deal out just desserts to the bad men who would destroy the town. The town is left a smoking ruin, but "Along the railroad track stiffened bodies hanging from the cross-bars of telegraph poles in the gloom of the breaking day told a ghastly story of justice summarily administered to the worst of the offenders" (307).

774. _____. "The Nerve of Foley." In *The Nerve of Foley,* 3–27. New York and London: Harcourt & Brace, 1900.

At a time when a labor strike threatens, "the railroad man sleeps like the soldier, with an ear alert—but just the same he sleeps, for with waking comes duty" (3). In this story the engineers strike on a winter night, paralyzing the road. Reed, the narrator, joins other managers in maintaining some service. Nevertheless, "Trainloads of fruit and meat rotted in the yards. The strikers grew more turbulent daily. They beat our new men and crippled our locomotives" (9). Foley, an engineer from the East, turns up at the yard seeking work. His veins run ice water: He is fearless when threatened, and further demonstrates his nerve when a striker's child falls into mortal danger. Spearman here portrays the strikers as misguided, but not evil. Enlightened railroaders, in Spearman's view, are company men, not strikers.

775. _____. "The Nightman's Story." *New England Magazine,* n.s., 29 (Feb. 1904): 740–748. Also in Spearman's *Held for Orders* (as "The Last Order— The Nightman's Story: Bullhead"). Garden City, NY: Doubleday, Page, 1912.

James Gillespie Blaine Lyons, better known as "Bullhead," is a brakeman on Pat Francis's passenger train. A gaffe, and then a fight, with a German tourist earn him a suspension. He returns to try freight work, but lurches from one job, and one disaster, to the next. At length he obtains work as a telegraph operator at Goose River, notorious for the presence of lunch-counter woman Nellie Cassidy, a cruel soul who admires engineers and conductors, but despises operators. Nellie sets poor Bullhead up for heartbreak, and strikes without mercy. Although all the West Enders—Francis, Bucks, Callahan—have told Bullhead he isn't cut out for railroad service, he becomes a true railroader, one dark and stormy night, even though the effort nearly kills him. The story is sentimental, yet engaging, even a century after publication, for readers never tire of the story of the congenital foul-up who rises to unexpected heroics.

776. _____. "The Operator's Story: DeMolay Four." In *Held for Orders*, 247–291. Garden City, NY: Doubleday, Page, 1912. *New England Magazine*, n.s., 29 (Nov. 1903): 357–370.

Martin Duffy rises quickly on the West End, from telegraph operator to division chief. His brother Bob, although able, exerts his ability only when the mood strikes him. One summer a large number of trains bound for a Knights Templar convention in San Francisco comes through on the division. The train De-Molay Four from Pittsburgh is the first of a series of fine trains the conventioneers ride. Duffy and crew manage nearly three dozen special trains that Sunday, but a slip-up on the orders down the line—by brother Bob—puts the DeMolay Four on collision course with another train. There seems to be nothing to do but to assemble the wrecking crew, when the rising moon intervenes in a most unlikely way.

777. _____. "The Roadmaster's Story: The Spider Water." In *Held for Orders*, 63–106. Garden City, NY: Doubleday, Page, 1912. *McClure's Magazine* 17 (Oct. 1901): 594–600. *Railroad Magazine* 92 (Nov. 1972): 42–48.

The Spider Water is a "villain stream"

named aptly by the Sioux: Ever since the railroad first bridged it, it has caused trouble. Brodie, a masterful construction engineer, comes to the West End to conquer the Spider Water. He fails, but trains the diligent and talented Phil Hailey to succeed him. Hailey does a brilliant job, but in an executive reorganization managed from the main office in Omaha, he is overlooked and unrewarded. "Nobody ever knows what Omaha will do next," says Bucks (80). Hailey is, in fact, terminated. The road president considers Hailey's lack of a formal engineering degree insurmountable, in spite of his wealth of practical expertise. Hailey steps down to the roadmaster's position, and a new, degreed engineer, with an eye to cost-cutting, assumes bridge superintendent duties. In frightful spring rains and snow melt, the railroad learns the value of practical wisdom versus formal education.

778. _____. "Sankey's Double-Header." *McClure's Magazine* 14 (March 1900): 456–460. Also in Spearman's *The Nerve of Foley*. New York and London: Harcourt & Brace, 1900.

Conductor Old Man Sankey, the oldest man in the train service, apparently came with the tracks. He is said to be a Sioux Indian. "I suppose every old traveler on the system knew Sankey," says the narrator. "He was not only always ready to answer questions; but, what is more, ready to answer the same question twice" (457). Sankey's wife died early; his adolescent daughter, Neeta, and the railroad were everything to him, and he is universally popular. In the terrible winter of "the Big Snow," Sankey and all the West Enders "worked like Americans" to keep the line going; "there were no cowards on our rolls" (458). Sankey himself is a model of steadfastness. He proves himself not only a ferocious foe of the elements, but heroic. At a critical point, he devises a snow-plowing technique using multiple engines (the "double-header"), and sacrifices his own life in a wreck. "There never was a funeral in McCloud like Sankey's ... and in time of blockade and desperation in the West End they still send out Sankey's double-header; though Sankey, as the conductors tell the children, traveling east or traveling west—Sankey isn't running any more" (460).

779. _____. "Second Seventy-Seven." In *The Nerve of Foley*, 29–44. New York and London: Harcourt & Brace, 1900.

Reed, the narrator, is a train dispatcher on the West End. In a busy summer month, he presses into service on Train 77 the naïve young Ben Buckley. Train 77 is an excursion run, with 500 passengers in Pullmans. On a night of bad weather, the 77's crew is caught between a washed-out bridge ahead, and a runaway freight—the second 77—bearing down on them from behind. Young Ben saves the day, and the train, in heroic fashion: "And on stormy nights switchmen in the Zanesville yards, smoking in their shanties, still tell of that night, that storm, and how Ben Buckley threw Second Seventy-Seven at the foot of Beverly Hill" (44).

780. _____. "Siclone Clark." In *The Nerve of Foley*, 211–235. New York and London: Harcourt & Brace, 1900.

Former striker Duck Middleton waxes nostalgic about the early days on the West End, when he worked as Siclone Clark's fireman. Siclone obtained his curious name from a misspelling when he entered the railroad service, stating his name as "Cyclone." During the big strike, Siclone threatened to kill any scab who would take over his engine, the 313. Siclone tried to carry out his threat, too, leaving the 313's new engineer, Fitzpatrick, for dead before disappearing. In an ironic reversal, Siclone later saved Fitzpatrick from a burning barracks before vanishing again. This story is a more interesting than average Spearman tale, owing to its concentration on elusive character rather than on railroading nuts and bolts.

781. _____. "The Sky-scraper." In *The Nerve of Foley*, 63–88. New York and London: Harcourt & Brace, 1900.

"Many locomotives as I have seen and ridden, a new one is always a wonder to me; chokes me up, even, it means so much," says this story's narrator (65). Engineer Foley pulls into the yard in a new engine, and the railroaders rhapsodize over his "sky-scraper" of an engine with "her" 90-inch driving wheels. Young Georgie McNeal draws the task of breaking in the new machine. A sudden hike in wheat prices in Chicago provokes frantic efforts to ship as much of the grain as possible. In the rush, a blunder leads to a head-on crash between the Sky-Scraper and another train. Dad Hamilton badly injures himself rescuing Georgie from the wreck, and the rescue leads to a shocking discovery about the two men.

782. _____. "Soda-water Sal." In *The Nerve of Foley*, 89–107. New York and London: Harcourt & Brace, 1900.

Dad Sinclair now runs the former Sky-Scraper, rebuilt after its collision, on a short connecting run. Several of the railroaders rename the engine Soda-Water Sal. Despite her less than imposing name, Sal has more left in her than meets the eye. When three coal cars break loose from a spur and go careening down the line toward an oncoming train, Dad and the green fireman Dick Burns leap into action aboard Sal. Burns is an Irishman, portrayed heroically as he fires Sal: "From the coal to the fire, the fire to the water, the water to the gauge, the gauge to the stack, and back again to the coal—that was Burns. Neither eyes nor ears nor muscles for anything but steam" (99).

783. _____. "The Striker's Story: McTerza." In *Held for Orders*, 107–140. Garden City, NY: Doubleday, Page, 1912. *McClure's Magazine* 17 (July 1901): 287–296.

Johnnie McTerza is a Reading Railroad engineer brought in as a scab on the West End during a strike. He stutters, and says little, but gives as good as he takes when strikers harass him. The strike turns ugly when a group of Polish workers vandalizes both railroad and city equipment. The narrator describes the gathering violence: "The detectives opened with their Winchesters, and a yell went up that took me back to the Haymarket" (126). The strikers torch the freight house and many railroad cars, and are on the verge of stoning McTerza to death. The story mingles credibly-described violence with a sentimental subplot concerning McTerza's interest in diner proprietress Kate Mullenix. Spearman portrays the Polish strikers—"polacks"—as brute and mindless.

784. _____. "The Switchman's Story: Shockley." In *Held for Orders*, 1–38. Garden City, NY: Doubleday, Page, 1912. Published as "Shockley: How He Helped the Russian Switchman to Celebrate Christmas." *McClure's Magazine* 16 (Dec. 1900): 174–182.

Callahan is dispatcher at the little Benkleton yard, at the edge of cattle country. Some of the local ruffians cause trouble for the railroad, especially for the yardmen. Cowboys with time on their hands use railroad lanterns, signals, and train lights for target practice. Sometimes they miss the hardware, and hit the yardmen. Shockley, a thin, unprepossessing chap, arrives from headquarters to assume yardmaster duties, and to tame the cowboys. Shockley is a good railroader, but has some darkness in his past: While striking in Chicago, he killed a man. Shockley gets a grip on the yard and the cowboys, and becomes a special hero to switchman Chris Oxen, one of the many Russian immigrant workers in the yard. The story ends in a believable tragedy stemming from routine yardwork left undone, and a moment's carelessness.

785. _____. "The Trainmaster's Story: Of the Old Guard." In *Held for Orders*, 293–325. Garden City, NY: Doubleday, Page, 1912. Published as "Of the Old Guard: Dave Hawk, Conductor: Looter and Hero." *McClure's Magazine* 17 (Sept. 1901): 450–456.

A former British soldier, Tommie Burnes, hooks on with the West End as a brakeman. Dave Hawk, a conductor, looks after the penniless fellow and gives him money for food until his first payday. Hawk, in spite of his railroading expertise, has not been above stealing from the road, like almost everyone else on the West End. When John Bucks takes over as superintendent, he cleans house—except for Hawk, whom he offers the trainmaster's job. Hawk, torn by guilt, doubts that he could discipline personnel knowing his own past. The issue turns moot when Hawk intervenes in a train robbery, and pays the price for his courage.

"He never hesitated with the other men high and low to loot the company," says Tommie. "The big looters were financiers: Dave was only a thief.... [but] When I was friendless, he was my friend" (325).

786. _____. *Whispering Smith*. New York: Scribner's, 1906. 421p.

The novel opens at the scene of a train wreck in the mountains, with Sinclair, a hard-nosed wrecking boss, ordering his men to ignore a hobo, Wickwire, badly injured in the wreck: "He'll find water fast enough. Let the damned hobo crawl down the creek after it," says Sinclair (5). In addition to his callousness, Sinclair helps himself to goods spilled in the wreck—cigars, wine, even silk dresses. His new boss, George McCloud, will not tolerate the looting, and fires Sinclair and his subordinates.

McCloud is a Boston college man, "an exception to every tradition that goes to make up a mountain railroad man" (33). His dismissal of Sinclair arouses popular protest, but the railroad stands firm. Sinclair embarks on a vengeful career of sabotage and train robbery. Enter Whispering Smith, railroad detective, "a man of patience and endurance and with courage and skill in dealing with lawless men ... terrible in resource and daring..." (208), but a gentleman, nevertheless.

Whispering Smith is a more than serviceable Western of B-movie values (it was filmed in 1915, 1926, and 1948, the last time with Alan Ladd in the title role). It features plenty of ridin,' shootin,' fightin' and lovin,' all springing from closely-observed Old West railroading. Spearman is better than most writers of this genre in creating credible characters, and, although the story is melodramatic, Spearman tells it well.

787. _____. "The Yellow Mail Story: Jimmie the Wind." In *Held for Orders*, 327–359. Garden City, NY: Doubleday, Page, 1912. Published as "Run of the Yellow Mail" in *McClure's Magazine* 17 (May 1901): 93–100. *Railroad Magazine* 91 (July 1972): 52–55.

Jimmie Bradshaw, long a freight engineer, hankers for one thing: a fast run with a passenger train. His chance begins to materialize when the road officials discuss a fast mail train to San Francisco. An agreement gives them three months to prepare the line for the Yellow Mail train. The train draws its name from its three cars, "done in varnished buttercup ... and they looked as pretty as cowslips" (342). Bradshaw fills in for a hung-over fireman on the train's test run, and takes command when the train derails. "The thing is to move the mail, not to stand here chewing about it!" he says (349). Bradshaw moves the mail so well that the local Sioux christen him with his nickname, Jimmie the Wind.

This is an archetypal story of railroading pulp fiction, with the frustrated engineer yearning for a chance; the drunken crew member; the wreck that seems to end all hope; the salvaging of hope when a real railroader takes charge; the just-did-make-it race to the finish; the fulfillment of the frustrated hero's dreams; and his earning legendary status—all couched in manly good humor.

788. Spielberg, Peter. "Among School Children." In *Bedrock: A Work of Fiction Composed of Fifteen Scenes from My Life*, 19–28. Trumansburg, NY: Crossing Press, 1973.

The fatigue and inanity of a long rail journey come through clearly in this story. The most memorable portion of the trip involves the annoying presence in the coach of five blind, loud children. After the children get off at a stop not noted on the schedule, the residue of their presence occupies the other passengers with banal chatter. The passengers complain about the children, the railroad, rude ticket agents, the ventilation, the delays, the lighting, and the service. The story also describes a convincing scene in which the passengers leave the train, "dragging their feet, half asleep, but moving along steadily, in single file, past muddied seats, soiled antimacassars, crumpled newspapers, half-eaten sandwiches, empty paper bags" (27). The author tries at the end to draw a parallel between the blind children and the adult passengers; the effort is not altogether successful, but the story remains effective.

789. _____. "The Architecture of the City." In *Bedrock: A Work of Fiction*

Composed of Fifteen Scenes from My Life, 179–184. Trumansburg, NY: Crossing Press, 1973.

In this ambiguous fantasy, the narrator lies tied to the railroad tracks that border a city. "The city began past the tracks, or, if you will, it ended at the tracks" (180). Apparently trains no longer run on the track. On the other hand, perhaps they do, for the narrator seems to detect a vibration in the rails, as if from an approaching train. The narrator hopes that his life will suddenly change.

790. Spike, Paul. "Bad News." In *Bad News*, 3–14. New York: Holt, Rinehart & Winston, 1971.

The narrator, Felix, is an American conductor on a train leaving Germany. Old Ronald, the black steward, works in the club car. Felix's brother is the engineer. A newspaper turns up on the train with bizarre news about money-eating ape packs scourging Scotland. The ape story is evidently a fabrication meant to conceal some natural disaster even more ominous. Things are bad: The whole train crew is summarily laid off. On its surface, the story makes no sense, but its evocation of dreadful, incomprehensible retribution from an offended Nature is persuasive.

791. Statham, Frances P. *The Silk Train*. New York: Fawcett, 1994. 377p.

A silk train heads from Seattle toward the Dakota Territory. In addition to the heavily-guarded cargo, the train carries Sarah Macauley, a schoolteacher bound for the remote town of Medova, and her new traveling companion, Anya Fodorsy. Anya has dark secrets about herself that she does not reveal to Sarah. In a holdup attempt, Sarah sustains a fatal wound, and Anya switches identities with her. Anya is fleeing her villainous husband, a Russian prince (it happens every day!), and will seek to disappear into her new identity as a schoolmarm. Except for a convenient and explosive attack on another silk train near this Western romance's conclusion, the chief railroading business is the trip at the book's beginning, which establishes the basis for the rest of the plot.

792. Steele, James W. "Brown's Revenge." In *Sons of the Border: Sketches of the Life and People of the Far Frontier*, 103–121. Topeka, KS: Commonwealth Printing, 1873.

Available at *Wright American Fiction*: http://www.letrs.indiana.edu/web/w/wright2/

This moral tale, although more than a little creaky in its construction, still packs some punch. The narrator describes the mysterious George Denham, the gentle yet haunted proprietor of what would today be called a health spa. The spa relies on the waters of a western hot spring. One day a world-worn fellow, William Brown, appears at Denham's spa, and the story he tells to the locals—of a robbery aboard a train just before Christmas in 1862—brings the source of Denham's perennial anxiety to light, and Denham to self-inflicted justice.

793. Steele, Wilbur D. "Due North." In *The Best Stories of Wilbur Daniel Steele*, 403–435. Garden City, NY: Doubleday, 1946.

May Coberly has spent her life in fear, from the time her brother made her sit on the back fence as the Chicago flier roared by on the Rock Island tracks. Her discomfort peaks when she is 17, when she must take the train from Des Moines to Ocean Grove, New Jersey, to represent her church at a convention. On the train, a young man flirts with her, and her fear subsides. May's trip, and her budding romance, collapse in Davenport, where appendicitis strikes her. This is the end of the railroad in the story, too, except in May's memories of what might have been in a life of romantic melodrama.

794. Sterling, P.M. "Hound of Cyclops." In *Selected Short Stories of Today*, edited by Dorothy Scarborough, 383–390. New York: Farrar & Rinehart, 1935. *Frontier and Midland*, Winter, 1934–35.

Paul, a small boy, gets out of bed to watch a train pass in the night. For Paul, the train's arrival is transfixing. His preoccupation with trains provokes a nightmare in which he stands between the rails, unable to move, with a train fast approaching. His father forbids him to watch the trains and his mother tells him that he can no longer walk along the tracks on his way to school. Parental adjuration does not constrain his obsession. In this psychological tale, Paul's mother figures prominently as a haven from the threatening power the train represents.

795. Stevens, James. "C.P.R." In *The Railroaders*, edited by Bill Pronzini and Martin H. Greenberg, 54–68. New York: Fawcett Gold Medal, 1986. Also in Stevens's *Homer in the Sagebrush*. New York and London: Knopf, 1928.

Shot McCune, a steel-gang boss on the Canadian Pacific Railroad, attempts to drink a rival under the table the night before the first scheduled arrival of a trans–Canada train in Vancouver. Although a bad piece of fiction, with heavy helpings of stereotyped French Canadian, Irish, and Chinese dialect, the story provides some insight into what the reading public found appealing in the way of he-man railroad yarns.

796. Stewart, Charles D. *Finerty of the Sand House*. New York: Century, 1913. 156p.

Michael Finerty, the Irish night keeper of the sand house and coal chutes in the Memphis, Tennessee, railroad yards, is the chief narrator of this collection of his adventures, and of his opinions on such topics as politics and women's rights. Thanks to its drenching in something intended as comical Irish dialect, the book is almost totally unreadable. Its concern with railroads is minimal: The only matter of interest here is the author's employment of a stereotypical Irish working man as the vehicle for patronizing ethnic humor.

797. _____. *The Fugitive Blacksmith*. New York: Century, 1905. 321p.

In this earlier treatment of Michael Finerty, he is also tending the locomotive sand supply in the Memphis yards. Here he shelters a one-legged tramp, thoughtfully nicknamed Stumpy, in his sand house. Stumpy relates a story of his riding the rails to Texas during a strike with a blacksmith fleeing the law. Railroad functionaries were particularly touchy about hoboes during the strike, and made the task of getting and keeping a free ride a challenge. Finerty's kind treatment of Stumpy is not unique: For the payment of a song and dance—literally—he allows hoboes to sleep in the sand house. The bulk of the novel, which falls into long, nearly impossible-to-read stretches of Irish dialect, concerns Stumpy's recitation of his adventures to the patient and interested Finerty.

798. Stewart, Donald O. *The Crazy Fool.* New York: Albert & Charles Boni, 1925. Also in *Best American Humorous Short Stories.* Edited by Robert N. Linscott. No place: Modern Library, 1945.

In a long (pp. 32–60) passage in this novel, young Charlie Hatch and old Mr. King are busy trying to leave New York City on a train. If the logic of *Alice in Wonderland* were transplanted into a pair of train passengers, this passage—which includes the heroes' writing the train engineer a letter offering him bicarbonate of soda—would surely be the result. With its absurd, hilarious dialog (see in particular the exchange with the engineer, pp. 48–49), and inspired nonsense from start to finish, the passage is a treat to read. As editor Robert N. Linscott realized, it stands well enough independently to pass muster as a short story.

799. Stoddard, Si. "Burning Mountain." *Railroad Magazine* 78 (Jan. 1966): 24–38.

The narrator runs the construction engine on a Montana track-laying project; Jimmy Shaw, a gangly kid, fires for him. Jimmy is smitten by Dorothy Morton, who lives in a local boarding house in the town of Hargan, and drives the railroaders "wild without signals" (35). Trouble surfaces when engineer Red Gaffney, with whom Jimmy previously tangled, becomes a rival for Dorothy's affections. A forest fire forces evacuation of Hargan, but Dorothy's uncle, railroad Superintendent Marsh, is unaccounted for. Jimmy heroically leads a rescue party into the inferno, and Gaffney slinks off, a coward—and without Dorothy.

800. Stong, Philip D. *Village Tale.* New York: Harcourt, Brace, 1934. 300p.

The village of Brunswick, Iowa, consisting of some 20 houses, lies between Keokuk and Des Moines. The Kaydee Railroad serving Brunswick has never amounted to anything, and now, given the Depression, it probably never will. Even so, the train's arrival from Keokuk remains the highlight of the village's life; however small and out-of-the-way Brunswick might be, the rails running through the town connect it with great cities and the ends of the continent. The "regular" 6:45 train, which might be hours late, is pulled by "one of the worst railroad engines in the world" (11). When it arrives on time, the moment is an occasion for wonder. The train limps into town at various points in the story, carrying with it a hint of the outside world—before the little community collapses in on itself again. Despite a contrived happy ending, the book ably depicts the incestuousness that can burden remote small town life.

801. Stratton, Frank N. "When the Train Was Held Up." *Munsey's Magazine* 32 (Oct. 1904): 19–24.

Harlan, a railroad express messenger, witnesses a hobo's beating by a brakeman one winter night. Harlan gives Jim, the hobo, shelter in his express car, which carries $50,000 cash. As Jim warms himself at the stove and eats a ham sandwich Harlan gives him, his talk of train robberies makes Harlan uneasy. Jim relates a story of how a crooked business group drove him out of business, and blacklisted him. He is on his way to Denver, hoping to find work in a sheet iron plant. When Harlan and Jim hear shots fired outside, Harlan fears that Jim is somehow involved in a robbery attempt. Jim denies it: "Why, pardner, didn't you invite me in when I was freezin' to death, an' warm me, an' feed me, an' treat me like I was human? Yes, you did! An' now, by the Eternal, I'll stay with you!" (22). The bandits cut the express car loose from the train; when it stops, Harlan and Jim leap out to face them.

The story's success lies in the bond between Harlan and Jim. No one can doubt that they will prevail, but their quick camaraderie, including conversation about their children, gives the tale some redeeming virtues.

802. Street, James H. "The Crusaders." *Saturday Evening Post* 212 (Nov. 11, 1939): 12–13+. Also in Street's *Short Stories*. New York: Dial Press, 1945.

In this pep-talk for a nation emerging from the Depression, Andy Wallace, editor of the Hillvale, Mississippi, newspaper, meets the southbound Cannonball at the local station every Saturday with his grandson, Pod. Pod has been living with Andy since his parents' deaths. The two are not alone at the station: "Just about everybody in town who didn't have work to do—and few did—was at the train, for the weekly visits of the train and the quarterly sessions of court were the biggest scheduled events in the little county seat" (13). Andy learns that the Cannonball will soon be replaced by a streamliner. The news sets him to reminiscing with Pod's teacher, Miss Beth, about the role the Cannonball has played in the life of the town. Miss Beth says that although many folks in town have never seen the interior of a luxury train, they will wait for an hour to see the Cannonball pass. "Trains represent escape," says Andy (88). Andy orchestrates for Miss Beth a visit to the World's Fair, and a return trip south with him and Pod aboard the new streamliner, leaving from Chicago.

The story blends conventional romance—we know that Andy and Miss Beth were made for each other—with earnest cheerleading for the greatness and variety of America. On the trip south, Andy points out the grandness of "the backbone of America" (91), from the stockyards and steel mills in the North to the breadbasket of the Midwest and the cotton country of the South, "a thousand miles of empire held together, not by a spiritual or a temporal boss but by folks with faith in one another" (91).

803. Street, Julian Leonard. "Mr. Bisbee's Princess." *Golden Book Magazine* 11 (April 1930): 66–83. Also in Street's *Mr. Bisbee's Princess, and Other Stories*. Garden City, NY: Doubleday, 1925; and in *O. Henry Memorial Award Prize Stories of 1925*. Edited by Blanche C. Williams. Garden City, NY: Doubleday, 1925.

The very conservative and cautious Chicago jeweler Mr. Bisbee is taking the train home after a brief vacation in California. On the observation platform, he meets an exotic and mysterious woman of foreign origin, and helps her remove a bit of cinder from her eye. Mr. Bisbee becomes taken with the woman, and, among other insights, tells her that "there's no place like a train to study human nature" (72). The woman proves to be a princess; upon his return to Chicago, Mr. Bisbee's chaste relationship with her aboard the train becomes blown out of proportion, both by himself and by others. This is an amusing "strangers on a train" variant, and a nicely written story of a man everywhere cautious but in his fantasy.

804. Stringer, Arthur. *Power.* New York: A.L. Burt, 1925. 308p. Indianapolis: Bobbs-Merrill, 1925.

Power rises above run-of-the-mill popular novels concerning railroading through its close examination of 57-year-old John Rusk, president of a transcontinental railroad with over 40 years of railroad work to his credit. Author Stringer presents the novel in the form of Rusk's memoirs dictated to his male secretary, young Wallie. In their course, Stringer does a creditable job of showing how railroad developers like Rusk stitched the nation together, following a hard-nosed business credo that sometimes cost its adherents appreciably in their personal lives even as it enabled them to contribute to the industrial and commercial growth of the nation.

"Serve, to Survive!" is one of the mottoes that hangs on Rusk's wall. It captures succinctly his belief that not merely success, but existence itself, depends on meeting the needs of the marketplace. Everything that he does in advancing his railroad from its inception as a backwoods Michigan line to a major national power reflects that motto.

As he looks back with pride in his part in building the nation's rail system, Rusk observes that "railroading in this New World of ours, all things considered, is the biggest and keenest battle that he-men can wade into. There's only one thing bigger: and that's war itself" (7–8). "It was our railroads that sewed up our ragged frontiers and made us one," he continues, "But for everything I got I worked, and worked hard" (9–10).

Rusk describes his rough boyhood in rural Michigan as tempered by his favorite authors—Twain, Dickens, Bret Harte—but literature soon succumbs to technical reading, "For even in those days I had an itch for power" (32). *Power* is an apt title for the novel, for the word appears regularly throughout, in various contexts. Rusk devotes his life to power, whether the motive power that makes his railroad, the D&B, go, or the power of will that allows him to meet and face down any challenge to his determination to make the railroad a success.

Rusk begins his railroading career in his early teens, soon advancing to machinist's helper, then to the cab of an engine at 18, his superior lying to qualify him for a job that requires a minimum age of 21. His rise is rapid. He reviews his career stops—telegrapher, station agent, superintendent—speaking with honesty of himself and those around him. He does not spare himself criticism, or portray himself as a hero; rather, as a practical, dedicated hardworking man. He is a railroader who cannot tolerate waste, laziness or sloppiness, and his relationship with union men is wary. Nevertheless, he admires and rewards good work, and strongly sympathizes with men at whatever level of the industry who dedicate themselves to the road's best interests.

Tragedy lurks in the tale, tragedy rooted in Rusk's devotion to his work. Although a generous provider for his family, he generally ignores his children, and when not ignoring them labors with little success to understand them. His troubled interaction with his family is convincing, and his children call him to accounts for his obliviousness to their needs and nature in favor of his tending the demands of the railroad. Not until a minor stroke fells him does Rusk take the time for these memoirs, and for reflection that brings him a better understanding of the people about whom he cares the most.

Power is an effective portrait, both sympathetic and critical, of a late–19th and early 20th century railroad mogul.

805. Strucinski, Mitchell J. "The Railroad in the Alley." *Atlantic* 198 (Nov. 1956): 78–80.

A retired railroad engineer, Jeff Doubleday, and amateur inventor is one of the few comparatively well-off people in his urban neighborhood during the Depression. For that reason, perhaps, and because he lives alone, he is a favorite target of abuse for neighborhood boys. One night the narrator, a local boy who has participated in Doubleday's torment, sneaks a look with his friend Mike into Doubleday's basement, and is amazed at the elaborate model railroad layout he sees. The model trains are Doubleday's means of continuing his working life, if in miniature; he labors exhaustively over their details. Mike, who irrationally blames Doubleday for his father's imprisonment, steals and destroys the old engineer's trains. There is no happy resolution here, merely a weary sadness in Doubleday's disappointment and pain.

806. Stuart, Jane. "Glory Train." *Saturday Evening Post* 246 (June/July 1974): 18–19+. Also in Stuart's *Gideon's Children*. New York: McGraw-Hill, 1976.

Can there be any trivial travel matter more annoying than being trapped in a train coach with a flock of Christian evangelists bellowing their praises of Jesus while their leader flails a guitar? (It has happened to this bibliographer, and he thinks not.) In car 1180 in this story, some 50 Born Again brothers and sisters exert their guilt-making skills on one Galen Millz, who, they all know, has some terrible hidden sin in his closet. The group's leader, Brother Sugg, presses Galen for a full confession. The confession comes, and proves a little more personal for Brother Sugg than he expected. The story suggests a degree of sadism in Sugg's character, to accompany his self-congratulatory sanctimony.

807. Stuart, Jesse. "The Anglo-Saxons of Auxierville." In *Clearing in the Sky, & Other Stories*, 206–218. Lexington, KY: University Press of Kentucky, 1984. *Profile* 11 (Spring 1950): 8–9+.

A stranger's arrival in the mountain town of Auxierville allows author Stuart to reveal, through young Billie Auxier, the details of life in this remote coal-mining town. The stranger talks with Billie and helps him dig for fishing worms. Billie describes the coal miner's shotgun houses, and the local railroaders' shacks. Billie is from a family of 14 children; three of them, and their mother, have died. One of Billie's brothers died when a train rolled over him. Billie's father works seven days a week in the roundhouse. Billie is relieved that the land on which many local families' shacks, including his own, though owned by the railroad, has been condemned—"and we won't have to move our shacks any more" (215). The Auxier shack sits on a plot of land so heavy with cinders that nothing will grow in the yard. Not more than three feet separates the back porch from the nearest railroad track, which is followed by ten more tracks.

The stranger studies Billie and his many siblings, and decides that they are Anglo-Saxons, "The last remnants of merry old England under the wide and spacious skies of great America!" (218). Not to mention in the filthy, merciless land, the brackish water, and the routine of early death that comes with what passes for life in Auxierville.

808. _____. "Fast-Train Ike." In *Nightmares in Dixie: Thirteen Horror Tales from the American South*, edited by F. McSherry, et al., 89–104. Little Rock: August House, 1987. Also in Stuart's *Come Gentle Spring*. New York: McGraw Hill, 1969.

Fast-Train Ike is a local character who has been riding the Old Line Special for at least 49 years. He wears an antiquated suit, and tends to fits of panic over his belief that the train will wreck, and kill him. Ike has been a decades-long pest to Conductor Harry, disturbing the other passengers with his "spells." Ike has been forewarned of the train's wreck by a dream. Here Ike flags down and boards the train, and proceeds to his standard visionary harangue; this time, however, fate accommodates Ike's vision, after he creates a mad scene aboard the train. "My worries are over," says Conductor Harry, "for the rest of my years on this road will be spent in peace" (104).

809. _____. "Huey, the Engineer." In *Headlights and Markers: An Anthology of American Railroad Stories*, edited by Frank P. Donovan, Jr., and Robert Selph Henry, 201–222. New York: Creative Age, 1946. Also in *Best Short Stories of 1938*. Edited by Edward J. O'Brien. Boston: Houghton Mifflin, 1938. *Esquire* 8 (Aug. 1937): 36–37+.

The narrator looks back from a long chronological distance to his childhood, when he idolized Huey, the engineer who ran a locomotive on the E-K, the Eastern Kentucky Railroad, along 36 miles of track. He wanted to be an engineer, like Huey, but his father was convinced that the E-K was doomed, even though it was booming after the Civil War. The narrator reminisces about the place Huey and his train played in the life of the rural area, from taking players and fans to a baseball game to pulling extra cars full of people to a hanging. During the depression of the 1890s, the train "hauled big loads of money" (212), that is, seed corn and other crops, when the locals' medium of exchange was in kind, not cash. When World War I comes, Huey is still there, taking men off to the Army: "Lord, them dark days. I was there when they loaded the boys on the train. So many of them so drunk they didn't know where they's a-going" (215).

Huey runs his engine for 50 years, and knows everyone around; he is one of the constants of the community, and for decades many wanted to be like him. Even constants fail, however, and one day Huey dies. "But now ... we stand and shed our tears unashamed of tears for our engineer that once pulled the train where no track now is—nothing but the wind and dents in the earth and cinders ground down and old bridges—but we remember—we'll always remember—and Huey—our engineer—we wonder on what silent train and to what silent land our engineer has gone" (222).

This touching, tender story's conclusion is not hard to anticipate, but Stuart writes of his rural Kentucky people with such absolute authenticity, and such honest feeling, that the anticipation heightens the impact of Huey's death, one of the saddest and most genuinely affecting in the fiction of the railroad.

810. Styron, William. *Lie Down in Darkness.* 1951. Reprint, New York: Viking, 1957. 400p.

This novel opens with a sketch of a train ride from Richmond to Port Warwick, Virginia, as any vaguely-engaged traveler might experience it. The train makes the transition from city to suburbs to country, past ordinary, unremarkable sights. A novelty salesman describes his hobbies and recites favorite jokes, but upon reaching the station, one promptly forgets both the salesman and the trip itself. It becomes clear that the train carried the body of young Peyton Loftis, who went mad and killed herself in New York City. Friends and family members waited at the station in Port Warwick for her body to arrive, so that they could take it for burial. The account of the train trip, with its focus on daily banalities, contrasts with the tragic cargo that affects one small group of people. The book ends with a passing train rumbling north, on the way to Richmond.

811. Sullivan, Oscar M. *The Empire-Builder: A Biographical Novel of the Life of James J. Hill.* New York: Century, 1928. 372p.

Sullivan uses the character of Lucien Ryder as a vehicle for laying out the life of the force behind the Great Northern Railroad. As a boy, Lucien immediately recognizes Hill's nature when Hill visits the Ryder family's store in St. Cloud, Minnesota. Hill becomes Lucien's idol. Lucien's father goes to work for Hill, and the Ryders move to St. Paul, Hill's home. The railroading begins in earnest with Hill's acquisition of the broken-down St. Paul & Pacific. Lucien studies law, and eventually secures a job in Hill's legal department. One especially interesting chapter, "Discord," relates the author's view of the mutually respecting manner in which Hill and the great labor leader Eugene V. Debs finessed a strike settlement on the Great Northern. Sullivan characterizes both men as visionary dreamers, and both rooted in practical concern for workers. The book's extensive financial and legal details and recitation of business make for historical credibility, but do not serve the purposes of fiction well. As a novel, this effort is not very satisfactory; as an historical artifact, it remains of interest.

812. Summerton, Winter. *Will He Find Her?: A Romance of New York and New Orleans.* New York: Derby & Jackson, 1860. 491p.

Available at *Wright American Fiction*: http://www.letrs.indiana.edu/web/w/wright2/

In a forgettable (and forgotten) romance, the author sets aside his story at a critical point to complain about the absence of railroad development in Alabama, especially between Mobile and Montgomery: "But when we consider that a railroad would shorten the mail time between those two points from thirty-six to eight hours, and that the entire travel would pass over the road, thereby yielding a rich percentage on the capital invested, it is indeed a matter of surprise that some of our capitalists have not yet turned their serious attention to the enterprise" (133). It would be a matter of surprise if today's romance novelist went on an irritated digression over, say, airport security practices, but seeing this sort of complaint wedged into a romance of the mid–19th century helps produce an understanding of the pressing importance of the railroad to American life of the period.

813. Sutter, Leona A. "Romance of the Little Conductor." *Sunset* (Central West Edition) 25 (Sept. 1910): 261–266.

Tom Percy, the much-liked conductor aboard the Limited, routinely gathers and bundles passengers' discarded newspapers and magazines; he drops them off for a woman who lives with her daughter at a remote spot on the desert route. With a passenger, Percy reflects on the hardy courage of this woman, living in such a forlorn place. Percy has over the years grown very fond of her, although he has never spoken to her, but has simply tossed the bundled periodicals from the rear of the train. One day a minor accident forces the Limited to halt for several hours near the woman's house, and Percy goes to visit her for the first time. He soon learns that she answers in kind his fantasies about her. The story is the sentimental opposite of Thomas Wolfe's "The Far and the Near"(Entry 940), in which an engineer's daydreams about a woman he has observed for years from his cab founder when tested by reality. This story has an exalted ending: "He would take her away from the desert and its cruelty to a world where the sun shone more kindly than anywhere else on earth, where the blossoms rioted and the sea crept up to California's Golden Land of the whole world's dream" (266).

814. Sutton, Stack. *End of the Tracks.* Garden City, NY: Doubleday, 1981. 183p.

In 1869, former U.S. marshal Creed Weatherall has an appointment with Col. Thompson of the Central Pacific Railroad in Thompson's San Francisco office. Thompson hires Weatherall to clean up, to a degree, the end-of-track "hell on wheels" tent-and-shack towns that follow the CP workers every mile of the way along the transcontinental route. The job's danger becomes immediately apparent: The assignment is a little more involved than airing out brothels and gambling dens, for unknown parties will stop at nothing to prevent the CP from meeting the Union Pacific. The novel contains more than adequate railroading passages, including a description of Creed's trip with Thompson aboard Thompson's private car: "They were hitting about thirty miles an hour..." (27) while drinking coffee prepared by the Chinese cook. (Considerable coffee-drinking goes on here; the author may have worked with a cup at hand.) In addition to the coffee, the reader enjoys runaway trains, sabotage, murdered railroaders, and occasional brawls in bare-knuckled, railroad-Western fun, better written than most entries in the present-day genre.

815. Swan, E.W. "The Dumb Luck of 'Wide-Open Jim.'" In *Along the Line ... or ... Western Railroad Stories,* 45–60. New York: Broadway Publishing, 1905.

Jim Hawkins, the youngest engineer on the division, won his nickname for his speedy runs. His regular route, a passenger run through wetlands, turns to little more than a swamp adventure one June. He and his fireman ignore the obvious as they try to take a frantic passenger to his deathly ill daughter, and sustain serious injury when they plow into a track

washout. The line fires Jim for his recklessness, but the passenger, a cattle baron, rewards Jim for his efforts—and Jim marries his recovered daughter. Dumb luck, indeed!

816. _____. "The Fate of the 368." In *Along the Line ... or ... Western Railroad Stories,* 61–73. New York: Broadway Publishing, 1905.

Duke is the railroad shoemaker, working in a shop next to the track. His shop is a hangout for story-telling railroaders. One day at the shop Windy Walker tells the story of the time he and engineer Jim Hawkins ran out of water for their engine crossing a desert. The tale is a tall one, with a Professor Nomuch who purports to make steam from "liquid air."

817. _____. "The Foreman's Order." In *Along the Line ... or ... Western Railroad Stories,* 117–121. New York: Broadway Publishing, 1905.

Foreman R.T. Ruggley is the most disliked man on the division. He owes his job to nepotism: He's the master mechanic's brother-in-law. "But it is ever the same in railroading. The man with a pull will inevitably outstrip the fellow with competence as his only promoter" (117). In this brief story, not even nepotism can stand up to lethal ineptitude.

818. _____. "The Golden Rule Trainmaster." In *Along the Line ... or ... Western Railroad Stories,* 74–84. New York: Broadway Publishing, 1905.

A squabble over procedures leads switchman Golden to wish Trainmaster Stoddard ill luck in the yards. Golden does not truly mean his bad wish, especially toward the kindly Stoddard, who goes against the common belief that railroaders won't do their duty unless hounded by their superiors. For his equitable conduct, Stoddard has earned the sobriquet "the Golden Rule Trainmaster." Out in the yard that night, Golden is seriously injured, and is trapped beneath an engine. Stoddard dies trying to save Golden. "After all, most railroad accidents are alike to a great degree. A man is beneath the cruel wheels; the news spreads like a flash, and somewhere at the little home that is waiting for his return the messenger of death knocks.... Some one inside cries: 'Yes, I knew it would come some time! I knew it would'" (82–83). Far too often, at the turn of the century, it did.

819. _____. "The Lap-Order at Kenton." In *Along the Line ... or ... Western Railroad Stories*, 85–108. New York: Broadway Publishing, 1905.

An amiable dispatcher tells the story of Jerry Conner, a skinny, chain-smoking prairie telegraph operator. Late one winter night as the two of them were on duty, Conner leaped to his feet from a doze, with bewildering shouts about "A lap-order at Kenton!" (A lap order is a dispatcher's nightmare: It gives two trains overlapping authority to run on the same track at the same time, in opposite directions. The likely consequences are obvious.) Conner dashes out into the snowy night and goes bounding out across the yards, with ticket-agent Lawton and the dispatcher far in his wake. Miles later, they find Conner unconscious in the snow. Carrying him back, they become lost. All ends well, in spite of Conner losing one leg to frostbite. The sense of fear accompanying being lost in the country on a freezing night is well evoked, and unsettling; in spite of its overall good humor, the story carries an undercurrent of anxiety. This anxiety manifests itself, as well, in Conner's conviction that he has sent a lap-order dooming two trains to collision; the "order" is naught but a product of his overtaxed mind.

820. _____. "The Passing of Fireman O'Leary." In *Along the Line ... or ... Western Railroad Stories*, 1–30. New York: Broadway Publishing, 1905.

Buster O'Leary's luck has been habitually bad, but he takes all his setbacks in stride. On his first chance at a preferred run, the officials inflict 10 demerit marks on his record for a dirty cab that he had no time to clean. O'Leary works for engineer "Dad" Grossman on a pusher engine assisting freights over the local mountain grades. O'Leary's luck holds: As he and Grossman are pushing a heavy freight up a hill, the freight train separates from its engine near the front of the train, leaving O'Leary and Grossman trying to hold back a loose train intent on rolling downhill. Grossman considers the situation, and jumps off the engine, leaving O'Leary "the lone, brave fireman who stayed by his post yet conscious of his perilous charge, willing to do or die" (18). Buster does: He heroically attaches the air brakes from the helper engine to the runaway train, and thwarts disaster. In a very unusual coda for such a story of heroism, O'Leary, basking in his glory, goes on a drunken binge and loses his job.

821. _____. "That 'Spotter' Deal." In *Along the Line ... or ... Western Railroad Stories*, 109–116. New York: Broadway Publishing, 1905.

A number of trainmen gossiping in the lobby of a Santa Fe division point listen to Conductor Effingham tell the story of the "spotter" deal in Dodge City, back when "there were some bold, bad men on the Santa Fe" (111), many of them heavy drinkers. Early in Effingham's career, another trainman pointed out a "spotter" aboard—an undercover railroad official looking for monkey business, or worse, among the crew or passengers. The crewmen tried an inspired, but stupid, practical joke on the spotter that landed them in hot water with the brass.

822. _____. "When the Texan Was Yardmaster." In *Along the Line ... or ... Western Railroad Stories*, 31–44. New York: Broadway Publishing, 1905.

Windy Walker, fireman promoted to switch-engine operator on the Pollywog branch line, tells about the Texas longhorn steer that one day ran wild in the yards. "Tell y' what, that critter was on a man-hunt ... every time he caught sight of a switchman, or any one else, for that matter, the dirt began to fly" (36). Walker saved the switchmen from playing bullfighter by running down the beast with his switcher—and then had to pay its owner $30 for the carcass.

823. Sweet, Clifford. "A Man of Imagination." *Railroad Magazine* 23 (Dec. 1937): 28–32. *Railroad Magazine* 77 (May 1965): 60–62.

An abandoned caboose in wretched condition has long annoyed officials of the St. Louis & Kansas City Railroad. The heap belongs to skinflint Henry Ball, who refuses to deal with it. When the old caboose burns down, railroad Superintendent Melcher is glad to be rid of it—until Ball hits him with a damages claim. An ironic twist involving Ball's acquisition of the caboose helps the road escape the legal knot he thinks he has tied around it, and Station Agent Abner Trumbull receives credit as a man of imagination for his thoughtful torching of the relic.

824. Tarkington, Booth. "Mary Smith." In *Harlequin and Columbine, and Other Stories*, 127–161. Garden City, NY: Doubleday, Page, 1922. *Saturday Evening Post* 185 (Aug. 17, 1912): 3–5+.

In this funny and charming look at an attenuated trainboard romance, young Henry Millick Chester is on his way to Richmond, Indiana. Alone in the Pullman washroom, he admires his smile in the room's angled mirrors. The porter, a "Libyan," observes quizzically. Henry has the solipsistic nature of the typical 19-year-old, and feels himself sophisticated well beyond the level of anyone else on the train. In the dining car, the steward places a lovely young woman opposite Henry. He becomes so besotted that he loses track of the train's progress, and is stunned when the porter tells him that Richmond is less than five minutes away. Henry, although lost in delightful conversation with this appealing girl, has yet to learn her name or her address. She provides both—after a fashion.

825. Taylor, John. "The Train Station." *World Letter* 7 (1996): 41.

In a one-page dream-like vignette, the narrator and three friends arrive at a European train station. It is cold. He and his friend Charlie go to examine a new type of boxcar in the yards. When they return, the train and their companions have vanished. The station is deserted and in ruins. The narrator turns to Charlie—but Charlie, too, has vanished. The narrator follows the tracks out into the country, where he sees the rails converge into a point on the horizon.

826. Taylor, Ross McLaury. *Brazos: An Historical Novel of the Southwest, 1876–1885*. Indianapolis: Bobbs-Merrill, 1938. 329p.

In spite of its subtitle, this book is less an historical novel than it is an engaging character study of a young man discovering himself, and the world. Brazos Bolton is a 16-year-old Texan in 1876 when he sets out to see the world, or at least a larger part of it, leaving his family behind on their cattle ranch. Brazos sees his first train from horseback, and is nearly as frightened as his horse by the steaming, shrieking engine. His education as a man on his own takes a sour turn, and he spends hard time in jail. When freed, he learns that his parents are dead, and the ranch lost. He has nowhere to go, and no one to think of when he hires on as a foreman in a railroad construction job. It proves to be rugged, dangerous work: "the skin on the men's hands, exposed to the cold, cracking until the blood ran, feet frosted, horses down, legs broken by suddenly shifting loads of ties, moving up from camp to camp..." (252). Brazos takes little satisfaction in the work. He sees into the future, thinking of how "not one of the thousands who worked there would be remembered" (253). He becomes hardened to the injuries the laborers suffer, seeing through them to the job's demands. The hardness he develops is called on by subsequent events, including a bridge washout that maims and kills a number of bridge gang workers. Brazos asks their foreman where to send the bodies. "Yuh know, Mister Bolton," says the foreman, "these men got no homes.... We just bury them where they die. No difference. Just the breaks. Lucked out. Bury 'em up on the right-of-way" (284–285). Yet not even Brazos's hardness protects him from nausea following his killing of a Mexican cook who has gone berserk and killed other railroaders.

Although Brazos is a tough man, he is also upright and inherently decent, as his romantic interest, Mary, recognizes. Their courtship, long-interrupted by Brazos's adventures, forms a tender counterpoint to the steely life Brazos leads. Railroad action comprises only about the book's final third, but it is as a railroader that Brazos realizes his abilities.

827. Teal, Valentine. "Trip by Train." *Woman's Home Companion* 77 (Jan. 1950): 26–27+.

In a story that combines comical passages

with pathos, a 12-year-old boy describes a 1945 train trip with his family. Almost everything that can go wrong does, including a wreck up the line that creates a delay of many hours. The mother of the family burdens her husband with non-stop chatter about the other passengers, offering bold assumptions, based on no evidence, about their personal lives. The nearby passengers include a young woman prone to tears and a soldier with one arm; Mother decides to play matchmaker between them. On the last day of the wearisome trip, the conductor enters the car to announce that World War II has ended. (The story's opening demonstrates that Mother's match-making is more effective than her instant character analysis.)

828. Terhune, Albert Payson. *Caleb Conover, Railroader*. New York and London: Authors and Newspapers Association, 1907. 322p.

In "the Mountain State," Caleb Conover, railroader and political boss, "owns the [convention] delegates and the newspapers and the Legislature as well as the railroads" (20). In a state of intoxication, he announces his intention to run for governor. He has crushed competitors like bugs beneath his heel. Conover is a flinty man, sometimes crude, unrelenting, and shaped by his history as a man who has struggled to overcome obstacles in an industry in which one gives no quarter. Despite the novel's title and Conover's past, however, there is little attention in the novel to railroading itself.

829. Thant, Octave. "The 'Scab.'" *Scribner's Magazine* 18 (Aug. 1895): 223–234. Also in Thant's *The Heart of Toil*. New York: Scribner's, 1898.

In July 1894, two commercial travelers are sweating their way by train between Joliet and Chicago. One swats a fly, and wishes it were labor leader Eugene V. Debs, whose followers are tying up railroad traffic with their strike. Pauls, the fireman on this train, is reputedly a scab, which explains the rocks hurled at the train at Spring Valley. An old woman who overhears the businessmen asks for the brakeman, Jerry Lyon, to tell her what a scab is. "Why, a scab's a feller that scabs—takes another feller's job!" he says (224). Lyon tries to explain the principles of the union to the old woman, but she cannot grasp them.

In spite of his union sympathies, Lyon fears for the scab fireman's safety, and offers to trade tasks with him for the trip. Pauls declines, saying that he doesn't want another man stoned in his place. Before the trip ends, Pauls performs heroically in a mob scene, and the fireman he supplanted cruelly assaults the old woman who expressed bafflement over union ideas. Thanet's own sympathy plainly goes not to the strikers, whom she presents as a ragged, snarling, violent bunch—including the women: "Scabs! Scabs! Kill the scabs! Pull 'em off the engine!" shrieks one woman (233).

830. Thomas, Carolyn [Actea Duncan]. *Narrow Gauge to Murder*. Philadelphia and New York: Lippincott, 1953. 256p.

Gail Rawson, a graduate student, comes to Glory Cloud, Colorado, for the summer to work on her thesis on a local writer. She also plans to help her adviser, Dr. Dahlberg, research narrow-gauge railroads, including the long-defunct Granger, Glory Cloud, & Western. Gail soon learns that circa 1921, the railroad was the focus of a scandal involving murder, suicide, and large sums lost. The road was born under a bad sign, with graft galore blighting its construction, and later criminal negligence leading to mass death. Murder rears its head afresh when someone demonstrates very plainly that further inquiries into the railroad's troubled past are unwelcome.

Some agreeable ingredients—an appealing heroine, a nicely-described setting, and interesting role of the vanished railroad in contemporary life—provoke reader interest, but convolutions in the narrative may tax one's patience.

831. Thompson, Maurice. "Hoiden." In *Hoosier Mosaics*, 127–161. New York: E.J. Hale & Son, 1875.

Available at *Wright American Fiction*: http://www.letrs.indiana.edu/web/w/wright2/

Luke Plunkett is the master of Rackenshack, an Indiana estate. He has let the house go to pieces, while investing heavily in his outbuildings. Plunkett's own appearance recalls that of his house: shambling and ill-kempt. When he learns that surveyors are to plot a railroad right-of-way straight across his farm, he is outraged. He doesn't want his land or his livestock troubled; "The truth is he was bitterly opposed to railroads anyhow. They were innovations. They were enemies to liberty. They brought fashion, and spendthrift ways, and all that along with them" (132). A confrontation in his fields with Elliot Pearl, the railroad's chief engineer, crumbles when Plunkett meets Pearl's beautiful daughter, Hoiden. As the railroad builds across the farm, Plunkett floats through the summer in a romantic haze. The romance is doomed, and Plunkett's joy is supplanted by a leaden heart. The story possesses an antiquated charm in spite of its overt sentimentality; one cannot help pitying poor Plunkett.

832. _____. "Stealing a Conductor." In *Hoosier Mosaics*, 114–126. New York: E.J. Hale & Son, 1875.

Available at *Wright American Fiction*: http://www.letrs.indiana.edu/web/w/wright2/

The local storyteller tells a stranger in town about how he "stole" a conductor named Fuller. The storyteller was broke, and walking back to Georgia from Florida. He jumped a train out in the wilds, but the conductor saw him and demanded a fare. The two tussled, and were both left behind when the train pulled away. The conductor spent some time tied to a tree in a swamp, and knew the thrill of being threatened with a gun. "I'm just going to shoot you a little bit for the fun o' the thing," says the conductor's nemesis. A funny story yet, with its humor deriving from the storyteller's sense of the absurd.

833. Thurber, James. "The Lady on 142." In *Thurber on Crime*, edited by Robert Lopresti, 202–208. New York: Mysterious Press, 1991. *New Yorker* 19 (Aug. 21, 1943): 19–21.

In a piece of characteristically Thurberian humor, a man and his wife are taking a short train trip to a small town in New York. While waiting to board, they overhear the stationmaster's end of a telephone conversation concerning a woman and a trainman on Train 142.

The man's imagination runs wild; soon he has convinced himself that the woman referred to in the overheard conversation is a spy. When he nods off in his seat, he has a vivid dream in which he and his wife are abducted from the train by foreign agents.

834. Titus, Harold. *Below Zero: A Romance of the North Woods*. Philadelphia: Macrae, Smith, 1932. 320p.

This undistinguished sentimental adventure of the logging business features occasional railroading scenes. The most important is a 10-page passage describing an engine derailment owing to sabotage in the dead of winter. The situation allows the hero, John Steele, to demonstrate his mastery of men and equipment in adverse conditions.

835. _____. "Hot Engine." In *Open Throttle: Stories of Railroads and Railroad Men*, edited by Phyllis R. Fenner, 51–74. New York: Morrow, 1966. *Saturday Evening Post* 206 (April 18, 1934): 12–13+.

Young engineer Danny Bryson is an upright, hardworking man who knows locomotives inside out. Already in trouble with railroad officials thanks to another worker's errors—or even sabotage—Danny is drafted to take "the Old Man," a top official, on a special run to meet some bankers. For the trip, he must use a defective engine that runs hot. Will Danny deliver the Old Man on time for the critical meeting? This Depression-era story dwells on the contrast between men who rise in the profession through self-service and brown-nosing, and those, like Danny, who wish only for a chance to make good through earnest labor.

836. _____. "A Little Action." *Railroad Magazine* 91 (Aug. 1972): 40–46. *Saturday Evening Post* 208 (Jan. 18, 1936): 14–15+.

George Hoskins, around 60 years old, has put in so many years as a dispatcher that his right shoulder is higher than his left from sitting hunched over the telegraph key. This deskbound railroader, although intimately involved in train operations, longs to be out on the line himself, aboard the trains, helping deal with problems on the spot. As he carries out his duties, his longing yields to realistic daydreams in which he is right there, sharing the action with the men on the line. "George galloped for the caboose with the flagman. He lifted the pin with the brakeman. He stood beside the switch with the baggageman" (43). The story is a nearly-perfect portrait of a knowledgeable, experienced worker in a sensitive position who identifies so powerfully with those dependent on him that he puts himself almost literally in their shoes as they go about their work, far out of his sight. This is a remarkable few pages of industrial fiction.

837. Tolman, Albert W. "Stopping the Cannon-Ball." In *Best Stories of Heroism I Know*, edited by John C. Minot, 126–134. Chicago: Wilcox & Follett, 1946.

Railroad tunnel patrolman Barry Parsons faces a tough-enough task in walking his half of a five-mile-long tunnel; making an especially nasty job of it, the tunnel ventilation system has failed, leaving the route full of noxious smoke and fumes. Could it get any worse? Indeed! A section of the ceiling collapses during Barry's patrol, leaving a lethal obstacle across the track, dead in the path of the onrushing Cannonball Express. Barry must dig through the rubble and plant a torpedo to alert the train's crew. Could any reader doubt that he would succeed?

838. Toomer, Jean. "Fern." In *Cane*, 14–17. 1923. Reprint, New York: Liveright, 1975.

The narrator, a Northern black, meditates on a young, mysterious black woman, Fernie May Rosen, of Georgia. Fern has a strange power over men; they feel compelled to provide her some tangible measure of their regard, even if anonymously. She is a mesmerizing woman. As he tries to illuminate for the reader the impenetrable essence of Fern's nature, the narrator turns to the railroad as a tool of inquiry: "I ask you, friend (it makes no difference if you sit in the Pullman or the Jim Crow as the train crosses the road), what thoughts would come to you ... had you seen her in a quick flash, keen and intuitively, as she sat there on her porch when your train thundered by" (16). So powerful is Fern's effect that a mere glimpse of her from a train window can rattle men's minds.

839. _____. "Love on a Train." In *A Jean Toomer Reader: Selected Unpublished Writings*, edited by Frederik L. Rusch, 146–165. New York and Oxford: Oxford University Press, 1993.

Young Dr. Coville is leaving his lucrative Chicago practice for a few months in Europe. He is tense with the demands of work; when he drops into his Pullman seat for the first leg of his journey, he can barely wait for the train to move. Much relieved at the train's departure, he goes to sit in the club car, where he studies the other passengers. Soon, his restlessness returns, and he goes to the observation car. There he sees an attractive young woman, and goes through protracted mental gyrations about whether and how to approach her. Her brief look of contempt at him does not help. That evening he finally speaks to her, and is troubled to hear her voice ideas about him that he himself has thought. She challenges him, provokes him, questions him, and strikes to the heart of his assumptions about himself—and leaves him dazed with admiration and confusion. The balance of this compelling and almost unbearably romantic story concerns Dr. Coville's effort not to lose track of this remarkable woman, and of his thunderstruck insight into his personal limitations. It is unfortunate that the story did not see publication in the author's lifetime. (Among its many pluses, it offers, through the woman, a fine explanation of why people tend to wave at those aboard passing trains, and at those who watch the trains pass.)

840. Tracy, F.B. "The Farmer's Railroad." *McClure's Magazine* 13 (May 1899): 35–42. Also in *The Railroad: Stories from McClure's.* New York: McClure, Phillips, 1901.

At a North Dakota town meeting, citizen Daniel Minds laments the local wheat farmers' exploitation at the hands of the Great Mogul Railroad "fer haulin' our stuff tuh Duluth" at inflated rates (36). Minds argues that the farmers of the Red River Valley should build their own railroad to Duluth. He receives little encouragement, but vows to go to St. Paul to speak to the head of the Great Mogul line. This magnate—evidently modeled on James Hill—"grabbed this line and that one, and extended them first to Duluth, then to Winnipeg, and then on to the West, until by buying, seizing, leasing, building, by any means getting lines and connections, his trains reached the Pacific.... His employees were peons, slaves" (38, 39).

Minds presents himself as a "railroad president," and secures from the amused rail titan a pass to ride the Great Mogul. Minds's devotion to the project takes him to New York City and Washington, D.C., and, amazingly, legislation falls into place to support his vision. Disaster strikes, however, through a combination of crop-wrecking weather, business intrigues, and influence exerted from St. Paul. The story ends with Minds "removed to the State Hospital for the Insane. Last Monday he announced that Christ would come in six days and he had been called to warn people of the event" (42). The moral: You can't buck the railroad.

841. Train, Arthur C. *Tassels on Her Boots.* New York: Scribner's, 1940. 301p.

Barry Carter works for tycoon Jim Fisk as part lawyer, part errand boy, and part personal companion. Carter is never sure whether he represents Fisk's Erie Railroad, or his steamship company, or Fisk personally. By midbook, however, he grows increasingly unhappy with Fisk's financial abuses of the Erie, including the printing of legally-approved unlimited stock certificates. Carter's disgust at his boss's underhanded ways eventually becomes intolerable, and one day he beats Fisk in Fisk's office. Chapter 15, "The Susquehanna War," finds Carter eating at Delmonico's, and eavesdropping on Commodore Vanderbilt and J.P. Morgan at the next table. The two great capitalists are discussing the threat that the Erie Railroad poses their own railroading interest, from Pennsylvania to New England. The crux of the issue concerns control of the Albany & Susquehanna Railroad. The chapter details the legal, barely-legal, and extra-legal maneuverings of the men competing for the road. It culminates in a head-on collision between two trains, one carrying an ad-hoc army of Erie railroaders, the other bearing a hostile Albany faction waving shovels, clubs, and firearms.

The novel's chief business is the corruption of the Tweed Ring; it tries to follow historical events faithfully. (The book's title is that of a song popular during the corruption-riddled presidential administration of U.S. Grant.)

842. Tucker, Wilson. *Last Stop.* Garden City, NY: Doubleday, 1963. 180p.

In this quick, readable mystery, a rainy day in Nebraska finds a small group of people intimately linked aboard a train jammed with vacationers. The group includes professional researcher Martin Davissey, young newspaper reporter Gee Churchill, and two men manacled together: Undersheriff Brace Tolley, and manslaughter convict Arthur Lang. Tolley is escorting Lang to prison. As is the common case in train-board mysteries, the train serves here as a means to coop up the main characters for an extended time. The novel features a vividly-described wreck and its immediate aftermath from the point of view of the passengers, as the train plunges into a river. The disaster sets the stage for the revelations of the mystery's previously-obscured details, and for its resolution.

843. Tully, Jim. *Emmett Lawler.* New York: Harcourt, Brace, 1922. 315 p.

This semi-autobiographical story of a young man's years as a hobo sustains a tone of romantic, genial goodwill at the same time as it addresses the dangers of life on the road—and on the rails—in the early part of the 20th century. Tully is an observant writer, and through Emmett's adventures offers glimpses of American life ranging from circus work to forced labor in a Southern prison.

When Emmett is a boy, his mother dies, and his impoverished Irish-American father packs him and two siblings off to an orphanage. Early in the book this fragment of the Lawler family boards a train for the orphanage—a fitting vehicle, for Emmett's later ramblings around the country come courtesy of countless rides hitched on trains.

Midway in the book, Tully composes a paean to the American hobo, an adventurer notable "in sheer capacity for suffering and endurance, daring and deviltry," who "shows qualities every day that are worthy of a higher cause" (136). Adding detail, Tully argues that "The young tramp must have initiative and originality. He must be self-reliant, and wage war with the organized system that would exterminate him with force, instead of leading him to the light with kindness" (137). Tully is sensitive to the way hoboes pass into, and out of, each other's lives with random chance. He portrays the hobo world as one marked by occasional fraternal violence, but also by friendship. At one hobo camp, the veteran rail rider Slim Eddie gives novice Emmett some practical counsel: "Allus watch yure clothes, Kid.... Some o' these tramps 'ud steal yure eyebrows while you sleep" (138).

Railroaders sometimes appear as heartless representatives of authority in railroad fiction, but in *Emmett Lawler* Tully often presents them as sympathetic to the struggles of the hoboes. One evening a conductor finds Lawler and some other hoboes hiding in an open gondola on his train. One of the 'boes, a bricklayer, seeks mercy by pulling out his union card. His solidarity with a brother laborer does not impress the conductor at first, but the bricklayer persists: "We are all three down and out, all on the bum, and you want to make us walk.... Will you sleep better at the end of the run if you ditch us?" (141) The conductor relents, and the men spend the night under the stars in the gondola. On another occasion, Emmett and a companion trudge on numb feet away from a train that they have ridden on a cold night. When the two young men enter a restaurant, a group of railroad men warm to them, and buy them a meal and a bed for the night.

The rigors of riding the rails help give Emmett a sense of the equality of races. At one point, black hoboes help Emmett board a moving train, and advise him on the best technique to perform that tricky task. The black hoboes are headed for a town which, in spite of its reputation as "hostile," inimical to vagrants, is a place where many "cullud fellahs" have been able to find work. Later, with another traveling companion, Emmett does jail time in Mississippi. On their release, determined to leave the state quickly, the two walk 50 miles in two days, and beg for food "in the negro settlements. As a rule, the negroes were humane. As has been said, 'a fellow feeling makes one wondrous kind.'"(261) Without extraneous comment, a short time later Tully has Emmett and his friend stumble onto a lynching scene near New Orleans. "The black man who had pleaded for his life now swung in the wind at the end of a rope.... His body was riddled with bullets, and his clothes were half torn from him. Many of the people, among them children, had carried away souvenirs of the occasion" (262).

In *Emmett Lawler*, the trains are never far off, and represent the readiest, most reliable way to escape present trouble or to seek future good fortune. The hoboes on whom Tully focuses are a diverse lot, and despite their material want and their run-ins with the law are not without goodness, a sense of their fellow men's suffering, and even a measure of nobility.

844. Twain, Mark. "Cannibalism in the Cars." In *The Complete Short Stories of Mark Twain*, edited by Charles Neider, 9–16. Garden City, NY: Doubleday, 1957. *The Broadway* (London), Nov. 1868.

The narrator boards the train in St. Louis, going west. A distinguished-looking man gets on at Terre Haute and joins him. He relates an account of a previous rail journey, in the winter of 1853, when he and his fellow passengers became marooned on the way to Chicago in a terrible blizzard. Days passed, the storm unrelenting, and hunger drove the men to an absurd series of parliamentary meetings in which they "elected" one of their number to serve as the next meal. "I liked Harris," says the storyteller. "He might have been better done, perhaps, but I am free to say that no man ever agreed with me better than Harris, or offered me so large a degree of satisfaction" (14). And then there was Morgan, "a perfect gentleman, and singularly juicy" (15).

Twain renders the story in a tone of horror, and it is very funny. In spite of its apocryphal nature, the story does evoke the dangers that could accompany rail travel in the mid-19th century.

845. _____. "The Danger of Lying in Bed." In *The Writings of Mark Twain*. Vol. 24, *The $30,000 Bequest, and Other Stories*, 257–261. Hartford, CT: American Publishing Co., 1907. *Buffalo Express*, Jan. 28, 1871.

Twain expresses disappointment in never having collected on the railroad accident insurance he has bought. In spite of the many thousands of miles he has racked up on the rails, he has never been lucky enough to be in an accident. A little calculation reveals to him that the real danger is much closer to home than on the nation's railroads: "Well, the Erie [Railroad] kills from thirteen to twenty-three persons out of its million [passengers] in six months; and in the same time 13,000 of New York's million die in their beds!" The answer is clear: "I will never sleep in a bed again" (259). Twain contends that the wonder is not that the railroads kill 300 people a year, "but that they do not kill three hundred times three hundred!" (261).

846. _____. "The Invalid's Story." In *The Complete Short Stories of Mark Twain*, edited by Charles Neider, 187–192. Garden City, NY: Doubleday, 1957. First published in Twain's *The Stolen White Elephant*. Boston: Osgood & Co., 1882; there it appears under its own title as part of "Some Rambling Notes of an Idle Excursion."

Twain hits and holds a note of outlandish hilarity in this tale of confused rail shipments. The narrator describes his efforts to escort a coffin containing the body of a deceased friend from Ohio to Wisconsin. The trip begins on a freezing winter night, and the coffin and a shipment of guns in an identical box are promptly confused. In the express car, the narrator accompanies the guns, and, without his knowledge, a fetid hunk of Limburger cheese. He shares the car with the railroad expressman. The two struggle to maintain decorum and presence of mind as the car, battened down against the weather and heated by the stove, begins to fill with the reek of the cheese, a scent they mistake for the fragrance of the narrator's late friend. "He's pretty ripe, *ain't* he!" says the expressman (189). The whole business affects the narrator

woefully: "The is my last trip: I am on my way home to die," he closes (192). Twain's mordant humor, rooted in colloquialisms and the absurd mix-up, carries the story from start to finish in a fine example of railroad comedy.

847. _____, and Charles Dudley Warner. *The Gilded Age: A Tale of To-Day*. Hartford, CT: American Publishing Co., 1873. 576p.

The Gilded Age must be the only novel whose title has come to represent the era it describes. In this satire of American business ethics during Reconstruction, Twain and Warner haul the reader through the cesspool of corruption, giddy delusion, and unmitigated greed that marked the period. Their targets range from the prototypical American dreamer—embodied by Col. Eschol Sellers— cooking up fantastic and frequently idiotic schemes that he can never bring to fruition, regardless of his professed faith in them— whose foolish blunders damage everyone around them, to politicians and businessmen so deliberate and purposeful in their venality that Dante would surely consign them to one of the lowest circles of the Inferno.

The railroad plays an important part in the novel. Philip Sterling (he of the suggestive surname) is a college lad with high standards of literary aspiration, and no particular cognizance of the necessity of grubby work as a precursor to success of any kind. His friend Henry Brierly's uncle is "a great railroad man" (120); Henry talks Philip into leaving New York City with him to work as a rodman in railroad surveying in Missouri. They travel to St. Louis with railroad contractor Duff Brown, who possesses "a certain vulgar swagger and insolence of money" that greatly impresses the St. Louis hotel clerk who waits on them (125). In St. Louis the young men stumble into the realm of Col. Sellers, who weaves his usual web of promotional malarkey around them, including a reference to laying the rails and going on from there.

Sellers sells Brierly a bill of dubious goods about running the Salt Lick Pacific Extension through an as-yet non-existent city built up from the settlement of Stone's Landing; Philip is less inclined to subscribe to the scheme.

Nevertheless, out they go to make a preliminary survey, "and the chief object of a preliminary survey was to get up an excitement about the road, to interest every town in that part of the state in it, under the belief that the road would run through it, and to get the aid of every planter upon the prospect that a station would be on his land" (160).

The "railroad" thus comes to Stone's Landing, minus only the track, a locomotive, and a train. After some excited laying out of the future city, the surveyors depart, leaving the locals to speculate.

"The next morning the camp moved on, followed till it was out of sight by the listless eyes of the group in front of the store, one of whom remarked that, 'he'd be doggoned if he ever expected to see *that* railroad any mo'" (167). Later, one of the locals confirms expectations: "A railroad come here last summer, but it haint been here no mo'" (190).

The Stone's Landing developers push a bill through Congress to support their project, but the bill produces no happy results: the bribes required to buy off congressional support left no funds for the Stone's Landing end of the deal. The railroad is nothing but fodder for Wall Street speculators.

One of the book's railroading highlights—or lowlights, to be more precise—occurs shortly after the Stone's Landing failure. Col. Sellers, constructing castles in the air as usual, demonstrates on a luncheon table what he sees as the inevitable success of the road. He lays out an imaginary right-of-way running from St. Louis to a potato, representing Slouchburg; a carving knife continues the route to Doodleville, signified by the black pepper. "Then we run along the—yes—the comb—to the tumbler ... ain't it a ripping road, though? I tell you, it'll make a stir when it gets along" (247).

Following the Stone's Landing debacle, the foul-tempered Conductor Slum throws Philip off an actual train when Philip attempts to defend the interests of a woman the conductor is ill treating. Philip lands in a swamp—a not symbolically inappropriate location, considering the swamp of corruption that marked the Stone's Landing "development." When Philip complains to someone familiar with the locale, wondering if some action against the

railroad might be worthwhile, he receives no encouragement. The fellow explains that "...suin's no use. The railroad company owns all these people along here, and the judges on the bench too.... You haint no chance with the company" (268).

In spite of some slow stretches, *The Gilded Age* remains a funny and instructive skewering of American business practices; the line between the Stone's Landing scam and the Enron scandal of the 21st century is even clearer than the railroad Col. Sellers constructs on the lunch table.

848. Tyler, Charles W. "The Angel of Canyon Pass." In *The Railroaders*, edited by Bill Pronzini and Martin H. Greenberg, 81–99. New York: Fawcett Gold Medal, 1986. *Railroad Magazine* 19 (April 1936): 24–35. *Railroad Magazine* 92 (Feb. 1973): 54–58.

Engineer Bill Carnegan is a noble railroader who has quit his job back East to bring his wife Ann to a more hospitable climate. He takes a job as a trackwalker in the desolate Canyon Pass. His wife, a kindly soul, feeds hungry hoboes, patches the clothes of Mexican gandy dancers, and earns a reputation as the "Angel of Canyon Pass." She dies tragically, but Bill soldiers on, his wife's grave in view of the track. The gravesite plays a critical part in Bill's saving a passenger train from disaster. Tyler spares nothing in his idealization of the brave Bill and his tender wife, both of whom are revered by railroaders and passengers alike for their heroic sacrifices.

849. Tyler, Sandra. *After Lydia.* New York: Harcourt, Brace, 1995. 306p.

Twenty-seven-year-old Vickie's mother Lydia grabbed the car keys one day and ran out on a gardening errand. On her trip, a train struck and killed her at the nearby crossing in her Massachusetts town. Vickie is suspicious that her mother's death was a suicide. She does not learn the truth, one way or another, and the railroad—aside from providing the means to Lydia's end—plays no further part in this talky novel.

Underhill, Edward F. *see* **Ockside, Knight Russ, M.D., and Q.K. Philander Doesticks, P.B.**

850. Underhill, Zoe Dana. "The Conductor's Story." *Harper's Weekly* 33 (July 27, 1889): 610–611.

In this gloomy ghost story, a traveling salesman who was acquainted with a conductor in the West years earlier is surprised to meet the fellow, Waring, on a little New England railroad. Waring is in bad shape, and that evening tells the salesman of his troubles. He feels responsible for the deaths of 150 passengers in a wreck out West; his guilt seems inexplicable, but as he relates his story, involving a cruel engineer's inability to listen to his mother, the reasons for his self-blame become clear.

851. Updike, David. "Agawam." In *Out on the Marsh; Stories*, 91–99. Boston: D.R. Godine, 1988.

The narrator prefers to return to his old hometown of Agawam, Massachusetts, by train. The train "moves along at the pace of passing thoughts, carrying me on the back of its vast, irresistible mass, as light as a feather … the chant of the conductor barking out a familiar litany of towns, is a song I have known since childhood" (92, 93). The narrator knows well the scenery along the route, from marshes and fields to children playing in their yards. The story concerns the narrator's gradual weaning, if not alienation, from his hometown; the train ride back, along the familiar route, forms a counterpoint to the separation and distancing that develops between the narrator and his youthful home.

852. Upson, William H. "Working on the Railroad." *Saturday Evening Post* 202 (June 21, 1930): 16–17+.

An American tractor salesman, Alexander Botts, has been sent by his firm to crack the Italian tractor market. The tractors are too costly for the typical Italian farmer, but Botts conceives the notion of selling them to Italian railroads to use for switching their lightly-built cars. An Italian railroad official admires the tractors, but balks at the expense of paying to operate them. Confusion ensues, but Botts perseveres like the good American businessman he is, winning the railroad's favor and the tractor contract.

853. Vance, Louis J. *The Trey O'Hearts*. New York: Grosset & Dunlap, 1914. 283p.

Written as the basis for a movie serial produced but now apparently lost, this novel features the cliffhanging, chapter-ending nonsense typical of such work. A 20+-page section involves the principals in a breathless train chase, biplane pursuit of a train, and heroic handcar antics. (Is it not always the case that the old handcar the hero spots abandoned beside the track needs nothing but a little elbow grease to send it flying down the rails?) Vance was a prolific popular writer who in this novel plugs into the widespread public fascination with motive power, both by air and rail.

854. Van Doren, Mark. "The Uncertain Glory." In *Home with Hazel, and Other Stories*, 19–37. New York: Harcourt, Brace, 1957. Also in Van Doren's *Collected Stories*. New York: Hill & Wang, 1962.

Gorman, an actuary with a quick imagination, is riding the train to Atlantic City, where he will deliver an address. He becomes obsessed with a young woman who boards his coach; his thoughts revolve around her, although she, to all appearances, is unaware of his existence. They never exchange a word. Yet something might "happen" between them, Gorman fears (hopes?), in spite of his loyalty to his wife and family. After he gives his paper, Gorman loiters on the beach, sure that the young woman is gone, but he bumps into her—almost literally. He is nearly beside himself when, on the return train, he sees her again in his car. In the end, she vanishes in the crowd at the station, and Gorman's overheated fantasies return to a familiar theme: accidents involving his wife and children. In this strangers-on-a-train tale, Gorman spins an elaborate, and wholly unprovoked, scenario involving his sub rosa relationship with a woman to whom he amounts to nothing more than another piece of furniture on the train.

855. Van Wert, William F. "Recycling Dante." In *Local: An Anthology of the Subway Experience*, edited by Jay Heller, 35–53. Brooklyn: Zonepress, 1977.

Local gathers photos, poems, and stories into an effort to portray life on the subway train. In the last category are a half-dozen pieces, most no more than a page long. By far the most substantial of the stories is Van Wert's. The hero here, such as he is, is Arnie Klandinsky, a New York City librarian who hates books but loves reading. The narrator, Claire Lumiere, also works at the library. She discovers that Arnie, whose relationships with women are wanting, is the notorious subway kissing bandit whose stolen smooches on the trains have been the preoccupation of the press. In this curious story of psychological ferment, Arnie devolves to the figure of a masked clown sitting on the subway platform of Times Square, and Claire, who at first seems so reserved, so unlikely to deviate from the daily routine, seduces a subway conductor under an assumed identity, and on her last night in New York City takes the subway to attend a midnight Easter mass.

Van Wyck, Francis *see* **Weaver, Ward**

856. Waldo, Harold. *The Magic Midland.* New York: Doran, 1923. 305p.

Young Larry McGraw grows up in the small mid–Michigan town of Sidney around the turn of the 19th century. Larry is an uncertain youth who benefits greatly from the friendship of locomotive engineer Ted Church, master of the "Old 1200." Church rescues Larry from an embarrassing situation before other local boys by asking Larry—who, his mother dead, does his own and his father's laundry—to wash his favorite silk shirts. He gives Larry his railroad watch as an advance payment for the work; Larry is so overcome that he cannot speak: He can only raise "his forefinger to his sandy shock of hair in the railroad man's hail of greeting and farewell" (74). Soon Church lets Larry ride in his engine, all the way to exotic Port Huron—"an incredible shining prospect!" (79). Larry's stern father forbids him to go, but Larry runs off to meet the train, and the trip proves even more exciting than Larry anticipated.

As Larry grows older and surer of himself, Church and the 1200 subside from the story. The railroad makes its final appearance in the last pages, when Larry, having recently joined the U.S. Navy, takes the train across Michigan from the Great Lakes Naval Training Station to report for destroyer duty on the East Coast. In the evening, the train passes through Sidney, and Larry stands on the rear platform to watch the sights of his old hometown slip past. He vows to himself that he will return. This is a gentle and somewhat idealized story of adolescence, but it has its merits, including its portrayal of Larry's friendship with Engineer Church.

857. Walsh, George E. "The Engineer Who Was Afraid." *Harper's Weekly* 53 (May 22, 1909): 22–23+.

This story is related by a fireman who left the Eastern roads "to enjoy the calm peacefulness of railroading up and down the slopes of the Rockies" (22). He and engineer Jim Bailey run a has-been 1879 engine. Jim is a competent engineer, but fears high speeds. Even 30 mph is enough to tighten his jaw; the narrator is contemptuous, until he learns of Jim's rough history. One day the pair must pull one section of the railroad president's train; the other section follows. Jim Bailey re-establishes his nerve with his heroics at a burning trestle, and everyone recognizes his valor: men groan and women sob and faint as they wait for Jim to save them. In the end, the railroad president falls to his knees in gratitude for Jim's fearless labors.

858. Walsh, Thomas. *Nightmare in Manhattan.* Boston: Little, Brown, 1950. 218p.

Frances Kennedy, personal secretary to an oil company executive, recognizes on the commuter train three men who forced her car off the road on the way to the station. She sees that one of the men has a gun, and tries to interest the conductor in the fact. "A lot of people see a lot of things happen on trains, or from trains—or imagine they do," he says, and suggests that she "forget it" (8). Railroad cop Lt. William Calhoun acts on Frances's urgings, and follows the three men at Manhattan Station. Before long, the pursuit grows serious: The men have kidnapped the six-year-old son of Frances's boss. In a crime story with frequent railroad station action, Lt. Calhoun prevails—and wins the affection of Frances Kennedy.

Ward, Elizabeth Stuart Phelps *see* Ward, Herbert D., Mrs.

859. Ward, Herbert D., Mrs. [Elizabeth Stuart Phelps Ward]. "The Semaphore." *Scribner's Magazine* 14 (Dec. 1893): 760–776. Also in Ward's *The White Crown*. New York: Houghton, Mifflin, 1894.

Mrs. Ward throws another story onto the pile of those detailing hard-working railroaders' selflessness. Sumach Junction, 14 miles from the city, is a miserable place in New England shunned by all but railroaders and unfortunate travelers. The community's heart centers on the railroad switch tower, where three men—Fred, Joe, and Matt—grapple with the junction's complex switching duties. On a cold winter night, Joe's infant son is deathly ill; Joe is already trading 12-hour shifts with Fred to cover for Matt, also down with illness. When he returns to spell Fred, Joe has had no sleep, and is in a daze. "I ain't no boy," insists Joe; "I say, I can stand it like a man tonight" (763). Joe's fatigue, and his anxiety over his son, leave him operating, just barely, on auto-pilot: He can barely grasp routines he knows in his blood. His weariness yields to adrenaline when he cannot move an ice-jammed semaphore to warn an oncoming train to stop before plowing into a stalled express. Joe stands on the track waving a lantern to signal the train to stop.

860. Warman, Cy. "Ar Ye Worth It?" In *Short Rails*, 219–224. New York: Scribner's, 1900.

Born in Illinois, Cy Warman (1855–1914) worked for many years on the Denver and Rio Grande. The Canadian National System named Warman Junction, Saskatchewan, after the author. Following stints as a journalist and poet, he focused on the railroad, in both fact and fiction—today, it is sometimes difficult to tell one from the other, so closely to actual events did Warman pin his stories. In this story, young Steve grows restless on his father's Michigan farm, and goes out West, where he enters railroading. Time passes, Steve excels in his work, and he becomes a general freight agent. After years of intending to do so, he returns for a visit to the farm, where he tells his father how much money he makes. The old man then asks him an astonished question (see the story's title).

861. _____. "The Brakeman and the Squaw." In *Frontier Stories*, 137–146. 1898. Reprint, Freeport, NY: Books for Libraries, 1969.

In a fiction that one might accept as fact, an elderly Indian woman once treated kindly by a conductor assists a party of rescuers in retrieving a brakeman being held for ransom (rum, chiefly) by a small group of Indians.

862. _____. "Catching a Runaway Engine." In *The Express Messenger, and Other Stories of the Rail*, 151–158. New York: Scribner's, 1900. *McClure's Magazine* 6 (May 1896): 589–590.

The heroic engineer Jakie Moyer uses his own engine to halt a runaway locomotive bearing down on him on a mountain downgrade. "When you cross La Veta Mountain again, ask for Jakie—Moyer,—he's the boy" (158).

863. _____. "Chasing the White Mail." In *The Last Spike, and Other Railroad Stories*, 107–117. New York: Scribner's, 1906.

Yank Hubbard, a reckless but so-far unwrecked engineer, aims to strike fear into the president of his railroad by following the old man's private car closely with his own freight engine. The two trains play something like a game of tag along the route, until the devilish Hubbard trades hijinks for heroism.

864. _____. "A Couple O' Captains." In *Frontier Stories*, 235–246. 1898. Reprint, Freeport, NY: Books for Libraries, 1969. *McClure's Magazine* 11 (Oct. 1898): 551–553.

Two cavalry captains thrown out of work at the end of the Sioux Indian wars search for jobs. One of them, Gene, goes on to a law career; the other, Tom, works as a brakeman with the Burlington in Iowa, on the edge of the wild

West, where Indians occasionally wreck stations and rob freight cars. As Tom rises on the railroad, the two old soldiers meet from time to time. At one point Tom and Gene meet at the station in Chicago. Tom is now general manager of the road, and "a smart black porter" tends dutifully to the commands of "his master" (243). The "black boy" (244) leads the two men to Tom's private drawing room aboard the train.

865. _____. "The Death Run." *Mc-Clure's Magazine* 3 (Aug. 1894): 248–251. Also in Warman's *Tales of an Engineer, with Rhymes of the Rail.* New York: Scribner's, 1896.

"The Death Run" is a long, dangerous stretch of mountain road on the Denver & Rio Grande, where large chunks of the "scenery" often slip from the mountainsides to fall on trains passing below. The narrator describes, with overtones of the supernatural, a fatal accident befalling one locomotive and its crew. Warman's emphasis is on the courage of the engineer, who thinks not at all of saving himself, and on parental anguish at the loss of railroading sons.

866. _____. "The Engineer's White Hair." In *Short Rails*, 73–85. New York: Scribner's, 1900.

A white-haired Southern engineer and a New England tourist who fought each other at Gettysburg recall their confrontation. Over cigars, the engineer tells the tale of how his hair turned white. (The event had nothing to do with railroading.)

867. _____. "The Express Messenger." In *The Express Messenger, and Other Stories of the Rail*, 1–37. New York: Scribner's, 1900.

In the Old West, a railroad express messenger charged with guarding a shipment of gold and money disappears with the loot in the aftermath of a train wreck. The popular conclusion: The messenger is a thief. This sentimental adventure features a noble bandit and a faithful railroader.

868. _____. "Fanny and the Fireman." In *Short Rails*, 299–310. New York: Scribner's, 1900.

Fanny McCann is head waitress at a railroad eatery, the Mint Julep diner. Fanny is romantically torn between the slick proprietor of the Mint Julep and an engine fireman, who fears that the eatery is merely the first step on the road to ruin for this "pure young girl" (303). The tears receive a good jerking in this mawkish tale; Fanny marries the Mint Julep cad, who leads a life of rapid dissipation; her infant dies—"And then she lay and sobbed above this mite of cold, cold clay" (309)—; and the fireman sustains horrible injuries in a wreck. Warman writes better when he stays on railroad property.

869. _____. "First Train Over the Bridge." In *Short Rails*, 285–297. New York: Scribner's, 1900.

Two questions wait ahead on the new engine's run out of St. Louis: What will it be like to be the first express train across the big bridge—and is there any substance to the rumor that a hold-up gang waits up the track? The old engineer and his young fireman are meticulous in preparing their beautiful engine for the run. The bridge-crossing, though a bit giddying, goes fine. Near Terre Haute, however, the train-robber warnings prove prescient. The trip ends in tragedy for the train crew. This piece appears to be a hybrid of fact and fiction; details before the hold-up have the ring of straight reporting, but a sentimental, parallel theme, involving the old engineer, his wife, and the fireman's sweetheart, has the flavor of mass-market fiction.

870. _____. "Flying through Flames." In *Tales of an Engineer, with Rhymes of the Rail*, 63–69. New York: Scribner's, 1896. *McClure's Magazine* 3 (Oct. 1894): 422–423.

This sketch—little more than a vignette—describes a passenger train's trip through forest-fire-ravaged mountain country. As the train reaches an intended stop, the surroundings burst into flame, and the engineer opens the throttle. "The engine-men were almost suffocated in the cab, while the paint was peeled from the Pullman cars..." (68). Back in the roundhouse, the engineer addresses his locomotive: "Well, old girl, we got through, didn't we? But it was a close call" (69).

871. _____. "Four-Flushing." *Railroad Man's Magazine*, no. 1, Oct. 1906.

Retrieved January 28, 2005, from http://home.mindspring.com/~railroadstories/rrmmv1n1/fflush.htm

Superintendent VanLaw of the P.D.&Q. is helping the railroad expand rapidly in the West in the 1870s. Here his road and the Illinois Western compete fiercely to be the first to build to the town of Spike Buck. The story dwells on the political and business infighting, including charges of corruption, connected to the railroads' efforts. The story's title alludes to a gambit VanLaw employs to facilitate the P.D.&Q.'s success.

872. _____. "A Ghost Train Illusion." In *The Express Messenger, and Other Stories of the Rail*, 117–131. New York: Scribner's, 1900.

On the Rio Grande Western, a special train is pulling the line's general manager. The train's engineer and fireman are convinced, first, that they will ram another train head-on; then, at the other train's apparent vanishing act, they suspect that they have seen a ghost. Warman has a more prosaic explanation for the averted collision.

873. _____. "The Great Wreck on the Pere Marquette." In *The Last Spike, and Other Railroad Stories*, 181–192. New York: Scribner's, 1906.

Kelly, an Irish section gang boss on the Pere Marquette in Michigan, is one of the apparent victims in a hand-car accident. One of the hands laments the fact that Kelly died a Republican. His death, like that of the other victims, proves a premature assumption. This humorous effort achieves mild success through its mockery of the stereotype of the stouthearted railroader.

874. _____. "Head On." *Saturday Evening Post* 182 (May 7, 1910): 22–23+.

On a stormy winter night, the Limited, running hard to make up time, is steaming toward an oncoming freight with 30 cars of tea. A confusion in orders has put the trains on collision course. Through blind luck, trainmens' keen reflexes, and, Warman suggests, the power of prayer, calamity is avoided.

875. _____. "In the Black Canon." In *The Last Spike, and Other Railroad Stories*, 151–164. New York: Scribner's, 1906.

Sometime in the 1880s, Buckingham, a cold-hearted gambler, contests with the admirable express messenger John Cassidy for the hand and heart of lovely Nora O'Neal. She manages a dining station, much like a Harvey House, on the R&W line in Colorado. Buckingham's motive is sinister: He aims to use Nora as a tool to facilitate his robbing Cassidy of his strongbox aboard the train through Black Canon.

876. _____. "In the Hospital." In *Frontier Stories*, 69–77. 1898. Reprint, Freeport, NY: Books for Libraries, 1969.

Frank, an engineer recuperating from a leg broken in a train wreck, reminisces for his friend and fellow patient about his work on the construction train laying track for the Kansas Pacific. He tells the story of how a band of "red devils" (75) trapped and killed a careless conductor who strayed from his train.

877. _____. "The Iron Horse and the Trolley." In *The Last Spike, and Other Railroad Stories*, 135–150. New York: Scribner's, 1906.

A disputed gold mine sale in the Klondike provokes a mad race for the Canadian border between an electric trolley and a train. American lawmen seek to arrest those aboard the train who would countenance the sale.

878. _____. "Jack Farley's Flying Switch." In *Short Rails*, 37–56. New York: Scribner's, 1900. *Lippincott's Monthly Magazine* 66 (Sept. 1900): 454–461.

The narrator rides in the caboose with conductor Jack Farley on a night run through the mountains. Farley, although a great storyteller, is also a notorious drunk, and judging by his behavior in the caboose is apparently suffering from the DTs. The superintendent indulges Farley because of his skilled work, when he approaches sobriety. Finally discharged, Farley struggles back into service, and fully redeems himself in an heroic act of self-sacrifice. (Such acts happen every day on pulp-fiction railroads.)

879. _____. "The Last Spike." In *The Last Spike, and Other Railroad Stories*, 1–29. New York: Scribner's, 1906.

J. Bradford, civil engineer, takes a humble laborer's job on the Pacific Railroad and shows exemplary mettle at every task. Heroic beyond limits, Bradford prevails against every obstacle in his service to the road, including an attempt by Sioux Indians to burn him alive. Strength, pluck, and an iron will carry him through in his efforts to help build the transcontinental railroad—and, yes, to win the hand of his beloved. This thoroughly sentimental story is redeemed by several pages focusing on the ceremony of driving the last spike to join the Union and Central Pacific Railroads in 1869.

880. _____. "A Locomotive as a War Chariot." In *The Express Messenger, and Other Stories of the Rail*, 101–115. New York: Scribner's, 1900.

Another story relating railroaders' problems with Sioux Indians, this narrative from an old engineer looks back at the days of the Kansas Pacific's construction. The Sioux attack a construction train; the narrator and train crew overcome the Indians and capture their leader, Bear Foot, thus further stoking "the wrath of the red men" (108). The Sioux later try to capture a roundhouse, to their regret. Bear Foot succumbs, and the railroaders "placed him alongside the depot where the sun would catch him early," and "the coroner came and sat on him and pronounced him a good [i.e., dead] Indian" (115).

881. _____. "The Locomotive That Lost Herself." In *The Express Messenger, and Other Stories of the Rail*, 39–68. New York: Scribner's, 1900. *McClure's Magazine* 7 (June 1896): 89–96. Also in *Short Lines: A Collection of Classic American Railroad Stories*. Edited by Rob Johnson. New York: St. Martin's, 1996.

Oscar Hansen designs and supervises the construction of a new locomotive. Hansen, a genius, lives for his work. The engine, tagged ominously as No. 13, begins its career in Colorado. Things go badly, and Hansen, obsessive over the engine, is its constant companion. "She is my life!" he insists. "I have put my soul into her..." (49). Hansen's bond with—or bondage to—the ill-fated engine takes first his reason, and then his life. The quaint tall tale emphasizes the link between the machine and its maker.

882. _____. "The Milwaukee Run." In *The Last Spike, and Other Railroad Stories*, 273–286. New York: Scribner's, 1906.

Henry Hautman, veteran engineer on the Chicago, Milwaukee & Wildwood, was near the road's mandatory retirement age. The more he reflected on his long service, "the more he dreaded the day when he must take his little personal effects from the cab of the La Salle and say good-bye to her, to the road, and hardest of all, to the 'old man,' as they called the master mechanic" (280). Henry makes a last inspection on Christmas Eve of his beloved La Salle locomotive; the other railroaders on hand give him a private moment with the old engine. He sits in the cab, lost in memories of his career. Eventually the lamp-lighters arrive, "but before their gleam reached his face the old engineer slid down and hurried away home with never a backward glance" (285). The story ends happily, as is almost inevitable, but Warman's depiction of the old engineer's leave-taking from his engine is touching.

883. _____. "The Mysterious Message." In *The Express Messenger, and Other Stories of the Rail*, 175–224. New York: Scribner's, 1900.

As the railroad's new president is about to make an inspection tour, the division superintendent insists that Goodlough, his trainmaster, take on a young woman, Miss Morgan, as a telegraph operator, owing to her engineer father's death in a wreck. Incensed at having the young woman forced upon him, the trainmaster makes a careless error at the telegraph, setting the stage for a disastrous collision. The usual trainman heroics prevent the wreck. In the aftermath, the trainmaster loses his faculties, and Miss Morgan becomes a dispatcher.

She excels at the work, but the railroaders in general are not pleased. "A woman operator was bad enough, but a woman despatcher was sure, they argued, to make trouble. A girl at twenty giving orders to gray-haired conductors and storm-faced engineers was a thing that ought not to be" (198–199).

When the trainmaster recovers, the road restores him to his post, and he must move Miss Morgan to the third trick, the night shift. She is humble: "If he could ... forgive her having been born a woman, she would be content to take whatever he had to offer her" (208). Inevitably, Goodlough and Miss Morgan fall in love, and she relinquishes her position with the road to become his wife. This in spite of her superb work, and what proves to be the message referred to in the story's title, the message she sent by telegraphy that prevented the wreck Goodlough nearly caused. All the occupational skill in the world does not, here, hold a candle to the satisfactions of marriage, the ultimate "promotion" for a woman in Warman's world.

884. _____. "The Mysterious Signal." In *The Last Spike, and Other Railroad Stories*, 85–106. New York: Scribner's, 1906.

On different railroads around the country, trainmen hear an inexplicable "stop" signal, and act on it. The phenomenon becomes so widespread that exasperated railroad officials threaten anyone who heeds the signal with a reprimand. The source of the signal proves not altogether ghostly—but not quite natural, either.

885. _____. "The New Ticket Agent." In *Short Rails*, 3–35. New York: Scribner's, 1900.

Lancing Cutter, Jr., the new ticket agent in a little Wisconsin town, has been a city man all his life. He is taken aback by what he considers the rural bumpkins in the town. When the agent he is replacing shows him around the station, Cutter is dismayed at the menial chores expected of him, including polishing the lanterns and sweeping the floor. All the new man needs is a little trial by fire, and he gets it in a funny passage in which the locals,

over-eager to board a train for a July 4th excursion, brawl with railroad personnel at the station. While trying to do his duty, Cutter is "insulted, beaten, and walked upon" (31). A little epilogue, set years later, reveals how both the old agent and the new have advanced with the railroad.

886. _____. "Number Three." In *The Last Spike, and Other Railroad Stories*, 237–251. New York: Scribner's, 1906.

Near Christmas, a drunken man boards the westbound express, leaving Omaha. The drunk, Charley Downs, tries to steal a coat that belongs to the railroad superintendent on the train. Upon learning of Downs's brave efforts to reform—the theft of the coat notwithstanding—the superintendent intervenes on his behalf. An unabashedly maudlin Yule tale.

887. _____. "On the Blacklist." In *Short Rails*, 257–283. New York: Scribner's, 1900.

Redmond Smith, a young orphan boy, lives restively with an uncle and helps work his uncle's farm. What he cares for is railroading. Redmond shucks off the farm life and hops a freight to Cleveland, where he lies about his age to land a job in the yards. Red's hot temper obstructs his career, and he finds himself dismissed. The roadmaster who fires him passes word among his peers, and Red has trouble finding work. He has been black-listed, and his experience "was the experience of hundreds of others, worthy and unworthy, who looked in vain for employment while their names were on the black-list" (276). Red goes west, where what counts is a man's ability, not his past—and prospers.

888. _____. "On the Limited." In *The Last Spike, and Other Railroad Stories*, 211–218. New York: Scribner's, 1906. *Canadian Magazine of Politics, Science, Art and Literature* 26 (1905–06): 65+.

The narrator describes pulling out of an Ontario station on the International Limited bound for Montreal—a dreadful 25 minutes (!) late. He repairs to the library car (!), to lounge, while the engineer pushes to make up for the lost time. "Along the shore of the sleeping lake our engine swept like a great, black, wingless bird of night" (217). It brings the train in on time. The story features little vignettes among the passengers.

889. _____. "Oppressing the Oppressor." In *The Last Spike, and Other Railroad Stories*, 119–133. New York: Scribner's, 1906. *Lippincott's Monthly Magazine* 67 (June 1901): 731–736.

One Buffalo Jones of Garden City comes to see the president of the Santa Fe Railroad. Jones insists that the road install a 50-car spur at his nonentity of a village. The official shrugs off Jones with gentle disdain, but Jones has friends in the California legislature, and knows how to employ them. Warman depicts this as standard operational procedure for aspiring towns near a rail line.

890. _____. "Out on the Road." In *Short Rails*, 57–71. New York: Scribner's, 1900.

During a train trip, the general manager relates to the narrator an account of how the black porter who waits on them suffered during a hold-up some years earlier. Although the "darky," as the general manager calls him, saved the GM's life in the incident, a particular train whistle still gives the porter the willies, recalling a whistle sounded on the night of the hold-up.

891. _____. "Perpendicular Railroad." In *Short Rails*, 103–114. New York: Scribner's, 1900.

The Calumet Branch line went in to ship coal; the grade is so steep that it would be unsafe for a passenger train. The run is, in one railroader's jest, so "infu'nal pu'pindiculah I can't find a place to set my dinnah pail" (108). "Hardluck" Leonard, who has been badly burned in a revival meeting fire and literally blown through the roof in an explosion at a soda fountain, finds the Calumet Branch just his speed. "Gi'me the death run an' the all-night saloon," he says, "but keep me away from camp meetin' an' sody-fountains" (109). A tall and funny tale.

892. _____. "A Railway Mail Clerk." In *The Express Messenger, and Other Stories of the Rail*, 159–174. New York: Scribner's, 1900.

Warman praises the wit and courage of railway mail clerks, who usually ride in the car behind the locomotive—"and they take whatever is left when the grim reaper has finished with the enginemen" (161). Here he tells the story of Doc Pippin, who began a career in law enforcement, but becomes a U.S. railway postal clerk: "His loyalty, bravery, and devotion to duty had been warmly commended in autograph letters from the highest officials in the mail service" (17). Doc proves his courage when he sustains a mortal injury in a train wreck, even as he seeks to save the mail from the resulting blaze.

893. _____. "A Running Switch." In *Short Rails*, 87–101. New York: Scribner's, 1900.

O'Grady, who runs a brickyard near Buffalo, believes that because he ships material on the railroad, he has a right to a free ride on the freight train. When he falls off a caboose one day, drunk, and lands on his precious pet dog—killing the pooch—O'Grady blames the engineer. O'Grady's follies continue in a slapstick vein, concluding with an accident involving a hard door, O'Grady's head, and a basket of eggs.

894. _____. "A Scalp for a Scalp." In *Frontier Stories*, 35–47. 1898. Reprint, Freeport, NY: Books for Libraries, 1969.

As their train steams across the prairie, a railroad superintendent tells his companion about a Sioux Indian attack that took place at a station years ago. Pawnee scouts helped the white men defeat "the wily Sioux" (46).

895. _____. "Scraptomania." In *The Express Messenger, and Other Stories of the Rail*, 225–238. New York: Scribner's, 1900.

Engineer John "Scrappy" Jones has a penchant for fisticuffs, and "had licked about half the engineers on the middle division" (230). Warman narrates the story of a succession of Jones's battles approvingly, with the clear implication that a good route to friendship lies in beating the other fellow bloody.

896. _____. *Snow on the Headlight: A Story of the Great Burlington Strike.* New York: Appleton, 1899. 249p.

In 1888, the Brotherhood of Locomotive Engineers and the Brotherhood of Locomotive Firemen struck the Burlington & Quincy Railroad Company, which ran from Chicago to Denver and Cheyenne. The strike lasted nearly a year, and resulted in the capitulation of the striking unions, although not before a bitterly fought, violent struggle. In this novel, which relies on the events of the strike for the framework of its plot, Warman takes a critical view of both labor and capital. He focuses on the men who are torn between supporting their unions and earning enough to allow their families to meet the necessities of life. Some, like the agitator George Cowels, are chiefly self-interested; others, like Dan Moran, agonize at a more selfless level: "They had not dreamed that the fight could become so bitter. Life-long friends became enemies. Family ties were severed, homes were ruined, men's lives were wrecked, women's hearts were broken, and out of the shadow of the awful strife came men fit for murder" (98).

Melodrama is plentiful in the story, from Cowels's fireman killing him in a row in the cab on the Denver Limited over Cowels's faithlessness to the brotherhood, to a dying man, nearly sliced in two by an engine's drivewheel, exonerating Dan Moran of bogus charges. Warman's sympathy goes partly to the strikers, and very little to the Burlington, but his great concern is for the strike's most innocent victims, the wives and children of strikers left to suffer at home. Warman relates nakedly emotional stories of women freezing to death while their striking husbands are in jail on false charges. These passages flow from Warman's genuine compassion, and there can be little doubt that they have a footing in actual events.

Warman comes down hard on union leaders who enjoyed power and its trappings, but who had no sound idea about how to advance the rank-and-file's interests. He also displays a clear contempt for the Pinkertons, here referred to as "the famous Watchem detective agency" (170), who helped the Burlington crush the strike. He describes, and implicitly condemns, the way railroad interests manipulated the press, being sure that every story reaching the public came with a slant favorable to the Burlington, and depicting the strikers as irrational, or worse.

A long coda follows what should probably be the proper conclusion of the book; it details the post-strike lives of some principal characters, and, in the end, gives full meaning to the novel's main title. *Snow on the Headlight* is not an artful book, but it is an interesting one; Warman's efforts to come to grips with a terrible episode in the industry he loves are earnest and impassioned, even if they do often lapse into melodrama.

897. _____. "The Story of Engine 107." In *The Express Messenger, and Other Stories of the Rail*, 133–150. New York: Scribner's, 1900. Published as "The Vicissitudes of Engine 107." *McClure's Magazine* 9 (June 1897): 717–721.

The Baldwin company ships twin engines to Colorado for service on a narrow-gauge road. One of them, the 107, suffers a series of fatal accidents, prompting the railroaders in her vicinity to exercise all their superstitions: rabbit-foot rubbing, wishing on the new moon, and so on. Warman produces a nice sentence in this story: "The train came in on time, drawn by the 109, and she stood with calm dignity on the siding, while her wild, wayward, and disreputable sister, all gaudy in her new paint, with clanging bell and blowing steam, with polished headlight and new flags fluttering at her shoulders, glided backward, like a gay girl on roller skates, to take her place" (144–145). Anthropomorphism is not uncommon in descriptions of locomotives, though no other can approach that of Edwin C. Washburn in "*The 17*" (Entry 905).

898. _____. "The Stuff that Stands." In *The Last Spike, and Other Railroad Stories*, 253–271. New York: Scribner's, 1906.

In the late 1850s, young Melvin Jewett, telegrapher, takes charge of a little way-station as agent, operator, yardmaster, and general factotum. Jewett is ambitious, "earnest, brave, and industrious" (255). His hard work leads to his appointment as train dispatcher in Bloomington; he works the midnight to morning "death trick," so called because of the many accidents during those hours. During the Civil War,

Jewett organizes a drill company, distinguishes himself in the war, overcomes false accusations, and carries off assorted what-not of an heroic sort, for he "is made of the stuff that stands" (271).

899. _____. "Sympathy Strike." In *Short Rails*, 173–186. New York: Scribner's, 1900.

The narrator, a railroader for some 48 hours, must crawl beneath an engine and hoe the ash-pan clean—while the engine is operational: "I could hear my scared heart pounding the ties on which I lay" (177). Some time after his tenure, he intervenes in the railroad's disciplinary action against a young yardman, Smith, and tries to dissuade the general manager from firing him. Smith is, however, plainly implicated in theft of freight.

900. _____. "The Wahsatch Band of Bandits." In *Frontier Stories*, 195–207. 1898. Reprint, Freeport, NY: Books for Libraries, 1969.

Train robbers, although often inept, harass the Denver and Rio Grande Railroad on the line to Salt Lake. Engineer Ed Maloney, in spite of his devotion to the rules, equips himself with a .45 revolver for extra protection in the cab. The revolver proves handy when the Wahsatch Gang jumps his train, but not nearly as handy as Maloney's precious railroad rule book, which he keeps in a pocket over his heart.

901. _____. "Wakalona." In *The Express Messenger, and Other Stories of the Rail*, 81–100. New York: Scribner's, 1900.

McAlester, a brakeman, falls in love with a young Pawnee Indian woman, Wakalona. One day Sioux Indians partially scalp her, and, in shame, she wanders the Nebraska wilderness. McAlester rescues her from her own people, who consider her abuse by the Sioux a sign of her "death." McAlester is heroic, and Wakalona—even her name is assigned to her by the railroaders—is helpless without him. Warman exploits popular ideas about Native Americans, and portrays the white railroaders as the hope of civilization.

902. _____. "A Wild Night at Wood River." In *The Express Messenger, and Other Stories of the Rail*, 69–80. New York: Scribner's, 1900.

In a piece presented as a tale of the early days of the Union Pacific, a family and the new schoolmarm hide in a boxcar from the Sioux, who burn their cottage and attack the depot. A courageous station agent and a valiant conductor figure in the defeat of the "red devils" (73).

903. _____. "The Wreck at Roubideau." In *Short Rails*, 115–124. New York: Scribner's, 1900.

One starlit night, Andy Degan, a former Burlington engineer, is running on the Denver and Rio Grande down a dangerous stretch of track. His fireman jumps out of the cab when both realize that they are fast-approaching a washed-out bridge over the Gunnison River. Degan takes action that saves the remaining crew, but he accompanies the engine into the torrent below. As the engine rolls in the powerful current, Degan frantically seeks escape.

Warner, Charles Dudley *see* **Twain, Mark, and Charles Dudley Warner**

904. Warren, Joseph. *The General*. New York: Grosset & Dunlap, 1927. 182p.

"It's the tale of a lad, a lass and a locomotive" (1), the novelization of the 1927 Buster Keaton film *The General*, itself a comedic take on the Andrews Raid of April 1862, when a group of Union soldiers led by Capt. James J. Andrews hijacked a Confederate train at Big Shanty, Georgia. Their intent: to burn Southern railroad bridges and to cut supply lines. The story's hero is Johnny Grey, engineer on the General for the Western and Atlantic Railroad. Johnny tries to enlist in the Confederate army to impress his sweetheart, Annabelle, but the army rejects him: He would be more valuable to the cause as an engineer. When Andrews' men steal the General from under Southern noses at a lunch stop, Johnny pursues the engine, first by handcar, then by another locomotive, the Texas. The raiders meet their fate in a flood, and Johnny redeems himself in Annabelle's eyes while history is mocked.

Described on the title page as "A farcical novel with an historical background," *The General* lives up—or down—to the description.

905. Washburn, Edwin C. *"The 17."* Englewood, NJ: Washburn, 1929. 290p.

The author describes this novel as the "memoirs of an old American eight wheeler" (vii). It features anthropomorphism unleashed. The opening chapter begins in the Baldwin Locomotive works in Philadelphia, where two engines under construction carry on a conversation with each other. According to Squatty the switch engine, "I heard the 1012 say to the 1151 that of course she made time with a good track and picked coal" (7). What engine would do otherwise? The novel's heroine is the 17, one of the new Baldwins introduced in the first chapter. The reader who follows the 17 on her career—as well as in her private thoughts and her conversations with both other engines and rolling stock—learns both substantial American railroad history and technical matters. Human beings, chiefly railroad laborers and officials, also have their say, but only as a means of further illustrating the picture of life on the rails drawn by the 17 and her sisters. One of the most dramatic passages, again, related among locomotives, concerns the efforts of engines and railroaders to save lives in a raging Minnesota forest fire.

The 17 flourishes in the late 19th century; at the end of her career, she moves from the Northwest to help build railroads in the far West. In spite of the fanciful premise on which the novel rests, the author clings resolutely to the details of railroading history. That he felt free to approach an adult audience in the manner of *"The 17"* suggests something of the public's fascination and romance with the railroad in its glory years. Numerous photos of locomotives and railroad scenes are a nice plus in the book.

906. Waters, Don. "Milepost 40." *Railroad Magazine* 38 (Sept. 1945): 30–39. Also in *Tales of the Rails*. Edited by Veronica Hutchinson. Cleveland and New York: World Publishing, 1952. Reprinted as "Mystery of Milepost 40." *Railroad Magazine* 84 (Feb. 1969): 36–39.

Young fireman Jack Barnes learns that his father, an engineer, has been pinned under his wrecked locomotive at milepost 40. Jack rides out on the wrecking train, thinking how all the modern safety improvements cannot prevent a derailment. He watches as rescuers pull his father—dead—from under the wrecked engine. A year later, in the aftermath of seeing his father blamed for the accident, Jack is an engineer himself, and on a run past milepost 40 finds a way to discover the real cause of his father's fatal wreck.

907. _____. *Pounding the Rails: An Adventure Story*. New York: Chelsea House, 1928. 247p.

Engineer Zeb White "had started railroading an ignorant mountain boy, had won his way to the engineer's side of the finest run on the division, had put poverty behind him, [and] had won greater riches in the love of a woman..." (15). Early in the story, White survives an accident that kills his fireman, giving the author a chance to remark on the mindset of railroaders: "Railroading breeds fatalism. Constant presence of danger attends all men who ride the moving trains" (25). Zeb is glad to be able to go home to a place, unlike the railroad boarding houses of his past, where he can talk of things other than the road. He is glad, too, that his son has "not grown up in an atmosphere of banging cars and pounding rails" (34).

Offered the post of road foreman of engines, Zeb reflects on his quarter-century with the company, and realizes that there are better jobs than pulling the throttle and brake valve. Railroading had changed, too, with a new emphasis on speed, and Zeb decides to take the new job. It proves a tough one, for lax work all across the division has led to poor service, accidents, and alibis.

Zeb White's new secretary is Ellen McCoy. He finds it awkward to confer with her on railroading details: "With that soft, warm flush on her cheeks, that sweet curve to her chin, those white, well-formed hands, she seemed out of place. Railroading was man's work" (54).

The novel is, as the subtitle promises, an adventure, but it is also the author's effort to outline, through Zeb White's experiences, how the railroader's life is changing in accord with the evolution of the business. The occasional life-taking wreck is no longer an unavoidable act of Nature, but the result of carelessness. Discipline, planning, one might even suggest scientific management, are the new necessities. The day of the engineer as cowboy is over.

White shows his commitment to fairness in his new position—"I propose to see absolute justice done to every man on the runs" (70)—when he dresses down an engineer for abusing his black fireman. White's preconceptions about women do not prevent Ellen McCoy from becoming a valuable assistant, far more than a secretary. Author Waters brings to the fore changes in the railroad work culture, from a time when men were proud to call themselves "railroaders" to one in which the railroad has become a "system," and "when you met them [i.e., young railroaders] uptown, you couldn't tell them from bank clerks!" (157).

With its sentimental subplot, the novel does not qualify overall as serious fiction, but Waters is serious in his discourse on the changing nature of railroading, industry, and even to some extent the working relationships of men and women, and in these respects *Pounding the Rails* is an interesting, insightful, and worthwhile work.

908. Waters, Frank. *The Woman at Otowi Crossing*. 1966. Reprint, Athens, Ohio: Sage/Swallow Press, 1981. 300p.

Helen Chalmers had long run a little tearoom serving patrons of a narrow-gauge outfit, the Chile Line, at the Otowi Crossing in New Mexico. The novel opens in 1941 with the little train pulling up to the crossing empty, the last passenger run having taken place a week earlier, its last run—period—this evening. The crew members are relieved to find Helen still there: "To pass by a dark station on our last run would of broke our hearts," says the brakeman (13). The wrecking crews follow, tearing up the rails. Helen gives the crew refreshments, and stands in the doorway, watching the train disappear in the distance. "There was a single last whistle—the voice of one of America's last baby railroads confiding its history to memory" (16). While the trainmen ate, some U.S.

Army personnel stopped at the tearoom to ask directions to nearby Los Alamos.

Not long after the attack on Pearl Harbor, Helen goes to a nearby town to meet her grown daughter, Emily. The little town boasts one of the most charming of the Fred Harvey railroad hotels. Helen tells a companion that such a beautiful establishment is what she always wanted at the Crossing. He informs her that the hotel is about to be closed and demolished. "No, they can't!" she says. "Oh, what's happening to the world?" (69).

Local journalist Jack Turner, searching for a peg on which to hang a syndicated column, conceives of "Whistle Stops on the Chile Line," exploiting the line's vanished character. The Manhattan Project is producing frantic activity at Los Alamos, as Helen finds in Jack's nostalgic columns a painful evocation of a world that has gone and will not return. From here, the novel moves on to describe the new world Helen finds in the Atomic Age, one in which her senses grow sharper, and a mystical quality marks her life. Indeed, she becomes known not as Helen, but as the Woman at Otowi Crossing, with a mythology of critical importance to a world on the cusp. The myth business may strike the reader as deeply felt, or as hokum—or both—but Waters very keenly grasps the sense of a way of life coming to an end with the demise of the Chile Line, and with Helen's struggle with this loss. The story is based on the real-life Edith Warner; Peggy P. Church's *The House at Otowi Bridge* (Albuquerque: University of New Mexico Press, 1960) is a non-fiction account of Warner's life.

909. Way, Charles J. "My New Home in Northern Michigan." In *My New Home in Northern Michigan, and Other Tales*, 15–55. Trenton, NJ: Printed by W.S. and E.W. Sharp, 1874.

Available at *Wright American Fiction*: http://www.letrs.indiana.edu/web/w/wright2/

Properly speaking, this piece more readily fits into the genre of travel writing than fiction, but let the author, who calls it a "tale," have his way. Travel writing or short story, "My New Home" provides an interesting account of the narrator's move from New Jersey to Michigan in 1871. His route to Michigan takes him by rail to Chicago and then Milwaukee, and on a steamer trip across Lake Michigan to Michigan's western shore. Comments on other passengers, especially the large number of immigrants bound for Wisconsin and Minnesota, lend an intimate historical touch: "It is a suggestive sight to stand at the depot and watch the arrival of the long lines of emigrant trains as they pour into Milwaukee. You see thousands of German men, women, and children ... clamber down from the cars to await the next trains toward their destination" (22). The narrator describes Chicago's vast ruins from the great fire as he views them from the train. He mocks the citizens of Trenton, New Jersey, for lacking "stamina enough to build a mile of railroad," in contrast to the energetic residents of Milwaukee (21).

In Michigan, the narrator takes a slow train from Muskegon to Whitehall. "By fastening the vision firmly upon a tree, you could satisfy yourself that the train was in motion" (25). Attention to railroad detail peters out at Whitehall, then the end of railroad connection with Northern Michigan in that part of the state.

910. Weaver, Ward [Francis Van Wyck]. *End of Track*. New York: Reynal & Hitchcock, 1943. 303p.

Robert Burton, a recently-discharged captain in the Confederate army, and a pal are rescued from marauding Cheyenne Indians by a passing Union Pacific train. The train's only passenger car is filled with assorted rough men, and a few rough women, headed for the end-of-track boom towns. The opening chapter ends with a train wreck, and angry Indians threatening the survivors. A detachment of U.S. Cavalry saves them in the nick of time. Burton continues by train to Julesburg, a wild-eyed, red-whiskey-drinking town, populated by loafers, teamsters, harlots, section hands, and various folk all instrumental (or, in the harlots' cases, at least accessory) to the building of the transcontinental railroad.

Union Pacific workers are busy fending off Indians, who see the railroad as a threat to their way of life. Burton works as a hunter for the UP, a position that puts him into direct conflict with "them red bastards" (115).

Eventually he works to thwart the bad guys intent on ruining the UP.

Romance, gunplay, Indian fighting, tough talk, and hard riding fill the book. Even a little labor unrest hits the fan: At one point the track workers reach the limit of abuse they can tolerate. "Them Eastern leeches are bleedin' us!... Are we goin' to take their double crossin' like a lot of greasers? Let's git after 'em! Show 'em we can hit back! Stop the trains! Kill the slave-driving bastards!" (280).

The novel is an uneven mix of historical milieu, including actual historical characters, and free-swinging railroad-cowboy funfest, with its pulp roots showing clearly.

911. Webb, Charles H. *John Paul's Book: Moral and Instructive: Consisting of Travels, Tales, Poetry and Like Fabrications*. Hartford, CT, and Chicago: Columbian Book Co., 1874. 621p.

Available at *Wright American Fiction*: http://www.letrs.indiana.edu/web/w/wright2/

In a compendium of observation, with a fictional patina, on a wide range of topics, Webb's titular character and narrator tackles the railroads from time to time—or they tackle him. His point of view runs from the comically ironic to the outraged. In the first category, Mr. Paul relates the harrowing adventure of his favorite trunk on a train trip to New York. The trunk has accompanied him everywhere; in his efforts to square away the trunk and his other baggage, he carries on a ridiculous, highfalutin, mock-elegant conversation with a Grand Central Depot railroad official. The official assures him that "a good many gentlemen ... are employed expressly to find out where you wish to go and keep you from going there..." (30). Mr. Paul then proceeds on a maddening and absurd ordeal ending in disaster for his beloved trunk.

In the outrage category, Mr. Paul later attacks railroad tycoons such as Jay Gould and Horace Clark for their crooked dealings. All of these men, he contends, have the same ambition: to rob stockholders and customers blind, by whatever method works. Mr. Paul writes with humorous irony of his financial ills stemming from the Panic of 1873 (spurred on by the collapse of Jay Cooke's investment house, heavily over-extended in the Northern Pacific Railroad); when he comes to the railroads, however, his humor vanishes: "Every road has been run," he says, "as though Wall Street were its beginning and its terminus—as if nothing was to be carried by it but their own selfish ends" (246).

912. Weidman, Jerome. "An Easy One." *New Yorker* 17 (Dec. 6, 1941): 32–36. Also in Weidman's *My Father Sits in the Dark, and Other Selected Stories.* New York: Random House, 1961.

A woman who claims to be a widow and her young son are traveling by train from Salt Lake City to New York. The boy, David, loudly interrogates his mother on the state capitals, drawing the attention of other passengers. One of them, a tall man, discards his magazine and ingratiates himself with David's mother. Terrific tension ensues as David, who regards the stranger with a blend of despair and terror, refuses to continue the game. Not even the intervention of a gentle and diplomatic porter can mollify the boy. There is plainly something going on below the surface in the young widow's life, of which her son is well aware, but at which the reader can only guess.

913. _____. "Gallantry in Action." In *My Father Sits in the Dark, and Other Selected Stories*, 173–182. New York: Random House, 1961.

Frank Loewenstein and his young son Bobby are traveling from California to New York during World War II on a train filled with American soldiers. The dining car is crowded; Loewenstein suggests that two airmen wait in his drawing room while he bribes the porter to bring them food there. The airmen drink liberally from Loewenstein's liquor, and—after he finally tells the men his name—a captain among them relates in a ghastly, mock–Yiddish accent the story of his winning a combat medal. The mockery goes over Bobby's head, although he knows he has missed something important. Loewenstein reacts firmly but subtly, and, in spite of the captain's behavior, goes out of his way to see that the two airmen are treated well. In the end,

"Mr. Loewenstein stared through the washroom window at the night smashing by outside, and he fingered the side of his strong face delicately, like a man probing for an old, forgotten bruise that has unexpectedly become painful again" (182).

914. Welch, Doug. "Mrs. Union Station." In *Great Railroad Stories of the World*, edited by Samuel Moskowitz, 131–154. New York: McBride, 1954. *Saturday Evening Post* 210 (Dec. 25, 1937): 8–9+.

Although this story, like most in massmarket magazines, reinforces popular stereotypes and assumptions, it remains mildly diverting. Newly-married Helene Appleby learns that her husband, Steve, is a fanatical model railroad buff who bases his modeling on close observation of the real thing. The conflict between the Applebys sums itself up in an exchange in which Mrs. Appleby asks her train-buff husband why he doesn't pay her more attention. The catalyst for this pat, middle-class spat could be golf, football, cars, bowling, or any other "male" activity. The complications and resolution are obvious, but the story is saved by author Welch's keen observations of railroading details.

915. Wellman, Manly Wade. "The Little Black Train." In *Best from Fantasy and Science Fiction: 4th Series*, edited by Anthony Boucher, 234–253. New York: Ace, 1955. Also in Wellman's *Who Fears the Devil?* Sauk City, WI: Arkham House, 1963. *Magazine of Fantasy and Science Fiction* 7 (Aug. 1954): 114–127.

Narrator John the Balladeer is an itinerant guitarist who picks up a gig at a High Fork country barbecue—or what guest of honor Donie Carawan calls the birthday of a curse. John is looking for local songs, and has heard of one about a little black train. The party guests seize up when John improvises an accompaniment as Donie sings the ominous lyrics of the song. Donie has been cursed to death by a train driven by her former lover, who at her urging murdered the owner of the High Fork Railroad, who left Donie everything. She has sold the railroad; the tracks have been torn up; and Donie laughs at the curse of the little black train that supposedly comes at midnight to carry sinners off to judgment. John the guitarist gives Donie some apt advice: "You act right, you won't be so apt to hear that whistle at midnight" (252).

916. Welty, Eudora. "Bride of the Innisfallen." In *The Bride of the Innisfallen, and Other Stories*, 47–83. New York: Harcourt, Brace, 1955. *New Yorker* 27 (Dec. 1, 1951): 53–56.

A young American woman—"the American girl"—sits in a crowded railway coach compartment. She is leaving gloomy, gray London for Ireland, without the knowledge of her husband. The story advances though a thicket of competing conversations and monologs as most of the compartment occupants talk incessantly. The resulting babble does not facilitate a flowing narrative, and is, in fact, annoying. Nevertheless, there is a nice passage in which the travelers share food, and Welty gives a good impression of travel with strangers who cannot be quiet. As for the American girl, who appears to be shedding a spiritual burden, one suspects that it hardly matters whether she is bound for Ireland or Iceland, as long as her husband is not there when she arrives. (The *Innisfallen* is the name of the ship that the train passengers will catch to reach Ireland.)

917. _____. *Delta Wedding*. 1946. Reprint, New York: Harcourt, Brace, Jovanavich, 1974. 247p.

This novel opens with a nicely-described scene on a coach on the Yazoo-Delta—more popularly known as the Yellow Dog—in early fall of 1923. Nine-year-old Laura McRaven is traveling alone from Jackson to Fairchilds, Mississippi. All the windows in the coach are propped open in passengers' hopes of catching a breeze; the train moves so slowly that it seems to be racing the butterflies that flit in and out of the open windows. At one point, the Dog stops in an open field, and Laura watches the engineer go out and pick a bunch of goldenrod. The train passes into the Delta, where "most of the world seemed sky" (4). When the train reaches the station in Fairchilds, Laura sees a half-dozen of her cousins hopping up and down in excitement at her visit.

918. _____. "The Key." In *A Curtain of Green, and Other Stories*, 56–73. New York: Harcourt, Brace, 1941. *Harper's Bazaar* 75 (Aug. 1941): 71+.

A group of insect-bitten would-be passengers waits for the late train at a backwater station. Albert and Ellie Morgan, a middle-aged couple, sit below an admonitory poster showing a train about to ram an open touring car. Nearby a young man drops a key that bounces toward Albert. He picks it up, and in an excited exchange with his wife reveals that neither can speak or hear. They treat the key like a sign, a symbol of a new future, and Albert pockets it. The young man does not interfere. Albert and Ellie miss their train, bound for Niagara Falls. "To work so many years, and then to miss the train," signs Ellie (71). In the now nearly-empty station, the young man who surrendered the key makes a concluding gesture of compassion, probably a futile one, toward the couple.

919. _____. "Lily Daw and the Three Ladies." In *A Curtain of Green, and Other Stories*, 3–20. New York: Harcourt, Brace, 1941. *Prairie Schooner* 11 (Winter 1937): 266–275.

Three self-appointed guardians—"the ladies"—of the nubile but retarded Lily Daw determine that the best place for Lily is the Ellisville Institute for the Feeble-Minded. They round her up and pack her onto the train at the Victory, Mississippi, station while the town band plays in Lily's honor on the platform. Lily's real ambition is to marry a half-deaf xylophone player, and, judging by the conclusion, it looks as though she will attain that happiness. Much of the town has gathered to see her off to the asylum. "Some of the people thought Lily was on the train, and some swore she wasn't. Everybody cheered, though, and a straw hat was thrown into the telephone wires" (20). The story is simultaneously funny and pathetic.

920. West, John. "The Vanishing Passenger." *Mysterious Traveler Magazine* 1 (June 1952): 62–76.

The narrator, a romance writer, describes her trip to Hollywood with her nephew,

Jonathan Duke, aboard the Twentieth Century. When a passenger dies—stabbed to death—all suspicion focuses on young Peggy Andrews. The conductor is especially convinced of her guilt, until a mysterious passenger turns up missing. Before the train reaches Chicago, Jonathan has sewn up the mystery neatly.

921. Westheimer, David. *Von Ryan's Express*. Garden City, NY: Doubleday, 1964. 327p.

American Colonel Joseph Ryan joins fellow prisoners at an Italian camp near the end of World War II. Following Italy's surrender, German troops force the prisoners aboard boxcars on a train bound for Germany. The last half of the novel concerns Col. Ryan's implausible but exciting hijacking of the train and his attempt to take it into neutral Switzerland, with the prisoners aboard. There is nothing of American railroading here, but Ryan's character is a classic of the American adventure-fiction type: tough, smart, brave, and determined.

922. Wharton, Edith. "A Journey." In *Midnight Specials: An Anthology for Train Buffs and Suspense Aficionados*, edited by Bill Pronzini, 35–47. Indianapolis: Bobbs-Merrill, 1977. Also in Wharton's *The Greater Inclination*. 1899. Reprint, New York: AMS Press, 1969.

A woman accompanies her mortally ill husband by train to their New York City home. They have been away seeking treatment for him, but it is clear that he is going home to die. The woman has come almost to resent her husband, for she remains in the prime of life, and he has become a tedious chore. Her yoke to the infirm breaks when she finds her husband dead in his berth one morning. Immediately she fears that she will be put off the train with his body should railroad officials learn of his death. With a long trip to New York remaining, she feels compelled to try to conceal the truth until the end of the journey. Wharton effectively portrays the woman's anguished mental state. Other passengers are hypocritically solicitous, evidently glad to relieve the boredom of their trip with an opportunity to offer aid to the interestingly afflicted. A woman urges that the woman's husband take his medicine more often; a religious pest—a Christian Scientist—wants the "sick" man to read one of his tracts. There is no real companionship in this coach of strangers: The woman is alone with her dead husband, but worse than alone, owing to the other passengers' insistence on "helping."

923. Wilcox, Wendell. "The Pleasures of Travel." In *O. Henry Memorial Award Prize Stories of 1944*, edited by Herschel Brickell, 225–233. Garden City, NY: Doubleday, 1944. *New Yorker* 19 (Nov. 13, 1943): 24–27.

Mr. and Mrs. Glaum must sit in the seat at the end of the coach, facing a mother and her two small children. Conversation with the young mother leads to revelation of fissures in the Glaums' marriage. In the club car with his wife Louisa back in the coach, Mr. Glaum, drunk, relates his unhappiness with his wife to another man. At length he returns to his wife and finds her asleep, "like a lovely girl laid out for burial" (232). One does not anticipate a happy future for the glum Glaums.

924. Williams, Ben A. "Man Afraid." *Saturday Evening Post* 202 (April 26, 1930): 8–9+. Also in *The Best American Mystery Stories of the Year*. Edited by Carolyn Wells. New York: John Day, 1931.

Timorous Simon Gary, a clerk in his father's Boston-area drugstore, fears many things, especially his wife, Alice. He has aroused her temper by repeatedly coming home late after missing the last train from the city. One winter night two bank robbers visit the drugstore, and in stupid confusion Simon pursues them to an express train to Chicago. The crooks seize Simon on the train. While he lies bound and gagged in an upper berth, he listens to the robbers debate his fate. Driven by fear of once again stoking his wife's ire by coming home late, Simon overcomes the felons in heroic but thoroughly modest fashion.

925. Williams, Charles X. "Bulletin 99." *Railroad Magazine* 83 (June 1968): 42–44+.

Boomer engineer Spike Nolan likes his job with the Kansas & California Railway, but the young, cold-eyed superintendent, P. Virgil Miller, makes him uneasy. Bulletin 99 takes Miller's unforgiving approach a step too far: It requires railroad personnel to report others who violate road rules. On a run some months later with Nolan, Miller learns that cooperation among trainmen is a better way to success than is surveillance. The author, a former boomer, displays extensive knowledge of train operations, although the story's emphasis on technical detail will leave the average non-railfan reader puzzled.

926. Williams, Jeanne. *Home Station.* New York: St. Martin's, 1995. 321p.

Ed Morland, a recent Spanish-American War veteran who lost an arm in the conflict, also loses his job as station agent when he takes the visiting Teddy Roosevelt to task publicly over the war's assorted injustices. Adam Benedict, who plans to build a railroad to the tumbledown village of Bountiful southwest of Dodge City, hires Ed to serve there as agent. Ed and his daughter, Lesley, take up residence in a sparsely-furnished boxcar in Bountiful. As the story progresses, Benedict presides over Bountiful's resurgence. He also falls in love, to the extent that this hardheaded business man can, with Lesley. She does not return the feeling, her heart going to young Jim Kelly.

When Ed is mortally wounded by thugs in an attempted payroll holdup, Lesley assumes station agent duties, and performs well. Ed's tombstone arrives by rail two weeks after his death, shortly before Benedict builds a new depot. The new depot notwithstanding, Benedict—in a vengeful snit over his rejection by Lesley—and losing control of the town he conceived as his personal establishment, decides to bypass Bountiful with his railroad, and leave it to a slow death. The townsfolk, led by Jim Kelly, vow to save the day, and the town, by building their own line, the Citizens' Railroad.

This historical romance rests in part on diligent research, and offers interesting details of both railroading and national life in the era of its setting. Historical facts, unfortunately, sometimes come through with an air of pedagogy, rather than as integral aspects of the

story. The characterization, however, is effective and reasonably complex, especially in Lesley's case. If the conclusion is too sweet to believe long after closing the book, it is touching while the reader remains in the grip of the main characters.

927. Williams, Joy. "Train." In *The Vintage Book of Contemporary American Short Stories*, edited by Tobias Wolff, 537–552. New York: Vintage, 1994. *Ms* 10 (March 1982): 66–67+. Also in Williams's *Taking Care; Short Stories*. New York: Random House, 1982.

Two little girls, Danica Anderson and Jane Muirhead, are riding a train from Washington, D.C., to Florida, accompanied by Jane's parents. The Muirheads are a quarreling pair. The girls explore the train, meet other passengers, and engage them in not-too believable conversation. Williams ascribes to the girls a coy sophistication and vocabulary that exceed the level appropriate to their age by a wide margin.

928. Williamson, Eric M. "Blue Train." *Virginia Quarterly Review* 74 (Spring, 1998): 263–278.

The narrator has just graduated from a California high school. He lives with his father in an old trailer near the service station where his father works. Both are jazz musicians; neither of them can bring himself to play for keeps. The boy's mother lives with her latest husband, John. John is younger than the narrator, and works for the Southern Pacific. The narrator goes to visit his mother and John at the caboose they share at the railroad switching yard in Oakland. The three of them get drunk; John and the narrator go to a bar and drink some more. In a parallel plot, the narrator associates with a Mr. Beasley as a demolition worker; Mr. Beasley is a catalyst for the narrator's reflections. His mother, meanwhile, stands on the caboose platform, looking "like she was posing for a dirty magazine" (270).

929. Williamson, Jack. "We Ain't Beggars." In *The Early Williamson*, 168–176. Garden City, NY: Doubleday, 1975. *New Mexico Quarterly* 3 (Aug. 1933): 162–172.

A boy, Lee Haskell, and his dog, Tige, are riding a boxcar through Texas with other hoboes during the Depression. The boy is hungry, but resists the encouragement of another hobo to beg. The source of Lee's pride is evident in a flashback to his relationship with his late father. Lee continues hopping freights and stubbornly refusing assistance from other hoboes. His pride proves his tragic undoing. In an interesting preface to the story, author Williamson—who is better known for his science fiction—describes his own hoboing early in the Depression, an experience on which he bases the story. "The editor [of the *New Mexico Quarterly*] had reservations, natural at the time, about soiling his academic pages with such a rude phrase as 'son of a bitch,' but finally decided to let it stand" (167). The story itself has merit in its depiction of down-and-out men struggling to survive, even if Lee's behavior is a bit too melodramatic to accept.

930. Wilner, Herbert. "On a Train in Germany." In *Dovisch in the Wilderness, and Other Stories*, 139–154. Indianapolis: Bobbs-Merrill, 1968.

An American television worker in Germany to collect film for editing travels by train from Munich to Zurich. A bombardier who saw Germany from the air in the war, he takes the train to see it from the ground up. His compartment is crowded with a mixed lot of passengers. The American looks out the window at the rail yards and buildings he bombed in the war, and remembers the terrible fear he felt on his missions. As the other passengers chat, snow begins to fall, and the American watches it whirl away from the window. A young woman in the compartment weeps, and talks inaudibly in the corridor with a male companion. The woman's anxiety fills the compartment, and the American feels cheated of the private experience he had hoped for on the train. His perceptions change when the distressed woman is revealed to be a Jew, and is escorted from the train by guards, apparently for a passport problem. The Jewish woman's trouble triggers in the American a surge of anguish and sympathetic terror. The war is over; the woman will come back; but the thin veneer of civility that covers the pit of historical awareness has been torn away, and for the American has come not personal resolution, but an awareness of others' fears.

931. Wilson, Bourdon. "While the Tracks Were Being Cleaned." *Sunset* (Central West Edition) 56 (Feb. 1926): 28–29+.

Old Man Williams is irate over recent accidents on the railroad, and is threatening to dismiss workers regardless of their blame, or lack of same. His young stenographer, Miss Andrews, is taking the brunt of his anger as he dictates threats to his subordinates, even as a landslide's remains are being cleared from a stretch of the railroad's track. The story's narrator, Billy, sees another side of the Old Man. Shortly after driving poor Miss Andrews from the office in tears, Williams takes Billy to visit a Civil War veteran, a man who treated Williams kindly during the war. The old veteran has fallen on hard times, and Williams intercedes generously. Back at the office, he begs Miss Andrews' forgiveness. Even a railroad magnate driven to distraction by acts natural and human can sometimes show his heart.

932. Wilson, Mrs. E.V. "The Story I Heard on the Cars." *McClure's Magazine* 1 (Aug. 1893): 224–234.

Although Lizzie Neff's "The Last Years" in the preceding issue depends to some extent on a railroad accident for its plot, this story is the first of many in *McClure's* to feature the railroad and train travel prominently. The narrator describes a tiresome train trip, "with the same monotonous stretch of prairie to be seen from the window" throughout the day (224). To relieve her boredom, she begins to listen to a conversation between two elderly women sitting ahead of her. She grows absorbed in their story, and is disappointed that the train reaches its destination, where the conductor escorts her from the car before she has heard the last detail. (Compare to Entry 333.)

933. Wilson, Sloan. "Drunk on the Train." *New Yorker* 23 (Jan. 3, 1948): 52–55.

Jim Murphy, an old, bloated, very drunk man aboard the train, focuses his attention on Miss Dorothy Upland. Dorothy, a Vassar-educated librarian, struggles to be civil to the reeking stranger, who insists on showing her his merchant seaman's papers, and on reciting inane verse to her. Murphy assaults a conductor, and is put off the train. Dorothy watches the scene on the platform where a railroad policeman takes Murphy in hand. As the train leaves the station, "Miss Upland kept her eyes on the old man and when she drew abreast of him, he looked up and their eyes met. She smiled. It suddenly seemed very important that he should smile back, but he just stared at her without any sign of recognition" (55).

934. Winslow, Thyra S. "Grandma." In *Picture Frames*, 21–49. New York: Knopf, 1923. Also in *Middle Age, Old Age: Short Stories, Poems, Plays, and Essays on Aging*. New York: Harcourt, Brace, 1980.

Grandma, 73, lives part-time with her son Fred and his family. She does her share of housework, and candidly evaluates the merits of all her immediate relatives, if only to herself. Early in this story she takes the train to other relatives' home, where she has a not terribly good time. On the train ride from this visit to yet another set of relatives, Grandma engages a stranger, a woman, in a conversation in which she favorably embroiders upon the reality of her relationships with her offspring and their families. She moves on to another stranger, a young mother, and continues her romantic gloss on her family life. All her accounts "made her children kind, considerate, affectionate, successful, capable" (43). Grandma's real pleasure is not in her family, but in the idealized portraits she draws of them for strangers on the train.

935. Wister, Owen. "Stanwick's Business." In *Short Lines: A Collection of Classic American Railroad Stories*, edited by Rob Johnson, 221–239. New York: St. Martin's, 1996. *Saturday Evening Post* 177 (Oct. 8, 1904): 3–5+. Also in Wister's *Safe in the Arms of Croesus*. New York: Macmillan, 1928.

While waiting for the Pennsylvania Railroad train to the New Jersey coast, the narrator is apprehended by the boorish and wildly popular author of railroad fiction, Stanwick.

Stanwick's latest story is out, and all over the cover of the magazine on the station newsstand. Stanwick buys the narrator a copy; when the engineer sees the magazine in the narrator's hand, he expresses contempt. "They've hired a prize liar to write for them," he says. "There's a railroad story in that thing. The call boy had it in the roundhouse, and we took it away from him.... We don't care to have him grow up on matinee-girl trash like that" (227). A conductor also sees the magazine. "Only one thing wrong with that story," he says: "The printed matter. The illustrations are all right" (231).

Everyone on the train seems to be reading Stanwick's latest. Called to account for his nonsensical tale, Stanwick, a former railroader, is sanguine. "I'm an author now, and I write for the sentimental million who don't want realism, but the unreal realistically described" (234).

A modest collision with a New York Central engine turns the trip into a lesson in the public's sentimentality. One good lesson emerges from this very funny satire of popular railroad fiction: In the words of the conductor, "Put your money in your pants, and don't ask questions" (239).

936. _____. "Twenty Minutes for Refreshments." In *Women and Things: America's Best Funny Stories*, 252–283. New York: Harper, 1906. Also in Wister's *The Jimmyjohn Boss, and Other Stories*. New York: Garrett Press, 1969.

On a train excursion to the Pacific, the narrator meets some curious characters on the rails, not the least of whom is a conductor, Gadsden, who runs side businesses in fly paper and razor stropping compound, and Mrs. Sedalia Preen, a haughty woman of means. On a Friday afternoon, they have 20 minutes for dinner at the station of Sharon. Here the narrator is drafted by the locals to judge a baby show, with Gadsden's help. Wister's "Stanwick's Business" is a funnier story, and has more to do with railroading.

937. _____. *The Virginian*. 1902. Revised edition, New York: Macmillan, 1930. 567p.

The Virginian established many archetypes

of the Western—from the classic line, "When you call me that, smile" (printed "SMILE" in the novel), to the show-down gunfight between the good guy and the bad guy, the mysterious, noble, straight-arrow cowboy, and other elements that have been recycled endlessly in fiction, motion pictures, and television. A lengthy passage in the novel concerns the title character's job playing foreman to a group of cowhands taking cattle to Chicago by train. After delivering two 10-car trains to Chicago, the Virginian was to return by St. Paul over the Northern Pacific, assigned to meet railroad officials in St. Paul and explain to them the benefits they would enjoy from offering low shipping rates to the Sunk Creek ranch. In an amusing passage on the return train trip, the Virginian embarrasses the villain, Trampas, in a scheme involving a meal of frogs' legs. In another passage, the narrator makes an observation reminiscent of Richard Reinhardt's remarks (see discussion in this bibliography's introduction) on the insular nature of railroaders: "A train-hand had arrived over the roof, and hanging the red lights out behind, left us again without remark or symptom of curiosity. The train-hands seemed interested in their own society and lived in their own caboose" (190).

Molly Wood, the Virginian's romantic interest, also enjoys a train experience. Molly, soon to be the new schoolmarm in Bear Creek, Wyoming, travels by train across the country to reach her new job. She leaves Bennington, Vermont, with tearful people waving goodbye to her at the station. Molly takes nothing with her but a few modest belongings and the craving for the unknown felt by so many fictional characters making their escape from settled homes to new worlds. Molly is convinced by the time the train reaches Ohio that she has indeed reached the "unknown," but the wilds of Ohio soon pale in scope as the train travels on across the Great Plains.

938. Wolcott, Richmond. "Coming from the Front." In *Stories and Sketches by Our Best Authors*, 281–292. Boston: Lee and Shepard, 1867.

Available at *Wright American Fiction*: http://www.letrs.indiana.edu/web/w/wright2/

An anonymous 1st lieutenant, honorably discharged from the Union Army in Georgia in 1864, recalls his difficult effort to return to the North by rail. He leaves Atlanta on a hot, dusty morning; rather than taking a place in a car full of drunken soldiers, he secures a spot in the cattle car, finding that "the company was good" (284). The train passes landmarks of Sherman's drive through the state, but there is little sense of security aboard: Confederate troops often harass trains under nominal Union control. Food is hard to find; crackers and cheese make a sumptuous meal aboard the train, although in the next morning's light "we discovered that both crackers and cheese had a singularly animated appearance" (291). Not until the train reaches Nashville, passing the broken, burned-out cars lining the roadside, do the travelers feel safe. Whether classified as fiction or memoir—it is uncertain which this story is—it bears the unmistakable stamp of careful observation.

939. Wolfe, Thomas. "Dark in the Forest, Strange As Time." In *From Death to Morning*, 98–113. New York: Grosset & Dunlap, 1935. *Scribner's Magazine* 96 (Nov. 1934): 273–278. Also in *The Complete Short Stories of Thomas Wolfe*. New York: Scribner's, 1987.

The story opens with a scene on the platform of a Munich train station. Wolfe captures the chaotic pre-departure moments of a train at a crowded station as boarding passengers and those who will stay behind call out last-second instructions and entreaties. A young American man watches the throng of people parting from each other, and senses in the universality of their "language of departure" something of the common human identity. He watches in particular the separation of an obviously ill man and a young woman. The train leaves Munich, "swift as dreams" (105), as the American and the ill man share a compartment. The American looks out the window, feeling at home as the train passes through the Alps. He willingly submits to an interrogation by his compartment mate, who is evidently dying. The sick man discounts the lure of travel, for everywhere "it iss ze same" (109).

In the dining car, the American contrasts

the experience of train travel in the U.S. with that in Europe: "In America, the train gives one a feeling of wild and lonely joy, a sense of the savage, unfenced, and illimitable wilderness of the country ... a wordless and unutterable hope as one thinks of the enchanted city toward which he is speeding; the unknown and fabulous promise of the life he is to find there" (111). In Europe, train travel evokes feelings of wealth, power, luxury, and love.

When the American returns to his compartment, he finds the man he left behind dead. He decides not to inform the authorities. After all, will there not "be silence for us all and silence only, nothing but silence, at the end?" (113). No doubt.

940. _____. "The Far and the Near." In *Great Railroad Stories of the World*, edited by Samuel Moskowitz, 49–55. New York: McBride, 1954. Also in Wolfe's *From Death to Morning*. New York: Grosset & Dunlap, 1935. Published as "The Cottage by the Tracks" in *Cosmopolitan* 99 (July 1935): 48–50.

A railroad engineer, unnamed here, for over 20 years never failed to blow his engine's whistle when he passed a little house outside a certain town. Nor did the woman, and in later years the woman's daughter, who lived in the house fail to wave boldly and cheerfully at the engineer as he passed. The sight of the two women "gave him the most extraordinary happiness he had ever known" (53). Upon his retirement, the engineer decides to visit the little house and its reliable occupants. The visit proves far less satisfying than the old engineer imagined.

Wolfe uses the train in this story as a tool to illustrate the illusory pleasures derived from safely shallow and distant relationships. Put to the test of face-to-face intimacy, these pleasures dissolve and run. The story achieves a surprising power in its compact few pages; its blow to the reader mirrors that sustained by the engineer, for the reader's expectations, too, are far more optimistic than the outcome justifies. Anyone who has gladly waved at an engineer on a passing train will find a chill in this story.

941. _____. *I Have a Thing to Tell You.* In *The Short Novels of Thomas Wolfe*, edited by C. Hugh Holman, 233–278. New York: Scribner's, 1961. *New Republic* 90 (March 10, 1937): 132–136; (March 17, 1937): 159–164; (March 24, 1937): 202–207.

Paul, an American writer visiting Germany, narrates this terrifically tense novella set chiefly aboard a German train bound for Belgium. Before Paul boards the train, his German friend Franz spills out a torrent of contempt for the "fools" presently running the German state. Franz frequently prefaces his remarks by saying "I will tell you something." Franz is not optimistic about his future in the Reich. When the train leaves the station, Paul watches Franz on the platform. "Then the train swept out around the curve. And he was lost" (250).

Paul shares a compartment with several other passengers, including an anxious little man who surveys the others with an air of suspicion. Paul strikes a quick bond with a young Polish-American, Johnnie Stefanowski, with whom he enjoys dinner and drinks in the spotless dining car. The passengers in the compartment loosen up a bit as the trip goes on, and by the time the train reaches the Belgian border, even the nervous little man seems to be enjoying himself.

At that point, things go sour. German authorities hold the train, and seize the nervous little man from the compartment after searching his belongings. They have discovered that he is a Jew, and that he is trying to flee Germany with his money. The German thugs march the poor man past his fellow passengers. The victim and the other passengers exchange looks. In the silent exchange there is anguish, "And we were all somehow naked and ashamed, and somehow guilty. We all felt somehow that we were saying farewell, not to a man but to humanity; not to some nameless little cipher out of life, but to the fading image of a brother's face. We lost him then. The train swept out and gathered speed—and so farewell" (274).

This powerful story closes with Paul echoing his friend Franz: "I have a thing to tell you ... a wind is rising, and the rivers flow"

(278). Today's reader of this novella appreciates in retrospect Wolfe's prescient anticipation of much worse to come.

I Have a Thing to Tell You also appears, in an expanded version, in Book VI of Wolfe's You Can't Go Home Again.

942. _____. *Look Homeward, Angel: A Story of the Buried Life.* 1929. Reprint, New York: Scribner's, 1957. 662p.

Wolfe turns again and again to the train as symbol and thematic vehicle in this novel. Born in 1900, Eugene Gant in 1904 goes with his mother and siblings to St. Louis from his boyhood home in Altamont (based on Asheville, North Carolina, Wolfe's boyhood home), leaving behind his worthless father. The children wave good-bye to the elder Gant from the coach window, and the pounding of the wheels lulls Eugene to sleep. The St. Louis sojourn ends when Eugene's brother Grover dies, and the family returns to Altamont on a train, escorting his coffin. At 15, Eugene takes a train trip to Charleston. The coach is hot and stuffy; passengers sleep fitfully as a baby wails. A hill-man shells peanuts and throws the shells into the aisle: "People trod through them with a sharp masty crackle.... There was a crushed litter of sanitary drinking-cups upon the floor, and a stale odor from the toilets" (381). The atmosphere is unappealing at this level, but to young Eugene the trip represents escape from the fetters of family and place that have buried his creative energy, and hints of something great that lies beyond: "the vast structure of the earth" seen from the windows, "the huge flowing lift of the earth-waves, cyclic intersections bewildering—the American earth—rude, immeasurable, formless, mighty" (381).

Whether as a symbol of escape, or destiny, or of the fundamental American obsession with movement for the sake of movement, Wolfe uses the train here and elsewhere in his work on many occasions. Sometimes he dwells on the bulk and power and rhythm of the train itself; sometimes on the suggestion of the journey, the escape, or the call of the future in a distant locomotive whistle. The railroad's presence in this novel is so frequent that it makes perfect sense for Douglas W. Gorsline's illustrations to depict locomotives steaming across the land.

943. _____. *The Lost Boy: A Novella.* Chapel Hill: University of North Carolina Press, 1992. 81p.

Readers whose interest in Thomas Wolfe matches or exceeds their interest in railroads will find editor James W. Clark's introduction a valuable look at the evolution and publishing history of this novella. In the story, the second part features Grover's mother's memories of the boy, then 11 years old, on a train trip through Indiana in 1904, on the way to the World's Fair in St. Louis. Mother is clearly proud of her serious, observant son, who sits with his nose pressed to the window, looking out at the farms the train passes. The most memorable passage here is what will be, for most contemporary readers, an account of racist confrontation. After the train enters Indiana, which has no Jim Crow laws, family retainer Simpson Featherstone strides into the coach where Grover rides with his mother. Featherstone, "that big old yellow, pockmarked darky," with a bearing "just as impudent and brazen as you please," takes off his coat, puts his bag up on the rack, and sits down, "as if he owned the railroad." He is so "nigger like, when we crossed over into Indiana he starts right back out of the nigger car into our own—well, the impudence of him" (40). Grover's mother demands that Featherstone return to the "nigger car," but he shows no inclination to do so; not, that is, until young Grover helps him see the light. Grover lectures Featherstone on how he was brought up, and how he "knows better" than to act so boldly. "You should have seen the expression on that darky's face," says Grover's mother. "I had to laugh when I thought about it later" (42). Cowed by the child's pompous assumption of authority, Featherstone retreats to the "nigger car," and Grover basks in the approbation of a "gentleman" passenger impressed by the boy's racial mastery. The chief focus is not on Grover's racist behavior, but what is, to his mother, his endearing air of "maturity" in taking responsibility for putting Featherstone in his place.

Wolfe reworked this story heavily, and, in

spite of identical titles, the version appearing here is not the same as those in Wolfe's collection, *The Hills Beyond*; in Scribner's 1987 anthology, *The Complete Short Stories of Thomas Wolfe*; or in the story's November, 1937, publication in *Redbook*.

944. _____. *Of Time and the River: A Legend of Man's Hunger in His Youth.* New York: Scribner's, 1935. 912p.

The novel's subtitle nearly says it all about this work. In this, his last novel published before his death, Wolfe's alter ego Eugene Gant goes to college and grows up. The major, although by no means the only, railroad business comes in the opening section, "Orestes: Flight Before Fury." In one of the longest train rides in American fiction, young Eugene leaves his sleepy Southern hometown of Altamont to attend college at Harvard. Eugene awaits the train at the station with the urgency of the schoolboy he still is. He stamps impatiently up and down the platform, and becomes exasperated with his mother when she launches a lugubrious guilt-laying declamation over Eugene's impending departure. "I hope we are all here when you come back again," she whimpers. "'I hope you find us all alive....' [ellipsis in original]. She smiled bravely, mysteriously, tearfully. 'You never know,' she whispered, 'you never know'" (21).

With his mother carrying on thus, it is a wonder that Eugene can bear to wait for the train, that he does not seize an idle handcar, haul it onto the track, and start pumping. The train does arrive, however, and Eugene's mother does not throw herself before it. As the train approaches, they watch "Across the golden pollenated [sic] haze of the warm autumnal afternoon ... with numb lips and an empty hollowness of fear, delight, and sorrow in their hearts" (22). Eugene's mother is in a state of semi-shock as the train halts before them, but Eugene is transported: "It was his train and it had come to take him to the strange and secret heart of the great North ... whose austere and lonely image, whose frozen heat and glacial fire, and dark stern beauty had blazed in his vision since he was a child" (23). The train to the North is Eugene's "escape," his "road to freedom," his "dream made real" (24).

Eugene recovers his senses sufficiently to board the train, and for most of the next 60 pages rides away from his boyhood. A visit to his dying father in Baltimore briefly interrupts his trip to Cambridge. When Eugene leaves, he knows that he will not see his father alive again. In a tidy experiential package, then, Eugene slips the skin of his early life: his hometown, his mother, his father—to begin a new existence. The "mighty station" in Boston is filled "with the ceaseless throngings of its illimitable life, and all of the murmurous, remote and mighty sounds of time forever held there...." (89).

There is no shortage of rhapsodic rail reverie in this section of the novel; any reader who wishes to know how seriously Wolfe took the railroad must read it. This mammoth novel contains many other interesting train-related passages, too many to dwell on here, but the beginning is the place to start.

945. _____. "The Sun and the Rain." In *The Complete Short Stories of Thomas Wolfe*, edited by Francis E. Skipp, 142–146. New York: Scribner's, 1987. *Scribner's Magazine* 95 (May 1934): 358–360. Also in *Best Short Stories of 1935*. Edited by Edward J. O'Brien. Boston: Houghton Mifflin, 1935.

In this story drawn from *Of Time and the River*, a young American on his way to Orleans, France, on a rainy day tries to talk with the peasant family sharing his train compartment. Language difficulties render the conversation clumsy. The peasant couple's daughter grows angry when her father, in her opinion, is embarrassingly obtuse about the American's speech. The young man, however, seems untroubled. He gives the peasant man some Lucky Strike cigarettes, and appears happy to accept his tutoring in a few French terms, including those for the sun and the rain.

946. _____. "The Train and the City." In *The Complete Short Stories of Thomas Wolfe*, edited by Francis E. Skipp, 10–29. New York: Scribner's, 1987. *Scribner's Magazine* 93 (May 1933): 285–294.

In this story the narrator carries on effusively about the glory of spring in New

York City. It is all so greenly wonderful! Sometimes he leaves the city, simply for the pleasure inherent in returning to it. One Saturday he boards the limited to head south, and, with his fellow passengers, thrills to discover the train racing, engine-to-engine, with another southbound train on the adjacent track. He sees the other train's engineer, leaning out his cab window, on his face "the character of courage, dignity, and an immense and expert knowledge" (18). The passengers and crews of both trains become caught up in the excitement of the impromptu competition; "a fat and enormous darkey" porter expresses dismay at the rival train's overtaking and passing the limited (19). The limited reasserts itself, however, and catches the other train. The passengers of each train observe one another good-naturedly from the train windows. The narrator's intense attention to his surroundings marks a memorable passage as he looks into the other train, where he sees the luxurious interiors of the Pullman cars, "...and the people fixed there for an instant in incomparably rich and vivid little pictures of their life and destiny, as we were all hurled onward, a thousand atoms, to our journey's end somewhere upon the mighty continent, across the immense and lonely visage of the everlasting earth" (20).

The passengers in the opposing train pass and vanish and are "gone forever," yet the narrator seems to know them with an astonishing intimacy. He sees in the opposite parlor car "a lovely girl, blonde haired, with a red silk dress, and slender shapely legs crossed carelessly, holding an opened magazine face downward in one hand, and with the slender tapering fingers of the other hand curved inward toward her belly where they fumbled with a charm or locket hanging from a chain..." (20).

Later in the journey, the narrator overhears an inscrutable exchange between the fat porter and a black railyard worker, and their "casual, incredible conversation" folds in with his indelible memories of the trip. He returns to New York with his sensibilities at a keener pitch than ever; the train has taken him away, but it has brought him back, revivified and ready for an even more exuberant rhapsody on the city and its place in the American scene.

This story's gushing tone is off-putting,

initially, but it develops an undeniable power at the point when the description of the train trip comes into play. The story's momentum builds not unlike that of a locomotive itself as it slowly gathers speed to become a potent force, a force sufficient to bear before it the narrator's nearly ecstatic vision of the great city in which he lives.

947. Wolff, Geoffrey. "Love Under the Clock." *Esquire* 114 (July 1990): 92–106.

Nathaniel Clay's grandparents put him on the Empire Builder in Seattle to go to Princeton. In the dining car he meets a beautiful but smug and pretentious young woman, Diana. She invites him to her compartment, where nothing much happens, although it leads Nathaniel to fancy that they have a "complex" relationship. (They haven't *any* relationship, but Nathaniel is a freshman.) Nathaniel reads Scott Fitzgerald's *The Great Gatsby* on the train. Diana dumps him in Chicago, although he is not alert enough to realize it, and he goes east on the 20th Century Limited. In his sophomore year at Princeton, he reconnects with Diana—and, thanks to his roommates, realizes her true character. "He wished he could be glad to know better than he knew on the *Empire Builder*, to see ... the common girl got up in such an uncommon face. He wasn't glad about any of it" (106). Thus the truth so often settles.

948. "A Woman's Courage." *Harper's Weekly* 17 (July 12, 1873): Supplement, p. 610.

Old New Englander Jonathan Beers warns his niece Dorothy against Israel Esmayne, a railroad switchman with a past habit of drunkenness. Dorothy is convinced that Israel has sworn off the bottle; he has not. A passing stranger gives Israel a flask, and by the time he is supposed to set the switches that day, he is too intoxicated to know what he is doing. He passes out, terrified that his relapse will cost the lives of people on the express train. Dorothy saves the moment by changing the switches herself, and when Israel comes to his gratitude overcomes his alcoholism: He and Dorothy marry, and he remains sober forever. (It happens every day, does it not?)

949. Wood, Frances G. "Turkey Red." In *O. Henry Memorial Award Prize Stories* *of 1919*, edited by Blanche C. Williams, 105–119. Garden City, NY: Doubleday, 1920. *Pictorial Review*, Nov. 1919, 18+.

In Dakota Territory one winter day, residents Hillas and Dan try to convince Smith, a visiting Eastern businessman, that the area would be livable if only it had a railroad. Out on the plains, a blizzard comes up, catching the three men exposed. They gain shelter—barely—in the hut of a woman whose infant is near death. Moved by the courage of the settlers, Smith promises to help bring a railroad through the area. "To bring a road here," says Dan, "would be like—playing God!" (119). Something of the almost unspeakable necessity of railroad service to a remote settlement marks this story; the reader can sense it in Dan's statement. Without the railroad, there is no future.

950. Wood, Jane R. *The Train to Estelline.* Denton, TX: University of North Texas, 2000. 210p.

In 1911, 17-year-old Lucinda Richards of Bonham, Texas, secures a teaching job in the town of White Star. On the novel's second page, she leaves on the Texas and Pacific Railroad for her new life; on the third, she travels on the Fort Worth and Denver: "At seven o'clock, the train left the station, rounded a bend, and, suddenly, all I had ever known of my home was gone from sight" (3). Lucinda gets off the train at Estelline, and goes to White Star by wagon. This enjoyable novel, told in epistolary form, shows Lucinda's growth during the school year in White Star. It closes, appropriately, with her last letter, written in May of 1912, once again aboard a Texas and Pacific train.

951. Woods, George B. "Marrying a Pickpocket." In *Essays, Sketches, and Stories*, 377–398. Boston: James R. Osgood, 1873.

Available at *Wright American Fiction*: http://www.letrs.indiana.edu/web/w/wright2/

Narrator Mary Gilman, a teacher, determines to take the train from her Massachusetts home to a better job in a Maine high school. She studies herself into a headache over the railroad guide to plot her trip, which must go through Boston. "I felt quite in the mood of a daring discoverer at the thought of making my way to Boston and through it on my own responsibility" (379). A schedule snag leaves her with nearly three idle hours in Boston. Her fellow travelers are "made up of all the inevitable characters ... whom my subsequent travelling experiences have taught me to look for in every railway journey" (380). In the Boston train station waiting room, she sees a sign alerting passengers to beware of pickpockets. She is unconcerned, having placed all her valuables, except her pocketbook, in a trunk stashed in the baggage room. Ensuing is a nightmarish adventure in which Mary is mistakenly arrested as a pick-pocket. Only through the unlikely intervention of an acquaintance is she able to resume her trip. The story achieves considerable tension, as well as fear and pity for an innocent traveler set upon by authorities. (The title follows from Mary's husband's subsequent joking about having "married a pickpocket.")

952. Woolrich, Cornell. "Death in the Air." In *Nightwebs*, 249–271. New York: Harper & Row, 1971. *Detective Fiction Weekly*, Oct. 10, 1936.

Detective Stephen "Step" Lively is taking his usual elevated train ride through the tenements of New York City when a man reading a newspaper in a nearby seat slumps over, dead, a bullet in his head. Lively is convinced that the shot came from a tenement window along the route. He takes a dangerous walk along the track back to the scene of the shooting, where he engages in some creditable ratiocination, with a touch of reefer madness for pulp flavoring. A nice passage describes the view from the elevated as it goes through the tenements: The train passes so close to the buildings that it is easy to look in through the windows. "A man in his underwear reading a paper by a lamp, a woman bent over a washtub in a steaming kitchen. Their heads never turned at the streaming, comet-like lights or the roar of the wheels going by. They were so used to it they never gave it a thought.... Nor did those on the train show any interest either, as a rule" (252). The passengers and the tenement dwellers are mutually oblivious, their lives sealed off from one another's.

953. _____. "The Phantom of the Subway." In *Midnight Specials: An Anthology for Train Buffs and Suspense Aficionados,* edited by Bill Pronzini, 118–138. Indianapolis: Bobbs-Merrill, 1977. Published as "You Pays Your Nickel." *Argosy,* Aug. 22, 1936.

A pulp-souled yarn that hurtles along at a breakneck pace, this story pits New York subway guard Delaney against "the Phantom," a thief and killer who tries to use Delaney's train as a means of escape.

954. Wright, Harold B. *The Winning of Barbara Worth.* Chicago: Book Supply, 1911. 511p.

Set in Colorado's Imperial Valley, this novel, meshing a romance with an account of industrial land development, is yet another concerned with railroad building in the West. Plans call for the Southwestern and Continental Railroad to pass through a Colorado basin that is barely more than a wasteland. A party reconnoitering the route, led by banker Jefferson Worth, rescues Barbara, a four-year-old girl, the survivor of a desert calamity. The Worths raise the child as their own. Much of the novel's attention focuses on the construction of the railroad, and a change in plans that leaves the town of Kingston, instead of happily situated on the right-of-way, a dozen miles off, thanks to a decision by Worth. Kingston's citizens are apoplectic. Worth reconsiders in an act of political gamesmanship, and sinks all of his personal fortune into the railroad, leaving observers confused and suspicious about his motives. The story moves at a stolid pace.

Wright, Mabel Osgood *see* **Barbara**

955. Wright, Richard. "Big Boy Leaves Home." In *Uncle Tom's Children,* 17–53. 1938. Reprint, New York: Harper & Row, 1969. Also in *The Literary South.*

Edited by Louis D. Rubin, Jr. New York: Wiley & Sons, 1979.

Four hooky-playing African-American boys, with Big Boy the clown and boss of the group, amble through the countryside on an early summer day, telling jokes and engaging in adolescent horseplay. Lying on the warm ground, they hear a distant train whistle—"Boun fer up Noth, Lawd, bound fer up Noth!" says one (19). The whistle inspires them to sing the Gospel tune, "This Train." Later, after a dip at a swimming hole, they hear another train, heading north. "Lawd, Ahm goin Noth some day," says one of the boys (27). A lethal confrontation with a white couple at the swimming hole shatters the boys' dreamy reflections, and forces Big Boy into a horrifying flight for his life. The passage of time since its composition has done nothing to mitigate this story's disturbing effects.

956. _____. "The Man Who Was Almost a Man." In *Eight Men,* 11–26. 1961. Reprint, New York: Thunder's Mouth, 1987.

Seventeen-year-old Dave Saunders, who thinks himself "Almost a man" (11), is a fieldworker who becomes preoccupied with a desire to own a gun. He buys a cheap revolver from a white store proprietor, and, in a passage of terrible absurdity, accidentally shoots to death a mule belonging to his employer, Jim Hawkins. Humiliated before his neighbors and forced to pay back Hawkins over a protracted time, Dave bolts. He retrieves the gun from the place he abandoned it after the shooting, and hops a freight train. "Ahead the long rails were glinting in the moonlight, stretching away, away to somewhere, somewhere where he could be a man..." (26). This is a chilling story of a boy who, although a long way from manhood, does not seem far from being in a man's trouble. (Wright published a variant of the story, "Almos' a Man," in *Harper's Bazaar* in 1941.)

APPENDIX:
PUBLICATIONS BY
DECADE

The entry placements below sometimes represent only a best guess regarding initial publication for short stories, owing to elusive or non-existent indexing of periodicals in which the stories may have appeared before their publication in anthologies. This problem is especially troublesome for stories published in anthologies at the beginning of a decade, but for which no indications of previous publication surface. Chances are good that an anthologized story published in 1900 or 1901, for example, appeared somewhere in print in the preceding decade; entry placements generally follow that assumption. Some items in the bibliography are not included in this decade-by-decade list, since even a "best guess" about their debuts would be too questionable to put forward. Nevertheless, the list will help readers isolate the novels and stories by period, and help give a sense of the way fiction with railroad concerns evolved over the years.

1840–1849 335, 664

1850–1859 336, 601, 646

1860–1869 29, 86, 160, 212, 321, 359, 428, 583, 662, 663, 696, 702, 707, 812, 844, 938

1870–1879 3, 80, 180, 242, 244, 322, 333, 385, 387, 416, 463, 616, 676, 708, 735, 792, 831, 832, 845, 847, 909, 911, 948, 951

1880–1889 30, 31, 172, 288, 338, 384, 386, 410, 551, 846, 850

1890–1899 7, 8, 27, 93, 94, 110, 120, 149, 182–184, 198, 239, 267, 274, 276, 289–291, 305, 357, 362–370, 393, 411, 453, 464, 473, 475, 493, 501, 522, 555, 642, 644, 686, 691, 717, 731, 732, 758, 829, 840, 859, 860–862, 864–870, 872, 876, 880, 881, 883, 885, 887, 890–897, 899–903, 922, 932

1900–1909 23, 26, 28, 41, 108, 109, 118, 122, 127, 132, 134, 138, 140, 142, 150, 151, 157, 158, 201, 237, 299, 301, 326, 352, 355, 405, 406, 426, 427, 429, 454, 474, 476, 480, 482–485, 488, 490–492, 496–499, 534, 553, 554, 598, 612, 631, 643, 647, 653, 654, 680, 683, 694, 733, 756, 757, 759–762, 765–770, 772, 774–787, 797, 801, 815–822, 828, 857, 863, 871, 873, 875, 877, 879, 882, 884, 886, 888, 889, 898, 935, 937

1910–1919 1, 5, 15, 16, 32, 53, 117, 133, 137, 141, 166, 230, 235, 236, 238, 297, 308, 314, 361, 378, 396, 398, 414, 415, 422, 432, 433, 457, 461, 477–479, 486, 487, 489, 494, 495, 500, 502, 505, 562,

617–626, 629, 630, 632–635, 637, 640, 641, 689, 692, 730, 734, 763, 769, 771, 773, 796, 813, 824, 853, 874, 949, 954

1920–1929 6, 75, 90, 102, 115, 121, 136, 139, 163, 175, 176, 200, 223, 241, 262, 265, 271, 292, 298, 302, 303, 344–346, 360, 418, 439, 440, 458, 459, 481, 503, 506, 507, 556, 565, 584, 593, 604, 606, 607, 681, 710, 738, 739, 741–744, 746, 748–751, 753, 754, 764, 795, 798, 804, 811, 838, 843, 856, 904, 905, 907, 931, 934, 942

1930–1939 14, 17, 42, 45–47, 50, 55, 65, 69–71, 74, 83, 92, 100, 106, 111, 143, 144, 152, 162, 164, 169, 173, 174, 179, 191–195, 205–208, 215, 217, 231, 240, 252, 254, 260, 261, 264, 270, 275, 282, 318–320, 330,

337, 339, 377, 381, 382, 397, 408, 413, 421, 423, 436, 437, 442, 443, 445, 452, 465, 504, 530, 532, 538, 552, 559, 564, 568, 586, 587, 590, 605, 614, 652, 673, 682, 688, 693, 700, 705, 740, 747, 752, 755, 794, 800, 802, 803, 809, 823, 826, 834–836, 848, 852, 914, 919, 924, 929, 939–941, 944–946, 952, 953, 955

1940–1949 4, 18, 25, 39, 40, 43, 44, 48, 49, 51, 54, 56–61, 63, 64, 67, 68, 77, 78, 89, 96, 107, 112, 119, 181, 185, 189, 204, 217, 219, 221, 257, 259, 263, 278, 286, 296, 312, 313, 317, 324, 331, 334, 340, 341, 358, 383, 391, 394, 395, 400, 404, 434, 435, 441, 444, 446, 449, 450, 466, 509, 510, 516, 529, 540, 541, 544, 548, 557, 561, 603, 608, 648, 649, 651, 665, 675, 685, 701, 704, 716, 719, 727, 833, 841, 906, 910, 912, 917, 918, 923, 933

1950–1959 35–38, 52, 66, 81, 85, 87, 91, 99, 101, 113, 146, 161, 196, 209, 211, 213, 216, 218, 225, 243, 246, 268, 273, 287, 293, 306, 307, 323, 356, 371, 372, 374, 375, 401, 403, 407, 409, 424, 425, 508, 513, 514, 523, 524, 528, 527, 535, 539, 542, 543, 566, 570, 595, 602, 611, 650, 674, 677, 678, 684, 690, 695, 715, 805, 807, 810, 827, 830, 858, 915, 916, 920

1960–1969 20, 21, 82, 128, 171, 178, 197, 214, 220, 222, 234, 245, 247, 253, 279, 373, 390, 392, 431, 471, 523, 525, 531, 546, 547, 575, 577, 578, 579, 580, 609, 610, 645, 657, 659, 667, 671, 679, 714, 737, 799, 808, 842, 908, 921, 925, 930, 956

1970–1979 2, 19, 24, 76, 97, 104, 105, 131, 155, 190, 232, 269, 300, 376, 420, 456, 470, 472, 512, 515, 517, 520, 572,

574, 581, 592, 613, 656, 666, 668, 672, 698, 709, 788–790, 806, 855

1980–1989 73, 98, 114, 116, 129, 130, 145, 147, 154, 186–188, 202, 227, 228, 256, 277, 284, 309, 310, 327, 343, 348, 349, 379, 399, 402, 438, 455, 460, 469, 511, 518, 519, 521, 526, 533, 563, 670, 697, 699, 711, 718, 723, 814, 851, 927

1990–1999 13, 22, 34, 72, 84, 95, 123, 124, 126, 153, 159, 165, 177, 210, 224, 226, 255, 272, 283, 285, 295, 329, 380, 419, 430, 517, 536, 545, 549, 550, 558, 560, 585, 588, 589, 591, 594, 597, 600, 658, 660, 661, 669, 703, 706, 722, 724, 726, 736, 791, 825, 849, 926, 928, 947

2000– 11, 33, 79, 88, 103, 125, 199, 229, 266, 280, 294, 311, 315, 316, 332, 388, 412, 417, 467, 655, 950

TITLE INDEX

SUBJECT INDEX